# Econometrics by Example

Damodar Gujarati, *Basic Econometrics* (McGraw-Hill, USA)
Damodar Gujarati, *Essentials of Econometrics* (McGraw-Hill, USA)
Damodar Gujarati, *Government and Business* (McGraw-Hill, USA)

# Econometrics by Example

## Damodar Gujarati

First published 2011 by
PALGRAVE MACMILLAN

Palgrave Macmillan in the UK is an imprint of Macmillan Publishers Limited, registered in England, company number 785998, of Houndmills, Basingstoke, Hampshire RG21 6XS.

Palgrave Macmillan in the US is a division of St Martin's Press LLC, 175 Fifth Avenue, New York, NY 10010.

Palgrave Macmillan is the global academic imprint of the above companies and has companies and representatives throughout the world.

Palgrave® and Macmillan® are registered trademarks in the United States, the United Kingdom, Europe and other countries

ISBN 978-0-230-29039-6

This book is printed on paper suitable for recycling and made from fully managed and sustained forest sources. Logging, pulping and manufacturing processes are expected to conform to the environmental regulations of the country of origin.

A catalogue record for this book is available from the British Library.

A catalog record for this book is available from the Library of Congress.

10   9   8   7   6   5   4
20   19   18   17   16   15   14   13   12

Printed in Great Britain by the MPG Books Group, Bodmin and King's Lynn

# Dedication

*For Joan Gujarati, Diane Gujarati-Chesnut, Charles Chesnut and my grandchildren "Tommy" and Laura Chesnut*

# Short contents

# Contents

# Preface

*Econometrics by Example* (EBE) is written primarily for undergraduate students in economics, accounting, finance, marketing, and related disciplines. It is also intended for students in MBA programs and for researchers in business, government, and research organizations.

There are several excellent textbooks in econometrics, written from very elementary to very advanced levels. The writers of these books have their intended audiences. I have contributed to this field with my own books, *Basic Econometrics* (McGraw-Hill, 5th edn, 2009) and *Essentials of Econometrics* (McGraw-Hill, 4th edn, 2009). These books have been well received and have been translated into several languages. EBE is different from my own books and those written by others in that it deals with major topics in econometrics from the point of view of their practical applications. Because of space limitations, textbooks generally discuss econometric theory and illustrate econometric techniques with just a few examples. But space does not permit them to deal with concrete examples in detail.

In EBE, each chapter discusses one or two examples in depth. To give but one illustration of this, Chapter 8 discusses binary dummy dependent variable regression models. This specific example relates to the decision to smoke or not to smoke, taking the value of 1 if a person smokes or the value of 0 if he/she does not smoke. The data consist of a random sample of 119 US males. The explanatory variables considered are age, education, income, and price of cigarettes. There are three approaches to modeling this problem: (1) ordinary least-squares (OLS), which leads to the linear probability model (LPM), (2) the logit model, based on the logistic probability distribution, and (3) the probit model, based on the normal distribution.

Which is a better model? In assessing this, we have to consider the pros and cons of all of these three approaches and evaluate the results based on these three competing models and then decide which one to choose. Most textbooks have a theoretical discussion about this, but do not have the space to discuss all the practical aspects of a given problem.

This book is self-contained in that the basic theory underlying each topic is discussed without complicated mathematics. It has an appendix that discusses the basic concepts of statistics in a user-friendly manner and provides the necessary statistical background to follow the concepts covered therein. In EBE all the examples I analyse look at each problem in depth, starting with model formulation, estimation of the chosen model, testing hypotheses about the phenomenon under study, and post-estimation diagnostics to see how well the model performs Due attention is paid to commonly encountered problems, such as multicollinearity, heteroscedasticity, autocorrelation, model specification errors, and non-stationarity of economic time series. This step-by-step approach, from model formulation, through estimation and hypothesis-testing, to post-estimation diagnostics will provide a framework for less experienced students and researchers. It will also help them to understand empirical articles in academic and professional journals.

The specific examples discussed in this book are:

1  Determination of hourly wages for a group of US workers

2  Cobb–Douglas production function for the USA

3  The rate of growth of real GDP, USA, 1960–2007

4  The relationship between food expenditure and total expenditure

5  Log-linear model of real GDP growth

6  Gross private investment and gross private savings, USA, 1959–2007

7  Quarterly retail fashion sales

8  Married women's hours of work

9  Abortion rates in the USA

10  US consumption function, 1947–2000

11  Deaths from lung cancer and the number of cigarettes smoked

12  Model of school choice

13  Attitude toward working mothers

14  Decision to apply to graduate school

15  Patents and R&D expenditure: an application of the Poisson probability distribution

16  Dollar/euro exchange rates: are they stationary?

17  Closing daily prices of IBM stock: are they a random walk?

18  Is the regression of consumption expenditure on disposable personal income spurious?

19  Are 3-month and 6-month US Treasury Bills cointegrated?

20  ARCH model of dollar/euro exchange rate

21  GARCH model of dollar/euro exchange rate

22  An ARMA model of IBM daily closing prices

23  Vector error correction model (VEC) of 3-month and 6-month Treasury Bill rates

24  Testing for Granger causality between consumption expenditure and per capita disposable income

25  Charitable donations using panel data

26  Duration analysis of recidivism

27  Instrumental variable estimation of schooling and socio-economic variables

28  The simultaneity between consumption expenditure and income

The book is divided into four parts:

Part I discusses the classical linear regression model, which is the workhorse of econometrics. This model is based on restrictive assumptions. The three chapters cover the linear regression model, functional forms of regression models, and qualitative (dummy) variables regression models.

Part II looks critically at the assumptions of the classical linear regression model and examines the ways these assumptions can be modified and with what effect. Specifically, we discuss the topics of multicollinearity, heteroscedasticity, autocorrelation, and model specification errors.

Part III discusses important topics in cross-section econometrics. These chapters discuss and illustrate several cross-sectional topics that are, in fact, not usually discussed in depth in most undergraduate textbooks. These are logit and probit models, multinomial regression models, ordinal regression models, censored and truncated regression models, and Poisson and negative binomial distribution models dealing with count data.

The reason for discussing these models is that they are increasingly being used in the fields of economics, education, psychology, political science, and marketing, largely due to the availability of extensive cross-sectional data involving thousands of observations and also because user-friendly software programs are now readily available to deal with not only vast quantities of data but also to deal with some of these techniques, which are mathematically involved.

Part IV deals primarily with topics in time series econometrics, such as stationary and nonstationary time series, cointegration and error-correction mechanisms, asset price volatility (the ARCH and GARCH models), and economic forecasting with regression (ARIMA and VAR models).

It also discusses three advanced topics. These are panel data regression models (that is, models that deal with repeated cross-sectional data over time; in particular we discuss the fixed effects and random effects models), survival or duration analysis of phenomena such as the duration of unemployment and survival time of cancer patients, and the method of instrumental variables (IV), which is used to deal with stochastic explanatory variables that may be correlated with the error term, which renders OLS estimators inconsistent.

In sum, as the title suggests, *Econometrics by Example* discusses the major themes in econometrics with detailed worked examples that show how the subject works in practice. With some basic theory and familiarity with econometric software, students will find that "learning by doing" is the best way to learn econometrics. The prerequisites are minimal. An exposure to the two-variable linear regression model, a beginning course in statistics, and facility in algebraic manipulations will be adequate to follow the material in the book. EBE does not use any matrix algebra or advanced calculus.

EBE makes heavy use of the *Stata* and *Eviews* statistical packages. The outputs obtained from these packages are reproduced in the book so the reader can see clearly the results in a compact way. Wherever necessary, graphs are produced to give a visual feel for the phenomenon under study. Most of the chapters include several exercises that the reader may want to attempt to learn more about the various techniques discussed. Although the bulk of the book is free of complicated mathematical derivations, in a few cases some advanced material is put in the appendices.

## Companion website

The data used in this textbook are posted on the companion website and notes within each chapter direct the reader to this at the relevant points. Students are encouraged to use these data in several end-of-chapter exercises to practice applying what they have learned to different scenarios. The instructor may also want to use these data for classroom assignments to develop and estimate alternative econometric models. For the instructor, solutions to these end-of-chapter exercises are posted on the companion website in the password protected lecturer zone. Here, (s)he will also find a collection of PowerPoint slides which correspond to each chapter for use in teaching.

# Acknowledgments

In preparing *Econometrics by Example* I have received invaluable help from Inas Kelly, Assistant Professor of Economics, Queens College of the City University of New York, and Professor Michael Grossman, Distinguished Professor of Economics at the Graduate Center of the City University of New York. I am indebted to them. I am also grateful to the following reviewers for their very helpful comments and suggestions:

▲ Professor Michael P. Clements, University of Warwick

▲ Professor Brendan McCabe, University of Liverpool

▲ Professor Timothy Park, University of Georgia

▲ Professor Douglas G. Steigerwald, University of California Santa Barbara

▲ Associate Professor Heino Bohn Nielsen, University of Copenhagen

▲ Assistant Professor Pedro André Cerqueira, University of Coimbra

▲ Doctor Peter Moffatt, University of East Anglia

▲ Doctor Jiajing (Jane) Sun, University of Liverpool

and to the other anonymous reviewers whose comments were invaluable. Of course, I alone am responsible for any errors that remain.

Without the encouragement and frequent feedback from Jaime Marshall, Associate Director of College Publishing at Palgrave Macmillan, I would not have been able to complete this book on time. Thanks Jaime. For their behind the scenes help, I am thankful to Aléta Bezuidenhout and Amy Grant.

The author and publishers are grateful to the following for their permission to reproduce data sets:

▲ MIT Press for data from Wooldridge, *Economic Analysis of Cross Section and Panel Data* (2010), and also from Mullay, "Instrumental-variable Estimation of count data models: an application to models of cigarette smoking behavior", *Review of Economics and Statistics* (1997), vol. 79, #4, pp. 586–93.

▲ SAS Institute, Inc. for data from Freund and Littell, *SAS System for Regression*, third edition (2000) pp. 65–6, copyright 2000, SAS Institute Inc., Cary, NC, USA. All rights reserved. Reproduced with permission of SAS Institute Inc., Cary, NC.

▲ American Statistical Association for data from Allenby, Jen and Leone, "Economic trends and being trendy: the influence of consumer confidence on retail fashion sales", *Journal of Business and Economic Statistics* (1996) vol. 14/1, pp. 103–11.

These data are hosted on the JBES archives. We also thank Professor Christiaan Heij for allowing us to use the quarterly averages he calculated from these data.

# A personal message from the author

## Dear student,

Firstly, thank you for buying *Econometrics by Example*. This book has been written and revised in response to feedback from lecturers around the world, so it has been designed with your learning needs in mind. Whatever your course, it provides a practical and accessible introduction to econometrics that will equip you with the tools to tackle econometric problems and to work confidently with data sets.

Secondly, I hope you enjoy studying econometrics using this book. It is still in fact a comparatively young field, and it may surprise you that until the late nineteenth and early twentieth century the statistical analysis of economic data for the purpose of measuring and testing economic theories was met with much skepticism. It was not until the 1950s that econometrics was considered a sub-field of economics, and then only a handful of economics departments offered it as a specialized field of study. In the 1960s, a few econometrics textbooks appeared on the market, and since then the subject has made rapid strides.

Nowadays, econometrics is no longer confined to economics departments. Econometric techniques are used in a variety of fields such as finance, law, political science, international relations, sociology, psychology, medicine and agricultural sciences. Students who acquire a thorough grounding in econometrics therefore have a head start in making careers in these areas. Major corporations, banks, brokerage houses, governments at all levels, and international organizations like the IMF and the World Bank, employ a vast number of people who can use econometrics to estimate demand functions and cost functions, and to conduct economic forecasting of key national and international economic variables. There is also a great demand for econometricians by colleges and universities all over the world.

What is more, there are now several textbooks that discuss econometrics from very elementary to very advanced levels to help you along the way. I have contributed to this growth industry with two introductory and intermediate level texts and now I have written this third book based on a clear need for a new approach. Having taught econometrics for several years at both undergraduate and graduate levels in Australia, India, Singapore, USA and the UK, I came to realize that there was clearly a need for a book which explains this often complex discipline in straightforward, practical terms by considering several interesting examples, such as charitable giving, fashion sales and exchange rates, **in depth**. This need has now been met with *Econometrics by Example*.

What has made econometrics even more exciting to study these days is the availability of user-friendly software packages. Although there are several software packages, in this book I primarily use *Eviews* and *Stata*, as they are widely available and easy to get started with. Student versions of these packages are available at reasonable cost and I have presented outputs from them throughout the book so you can see the results of the analysis very clearly. I have also made this text easy to navigate by dividing it into four parts, which are described in detail in the Preface. Each chapter follows a similar structure, ending with a summary and conclusions section to draw together the main points in an easy-to-remember format. I have put the data sets used in the examples in the book up on the companion website, which you can find at www.palgrave.com/economics/gujarati.

I hope you enjoy my hands-on approach to learning and that this textbook will be a valuable companion to your further education in economics and related disciplines and your future career. I would welcome any feedback on the text; please contact me via my email address on the companion website.

# List of tables

Tables not included in this list may be found on the companion website. See Appendix 1 for details of these tables.

# List of figures

**I**

# The linear regression model

# 1

# The linear regression model: an overview

As noted in the Preface, one of the important tools of econometrics is the **linear regression model** (**LRM**). In this chapter we discuss the general nature of the LRM and provide the background that will be used to illustrate the various examples discussed in this book. We do not provide proofs, for they can be found in many textbooks.[1]

## 1.1 The linear regression model

The LRM in its general form may be written as:

$$Y_i = B_1 + B_2 X_{2i} + B_3 X_{3i} + \ldots + B_k X_{ki} + u_i \tag{1.1}$$

The variable $Y$ is known as the dependent variable, or **regressand**, and the $X$ variables are known as the explanatory variables, predictors, covariates, or **regressors**, and $u$ is known as a random, or stochastic, error term. The subscript $i$ denotes the $i$th observation. For ease of exposition, we will write Eq. (1.1) as:

$$Y_i = BX + u_i \tag{1.2}$$

where $BX$ is a short form for $B_1 + B_2 X_{2i} + B_3 X_{3i} + \ldots + B_k X_{ki}$.

Equation (1.1), or its short form (1.2), is known as the **population or true model**. It consists of two components: (1) a **deterministic** component, $BX$, and (2) a **nonsystematic**, or **random** component, $u_i$. As shown below, $BX$ can be interpreted as the **conditional mean** of $Y_i$, $E(Y_i \mid X)$, conditional upon the given $X$ values.[2] Therefore, Eq. (1.2) states that an individual $Y_i$ value is equal to the mean value of the population of which he or she is a member plus or minus a random term. The concept of population is general and refers to a well-defined entity (people, firms, cities, states, countries, and so on) that is the focus of a statistical or econometric analysis.

For example, if $Y$ represents family expenditure on food and $X$ represents family income, Eq. (1.2) states that the food expenditure of an individual family is equal to the mean food expenditure of all the families with the same level of income, plus or minus

---

1  See, for example, Damodar N. Gujarati and Dawn C. Porter, *Basic Econometrics*, 5th edn, McGraw-Hill, New York, 2009 (henceforward, Gujarati/Porter text); Jeffrey M. Wooldridge, *Introductory Econometrics: A Modern Approach*, 4th edn, South-Western, USA, 2009; James H. Stock and Mark W. Watson, *Introduction to Econometrics*, 2nd edn, Pearson, Boston, 2007; and R. Carter Hill, William E. Griffiths and Guay C. Lim, *Principles of Econometrics*, 3rd edn, John Wiley & Sons, New York, 2008.

2  Recall from introductory statistics that the unconditional expected, or mean, value of $Y_i$ is denoted as $E(Y)$, but the conditional mean, conditional on given $X$, is denoted as $E(Y \mid X)$.

a random component that may vary from individual to individual and that may depend on several factors.

In Eq. (1.1) $B_1$ is known as the intercept and $B_2$ to $B_k$ are known as the slope coefficients. Collectively, they are called **regression coefficients or regression parameters**. In regression analysis our primary objective is to explain the *mean*, or average, behavior of $Y$ in relation to the regressors, that is, how *mean* $Y$ responds to changes in the values of the $X$ variables. An individual $Y$ value will hover around its mean value.

*It should be emphasized that the causal relationship between Y and the Xs, if any, should be based on the relevant theory.*

Each slope coefficient measures the (partial) rate of change in the *mean value* of $Y$ for a unit change in the value of a regressor, holding the values of all other regressors constant, hence the adjective partial. How many regressors are included in the model depends on the nature of the problem and will vary from problem to problem.

The error term $u_i$ is a catchall for all those variables that cannot be introduced in the model for a variety of reasons. However, the average influence of these variables on the regressand is assumed to be negligible.

## The nature of the $Y$ variable

It is generally assumed that $Y$ is a random variable. It can be measured on four different scales: **ratio scale**, **interval scale**, **ordinal scale**, and **nominal scale**.

▲ **Ratio scale**: A ratio scale variable has three properties: (1) ratio of two variables, (2) distance between two variables, and (3) ordering of variables. On a ratio scale if, say, $Y$ takes two values, $Y_1$ and $Y_2$, the ratio $Y_1/Y_2$ and the distance $(Y_2 - Y_1)$ are meaningful quantities, as are comparisons or ordering such as $Y_2 \leq Y_1$ or $Y_2 \geq Y_1$. Most economic variables belong to this category. Thus we can talk about whether GDP is greater this year than the last year, or whether the ratio of GDP this year to the GDP last year is greater than or less than one.

▲ **Interval scale**: Interval scale variables do not satisfy the first property of ratio scale variables. For example, the distance between two time periods, say, 2007 and 2000 (2007 – 2000) is meaningful, but not the ratio 2007/2000.

▲ **Ordinal scale**: Variables on this scale satisfy the *ordering* property of the ratio scale, but not the other two properties. For examples, grading systems, such as A, B, C, or income classification, such as low income, middle income, and high income, are ordinal scale variables, but quantities such as grade A divided by grade B are not meaningful.

▲ **Nominal scale**: Variables in this category do not have any of the features of the ratio scale variables. Variables such as gender, marital status, and religion are nominal scale variables. Such variables are often called **dummy** or **categorical variables**. They are often "quantified" as 1 or 0, 1 indicating the presence of an attribute and 0 indicating its absence. Thus, we can "quantify" gender as male = 1 and female = 0, or vice versa.

Although most economic variables are measured on a ratio or interval scale, there are situations where ordinal scale and nominal scale variables need to be considered. That requires specialized econometric techniques that go beyond the standard LRM. We will have several examples in Part III of this book that will illustrate some of the specialized techniques.

## The nature of $X$ variables or regressors

The regressors can also be measured on any one of the scales we have just discussed, although in many applications the regressors are measured on ratio or interval scales. In the standard, or **classical linear regression model (CLRM)**, which we will discuss shortly, it is assumed that the regressors are *nonrandom*, in the sense that their values are fixed in repeated sampling. As a result, our regression analysis is *conditional*, that is, conditional on the given values of the regressors.

We can allow the regressors to be random like the $Y$ variable, but in that case care needs to be exercised in the interpretation of the results. We will illustrate this point in Chapter 7 and consider it in some depth in Chapter 19.

## The nature of the stochastic error term, $u$

The stochastic error term is a catchall that includes all those variables that cannot be readily quantified. It may represent variables that cannot be included in the model for lack of data availability, or errors of measurement in the data, or intrinsic randomness in human behavior. Whatever the source of the random term $u$, it is assumed that the *average* effect of the error term on the regressand is marginal at best. However, we will have more to say about this shortly.

## The nature of regression coefficients, the $B$s

In the CLRM it is assumed that the regression coefficients are some fixed numbers and not random, even though we do not know their actual values. It is the objective of regression analysis to estimate their values on the basis of sample data. A branch of statistics known as **Bayesian** statistics treats the regression coefficients as random. In this book we will not pursue the Bayesian approach to the linear regression models.[3]

## The meaning of linear regression

For our purpose the term "linear" in the linear regression model refers to *linearity in the regression coefficients*, the $B$s, and *not* linearity in the $Y$ and $X$ variables. For instance, the $Y$ and $X$ variables can be logarithmic (e.g. $\ln X_2$), or reciprocal ($1/X_3$) or raised to a power (e.g. $X_2^3$), where ln stands for natural logarithm, that is, logarithm to the base e.[4]

Linearity in the $B$ coefficients means that they are not raised to any power (e.g. $B_2^2$) or are divided by other coefficients (e.g. $B_2/B_3$) or transformed, such as $\ln B_4$. There are occasions where we may have to consider regression models that are not linear in the regression coefficients.[5]

---

3  Consult, for instance, Gary Koop, *Bayesian Econometrics*, John Wiley & Sons, West Sussex, England, 2003.

4  By contrast, logarithm to base 10 is called common log. But there is a fixed relationship between the common and natural logs, which is: $\ln_e X = 2.3026 \log_{10} X$.

5  Since this is a specialized topic requiring advanced mathematics, we will not cover it in this book. But for an accessible discussion, see Gujarati/Porter, *op cit.*, Chapter 14.

## 1.2     The nature and sources of data

To conduct regression analysis, we need data. There are generally three types of data that are available for analysis: (1) time series, (2) cross-sectional, and (3) pooled or panel (a special kind of pooled data).

### Time series data

A time series is a set of observations that a variable takes at different times, such as *daily* (e.g. stock prices, weather reports), *weekly* (e.g. money supply), *monthly* (e.g. the unemployment rate, the consumer price index CPI), *quarterly* (e.g. GDP), *annually* (e.g. government budgets), *quinquenially* or every five years (e.g. the census of manufactures), or *decennially* or every ten years (e.g. the census of population). Sometimes data are collected both quarterly and annually (e.g. GDP). So-called **high-frequency data** are collected over an extremely short period of time. In **flash trading** in stock and foreign exchange markets such high-frequency data have now become common.

Since successive observations in time series data may be correlated, they pose special problems for regressions involving time series data, particularly, the problem of **autocorrelation**. In Chapter 6 we will illustrate this problem with appropriate examples.

Time series data pose another problem, namely, that they may not be **stationary**. Loosely speaking, *a time series data set is stationary if its mean and variance do not vary systematically over time.* In Chapter 13 we examine the nature of stationary and nonstationary time series and show the special estimation problems created by the latter.

If we are dealing with time series data, we will denote the observation subscript by $t$ (e.g. $Y_t$, $X_t$).

### Cross-sectional data

Cross-sectional data are data on one or more variables collected at *the same point in time*. Examples are the census of population conducted by the Census Bureau, opinion polls conducted by various polling organizations, and temperature at a given time in several places, to name a few.

Like time series data, cross-section data have their particular problems, particularly the problem of **heterogeneity**. For example, if you collect data on wages in several firms in a given industry at the same point in time, heterogeneity arises because the data may contain small, medium, and large size firms with their individual characteristics. We show in Chapter 5 how the **size** or **scale effect** of heterogeneous units can be taken into account.

Cross-sectional data will be denoted by the subscript $i$ (e.g. $Y_i$, $X_i$).

### Panel, longitudinal or micro-panel data

Panel data combines features of both cross-section and time series data. For example, to estimate a production function we may have data on several firms (the cross-sectional aspect) over a period of time (the time series aspect). Panel data poses several challenges for regression analysis. In Chapter 17 we present examples of panel data regression models.

Panel observations will be denoted by the double subscript $it$ (e.g. $Y_{it}$, $X_{it}$).

### Sources of data

The success of any regression analysis depends on the availability of data. Data may be collected by a governmental agency (e.g. the Department of Treasury), an international agency (e.g. the International Monetary Fund (IMF) or the World Bank), a private organization (e.g. the Standard & Poor's Corporation), or individuals or private corporations.

These days the most potent source of data is the Internet. All one has to do is "Google" a topic and it is amazing how many sources one finds.

### *The quality of data*

The fact that we can find data in several places does not mean it is good data. One must check carefully the quality of the agency that collects the data, for very often the data contain errors of measurement, errors of omission or errors of rounding and so on. Sometime the data are available only at a highly aggregated level, which may not tell us much about the individual entities included in the aggregate. *The researchers should always keep in mind that the results of research are only as good as the quality of the data.*

Unfortunately, an individual researcher does not have the luxury of collecting data anew and has to depend on secondary sources. But every effort should be made to obtain reliable data.

## 1.3 Estimation of the linear regression model

Having obtained the data, the important question is: how do we estimate the LRM given in Eq. (1.1)? Suppose we want to estimate a wage function of a group of workers. To explain the hourly wage rate ($Y$), we may have data on variables such as gender, ethnicity, union status, education, work experience, and many others, which are the $X$ regressors. Further, suppose that we have a random sample of 1,000 workers. How then do we estimate Eq. (1.1)? The answer follows.

### The method of ordinary least squares (OLS)

A commonly used method to estimate the regression coefficients is the method of **ordinary least squares (OLS)**.[6] To explain this method, we rewrite Eq. (1.1) as follows:

$$u_i = Y_i - (B_1 + B_2 X_{2i} + B_3 X_{3i} + \ldots + B_k X_{ki})$$
$$= Y_i - \mathbf{BX} \tag{1.3}$$

Equation (1.3) states that the error term is the difference between the actual $Y$ value and the $Y$ value obtained from the regression model.

One way to obtain estimates of the $B$ coefficients would be to make the sum of the error term $u_i (=\Sigma u_i)$ as small as possible, ideally zero. For theoretical and practical reasons, the method of OLS does not minimize the sum of the error term, but minimizes the sum of the squared error term as follows:

---

6 OLS is a special case of the generalized least squares method (GLS). Even then OLS has many interesting properties, as discussed below. An alternative to OLS that is of general applicability is the **method of maximum likelihood (ML)**, which we discuss briefly in the Appendix to this chapter.

$$\sum u_i^2 = \sum (Y_i - B_1 - B_2 X_{2i} - B_3 X_{3i} - \ldots - B_k X_{ki})^2 \qquad (1.4)$$

where the sum is taken over all observations. We call $\sum u_i^2$ the **error sum of squares** (**ESS**).

Now in Eq. (1.4) we know the sample values of $Y_i$ and the Xs, but we do not know the values of the B coefficients. Therefore, to minimize the error sum of squares (ESS) we have to find those values of the $B$ coefficients that will make ESS as small as possible. Obviously, ESS is now a function of the $B$ coefficients.

The actual minimization of ESS involves calculus techniques. We take the (partial) derivative of ESS with respect to each $B$ coefficient, equate the resulting equations to zero, and solve these equations simultaneously to obtain the estimates of the $k$ regression coefficients.[7] Since we have $k$ regression coefficients, we will have to solve $k$ equations simultaneously. We need not solve these equations here, for software packages do that routinely.[8]

We will denote the estimated B coefficients with a lower case $b$, and therefore the estimating regression can be written as:

$$Y_i = b_1 + b_2 X_{2i} + b_3 X_{3i} + \ldots + b_k X_{ki} + e_i \qquad (1.5)$$

which may be called the **sample regression model**, the counterpart of the population model given in Eq. (1.1).

Letting

$$\hat{Y}_i = b_1 + b_2 X_{2i} + b_3 X_{3i} + \ldots + b_k X_{ki} = \boldsymbol{bX} \qquad (1.6)$$

we can write Eq. (1.5) as

$$Y_i = \hat{Y}_i + e_i = \boldsymbol{bX} + e_i \qquad (1.7)$$

where $\hat{Y}_i$ is an estimator of $\boldsymbol{BX}$. Just as $\boldsymbol{BX}$ (i.e. $E(Y|X)$) can be interpreted as the **population regression function** (**PRF**), we can interpret $\boldsymbol{bX}$ as the **sample regression function** (**SRF**).

We call the $b$ coefficients the **estimators** of the B coefficients and $e_i$, called the **residual**, an estimator of the error term $u_i$. *An estimator is a formula or rule that tells us how we go about finding the values of the regression parameters.* A numerical value taken by an estimator in a sample is known as an **estimate**. Notice carefully that the estimators, the $b$s, are *random variables*, for their values will change from sample to sample. On the other hand, the (population) regression coefficients or parameters, the Bs, are fixed numbers, although we do not what they are. On the basis of the sample we try to obtain the best guesses of them.

The distinction between population and sample regression function is important, for in most applications we may not be able to study the whole population for a variety of reasons, including cost considerations. It is remarkable that in Presidential elections in the USA, polls based on a random sample of, say, 1,000 people often come close to predicting the actual votes in the elections.

---

7  Those who know calculus will recall that to find the minimum or maximum of a function containing several variables, the *first-order condition* is to equate the derivatives of the function with respect to each variable equal to zero.

8  Mathematically inclined readers may consult Gujarati/Porter, *op cit.*, Chapter 2.

In regression analysis our objective is to draw inferences about the population regression function on the basis of the sample regression function, for in reality we rarely observe the population regression function; we only guess what it might be. This is important because our ultimate objective is to find out what the true values of the $B$s may be. For this we need a bit more theory, which is provided by the **classical linear regression model (CLRM)**, which we now discuss.

## 1.4　The classical linear regression model (CLRM)

The CLRM makes the following assumptions:

**A-1:** The regression model is *linear in the parameters* as in Eq. (1.1); it may or may not be linear in the variables $Y$ and the $X$s.

**A-2:** The regressors are assumed to be fixed or **nonstochastic** in the sense that their values are fixed in repeated sampling. This assumption may not be appropriate for all economic data, but as we will show in Chapters 7 and 19, if $X$ and $u$ are *independently distributed* the results based on the classical assumption discussed below hold true provided our analysis is conditional on the particular $X$ values drawn in the sample. However, if $X$ and $u$ are *uncorrelated*, the classical results hold true asymptotically (i.e. in large samples.)[9]

**A-3:** Given the values of the $X$ variables, the expected, or mean, value of the error term is zero. That is,[10]

$$E(u_i \mid X) = 0 \tag{1.8}$$

where, for brevity of expression, $X$ (the bold $X$) stands for all $X$ variables in the model. In words, the **conditional expectation** of the error term, given the values of the $X$ variables, is zero. Since the error term represents the influence of factors that may be essentially random, it makes sense to assume that their mean or average value is zero.

As a result of this *critical* assumption, we can write (1.2) as:

$$E(Y_i \mid X) = BX + E(u_i \mid X)$$
$$= BX \tag{1.9}$$

which can be interpreted as the model for *mean* or *average* value of $Y_i$ conditional on the $X$ values. **This is the population (mean) regression function (PRF)** mentioned earlier. In regression analysis our main objective is to estimate this function. If there is only one $X$ variable, you can visualize it as the (population) regression line. If there is more than one $X$ variable, you will have to imagine it to be a curve in a multi-dimensional graph. The estimated PRF, the sample counterpart of Eq. (1.9), is denoted by $\hat{Y}_i = bx$. That is, $\hat{Y}_i = bx$ is an estimator of $E(Y_i \mid X)$.

**A-4:** The variance of each $u_i$, given the values of $X$, is constant, or **homoscedastic** (*homo* means equal and *scedastic* means variance). That is,

$$\mathrm{var}(u_i \mid X) = \sigma^2 \tag{1.10}$$

---

**9** Note that independence implies no correlation, but no correlation does not necessarily imply independence.

**10** The vertical bar after $u_i$ is to remind us that the analysis is conditional on the given values of $X$.

*Note*: There is no subscript on $\sigma^2$.

**A-5**: There is no correlation between two error terms. That is, there is no **autocorrelation**. Symbolically,

$$\text{cov}(u_i, u_j \mid X) = 0 \quad i \neq j \tag{1.11}$$

where Cov stands for covariance and $i$ and $j$ are two different error terms. Of course, if $i$ = $j$, Eq. (1.11) will give the variance of $u_i$ given in Eq. (1.10).

**A-6**: There are no perfect linear relationships among the $X$ variables. This is the assumption of **no multicollinearity**. For example, relationships like $X_5 = 2X_3 + 4X_4$ are ruled out.

**A-7**: The regression model is *correctly specified*. Alternatively, there is no **specification bias** or **specification error** in the model used in empirical analysis. It is implicitly assumed that the number of observations, $n$, is greater than the number of parameters estimated.

Although it is not a part of the CLRM, it is assumed that the error term follows the **normal distribution** with zero mean and (constant) variance $\sigma^2$. Symbolically,

**A-8**:     $u_i \sim N(0, \sigma^2)$                                   (1.12)

On the basis of Assumptions A-1 to A-7, it can be shown that the method of **ordinary least squares (OLS)**, the method most popularly used in practice, provides estimators of the parameters of the PRF that have several *desirable statistical properties*, such as:

1  The **estimators are** *linear, that is, they are linear functions of the dependent variable Y.* **Linear estimators are easy to understand and deal with compared to nonlinear estimators.**

2  The **estimators are** *unbiased, that is, in repeated applications of the method, on average, the estimators are equal to their true values.*

3  In the class of linear unbiased estimators, OLS estimators have minimum variance. As a result, the true parameter values can be estimated with least possible uncertainty; an unbiased estimator with the least variance is called an *efficient estimator.*

In short, under the assumed conditions, OLS estimators are **BLUE: best linear unbiased estimators**. This is the essence of the well-known **Gauss–Markov theorem**, which provides a theoretical justification for the method of least squares.

With the added Assumption **A-8**, it can be shown that the OLS estimators are themselves normally distributed. As a result, we can draw inferences about the true values of the population regression coefficients and test statistical hypotheses. With the added assumption of normality, the OLS estimators are **best unbiased estimators (BUE)** in the entire class of unbiased estimators, whether linear or not. With normality assumption, CLRM is known as the **normal classical linear regression model (NCLRM)**.

Before proceeding further, several questions can be raised. How realistic are these assumptions? What happens if one or more of these assumptions are not satisfied? In that case, are there alternative estimators? Why do we confine to linear estimators only? All these questions will be answered as we move forward (see Part II). But it may be added that in the beginning of any field of enquiry we need some building blocks. The CLRM provides one such building block.

## 1.5   Variances and standard errors of OLS estimators

As noted before, the OLS estimators, the *b*s, are random variables, for their values will vary from sample to sample. Therefore we need a measure of their variability. In statistics the variability of a random variable is measured by its **variance** $\sigma^2$, or its square root, the **standard deviation** $\sigma$. In the regression context the standard deviation of an estimator is called the **standard error**, but conceptually it is similar to standard deviation. For the LRM, an estimate of the variance of the error term $u_i$, $\sigma^2$, is obtained as

$$\hat{\sigma}^2 = \frac{\Sigma e_i^2}{n-k} \tag{1.13}$$

that is, the residual sum of squares (**RSS**) divided by $(n-k)$, which is called the **degrees of freedom** (df), *n* being the sample size and *k* being the number of regression parameters estimated, an intercept and $(k-1)$ slope coefficients. $\hat{\sigma}$ is called the **standard error of the regression** (SER) or **root mean square**. It is simply the standard deviation of the *Y* values about the estimated regression line and is often used as a summary measure of "goodness of fit" of the estimated regression line (see Sec. 1.6). *Note that a "hat" or caret over a parameter denotes an estimator of that parameter.*

It is important to bear in mind that the standard deviation of *Y* values, denoted by $S_Y$, is expected to be greater than SER, unless the regression model does not explain much variation in the *Y* values.[11] If that is the case, there is no point in doing regression analysis, for in that case the *X* regressors have no impact on *Y*. Then the best estimate of *Y* is simply its mean value, $\overline{Y}$. Of course we use a regression model in the belief that the *X* variables included in the model will help us to better explain the behavior of *Y* that $\overline{Y}$ alone cannot.

Given the assumptions of the CLRM, we can easily derive the variances and standard errors of the *b* coefficients, but we will not present the actual formulas to compute them because statistical packages produce them easily, as we will show with an example.

### Probability distributions of OLS estimators

If we invoke Assumption A-8, $u_i \sim N(0, \sigma^2)$, it can be shown that each OLS estimator of regression coefficients is itself normally distributed with mean value equal to its corresponding population value and variance that involves $\sigma^2$ and the values of the *X* variables. In practice, $\sigma^2$ is replaced by its estimator $\hat{\sigma}^2$ given in Eq. (1.13). In practice, therefore, we use the *t* **probability distribution** rather than the normal distribution for statistical inference (i.e. hypothesis testing). But remember that as the sample size increases, the *t* distribution approaches the normal distribution. The knowledge that the OLS estimators are normally distributed is valuable in establishing confidence intervals and drawing inferences about the true values of the parameters. How this is done will be shown shortly.

---

**11**  The sample variance of *Y* is defined as: $S_Y^2 = \Sigma(Y_i - \overline{Y})^2/(n-1)$ where $\overline{Y}$ is the sample mean. The square root of the variance is the standard deviation of *Y*, $S_Y$.

## 1.6    Testing hypotheses about the true or population regression coefficients

Suppose we want to test the hypothesis that the (population) regression coefficient $B_k$ = 0. To test this hypothesis, we use the ***t* test** of statistics,[12] which is:

$$t = \frac{b_k}{se(b_k)}$$

where $se(b_k)$ is the standard error of $b_k$. This $t$ value has $(n - k)$ degrees of freedom (df); recall that associated with a $t$ statistic is its degrees of freedom. In the $k$ variable regression, df is equal to the number of observations minus the number of coefficients estimated.

Once the $t$ statistic is computed, we can look up the $t$ table to find out the probability of obtaining such a $t$ value or greater. If the probability of obtaining the computed $t$ value is small, say 5% or less, we can reject the null hypothesis that $B_k$ = 0. In that case we say that the estimated $t$ value is *statistically significant*, that is, *significantly different from zero*.

The commonly chosen probability values are 10%, 5%, and 1%. These values are known as the **levels of significance** (usually denoted by the Greek letter $\alpha$ (alpha) and also known as a Type I error), hence the name ***t* tests of significance.**

We need not do this labor manually as statistical packages provide the necessary output. These software packages not only give the estimated $t$ values, but also their $p$ (probability) values, which are the **exact level of significance** of the $t$ values. If a *p value* is computed, there is no need to use arbitrarily chosen $\alpha$ values. In practice, a low $p$ value suggests that the estimated coefficient is statistically significant.[13] This would suggest that the particular variable under consideration has a statistically significant impact on the regressand, holding all other regressor values constant.

Some software packages, such as *Excel* and *Stata*, also compute **confidence intervals** for individual regression coefficients – usually a 95% confidence interval (CI). Such intervals provide a range of values that has a 95% chance of including the true population value. 95% (or similar measure) is called the **confidence coefficient (CC)**, which is simply one minus the value of the level of significance, $\alpha$, times 100 – that is, CC = $100(1 - \alpha)$.

The $(1 - \alpha)$ confidence interval for any population coefficient $B_k$ is established as follows:

$$\Pr\left[b_k \pm t_{\alpha/2}\, se(b_k)\right] = (1 - \alpha) \qquad\qquad (1.14)$$

where Pr stands for probability and where $t_{\alpha/2}$ is the value of the $t$ statistic obtained from the $t$ distribution (table) for $\alpha/2$ level of significance with appropriate degrees of freedom, and $se(b_k)$ is the standard error of $b_k$. In other words, we subtract or add $t_{\alpha/2}$ times the standard error of $b_k$ to $b_k$ to obtain the $(1 - \alpha)$ confidence interval for true $B_k$.

---

**12**  If the true $\sigma^2$ is known, we can use the standard normal distribution to test the hypothesis. Since we estimate the true error variance by its estimator, $\hat{\sigma}^2$, statistical theory shows that we should use the $t$ distribution.

**13**  Some researchers choose $\alpha$ values and reject the null hypothesis if the *p value* is lower than the chosen $\alpha$ value.

$[b_k - t_{\alpha/2} se(b_k)]$ is called the **lower limit** and $[b_k + t_{\alpha/2} se(b_k)]$ is called the **upper limit** of the confidence interval. This is called the two-sided confidence interval.

Confidence intervals thus obtained need to be interpreted carefully. In particular note the following:

1  The interval in Eq. (1.14) does not say that the probability of the true $B_k$ lying between the given limits is $(1 - \alpha)$. Although we do not know what the actual value of $B_k$ is, it is assumed to be some fixed number.

2  The interval in Eq. (1.14) is a **random interval** – that is, it will vary from sample to sample because it is based on $b_k$, which is random.

3  Since the confidence interval is random, a probability statement such as Eq. (1.14) should be understood in the long-run sense – that is in repeated sampling: if, in repeated sampling, confidence intervals like Eq. (1.14) are constructed a large number of times on the $(1 - \alpha)$ probability basis, then in the long run, on average, such intervals will enclose in $(1 - \alpha)$ of the cases the true $B_k$. Any single interval based on a single sample may or may not contain the true $B_k$.

4  As noted, the interval in Eq. (1.14) is random. But once we have a specific sample and once we obtain a specific numerical value of $B_k$, the interval based on this value is not random but is fixed. So we cannot say that the probability is $(1 - \alpha)$ that the given fixed interval includes the true parameter. In this case $B_k$ either lies in this interval or it does not. Therefore the probability is 1 or 0.

We will illustrate all this with a numerical example discussed in Section 1.8.

Suppose we want to test the hypothesis that *all the slope coefficients in Eq. (1.1) are simultaneously equal to zero*. This is to say that all regressors in the model have no impact on the dependent variable. In short, the model is not helpful to explain the behavior of the regressand. This is known in the literature as the **overall significance of the regression**. This hypothesis is tested by the *F* test of statistics. Verbally the *F* statistic is defined as:

$$F = \frac{\text{ESS}/\text{df}}{\text{RSS}/\text{df}} \tag{1.15}$$

where ESS is the part of the variation in the dependent variable $Y$ explained by the model and RSS is the part of the variation in $Y$ not explained by the model. The sum of these is the total variation in $Y$, call the total sum of squares (**TSS**).

As Eq. (1.15) shows, the $F$ statistic has two sets of degrees of freedom, one for the numerator and one for the denominator. The denominator df is always $(n - k)$ – the number of observations minus the number of parameters estimated, including the intercept – and the numerator df is always $(k - 1)$ – that is, the total number of regressors in the model excluding the constant term, which is the total number of slope coefficients estimated.

The computed $F$ value can be tested for its significance by comparing it with the $F$ value from the $F$ tables. If the computed $F$ value is greater than its **critical** or **benchmark** *F value* at the chosen level of $\alpha$, we can reject the null hypothesis and conclude that at least one regressor is statistically significant. Like the $p$ value of the $t$ statistic, most software packages also present the $p$ value of the $F$ statistic. All this information can be gleaned from the **Analysis of Variance (AOV)** table that usually accompanies regression output; an example of this is presented shortly.

It is very important to note that the use of the $t$ and $F$ tests is explicitly based on the assumption that the error term, $u_i$, is normally distributed, as in Assumption A-8. If this assumption is not tenable, the $t$ and $F$ testing procedure is invalid in small samples, although they can still be used if the sample is sufficiently large (technically infinite), a point to which we will return in Chapter 7 on specification errors.

## 1.7  $R^2$: a measure of goodness of fit of the estimated regression

The **coefficient of determination**, denoted by $R^2$, is an overall measure of goodness of fit of the estimated regression line (or plane, if more than one regressor is involved), that is, it gives the proportion or percentage of the total variation in the dependent variable $Y$ (TSS) that is explained by all the regressors. To see how $R^2$ is computed, let us define:

$$\text{Total Sum of Squares (TSS)} = \Sigma y_i^2 = \Sigma(Y_i - \overline{Y})^2$$

$$\text{Explained Sum of Squares (ESS)} = \Sigma(\hat{Y}_i - \overline{Y})^2$$

$$\text{Residual Sum of Squares (RSS)} = \Sigma e_i^2$$

Now it can be shown that

$$\Sigma y_i^2 = \Sigma \hat{y}_i^2 + \Sigma e_i^2 \tag{1.16}[14]$$

This equation states that the total variation of the actual $Y$ values about their sample mean (TSS) is equal to sum of the total variation of the estimated $Y$ values about their mean value (which is the same as $\overline{Y}$) and the sum of residuals squared. In words,

$$\text{TSS} = \text{ESS} + \text{RSS} \tag{1.17}$$

Now we define $R^2$ as:

$$R^2 = \frac{\text{ESS}}{\text{TSS}} \tag{1.18}$$

Thus defined, the coefficient of determination is simply the proportion or percentage of the total variation in $Y$ explained by the regression model.

$R^2$ therefore lies between 0 and 1, *provided there is an intercept term in the model*. The closer it is to 1, the better is the fit, and the closer it is to 0, the worse is the fit. Remember that in regression analysis one of the objectives is to explain as much variation in the dependent variable as possible with the help of the regressors.

Alternatively, $R^2$ can also be defined as:

$$R^2 = 1 - \frac{\text{RSS}}{\text{TSS}} \tag{1.19}[15]$$

---

**14**  Hint: Start with $y_i = \hat{y}_i + e_i$, take the sum of square of this term on both sides and keep in mind that $\Sigma \hat{y}_i e_i = 0$ as a result of OLS estimation.

**15**  TSS = ESS + RSS. Therefore, 1=ESS/TSS + RSS/TSS. That is, $1 = R^2 - \text{RSS}/\text{TSS}$. Rearranging this, we get Eq. (1.19).

One disadvantage of $R^2$ is that it is an increasing function of the number of regressors. That is, if you add a variable to model, the $R^2$ values increases. So sometimes researchers pay the game of "maximizing" $R^2$, meaning the higher the $R^2$, the better the model.

To avoid this temptation, it is suggested that we use an $R^2$ measure that explicitly takes into account the number of regressors included in the model. Such an $R^2$ is called an **adjusted** $R^2$, denoted as $\overline{R}^2$ ($R$-bar squared), and is computed from the (unadjusted) $R^2$ as follows:

$$\overline{R}^2 = 1 - (1 - R^2)\frac{n-1}{n-k} \tag{1.20}$$

The term "adjusted" means adjusted for the degrees of freedom, which depend on the number of regressors ($k$) in the model.

Notice two features of $\overline{R}^2$:

1 If $k > 1$, $\overline{R}^2 < R^2$, that is, as the number of regressors in the model increases, the adjusted $R^2$ becomes increasingly smaller than the unadjusted $R^2$. Thus, $\overline{R}^2$ imposes a "penalty" for adding more regressors.

2 The unadjusted $R^2$ is always positive, but the adjusted $R^2$ can sometimes be negative.

Adjusted $R^2$ is often used to compare two or more regression models that have the same dependent variable. Of course, there are other measures of comparing regression models, which we will discuss in Chapter 7.

Having covered the basic theory underlying the CLRM, we now provide a concrete example illustrating the various points discussed above. This example is a prototype of multiple regression models.

## 1.8    An illustrative example: the determinants of hourly wages

The *Current Population Survey* (CPS), undertaken by the U.S. Census Bureau, periodically conducts a variety of surveys on a variety of topics. In this example we look at a cross-section of 1,289 persons interviewed in March 1995 to study the factors that determine hourly wage (in dollars) in this sample.[16] Keep in mind that these 1,289 observations are a sample from a much bigger population

The variables used in the analysis are defined as follows:

*Wage*: Hourly wage in dollars, which is the dependent variable.

The explanatory variables, or regressors, are as follows:

*Female*: Gender, coded 1 for female, 0 for male

*Nonwhite*: Race, coded 1 for nonwhite workers, 0 for white workers

*Union*: Union status, coded 1 if in a union job, 0 otherwise

*Education*: Education (in years)

---

16  The data used here are from the Current Population Survey which is obtained from the US Census Bureau. It also appears in Paul A. Ruud, *An Introduction to Classical Econometric Theory*, Oxford University Press, New York, 2000.

*Exper*: Potential work experience (in years), defined as age minus years of schooling minus 6. (It is assumed that schooling starts at age 6).

Although many other regressors could be added to the model, for now we will continue with these variables to illustrate a prototype multiple regression model.

Note that wage, education, and work experience are ratio scale variables and female, nonwhite, and union are nominal scale variables, which are coded as **dummy variables**. Also note that the data here are cross-section data. The data are given in **Table 1.1**, which can be found on the companion website.

In this book we will use the *Eviews* and *Stata* software packages to estimate the regression models. Although for a given data set they give similar results, there are some variations in the manner in which they present them. To familiarize the reader with these packages, in this chapter we will present results based on both these packages. In later chapters we may use one or both of these packages, but mostly *Eviews* because of its easy accessibility.[17]

Using *Eviews* 6, we obtained the results in Table 1.2.

**Table 1.2  Wage regression.**

Dependent Variable: WAGE
Method: Least Squares
Sample: 1 1289
Included observations: 1289

|  | Coefficient | Std. Error | t-Statistic | Prob. |
|---|---|---|---|---|
| C | −7.183338 | 1.015788 | −7.071691 | 0.0000 |
| FEMALE | −3.074875 | 0.364616 | −8.433184 | 0.0000 |
| NONWHITE | −1.565313 | 0.509188 | −3.074139 | 0.0022 |
| UNION | 1.095976 | 0.506078 | 2.165626 | 0.0305 |
| EDUCATION | 1.370301 | 0.065904 | 20.79231 | 0.0000 |
| EXPER | 0.166607 | 0.016048 | 10.38205 | 0.0000 |

| | | | |
|---|---|---|---|
| R-squared | 0.323339 | Mean dependent var | 12.36585 |
| Adjusted R-squared | 0.320702 | S.D. dependent var | 7.896350 |
| S.E. of regression | 6.508137 | Akaike info criterion | 6.588627 |
| Sum squared resid | 54342.54 | Schwarz criterion | 6.612653 |
| Log likelihood | −4240.370 | Durbin–Watson stat | 1.897513 |
| F-statistic | 122.6149 | Prob(F-statistic) | 0.000000 |

The format of *Eviews* is highly standardized. The *first* part of the table shows the name of the dependent variable, the estimation method (least squares), the number of observations, and the sample range. Sometimes we may not use all the sample observations, and save some observations, called **holdover observations**, for forecasting purposes.

The *second* part of the table gives the names of the explanatory variables, their estimated coefficients, the standard errors of the coefficients, the *t* statistic of each coeffi-

---

17  *Excel* can also estimate multiple regressions, but it is not as extensive as the other two packages.

cient, which is simply the ratio of estimated coefficient divided by its standard error,[18] and the $p$ value, or the **exact level of significance** of the $t$ statistic. For each coefficient, the null hypothesis is that the population value of that coefficient (the big $B$) is zero, that is, the particular regressor has no influence on the regressand, after holding the other regressor values constant.

The smaller the $p$ value, the greater the evidence against the null hypothesis. For example, take the variable experience, *Exper*. Its coefficient value of about 0.17 has a $t$ value of about 10.38. If the hypothesis is that the coefficient value of this variable in the PRF is zero, we can soundly reject that hypothesis because the $p$ value of obtaining such a $t$ value or higher is practically zero. In this situation we say that the coefficient of the experience variable is highly statistically significant, meaning that it is highly significantly different from zero. To put it differently, we can say work experience is an important determinant of hourly wage, after allowing for the influence of the other variables in the model – an unsurprising finding.

If we choose a $p$ value of 5%, Table 1.2 shows that each of the estimated coefficients is statistically significantly different from zero, that is, each is an important determinant of hourly wage.

The *third* part of Table 1.2 gives some descriptive statistics. The $R^2$ (the coefficient of determination) value of $\approx 0.32$ means about 32% of the variation in hourly wages is explained by the variation in the five explanatory variables. It might seem that this $R^2$ value is rather low, but keep in mind that we have 1,289 observations with varying values of the regressand and regressors. In such a diverse setting the $R^2$ values are typically low, and they are often low when individual-level data are analyzed. This part also gives the adjusted $R^2$ value, which is slightly lower than the unadjusted $R^2$ values, as noted before. Since we are not comparing our wage model with any other model, the adjusted $R^2$ is not of particular importance.

If we want to test the hypothesis that all the slope coefficients in the wage regression are simultaneously equal to zero, we use the $F$ test discussed previously. In the present example this $F$ value is $\approx 123$. This null hypothesis can be rejected if the $p$ value of the estimated $F$ value is very low. In our example, the $p$ value is practically zero, suggesting that we can strongly reject the hypothesis that collectively all the explanatory variables have no impact on the dependent variable, hourly wages here. At least one regressor has significant impact on the regressand.

The table also lists several other statistics, such as Akaike and Schwarz information criteria, which are used to choose among competing models, the Durbin–Watson statistic, which is a measure of correlation in the error term, and the **log likelihood statistic**, which is useful if we use the ML method (see the Appendix to this chapter). We will discuss the use of these statistics as we move along.[19]

Although *Eviews* does not do so, other software packages present a table known as the **Analysis of Variance (AOV) table**, but this table can be easily derived from the information provided in the third part of Table 1.2. However, *Stata* produces not only the coefficients, their standard errors, and the aforementioned information, but also

---

18    The implicit null hypothesis here is that the true population coefficient is zero. We can write the $t$ ratio as: $t = (b_k - B_k) / se(b_k)$, which reduces to $t = b_k / se(b_k)$ if $B_k$ is in fact zero. But you can test any other hypothesis for $B_k$ by putting that value in the preceding $t$ ratio.

19    *Eviews* also gives the Hannan–Quinn information criterion, which is somewhere between the Akaike and Schwarz information criteria.

**Table 1.3** *Stata* **output of the wage function.**

| w | Coef. | Std. Err. | t | P>\|t\| | [95% Conf. Interval] | |
|---|---|---|---|---|---|---|
| female | −3.074875 | .3646162 | −8.43 | 0.000 | −3.790185 | −2.359566 |
| nonwhite | −1.565313 | .5091875 | −3.07 | 0.002 | −2.564245 | −.5663817 |
| union | 1.095976 | .5060781 | 2.17 | 0.031 | .1031443 | 2.088807 |
| education | 1.370301 | .0659042 | 20.79 | 0.000 | 1.241009 | 1.499593 |
| experience | .1666065 | .0160476 | 10.38 | 0.000 | .1351242 | .1980889 |
| _cons | −7.183338 | 1.015788 | −7.07 | 0.000 | −9.176126 | −5.190551 |

*Note*: |t| means the absolute t value because t can be positive or negative.

the AOV table. It also gives the 95% confidence interval for each estimated coefficient, as shown in Table 1.3.

As you can see, there is not much difference between *Eviews* and *Stata* in the estimates of the regression coefficients. A unique feature of *Stata* is that it gives the 95% *confidence interval* for each coefficient, computed from Eq. (1.14). Consider, for example, the education variable. Although the single best estimate of the true education coefficient is 1.3703, the 95% confidence interval is (1.2410 to 1.4995). Therefore, we can say that we are 95% confident that the impact of an additional year of schooling on hourly earnings is at least $1.24 and at most $1.49, *ceteris paribus* (holding other things constant).

So, if you hypothesize that the true education coefficient is, say, 1.43, as noted earlier, we cannot say that 1.43 lies in this interval because this interval is fixed. Therefore, 1.43 either lies in this interval or does not. All we can say is that if we follow the procedure of establishing confidence intervals in the manner of Eq. (1.14) in repeated sampling we will be reasonably sure that the confidence interval includes the true $B_k$. Of course, we will be wrong 5% of the time.

### Impact on mean wage of a unit change in the value of a regressor

The female coefficient of $\approx -3.07$ means, holding all other variables constant, that the average female hourly wage is lower than the average male hourly wage by about 3 dollars. Similarly, *ceteris paribus*, the average hourly wages of a nonwhite worker is lower by about $1.56 than a white worker's wage. The education coefficient suggests that the average hourly wages increases by about $1.37 for every additional year of education, *ceteris paribus*. Similarly, for every additional year of work experience, the average hourly wage goes up by about 17 cents, *ceteris paribus*.

### Test of the overall significance of the regression

To test the hypothesis that all slope coefficients are simultaneously equal to zero (i.e. all the regressors have zero impact on hourly wage), *Stata* produced Table 1.4.

The AOV gives the breakdown of the **total sum of squares** (**TSS**) into two components: one explained by the model, called the **explained sum of squares** (**ESS**) – that is the sum of squares explained by the chosen model, and the other not explained by the model, called the **residual sum of squares** (**RSS**), terms we have encountered before.

Now each sum of squares has its associated degrees of freedom. The TSS has $(n-1)$ df, for we lose one df in computing the mean value of the dependent variable $Y$ from

**Table 1.4  The AOV table.**

| Source | SS | df | MS | |
|---|---|---|---|---|
| Model | 25967.2805 | 5 | 5193.45611 | Number of obs = 1289 |
| Residual | 54342.5442 | 1283 | 42.3558411 | F(5, 1283) = 122.61 |
| Total | 80309.8247 | 1288 | 62.3523484 | Prob > F = 0.0000 |
| | | | | R-squared = 0.3233 |
| | | | | Adj R-squared = 0.3207 |
| | | | | Root MSE = 6.5081 |

the same data. ESS has $(k-1)$ degrees of freedom, the $k$ regressors *excluding* the intercept term, and RSS has $(n-k)$ degrees of freedom, which is equal to the number of observations, $n$, minus the number of parameters estimated (including the intercept).

Now if you divide the ESS by its df and divide RSS by its df, you obtain the mean sums of squares (MS) of ESS and RSS. And if you take the ratio of the two MS, you obtain the $F$ value. It can be shown that under the null hypothesis all slope coefficients are simultaneously equal to zero, and assuming the error term $u_i$ is normally distributed, the computed $F$ value follows the $F$ distribution with numerator df of $(k-1)$ and denominator df of $(n-k)$.

In our example, this $F$ value is about 123, which is the same as that obtained from *Eviews* output. As the table shows, the probability of obtaining such an $F$ or greater is practically zero, suggesting that the null hypothesis can be rejected. There is at least one regressor that is significantly different from zero.

If the AOV table is not available, we can test the null hypothesis that all slope coefficients are simultaneously equal to zero, that is, $B_2 = B_3 = ... = B_k = 0$, by using an interesting relationship between $F$ and $R^2$, which is as follows:

$$F = \frac{R^2/(k-1)}{(1-R^2)/(n-k)} \tag{1.18}[20]$$

Since the $R^2$ value is produced by all software packages, it may be easier to use Eq. (1.18) to test the null hypothesis. For our example the computed $R^2$ is 0.3233. Using this value, we obtain:

$$F = \frac{0.3233/5}{(1-0.3233)/1283} \approx 122.60 \tag{1.19}$$

This value is about the same as that shown in the *Stata* AOV table.

It should be emphasized that the formula given in Eq. (1.18) is to be used only if we want to test that *all* explanatory variables have zero impact on the dependent variable.

As noted before, $R^2$ is the proportion of the variation in the dependent variable explained by the regressor included in the model. This can be verified if you take the ratio of ESS to TSS from the AOV table (= 25967.2805/80309.8247) = $R^2$ = 0.3233.

---

20  For proof, see Gujarati/Porter, *op cit.*, p. 241.

## 1.9    Forecasting

Sometimes we may want to use the estimated regression model for forecasting purposes. Return to our wage regression given in Table 1.2. Suppose we are given information about a prospective wage earner concerning his or her $X$ values. Given that information and the regression coefficients given in Table 1.2 we can easily calculate the expected (average) wage of this person. Whether that prospective wage earner will actually get the wages calculated from the regression in Table 1.2 cannot be told with certainty. All we can say is what a person with the given ($X$) characteristics might earn. This is the essence of forecasting.

Forecasting is generally used in the context of time series analysis. In Chapter 16 we will explore this topic more fully with illustrative examples.

## 1.10    The road ahead

Now that we have presented the basics of the CLRM, where do we go from here? The answer follows.

The wage regression given in Table 1.2 is based on the assumptions of the CLRM. The question that naturally arises is: how do we know that this model satisfies the assumptions of the CLRM? We need to know answers to the following questions:

1   The wage model given in Table 1.2 is linear in variables as well as parameters. Could the wage variable, for instance, be in logarithmic form? Could the variables for education and experience be also in logarithmic form? Since wages are not expected to grow linearly with experience forever, could we include experience squared as an additional regressor? All these questions pertain to the **functional form** of the regression model, and there are several of them. We consider this topic in Chapter 2.

2   Suppose some of the regressors are quantitative and some are qualitative or nominal scale variables, also called dummy variables. Are there special problems in dealing with dummy variables? How do we handle the interaction between quantitative and dummy variables in a given situation? In our wage regression we have three dummy variables, *female*, *nonwhite*, and *union*. Do female union workers earn more than non-union female workers? We will deal with this and other aspects of **qualitative regressors** in Chapter 3.

3   If we have several regressors in a regression model, how do we find out that we do not have the problem of **multicollinearity**? If we have that problem, what are the consequences? And how do we deal with them? We discuss this topic in Chapter 4.

4   In cross-sectional data the error variance may be **heteroscedastic** rather than homoscedastic. How do we find that out? And what are the consequences of heteroscedasticity? Are OLS estimators still BLUE? How do we correct for heteroscedasticity? We answer these questions in Chapter 5.

5   In time series data the assumption of no **autocorrelation** in the error term is unlikely to be fulfilled. How do we find that out? What are the consequences of

autocorrelation? How do we correct for autocorrelation? We will answer these questions in Chapter 6.

6   One of the assumptions of the CLRM is that the model used in empirical analysis is "correctly specified" in the sense that all relevant variables are included in the model, no superfluous variables are included in the model, the probability distribution of the error term is correctly specified, and there are no errors of measurement in the regressors and regressand. Obviously, this is a tall order. But it is important that we find out the consequences of one or more of these situations if they are suspected in a concrete application. We discuss the **problem of model specification** in some detail in Chapter 7. We also discuss briefly in this chapter the case of stochastic regressors instead of fixed regressors, as assumed in the CLRM.

7   Suppose the dependent variable is not a ratio or interval scale variable but is a nominal scale variable, taking values of 1 and 0. Can we still apply the usual OLS techniques to estimate such models? If not, what are the alternatives? The answer to these questions can be found in Chapter 8, where we discuss the **logit** and **probit** models, which can handle a nominal dependent variable.

8   Chapter 9 extends the bivariate logit and probit models to multi-category nominal scale variables, where the regressand has more than two nominal values. For example, consider the means of transportation to work. Suppose we have three choices: private car, public bus, or train. How do we decide among these choices? Can we still use OLS? As we will show in this chapter, such problems require non-linear estimation techniques. **Multinomial conditional logit or multinomial probit models** discussed in this chapter show how multi-category nominal scale variables can be modeled.

9   Although nominal scale variables cannot be readily quantified, they can sometimes be ordered or ranked. **Ordered logit** and **ordered probit models**, discussed in Chapter 10, show how ordered or ranked models can be estimated.

10  Sometimes the regressand is restricted in the values it takes because of the design of the problem under study. Suppose we want to study expenditure on housing by families making income under $50,000 a year. Obviously, this excludes families with income over this limit. The **censored sample** and **truncated sample modeling** discussed in Chapter 11 show how we can model phenomena such as this.

11  Occasionally we come across data that is of the *count type*, such as the number of visits to a doctor, the number of patents received by a firm, the number customers passing through a check-out counter in a span of 15 minutes, and so on. To model such count data, the **Poisson probability distribution (PPD)** is often used. Because the assumption underlying the PPD may not always be fulfilled, we will discuss briefly an alternative model, knows as the **negative binomial distribution (NBD)**. We discuss these topics in Chapter 12.

12  In cases of time series data, an underlying assumption of the CLRM is that the time series are **stationary**. If that is not the case, is the usual OLS methodology still applicable? What are the alternatives? We discuss this topic in Chapter 13.

13  Although heteroscedasticity is generally associated with cross-sectional data, it can also arise in time series data in the so-called **volatility** clustering phenomenon

observed in financial time series. The **ARCH** and **GARCH** models discussed in Chapter 14 will show how we model volatility clustering.

14 If you regress a nonstationary time series on one or more nonstationary time series, it might lead to the so-called **spurious** or **nonsense regression phenomenon**. However, if there is a stable long-term relationship between variables, that is if the variables are **cointegrated**, there need not be spurious regression. In Chapter 15 we show how we find this out and what happens if the variables are not cointegrated.

15 Forecasting is a specialized field in time series econometrics. In Chapter 16 we discuss the topic of economic forecasting using the LRM as well as two prominently used methods of forecasting, namely, **ARIMA** (autoregressive integrated moving average) and **VAR** (vector autoregression). With examples, we show how these models work.

16 The models discussed in the preceding chapters dealt with cross-sectional or time series data. Chapter 17 deals with models that combine cross-sectional and time series data. These models are known as **panel data regression models**. We show in this chapter how such models are estimated and interpreted.

17 In Chapter 18 we discuss the topic of **duration or survival analysis**. Duration of a marriage, duration of a strike, duration of an illness, and duration of unemployment are some examples of duration data.

18 In Chapter 19, the final chapter, we discusses a topic that has received considerable attention in the literature, namely, the method of **Instrumental Variables (IV)**. The bulk of this book has been devoted to the case of nonstochastic or fixed regressors, but there are situations where we have to consider stochastic, or random, regressors. If the stochastic regressors are correlated with the error term, the OLS estimators are not only biased but are also inconsistent – that is, the bias does not diminish no matter how large the sample. The basic principle of IV is that it replaces the stochastic regressors with another set of regressors, called **instrumental variables** (or simply **instruments**), that are correlated with the stochastic regressors but are uncorrelated with the error term. As a result, we can obtain consistent estimates of the regression parameters. In this chapter we show how this can be accomplished.

In the remainder of the book, we will discuss all these topics with concrete examples. Of course, the list of topics discussed does not by any means exhaust all the econometric techniques, which are continuously evolving. But I hope the topics and examples discussed in this book will provide beginning students and researchers a broad exposure to the commonly used econometric techniques. I further hope that the examples discussed in the book will whet the reader's appetite to study more advanced econometric techniques.

## Exercise

1.1   Consider the regression results given in Table 1.2.

(*a*)   Suppose you want to test the hypothesis that the true or population regression coefficient of the education variable is 1. How would you test this hypothesis? Show the necessary calculations.

(b) Would you reject or not reject the hypothesis that the true union regression coefficient is 1?

(c) Can you take the logs of the nominal variables, such as gender, race, and union status? Why or why not?

(d) What other variables are missing from the model?

(e) Would you run separate wage regressions for white and nonwhite workers, male and female workers, and union and non-union workers? And how would you compare them?

(f) Some states have right-to-work laws (i.e. union membership is not mandatory) and some do not have such laws (i.e. mandatory union membership is permitted). Is it worth adding a dummy variable taking the value of 1 if the right-to-work laws are present and 0 otherwise? A priori, what would you expect if this variable is added to the model?

(h) Would you add the age of the worker as an explanatory variable to the model? Why or why not?

## Appendix

# The method of maximum likelihood (ML)

As noted earlier, an alternative to OLS is the method of maximum likelihood (ML). This method is especially useful in estimating the parameters of nonlinear (in parameter) regression models, such as the logit, probit, multinomial logit, and multinomial probit models. We will encounter ML in the chapters where we discuss these models.

To minimize the algebra, we consider a two-variable regression model:

$$Y_i = B_1 + B_2 X_i + u_i \tag{1}$$

where

$$u_i \sim IIDN(0, \sigma^2) \tag{2}$$

That is, the error term is *independently and identically distributed as a normal distribution* with zero mean and constant variance (i.e. standard normal distribution).

Since $B_1$ and $B_2$ are constants and $X$ is assumed to be fixed in repeated sampling, Eq. (2) implies:

$$Y_i \sim IIDN(B_1 + B_2 X_i, \sigma^2) \tag{3}[21]$$

that is, $Y_i$ is also independently and identically distributed as a normal distribution with the stated parameters. Therefore we can write

$$f(Y_i) = \frac{1}{\sigma\sqrt{2\pi}} \exp\left[-\frac{1}{2\sigma^2}(Y_i - B_1 - B_2 X_i)^2\right] \tag{4}$$

---

[21] Recall from introductory statistics that the density of a random normal variable $X$ with mean $\mu$ and variance $\sigma^2$ is

$$f(X) = \frac{1}{\sigma\sqrt{2\pi}} \exp\left[-\frac{1}{2\sigma^2}(X - \mu)^2\right], \quad -\infty < X < \infty, \ \sigma^2 > 0.$$

which is the density function of a normally distributed $Y_i$ with mean and variance given in Eq. (3). Note: exp means e raised to the power of the expression in the curly brackets, e being the base of the natural logarithm.

Since each $Y_i$ is distributed as in Eq. (4), the joint density (i.e. joint probability) of the $Y$ observations can be written as the product of $n$ such terms, one for each $Y_i$. This product gives:

$$f(Y_1, Y_2, \ldots Y_n) = \frac{1}{\sigma^n (\sqrt{2\pi})^n} \exp\left[ -\frac{1}{2} \sum \frac{(Y_i - B_1 - B_2 X_i)^2}{\sigma^2} \right] \qquad (5)$$

If $Y_1, Y_2, \ldots, Y_n$ are given or known but $B_1, B_2$, and $\sigma^2$ are unknown, the function in Eq. (5) is called a **likelihood function**, denoted by LF.

The **method of maximum likelihood**, as the name suggests, consists of estimating the unknown parameters in such a way that the probability of observing the sample $Y$s is the maximum possible. Therefore, we have to find the maximum of Eq. (5). It is easy to find the maximum if we take the logarithm of this function on both sides to yield:

$$-\frac{n}{2} \ln \sigma^2 - \frac{n}{2} \ln(2\pi) - \frac{1}{2} \sum \frac{(Y_i - B_1 - B_2 X_i)^2}{\sigma^2} \qquad (6)$$

Since the last term in Eq. (6) enters negatively, to maximize (6) we have to minimize this last term. Apart from $\sigma^2$, this term is nothing but the squared error term of OLS. If you differentiate the last term with respect to the intercept and slope coefficient, you will find that the estimators of $B_1$ and $B_2$ are the same as the least squares estimators discussed in the text.

There is, however, a difference in the estimator of $\sigma^2$. It can be shown that this estimator is:

$$\hat{\sigma}^2_{ML} = \frac{\sum e_i^2}{n} \qquad (7)$$

whereas the OLS estimator is:

$$\hat{\sigma}^2 = \frac{\sum e_i^2}{n - k} \qquad (8)$$

In other words, the ML estimator of the unknown variance is not adjusted for the degrees of freedom, whereas the OLS estimator is. In large samples, however, the two estimators give about the same value, although in small sample the ML estimator is a biased estimator of the true error variance.

If you look at the regression results of our wage example given in Table 1.2, you will see the ln LF value is −4240.37. This is the maximized value of the log likelihood function. If you take the anti-log of this value, you will see it to be close to zero. Also note that the values of all the regression coefficients given in that table are also ML estimates under the assumption that the error term is normally distributed.

So, for all practical purposes, the OLS and ML estimates of the regression coefficients are the same, assuming the error term is normally distributed. That is why it is important to find out if the error term is in fact normally distributed in any application. We will discuss this topic further in Chapter 7.

The ML estimators have many desirable large sample properties: (1) they are asymptotically unbiased; (2) they are consistent; (3) they are asymptotically efficient – that is, in large samples they have the smallest variance among all consistent estimators; and (4) they are asymptotically normally distributed.

Keep in mind the distinction between an unbiased estimator and a consistent estimator. Unbiasedness is a property of repeated sampling: keeping the sample size fixed, we draw several samples and from each sample we obtain an estimate of the unknown parameter. If the average value of all these estimates is equal to the true value of the parameter, then that estimator (or that method of estimation) produces an unbiased estimator.

An estimator is said to be consistent if it approaches the true value of the parameter as the sample size gets larger and larger.

As noted previously, in OLS we use $R^2$ as a measure of goodness of fit of the estimated regression line. The equivalent of $R^2$ in the ML method is the **pseudo $R^2$**, which is defined as:[22]

$$\text{pseudo-}R^2 = 1 - \frac{lfL}{lfL_0} \tag{9}$$

where $lfL$ is the log likelihood of the model under consideration and $lfL_0$ is the log likelihood without any regressors in the model (except the intercept). The pseudo-$R^2$ thus measures the proportion by which $lfL$ is smaller (in absolute size) than $lfL_0$.

Since likelihood represents joint probability, it must lie between 0 and 1. Therefore the value of $lfL$ must be negative, as in our illustrative example.

In OLS we test the overall significance of the regression model by the $F$ test. The equivalent test under ML is the **likelihood ratio statistic** $\lambda$.

This is defined as:

$$\lambda = 2(lfL - lfL_0) \tag{10}$$

Under the null hypothesis that the coefficients of all regressors are jointly equal to zero, this statistic is distributed as a $\chi^2$ (chi-square) distribution with $(k-1)$ df, where $(k-1)$ is the number of regressors. As with other tests of significance, if the computed chi-square value exceeds the critical chi-square value at the chosen level of significance, we reject the null hypothesis.

---

22 The following discussion follows Christopher Dougherty, *Introduction to Econometrics*, 3rd edn, Oxford University Press, Oxford, 2007, pp. 320–1.

# 2

# Functional forms of regression models

You will recall that our concern in this book is primarily with linear regression models, that is, models linear in parameters; they may or may not be linear in variables. In this chapter we consider several models that are linear in parameters but are not necessarily so in the variables. In particular, we will discuss the following models, which are frequently used in empirical analysis.

1  Log-linear or double-log models where the regressand as well as the regressors are all in logarithmic form.

2  Log-lin models in which the regressand is logarithmic but the regressors can be in log or linear form.

3  Lin-log models in which the regressand is in linear form, but one or more regressors are in log form.

4  Reciprocal models in which the regressors are in inverse form.

5  Standardized variable regression models

We will use several examples to illustrate the various models.

## 2.1    Log-linear, double log or constant elasticity models

We consider the celebrated Cobb–Douglas (CD) production function, which may be expressed as:[1]

$$Q_i = B_1 L_i^{B_2} K_i^{B_3} \tag{2.1}$$

where $Q$ = output, $L$ = labor input, $K$ = capital, and $B_1$ is a constant.

This model is nonlinear in the parameters and to estimate it as it stands requires nonlinear estimation techniques. However, if we take the logarithm of this function, we obtain

$$\ln Q_i = \ln B_1 + B_2 \ln L_i + B_3 \ln K_i \tag{2.2}$$

where ln denotes natural logarithm.

Writing $\ln B_1 = A$, we can write Eq. (2.2) as:

$$\ln Q_i = A + B_2 \ln L_i + B_3 \ln K_i \tag{2.3}$$

---

1  See any microeconomics textbook for the history and details of the Cobb–Douglas production function.

Equation (2.3) is linear in the parameters $A$, $B_2$, and $B_3$ and is therefore a linear equation, although it is nonlinear in the variables $Q$, $L$, and $K$.[2]

Adding the error term $u_i$ to Eq. (2.3), we obtain the following LRM:

$$\ln Q_i = A + B_2 \ln L_i + B_3 \ln K_i + u_i \tag{2.4}$$

Equation (2.4) is known as a **log-log**, **double-log**, **log-linear**, or **constant elasticity model**, because both the regressand and regressors are in the log form.

An interesting feature of the log-linear model is that the slope coefficients can be interpreted as elasticities.[3] Specifically, $B_2$ is the (partial) elasticity of output with respect to the labor input, holding all other variables constant (here capital, or $K$). That is, it gives the percentage change in output for a percentage change in the labor input, *ceteris paribus*.[4] Similarly, $B_3$ gives the (partial) elasticity of output with respect to the capital input, holding all other inputs constant. Since these elasticities are constant over the range of observations, the double-log model is also known as constant elasticity model.

An advantage of elasticities is that they are *pure* numbers, that is, devoid of units in which the variables are measured, such as dollars, person-hours, or capital-hours, because they are ratios of percentage changes.

Another interesting property of the CD function is that the sum of the partial slope coefficients, $(B_2 + B_3)$, gives information about **returns to scale**, that is, the response of output to a proportional change in the inputs. If this sum is 1, then there are **constant returns to scale** – that is, doubling the inputs will double the output, tripling the inputs will triple the output, and so on. If this sum is less than 1, then there are **decreasing returns to scale** – that is, doubling the inputs less than doubles the output. Finally, if this sum is greater than 1, there are **increasing returns to scale** – that is, doubling the inputs more than doubles the output.

Before presenting a concrete example, it should be noted that in a log-linear regression model involving several variables, the slope coefficient of each regressor gives the partial elasticity of the dependent variable with respect to that variable, holding all other variables constant.

## The Cobb–Douglas production function for the USA

To illustrate the CD function, we present in **Table 2.1** data on output (as measured by value added, in thousands of dollars), labor input (worker hours, in thousands), and capital input (capital expenditure, in thousands of dollars) for the US manufacturing sector. The data is cross-sectional, covering 50 states and Washington, DC, for the year 2005. The table can be found on the companion website.

The OLS regression results are given in Table 2.2.

---

2  Note that $A = \ln B_1$. Therefore, $B_1 = $ anti-log $(A)$, which is nonlinear. However, in most applications the intercept may not have any viable economic interpretation.

3  An elasticity is simply the ratio of the percentage change in one variable divided by the percentage in another variable. For example, if $Q$ is quantity and $P$ is price, then the percentage change in quantity divided by the percentage in price is called the price elasticity.

4  That is,

$$B_2 = \frac{\partial \ln Q}{\partial \ln L} = \frac{\partial Q / Q}{\partial L / L} = \frac{\partial Q}{\partial L} \cdot \frac{L}{Q},$$

where we are using the curly $d$ to indicate that we are taking the partial derivative.

**Table 2.2  Cobb–Douglas function for USA, 2005.**

Dependent Variable: LOUTPUT
Method: Least Squares
Sample: 1 51
Included observations: 51

|  | Coefficient | Std. Error | t-Statistic | Prob. |
|---|---|---|---|---|
| C | 3.887600 | 0.396228 | 9.811514 | 0.0000 |
| lnLABOR | 0.468332 | 0.098926 | 4.734170 | 0.0000 |
| lnCAPITAL | 0.521279 | 0.096887 | 5.380274 | 0.0000 |

| | | | | |
|---|---|---|---|---|
| R-squared | 0.964175 | Mean dependent var | 16.94139 |
| Adjusted R-squared | 0.962683 | S.D. dependent var | 1.380870 |
| S.E. of regression | 0.266752 | Akaike info criterion | 0.252028 |
| Sum squared resid | 3.415520 | Schwarz criterion | 0.365665 |
| Log likelihood | −3.426721 | Durbin–Watson stat | 1.946387 |
| F-statistic | 645.9311 | Prob(F-statistic) | 0.000000 |

*Note*: L stands for the log of.

## Interpretation of the results

The first point to notice is that all the regression coefficients (i.e. elasticities) are individually statistically highly significant, for their $p$ values are quite low. Secondly, on the basis of the $F$ statistic we can also conclude that collectively the two factor inputs, labor and capital, are highly statistically significant, because its $p$ value is also very low. The $R^2$ value of 0.96 is also quite high, which is unusual for cross-sectional data involving heterogeneous states. The Akaike and Schwarz criteria are alternatives to $R^2$, which are further discussed later in the chapter. The Durbin–Watson statistic, although routinely produced by *Eviews*, may not always be useful in cross-sectional data, although sometimes it is an indication of model specification errors, as we will show in Chapter 7 on specification errors.

The interpretation of the coefficient of lnLABOR of about 0.47 is that if we increase the labor input by 1%, on average, output goes up by about 0.47 %, holding the capital input constant. Similarly, holding the labor input constant, if we increase the capital input by 1%, on average, the output increases by about 0.52 %. Relatively speaking, it seems a percentage increase in the capital input contributes more towards the output than a percentage increase in the labor input.

The sum of the two slope coefficients is about 0.9896, which is close to 1. This would suggest that the US Cobb–Douglas production function was characterized by constant returns to scale in 2005.[5]

Incidentally, if you want to get back to the original production function given in Eq. (2.1), it is as follows:

$$Q_i = 48.79L^{0.47}K^{0.51} \qquad\qquad (2.5)$$

Note: 48.79 is approximately the anti-log of 3.8876.[6]

---

5  We will not discuss here the question of whether a production function for the USA as a whole is meaningful or not. There is a vast literature about this topic. Our main objective here is to illustrate the double-log model.

6  Remember that $A = \ln B_1$, therefore $B_1 = $ anti-log of $A$.

## Evaluation of the results

Although, judged by the usual statistical criteria, the results of the Cobb–Douglas production function given in Table 2.2 look impressive, we have to guard against the possibility of *heteroscedasticity*. This is because our "sample" consists of very diverse states, with diverse manufacturing sectors. Also, the physical size and population density varies from state to state. In Chapter 5, on heteroscedasticity, we will reconsider the Cobb–Douglas production function to see if we have the problem of heteroscedasticity.

In Chapter 7, on specification errors, we will also find out if the error term is normally distributed, for the $t$ and $F$ tests dependent critically on the normality assumption, especially if the sample size is small. In that chapter we will also consider if there is any specification error in the Cobb–Douglas production function used in our example.

Although the double-log specification of the Cobb–Douglas production function is standard in the literature, for comparative purposes we also present the results of the linear production function, namely,

$$\text{Output}_i = A_1 + A_2\text{Labor}_i + A_3\text{Capital}_i + u_i \tag{2.6}$$

The results of this regression are shown in Table 2.3.

The labor and capital coefficients in this regression are statistically highly significant. If labor input increases by a unit, the average output goes up by about 48 units, holding capital constant. Similarly, if capital input goes up by a unit, output, on average, goes up by about 10 units, *ceteris paribus*. Notice that the interpretations of the slope coefficients in the log-linear production function and those in the linear production function are different.

Which is a better model, the linear model or the log-linear one? Unfortunately, we cannot compare the two models directly, as the dependent variables in the two models are different. Also, we cannot compare the $R^2$ values of the two models, because to compare the $R^2$s of any two models the dependent variable must be the same in the two models. In Section 2.8 we will show how we can compare the linear and log-linear models.

**Table 2.3  Linear production function.**

Dependent Variable: OUTPUT
Method: Least Squares
Sample: 1 51
Included observations: 51

|        | Coefficient | Std. Error | t-Statistic | Prob.  |
|--------|-------------|------------|-------------|--------|
| C      | 233621.5    | 1250364.   | 0.186843    | 0.8526 |
| LABOR  | 47.98736    | 7.058245   | 6.798766    | 0.0000 |
| CAPITAL| 9.951890    | 0.978116   | 10.17455    | 0.0000 |

| | | | |
|---|---|---|---|
| R-squared | 0.981065 | Mean dependent var | 43217548 |
| Adjusted R-squared | 0.980276 | S.D. dependent var | 44863661 |
| S.E. of regression | 6300694. | Akaike info criterion | 34.20724 |
| Sum squared resid | 1.91E+15 | Schwarz criterion | 34.32088 |
| Log likelihood | −869.2846 | Durbin–Watson stat | 1.684519 |
| F-statistic | 1243.514 | Prob(F-statistic) | 0.000000 |

## 2.2    Testing validity of linear restrictions

The log-linear Cobb–Douglas production function fitted to the production data showed that the sum of the output–labor and output–capital elasticities is 0.9896, which is about 1. This would suggest that there were constant returns to scale. How do we test this explicitly?

If in fact $B_2 + B_3 = 1$, which is an example of a **linear restriction**, one way of testing for constant returns to scale is to incorporate this restriction directly into the estimating procedure. To see how this is done, we can write

$$B_2 = 1 - B_3 \qquad\qquad (2.7)^7$$

As a result, we can write the log-linear Cobb–Douglas production function as:

$$\ln Q_i = A + (1 - B_3)\ln L_i + B_3 \ln K_i + u_i \qquad\qquad (2.8)$$

Collecting terms, we can write Eq. (2.8) as:

$$\ln Q_i - \ln L_i = A + B_3 (\ln K_i - \ln L_i) + u_i \qquad\qquad (2.9)$$

Using the properties of logarithms, we can write this equation as:[8]

$$\ln\left(\frac{Q_i}{L_i}\right) = A + B_3 \ln\left(\frac{K_i}{L_i}\right) + u_i \qquad\qquad (2.10)$$

where $Q_i / L_i$ output–labor ratio, or labor productivity, and $K_i / L_i$ capital–labor ratio, two of the "great" ratios of economic development and growth.

In words, Eq. (2.10) states that labor productivity is a function of capital labor ratio. We call Eq. (2.10) the **restricted regression (RS)** and the original Eq. (2.4) the **unrestricted regression (URS)** for obvious reasons.

Once we estimate Eq. (2.10) by OLS, we can obtain the estimated value of $B_3$, from which we can easily obtain the value of $B_2$ because of the linear restriction ($B_2 + B_3 = 1$). How do we decide if the linear restriction is valid? To answer this question, we first present the results of the regression based on Eq. (2.10): Table 2.4.

These results suggest that if the capital–labor ratio goes up by 1%, labor productivity goes up by about ½%. In other words, the elasticity of labor productivity with respect to capital–labor ratio is ½, and this elasticity coefficient is highly significant. Note that the $R^2$ of about 0.38 is not directly comparable with the $R^2$ value of Table 2.2 because the dependent variables in the two models are different.

To test the validity of the linear regression, we first define:

$RSS_R$ = residual sum of squares from the restricted regression, Eq. (2.10)

$RSS_{UR}$ = residual sum of squares from the unrestricted regression, Eq. (2.4)

$m$ = number of linear restrictions (1 in the present example)

$k$ = number of parameters in the unrestricted regression (3 in the present example)

$n$ = number of observations (51 in the present example).

---

7   We can also express the linear restriction as $B_3 = 1 - B_2$.

8   Note that $\ln XY = \ln X + \ln Y$; $\ln(X/Y) = \ln X - \ln Y$; $\ln X^k = k \ln X$ (where $k$ is a constant), but note that $\ln (X + Y) \neq \ln X + \ln Y$.

**Table 2.4 Cobb–Douglas production function with linear restriction.**

Dependent Variable: LOG(OUTPUT/LABOR)
Method: Least Squares
Sample: 1 51
Included observations: 51

| Variable | Coefficient | Std. Error | t-Statistic | Prob. |
|---|---|---|---|---|
| C | 3.756242 | 0.185368 | 20.26372 | 0.0000 |
| LOG(CAPITAL/LABOR) | 0.523756 | 0.095812 | 5.466486 | 0.0000 |

| | | | |
|---|---|---|---|
| R-squared | 0.378823 | Mean dependent var | 4.749135 |
| Adjusted R-squared | 0.366146 | S.D. dependent var | 0.332104 |
| S.E. of regression | 0.264405 | Akaike info criterion | 0.215754 |
| Sum squared resid | 3.425582 | Schwarz criterion | 0.291512 |
| Log likelihood | −3.501732 | Prob(F-statistic) | 0.000002 |
| F-statistic | 29.88247 | Durbin–Watson stat | 1.93684 |

Now to test the validity of the linear restriction, we use a variant of the $F$ statistic discussed in Chapter 1.[9]

$$F = \frac{(RSS_R - RSS_{UR})/m}{RSS_{UR}/(n-k)} \sim F_{m,(n-k)} \qquad (2.11)$$

which follows the $F$ probability distribution of statistics, where $m$ and $(n-k)$ are the numerator and denominator degrees of freedom. It should be noted that $RSS_R$ is never smaller than $RSS_{UR}$, so the $F$ ratio is always nonnegative.

As usual, if the computed $F$ exceeds the critical $F$ value at the chosen level of significance and the appropriate degrees of freedom, we reject the null hypothesis; otherwise, we do not reject it.

From Table 2.2 we obtain $RSS_{UR} = 3.4155$, and from Table 2.4 we obtain $RSS_R = 3.4255$. We know that $m = 1$ and $n = 51$. Putting these values in Eq. (2.11), the reader will find that the estimated $F$ value is about 0.142. For 1 df in the numerator and 48 df in the denominator, this $F$ value is not significant; actually the $p$ value of obtaining such an $F$ (the exact level of significance) is about 0.29. Therefore the conclusion in the present example is that the estimated Cobb–Douglas production function in Table 2.2 probably exhibits constant returns to scale. So there is no harm in using the production function given in Eq. (2.10). *But it should be emphasized that the F testing procedure outlined above is valid only for linear restriction; it is not valid for testing nonlinear restriction(s), such as $B_2B_3 = 1$.*

## 2.3 Log-lin or growth models

A topic of great interest to economists, the government, the business sector, and policy makers is the rate of growth of key economic variables, such as GDP, money supply, population, employment, productivity and interest rates, to name a few.

---

9 For details, see Gujarati/Porter, *op cit.*, pp. 243–6.

To see how the growth rate of an economic variable can be measured, we proceed as follows. To be specific, suppose we want to measure the rate of growth of real GDP (i.e. GDP adjusted for inflation) for the USA for the period 1960–2007. For this purpose, suppose we use the following model:

$$RGDP_t = RGDP_{1960}(1+r)^t \qquad (2.12)$$

where $RGDP$ stands for real GDP, $r$ is the rate of growth, and $t$ is time measured chronologically.

Equation (2.12) is the well-known compound interest formula from basic finance. Taking the natural log of both sides of Equation (2.12), we obtain

$$\ln RGDP_t = \ln RGDP_{1960} + t \ln(1+r) \qquad (2.13)$$

Now letting $B_1 = \ln RGDP_{1960}$ and $B_2 = \ln(1 + r)$, we can write Equation (2.13) as

$$\ln RGDP_t = B_1 + B_2 t \qquad (2.14)$$

Adding the error term $u_t$ to (2.14), we obtain the following regression model:[10]

$$\ln RGDP_t = B_1 + B_2 t + u_t \qquad (2.15)$$

Equation (2.15) is like any other regression model; the only difference is that here the regressor is "time", which takes values of 1, 2, ..., 47.

Model (2.15) is called a **semilog model** because only one variable (in this case the regressand) appears in the logarithmic form, whereas the regressor (time here) is in the level or linear form. For descriptive purposes we can call (2.15) a **log-lin model**.

Equation (2.15) can be estimated by the usual OLS routine. But before we present the regression results, it may be noted that the slope coefficient $B_2$ in (2.14) measures *the constant proportional or relative change in the regressand for a given absolute change in the value of the regressor.* That is,

$$B_2 = \frac{\text{relative change in regressand}}{\text{absolute change in regressor}} \qquad (2.16)^{11}$$

In practice we multiply $B_2$ by 100 to compute the percentage change, or the **growth rate**; 100 times $B_2$ is also known as the **semi-elasticity** of the regressand with respect to the regressor.

## Regression results

Using the data on Real GDP for the USA for 1960–2007, we obtain the results given in Table 2.6. **Table 2.5**, containing the data, can be found on the companion website.

---

10  We add the error term to take into account the possibility that the compound interest formula may not hold exactly.

11  Readers familiar with calculus can differentiate Equation (2.15) with respect to $t$, to obtain: $d(\ln RGDP)/dt = B_2$. But $d(\ln RGDP)/dt = (1/RGDP)(d(RGDP)/dt)$, which is a relative change in $RGDP$.

**Table 2.6  Rate of growth of real GDP, USA, 1960–2007.**

Dependent Variable: LRGDP
Method: Least Squares
Sample: 1960 2007
Included observations: 48

|  | Coefficient | Std. Error | t-Statistic | Prob. |
|---|---|---|---|---|
| C | 7.875662 | 0.009759 | 807.0072 | 0.0000 |
| TIME | 0.031490 | 0.000347 | 90.81657 | 0.0000 |

| | | | | |
|---|---|---|---|---|
| R-squared | 0.994454 | Mean dependent var | 8.647156 |
| Adjusted R-squared | 0.994333 | S.D. dependent var | 0.442081 |
| S.E. of regression | 0.033280 | Akaike info criterion | −3.926969 |
| Sum squared resid | 0.050947 | Schwarz criterion | −3.849003 |
| Log likelihood | 96.24727 | Durbin–Watson stat | 0.347740 |
| F-statistic | 8247.650 | Prob(F-statistic) | 0.000000 |

### Interpretation of the results

These results show that over the period of 1960–2007 the USA's real GDP had been in-creasing at the rate of 3.15% per year. This growth rate is statistically significant, for the estimated $t$ value of about 90.82 is highly significant.

What is the interpretation of the intercept? If you take the anti-log of 7.8756, you will obtain anti-log (7.8756) = 2632.27, which is the beginning value of real GDP, that is, the value at the beginning of 1960, our starting point. The actual value of RGDP for 1960 was about \$2501.8 billion.

Figure 2.1 shows the scatter diagram of the log of real GDP and time and the fitted regression line:

*A technical note*: The coefficient $B_2$ gives the **instantaneous** (at a point in time) rate of growth and not the **compound** (over a period of time) rate of growth, $r$. But it is easy to compute the latter, noting that $B_2 = \ln(1 + r)$. Therefore, $r = $ anti-log$(B_2) - 1$. Now anti-log $(B_2) = 1.03199$. Therefore the compound rate of growth is 0.03199 or about

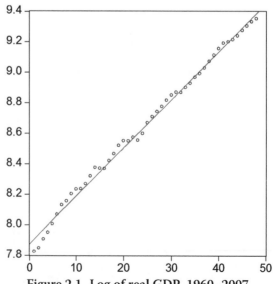

**Figure 2.1  Log of real GDP, 1960–2007.**

3.2%, which is slightly greater than the instantaneous rate of growth of about 3.1%. The difference is due to compounding.

## The linear trend model

Suppose that, instead of estimating the growth model (2.14), we estimate the following model:

$$RGDP_t = A_1 + A_2 time + u_t \qquad (2.17)$$

This is known as the **linear trend model** and the time variable is known as the **trend variable**. The slope coefficient $A_2$ in this model gives the absolute (*not* relative or percentage) change in RGDP per unit time period. If $A_2$ is positive, there is an **upward trend in** RGDP, but if it is negative, there is a **downward trend** in RGDP or any regressand.

Using the data given in **Table 2.5**, we obtain the results in Table 2.7.

These results show that over the period 1960–2007, real GDP in the USA increased by about $187 billion per year, showing an upward trend – not a surprising finding.

The choice between the growth model of (2.15) and the linear trend model of (2.17) is up to the individual researcher, although for comparing RGDP across regions or countries it is the relative growth that may be more relevant. Note that since the dependent variables in the log-linear and linear trend models are not the same, it is not appropriate to compare the two $R^2$ values in determining which model to choose. But more on this in Section 2.7.

Since we are dealing with time series data, the Durbin–Watson statistic, which is a measure of autocorrelation in the error term, is an important statistic. In Chapter 6 on autocorrelation we will see how we interpret this statistic. Suffice to note here that if there is no autocorrelation the value of the Durbin–Watson statistic is about 2;[12] the closer it is to zero, the greater the evidence of autocorrelation.

Table 2.7  Trend in Real US GDP, 1960–2007.

Dependent Variable: RGDP
Method: Least Squares
Sample: 1960 2007
Included observations: 48

|  | Coefficient | Std. Error | t-Statistic | Prob. |
| --- | --- | --- | --- | --- |
| C | 1664.218 | 131.9990 | 12.60781 | 0.0000 |
| TIME | 186.9939 | 4.689886 | 39.87174 | 0.0000 |

| | | | | |
| --- | --- | --- | --- |
| R-squared | 0.971878 | Mean dependent var | 6245.569 |
| Adjusted R-squared | 0.971267 | S.D. dependent var | 2655.520 |
| S.E. of regression | 450.1314 | Akaike info criterion | 15.09773 |
| Sum squared resid | 9320440. | Schwarz criterion | 15.17570 |
| Log likelihood | −360.3455 | Durbin–Watson stat | 0.069409 |
| F-statistic | 1589.756 | Prob(F-statistic) | 0.000000 |

---

12  As we will show in Chapter 6, this statistic is based on several assumptions.

## 2.4    Lin-log models

In the log-lin, or growth, models, we are interested in finding the percent growth in the regressand for a unit change in the regressor. What about measuring the absolute change in the regressand for a percentage change in the regressor? If that is the objective of analysis, we can estimate the following model:

$$Y_i = B_1 + B_2 \ln X_i + u_i \qquad (2.18)$$

We call Eq. (2.18) a **lin-log model**, for obvious reasons.

What does the slope coefficient $B_2$ tell us in this model? As we know, the slope coefficient gives the change in $Y$ for a unit change in the regressor. So,

$$B_2 = \frac{\text{Absolute change in } Y}{\text{Change in } \ln X} = \frac{\text{Absolute change in } Y}{\text{Relative change in } X} \qquad (2.19)$$

Remember that *a change in the log of a number is a relative change, or percentage change, after multiplication by 100.*

Letting $\Delta$ denote a small change, we can write (2.19) as

$$B_2 = \frac{\Delta Y}{\Delta X / X} \qquad (2.20)$$

Or,

$$\Delta Y = B_2 (\Delta X / X) \qquad (2.21)$$

Equation (2.21) states that the absolute change in $Y$ ($= \Delta Y$) is equal to slope times the relative change in $X$. Thus, if $(\Delta X / X)$ changes by 0.01 unit (or 1%), the absolute change in $Y$ is $0.01(B_2)$. If in an application one finds $B_2 = 200$, the absolute change in $Y$ is $(0.01)(200) = 2$.

Therefore, when we estimate an equation like (2.18), *do not forget to multiply the value of the estimated slope coefficient by 0.01 or (what amounts to the same thing) divide it by 100. If you do not follow this procedure, you may be drawing misleading conclusions from your results.*

The lin-log model has been used in **Engel expenditure functions**, named after the German statistician Ernst Engel (1821–1896). Engel postulated that "the total expenditure that is devoted to food tends to increase in arithmetic progression as total expenditure increases in geometric proportion".[13] Another way of expressing this is that the share of expenditure on food decreases as total expenditure increases.

To shed light on this, **Table 2.8** gives data on food and nonalcoholic beverages consumed at home (Expfood) and total household expenditure (Expend), both in dollars, for 869 US households in 1995.[14] This table can be found on the companion website.

Regression of the share of food expenditure (SFDHO) in total expenditure gives Table 2.9.

---

13  This quote is attributed to H. Working (1943) Statistical laws of family expenditure, *Journal of the American Statistical Association*, vol. 38, pp. 43–56.

14  This is a random sample from data collected for about 5,000 households in the Quarterly Interview Survey of the Consumer Expenditure Survey conducted by the US Department of Labor, Bureau of Labor Statistics. The data used here are discussed in Christopher Dougherty, *Introduction to Econometrics*, 3rd edn, Oxford University Press.

**Table 2.9  Lin-log model of expenditure on food.**

Dependent Variable: SFDHO
Method: Least Squares
Sample: 1 869
Included observations: 869

|  | Coefficient | Std. Error | t-Statistic | Prob. |
|---|---|---|---|---|
| C | 0.930387 | 0.036367 | 25.58359 | 0.0000 |
| LOG(EXPEND) | −0.077737 | 0.003591 | −21.64822 | 0.0000 |

| | | | |
|---|---|---|---|
| R-squared | 0.350876 | Mean dependent var | 0.144736 |
| Adjusted R-squared | 0.350127 | S.D. dependent var | 0.085283 |
| S.E. of regression | 0.068750 | Akaike info criterion | −2.514368 |
| Sum squared resid | 4.097984 | Schwarz criterion | −2.503396 |
| Log likelihood | 1094.493 | Durbin–Watson stat | 1.968386 |
| F-statistic | 468.6456 | Prob(F-statistic) | 0.000000 |

*Note*: SFDHO = share of expenditure on food and nonalcoholic beverages in the total expenditure and Expend = total household expenditure.

All the estimated coefficents are individually highly statistically significant. The interpretation of the slope coefficient of about −0.08 is that if total expenditure increases by 1%, on average, the share of expenditure on food and nonalcoholic beverages goes down by about 0.0008 units, thus supporting the Engel hypothesis. This can be seen more clearly in Figure 2.2. (*Note*: Do not forget to divide the slope coefficient by 100). Alternatively, the slope coefficient can be interpreted as: If total expenditure increases by 100%, on average, the share of expenditure on food and nonalcoholic beverages goes down by about 0.08 units.

Although we have fitted a lin-log model, Figure 2.2 shows that the relationship between SFDHO and log (EXPEND) seems nonlinear. There are methods of capturing

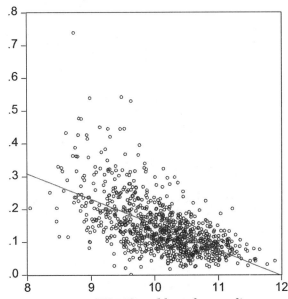

**Figure 2.2  SFDHO and log of expenditure.**

nonlinear relationships among variables, such as the reciprocal models or polynomial regression models, which we now discuss.

## 2.5 Reciprocal models

Sometimes we come across situations where the relationship between the regressand and regressor(s) is reciprocal or inverse, as in the following regression model:

$$Y_i = B_1 + B_2 \left( \frac{1}{X_i} \right) + u_i \tag{2.22}$$

This model is *nonlinear* in $X$ because it enters the model inversely or reciprocally, but it is an LRM because the parameters, the $B$s, are linear.

Some of the properties of this model are as follows. As $X$ increases indefinitely, the term $B_2(1/X_i)$ approaches zero (*note:* $B_2$ is a constant) and $Y$ approaches the limiting or asymptotic value $B_1$. The slope of Eq. (2.22) is given by

$$\frac{dY_i}{dX_i} = -B_2 \left( \frac{1}{X_i^2} \right).$$

Therefore, if $B_2$ is positive, the slope is negative throughout, and if $B_2$ is negative, the slope is positive throughout.

### Illustrative example: food expenditure revisited

In the previous section we fitted the lin-log model to food expenditure in relation to total expenditure. Let us see if the reciprocal model can also be fitted to the same data. So we estimate (Table 2.10)

$$\text{SFDHO} = B_1 + B_2 \left( \frac{1}{Expend_i} \right) + u_i \tag{2.23}$$

**Table 2.10  Reciprocal model of food expenditure.**

Dependent Variable: SFDHO
Method: Least Squares
Sample: 1 869
Included observations: 869

|  | Coefficient | Std. Error | t-Statistic | Prob. |
|---|---|---|---|---|
| C | 0.077263 | 0.004012 | 19.25950 | 0.0000 |
| 1/EXPEND | 1331.338 | 63.95713 | 20.81610 | 0.0000 |

| | | | |
|---|---|---|---|
| R-squared | 0.333236 | Mean dependent var | 0.144736 |
| Adjusted R-squared | 0.332467 | S.D. dependent var | 0.085283 |
| S.E. of regression | 0.069678 | Akaike info criterion | −2.487556 |
| Sum squared resid | 4.209346 | Schwarz criterion | −2.476584 |
| Log likelihood | 1082.843 | Durbin–Watson stat | 1.997990 |
| F-statistic | 433.3100 | Prob(F-statistic) | 0.000000 |

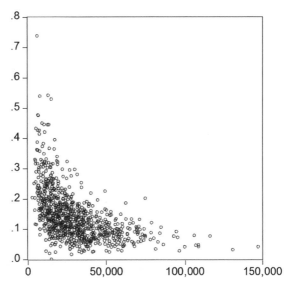

**Figure 2.3  Share of food expenditure in total expenditure.**

### Interpretation of the results

Both regression coefficients are statistically highly significant, for their $p$ values are practically zero. The intercept value of about 0.08 suggests that if total expenditure increases indefinitely, the share of food and nonalcoholic expenditure in total expenditure will eventually settle down to about 8%. The slope coefficient $B_2$ is positive, suggesting that the rate of change of SFDHO with respect to total expenditure will be negative throughout. This can be seen more vividly from Figure 2.3.

If you compare Figures 2.2 and 2.3, you will see that they are similar in appearance. The practical question is: which is a better model – lin-log or reciprocal?

This is a common problem in empirical work – the choice of the appropriate model. Since both models fit the data reasonably well, it is hard to choose between the two. On the basis of the $R^2$ criterion, the lin-log model gives a slightly higher value, but the difference in the two $R^2$s is not very large. *Incidentally note that we can compare the two $R^2$ values because the dependent variable in the two models is the same.*

## 2.6  Polynomial regression models

Let us revisit the linear trend model considered in Eq. (2.17) in which we regressed real GDP (RGDP) on the trend variable, *time*. Now consider the following model:

$$RGDP_t = A_1 + A_2 time + A_3 time^2 + u_t \qquad (2.24)$$

Equation (2.24) is an example of a **quadratic function**, or more generally, a **second-degree polynomial** in the variable *time*. If we had added $time^3$ to the model, it would have been a third-degree polynomial equation, the highest power of the regressor representing the degree of the polynomial.

The *first* point to note about Eq. (2.24) is that it is an LRM, that is, linear in the parameters, although the time variable enters the model linearly as well as quadratically. *Second*, the variables *time* and $time^2$ are functionally related and will be

Table 2.11  Polynomial model of US GDP, 1960–2007.

Dependent Variable: RGDP
Method: Least Squares
Sample: 1960 2007
Included observations: 48

|  | Coefficient | Std. Error | t-Statistic | Prob. |
|---|---|---|---|---|
| C | 2651.381 | 69.49085 | 38.15439 | 0.0000 |
| TIME | 68.53436 | 6.542115 | 10.47587 | 0.0000 |
| TIME^2 | 2.417542 | 0.129443 | 18.67647 | 0.0000 |

| | | | | |
|---|---|---|---|---|
| R-squared | 0.996787 | Mean dependent var | 6245.569 |
| Adjusted R-squared | 0.996644 | S.D. dependent var | 2655.520 |
| S.E. of regression | 153.8419 | Akaike info criterion | 12.97019 |
| Sum squared resid | 1065030. | Schwarz criterion | 13.08714 |
| Log likelihood | −308.2845 | Durbin–Watson stat | 0.462850 |
| F-statistic | 6979.430 | Prob(F-statistic) | 0.000000 |

highly correlated. Will this create the collinearity problem, which will violate one of the assumptions of the CLRM that there are no *exact linear* relationships among the regressors? No, because *time²* is a *non*linear function of time.

Using the data on RGDP, we obtained the results in Table 2.11.

First, notice that all the estimated coefficients are statistically significant, assuming the usual assumptions of the classical models hold. How do we interpret these results? In Eq. (2.17) with only the time variable as regressor, the coefficient of time was about 186.99, suggesting that RGDP was increasing by a *constant* amount of $186.99 billion per year.

But for the quadratic model RGDP is increasing at an increasing rate because both the coefficients of time and time-squared are positive. To see this differently, for the quadratic model given in Eq. (2.24), the rate of change of RGDP is given as

$$\frac{dRGDP}{dtime} = A_2 + 2A_3 time \qquad (2.25)$$

which is positive because both $A_2$ and $A_3$ are positive.

*Note*: The left-hand side of this equation is the derivative of RGDP with respect to time.

Using the results in Table 2.11, we obtain:

$$\frac{dRGDP}{dt} = 68.53 + 2(2.42) time \qquad (2.26)$$

$$= 68.53 + 4.84 time$$

As Eq. (2.26) shows, the rate of change of RGDP depends on the time at which the rate of change is measured. This is in strong contrast to the linear trend model, Eq. (2.17), which showed a constant rate of change of about $187 billion per year.[15]

---

15  If you take the second derivative of Eq. (2.24) with respect to time, you will obtain the value of 4.84. So it is the rate of change of the rate of change that is constant over time. (Note that the positive second derivative implies that the RGDP is increasing at an increasing rate.)

**Table 2.12  Polynomial model of log US GDP, 1960–2007.**

Dependent Variable: LRGDP
Method: Least Squares
Sample: 1960 2007
Included observations: 48

|  | Coefficient | Std. Error | t-Statistic | Prob. |
|---|---|---|---|---|
| C | 7.833480 | 0.012753 | 614.2239 | 0.0000 |
| TIME | 0.036551 | 0.001201 | 30.44292 | 0.0000 |
| TIME^2 | −0.000103 | 2.38E-05 | −4.348497 | 0.0001 |

| | | | | |
|---|---|---|---|---|
| R-squared | 0.996095 | Mean dependent var | 8.647157 | |
| Adjusted R-squared | 0.995921 | S.D. dependent var | 0.442081 | |
| S.E. of regression | 0.028234 | Akaike info criterion | −4.236106 | |
| Sum squared resid | 0.035873 | Schwarz criterion | −4.119156 | |
| Log likelihood | 104.6665 | Durbin–Watson stat | 0.471705 | |
| F-statistic | 5738.826 | Prob(F-statistic) | 0.000000 | |

## Log-lin model with quadratic trend variable

Suppose instead of estimating Eq. (2.24) that we estimate the following model:

$$\ln RGDP_t = B_1 + B_2 t + B_3 t^2 + u_t \tag{2.27}$$

The regression results of this model are shown in Table 2.12.

It is interesting to note that in Table 2.11 the trend and trend-squared coefficients are positive, whereas in Table 2.12 the trend coefficient is positive but the trend-squared term is negative. This suggests that although the rate of growth of RGDP is positive, it is increasing at a decreasing rate. To see this clearly, differentiating Eq. (2.27) with respect to time, we obtain (after suppressing the error term)

$$\frac{d\ln RGDP}{dt} = B_2 + 2B_3 t \tag{2.28}[16]$$

That is,

$$\frac{1}{RGDP}\frac{dRGDP}{t} = B_2 + 2B_3 t \tag{2.29}$$

But the left-hand side of this equation is the rate of growth of RGDP.

$$\text{Rate of growth of } RGDP = B_2 + 2B_3 t$$
$$= 0.0365 - 0.0002t \tag{2.30}$$

As Eq. (2.30) shows, the rate of growth of RGDP decreases at the rate of 0.0002 per unit of time.

Notice carefully that in Eq. (2.24) we are measuring *the rate of change in RGDP*, but in Eq. (2.27) we are measuring the *rate of growth in RGDP*. Dimensionally, these are different measures.

---

16  Recall that $d\ln Y / dX = (1/Y)dY / dX$, which is a relative change in $Y$. If it is multiplied by 100, it will become percentage change in $Y$ or the growth rate in $Y$. The point to keep in mind is that the change in the log of a variable is a relative change.

## 2.7    Choice of the functional form

The practical problem in doing empirical work is to decide on the functional form of the regression model that may be appropriate in a given situation. In the two-variable regression model this choice is very often not difficult because we can always plot the regressand and the (single) regressor and visually decide the functional form. But when it comes to the multiple regression models this choice is not easy, for it is difficult to draw a multi-dimensional plot.

In practice, therefore, we need to know the properties of the models we have discussed in this chapter. One way of accomplishing this is to consider the slope and the elasticity coefficients of the various models, which are summarized in Table 2.13.

If there is more than one regressor in the model, one can compute the partial slope and partial elasticity coefficients, holding other variables in the model constant.[17]

**Table 2.13  Summary of functional forms.**

| Model | Form | Slope $\left(\dfrac{dY}{dX}\right)$ | Elasticity $\left(\dfrac{dY}{dX}\right)\cdot\dfrac{X}{Y}$ |
|---|---|---|---|
| Linear | $Y = B_1 + B_2 X$ | $B_2$ | $B_2\left(\dfrac{X}{Y}\right)$* |
| Log-linear | $\ln Y = B_1 + B_2 \ln X$ | $B_2\left(\dfrac{Y}{X}\right)$ | $B_2$ |
| Log-lin | $\ln Y = B_1 + B_2 X$ | $B_2(Y)$ | $B_2(X)$* |
| Lin-log | $Y = B_1 + B_2 \ln X$ | $B_2\left(\dfrac{1}{X}\right)$ | $B_2\left(\dfrac{1}{Y}\right)$* |
| Reciprocal | $Y = B_1 + B_2\left(\dfrac{1}{X}\right)$ | $-B_2\left(\dfrac{1}{X^2}\right)$ | $-B_2\left(\dfrac{1}{XY}\right)$* |

*Note:* * indicates that the elasticity coefficient is variable, depending on the values taken by $X$ or $Y$ or both. If no $X$ and $Y$ are specified, these elasticities are often evaluated at the mean values of $X$ and $Y$, namely $\overline{X}$ and $\overline{Y}$.

## 2.8    Comparing linear and log-linear models

A frequently encountered problem in research is the choice between linear and log-linear models.[18] Consider our discussion about the production function for the US economy. Equation (2.4) is an example of a log-linear production function, the Cobb–Douglas function, whereas Eq. (2.6) is an example of a linear production function. Which is a better model for the data given in **Table 2.1**? We have already given the results of fitting these models in Tables 2.2 and 2.3, respectively.

On their own, both models fit the data well. But we cannot directly compare the two models, for the dependent variables in the two models are different. But a simple

---

17  For example, for the model $Y = B_1 + B_2 X + B_3 X^2$, the slope coefficient is $dY/dX = B_2 + 2B_3 X$ and the elasticity coefficient is $(dY/dX)(X/Y) = (B_2 + 2B_3 X)(X/Y)$ and this elasticity will depend on the values of $X$ and $Y$.

18  In the log-linear model the regressand is in log form, but the regressors could be in log form or linear form.

transformation of the dependent variable can render the two models comparable. We proceed as follows:

Step 1:     Compute the geometric mean (GM) of the dependent variable; call it $Q^*$.[19] For the data in **Table 2.1**, the GM of the output variable is $e^{16.94139} = 22842628$.

Step 2:     Divide $Q_i$ by $Q^*$ to obtain: $(Q_i/Q^*) = \tilde{Q}_i$

Step 3:     Estimate Eq. (2.4) using $\tilde{Q}_i$ in lieu of $Q_i$ as the dependent variable (i.e. use $\ln \tilde{Q}_i$ as the dependent variable).

Step 4:     Estimate Eq. (2.6) using $\tilde{Q}_i$ as the dependent variable instead of $Q_i$.

The dependent variables thus transformed are now comparable. Run the transformed regressions, obtaining their residual sum of squares (RSS) (say $RSS_1$ for the linear model and $RSS_2$ for the log-linear model) and choose the model that has the lowest RSS. To save space, we will not reproduce the results of these transformed regressions except for the following statistics:

|  | RSS |
|---|---|
| log-linear model | 3.4155 |
| linear model | 3.6519 |

Since the RSS of the log-linear model is lower, we may choose it over the linear model, although the two RSS are quite close. But a more formal test is available.

If the *null hypothesis* is that both models fit the data equally well, we can compute[20]

$$\lambda = \frac{n}{2} \ln \left( \frac{RSS_1}{RSS_2} \right) \sim \chi_1^2 \qquad (2.31)$$

where $RSS_1$ is the RSS from the linear model and $RSS_2$ is the RSS from the log-linear model. If the computed $\lambda$ (lambda) exceeds the critical chi-square value for 1 df, we can reject the null hypothesis and conclude that it is the log-linear production function that is a better model. If, however, the computed $\lambda$ is less than the critical value, we fail to reject the null hypothesis, in which case both models perform equally well.[21]

For our example, it can be shown that $\lambda = 74.2827$. The 5% critical chi-square value for 1 df. is 3.841. Since the computed chi-square value of 74.2827 is much greater than the critical chi-square value, we can conclude that the log-linear model performs better than the linear model.

Since the log-linear model is easy to interpret in terms of elasticities of labor and capital and the returns to scale parameter, we may choose that model in practice.

## 2.9     Regression on standardized variables

In the various examples discussed so far the regressand and regressors were not necessarily expressed in the same unit of measurement. Thus in the Cobb–Douglas

---

19   The geometric mean of $Y_1$ and $Y_2$ is $(Y_1 Y_2)^{1/2}$, the GM of $Y_1$, $Y_2$ and $Y_3$ is $(Y_1 Y_2 Y_3)^{1/3}$ and so on.

20   See Gary Koop, *Introduction to Econometrics*, John Wiley & Sons Ltd, England, 2008, pp. 114–15.

21   If $RSS_2 > RSS_1$, put the former in the numerator of Eq. (2.31) and $RSS_1$ in the denominator. The null hypothesis here is that both models perform equally well. If this hypothesis is rejected, then it is the linear model that is preferable to the log-linear model.

production function discussed earlier output, labor input and capital input were measured in different units of measurement. This affects the interpretation of regression coefficients, because the size of the (partial) regression coefficient depends on the units of measurement of the variable.

But this problem can be avoided if we express all variables in the *standardized form*. In the standardized form we express the value of each variable as deviation from its mean value and divide the difference by the standard deviation of that variable, such as

$$Y_i^* = \frac{Y_i - \overline{Y}}{S_Y}; \quad X_i^* = \frac{X_i - \overline{X}}{S_X} \tag{2.32}$$

where $S_Y$ and $S_X$ are the sample standard deviations and $\overline{Y}$ and $\overline{X}$ are the sample means of $Y$ and $X$, respectively. $Y_i^*$ and $X_i^*$ are called **standardized variables**.

It is easy to prove that the mean value of a standardized variable is always zero and its standard deviation value is always 1, no matter what its original mean and standard deviation values are. It is also interesting to note that the standardized variables are what are called **pure** (i.e. unit-free) **numbers**. This is because the numerator and denominator of the standardized variables are measured in the same unit of measurement.

If you now run the following regression:

$$Y_i^* = B_1^* + B_2^* X_i^* + u_i^* \tag{2.33}$$

you will find that $b_1^*$ is zero.[22]

The starred regression coefficients are called the **beta coefficients**, or **standardized coefficients**, whereas the regression coefficients of unstandardized variables are called **unstandardized coefficients**.

The slope coefficient in this regression is interpreted as follows: if the standardized regressor increases by one standard deviation unit, on average, the standardized regressand increases by $B_2^*$ standard deviation units. The point to remember is that, unlike the usual OLS regression, we measure the impact of a regressor not in terms of the original units in which $Y$ and $X$ are measured, but in standard deviation units.

It should be added that if we have more than one regressor, we can standardize all the regressors. To illustrate, we revisit the linear production function for the USA considered earlier (see Table 2.3) and reestimate it using standardized output, labor and capital variables. The results are shown in Table 2.14.

As expected, the intercept term is zero. The two standardized variables have individually significant impacts on (standardized) output. The interpretation of a coefficient of about 0.40 is that if the labor input increases by one standard deviation unit, the average value of output goes up by about 0.40 standard deviation units, *ceteris paribus*. The interpretation of the capital coefficient of about 0.60 is that if the capital input increases by one standard deviation unit, on average, output increases by about 0.60 standard deviation units. Relatively speaking, capital has more impact on output than labor. The regression coefficients in Table 2.3, by contrast, are unstandardized coefficients.

---

**22** Note that: $b_1^* = \overline{Y} - b_2^* \overline{X}^*$, but the mean values of the standardized variables are zero, so $b_i^*$ is zero *ipso facto*.

**Table 2.14  Linear production function using standardized variables.**

Dependent Variable: OUTPUTSTAR
Method: Least Squares
Sample: 1 51
Included observations: 51

|  | Coefficient | Std. Error | t-Statistic | Prob. |
|---|---|---|---|---|
| C | 2.52E–08 | 0.019666 | 1.28E–06 | 1.0000 |
| LABORSTAR | 0.402388 | 0.059185 | 6.798766 | 0.0000 |
| CAPITALSTAR | 0.602185 | 0.059185 | 10.17455 | 0.0000 |

| | | | |
|---|---|---|---|
| R-squared | 0.981065 | Mean dependent var | 5.24E-09 |
| Adjusted R-squared | 0.980276 | S.D. dependent var | 1.000000 |
| S.E. of regression | 0.140441 | Akaike info criterion | –1.031037 |
| Sum squared resid | 0.946735 | Schwarz criterion | –0.917400 |
| Log likelihood | 29.29145 | Durbin–Watson stat | 1.684519 |
| F-statistic | 1243.514 | Prob(F-statistic) | 0.000000 |

*Note*: STAR variables are standardized variables.

If you look at the results shown in Table 2.3, you might think that labor has relatively more impact on output than capital. But since labor and capital are measured in different units of measurement, such a conclusion would be misleading. But in a regression on standardized variables, it may be easier to assess the relative importance of the various regressors, because by standardizing we put all regressors on an equal footing.

*But note that whether we use standardized or unstandardized variables, the t, F, and $R^2$ values remain the same, thus not affecting statistical inference.*

## 2.10    Measures of goodness of fit

If you look at the various computer printouts given in the preceding tables, you will observe that there are several measures of "goodness of fit" of the estimated model; that is, how well the model explains the variation in the regressand. These measures include: (1) coefficient of determination, $R^2$, (2) adjusted $R^2$, usually denoted by $\overline{R}^2$, (3) Akaike's Information Criterion, and (4) Schwarz's Information Criterion.

### 1  $R^2$ measure

As noted earlier, this measures the proportion of the variation in the regressand explained by the regressors. It lies between 0 and 1, 0 indicating complete lack of fit and 1 indicating a perfect fit. $R^2$ usually lies within these limits; the closer it is to 0, worse is the fit, and the closer it is to 1, the better is the fit. A drawback of this measure is that by including more regressors in the model we can generally increase the $R^2$ value. This is because $R^2$ is an increasing function of the number of regressors in the model.

Although we have defined $R^2$ as the ratio of ESS to TSS, it can also be computed as the squared correlation coefficient between the actual $Y$ and the estimated $Y (= \hat{Y})$ from the regression model, where $Y$ is the regressand, that is:

$$r^2 = \frac{(\Sigma y_i \hat{y}_i)^2}{\Sigma y_i^2 \Sigma \hat{y}_i^2} \tag{2.34}$$

where $y_i = (Y_i - \overline{Y})$ and $\hat{y}_i = (\hat{Y}_i - \overline{Y})$.

## 2 Adjusted $R^2$

We have already discussed the adjusted $R^2$ ($= \overline{R}^2$). The adjusted $R^2$ is used to compare two or more regression models that have the same dependent variable, but differing numbers of regressors. Since the adjusted $R^2$ is usually smaller than the unadjusted $R^2$, it seems it imposes a penalty for adding more regressors to the model.

## 3 Akaike's Information Criterion (AIC)

Like the adjusted $R^2$, the AIC criterion adds a somewhat harsher penalty for adding more variables to the model. In its logarithmic form, AIC is defined as follows:

$$\ln \text{AIC} = \frac{2k}{n} + \ln\left(\frac{RSS}{n}\right) \tag{2.35}$$

where $RSS$ = residual sum of squares and $2k/n$ is the penalty factor.

The AIC criterion is useful in comparing two or more models. *The model with the lowest AIC is usually chosen.* The AIC criterion is also used for both in-sample and out-of-sample forecasting performance of a regression model.

## 4 Schwarz's Information Criterion (SIC)

This is an alternative to the AIC criterion, which in its log form can be expressed as:

$$\ln \text{SIC} = \frac{k}{n} \ln n + \ln\left(\frac{RSS}{n}\right) \tag{2.36}$$

The penalty factor here is $[(k/n)\ln n]$, which is harsher than that of AIC. Like AIC, the lower the value of SIC, the better the model. Also, like AIC, SIC can be used to compare in-sample or out-of-sample forecasting performance of a model.

It should be added that the idea behind adding the penalty factor is **Occam's razor**, according to which "descriptions should be kept as simple as possible until proved inadequate". This is also known as the *principle of parsimony*.

On the basis of this principle, which is a better criterion, AIC or SIC? Most often both these criteria select the same model, but not always. On theoretical grounds, AIC may be preferable, but in practice one may choose the SIC criterion, for it may select a more parsimonious model, other things remaining the same.[23] *Eviews* presents both these criteria.

If you compare the linear trend model given in Table 2.7 with the quadratic trend model given in Table 2.12, you will find that for the linear model the Akaike value is 15.0 and for the quadratic model it is −4.23. Here you would choose the quadratic trend model. On the basis of the Schwarz criterion, these values are 15.17 for the linear trend model and −4.12 for the quadratic trend model. Again, you would choose the latter model on the basis of this criterion. However, for the quadratic trend model, the Akaike value of −4.23 is more negative than the Schwarz value of −4.12, giving Akaike a slight edge in the choice.

It may be interesting to note that for the LRM both these criteria are related to the $F$ test as follows: "For a large enough sample size $n$, the comparison of AIC values

---

23 For a discussion about the relative merits of the various model selection criteria, see Francis X. Diebold, *Elements of Forecasting*, 3rd edn, Thomson/South-Western Publishers, 2004, pp. 87–90.

corresponds to an $F$ test with critical value 2 and SIC corresponds to an $F$ test with critical value $\log(n)$."[24]

If we are dealing with nonlinear-in-parameter regression models, estimated by the method of maximum likelihood (ML), the goodness of fit is measured by the likelihood ration (LR) statistic $\lambda$, which is explained in the Appendix to Chapter 1, which discusses the ML method. In Part III we will discuss models in which we use the LR statistic.

## 2.11    Summary and conclusions

In this chapter we considered a variety of linear regression models – that is, models that are linear in the parameters or can be made linear with suitable transformations. Each model is useful in specific situations. In some applications more than one model may fit the data. We discussed the unique features of each model in terms of slope and elasticity coefficients.

In comparing two or more models on the basis of $R^2$ we pointed out that the dependent variable in these models must be the same. In particular, we discussed the choice between a linear and a log-linear model, two of the commonly used models in research.

Although we have discussed the various models in terms of two-variable or three-variable linear regression models for expository purposes, they can be easily extended to regression models involving any number of regressors.[25] We can also have models in which some regressors are linear and some are log-linear.

We briefly discussed the role of standardized variables in regression analysis. Since a standardized variable has zero mean and unit standard deviation, it is easier to compare the relative influence of various regressors on the regressand.

We can evaluate a model in terms of the expected signs of the regression coefficients, their statistical significance in terms of the $t$ value of the coefficients, or the $F$ test if we are interested in the joint significance of two or more variables. We can judge the overall performance of a model in terms of $R^2$. If we are comparing two or more regression models, we can use the adjusted $R^2$ or the Akaike or Schwarz information criteria.

In this chapter we also discussed how we can incorporate linear restrictions in estimating regression models. Such restrictions are often suggested by economic theory.

## Exercises

**2.1**    Consider the following production function, known in the literature as the transcendental production function (TPF).

$$Q_i = B_1 L_i^{B_2} K_i^{B_3} e^{B_4 L_i + B_5 K_i}$$

where $Q$, $L$, and $K$ represent output, labor, and capital, respectively.

(*a*)  How would you linearize this function? (Hint: logarithms.)

---

24  See Christiaan Heij, Paul de Boer, Philip Hans Franses, Teun Kloek, and Herman K. van Dijk, *Econometrics Methods with Applications in Business and Economics*, Oxford University Press, Oxford, UK, 2004, p. 280.

25  To handle such multivariable regression models, we need to use matrix algebra.

(b) What is the interpretation of the various coefficients in the TPF?

(c) Given the data in **Table 2.1**, estimate the parameters of the TPF.

(d) Suppose you want to test the hypothesis that $B_4 = B_5 = 0$. How would you test these hypotheses? Show the necessary calculations. (Hint: restricted least squares.)

(e) How would you compute the output–labor and output–capital elasticities for this model? Are they constant or variable?

**2.2** How would you compute the output–labor and output–capital elasticities for the linear production function given in Table 2.3?

**2.3** For the food expenditure data given in Table 2.6, see if the following model fits the data well:

$$\text{SFDHO}_i = B_1 + B_2 \, \text{Expend}_i + B_3 \, \text{Expend}_i^2$$

and compare your results with those discussed in the text.

**2.4** Would it make sense to standardize variables in the log-linear Cobb–Douglas production function and estimate the regression using standardized variables? Why or why not? Show the necessary calculations.

**2.5** Show that the coefficient of determination, $R^2$, can also be obtained as the squared correlation between actual $Y$ values and the $Y$ values estimated from the regression model ($= \hat{Y}_i$), where $Y$ is the dependent variable. Note that the coefficient of correlation between variables $Y$ and $X$ is defined as:

$$r = \frac{\Sigma y_i x_i}{\sqrt{\Sigma x_i^2 \Sigma y_i^2}}$$

where $y_i = Y_i - \overline{Y}$; $x_i = X_i - \overline{X}$. Also note that the mean values of $Y_i$ and $\hat{Y}$ are the same, namely, $\overline{Y}$.

**2.6** **Table 2.15** gives cross-country data for 83 countries on per worker GDP for 1997 and Corruption Index for 1998.[26]

(a) Plot the index of corruption against per worker GDP.

(b) Based on this plot what might be an appropriate model relating corruption index to per worker GDP?

(c) Present the results of your analysis.

(d) If you find a positive relationship between corruption and per capita GDP, how would you rationalize this outcome?

26 Source: http://www.transparency.org/pressreleases_archive/1998/1998.09.22.cpi.html (for corruption index; Source: http://www.worldbank.org/research/growth/ (for per worker GDP).

# 3

# Qualitative explanatory variables regression models[1]

Most of the linear regression models we have discussed so far involved a quantitative regressand and quantitative regressors. We will continue to assume that the regressand is quantitative, but we will now consider models in which the regressors are quantitative as well as qualitative. In Chapter 8 we will consider regressands that are also qualitative in nature.

In regression analysis we often encounter variables that are essentially qualitative in nature, such as gender, race, color, religion, nationality, geographical region, party affiliation, and political upheavals. For example, in the wage function we discussed in Chapter 1, we had gender, union affiliation, and minority status among the regressors because these qualitative variables play an important role in wage determination.

These qualitative variables are essentially **nominal scale variables** which have no particular numerical values. But we can "quantify" them by creating so-called **dummy variables**, which take values of 0 and 1, 0 indicating the absence of an attribute and 1 indicating its presence. Thus the gender variable can be quantified as female = 1 and male = 0, or vice versa. In passing, note that dummy variables are also called **indicator variables**, **categorical variables**, and **qualitative variables**.

In this chapter we show how the dummy variables can be handled within the framework of the classical linear regression model (CLRM). For notational convenience, we will indicate the dummy variables by the letter $D$.

To set the stage, we start with a concrete example.

## 3.1   Wage function revisited

In Chapter 1 we considered the determination of hourly wage for a cross-section of 1,289 persons based on the data obtained from the *Current Population Survey* (CPS) for March 1995. The variables used in the analysis and the regression results are given in Table 1.2.

Let us write the wage function in a different format to emphasize the role of dummy variables in the regression.

$$Wage_i = B_1 + B_2 D_{2i} + B_3 D_{3i} + B_4 D_{4i} + B_5 Educ_i + B_6 Exper_i + u_i \quad (3.1)$$

---

1  For more details, see Gujarati/Porter, *op cit.*, Chapter 9.

Table 3.1  A model of wage determination.

Dependent Variable: WAGE
Method: Least Squares
Sample: 1 1289
Included observations: 1289

|  | Coefficient | Std. Error | t-Statistic | Prob. |
|---|---|---|---|---|
| C | −7.183338 | 1.015788 | −7.071691 | 0.0000 |
| FEMALE | −3.074875 | 0.364616 | −8.433184 | 0.0000 |
| NONWHITE | −1.565313 | 0.509188 | −3.074139 | 0.0022 |
| UNION | 1.095976 | 0.506078 | 2.165626 | 0.0305 |
| EDUCATION | 1.370301 | 0.065904 | 20.79231 | 0.0000 |
| EXPER | 0.166607 | 0.016048 | 10.38205 | 0.0000 |

| | | | | |
|---|---|---|---|---|
| R-squared | 0.323339 | Mean dependent var | 12.36585 |
| Adjusted R-squared | 0.320702 | S.D. dependent var | 7.896350 |
| S.E. of regression | 6.508137 | Akaike info criterion | 6.588627 |
| Sum squared resid | 54342.54 | Schwarz criterion | 6.612653 |
| Log likelihood | −4240.370 | Durbin–Watson stat | 1.897513 |
| F-statistic | 122.6149 | Prob(F-statistic) | 0.000000 |

where $D_{2i} = 1$ if female, 0 for male; $D_{3i} = 1$ for nonwhite, 0 for white; and $D_{4i} = 1$ if union member, 0 for non-union member, where the $D$s are the dummy variables.

For convenience, we are reproducing the results of the regression given in Table 1.2, using the notation given in Eq. (3.1) (Table 3.1).

Before we interpret the dummy variables, some general comments about these variables are in order.

*First*, if an intercept is included in the model and *if a qualitative variable has m categories, then introduce only (m − 1) dummy variables.* For example, gender has only two categories; hence we introduce only one dummy variable for gender. This is because if a female gets a value of 1, *ipso facto* a male get a value of zero. Of course, if an attribute has only two categories, it does not matter which category gets the value of 1 or zero. So we could code male as 1 and female as 0.

If, for example, we consider political affiliation as choice among Democratic, Republican, and Independent parties, we can have at most two dummy variables to represent the three parties. If we do not follow this rule, we will fall into what is called the **dummy variable trap**, that is, the situation of perfect collinearity. Thus, if we have three dummies for the three political parties and an intercept, the sum of the three dummies will be 1, which will then be equal to the common intercept value of 1, leading to perfect collinearity.[2]

*Second*, if a qualitative variable has *m* categories, you may include *m* dummies, *provided you do not include the (common) intercept in the model.* This way we do not fall into the dummy variable trap.

*Third*, the category that gets the value of 0 is called the **reference**, **benchmark** or **comparison category**. All comparisons are made in relation to the reference category, as we will show with our example.

---

2  Note that including an intercept in the model is equivalent to including a regressor in the model whose value is always one.

*Fourth*, if there are several dummy variables, you must keep track of the reference category; otherwise, it will be difficult to interpret the results.

*Fifth*, at times we will have to consider **interactive dummies**, which we will illustrate shortly.

*Sixth*, since dummy variables take values of 1 and 0, we cannot take their logarithms. That is, we cannot introduce the dummy variables in log form.[3]

*Seventh*, if the sample size is relatively small, do not introduce too many dummy variables. Remember that each dummy coefficient will cost one degree of freedom.

### Interpretation of dummy variables

Returning to the wage function given in Table 3.1, let us interpret the female dummy coefficient of −3.0748. Its interpretation is that the average hourly salary of a female worker is lower by about $3.07 as compared to the average salary of a male worker, which is the reference category here, of course holding all other variables constant. Similarly, the average hourly wage of union workers is higher by about $1.10 as compared to the average pay of non-union workers, which is the reference category. Likewise, the average hourly wage of a nonwhite worker is lower by about −$1.57 than a white worker, which is the reference category.

In passing, note that all the dummy coefficients are individually statistically highly significant, for their *p* values are practically 0. These dummy coefficients are often called **differential intercept dummies**, for they show the differences in the intercept values of the category that gets the value of 1 as compared to the reference category.

What does the common intercept value of about −7.18 denote? It is the expected hourly wage for white, non-union, male worker. That is, *the common intercept value refers to all those categories that take a value of* 0. Of course, this is the mechanical interpretation of the intercept term.[4] As we have remarked on several occasions, a negative intercept value very often does not have a viable economic interpretation.

The interpretation of the quantitative regressors is straightforward. For example, the education coefficient of 1.37 suggests that holding all other factors constant, for every additional year of schooling the average hourly wage goes up by about $1.37. Similarly, for every additional year of work experience, the average hourly wage goes up by about $0.17, *ceteris paribus*.

## 3.2    Refinement of the wage function

We have found that the average salary of a female worker is lower than that of her male counterpart and we also found that the average salary of a nonwhite worker is lower than that of his white counterpart. Is it possible that the average salary of a female nonwhite worker is different from the average salary of a female worker alone or a nonwhite worker alone? If that turns out to be the case, does it say something about possible discrimination against nonwhite female workers?

---

3  However, if instead of 1 and 0 you choose 10 and 1 as the dummy values, you may take their logs.

4  Basically, it shows where the regression line (or plane) lies along the *Y*-axis, which represents the dependent variable.

Table 3.2  Wage function with interactive dummies.

Dependent Variable: WAGE
Method: Least Squares
Sample: 1 1289
Included observations: 1289

| | Coefficient | Std. Error | t-Statistic | Prob. |
|---|---|---|---|---|
| C | −7.088725 | 1.019482 | −6.953264 | 0.0000 |
| D2(Gender) | −3.240148 | 0.395328 | −8.196106 | 0.0000 |
| D3(Race) | −2.158525 | 0.748426 | −2.884087 | 0.0040 |
| D4(Union) | 1.115044 | 0.506352 | 2.202113 | 0.0278 |
| EDUC | 1.370113 | 0.065900 | 20.79076 | 0.0000 |
| EXPERI | 0.165856 | 0.016061 | 10.32631 | 0.0000 |
| D2*D3(GenderRace) | 1.095371 | 1.012897 | 1.081424 | 0.2797 |

| | | | |
|---|---|---|---|
| R-squared | 0.323955 | Mean dependent var | 12.36585 |
| Adjusted R-squared | 0.320791 | S.D. dependent var | 7.896350 |
| S.E. of regression | 6.507707 | Akaike info criterion | 6.589267 |
| Sum squared resid | 54293.02 | Schwarz criterion | 6.617298 |
| Log likelihood | −4239.783 | Durbin–Watson stat | 1.898911 |
| F-statistic | 102.3875 | Prob(F-statistic) | 0.000000 |

To find this out, we reestimate the wage function by adding to it the *product* of the female and nonwhite dummies. Such a product is called an **interactive dummy**, for it interacts the two qualitative variables. Adding the interactive dummy, we obtain the results in Table 3.2.

The coefficient of the interactive dummy (D2 × D3) is about 1.10, but it is not statistically significant, for its $p$ value is about 28%.

But how do we interpret this value? *Ceteris paribus*, being a female has a lower average salary by about \$3.24, being a nonwhite has a lower average salary by about \$2.16 and being both has an average salary lower by about \$4.30 (= −3.24 − 2.16 + 1.10). In other words, compared to the reference category, a nonwhite female earns a lower average wage than being a female alone or being a nonwhite alone.

We leave it for the reader to find out if a female union worker or a nonwhite union worker earns an average wage that is different from the reference category. You can also interact female and union dummies, female and experience dummies, nonwhite and union dummies, and nonwhite and experience dummies.

## 3.3    Another refinement of the wage function

We implicitly assumed that the slope coefficients of the quantitative regressors, education, and experience, remain the same between male and female, and between white and nonwhite wage earners. For example, this assumption would imply that for every additional year of schooling or every additional year of work experience, male and female workers earn the same incremental amount of hourly wage. Of course this is an assumption. But with dummy variables, we can test this assumption explicitly.

Let us express the wage function as follows:

$$Wage_i = B_1 + B_2 D_{2i} + B_3 D_{3i} + B_4 D_{4i} + B_5 Educ_i$$
$$+ B_6 Exp_i + B_7 (D_{2i} Educ_i) + B_8 (D_{3i} Educ_i)$$
$$+ B_9 (D_{4i} Educ_i) + B_{10} (D_{2i} Exp_i) + B_{11} (D_{3i} Exp_i) \qquad (3.2)$$
$$+ B_{12} (D_{4i} Expr_i) + u_i$$

In Eq. (3.2) $B_2$, $B_3$, and $B_4$ are **differential intercept dummies,** as before, and $B_7$ through $B_{11}$ are **differential slope dummies.** If, for example, $b_7$, the estimated coefficient of $B_7$, is statistically significant, it would suggest that the rate of average salary progression per additional year of education is different for female than the reference group, which is white male, whose slope coefficient is $B_5$. Other differential slope coefficients are to be interpreted similarly.

The results of regression (3.2) are shown in Table 3.3. Compared to the results in Tables 3.1 and 3.2, the results in Table 3.3 are revealing. The differential slope coefficients for females with respect to education and experience are negative and statistically significant, suggesting that the rate of progression of average hourly wage for female workers *vis à vis* male workers is smaller with respect to education and experience. For nonwhite workers the rate of wage progression with respect to education is negative and lower than for white workers and it is statistically significant at the 10% level. The other differential slope coefficients are not statistically significant.

For discussion purposes we will drop the differential slope coefficients D3*EX and D4*ED and D4*EX. The results are given in Table 3.4.

**Table 3.3  Wage function with differential intercept and slope dummies.**

Dependent Variable: W
Method: Least Squares
Sample: 1 1289
Included observations: 1289

|  | Coefficient | Std. Error | t-Statistic | Prob. |
|---|---|---|---|---|
| C | −11.09129 | 1.421846 | −7.800623 | 0.0000 |
| D2 | 3.174158 | 1.966465 | 1.614144 | 0.1067 |
| D3 | 2.909129 | 2.780066 | 1.046424 | 0.2956 |
| D4 | 4.454212 | 2.973494 | 1.497972 | 0.1344 |
| ED | 1.587125 | 0.093819 | 16.91682 | 0.0000 |
| EX | 0.220912 | 0.025107 | 8.798919 | 0.0000 |
| D2*ED | −0.336888 | 0.131993 | −2.552314 | 0.0108 |
| D2*EX | −0.096125 | 0.031813 | −3.021530 | 0.0026 |
| D3*ED | −0.321855 | 0.195348 | −1.647595 | 0.0997 |
| D3*EX | −0.022041 | 0.044376 | −0.496700 | 0.6195 |
| D4*ED | −0.198323 | 0.191373 | −1.036318 | 0.3003 |
| D4*EX | −0.033454 | 0.046054 | −0.726410 | 0.4677 |

| | | | |
|---|---|---|---|
| R-squared | 0.332811 | Mean dependent var | 12.36585 |
| Adjusted R-squared | 0.327064 | S.D. dependent var | 7.896350 |
| S.E. of regression | 6.477589 | Akaike info criterion | 6.583840 |
| Sum squared resid | 53581.84 | Schwarz criterion | 6.631892 |
| Log likelihood | −4231.285 | Durbin–Watson stat | 1.893519 |
| F-statistic | 57.90909 | Prob(F-statistic) | 0.000000 |

*Note*: The symbol * denotes multiplication.

**Table 3.4  Reduced wage function.**

Dependent Variable: W
Method: Least Squares
Sample: 1 1289
Included observations: 1289

|  | Coefficient | Std. Error | t-Statistic | Prob. |
|---|---|---|---|---|
| C | −10.64520 | 1.371801 | −7.760020 | 0.0000 |
| FE | 3.257472 | 1.959253 | 1.662609 | 0.0966 |
| NW | 2.626952 | 2.417874 | 1.086472 | 0.2775 |
| UN | 1.078513 | 0.505398 | 2.133988 | 0.0330 |
| ED | 1.565800 | 0.091813 | 17.05422 | 0.0000 |
| EX | 0.212623 | 0.022769 | 9.338102 | 0.0000 |
| FE*ED | −0.346947 | 0.131487 | −2.638639 | 0.0084 |
| FE*EX | −0.094908 | 0.031558 | −3.007409 | 0.0027 |
| NW*ED | −0.329365 | 0.186628 | −1.764817 | 0.0778 |

| | | | | |
|---|---|---|---|---|
| R-squared | 0.331998 | Mean dependent var | 12.36585 |
| Adjusted R-squared | 0.327823 | S.D. dependent var | 7.896350 |
| S.E. of regression | 6.473933 | Akaike info criterion | 6.580402 |
| Sum squared resid | 53647.11 | Schwarz criterion | 6.616442 |
| Log likelihood | −4232.069 | Durbin–Watson stat | 1.889308 |
| F-statistic | 79.52030 | Prob(F-statistic) | 0.000000 |

From these results we can derive wage functions for male, female and nonwhite, and non-union workers, which are as follows:

**Wage function of white male non-union wage earners:**

$$\hat{Wage_i} = -10.6450 + 1.5658\, Educ_i + 0.2126\, Exper_i \qquad (3.3)$$

**Wage function of white non-union female wage earners**

$$\hat{Wage_i} = (-10.6450 + 3.2574) + (1.5658 - 0.3469)Educ_i$$
$$+ (0.2126 - 0.0949)Exper_i \qquad (3.4)$$
$$= -7.3876 + 1.2189 Educ_i + 0.1177 Exper_i$$

**Wage function for nonwhite male non-union workers**

$$\hat{Wage_i} = (-10.6450 - 2.6269) + (1.5658 - 0.3293)Educ_i$$
$$+ 0.2126 Exper_i \qquad (3.5)$$
$$= -8.0181 + 1.2365 Educ_i + 0.2126 Exper_i$$

**Wage function for white male union workers**

$$\hat{Wage_i} = (-10.6450 + 1.0785) + 1.5658 Educ_i + 0.2126 Exper_i \qquad (3.6)$$
$$= 9.5665 + 1.5658 Educ_i + 0.2126 Exper_i$$

Of course, there are other possibilities to express the wage function.

For example, you may want to interact female with union and education (female*union*education), which will show whether the females who are educated and belong to unions have differential wages with respect to education or union status. *But beware of introducing too many dummy variables, for they can rapidly consume degrees of freedom.* In the present example this is not a serious problem, because we have 1,289 observations.

## 3.4    Functional form of the wage regression

It is common in labor economics to use the logarithm of wages instead of wages as the regressand because the distribution of wages tends to be highly skewed, which can be seen from Figure 3.1.

This histogram of wage rates shows that it is right-skewed and is far from the normal distribution. If a variable is normally distributed, its **skewness** coefficient (a measure of symmetry) is 0 and its **kurtosis** coefficient (a measure of how tall or flat the normal distribution is) is 3. As the statistics accompanying this figure shows, in the present case skewness is about 1.85 and kurtosis is about 7.84, both values being far different than those of a normal distribution. The **Jarque–Bera (JB) statistic**, which is based on the skewness and kurtosis measures, will be discussed in Chapter 7. Suffice it to note here that for a normally distributed variable the value of the JB statistic is expected to be zero, which is obviously not the case here, for the estimated JB value is about 1990, which is far from zero and the probability of obtaining such a value is practically zero.[5]

On the other hand, the distribution of log of wages shows that it is symmetrical and normally distributed, as can be seen from Figure 3.2.

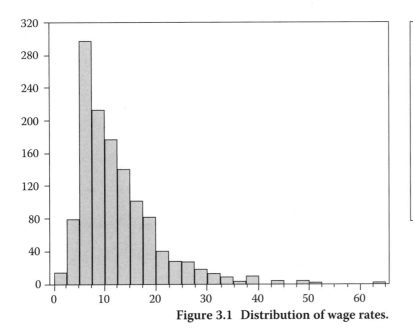

| Series: W | |
| --- | --- |
| Sample 1 1289 | |
| Observations 1289 | |
| | |
| Mean | 12.36585 |
| Median | 10.08000 |
| Maximum | 64.08000 |
| Minimum | 0.840000 |
| Std. Dev. | 7.896350 |
| Skewness | 1.848114 |
| Kurtosis | 7.836565 |
| | |
| Jarque–Bera | 1990.134 |
| Probability | 0.000000 |

**Figure 3.1  Distribution of wage rates.**

---

5  Under the hypothesis that a variable is normally distributed, Jarque–Bera have shown that in large samples the JB statistic follows the chi-square distribution with 2 df.

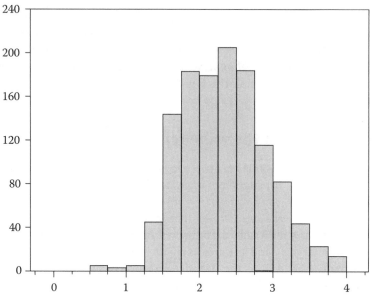

Figure 3.2 Distribution of log of wages.

That is why it is preferable to use the log of wage rates as the regressand. Also, in the log-transform the problem of heteroscedasticity is usually less severe.

Using the log of wage rate as the regressand (LW), the estimate of Eq. (3.1) is shown in Table 3.5. This shows that all the estimated coefficients are individually (on the basis of the $t$ test) as well as collectively (on the basis of the $F$ test) highly significant, because their $p$ values are so low. But how do we interpret these coefficients?

Table 3.5 Semi-log model of wages.

Dependent Variable: LW
Method: Least Squares
Sample: 1 1289
Included observations: 1289

| | Coefficient | Std. Error | t-Statistic | Prob. |
|---|---|---|---|---|
| C | 0.905504 | 0.074175 | 12.20768 | 0.0000 |
| D2 | −0.249154 | 0.026625 | −9.357891 | 0.0000 |
| D3 | −0.133535 | 0.037182 | −3.591399 | 0.0003 |
| D4 | 0.180204 | 0.036955 | 4.876316 | 0.0000 |
| EDUC | 0.099870 | 0.004812 | 20.75244 | 0.0000 |
| EXPER | 0.012760 | 0.001172 | 10.88907 | 0.0000 |

| | | | | |
|---|---|---|---|---|
| R-squared | 0.345650 | Mean dependent var | 2.342416 | |
| Adjusted R-squared | 0.343100 | S.D. dependent var | 0.586356 | |
| S.E. of regression | 0.475237 | Akaike info criterion | 1.354639 | |
| Sum squared resid | 289.7663 | Schwarz criterion | 1.378666 | |
| Log likelihood | −867.0651 | Durbin–Watson stat | 1.942506 | |
| F-statistic | 135.5452 | Prob(F-statistic) | 0.000000 | |

Recall from our discussion of functional forms of regression models in Chapter 2 that in Table 3.5 we are estimating a **semi-log** model where the wage rate variable is in the log form whereas the regressors are in linear form. As we know, with respect to the quantitative variables, education and work experience, their coefficients represent **semi-elasticities** – that is, relative (or percentage) change in the wage rate for a unit change in the regressor. Thus, the education coefficient of 0.0999 suggests that for every additional year of schooling, the average wage rate goes up by about 9.99%, *ceteris paribus*. Likewise, for every additional year of work experience, the average wage rate goes up by about 1.3%, *ceteris paribus*.

What about the dummy coefficients? One could interpret the female dummy coefficient of −0.2492 as suggesting that the average female wage rate is lower by 24.92% as compared to the male average wage rate. But if one wants to get a correct percentage change, we have to take the antilog (to base e) of the coefficient of the dummy variable, subtract 1 from it and multiply the difference by 100.[6] Following this procedure, we find that $e^{-0.2492} = 0.7794$. Subtracting 1 from this, we obtain −0.2206. Multiplying this by 100, we find −22.06%. That is, holding all other variables constant, the female average wage rate is lower than the male average wage rate by about 22.06%, which is different from 24.92%.

Therefore, the dummy coefficients given in Table 3.5 can be interpreted as percentage changes only as approximations. To get the correct percentage change we have to follow the procedure just described.

The results of the linear and log-linear regressions given in Tables 3.1 and 3.5 show that in both cases the coefficients of the regressors are highly significant, although their interpretations are different. But one important point to remember is that the $R^2$ value given in Table 3.1 (0.3233) and that given in Table 3.5 (0.3457) are not directly comparable for reasons already discussed in the chapter on functional forms of regression models. To wit, in the linear model the $R^2$ measures the proportion of the variation in the regressand explained by all the regressors, whereas in the log-linear model it measures the proportion of the variation in the log of the regressand. And the two are not the same. Recall that a change in the log of a variable is a proportional or relative change.

It is left for the reader to replicate the results of Tables 3.2, 3.3, and 3.4, using log of wage rate as the regressand.

## 3.5    Use of dummy variables in structural change

Suppose we want to study the relationship between gross private investments (GPI) and gross private savings (GPS) in the USA over the period 1959–2007, a span of 49 years. For this purpose let us consider the following investment function:

$$\text{GPI}_t = B_1 + B_2\text{GPS}_t + u_t, \qquad B_2 > 0 \tag{3.7}$$

where $B_2$ is the *marginal propensity to invest* (MPI) – that is, additional investment out of an additional dollar of savings. See **Table 3.6** on the companion website.

In 1981–1982 the US suffered its worst peace-time recession, until the severe recession of 2007–2008. It is quite likely that the investment-savings relationship postulated in Eq. (3.7) may have gone a structural change since then. To see if in fact the US

---

6  For a technical discussion, see Gujarati/Porter, *op cit.*, Chapter 9, p. 298.

Table 3.7  Regression of GPI on GPS, 1959–2007.

Dependent Variable: GPI
Method: Least Squares
Date: 07/06/10 Time: 15:27
Sample: 1959 2007
Included observations: 49

| Variable | Coefficient | Std. Error | t-Statistic | Prob. |
|---|---|---|---|---|
| C | −78.72105 | 27.48474 | −2.864173 | 0.0062 |
| GPS | 1.107395 | 0.029080 | 38.08109 | 0.0000 |

| | | | | |
|---|---|---|---|---|
| R-squared | 0.968607 | Mean dependent var | 760.9061 | |
| Adjusted R-squared | 0.967940 | S.D. dependent var | 641.5260 | |
| S.E. of regression | 114.8681 | Akaike info criterion | 12.36541 | |
| Sum squared resid | 620149.8 | Schwarz criterion | 12.44262 | |
| Log likelihood | −300.9524 | Hannan–Quinn criter. | 12.39470 | |
| F-statistic | 1450.170 | Durbin–Watson stat | 0.372896 | |
| Prob(F-statistic) | 0.000000 | | | |

economy has undergone a structural change, we can use dummy variables to shed light on this. Before we do that, let us present the results of regression (3.7) without taking into account any structural breaks. The results are shown in Table 3.7.

These results shows that the MPI is about 1.10, meaning that if GPS increases by a dollar, the average GPI goes up by about $1.10. The MPI is highly significant, although we may have to worry about the problem of autocorrelation, which we will address in another chapter.

To see if there is a structural break, we can express the investment function as:

$$GPI_t = B_1 + B_2 GPS_t + B_3 Recession81_t + u_t \tag{3.8}$$

where Recession81 is a dummy variable taking a value of 1 for observations beginning in 1981 and 0 before that year. As you will recognize, $B_3$ is a *differential intercept*, telling us how much the average level of investment has changed since 1981. The regression results are shown in Table 3.8.

The recession dummy coefficient is not significant, suggesting that there has been no statistically visible change in the level of investment pre- and post-1981 recession. In other words, the results would suggest that there is no structural break in the US economy. We have to accept this conclusion cautiously, for it is quite likely that not only the intercept but the slope of the investment–savings regression might have changed. To allow for this possibility, we can introduce both differential intercept and differential slope dummies. So we estimate the following model:

$$GPI_t = B_1 + B_2 GPS_t + B_3 Recession81$$
$$+ B_4 GPS^* Recession81_t + u_t \tag{3.9}$$

In this equation $B_3$ represents the differential intercept and $B_4$ the differential slope coefficient; see how we have interacted the dummy variable with the GPS variable.

The results of this regression are shown in Table 3.9. The results in this table are quite different from those in Table 3.8: now both the differential intercept and slope coefficients are statistically significant. This means that the investment–savings relationship has gone structural change since the recession of 1981. From this table we can

**Table 3.8  Regression of GPI on GPS with 1981 recession dummy.**

Dependent Variable: GPI
Method: Least Squares
Sample: 1959 2007
Included observations: 49

| Variable | Coefficient | Std. Error | t-Statistic | Prob. |
|---|---|---|---|---|
| C | −77.89198 | 27.72938 | −2.809006 | 0.0073 |
| GPS | 1.099832 | 0.032306 | 34.04453 | 0.0000 |
| RECESSION81 | 6.496153 | 11.69500 | 0.555464 | 0.5813 |

| | | | |
|---|---|---|---|
| R-squared | 0.968817 | Mean dependent var | 760.9061 |
| Adjusted R-squared | 0.967461 | S.D. dependent var | 641.5260 |
| S.E. of regression | 115.7225 | Akaike info criterion | 12.39954 |
| Sum squared resid | 616017.9 | Schwarz criterion | 12.51536 |
| Log likelihood | −300.7887 | Hannan−Quinn criter. | 12.44348 |
| F-statistic | 714.5717 | Durbin−Watson stat | 0.385512 |
| Prob(F-statistic) | 0.000000 | | |

**Table 3.9  Regression of GPI on GPS with interactive dummy.**

Dependent Variable: GPI
Method: Least Squares
Sample: 1959 2007
Included observations: 49

| Variable | Coefficient | Std. Error | t-Statistic | Prob. |
|---|---|---|---|---|
| C | −32.49016 | 23.24972 | −1.397443 | 0.1691 |
| GPS | 1.069202 | 0.025916 | 41.25623 | 0.0000 |
| DUMMY81 | −327.8491 | 61.75397 | −5.308955 | 0.0000 |
| GPS*DUMMY81 | 0.244142 | 0.044594 | 5.474721 | 0.0000 |

| | | | |
|---|---|---|---|
| R-squared | 0.981283 | Mean dependent var | 760.9061 |
| Adjusted R-squared | 0.980035 | S.D. dependent var | 641.5260 |
| S.E. of regression | 90.64534 | Akaike info criterion | 11.92989 |
| Sum squared resid | 369746.0 | Schwarz criterion | 12.08433 |
| Log likelihood | −288.2824 | Hannan−Quinn criter. | 11.98849 |
| F-statistic | 786.4151 | Durbin−Watson stat | 0.828988 |
| Prob(F-statistic) | 0.000000 | | |

derive the investment–savings regressions for the period pre- and post-1981 as follows:

**Investment–savings relationship before 1981**

$$\hat{GPI}_t = -32.4901 + 1.0692 GPS_t$$

**Investment–savings relationship after 1981**

$$\hat{GPI}_t = (-32.4901 - 327.8491) + (1.0692 + 0.2441) GPS_t$$

$$= -360.3392 + 1.3133 GPS_t$$

This example is a reminder that we have to be careful in using the dummy variables. It should also be added that there might be more than one structural break in the economy. For example, the USA underwent another recession right after the 1973 oil embargo imposed by the OPEC oil cartel. So we could have another dummy to reflect that event. The only precaution you have to exercise is that if you do not have a large enough samples, introducing too many dummy variables will cost you several degrees of freedom. And as the degrees of freedom dwindle, statistical inference becomes less reliable. This example also reminds us that in estimating a regression model we should be wary of mechanically estimating it without paying due attention to the possibility of structural breaks, especially if we are dealing with time series data.

## 3.6    Use of dummy variables in seasonal data

An interesting feature of many economic time series based on weekly, monthly, and quarterly data is that they exhibit seasonal patterns (oscillatory movements). Some frequently encountered examples are sales at Christmas time, demand for money by households at vacation times, demand for cold drinks in the summer, demand for air travel at major holidays such as Thanksgiving and Christmas, and demand for chocolate on Valentine's Day.

The process of removing the seasonal component from a time series is called **deseasonlization** or **seasonal adjustment** and the resulting time series is called a **deseasonalized** or seasonally adjusted time series.[7]

Important time series, such as the consumer price index (CPI), producer's price index (PPI), unemployment rate, housing starts, and index of industrial production are usually published in seasonally adjusted basis.

There are various methods of deseasonalizing a time series, but one simple and rough and ready method is the method of dummy variables.[8]

We illustrate this method with a concrete example. See **Table 3.10** on the companion website.[9]

Since sales of fashion clothing are season-sensitive, we would expect a good deal of seasonal variation in the volume of sales. The model we consider is as follows:

$$Sales_t = A_1 + A_2 D_{2t} + A_3 D_{3t} + A_4 D_{4t} + u_t \qquad (3.10)$$

where $D_2 = 1$ for second quarter, $D_3 = 1$ for third quarter, $D_4 = 1$ for fourth quarter, $Sales$ = real sales per thousand square feet of retail space. Later we will expand this model to include some quantitative regressors.

Notice that we are treating the first quarter of the year as the reference quarter. Therefore $A_2, A_3,$ and $A_4$ are *differential* intercept coefficients, showing how the mean sales in the second, third, and fourth quarters differ from the mean sales in the first quarter. $A_1$ is the mean sales value in the first quarter. Also note that we assume that each quarter is associated with a different season.

---

7   It may be noted that a time series may contain four components: seasonal, cyclical, trend, and random.

8   For an accessible discussion of the various methods, see Francis X. Diebold, *Elements of Forecasting*, 4th edn, South Western Publishing, 2007.

9   The data used here are taken from Christiaan Heij, Paul de Boer, Philip Hans Franses, Teun Kloek, Herman K. van Dijk, *Econometric Methods with Applications in Business and Economics*, Oxford University Press, 2004, but the original source is: G.M. Allenby, L. Jen, and R.P. Leone, Economic Trends and Being Trendy: The influence of Consumer Confidence on Retail Fashion Sales, *Journal of Business and Economic Statistics*, 1996, pp. 103–111.

**Table 3.11  Results of regression (3.10).**

Dependent Variable: SALES
Method: Least Squares
Sample: 1986Q1 1992Q4
Included observations: 28

|  | Coefficient | Std. Error | t-Statistic | Prob. |
|---|---|---|---|---|
| C | 73.18343 | 3.977483 | 18.39943 | 0.0000 |
| D2 | 14.69229 | 5.625010 | 2.611957 | 0.0153 |
| D3 | 27.96471 | 5.625010 | 4.971496 | 0.0000 |
| D4 | 57.11471 | 5.625010 | 10.15371 | 0.0000 |

| R-squared | 0.823488 | Mean dependent var | 98.12636 |
|---|---|---|---|
| Adjusted R-squared | 0.801424 | S.D. dependent var | 23.61535 |
| S.E. of regression | 10.52343 | Akaike info criterion | 7.676649 |
| Sum squared resid | 2657.822 | Schwarz criterion | 7.866964 |
| Log likelihood | −103.4731 | Durbin–Watson stat | 1.024353 |
| F-statistic | 37.32278 | Prob(F-statistic) | 0.000000 |

The data for estimating Eq. (3.10) are given in Table 3.10 along with data on some other variables, which can be found on the companion website.

The results of the regression (3.10) are given in Table 3.11. These results show that individually each differential intercept dummy is highly statistically significant, as shown by its $p$ value. The interpretation of, say, $D_2$ is that the mean sales value in the second quarter is greater than the mean sales in the first, or reference, quarter by 14.69229 units; the actual mean sales value in the second quarter is (73.18343 + 14.69229) = 87.87572. The other differential intercept dummies are to be interpreted similarly.

As you can see from Table 3.11, fashion sales are highest in the fourth quarter, which includes Christmas and other holidays, which is not a surprising finding.

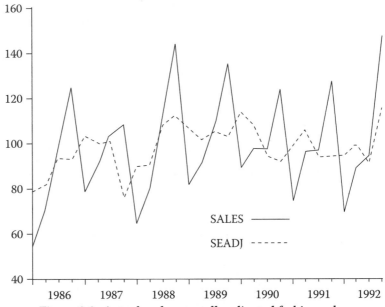

**Figure 3.3  Actual and seasonally adjusted fashion sales.**

**Table 3.12  Sales, forecast sales, residuals, and seasonally adjusted sales.**

| obs | SALES | SALESF | RESID | SEADJ |
|---|---|---|---|---|
| 1986Q1 | 53.71400 | 73.18343 | −19.46943 | 78.65417 |
| 1986Q2 | 71.50100 | 87.87572 | −16.37471 | 81.74889 |
| 1986Q3 | 96.37400 | 101.1481 | −4.774143 | 93.34946 |
| 1986Q4 | 125.0410 | 130.2981 | −5.257143 | 92.86646 |
| 1987Q1 | 78.61000 | 73.18343 | 5.426571 | 103.5502 |
| 1987Q2 | 89.60900 | 87.87572 | 1.733286 | 99.85689 |
| 1987Q3 | 104.0220 | 101.1481 | 2.873857 | 100.9975 |
| 1987Q4 | 108.5580 | 130.2981 | −21.74014 | 76.38345 |
| 1988Q1 | 64.74100 | 73.18343 | −8.442429 | 89.68118 |
| 1988Q2 | 80.05800 | 87.87572 | −7.817714 | 90.30589 |
| 1988Q3 | 110.6710 | 101.1481 | 9.522857 | 107.6465 |
| 1988Q4 | 144.5870 | 130.2981 | 14.28886 | 112.4125 |
| 1989Q1 | 81.58900 | 73.18343 | 8.405571 | 106.5292 |
| 1989Q2 | 91.35400 | 87.87572 | 3.478286 | 101.6019 |
| 1989Q3 | 108.1330 | 101.1481 | 6.984857 | 105.1085 |
| 1989Q4 | 135.1750 | 130.2981 | 4.876857 | 103.0005 |
| 1990Q1 | 89.13400 | 73.18343 | 15.95057 | 114.0742 |
| 1990Q2 | 97.76500 | 87.87572 | 9.889286 | 108.0129 |
| 1990Q3 | 97.37400 | 101.1481 | −3.774143 | 94.34946 |
| 1990Q4 | 124.0240 | 130.2981 | −6.274143 | 91.84946 |
| 1991Q1 | 74.58900 | 73.18343 | 1.405571 | 99.52917 |
| 1991Q2 | 95.69200 | 87.87572 | 7.816286 | 105.9399 |
| 1991Q3 | 96.94200 | 101.1481 | −4.206143 | 93.91746 |
| 1991Q4 | 126.8170 | 130.2981 | −3.481143 | 94.64246 |
| 1992Q1 | 69.90700 | 73.18343 | −3.276428 | 94.84717 |
| 1992Q2 | 89.15100 | 87.87572 | 1.275286 | 99.39889 |
| 1992Q3 | 94.52100 | 101.1481 | −6.627143 | 91.49646 |
| 1992Q4 | 147.8850 | 130.2981 | 17.58686 | 115.7105 |

*Note*: Residuals = actual sales − forecast sales; seadj = seasonally adjusted sales, which are obtained by adding to the residuals the average value of sales over the sample period, which is 98.1236.

Since the sales volume differs from quarter to quarter, how do we obtain the values of the fashion sales time series that take into account the observed seasonal variation? In other words, how do we deseasonalize this time series?

In order to deseasonalize the sales time series, we proceed as follows:

1  From the estimated model (3.10) we obtain the estimated sales volume.

2  Subtract the estimated sales value from the actual sales volume and obtain the residuals.

3  To the estimated residuals, we add the (sample) mean value of sales, which is 98.1236 in the present case. The resulting values are the deseasonalized sales values. We show the calculations in Table 3.12.

Figure 3.3 (p. 59) shows the actual and adjusted fashion sales. As you can see from this figure, the seasonally adjusted sales series is much smoother than the original series. Since the seasonal factor has been removed from the adjusted sales series, the ups and downs in the adjusted series may reflect the cyclical, trend, and random components that may exist in the series (see Exercise 3.12).

From the retailers' point of view, knowledge of seasonal factors is important as it enables them to plan their inventory according to the season. This also helps manufacturers to plan their production schedule.

## 3.7   Expanded sales function

Besides sales volume, we have data on real personal disposable income (RPDI) and consumer confidence index (CONF). Adding these variables to regression (3.10), we obtain Table 3.13.

The first point to note is that all the differential dummy coefficients are highly significant (the $p$ values being very low in each case), suggesting that there is seasonal factor associated with each quarter. The quantitative regressors are also highly significant and have *a priori* expected signs; both have positive impact on sales volume.

Following the procedure laid out for deseasonalizing a time series, for the expanded sales function we obtain the seasonally adjusted sales as shown in Table 3.14. Figure 3.4 shows the results graphically.

As you would expect, the seasonally adjusted sales figures are much smoother than the original sales figures.

**A technical note:** We found seasonality in the fashion sales time series. Could there be seasonality in the PPDI and CONF series? If so, how do we deseasonalize the latter two series? Interestingly, the dummy variables used to deseasonalize the sales time series also deseasonalize the other two time series. This is due to a well-known

**Table 3.13  Expanded model of fashion sales.**

Dependent Variable: SALES
Method: Least Squares
Sample: 1986Q1 1992Q4
Included observations: 28

|       | Coefficient | Std. Error | t-Statistic | Prob. |
|-------|-------------|------------|-------------|-------|
| C     | −152.9293   | 52.59149   | −2.907871   | 0.0082 |
| RPDI  | 1.598903    | 0.370155   | 4.319548    | 0.0003 |
| CONF  | 0.293910    | 0.084376   | 3.483346    | 0.0021 |
| D2    | 15.04522    | 4.315377   | 3.486421    | 0.0021 |
| D3    | 26.00247    | 4.325243   | 6.011795    | 0.0000 |
| D4    | 60.87226    | 4.427437   | 13.74887    | 0.0000 |

| | | | | |
|---|---|---|---|---|
| R-squared | 0.905375 | Mean dependent var | 98.12636 | |
| Adjusted R-squared | 0.883869 | S.D. dependent var | 23.61535 | |
| S.E. of regression | 8.047636 | Akaike info criterion | 7.196043 | |
| Sum squared resid | 1424.818 | Schwarz criterion | 7.481516 | |
| Log likelihood | −94.74461 | Durbin–Watson stat | 1.315456 | |
| F-statistic | 42.09923 | Prob(F-statistic) | 0.000000 | |

Table 3.14  Actual sales, forecast sales, residuals, and seasonally adjusted sales.

| SALES | FORECAST SALES | RESIDUALS | SADSALES |
|---|---|---|---|
| 53.71400 | 65.90094 | −12.18694 | 85.93666 |
| 71.50100 | 83.40868 | −11.90768 | 86.21592 |
| 96.37400 | 91.90977 | 4.464227 | 102.5878 |
| 125.0410 | 122.7758 | 2.265227 | 100.3888 |
| 78.61000 | 66.77385 | 11.83615 | 109.9598 |
| 89.60900 | 78.80558 | 10.80342 | 108.9270 |
| 104.0220 | 95.25996 | 8.762036 | 106.8856 |
| 108.5580 | 122.1257 | −13.56774 | 84.55586 |
| 64.74100 | 73.55222 | −8.811222 | 89.31238 |
| 80.05800 | 86.16732 | −6.109321 | 92.01428 |
| 110.6710 | 104.9276 | 5.743355 | 103.8670 |
| 144.5870 | 133.7971 | 10.78986 | 108.9135 |
| 81.58900 | 83.36707 | −1.778069 | 96.34553 |
| 91.35400 | 92.49550 | −1.141502 | 96.98210 |
| 108.1330 | 111.1844 | −3.051364 | 95.07224 |
| 135.1750 | 140.9760 | −5.801002 | 92.32260 |
| 89.13400 | 81.99727 | 7.136726 | 105.2603 |
| 97.76500 | 92.76732 | 4.997684 | 103.1213 |
| 97.37400 | 97.34940 | 0.024596 | 98.14819 |
| 124.0240 | 121.5858 | 2.438186 | 100.5618 |
| 74.58900 | 70.90284 | 3.686156 | 101.8098 |
| 95.69200 | 90.00940 | 5.682596 | 103.8062 |
| 96.94200 | 104.7525 | −7.810495 | 90.31310 |
| 126.8170 | 127.3469 | −0.529909 | 97.59369 |
| 69.90700 | 69.78981 | 0.117194 | 98.24079 |
| 89.15100 | 91.47620 | −2.325197 | 95.79840 |
| 94.52100 | 102.6534 | −8.132355 | 89.99124 |
| 147.8850 | 143.4796 | 4.405374 | 102.5290 |

*Note*: Seasonally adjusted sales (SADSALES) = residual + 98.1236

theorem in statistics, known as the **Frisch–Waugh Theorem**[10] (see Exercise 3.9). So by introducing the seasonal dummies in the model we deseasonalize all the time series used in the model. So to speak, we kill (deseasonalize) three birds (three time series) with one stone (a set of dummy variables).

The results given in Table 3.13 assume that the intercepts, reflecting seasonal factors, vary from quarter to quarter, but the slope coefficients of RPDI and CONF remain constant throughout. But we can test this assumption, by introducing differential slope dummies as follows:

---

10  "In general the theorem shows that if variables are subject to prior adjustment by ordinary least squares and the residuals subsequently used in a regression equation then the resulting estimates are identical to those from a regression which uses unadjusted data but uses the adjustment variables explicitly." Adrian C. Darnell, *A Dictionary of Econometrics*, Edward Elgar, UK, 1997, p. 150.

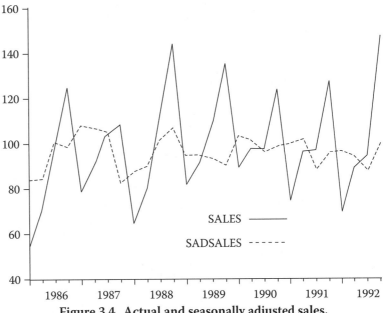

**Figure 3.4  Actual and seasonally adjusted sales.**

$$Sales_t = A_1 + A_2 D_{2t} + A_3 D_{3t} + A_4 D_{4t} + B_1 RPDI_t + B_2 CONF$$

$$+ B_3 (D_2 {}^* RPDI_t) + B_4 (D_3 {}^* RPDI_t) + B_5 (D_4 {}^* RPDI_t) \qquad (3.11)$$

$$+ B_6 (D_2 {}^* CONF_t) + B_7 (D_3 {}^* CONF_t) + B_8 (D_4 {}^* CONF_t) + u_t$$

In this formulation, the differential slope coefficients $B_3$ through $B_8$ allow us to find out if the slope coefficients of the two quantitative regressors vary from quarter to quarter. The results are shown in Table 3.15.

Since none of the differential slope coefficients are statistically significant, these results show that the coefficients of RPDI and CONF do not vary over the seasons. Since these results also show that none of the seasonal dummies are significant, there are no seasonal variations in the fashion sales. But if we drop the differential slope coefficients from the model, all the (differential) intercept dummies are statistically significant, as we saw in Table 3.13. This strongly suggests that there is a strong seasonal factor in fashion sales.

What this implies is that the differential slope dummies do not belong in the model. So we will stick with the model given in Table 3.12.

Even then the exercise in Table 3.15 is not futile because it shows that in modeling a phenomenon we must take into account the possibility of the differences in both the intercepts and slope coefficients. It is only when we consider the full model, as in Eq. (3.11), that we will be able to find out whether there are differences in the intercepts or slopes or both.

**Table 3.15  Fashion sales regression with differential intercept and slope dummies.**

Dependent Variable: SALES
Method: Least Squares
Sample: 1986Q1 1992Q4
Included observations: 28

|  | Coefficient | Std. Error | t-Statistic | Prob. |
|---|---|---|---|---|
| C | −191.5847 | 107.9813 | −1.774239 | 0.0951 |
| D2 | 196.7020 | 221.2632 | 0.888995 | 0.3872 |
| D3 | 123.1388 | 163.4398 | 0.753420 | 0.4621 |
| D4 | 50.96459 | 134.7884 | 0.378108 | 0.7103 |
| RPDI | 2.049795 | 0.799888 | 2.562601 | 0.0209 |
| CONF | 0.280938 | 0.156896 | 1.790602 | 0.0923 |
| D2*RPDI | −1.110584 | 1.403951 | −0.791042 | 0.4405 |
| D3*RPDI | −1.218073 | 1.134186 | −1.073963 | 0.2988 |
| D4*RPDI | −0.049873 | 1.014161 | −0.049176 | 0.9614 |
| D2*CONF | −0.294815 | 0.381777 | −0.772219 | 0.4512 |
| D3*CONF | 0.065237 | 0.259860 | 0.251046 | 0.8050 |
| D4*CONF | 0.057868 | 0.201070 | 0.287803 | 0.7772 |

| | | | |
|---|---|---|---|
| R-squared | 0.929307 | Mean dependent var | 98.12636 |
| Adjusted R-squared | 0.880706 | S.D. dependent var | 23.61535 |
| S.E. of regression | 8.156502 | Akaike info criterion | 7.333035 |
| Sum squared resid | 1064.456 | Schwarz criterion | 7.903980 |
| Log likelihood | −90.66249 | Hannan–Quinn criter. | 7.507578 |
| F-statistic | 19.12102 | Durbin–Watson stat | 1.073710 |
| Prob(F-statistic) | 0.000000 | | |

## 3.8　Summary and conclusions

Qualitative, or dummy, variables taking values of 1 and 0 show how qualitative regressors can be "quantified" and the role they play in regression analysis.

If there are differences in the response of the regressand because of qualitative regressors, they will be reflected in the differences in the intercepts, or slope coefficients, or both of the various subgroup regressions.

Dummy variables have been used in a variety of situations, such as (1) comparing two or more regressions, (2) structural break(s) in time series, and (3) deseasonalizing time series.

Despite their useful role in regression analysis, dummy variables need to be handled carefully. *First*, if there is an intercept in the regression model, the number of dummy variables must be one less than the number of classifications of each qualitative variable. *Second*, of course, if you drop the (common) intercept from the model, you can have as many dummy variables as the number of categories of the dummy variable. *Third*, the coefficient of a dummy variable must always be interpreted in relation to the reference category, that is, the category that receives the value of 0. The choice of the reference category depends on the purpose of research at hand. *Fourth*, dummy variables can interact with quantitative regressors as well as with qualitative regressors. *Fifth*, if a model has several qualitative variables with several categories, introduction of dummies for all the combinations can consume a large number of degrees of freedom, especially if the sample size is relatively small. *Sixth*, keep in mind that there are other more sophisticated methods of deseasonalizing a time series, such as the Census X-12 method used by the US Department of Commerce.

# Exercises

**3.1**  How would you compare the results of the linear wage function given in Table 3.1 with the semi-log wage regression given in Table 3.5? How would you compare the various coefficients given in the two tables?

**3.2**  Replicate Table 3.4, using log of wage rate as the dependent variable and compare the results thus obtained with those given in Table 3.4.

**3.3**  Suppose you regress the log of the wage rate on the logs of education and experience and the dummy variables for gender, race, and union status. How would you interpret the slope coefficients in this regression?

**3.4**  Besides the variables included in the wage regression in Tables 3.1 and 3.5, what other variables would you include?

**3.5**  Suppose you want to consider the geographic region in which the wage earner resides. Suppose we divide US states into four groups: east, south, west, and north. How would you extend the models given in Tables 3.1 and 3.5?

**3.6**  Suppose instead of coding dummies as 1 and 0, you code them as −1 and +1. How would you interpret the regression results using this coding?

**3.7**  Suppose somebody suggests that in the semi-log wage function instead of using 1 and 0 values for the dummy variables, you use the values 10 and 1. What would be the outcome?

**3.8**  Refer to the fashion data given in Table 3.10. Using log of sales as the dependent variable, obtain results corresponding to Tables 3.11, 3.12, 3.13, 3.14, and 3.15 and compare the two sets of results.

**3.9**  Regress Sales, RPDI, and CONF individually on an intercept and the three dummies and obtain residuals from these regressions, say $S_1$, $S_2$, $S_3$. Now regress $S_1$ on $S_2$ and $S_3$ (no intercept term in this regression)[11] and show that slope coefficients of $S_2$ and $S_3$ are precisely the same as those of RPDI and CONF obtained in Table 3.13, thus verifying the *Frisch–Waugh theorem*.

**3.10**  Collect quarterly data on personal consumption expenditure (PCE) and disposable personal income (DPI), both adjusted for inflation, and regress personal consumption expenditure on personal disposable income. If you think there is a seasonal pattern in the data, how would you deseasonalize the data using dummy variables? Show the necessary calculations.

---

11  Since the mean value of OLS residuals is always zero, there is no need for the intercept in this regression.

12  This is taken from Table 4 of Rashad (Kelly), Inas, Obesity and diabetes: the roles that prices and policies play. *Advances in Health Economics and Health Services Research*, vol. 17, pp. 113–28, 2007. Data come from various years.

**3.11** Continuing with Exercise 3.10, how would you find out if there are structural breaks in the relationship between PCE and DPI? Show the necessary calculations.

**3.12** Refer to the fashion sales example discussed in the text. Reestimate Eq. (3.10) by adding the trend variable, taking values of 1, 2, and so on. Compare your results with those given in Table 3.10. What do these results suggest?

**3.13** Continue with the preceding exercise. Estimate the sales series after removing the seasonal and trend components from it and compare your analysis with that discussed in the text.

**3.14** Estimate the effects of *ban* and *sugar_sweet_cap* on *diabetes* using the data in **Table 3.16**, which can be found on the companion website,[12] where

  *diabetes* = diabetes prevalence in country

  *ban* = 1 if some type of ban on genetically modified goods is present, 0 otherwise

  *sugar_sweet_cap* = domestic supply of sugar and sweeteners per capita, in kg

  What other variables could have been included in the model?

# Critical evaluation of the classical linear regression model

# 4

# Regression diagnostic I: multicollinearity

One of the assumptions of the classical linear regression model (CLRM) is that there is no *exact linear* relationship among the regressors. If there are one or more such relationships among the regressors we call it multicollinearity or collinearity, for short. At the outset, we must distinguish between **perfect collinearity** and **imperfect collinearity**.[1] To explain, consider the $k$-variable linear regression model:

$$Y_i = B_1 + B_2 X_{2i} + \ldots + B_k X_{ki} + u_i \tag{4.1}$$

If, for example, $X_{2i} + 3X_{3i} = 1$ we have a case of perfect collinearity for $X_{2i} = 1 - 3X_{3i}$. Therefore, if we were to include both $X_{2i}$ and $X_{3i}$ in the same regression model, we will have perfect collinearity, that is, a perfect linear relationship between the two variables. In situations like this we cannot even estimate the regression coefficients, let alone perform any kind of statistical inference.

On the other hand, if we have $X_{2i} + 3X_{3i} + v_i = 1$, where $v_i$ is a random error term, we have the case of imperfect collinearity, for $X_{2i} = 1 - 3X_{3i} - v_i$. Therefore, in this case there is no perfect linear relationship between the two variables; so to speak, the presence of the error term $v_i$ dilutes the perfect relationship between these variables.

In practice, exact linear relationship(s) among regressors is a rarity, but in many applications the regressors may be highly collinear. This case may be called **imperfect collinearity** or **near-collinearity**. Therefore, in this chapter we focus our attention on imperfect collinearity.[2]

---

1  If there is just one perfect linear relationship between two more regressors, we call it collinearity, but if there is more than one perfect linear relationship, we call it multicollinearity. However, we will use the terms *collinearity* and *multicollinearity* interchangeably. The context of the problem at hand will tell us which one we are dealing with.

2  To give an extreme example of perfect collinearity, suppose we introduce income variables in both dollars and cents in the consumption function, relating consumption expenditure to income. Since a dollar is equal to 100 cents, including this will lead to perfect collinearity. Another example is the so-called dummy variable trap, which, as we saw in Chapter 3, results if we include both an intercept term and all categories of the dummy variables. For example, in a regression explaining hours of work in relation to several economic variables, we include two dummies, one for male and one for female, and also retain the intercept term. This will lead to perfect collinearity. Of course, if we suppress the intercept term in this situation, we will avoid the dummy variable trap. In practice it is better to retain the intercept but include just one gender dummy; if the dummy takes a value of 1 for females, it will take a value of 0 whenever a male worker is involved.

## 4.1    Consequences of imperfect collinearity

1  OLS estimators are still BLUE, but they have large variances and covariances, making precise estimation difficult.

2  As a result, the confidence intervals tend to be wider. Therefore, we may not reject the "zero null hypothesis" (i.e. the true population coefficient is zero).

3  Because of (1), the $t$ ratios of one or more coefficients tend to be statistically insignificant.

4  Even though some regression coefficients are statistically insignificant, the $R^2$ value may be very high.

5  The OLS estimators and their standard errors can be sensitive to small changes in the data (see Exercise 4.6).

6  Adding a collinear variable to the chosen regression model can alter the coefficient values of the other variables in the model.

In short, when regressors are collinear, statistical inference becomes shaky, especially so if there is near-collinearity. This should not be surprising, because if two variables are highly collinear it is very difficult to isolate the impact of each variable separately on the regressand.

To see some of these consequences, we consider a three-variable model, relating the dependent variable $Y$ to two regressors, $X_2$ and $X_3$. That is, we consider the following model:

$$Y_i = B_1 + B_2 X_{2i} + B_3 X_{3i} + u_i \tag{4.1}$$

Using OLS, it can be shown that the OLS estimators are as follows[3]

$$b_2 = \frac{(\Sigma y_i x_{2i})(\Sigma x_{3i}^2) - (\Sigma y_i x_{3i})(\Sigma x_{2i} x_{3i})}{(\Sigma x_{2i}^2)(\Sigma x_{3i}^2) - (\Sigma x_{2i} x_{3i})^2} \tag{4.2}$$

$$b_3 = \frac{(\Sigma y_i x_{3i})(\Sigma x_{2i}^2) - (\Sigma y_i x_{2i})(\Sigma x_{2i} x_{3i})}{(\Sigma x_{2i}^2)(\Sigma x_{3i}^2) - (\Sigma x_{2i} x_{3i})^2} \tag{4.3}$$

$$b_1 = \overline{Y} - b_2 \overline{X}_2 - b_3 \overline{X}_3 \tag{4.4}$$

where the variables are expressed as deviations from their mean values – that is, $y_i = Y_i - \overline{Y}$, $x_{2i} = X_{2i} - \overline{X}_2$ and $X_{3i} - \overline{X}_3$.

Notice that the formulae for the two slope coefficients are symmetrical in the sense that one can be obtained form the other by interchanging the names of the variables.

It can be further shown that

$$\text{var}(b_2) = \frac{\sigma^2}{\Sigma x_{2i}^2 (1 - r_{23}^2)} = \frac{\sigma^2}{\Sigma x_{2i}^2} \text{VIF} \tag{4.5}$$

and

$$\text{var}(b_3) = \frac{\sigma^2}{\Sigma x_{3i}^2 (1 - r_{23}^2)} = \frac{\sigma^2}{\Sigma x_{3i}^2} \text{VIF} \tag{4.6}$$

---

3  See Gujarati/Porter, *op cit.*, pp. 193–4.

**Table 4.1  The effect of increasing $r_{23}$ on the variance of OLS estimator $b_2$.**

| Value of $r_{23}$ | VIF | Var($b_2$) |
|---|---|---|
| 0.0 | 1.00 | $\sigma^2 / \Sigma x_{2i}^2 = K$ |
| 0.50 | 1.33 | $1.33 \times K$ |
| 0.70 | 1.96 | $1.96 \times K$ |
| 0.80 | 2.78 | $2.78 \times K$ |
| 0.90 | 5.26 | $5.26 \times K$ |
| 0.95 | 10.26 | $10.26 \times K$ |
| 0.99 | 50.25 | $50.25 \times K$ |
| 0.995 | 100.00 | $100 \times K$ |
| 1.00 | Undefined | Undefined |

Note: A similar table can be shown for the variance of $b_3$.

where

$$\text{VIF} = \frac{1}{1 - r_{23}^2} \tag{4.7}$$

where $\sigma^2$ is the variance of the error term $u_i$ and $r_{23}$ is the coefficient of correlation between $X_2$ and $X_3$ and *VIF* is the **variance-inflating factor**: a measure of the degree to which the variance of the OLS estimator is inflated because of collinearity. To see this, consider Table 4.1.

It is clear from this table that as the correlation coefficient between $X_2$ and $X_3$ increases, the variance of $b_2$ increases rapidly in a nonlinear fashion. As a result, the confidence intervals will be progressively wider and we may mistakenly conclude that the true $B_2$ is indifferent from zero.

It may be noted that the inverse of the VIF is called **tolerance** (**TOL**) – that is

$$\text{TOL} = \frac{1}{\text{VIF}} \tag{4.8}$$

When $r_{23}^2 = 1$ (i.e. perfect collinearity ), TOL is zero, and when it is 0 (i.e. no collinearity), TOL is 1.

The VIF formula given for the two-variable regression can be generalized to the $k$-variable regression model (an intercept and $(k-1)$ regressors) as follows:

$$\text{var}(b_k) = \frac{\sigma^2}{\Sigma x_k^2} \left( \frac{1}{1 - R_k^2} \right) = \frac{\sigma^2}{\Sigma x_k^2} \text{VIF} \tag{4.9}$$

where $R_k^2$ is the $R^2$ from the regression of the $k$th regressor on all other regressors in the model and where $\Sigma x_k^2 = \Sigma(X_k - \overline{X}_k)^2$ is the variation in the $k$th variable about its mean value. The regression of the $k$th regressor on the other regressors in the model is called an **auxiliary regression**, so if we have 10 regressors in the model, we will have 10 auxiliary regressions.

The *Stata* statistical package computes the *VIF* and *TOL* factors by issuing the command **estat vif** after estimating an OLS regression, as we show in the following example.

## 4.2    An example: married women's hours of work in the labor market

To shed light on the nature of multicollinearity, we use the data from the empirical work done by Mroz[4] – see **Table 4.2** on the companion website. He wanted to assess the impact of several socio-economic variables on married women's hours of work in the labor market. This is cross-sectional data on 753 married women for the year 1975. It should be noted that there were 325 married women who did not work and hence had zero hours of work.

Some of the variables he used are as follows:

Hours: hours worked in 1975 (dependent variable)

Kidslt6: number of kids under age 6

Kidsge6: number of kids between ages 6 and 18

Age: woman's age in years

Educ: years of schooling

Wage: estimated wage from earnings

Hushrs: hours worked by husband

Husage: husband's age

Huseduc: husband's years of schooling

Huswage: husband's hourly wage, 1975

Faminc: family income in 1975

Mtr: federal marginal tax rate facing a woman

motheduc: mother's years of schooling

fatheduc: father's years of schooling

Unem: unemployment rate in county of residence

exper: actual labor market experience

As a starting point, we obtained the regression results of Table 4.3.

*A priori*, we would expect a positive relation between hours of work and education, experience, father's education and mother's education, and a negative relationship between hours of work and age, husband's age, husband's hours of work, husband's wages, marginal tax rate, unemployment rate and children under 6. Most of these expectations are borne out by the statistical results. However, a substantial number of coefficients are statistically insignificant, perhaps suggesting that some of these variables are collinear, thus leading to higher standard errors and reduced $t$ ratios.

## 4.3    Detection of multicollinearity

As we will see in the chapters on autocorrelation and heteroscedasticity, there is no unique test of multicollinearity. Some of the diagnostics discussed in the literature are as follows.

---

4  See T. A. Mroz, The sensitivity of an empirical model of married women's hours of work to economic and statistical assumptions, *Econometrica*, 1987, vol. 55, pp. 765–99.

**Table 4.3  Women's hours worked regression.**

Dependent Variable: HOURS
Method: Least Squares
Sample (adjusted): 1 428
Included observations: 428 after adjustments

| | Coefficient | Std. Error | t-Statistic | Prob. |
|---|---|---|---|---|
| C | 8595.360 | 1027.190 | 8.367842 | 0.0000 |
| AGE | −14.30741 | 9.660582 | −1.481009 | 0.1394 |
| EDUC | −18.39847 | 19.34225 | −0.951207 | 0.3421 |
| EXPER | 22.88057 | 4.777417 | 4.789319 | 0.0000 |
| FAMINC | 0.013887 | 0.006042 | 2.298543 | 0.0220 |
| FATHEDUC | −7.471447 | 11.19227 | −0.667554 | 0.5048 |
| HUSAGE | −5.586215 | 8.938425 | −0.624966 | 0.5323 |
| HUSEDUC | −6.769256 | 13.98780 | −0.483940 | 0.6287 |
| HUSHRS | −0.473547 | 0.073274 | −6.462701 | 0.0000 |
| HUSWAGE | −141.7821 | 16.61801 | −8.531837 | 0.0000 |
| KIDSGE6 | −24.50867 | 28.06160 | −0.873388 | 0.3830 |
| KIDSLT6 | −191.5648 | 87.83198 | −2.181038 | 0.0297 |
| WAGE | −48.14963 | 10.41198 | −4.624447 | 0.0000 |
| MOTHEDUC | −1.837597 | 11.90008 | −0.154419 | 0.8774 |
| MTR | −6272.597 | 1085.438 | −5.778864 | 0.0000 |
| UNEM | −16.11532 | 10.63729 | −1.514984 | 0.1305 |

| | | | |
|---|---|---|---|
| R-squared | 0.339159 | Mean dependent var | 1302.930 |
| Adjusted R-squared | 0.315100 | S.D. dependent var | 776.2744 |
| S.E. of regression | 642.4347 | Akaike info criterion | 15.80507 |
| Sum squared resid | 1.70E+08 | Schwarz criterion | 15.95682 |
| Log likelihood | −3366.286 | Durbin–Watson stat | 2.072493 |
| F-statistic | 14.09655 | Prob(F-statistic) | 0.000000 |

1  **High $R^2$ but few significant $t$ ratios.** In our example the $R^2$ value of 0.34 is not particularly high. But this should not be surprising in cross-sectional data with several diverse observations. However, quite a few $t$ ratios are statistically insignificant, perhaps due to collinearity among some regressors.

2  **High pairwise correlations among explanatory variables or regressors.** Recall that the sample correlation coefficient between variables $Y$ and $X$ is defined as:

$$r_{XY} = \frac{\Sigma x_i y_i}{\sqrt{\Sigma x_i^2 \Sigma y_i^2}} \tag{4.10}$$

where the variables are defined as deviations from their mean values (e.g. $y_i = Y_i - \bar{Y}$). Since we have 15 regressors, we will have 105 pairwise correlations.[5] We will not produce all these correlations. Most of the correlation coefficients are not particularly high, but some are in excess of 0.5. For example, the correlation between husband's age and family income is about 0.67, that between mother's

---

5  Of course not all these correlations will be different because the correlation between $Y$ and $X$ is the same as that between $X$ and $Y$.

education and father's education is about 0.55, and that between the marginal tax rate and family income is about −0.88.

It is believed that high pairwise correlations between regressors are a sign of collinearity. Therefore one should drop highly correlated regressors. But it is not a good practice to rely on simple or bivariate correlation coefficients, because they do not hold the other variables in the model constant while computing the pairwise correlations.

3 **Partial correlation coefficients**: To hold the other variables constant, we have to compute partial correlation coefficients. Suppose we have three variables $X_1$, $X_2$, and $X_3$. Then we will have three pairwise correlations, $r_{12}$, $r_{13}$, and $r_{23}$ and three partial correlations, $r_{12.3}$, $r_{13.2}$, and $r_{23.1}$; $r_{23.1}$, for example, means the correlation between variables $X_2$ and $X_3$, holding the value of variable $X_1$ constant (see Exercise 4.4 about computing partial correlation coefficients). It is quite possible that the correlation between $X_2$ and $X_3$ ($= r_{23}$) is high, say, 0.85. But this correlation does not take into account the presence of the third variable $X_1$. If the variable $X_1$ influences both $X_2$ and $X_3$, the high correlation between the latter two may in fact be due to the common influence of $X_1$ on both these variables. The partial correlation $r_{23.1}$ computes the net correlation between $X_2$ and $X_3$ after removing the influence of $X_1$. In that case it is quite possible that the high observed correlation of 0.85 between $X_2$ and $X_3$ may be reduced to, say, 0.35.

However, there is no guarantee that the partial correlations will provide an infallible guide to multicollinearity. To save space, we will not present the actual values of the partial correlations for our example. *Stata* can compute partial correlations for a group of variables with simple instructions.

Table 4.4  **The VIF and TOL factors.**

| Variable | VIF | TOL = 1/VIF |
|---|---|---|
| mtr | 7.22 | 0.138598 |
| age | 5.76 | 0.173727 |
| husage | 5.22 | 0.191411 |
| faminc | 5.14 | 0.194388 |
| huswage | 3.64 | 0.274435 |
| educ | 2.02 | 0.494653 |
| hushrs | 1.89 | 0.529823 |
| huseduc | 1.86 | 0.536250 |
| fatheduc | 1.61 | 0.621540 |
| motheduc | 1.60 | 0.623696 |
| exper | 1.53 | 0.652549 |
| kidsge6 | 1.41 | 0.708820 |
| wage | 1.23 | 0.813643 |
| kidslt6 | 1.23 | 0.815686 |
| unem | 1.08 | 0.928387 |
| Mean VIF | 2.83 | |

4 **Auxiliary regressions**: To find out which of the regressors are highly collinear with the other regressors included in the model, we can regress each regressor on the remaining regressors and obtain the auxiliary regressions mentioned earlier.

Since we have 15 regressors, there will be 15 auxiliary regressions. We can test the overall significance of each regression by the $F$ test discussed in Chapter 2. The null hypothesis here is that all the regressor coefficients in the auxiliary regression are zero. If we reject this hypothesis for one or more of the auxiliary regressions, we can conclude that the auxiliary regressions with significant $F$ values are collinear with the other variables in the model. Of course, if we have several regressors, as in our example, calculating several auxiliary regressors in practice will be tedious, if not computationally impossible.

5 **The variance inflation (VIF) and tolerance (TOL) factors**
The VIF and TOL factors for our example, which are obtained from *Stata*, are given in Table 4.4.

This table clearly shows that there is high degree of collinearity among several variables; even the average VIF is in excess of 2.

## 4.4 Remedial measures

There are several remedies suggested in the literature.[6] Whether any of them will work in a specific situation is debatable. Since the OLS estimators are BLUE as long as collinearity is not perfect, it is often suggested that the best remedy is to do nothing but simply present the results of the fitted model. This is so because very often collinearity is essentially a data deficiency problem, and in many situations we may not have choice over the data we have available for research.[7]

But sometimes it is useful to rethink the model we have chosen for analysis to make sure that all the variables included in the model may not be essential. Turning to the model given in Table 4.3, the variables father's education and mother's education are likely to be correlated, which in turn would mean that the daughter's education may also be correlated with these two variables. One can also question whether including children over the age of six as an explanatory variable makes any sense. Also, wife's and husband's ages are also correlated. Therefore if we exclude these variables from the model, maybe the collinearity problem may not be as serious as before.[8]

The results of the revised model are given in Table 4.5.

As you can see, most of the variables are now statistically significant at the 10% or lower level of significance and they make economic sense, the exception being the unemployment rate, which is significant at about the 11% level of significance. The corresponding VIF and TOL factors for the coefficients in this table are given in Table 4.6.

Although the average VIF has dropped, there is still considerable collinearity among the regressors included in the revised model. We could estimate more such models using various combinations of the explanatory variables given in Table 4.3 to

---

6 For a detailed discussion, see Gujarati/Porter, *op cit.*, pp. 342–6.

7 The econometrician Arthur Goldberger called this the problem of "micronumerosity", which simply means small sample size and or lack of sufficient variability in the values of the regressors. See his *A Course in Econometrics*, Harvard University Press, Cambridge, MA, 1991, p. 249.

8 But beware of specification bias. One should not exclude variables just to get rid of collinearity. If a variable belongs in the model, it should be retained even if it is not statistically significant.

**Table 4.5  Revised women's hours worked regression.**

Dependent Variable: HOURS
Method: Least Squares
Sample (adjusted): 1 428
Included observations: 428 after adjustments

|  | Coefficient | Std. Error | t-Statistic | Prob. |
|---|---|---|---|---|
| C | 8484.523 | 987.5952 | 8.591094 | 0.0000 |
| AGE | −17.72740 | 4.903114 | −3.615540 | 0.0003 |
| EDUC | −27.03403 | 15.79456 | −1.711604 | 0.0877 |
| EXPER | 24.20345 | 4.653332 | 5.201315 | 0.0000 |
| FAMINC | 0.013781 | 0.005866 | 2.349213 | 0.0193 |
| HUSHRS | −0.486474 | 0.070462 | −6.904046 | 0.0000 |
| HUSWAGE | −144.9734 | 15.88407 | −9.126972 | 0.0000 |
| KIDSLT6 | −180.4415 | 86.36960 | −2.089178 | 0.0373 |
| WAGE | −47.43286 | 10.30926 | −4.600995 | 0.0000 |
| MTR | −6351.293 | 1029.837 | −6.167278 | 0.0000 |
| UNEM | −16.50367 | 10.55941 | −1.562935 | 0.1188 |

| | | | | |
|---|---|---|---|---|
| R-squared | 0.335786 | Mean dependent var | 1302.930 | |
| Adjusted R-squared | 0.319858 | S.D. dependent var | 776.2744 | |
| S.E. of regression | 640.1992 | Akaike info criterion | 15.78680 | |
| Sum squared resid | 1.71E+08 | Schwarz criterion | 15.89112 | |
| Log likelihood | −3367.375 | Durbin–Watson stat | 2.078578 | |
| F-statistic | 21.08098 | Prob(F-statistic) | 0.000000 | |

see which model may be least collinear. But this strategy, called "**data mining**" or "**data fishing**", is not recommended. If we have a model containing several variables that legitimately belong in the model, it is better to leave them in the model. If some coefficients in this model are not statistically significant, so be it. There is very little we can do to the data short of collecting new data or a different set of data, if that is feasible.

**Table 4.6  VIF and TOL for coeficients in Table 4.5.**

| Variable | VIF | TOL =1/VIF |
|---|---|---|
| mtr | 6.54 | 0.152898 |
| faminc | 4.88 | 0.204774 |
| huswage | 3.35 | 0.298295 |
| hushrs | 1.76 | 0.568969 |
| age | 1.49 | 0.669733 |
| exper | 1.46 | 0.683036 |
| educ | 1.36 | 0.736669 |
| wage | 1.21 | 0.824171 |
| kidslt6 | 1.19 | 0.837681 |
| unem | 1.07 | 0.935587 |
| Mean VIF | 2.43 | |

## 4.5   The method of principal components (PC)

A statistical method, known as the **principal component analysis (PCA)**, can transform correlated variables into *orthogonal or uncorrelated variables*.[9] The orthogonal variables thus obtained are called the **principal components**. Returning to our hours-worked regression given in Table 4.3, we have 15 regressors. The method of PC will in principle compute 15 principal components, *PCs*, denoted as $PC_1, PC_2, ..., PC_{15}$, such that they all are mutually uncorrelated. These PCs are linear combinations of the original regressors. In practice we need not use all the 15 PCs, because a smaller number will often be adequate to explain the phenomenon under study, as we show below.

The basic idea behind PCA is simple. It groups the correlated variables into sub-groups so that variables belonging to any sub-group have a "common" factor that moves them together. This common factor may be skill, ability, intelligence, ethnicity, or any such factor. That common factor, which is not always easy to identify, is what we call a principal component. There is one PC for each common factor. Hopefully, these common factors or PCs are fewer in number than the original number of regressors.

The starting point of the PC analysis is the correlation matrix of the original variables. The $15 \times 15$ correlation matrix is too big to reproduce here, but any statistical package will produce them. From the correlation matrix, using *Minitab 15*, we obtained the following PCs (Table 4.7), 15 in total. We will not discuss the actual mathematics of extracting the PCs, for it is rather involved.

### Interpretation of the PCs

The first part of the above table gives the estimated 15 PCs. $PC_1$, the first principal component, has a variance (= eigenvalue) of 3.5448 and accounts for 24% of the total variation in all the regressors. $PC_2$, the second principal component, has a variance of 2.8814, accounting for 19% of the total variation in all 15 regressors. These two PCs account for 42% of the total variation. In this manner you will see the first six PCs cumulatively account for 74% of the total variation in all the regressors. So although there are 15 PCs, only six seem to be quantitatively important. This can be seen more clearly in Figure 4.1 obtained from *Minitab 15*.

Now look at the second part of Table 4.7. For each PC it gives what are called **loadings or scores or weights** – that is, how much each of the original regressors contributes to that PC. For example, Take $PC_1$: education, family income, father's education, mother's education, husband's education, husband's wage, and MTR load heavily on this PC. But if you take $PC_4$ you will see that husband's hours of work contribute heavily to this PC.

Although mathematically elegant, the interpretation of PCs is subjective. For instance, we could think of $PC_1$ as representing the overall level of education, for that variable loads heavily on this PC.

Once the principal components are extracted, we can then regress the original regressand (hours worked) on the principal components, bypassing the original

---

9   Literally interpreted, the term orthogonal means intersecting or lying at right angles. Uncorrelated variables are said to be orthogonal because when plotted on a graph, they form right angles to one of the axes.

**Table 4.7  Principal components of the hours-worked example.**

**Eigenanalysis of the Correlation Matrix**
428 cases used, 325 cases contain missing values

| Eigenvalue | 3.5448 | 2.8814 | 1.4598 | 1.2965 | 1.0400 | 0.8843 | 0.8259 | 0.6984 |
|---|---|---|---|---|---|---|---|---|
| Proportion | 0.236 | 0.192 | 0.097 | 0.086 | 0.069 | 0.059 | 0.055 | 0.047 |
| Cumulative | 0.236 | 0.428 | 0.526 | 0.612 | 0.682 | 0.740 | 0.796 | 0.842 |
| Eigenvalue | 0.6495 | 0.5874 | 0.4151 | 0.3469 | 0.1823 | 0.1046 | 0.0830 | |
| Proportion | 0.043 | 0.039 | 0.028 | 0.023 | 0.012 | 0.007 | 0.006 | |
| Cumulative | 0.885 | 0.925 | 0.952 | 0.975 | 0.987 | 0.994 | 1.000 | |

| Variable | PC1 | PC2 | PC3 | PC4 | PC5 | PC6 |
|---|---|---|---|---|---|---|
| AGE | 0.005 | 0.528 | 0.114 | 0.021 | −0.089 | 0.075 |
| EDUC | 0.383 | −0.073 | 0.278 | −0.064 | 0.188 | 0.150 |
| EXPER | −0.039 | 0.373 | 0.267 | 0.025 | 0.255 | 0.058 |
| FAMINC | 0.424 | 0.106 | −0.314 | 0.179 | −0.029 | −0.026 |
| FATHEDUC | 0.266 | −0.142 | 0.459 | −0.081 | −0.289 | −0.142 |
| HUSAGE | −0.008 | 0.513 | 0.106 | 0.021 | −0.141 | 0.033 |
| HUSEDUC | 0.368 | −0.091 | 0.129 | 0.015 | 0.069 | 0.230 |
| HUSHRS | 0.053 | −0.129 | 0.099 | 0.718 | 0.049 | 0.461 |
| HUSWAGE | 0.382 | 0.093 | −0.373 | −0.240 | −0.141 | −0.185 |
| KIDSGE6 | −0.057 | −0.320 | −0.309 | 0.062 | −0.292 | 0.101 |
| KIDSLT6 | 0.014 | −0.276 | 0.018 | −0.278 | 0.515 | 0.163 |
| WAGE | 0.232 | 0.052 | −0.031 | −0.054 | 0.526 | −0.219 |
| MOTHEDUC | 0.224 | −0.214 | 0.450 | −0.031 | −0.299 | −0.238 |
| MTR | −0.451 | −0.127 | 0.228 | −0.197 | 0.018 | −0.003 |
| UNEM | 0.086 | 0.071 | −0.039 | −0.508 | −0.208 | 0.711 |

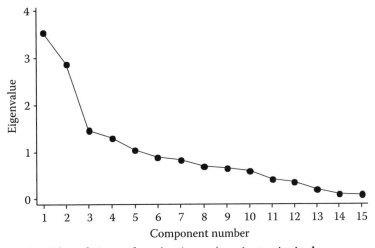

**Figure 4.1  Plot of eigenvalues (variances) against principal components.**

**Table 4.8  Principal components regression.**

Hours = 1303 − 1.5 C23 + 84.0 C24 + 18.6 C25 + 106 C26 + 4.8 C27 − 56.4 C28
428 cases used, 325 cases contain missing values*

| Predictor | Coef | SE | Coef t | P(P value) |
|---|---|---|---|---|
| Constant | 1302.93 | 36.57 | 35.63 | 0.000 |
| PC1 | −1.49 | 19.45 | −0.08 | 0.939 |
| PC2 | 84.04 | 21.57 | 3.90 | 0.000 |
| PC3 | 18.62 | 30.30 | 0.61 | 0.539 |
| PC4 | 105.74 | 32.16 | 3.29 | 0.001 |
| PC5 | 4.79 | 35.90 | 0.13 | 0.894 |
| PC6 | −56.36 | 38.94 | −1.45 | 0.149 |

$S^{**}$ = 756.605 R-Sq = 6.3% R-Sq(adj) = 5.0%
*Note*: * 325 married women had zero hours of work.
** This is the standard error of the regression (= $\hat{\sigma}$)
*Note*: The first column gives the name of the regressors – that is, the PCs, the third column gives their estimated standard errors, the fourth column gives the estimated $t$ values, and the last column gives the $p$ values (i.e. the exact level of significance.)

regressors: To illustrate, suppose we use only the first six PCs, as they seem to be the most important. Regressing hours worked on these six PCs, we obtain the results in Table 4.8 from *Minitab15*.

From these results it seems that PC2 and PC4 seem to explain the behavior of women's hours worked best. Of course, the rub here is that we do not know how to interpret these principal components. However, the method of principal components is a useful way of reducing the number of correlated regressors into a few components that are uncorrelated. As a result, we do not face the collinearity problem. Since there is no such thing as a free lunch, this simplification comes at a cost because we do not know how to interpret the PCs in a meaningful way in practical applications. If we can identify the PCs with some economic variables, the principal components method would prove very useful in identifying multicollinearity and also provide a solution for it.

In passing it may be mentioned that the method of **ridge regression** is another method of dealing with correlated variables. The estimators produced by ridge regression are biased, but they have smaller mean squared error (MSE) than the OLS estimators.[10] A discussion of ridge regression is beyond the scope of this book.[11]

## 4.6  Summary and conclusions

In this chapter we examined the problem of multicollinearity, a problem commonly encountered in empirical work, especially if there are several correlated explanatory variables in the model. As long as collinearity is not perfect, we can work within the

---

**10** The MSE of an estimator, say $\hat{\lambda}$ of $\lambda$, is equal to its variance plus the square of the bias in estimating it.
**11** For a user-friendly discussion, see Samprit Chatterjee and Ali S. Hadi, *Regression Analysis by Example*, 4th edn, John Wiley &Sons, New York, 2006, pp. 266–75.

framework of the classical linear regression model, provided the other assumptions of the CLRM are satisfied.

If collinearity is not perfect, but high, several consequences ensue. The OLS estimators are still BLUE, but one or more regression coefficients have large standard errors relative to the values of the coefficients, thereby making the $t$ ratios small. Therefore one may conclude (misleadingly) that the true values of these coefficients are not different from zero. Also, the regression coefficients may be very sensitive to small changes in the data, especially if the sample is relatively small (see Exercise 4.6).

There are several diagnostic tests to detect collinearity, but there is no guarantee that they will yield satisfactory results. It is basically a trial and error process.

The best practical advice is to do nothing if you encounter collinearity, for very often we have no control over the data. However, it is very important that the variables included in the model are chosen carefully. As our illustrative example shows, redefining a model by excluding variables that may not belong in the model may attenuate the collinearity problem, provided we do not omit variables that are relevant in a given situation. Otherwise, in reducing collinearity we will be committing model specification errors, which are discussed in Chapter 7. So, think about the model carefully before you estimate the regression model.

There is one caveat. If there is multicollinearity in a model and if your objective is forecasting, multicollinearity may not be bad, provided the collinear relationship observed in the sample continues to hold in the forecast period.

Finally, there is a statistical technique, called **principal components analysis**, which will "resolve" the problem of near-collinearity. In PCA we construct artificial variables in such a way that they are orthogonal to each other. These artificial variables, called principal components (PC), are extracted from the original $X$ regressors. We can then regress the original regressand on the principal components. We showed how the PCs are computed and interpreted, using our illustrative example.

One advantage of this method is that the PCs are usually smaller in number than the original number of regressors. But one practical disadvantage of the PCA is that the PCs very often do not have viable economic meaning, as they are (weighted) combinations of the original variables which may be measured in different units of measurement. Therefore, it may be hard to interpret the PCs. That is why they are not much used in economic research, although they are used extensively in psychological and education research.

## Exercises

**4.1**  For the hours example discussed in the chapter, try to obtain the correlation matrix for the variables included in Table 4.3. *Eviews*, *Stata*, and several other programs can compute the correlations with comparative ease. Find out which variables are highly correlated.

**4.2**  Do you agree with the following statement and why? *Simple correlations between variables are a sufficient but not a necessary condition for the existence of multicollinearity.*

**4.3**  Continuing with Exercise 4.1, find out the partial correlation coefficients for the variables included in Table 4.2, using *Stata* or any other software you have. Based on the partial correlations, which variables seem to be highly correlated?

**4.4**   In the three-variable model, $Y$ and regressors $X_2$ and $X_3$, we can compute three partial correlation coefficients. For example, the partial correlation between $Y$ and $X_2$, holding $X_3$ constant, denoted as $r_{12.3}$, is as follows:

$$r_{12.3} = \frac{r_{12} - r_{13} r_{23}}{\sqrt{(1-r_{13}^2)(1-r_{23}^2)}}$$

where the subscripts 1, 2, and 3 denote the variables $Y$, $X_2$, and $X_3$, respectively and $r_{12}$, $r_{13}$ and $r_{23}$ are simple correlation coefficients between the variables.

(a)   When will $r_{12.3}$ be equal to $r_{12}$? What does that mean?

(b)   Is $r_{12.3}$ less than, equal to or greater than $r_{12}$? Explain.

**4.5**   Run the 15 auxiliary regressions mentioned in the chapter and determine which explanatory variables are highly correlated with the rest of the explanatory variables.

**4.6**   Consider the sets of data given in the following two tables:

| Table 1 | | | | Table 2 | | |
|---|---|---|---|---|---|---|
| $Y$ | $X_2$ | $X_3$ | | $Y$ | $X_2$ | $X_3$ |
| 1 | 2 | 4 | | 1 | 2 | 4 |
| 2 | 0 | 2 | | 2 | 0 | 2 |
| 3 | 4 | 12 | | 3 | 4 | 0 |
| 4 | 6 | 0 | | 4 | 6 | 12 |
| 5 | 8 | 16 | | 5 | 8 | 16 |

The only difference between the two tables is that the third and fourth values of $X_3$ are interchanged.

(a)   Regress $Y$ on $X_2$ and $X_3$ in both tables, obtaining the usual OLS output.

(b)   What difference do you observe in the two regressions? And what accounts for this difference?

**4.7**   The following data describes the manpower needs for operating a US Navy bachelor officers' quarters, consisting of 25 establishments. The variables are described below and the data is given in **Table 4.9**,[12] which can be found on the companion website:

Y: Monthly manhours needed to operate an establishment

X1: Average daily occupancy

X2: Monthly average number of check-ins

X3: Weekly hours of service desk operation

X4: Common use area (in square feet)

X5: Number of building wings

X6: Operational berthing capacity

X7: Number of rooms

**Questions:**

Are the explanatory variables, or some subset of them, collinear? How is this detected? Show the necessary calculations.

---

12  Source: R. J. Freund and R. C. Littell (1991) *SAS System for Regression*. SAS Institute Inc.

*Optional*: Do a principal component analysis, using the data in the above table.

**4.8**     Refer to Exercise 4.6. First regress $Y$ on $X_3$ and obtain the residuals from this regression, say $e_{1i}$. Then regress $X_2$ on $X_3$ and obtain the residuals from this regression, say $e_{2i}$. Now regress $e_{1i}$ on $e_{2i}$. This regression will give the partial regression coefficient given in Eq. (4.2). What does this exercise show? And how would you describe the residuals $e_{1i}$ and $e_{2i}$?

II

# 5

# Regression diagnostic II: heteroscedasticity

One of the problems commonly encountered in cross-sectional data is *hetero-scedasticity* (unequal variance) in the error term. There are various reasons for heteroscedasticity, such as the presence of outliers in the data, or incorrect functional form of the regression model, or incorrect transformation of data, or mixing observations with different measures of scale (e.g. mixing high-income households with low-income households) etc.

## 5.1    Consequences of heteroscedasticity[1]

The classical linear regression model (CLRM) assumes that the error term $u_i$ in the regression model has *homoscedasticity* (equal variance) across observations, denoted by $\sigma^2$. For instance, in studying consumption expenditure in relation to income, this assumption would imply that low-income and high-income households have the same disturbance variance even though their average level of consumption expenditure is different.

However, if the assumption of homoscedasticity, or equal variance, is not satisfied, we have the problem of heteroscedasticity, or unequal variance, denoted by $\sigma_i^2$ (note the subscript $i$). Thus, compared to low-income households, high-income households have not only higher average level of consumption expenditure but also greater variability in their consumption expenditure. As a result, in a regression of consumption expenditure in relation to household income we are likely to encounter heteroscedasticity.

Heteroscedasticity has the following consequences:

1  Heteroscedasticity does not alter the *unbiasedness* and *consistency* properties of OLS estimators.

2  But OLS estimators are no longer of minimum variance or efficient. That is, they are not best linear unbiased estimators (BLUE); they are simply linear unbiased estimators (LUE).

3  As a result, the $t$ and $F$ tests based under the standard assumptions of CLRM may not be reliable, resulting in erroneous conclusions regarding the statistical significance of the estimated regression coefficients.

---

1  For details, see Gujarati/Porter text, *op cit.*, Chapter 11.

4 In the presence of heteroscedasticity, the BLUE estimators are provided by the method of *weighted least squares* (WLS).

Because of these consequences, it is important that we check for heteroscedasticity, which is usually found in cross-sectional data. Before we do that, let us consider a concrete example.

## 5.2    Abortion rates in the USA

What are the factors that determine the abortion rate across the 50 states in the USA? To study this, we obtained the data shown in **Table 5.1**, which can be found on the companion website.[2]

The variables used in the analysis are as follows:

*State* = name of the state (50 US states).

*ABR* = Abortion rate, number of abortions per thousand women aged 15–44 in 1992.

*Religion* = the percent of a state's population that is Catholic, Southern Baptist, Evangelical, or Mormon.

*Price* = the average price charged in 1993 in non-hospital facilities for an abortion at 10 weeks with local anesthesia (weighted by the number of abortions performed in 1992).

*Laws* = a variable that takes the value of 1 if a state enforces a law that restricts a minor's access to abortion, 0 otherwise.

*Funds* = a variable that takes the value of 1 if state funds are available for use to pay for an abortion under most circumstances, 0 otherwise.

*Educ* = the percent of a state's population that is 25 years or older with a high school degree (or equivalent), 1990.

*Income* = disposable income per capita, 1992.

*Picket* = the percentage of respondents that reported experiencing picketing with physical contact or blocking of patients.

### The model

As a starting point, we consider the following linear regression model:

$$\text{ABR}_i = B_1 + B_2 Rel_i + B_3 Price_i + B_4 Laws_i + B_5 Funds_i$$
$$+ B_6 Educ_i + B_7 Income_i + B_8 Picket_i + u_i \qquad (5.1)$$
$$i = 1, 2, \ldots, 50$$

*A priori*, we would expect ABR to be negatively related to religion, price, laws, picket, education, and positively related to fund and income. We assume the error term satisfies the standard classical assumptions, including the assumption of homoscedasticity. Of course, we will do a post-estimation analysis to see if this assumption holds in the present case.

Using *Eviews6*, we obtained the results of Table 5.2, which are given in the standard *Eviews* format.

---

2  The data were obtained from the website of Leo H. Kahane, http://www.cbe.csueastbay.edu/~kahane.

**Table 5.2  OLS estimation of the abortion rate function.**

Dependent Variable: ABORTION
Method: Least Squares
Sample: 1 50
Included observations: 50

|          | Coefficient | Std. Error | t-Statistic | Prob.  |
|----------|-------------|------------|-------------|--------|
| C        | 14.28396    | 15.07763   | 0.947361    | 0.3489 |
| RELIGION | 0.020071    | 0.086381   | 0.232355    | 0.8174 |
| PRICE    | −0.042363   | 0.022223   | −1.906255   | 0.0635 |
| LAWS     | −0.873102   | 2.376566   | −0.367380   | 0.7152 |
| FUNDS    | 2.820003    | 2.783475   | 1.013123    | 0.3168 |
| EDUC     | −0.287255   | 0.199555   | −1.439483   | 0.1574 |
| INCOME   | 0.002401    | 0.000455   | 5.274041    | 0.0000 |
| PICKET   | −0.116871   | 0.042180   | −2.770782   | 0.0083 |

| | | | |
|---|---|---|---|
| R-squared | 0.577426 | Mean dependent var | 20.57800 |
| Adjusted R-squared | 0.506997 | S.D. dependent var | 10.05863 |
| S.E. of regression | 7.062581 | Akaike info criterion | 6.893145 |
| Sum squared resid | 2094.962 | Schwarz criterion | 7.199069 |
| Log likelihood | −164.3286 | Durbin–Watson stat | 2.159124 |
| F-statistic | 8.198706 | Prob(F-statistic) | 0.000003 |

As these results show, on the basis of the $t$ statistic, price, income, and picket are statistically significant at the 10% or lower level of significance, whereas the other variables are not statistically significant, although some of them (laws and education) have the correct signs. *But remember that if there is heteroscedasticity, the estimated t values may not be reliable.*

The $R^2$ value shows that 58% of the variation in the abortion rate is explained by the model. The $F$ statistic, which tests the hypothesis that all the slopes' coefficients are simultaneously zero, clearly rejects this hypothesis, for its value of 8.199 is highly significant; its $p$ value is practically zero. *Again, keep in mind that the F statistic may not be reliable if there is heteroscedasticity.*

Note that the significant $F$ does not mean that each explanatory variable is statistically significant, as the $t$ statistic shows that only some of the explanatory variables are individually statistically significant.

## Analysis of results

As noted, a commonly encountered problem in cross-sectional data is the problem of heteroscedasticity. In our example, because of the diversity of the states we suspect heteroscedasticity.

As a simple test of heteroscedasticity, we can plot the histogram of squared residuals (S1S) from the regression given in Table 5.2; see Figure 5.1.

It is obvious from this figure that squared residuals, a proxy for the underlying squared error terms, do not suggest that the error term is homoscedastic.[3]

---

3  Recall that the OLS estimate of the error variance is given as: $\hat{\sigma}^2 = \Sigma e_t^2 / (n - k)$ – that is, residual sum of squares divided by the degrees of freedom.

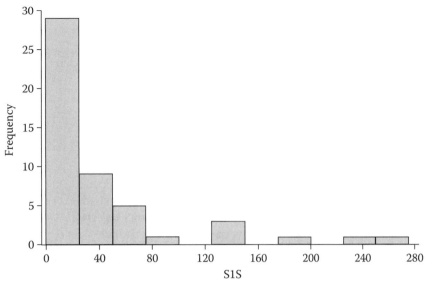

**Figure 5.1  Histogram of squared residuals from Eq. (5.1).**

We can get a better glimpse of heteroscedasticity if we plot the squared residuals (S1S) against the estimated abortion rate from the regression model (Figure 5.2).

*Note*: ABORTIONF is the estimated abortion rate from model (5.1).

It seems that there is a systematic relationship between the squared residuals and the estimated values of the abortion rate, which can be checked by some formal tests of heteroscedasticity (see also Eq. (5.3) below).

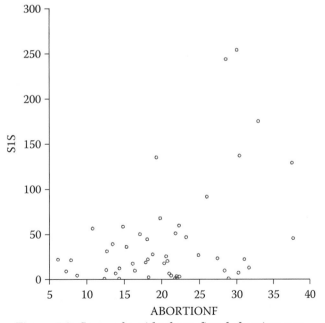

**Figure 5.2  Squared residuals vs. fitted abortion rate.**

## 5.3    Detection of heteroscedasticity

Besides the graphic methods described in the previous section, we can use two commonly used tests of heteroscedasticity, namely, the Breusch–Pagan and White tests.[4]

### Breusch–Pagan (BP) test

This test involves the following steps:

1 Estimate the OLS regression, as in Table 5.2, and obtain the squared OLS residuals, $e_i^2$, from this regression.

2 Regress $e_i^2$ on the $k$ regressors included in the model; the idea here is to see if the squared residuals (a proxy for true squared error term) are related to one or more $X$ variables.[5] You can choose other regressors also that might have some bearing on the error variance. Now run the following regression:

$$e_i^2 = A_1 + A_2 Rel_i + A_3 Price_i + A_4 Laws_i + A_5 Funds_i + A_6 Educ_i \\ + A_7 Income_i + A_8 Picket_i + v_i \tag{5.2}$$

where $v_i$ is the error term.

Save $R^2$ from regression (5.2); call it $R_{aux}^2$, where *aux* stands for auxiliary, since Eq. (5.2) is auxiliary to the primary regression (5.1) (see Table 5.3). The idea behind Eq. (5.2) is to find out if the squared error term is related to one or more of the regressors, which might indicate that perhaps heteroscedasticity is present in the data.

3 The null hypothesis here is that the error variance is homoscedastic – that is, all the *slope* coefficients in Eq. (5.2) are simultaneously equal to zero.[6] You can use the $F$ statistic from this regression with $(k-1)$ and $(n-k)$ in the numerator and denominator df, respectively, to test this hypothesis. If the computed $F$ statistic in Eq. (5.2) is statistically significant, we can reject the hypothesis of homoscedasticity. If it is not, we may not reject the null hypothesis.

As the results in Table 5.3 show, the $F$ statistic (7 df in the numerator and 42 df in the denominator) is highly significant, for its $p$ value is only about 2%. Thus we can reject the null hypothesis.

4 Alternatively, you can use the chi-square statistic. It can be shown that under the null hypothesis of homoscedasticity, the product of $R_{aux}^2$ (computed in step 2) and the number of observations follows the chi-square distribution, with df equal to the number of regressors in the model. If the computed chi-square value has a low $p$ value, we can reject the null hypothesis of homoscedasticity.[7] As the results in Table 5.3 show, the observed chi-square value $(=nR_{aux}^2)$ of about 16 has a very low $p$ value, suggesting that we can reject the null hypothesis of homoscedasticity. To

---

4  The details of these and other tests can be found in Gujarati/Porter text, *op cit.*, Chapter 11.
5  Although $e_i^2$ are not the same thing as $u_i^2$, in large samples the former are a good proxy.
6  If that is the case, the constant $A_1$ would suggest that the error variance is constant or homoscedastic.
7  Recall the relationship between $F$ and $\chi^2$ statistics, which is: $mF_{m,n} = \chi_m^2$ as $n \to \infty$; that is, for large denominator df, the numerator df times the $F$ value is approximately equal to the chi-square value with the numerator df, where $m$ and $n$ are the numerator and denominator df, respectively (see Statistical Appendix).

**Table 5.3  The Breusch–Pagan test of heteroscedasticity.**

Heteroskedasticity Test: Breusch–Pagan–Godfrey

| | | | |
|---|---|---|---|
| F-statistic | 2.823820 | Prob. F(7,42) | 0.0167 |
| Obs*R-squared | 16.00112 | Prob. Chi-Square(7) | 0.0251 |
| Scaled explained SS | 10.57563 | Prob. Chi-Square(7) | 0.1582 |

Test Equation:
Dependent Variable: RESID^2
Method: Least Squares
Date: 10/05/09 Time: 13:14
Sample: 1 50
Included observations: 50

| | Coefficient | Std. Error | t-Statistic | Prob. |
|---|---|---|---|---|
| C | 16.68558 | 110.1532 | 0.151476 | 0.8803 |
| RELIGION | −0.134865 | 0.631073 | −0.213707 | 0.8318 |
| PRICE | 0.286153 | 0.162357 | 1.762492 | 0.0853 |
| LAWS | −8.566472 | 17.36257 | −0.493387 | 0.6243 |
| FUNDS | 24.30981 | 20.33533 | 1.195447 | 0.2386 |
| EDUC | −1.590385 | 1.457893 | −1.090879 | 0.2815 |
| INCOME | 0.004710 | 0.003325 | 1.416266 | 0.1641 |
| PICKET | −0.576745 | 0.308155 | −1.871606 | 0.0682 |

| | | | |
|---|---|---|---|
| R-squared | 0.320022 | Mean dependent var | 41.89925 |
| Adjusted R-squared | 0.206693 | S.D. dependent var | 57.93043 |
| S.E. of regression | 51.59736 | Akaike info criterion | 10.87046 |
| Sum squared resid | 111816.1 | Schwarz criterion | 11.17639 |
| Log likelihood | −263.7616 | Durbin–Watson stat | 2.060808 |
| F-statistic | 2.823820 | Prob(F-statistic) | 0.016662 |

put it differently, the regression in Table 5.2 suffers from the problem of heteroscedasticity.

*A cautionary note*: this test is a large sample test and may not be appropriate in small samples.[8]

*In sum*, it probably seems that the abortion rate regression suffers from heteroscedasticity.

Returning to our example, we obtain the results shown in Table 5.3.

## White's test of heteroscedasticity

We proceed in the spirit of the BP test and regress the squared residuals on the seven regressors, the squared terms of these regressors, and the pairwise cross-product term of each regressor, for a total of 33 coefficients.

As in the BP test, we obtain the $R^2$ value from this regression and multiply it by the number of observations. Under the null hypothesis that there is homoscedasticity, this

---

**8** One might argue that the data we have is not really a random sample, for we have all the states in the Union. So, we actually have the whole population. But remember that the abortion rate data are only for one year. It is quite possible that this rate will vary from year to year. Hence we can treat the data used for a single year as a sample from all possible abortion rates for all the years that we have data.

product follows the chi-square distribution with df equal to the number of coefficients estimated. The White test is more general and more flexible than the BP test.

In the present example, if we *do not add* the squared and cross-product terms to the auxiliary regression, we obtain $nR^2 = 15.7812$, which has a chi-square distribution with 7 df. The probability of obtaining such a chi-square value or greater is about 0.03, which is quite low. This would suggest that we can reject the null hypothesis of homoscedasticity.

If we add the squared and cross-product terms to the auxiliary regression, we obtain $nR^2 = 32.1022$, which has a chi-square value with 33 df.[9] The probability of obtaining such a chi-square value is about 0.51. In this case, we will not reject the null hypothesis.

As this exercise shows, White's chi-square test is sensitive to whether we add or drop the squared and cross-product terms from the auxiliary regression.[10] Remember that the White test is a large sample test. Therefore, when we include the regressors and their squared and cross-product terms, which results in a loss of 33 df, the results of the auxiliary regression are likely to be very sensitive, which is the case here.

To avoid the loss of so many degrees of freedom, White's test could be shortened by regressing the squared residuals on the estimated value of the regressand and its squares.[11] That is, we regress:

$$e_i^2 = \alpha_1 + \alpha_2 Abortionf + \alpha_3 Abortionf^2 + v_i \qquad (5.3)$$

where *Abortionf* = forecast value of abortion rate from Eq. (5.1). Since the estimated abortion rate is a linear function of the regressors included in the model of Eq. (5.1), in a way we are indirectly incorporating the original regressor and their squares in estimating Eq. (5.3), which is in the spirit of the original White test. But note that in Eq. (5.3) there is no scope for the cross-product term, thus obviating the cross-product terms as in the original White test. Therefore the abridged White test saves several degrees of freedom.

The results of this regression are given in Table 5.4. The interesting statistic in this table is the *F* statistic, which is statistically highly significant, for its *p* value is very low. So the abridged White test reinforces the BP test and concludes that the abortion rate function does indeed suffer from heteroscedasticity. And this conclusion is arrived at with the loss of fewer degrees of freedom.

Notice that even though the *F* statistic is significant, the two partial slope coefficients are individually not significant. Incidentally, if you drop the squared ABORTIONF term from Eq. (5.3), you will find that the ABORTIONF term is statistically significant.[12] The reason for this is that the terms ABORTIONF and its square are functionally related, raising the spectre of multicollinearity. But keep in mind that multicollinearity refers to linear relationships between variables and not nonlinear relationships, as in Eq. (5.3).

---

9  This is because we have 7 regressors, 5 squared regressors and the cross-product of each regressor with the other regressors. But note that we do not add the squared values of the dummy variables, for the square of a dummy that takes a value of 1 is also 1. Also note that the cross-product of religion and income is the same as the cross-product of income and religion, so avoid double-counting

10  That is why it is noted that the White test has weak (statistical) power. The power of a (statistical) test is the probability of rejecting the null hypothesis when it is false.

11  See Jeffrey M. Wooldridge, *Introductory Econometrics: A Modern Approach*, 4th edn, South-Western Publishing, 2009, p. 275.

12  The coefficient of Abortionf is 3.1801 with a *t* value of 3.20, which is significant at the 0.002 level.

**Table 5.4  Abridged White test.**

Dependent Variable: RES^2
Method: Least Squares
Sample: 1 50
Included observations: 50
White Heteroskedasticity-Consistent Standard Errors & Covariance

|  | Coefficient | Std. Error | t-Statistic | Prob. |
|---|---|---|---|---|
| C | 20.20241 | 27.09320 | 0.745663 | 0.4596 |
| ABORTIONF | −1.455268 | 3.121734 | −0.466173 | 0.6432 |
| ABORTIONF^2 | 0.107432 | 0.081634 | 1.316014 | 0.1946 |

| | | | | |
|---|---|---|---|---|
| R-squared | 0.193083 | Mean dependent var | 41.89925 |
| Adjusted R-squared | 0.158746 | S.D. dependent var | 57.93043 |
| S.E. of regression | 53.13374 | Akaike info criterion | 10.84163 |
| Sum squared resid | 132690.1 | Schwarz criterion | 10.95635 |
| Log likelihood | −268.0406 | Durbin–Watson stat | 1.975605 |
| F-statistic | 5.623182 | Prob(F-statistic) | 0.006464 |

It should be noted that whether we use the BP or White or any other test of heteroscedasticity, these tests will only indicate whether the error variance in a specific case is heteroscedastic or not. But these tests do not necessarily suggest what should be done if we do encounter heteroscedasticity.

## 5.4    Remedial measures

Knowing the consequences of heteroscedasticity, it may be necessary to seek remedial measures. The problem here is that we do not know the true heteroscedastic variances, $\sigma_i^2$, for they are rarely observed. If we could observe them, then we could obtain BLUE estimators by dividing each observation by the (heteroscedastic) $\sigma_i$ and estimate the transformed model by OLS. This method of estimation is known as the method of **weighted least squares** (**WLS**).[13] Unfortunately, the true $\sigma_i^2$ is rarely known. Then what is the solution?

In practice, we make educated guesses about what $\sigma_i^2$ might be and transform the original regression model in such a way that in the transformed model the error variance might be homoscedastic. Some of the transformations used in practice are as follows:[14]

1  If the true error variance is proportional to the *square* of one of the regressors, we can divide both sides of Eq. (5.1) by that variable and run the transformed regression. Suppose in Eq. (5.1) the error variance is proportional to the square of income. We therefore divide Eq. (5.1) by the income variable on both sides and estimate this regression. We then subject this regression to heteroscedasticity tests, such as the BP and White tests. If these tests indicate that there is no evidence of heteroscedasticity, we may then assume that the transformed error term is homoscedastic.

---

**13**  Since each observation is divided (i.e. weighted) by $\sigma_i$, an observation with large $\sigma_i$ will be discounted more heavily than an observation with low $\sigma_i$.

**14**  For details, see Gujarati/Porter, *op cit.*, pp. 392–5.

2 If the true error variance is proportional to one of the regressors, we can use the so-called **square transformation**, that is, we divide both sides of (5.1) by the square root of the chosen regressor. We then estimate the regression thus transformed and subject that regression to heteroscedasticity tests. If these tests are satisfactory, we may rely on this regression.

There are practical problems in the applications of these procedures. *First,* how do we know which regressor to pick for transformation if there are several regressors? We can proceed by trial and error, but that would be a time-consuming procedure. *Second,* if some of the values of the chosen regressor are zero, then dividing by zero obviously will be problematic.

The choice of the regressor problem can sometimes be avoided by using the estimated $Y$ value (i.e. $\hat{Y}_i$), which is a weighted average value of all the regressors in the model, the weights being their regression coefficients, the $bs$.

It may be noted that all these methods of transformations are somewhat *ad hoc.* But there is not much we can do about it, for we are trying to guess what the true error variances are. All we can hope for is that the guess turns out to be reasonably good.

To illustrate all these transformations would be time- and space-consuming. However, we will illustrate just one of these transformations. If we divide (5.1) by the estimated abortion rate from (5.1), we obtain results in Table 5.5.

We subjected this regression to Breusch–Pagan and White's tests, but both tests showed that the problem of heteroscedasticity still persisted.[15]

It should be added that we do the transformations for the purpose of getting rid of hetersoscedasticity. We can get back to the original regression by multiplying through by ABORTIONF the results in Table 5.5.

3 The logarithmic transformation: sometimes, instead of estimating regression (5.1), we can regress the logarithm of the dependent variable on the regressors, which may be linear or in log form. The reason for this is that the log transformation compresses the scales in which the variables are measured, thereby reducing a tenfold difference between two values to a twofold difference. For example, the number 80 is 10 times the number 8, but ln 80 (= 4.3280) is about twice as large as ln 8 (= 2.0794).

The one caveat about using the log transformation is that we can take logs of positive numbers only.

Regressing the log of the abortion rate on the variables included in Eq. (5.1), we obtain the following results in Table 5.6.

Qualitatively these results are similar to those given in Table 5.1, in that the price, income, and picket variables are statistically significant. However, the interpretation of the regression coefficients is different from that in Table 5.1. The various slope coefficient measure **semi-elasticities** – that is, the relative changes in the abortion rate for a unit change in the value of the regressor.[16] Thus the price coefficient of −0.003 means if price goes up by a dollar, the relative change in the

---

**15** To save space, we do not present the detailed results. Readers can verify the conclusion by running their own tests, using the data given in Table 5.1.

**16** Recall our discussion about the semi-log models.

**Table 5.5  Transformed Eq. (5.1).**

Dependent Variable: ABORTION/ABORTIONF
Method: Least Squares
Sample: 1 50
Included observations: 50

|  | Coefficient | Std. Error | t-Statistic | Prob. |
|---|---|---|---|---|
| 1/ABORTIONF | 12.81786 | 11.22852 | 1.141545 | 0.2601 |
| RELIGION/ABORTIONF | 0.066088 | 0.068468 | 0.965239 | 0.3400 |
| PRICE/ABORTIONF | −0.051468 | 0.017507 | −2.939842 | 0.0053 |
| LAWS/ABORTIONF | −1.371437 | 1.819336 | −0.753812 | 0.4552 |
| FUNDS/ABORTIONF | 2.726181 | 3.185173 | 0.855897 | 0.3969 |
| EDUC/ABORTIONF | −0.228903 | 0.147545 | −1.551408 | 0.1283 |
| INCOME/ABORTIONF | 0.002220 | 0.000481 | 4.616486 | 0.0000 |
| PICKET/ABORTIONF | −0.082498 | 0.031247 | −2.640211 | 0.0116 |

| | | | |
|---|---|---|---|
| R-squared | 0.074143 | Mean dependent var | 1.011673 |
| Adjusted R-squared | −0.080166 | S.D. dependent var | 0.334257 |
| S.E. of regression | 0.347396 | Akaike info criterion | 0.868945 |
| Sum squared resid | 5.068735 | Schwarz criterion | 1.174869 |
| Log likelihood | −13.72363 | Durbin–Watson stat | 2.074123 |

*Note*: Abortionf is the abortion rate forecast from Eq. (5.1)

**Table 5.6  Logarithmic regression of the abortion rate.**

Dependent Variable: LABORTION
Method: Least Squares
Date: 10/09/09 Time: 14:45
Sample: 1 50
Included observations: 50

|  | Coefficient | Std. Error | t-Statistic | Prob. |
|---|---|---|---|---|
| C | 2.833265 | 0.755263 | 3.751362 | 0.0005 |
| RELIGION | 0.000458 | 0.004327 | 0.105742 | 0.9163 |
| PRICE | −0.003112 | 0.001113 | −2.795662 | 0.0078 |
| LAWS | −0.012884 | 0.119046 | −0.108226 | 0.9143 |
| FUNDS | 0.087688 | 0.139429 | 0.628907 | 0.5328 |
| EDUC | −0.014488 | 0.009996 | −1.449417 | 0.1546 |
| INCOME | 0.000126 | 2.28E−05 | 5.546995 | 0.0000 |
| PICKET | −0.006515 | 0.002113 | −3.083638 | 0.0036 |

| | | | |
|---|---|---|---|
| R-squared | 0.589180 | Mean dependent var | 2.904263 |
| Adjusted R-squared | 0.520710 | S.D. dependent var | 0.511010 |
| S.E. of regression | 0.353776 | Akaike info criterion | 0.905342 |
| Sum squared resid | 5.256618 | Schwarz criterion | 1.211266 |
| Log likelihood | −14.63355 | Durbin–Watson stat | 1.929785 |
| F-statistic | 8.604924 | Prob(F-statistic) | 0.000002 |

*Note* : Labortion = log of abortion

abortion rate is –0.003 or about –0.3%. All other coefficients are to be interpreted similarly.[17]

When this regression was subjected to Breusch–Pagan and White's test (without squared and cross-product terms), it was found that this regression did not suffer from heteroscedasticity. Again, this result should be accepted cautiously, for our "sample" of 51 observations may not be large enough.

This conclusion raises an important point of about heteroscedasticity tests. If one or more of these tests indicate that we have the problem of heteroscedasticity, it may not be heteroscedasticity *per se* but a model specification error, a topic we will discuss in Chapter 7 in some detail.

## White's heteroscedasticity-consistent standard errors or robust standard errors[18]

If the sample size is large, White has suggested a procedure to obtain heteroscedasticity-corrected standard errors. In the literature these are known as **robust standard errors**. White's routine is now built in several software packages. The procedure does not alter the values of the coefficients given in Table 5.2, but corrects the standard errors to allow for heteroscedasticity. Using *Eviews*, we obtain the results shown in Table 5.7.

If you compare these results with those given in Table 5.2, you will see some changes. The price variable is now less significant than before, although the income and picket coefficients have about the same level of significance. But notice that the estimated regression coefficients remain the same in the two tables.

But do not forget that the White procedure is valid in large samples, which may not be the case in the present example. Let us revisit the wage function first considered in Chapter 1 and the hours worked function discussed in Chapter 4; in both cases our samples are reasonably large.

### Wage function revisited

In Table 1.2 we presented a wage function of 1,289 workers. Since the data used in this table are cross-sectional, it is quite likely that the regression results suffer from heteroscedasticity. To see if this is the case, we used the BP and White's tests, which gave the following results.

**BP test**: When the squared residuals obtained from the model in Table 1.2 were regressed on the variables included in the wage regression, we obtain an $R^2$ value of 0.0429. Multiplying this value by the number of observations, 1,289, we obtained a chi-square value of about 55. For 5 df, the number of regressors in the wage function, the probability of obtaining such a chi-square value or greater was practically zero, suggesting that the wage regression in Table 1.2 did indeed suffer from heteroscedasticity.

**White's test of heteroscedasticity**: To see if the BP test results are reliable, we used White's test, both excluding and including the cross-product terms. The results were as follows. Excluding the cross-product terms, $nR^2 = 62.9466$, which has the

---

17  But recall the warning given in the previous chapter about interpreting dummy variables in semi-log regressions.

18  Details can be found in Gujarati/Porter, *op cit.*, p. 391.

**Table 5.7  Robust standard errors of the abortion rate regression.**

Dependent Variable: ABORTION RATE
Method: Least Squares
Sample: 1 50
Included observations: 50
White Heteroskedasticity-Consistent Standard Errors & Covariance

|  | Coefficient | Std. Error | t-Statistic | Prob. |
|---|---|---|---|---|
| C | 14.28396 | 14.90146 | 0.958561 | 0.3433 |
| RELIGION | 0.020071 | 0.083861 | 0.239335 | 0.8120 |
| PRICE | −0.042363 | 0.025944 | −1.632868 | 0.1100 |
| LAWS | −0.873102 | 1.795849 | −0.486178 | 0.6294 |
| FUNDS | 2.820003 | 3.088579 | 0.913042 | 0.3664 |
| EDUC | −0.287255 | 0.176628 | −1.626329 | 0.1114 |
| INCOME | 0.002401 | 0.000510 | 4.705512 | 0.0000 |
| PICKET | −0.116871 | 0.040420 | −2.891415 | 0.0060 |

| | | | |
|---|---|---|---|
| R-squared | 0.577426 | Mean dependent var | 20.57800 |
| Adjusted R-squared | 0.506997 | S.D. dependent var | 10.05863 |
| S.E. of regression | 7.062581 | Akaike info criterion | 6.893145 |
| Sum squared resid | 2094.962 | Schwarz criterion | 7.199069 |
| Log likelihood | −164.3286 | Durbin–Watson stat | 2.159124 |
| F-statistic | 8.198706 | Prob(F-statistic) | 0.000003 |

chi-square distribution with 5 df. The probability of obtaining such a chi-square value or greater is practically zero, thus confirming that the wage regression did in fact have heteroscedasticity. When we added the squared and cross-product terms of the regressors, we obtained $nR^2 = 79.4311$, which has a chi-square distribution with 17 df (5 regressors, 2 squared regressors, and 10 cross-product terms of the regressors). The probability of obtaining a chi-square value of as much as 79.4311 or greater is practically zero.

In sum, there is strong evidence that the wage regression in Table 1.2 suffered from heteroscedasticity.

Instead of transforming the wage regression in Table 1.2 by dividing it by one or more regressors, we can simply correct the problem of heteroscedasticity by computing White's robust standard errors. The results are given in Table 5.8.

If you compare these results with those in Table 1.2, you will see that the regression coefficients are the same, but some standard errors have changed, which then changed the $t$ values.

## Hours worked function revisited

Consider the results given in Table 4.2 about hours worked by 753 married women. These results are not corrected for heteroscedasticity. On the basis of the BP test and the White test, with or without squared and cross-product terms, it was found that the hours worked function in Table 4.2 was plagued by heteroscedasticity.[19]

---

**19**  For the BP test $nR^2 = 38.76$, which has a chi-square distribution with 10 df. The probability of obtaining such a chi-square value or greater is almost zero.  For the White test, $nR^2 = 40.19$ without the

**Table 5.8  Heteroscedasticity-corrected wage function.**

Dependent Variable: W
Method: Least Squares
Sample: 1 1289
Included observations: 1289
White Heteroskedasticity-Consistent Standard Errors & Covariance

|  | Coefficient | Std. Error | t-Statistic | Prob. |
|---|---|---|---|---|
| C | −7.183338 | 1.090064 | −6.589834 | 0.0000 |
| FEMALE | −3.074875 | 0.364256 | −8.441521 | 0.0000 |
| NONWHITE | −1.565313 | 0.397626 | −3.936647 | 0.0001 |
| UNION | 1.095976 | 0.425802 | 2.573908 | 0.0102 |
| EDUC | 1.370301 | 0.083485 | 16.41372 | 0.0000 |
| EXPER | 0.166607 | 0.016049 | 10.38134 | 0.0000 |

| | | | | |
|---|---|---|---|---|
| R-squared | 0.323339 | Mean dependent var | 12.36585 |
| Adjusted R-squared | 0.320702 | S.D. dependent var | 7.896350 |
| S.E. of regression | 6.508137 | Akaike info criterion | 6.588627 |
| Sum squared resid | 54342.54 | Schwarz criterion | 6.612653 |
| Log likelihood | −4240.370 | Durbin–Watson stat | 1.897513 |
| F-statistic | 122.6149 | Prob(F-statistic) | 0.000000 |

Since the sample is reasonably large, we can use the White procedure to obtain heteroscedasticity-corrected standard errors. The results are given in Table 5.9.

If you compare these results with those given in Table 4.2, you will see a few changes in the estimated standard errors and $t$ values. Family income and kids under 6 variables are now less significant than before, whereas the unemployment rate variable is a bit more significant.

The point to note here is that if the sample size is reasonably large, we should produce White's heteroscedasticity-corrected standard errors along with the usual OLS standard errors to get some idea about the presence of heteroscedasticity.

## 5.5    Summary and conclusions

In this chapter we considered one of the violations of the classical linear regression model, namely, heteroscedasticity, which is generally found in cross-sectional data. Although heteroscedasticity does not destroy the unbiasedness and consistency properties of OLS estimators, the estimators are less efficient, making statistical inference less reliable if we do not correct the usual OLS standard errors.

Before we solve the problem of heteroscedasticity, we need to find out if we have the problem in any specific application. For this purpose we can examine the squared residuals from the original model or use some formal tests of heteroscedasticity, such as the Breusch–Pagan and White's tests. If one or more of these tests show that we have the heteroscedasticity problem, we can then proceed to remediation of the problem.

squared and cross-product terms, and 120.23 when such terms are added. In both cases, the probability of obtaining such chi-square values or greater is practically zero.

**Table 5.9  Heteroscedasticity-corrected hours function.**

Dependent Variable: HOURS
Method: Least Squares
Sample (adjusted): 1 428
Included observations: 428 after adjustments
White Heteroskedasticity-Consistent Standard Errors & Covariance

|         | Coefficient | Std. Error | t-Statistic | Prob.  |
|---------|-------------|------------|-------------|--------|
| C       | 8484.523    | 1154.479   | 7.349222    | 0.0000 |
| AGE     | −17.72740   | 5.263072   | −3.368262   | 0.0008 |
| EDUC    | −27.03403   | 15.70405   | −1.721468   | 0.0859 |
| EXPER   | 24.20345    | 4.953720   | 4.885914    | 0.0000 |
| FAMINC  | 0.013781    | 0.007898   | 1.744916    | 0.0817 |
| HUSHRS  | −0.486474   | 0.073287   | −6.637928   | 0.0000 |
| HUSWAGE | −144.9734   | 17.58257   | −8.245293   | 0.0000 |
| KIDSLT6 | −180.4415   | 105.0628   | −1.717462   | 0.0866 |
| WAGE    | −47.43286   | 9.832834   | −4.823925   | 0.0000 |
| MTR     | −6351.293   | 1206.585   | −5.263859   | 0.0000 |
| UNEM    | −16.50367   | 9.632981   | −1.713246   | 0.0874 |

| | | | | |
|---|---|---|---|---|
| R-squared          | 0.335786  | Mean dependent var    | 1302.930 |
| Adjusted R-squared | 0.319858  | S.D. dependent var    | 776.2744 |
| S.E. of regression | 640.1992  | Akaike info criterion | 15.78680 |
| Sum squared resid  | 1.71E+08  | Schwarz criterion     | 15.89112 |
| Log likelihood     | −3367.375 | Durbin–Watson stat    | 2.078578 |
| F-statistic        | 21.08098  | Prob(F-statistic)     | 0.000000 |

The problem of heteroscedasticity can be solved if we know the heteroscedastic variances, $\sigma_i^2$, for in that case we can transform the original model (5.1) by diving it through by $\sigma_i$ and estimate the transformed model by OLS, which will produce estimators that are BLUE. This method of estimation is known as weighted least squares (WLS). Unfortunately, we rarely, if ever, know the true error variances. Therefore we need to find the second best solution.

Using some educated guesses of the likely nature of $\sigma_i^2$ we transform the original model, estimate it, and subject it to heteroscedasticity tests. If these tests suggest that there is no heteroscedasticity problem in the transformed model, we may not reject the transformed model. If, however, the transformed model shows that the problem of heteroscedasticity still persists, we can look for another transformation and repeat the cycle again.

However, all this labor can be avoided if we have a sufficiently large sample, because in that case we can obtain heteroscedasticity-corrected standard errors, using the procedure suggested by White. The corrected standard errors are known as **robust standard errors**. Nowadays there are several micro data sets that are produced by several agencies that have a large number of observations, which makes it possible to use the robust standard errors in regression models suspected of the heteroscedasticity problem.

## Exercises

**5.1**    Consider the wage model given in Table 1.2. Replicate the results of this table, using log of wage rates as the regressand. Apply the various diagnostic tests discussed in the chapter to find out if the log wage function suffers from heteroscedasticity. If so, what remedial measures would you take? Show the necessary calculations.

**5.2**    Refer to the hours worked regression model given in Table 4.2. Use log of hours worked as the regressand and find out if the resulting model suffers from heteroscedasticity. Show the diagnostic tests you use. How would you resolve the problem of heteroscedasticity, if it is present in the model? Show the necessary calculations.

**5.3**    Do you agree with the following statement: "Heteroscedasticity has never been a reason to throw out an otherwise good model"?[20]

**5.4**    Refer to any textbook on econometrics and learn about the Park, Glejser, Spearman's rank correlation, and Goldfeld–Quandt tests of heteroscedasticity. Apply these tests to the abortion rate, wage rate, and hours of work regressions discussed in the chapter. Find out if there is any conflict between these tests and the BP and White tests of heteroscedasticity.

**5.5**    Refer to Table 5.5. Assume that the error variance is related to the square of income instead of to the square of ABORTIONF. Transform the original abortion rate function replacing ABORTIONF by income and compare your results with those given in Table 5.5. *A priori*, would you expect a different conclusion about the presence of heteroscedasticity? Why or why not. Show the necessary calculations.

---

**20**  N. Gregory Mankiw, A quick  refresher course in macroeconomics, *Journal of Economic Literature*, vol. XXVIII, , p. 1648.

# 6

# Regression diagnostic III: autocorrelation

A common problem in regression analysis involving time series data is autocorrelation. Recall that one of the assumptions of the classical linear regression model (CLRM) is that the error terms, $u_t$, are uncorrelated – that is the error term at time $t$ is not correlated with the error term at time $(t-1)$ or any other error term in the past. If the error terms are correlated, the following consequences follow:[1]

1  The OLS estimators are still unbiased and consistent.

2  They are still normally distributed in large samples.

3  But they are no longer efficient. That is, they are no longer BLUE (best linear unbiased estimator). In most cases OLS standard errors are underestimated, which means the estimated $t$ values are inflated, giving the appearance that a coefficient is more significant than it actually may be.

4  As a result, as in the case of heteroscedasticity, the hypothesis-testing procedure becomes suspect, since the estimated standard errors may not be reliable, even asymptotically (i.e. in large samples). In consequence, the usual $t$ and $F$ tests may not be valid.

As in the case of heteroscedasticity, we need to find out if autocorrelation exists in a specific application and take corrective action or find alternative estimating procedures that will produce BLUE estimators. Before we undertake this task, let us consider a concrete example.

## 6.1    US consumption function, 1947–2000

Table 6.1 gives data on real consumption expenditure (C), real disposable personal income (DPI), real wealth (W) and real interest rate (R) for the USA for the years 1947–2000, the term "real" meaning "adjusted for inflation".[2] Table 6.1 can be found on the companion website.

Now consider the following regression model:

$$\ln C_t = B_1 + B_2 \ln DPI_t + B_3 \ln W_t + B_4 R_t + u_t \qquad (6.1)$$

---

1  For details, see Gujarati/Porter, *op cit.*, Chapter 12.

2  The data were obtained from various government sources, such as the Department of Commerce, Federal Reserve Bank and the *Economic Report of the President*.

Notice that we have put the subscript $t$ to indicate that we are dealing with time series data. Also note that ln stands for natural logarithm.

For simplicity of explanation we will call Eq. (6.1) the consumption function. The explanatory variables, or regressors, in this equation are the commonly used variables in the consumption function, although there may be variations in the choice of DPI, wealth, and interest rate. Refer to any macroeconomics textbook for the theory behind the consumption function.

Observe that we have introduced $C$, $DPI$, and $W$ in log forms but $R$ in linear form because some of the real interest rates were negative. $B_2$ and $B_3$ are the *elasticities* of consumption expenditure with respect to disposable income and wealth, respectively, and $B_4$ is semi-elasticity with respect to real interest rate (recall our discussion about functional forms of regression models in Chapter 2).[3] *A priori*, we expect the income and wealth elasticities to be positive and the interest rate semi-elasticity to be negative.

## Regression results

The results of the estimated regression are given in Table 6.2.

## Evaluation of results

As expected, the slope coefficients have the expected signs. *If the standard assumptions of CLRM hold*, all the estimated coefficients are "highly" statistically significant, for the estimated $p$ values are so low. The income elasticity of 0.8 suggests that, holding other variables constant, if real personal disposal income goes up by 1%, mean real consumption expenditure goes up by about 0.8%. The wealth coefficient of about 0.20 suggests that if real wealth goes up by 1%, mean real consumption expenditure goes up by about 0.2%, *ceteris paribus*. The interest semi-elasticity suggests that if interest rate

**Table 6.2  Regression results of the consumption function.**

Dependent Variable: LOG(C)
Method: Least Squares
Sample: 1947 2000
Included observations: 54

|  | Coefficient | Std. Error | t-Statistic | Prob. |
|---|---|---|---|---|
| C | −0.467711 | 0.042778 | −10.93343 | 0.0000 |
| L(DPI) | 0.804873 | 0.017498 | 45.99836 | 0.0000 |
| L(W) | 0.201270 | 0.017593 | 11.44060 | 0.0000 |
| R | −0.002689 | 0.000762 | −3.529265 | 0.0009 |

| | | | | |
|---|---|---|---|---|
| R-squared | 0.999560 | Mean dependent var | 7.826093 |
| Adjusted R-squared | 0.999533 | S.D. dependent var | 0.552368 |
| S.E. of regression | 0.011934 | Akaike info criterion | −5.947703 |
| Sum squared resid | 0.007121 | Schwarz criterion | −5.800371 |
| Log likelihood | 164.5880 | Durbin–Watson stat | 1.289219 |
| F-statistic | 37832.59 | Prob(F-statistic) | 0.000000 |

Note: L stands for natural log.

---

3  In the analysis of the consumption function it is common to use the log or semi-log forms, for the coefficients can be interpreted as elasticities or semi-elasticities.

goes up by *one percentage point* (not 1%), mean real consumption expenditure goes down by about 0.26%, *ceteris paribus*.

The high $R^2$ and other statistics given in the above table would suggest that the fitted model gives an excellent fit, although we should be wary of an $R^2$ value of practically one. This is because of the possibility of **spurious correlation** which arises when both the regressand and regressors are growing over time. But we will discuss this topic in greater detail in the chapter on time series econometrics (Chapter 13).

Since we are dealing with time series data, we have to guard against auto-, or serial, correlation. If there is autocorrelation in the error term, the estimated standard errors and, *ipso facto*, the estimated $t$ values will be suspect. Therefore, before we accept the results given in the preceding table, we need to check for the presence of autocorrelation.

## 6.2    Tests of autocorrelation

Although there are several tests of autocorrelation, we will discuss only a few here, namely, the **graphical method**, the **Durbin–Watson test**, and the **Breusch–Godfrey (BG) test**.[4]

### Graphical method

In evaluating regression results it is always good practice to plot the residuals from the estimated model for clues regarding possible violation of one or more OLS assumptions. As one author notes: "Anyone who tries to analyse a time series without plotting it is asking for trouble."[5]

For example, in our discussion of heteroscedasticity, we plotted the squared residuals against the estimated value of the regressand to find some pattern in these residuals, which may suggest the type of transformation one can make of the original model so that in the transformed model we do not face heteroscedasticity.

Since autocorrelation refers to correlation among the error terms, $u_t$, a rough and ready method of testing for autocorrelation is to simply plot the values of $u_t$ chronologically. Unfortunately, we do not observe $u_t$s directly. What we observe are their proxies, the $e_t$s, which we can observe after we estimate the regression model.

Although the $e_t$s are not the same thing as $u_t$s, they are *consistent* estimators of the latter, in the sense that as the sample size increases, $e_t$s converge to their true values, $u_t$s. Our sample of 54 observations may not be technically large, but they cover the bulk of the post-Second World War period data. Even if we extend our sample to the end of 2009, we will have at most nine more observations. Therefore we cannot do much about our sample size.

By plotting the data on $e_t$s chronologically we can get a visual impression of the possibility of autocorrelation. Doing so, we obtain Figure 6.1.

This figure shows the residuals $S_1$ obtained from regression (6.1) and the standardized residual, $S_2$, which are simply $S_1$ divided by the standard error of the regression. For scale comparability, we have multiplied $S_1$ by 100.

---

4  For the various methods of detecting autocorrelation, see Gujarati/Porter, *op cit.*, Chapter 12, pp. 429–40.

5  Chris Chatfield, *The Analysis of Time Series: An Introduction*, 6th edn, Chapman and Hall, 2004, p. 6.

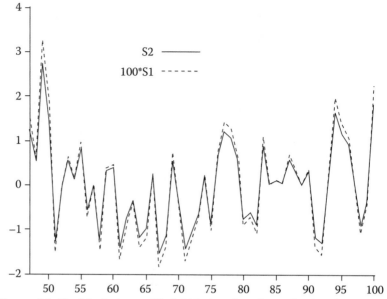

**Figure 6.1  Residuals (magnified 100 times) and standardized residuals.**

The $S_1$ and $S_2$ curves show a see-saw pattern, suggesting that the residuals are correlated. This can be seen more clearly if we plot residuals at time $t$ against residuals at time $(t-1)$, as in Figure 6.2.

The sketched regression line in Figure 6.2 suggests that the residuals are positively correlated.

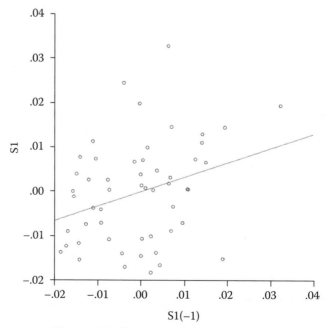

**Figure 6.2  Current vs. lagged residuals.**

### Durbin–Watson $d$ test[6]

The most celebrated, and often over-used, test for detecting serial correlation was developed by statisticians Durbin and Watson, and is popularly known as the **Durbin–Watson $d$ statistic,** *which is defined as:*

$$d = \frac{\sum_{t=2}^{t=n}(e_t - e_{t-1})^2}{\sum_{t=1}^{t=n} e_t^2} \tag{6.2}$$

This is the ratio of the sum of squared differences in successive residuals to the residual sum of squares. Note that the df in the numerator is $(n-1)$, as we lose one observation in taking successive differences of residuals. *Also note that the d value always lies between 0 and 4.*[7]

The $d$ value for our example is $1.2829 \approx 1.28$. What do we do with this value?

Before we see how the $d$ statistic works, *it is very important to bear in mind the assumptions underlying the d statistic.* These assumptions are:

1  The regression model includes an intercept term.[8]

2  The explanatory variables, or regressors, are fixed in repeated sampling.

3  The error term $u_t$ follows the **first-order autoregressive (AR1)** scheme:

$$u_t = \rho u_{t-1} + v_t \tag{6.3}$$

where $\rho$ (rho) is **the coefficient of autocorrelation** and it lies in the range $-1 \leq \rho \leq 1$. It is called first-order AR because it involves only the current and one-period lagged error term. $v_t$ is a random error term.

4  The error term $u_t$ is normally distributed.

5  The regressors do not include the lagged value(s) of the dependent variable, $Y_t$, that is, regressors do not include $Y_{t-1}, Y_{t-2}$ and other lagged terms of $Y$.

As you can see, these assumptions may be quite restrictive in practice.

The exact probability distribution of $d$ is difficult to derive because it depends in a complicated way on the values taken by the regressors. And since the values taken by regressors are sample-specific, there is no unique way to derive the sampling distribution of $d$.

However, based on the sample size and the number of regressors, Durbin and Watson were able to establish two *critical values* of the $d$ statistic, $d_L$ and $d_U$, called the lower and upper limits, so that if the computed $d$ value lies below the lower limit, or above the upper limit, or in between the two limits, a decision could be made about the presence of autocorrelation.

The *decision rules are as follows*:

1  If $d < d_L$, there probably is evidence of positive autocorrelation.

2  If $d > d_U$, there probably is no evidence of positive autocorrelation.

---

6  For details, see Gujarati/Porter, *op cit.*, Chapter 12.

7  For details, see Gujarati/Porter, *op cit.*, Chapter 12, pp. 435–6.

8  If the constant term is absent, Farebrother has modified the $d$ test to take this into account. For further details, see Gujarati/Porter, *op cit.*, p. 434.

3  If $d_L < d < d_U$, no definite conclusion about positive autocorrelation may be made.

4  If $d_U < d < 4-d_U$, there is probably no evidence of positive or negative autocorrelation.

5  If $4-d_U < d < 4-d_L$, no definite conclusion about negative autocorrelation may be made.

6  If $4-d_L < d < 4$, there probably is evidence of negative autocorrelation.

As noted, the $d$ value lies between 0 and 4. The closer it is to zero, the greater is the evidence of positive autocorrelation, and the closer it is to 4, the greater is the evidence of negative autocorrelation. If $d$ is about 2, there is no evidence of positive or negative (first-) order autocorrelation.

Durbin and Watson prepared tables that give the lower and upper limits of the $d$ statistic for a selected number of observations (up to 200) and a number of regressors (up to 10) and for 5% and 1% levels of significance.

Returning to our consumption function, we have $n = 54$, $X$ (number of regressors) = 3. The 5% critical $d$ values for this combination are (using $n = 55$): (1.452, 1.681). Since the computed $d$ value is about 1.28, it lies below the lower limit, leading to the conclusion that we probably have positive autocorrelation in the error term.

The 1% critical $d$ values are (1.284, 1.506). The computed $d$ value is slightly below the lower limit, again suggesting that our regression probably suffers from positive (first-order) autocorrelation.

## Breusch–Godfrey (BG) general test of autocorrelation[9]

To avoid some of the restrictive features of the $d$ test, Breusch and Godfrey have developed a test of autocorrelation that is more general in that it allows for (1) lagged values of the dependent variables to be included as regressors, (2) higher-order autoregressive schemes, such as AR (2) and AR (3), and (3) moving average terms of the error term, such as $u_{t-1}, u_{t-2}$ and so on.[10]

To illustrate the BG test, suppose in Eq. (6.1), the error term follows the following structure:

$$u_t = \rho_1 u_{t-1} + \rho_2 u_{t-2} + \ldots + \rho_p u_{t-p} + v_t \tag{6.4}$$

where $v_t$ is the error term that follows the usual classical assumptions.

Equation (6.4) is an **AR ($p$) autoregressive structure** where the current error term depends on previous error terms up to $p$ lags. The precise value of $p$ is often a trial and error process, although in most economic time series one does not have to choose a high value of $p$.

The null hypothesis $H_0$ is:

$$\rho_1 = \rho_2 = \ldots = \rho_p = 0 \tag{6.5}$$

That is, there is no serial correlation of any order.

---

9  For details, see Gujarati/Porter, *op cit.*, pp. 438–40.

10  An AR(2) scheme, for example, involves regressing the current value of variable on its values lagged one and two periods. In an MA(1), for example, the current error term and its immediate previous value are involved. MA is discussed further in Chapter 16.

In practice we only observe $e_t$s, the residuals, which are estimators of the $u_t$s. Therefore the BG test involves the following steps:

1  Estimate (6.1) by OLS and obtain the residuals, $e_t$.

2  Regress $e_t$ on the regressors in model (6.1) and the $p$ autoregressive terms given in (6.4), that is, run the following regression

$$e_t = A_1 + A_2 \ln DPI_t + A_3 \ln W_t + A_4 R_t + C_1 e_{t-1}$$
$$+ C_2 e_{t-2} + \ldots + C_p e_{t-p} + v_t \tag{6.6}$$

and obtain $R^2$ from this *auxiliary regression*.

3  If the sample size is large (technically, infinite), BG have shown that

$$(n-p)R^2 \sim \chi_p^2 \tag{6.7}$$

That is, in large sample, $(n-p)$ times $R^2$ follows the chi-square distribution with $p$ degrees of freedom.

4  As an alternative, we can use the $F$ value obtained from regression (6.6) to test the null hypothesis given in (6.5). This $F$ value has $(p, n-k-p)$ degrees of freedom in the numerator and denominator, respectively, where $k$ represents the number of parameters in (6.1) (including the intercept term).

Therefore, if in an application the chi-square value thus computed exceeds the critical chi-square value at the chosen level of significance, we can reject the null hypothesis of no autocorrelation, in which case at least one $p$ value in (6.6) is statistically significantly different from zero. In other words, we have some form of auto-correlation. Most statistical packages now present the $p$ value of the estimated chi-square value, so we need not choose the level of significance arbitrarily.

Similarly, if the computed $F$ value exceeds the critical $F$ value for a given level of significance, we can also reject the null hypothesis of no autocorrelation. Instead of choosing the level of significance, we can rely on the $p$ value of the estimated $F$ statistic and reject the null hypothesis if this $p$ value is low.

These two tests give similar results, which should not be surprising in view of the relationship between the $F$ and $\chi^2$ statistics.[11]

Before we illustrate the test, the following features of the BG test may be noted:

1  The test requires that the error variance of $u_t$, given the values of the regressors and the lagged values of the error term, is homoscedastic. If that is not the case, we will have to use heteroscedasticity-corrected variance, such as the White's robust error terms.

2  A practical problem in the application of the BG test is the choice of the number of lagged error terms, $p$, in Eq. (6.4). The value of $p$ may depend on the type of time series. For monthly data, we may include 11 lagged error terms, for quarterly data we may include three lagged error terms, and for annual data, one lagged error term may suffice. Of course, we can choose the lag length by trial and error and

---

11  This relationship is as follows: For large denominator df, the numerator df times the $F$ value is approximately equal to the chi-square value with the numerator df, where $m$ and $n$ are denominator and numerator df. respectively.

**Table 6.3  BG test of autocorrelation of the consumption function.**

Breusch–Godfrey Serial Correlation LM Test:

| | | | |
|---|---|---|---|
| F-statistic | 5.345894 | Prob. F(1,49) | 0.0250 |
| Obs*R-squared | 5.311869 | Prob. Chi-Square(1) | 0.0212 |

Test Equation:
Dependent Variable: RESID ($e_t$)
Method: Least Squares
Sample: 1947 2000
Presample missing value lagged residuals set to zero.

| | Coefficient | Std. Error | t-Statistic | Prob. |
|---|---|---|---|---|
| C | 0.000739 | 0.041033 | 0.018016 | 0.9857 |
| L(DPI) | −0.000259 | 0.016784 | −0.015433 | 0.9877 |
| L (w) | 0.000131 | 0.016875 | 0.007775 | 0.9938 |
| R | 0.000181 | 0.000735 | 0.246196 | 0.8066 |
| RESID(-1) | 0.330367 | 0.142885 | 2.312119 | 0.0250 |

| | | | |
|---|---|---|---|
| R-squared | 0.098368 | Mean dependent var | −7.07E−19 |
| Adjusted R-squared | 0.024765 | S.D. dependent var | 0.011591 |
| S.E. of regression | 0.011447 | Akaike info criterion | −6.014218 |
| Sum squared resid | 0.006420 | Schwarz criterion | −5.830053 |
| Log likelihood | 167.3839 | Durbin–Watson stat | 1.744810 |
| F-statistic | 1.336473 | Prob(F-statistic) | 0.269759 |

choose the value of $p$ based on the **Akaike** and **Schwarz information criteria** (see Chapter 2). The lower the value of these criteria, the better is the model.

Returning to our consumption function, the results of regression (6.6) are as follows: For illustration, we only include one lagged value of the residuals in this regression because we have annual data. The results are shown in Table 6.3.

As these results show, there is strong evidence of (first-order) autocorrelation, for both the $F$ and $\chi^2$ values are highly significant because their $p$ values are so low.

We also estimated the model including 2 and 3 lagged error terms. The Akaike information criterion gave these values as −6.01, −6.00, and −5.96 for one, two, and three lagged error terms in Eq. (6.6). Although there is not a substantial difference in these values, on the basis of the Akaike criterion, we choose the model with the largest negative value, which is −6.01, thus justifying the use of one lagged error term in Eq. (6.6).[12] Also, the coefficients of the second and third lagged terms were statistically insignificant.

## 6.3   Remedial measures

If we find autocorrelation in an application, we need to take care of it, for depending on its severity, we may be drawing misleading conclusions because the usual OLS standard errors could be severely biased. Now the problem we face is that we do not know the correlation structure of the error terms $u_t$, since they are not directly observable.

---

12  Note that −5.96 is greater than −6.0, which is greater than −6.1.

Hence, as in the case of heteroscedasticity, we need to resort to some educated guesswork or some kind of transformation of the original regression model so that in the transformed model we do not face the serial correlation problem. There are several methods that we could try.

## First-difference transformation

Suppose autocorrelation is of AR(1) type, as in Eq. (6.3), which we can write as:

$$u_t - \rho u_{t-1} = v_t \tag{6.8}$$

If we know the value of $\rho$, we can subtract from the current value of the error term $\rho$ times the previous value of the error term. The resulting error term, $v_t$ will satisfy the standard OLS assumptions. Therefore we can transform the original regression as:

$$\ln C_t - \rho \ln C_{t-1} = B_1(1-\rho) + B_2(\ln DPI_t - \rho \ln DPI_{t-1})$$
$$+ B_3(\ln W_t - \rho \ln W_{t-1}) + B_4(R_t - \rho R_{t-1}) \tag{6.9}$$
$$+ (u_t - \rho u_{t-1})$$

The last term in this equation is simply $v_t$, which now is free from serial correlation.

The transformed model can therefore be estimated by OLS. All we have to do is transform each variable by subtracting from its current value $\rho$ times its previous value and run the regression. The estimators obtained from the transformed model are BLUE.

But note that in this transformation we lose one observation, because for the very first observation there is no antecedent. If the sample is reasonably large, loss of one observation may not matter much. But if the sample size is small, the loss of the first observation means the estimators will not be BLUE. However, there is a procedure, called the **Prais–Winsten transformation**, that can take into account the first observation.[13]

Now the question is: how do we estimate $\rho$? We know that $-1 \le \rho \le 1$. Therefore, any value in this range can be used to transform the original model, as in (6.9). But which one value should we choose, for literally there is an infinite number of values in this range?

Many economic time series are highly inter-correlated, suggesting that perhaps a value $\rho = 1$ may be appropriate to transform the original model. If this is indeed the case, Eq. (6.9) can be written as:

$$\Delta \ln C_t = B_2 \Delta \ln DPI_t + B_3 \Delta \ln W_t + B_4 \Delta R_t + v_t \tag{6.10}$$

where $\Delta$ is the **first-difference operator**. $\Delta \ln C_t = (\ln C_t - \ln C_{t-1})$, etc.

Equation (6.10) is called, appropriately, the **first-difference transformation**. By contrast, Eq. (6.1) is called the **level form** regression.

In estimating (6.10), notice that there is no intercept in it. Therefore, in estimating this model you have to suppress the intercept term. Most software packages can do that without much trouble.

Using *Eviews*, the empirical counterpart of Eq. (6.10) is shown in Table 6.4.

---

[13] We will not pursue this transformation here, which is now built into software packages. For details, see Gujarati/Porter, *op cit.*, pp. 442–3.

**Table 6.4 First difference transform of the consumption function.**

Dependent Variable: D(LC)
Method: Least Squares
Sample (adjusted): 1948 2000
Included observations: 53 after adjustments

|          | Coefficient | Std. Error | t-Statistic | Prob. |
|----------|-------------|------------|-------------|-------|
| D(LDPI)  | 0.848988    | 0.051538   | 16.47313    | 0.0000 |
| D(LW)    | 0.106360    | 0.036854   | 2.885941    | 0.0057 |
| D(R)     | 0.000653    | 0.000826   | 0.790488    | 0.4330 |

| | | | |
|---|---|---|---|
| R-squared | 0.614163 | Mean dependent var | 0.035051 |
| Adjusted R-squared | 0.598730 | S.D. dependent var | 0.017576 |
| S.E. of regression | 0.011134 | Akaike info criterion | −6.102765 |
| Sum squared resid | 0.006198 | Schwarz criterion | −5.991239 |
| Log likelihood | 164.7233 | Hannan–Quinn criter. | −6.059878 |
| Durbin–Watson stat | 2.026549 | | |

*Note*: D stands for the first difference operator $\Delta$ and L stands for natural logarithm.

If we test this regression for autocorrelation using the BG test, we find that there is no evidence of autocorrelation, whether we use 1, 2, or more lagged error terms in Eq. (6.4).

If we compare the regression results of the original regression given in Table 6.2 and those obtained from first difference transformation given in Table 6.4, we see that the income elasticity is more or less the same, but the wealth elasticity, although statistically significant, is almost half in value and the interest rate semi-elasticity is practically zero and has the wrong sign. This outcome could be due to the wrong value of $\rho$ chosen for transformation. But more fundamentally it may have to do with the **stationarity** of one or more variables, a topic that we explore in depth in the chapter on time series econometrics (Chapter 13).

It should be emphasized that the $R^2$ values in the level form (i.e. given in Table 6.2) and in the first-difference form (i.e. Table 6.4) are not directly comparable because the dependent variable in the two models is different. As noted before, to compare two or more $R^2$ values, the dependent variable must be the same.

## Generalized transformation

Since it will be a waste of time to try several values of $\rho$ to transform the original model, we may proceed somewhat analytically. For instance, if the AR(1) assumption is appropriate, we can regress $e_t$ on $e_{t-1}$, using $e_t$ as a proxy for $u_t$, an assumption that may be appropriate in large samples, because in large samples $e_t$ is a consistent estimator of $\rho$. That is we estimate:

$$e_t = \hat{\rho} e_{t-1} + \text{error} \tag{6.11}$$

where $\hat{\rho}$ is an estimator of $\rho$ given in (6.8).

Once we obtain an estimate of $\rho$ from Eq. (6.11), we can use it to transform the model as in Eq. (6.9) and estimate the model thus transformed.

The estimates of the parameters thus obtained are known as **feasible generalized least squares (FGLS) estimators**.

Using our data, it can be shown that $\hat{\rho} = 0.3246$.

Another method of obtaining an estimate of $\rho$, especially in large samples, is to use the following relationship between $\rho$ and Durbin–Watson $d$, which is:

$$\rho \approx 1 - \frac{d}{2} \tag{6.12}$$

where $d$ is the DW $d$ obtained from the original regression. In our example, $d$ was found to be 1.2892. Therefore we get

$$\hat{\rho} = 1 - \frac{1.2892}{2} = 0.3554$$

We can use this estimated value of $\rho$ to transform the original model.

The estimates obtained from Eqs. (6.11) and (6.12) are about the same. It should be noted that $\hat{\rho}$ estimated from (6.11) or (6.12) provides a *consistent estimate* of the true $\rho$. For illustration we use $\hat{\rho} = 0.3246$ and obtain the results shown in Table 6.5.

Now we analyze the residuals from this regression for serial correlation, using, say, the BG test. Using 1 and 2 lagged terms in Eq. (6.6), it was found that the estimated BG statistic was not statistically significant, indicating that the residuals in the AR(1) transformation were not autocorrelated: the BG chi-square value allowing for one lagged residual term was 0.0094, whose probability was about 92%.

If you compare the results in this table with those given in Table 6.2, you will see that the standard errors of the coefficients in the two tables are substantially different, but keep in mind that Table 6.2 does not correct for autocorrelation, whereas Table 6.5 does. The magnitudes of the income and wealth elasticities are about the same in the two tables, although the standard errors, and therefore the $t$ values, are different.

The lower absolute $t$ values in Table 6.5 suggest that the original OLS standard errors were underestimated, which follows our discussion of the consequences of OLS estimation in the presence of autocorrelation.

The interest rate coefficient in the transformed model has the correct sign, but it is statistically insignificant. Again this may be due to the reasons discussed previously.

**Table 6.5  Transformed consumption function using $\hat{\rho} = 0.3246$.**

Method: Least Squares
Date: 10/18/09 Time: 19:12
Sample (adjusted): 1948 2000
Included observations: 53 after adjustments

|  | Coefficient | Std. Error | t-Statistic | Prob. |
|---|---|---|---|---|
| C | −0.279768 | 0.033729 | −8.294681 | 0.0000 |
| LDPI−0.3246*LDPI(−1) | 0.818700 | 0.021096 | 38.80871 | 0.0000 |
| LW−0.3246*LW(−1) | 0.183635 | 0.020986 | 8.750235 | 0.0000 |
| R−0.3246*R(−1) | −1.84E−05 | 0.000969 | −0.019017 | 0.9849 |

| | | | | |
|---|---|---|---|---|
| R-squared | 0.999235 | Mean dependent var | 5.309128 | |
| Adjusted R-squared | 0.999188 | S.D. dependent var | 0.365800 | |
| S.E. of regression | 0.010423 | Akaike info criterion | −6.217159 | |
| Sum squared resid | 0.005323 | Schwarz criterion | −6.068458 | |
| Log likelihood | 168.7547 | Hannan–Quinn criter. | −6.159976 | |
| F-statistic | 21333.54 | Durbin–Watson stat | 1.448914 | |
| Prob(F-statistic) | 0.000000 | | | |

The $R^2$ values in the two tables are about the same, but we cannot compare them directly for reasons already discussed.

Before proceeding further, it should be noted that the AR(1) transform is a specific case of the more general transformation, AR($p$) shown in Eq. (6.4). If, for example, the error term follows AR(2),

$$u_t = \rho_1 u_{t-1} + \rho_2 u_{t-2} + v_t \qquad (6.13)$$

then

$$u_t - \rho_1 u_{t-1} - \rho_2 u_{t-2} = v_t \qquad (6.14)$$

where $v_t$ now follows the standard OLS assumptions. In this case we will have to transform the regressand and regressors by subtracting from the current value of each variable their previous two values, each multiplied by the autocorrelation coefficients $\rho_1$ and $\rho_2$, respectively.

In practice, of course we replace the unobserved $u$s by their counterparts, the $e$s. But there is no need to do this manually. In *Eiews*, for example, if you add the terms AR(1) and AR(2) when running the OLS regression, you will get the results practically instantly.

In deciding how many AR terms to add, we may have to use the Akaike or similar information criterion to decide the value of $p$. If your sample is not very large, you may not want to add too many AR terms, for each added AR term will consume one degree of freedom.

### The Newey–West method of correcting OLS standard errors

All the methods of searching for autocorrelation coefficient(s) discussed thus far are essentially *trial and error methods*. Which method will succeed in a concrete application will depend on the nature of the problem and on the sample size.

But if the sample size is large (technically infinite), one can estimate an OLS regression in the usual manner but correct the standard errors of the estimated coefficients, by a method developed by Newey and West. The standard errors corrected by their procedure are also known as **HAC** (heteroscedasticity and autocorrelation consistent) standard errors.[14] Generally speaking, if there is autocorrelation, the HAC standard errors are found to be larger than the usual OLS standard errors.

The HAC procedure is now incorporated in several software packages. We illustrate this procedure for our consumption function. Using *Eviews*, we obtained the results in Table 6.6.

If you compare the HAC standard errors with the OLS standard errors given in Table 6.2, you will observe that they do not differ substantially. This would suggest that despite the evidence of autocorrelation based on several autocorrelation tests, the autocorrelation problem does not seem to be very serious. This may be due the fact that the observed correlation found in the error term, of between 0.32 and 0.35, may not be very high. Of course, this answer is specific to our data set and there is no guarantee that this will happen in every case.

---

14  The mathematics behind this method is rather complicated. If you are familiar with matrix algebra, you can consult William H. Greene, *Econometric Analysis*, 6th edn, Pearson/Prentice Hall, New Jersey, 2008, Chapter 19.

**Table 6.6** HAC standard errors of the consumption function.

Dependent Variable: LC
Method: Least Squares
Sample: 1947 2000
Included observations: 54
Newey–West HAC Standard Errors & Covariance (lag truncation=3)

|        | Coefficient | Std. Error | t-Statistic | Prob. |
|--------|-------------|------------|-------------|--------|
| C      | −0.467714   | 0.043937   | −10.64516   | 0.0000 |
| LDPI   | 0.804871    | 0.017117   | 47.02132    | 0.0000 |
| LW     | 0.201272    | 0.015447   | 13.02988    | 0.0000 |
| R      | −0.002689   | 0.000880   | −3.056306   | 0.0036 |

| | | | |
|---|---|---|---|
| R-squared | 0.999560 | Mean dependent var | 7.826093 |
| Adjusted R-squared | 0.999533 | S.D. dependent var | 0.552368 |
| S.E. of regression | 0.011934 | Akaike info criterion | −5.947707 |
| Sum squared resid | 0.007121 | Schwarz criterion | −5.800374 |
| Log likelihood | 164.5881 | Durbin–Watson stat | 1.289237 |
| F-statistic | 37832.71 | Prob(F-statistic) | 0.000000 |

Incidentally, observe that the estimated coefficient values in the two tables are the same, as are the other summary statistics. In other words, the HAC procedure only changes the standard errors, and hence the $t$ statistics and their $p$ values. This is similar to White's robust error terms which also do not affect the original regression coefficients and other summary statistics.

*But keep in mind that the HAC procedure is valid in large samples only.*[15]

## 6.4   Model evaluation

An important assumption of the CLRM is that the model used in the analysis is "correctly specified". This is often a tall order, for searching for the correct model is like searching for the Holy Grail. In practice we use prior empirical work that has been published in the field as a guide, obtain the best available data, and use the best possible method of estimation.

Even then, model building is an art. In the context of this chapter, autocorrelation can arise for several reasons, such as *inertia, specification error, Cobweb phenomenon, data manipulation,* and *nonstationarity.*[16]

To illustrate, we will consider the case of model specification error. Now consider a re-specification of model (6.1):

$$\ln C_t = A_1 + A_2 \ln DPI_t + A_3 \ln W_t + A_4 R_t + A_5 \ln C_{t-1} + u_t \qquad (6.15)$$

This model differs from (6.1) in that we have added the log of consumption expenditure lagged one period as an additional regressor and changed the coefficient notation from B to A to see if there is any difference between them.

Model (6.15) is called an **autoregressive model** because one of the regressors is the lagged value of the regressand. The reason for adding the lagged consumption

---

15 For some of the limitations of the HAC procedure, see Jeffrey M. Wooldridge, *Introductory Econometrics,* 4th edn, South-Western, Ohio, 2009, pp. 428–31.

16 For a brief discussion about this, see Gujarati/Porter, *op cit.,* pp. 414–18.

Table 6.7  Autoregressive consumption function.

Dependent Variable: LC
Method: Least Squares
Sample (adjusted): 1948 2000
Included observations: 53 after adjustments

|  | Coefficient | Std. Error | t-Statistic | Prob. |
|---|---|---|---|---|
| C | −0.316023 | 0.055667 | −5.677048 | 0.0000 |
| LINC | 0.574832 | 0.069673 | 8.250418 | 0.0000 |
| LW | 0.150289 | 0.020838 | 7.212381 | 0.0000 |
| R | −0.000675 | 0.000894 | −0.755458 | 0.4537 |
| LC(−1) | 0.276562 | 0.080472 | 3.436754 | 0.0012 |

| | | | | |
|---|---|---|---|---|
| R-squared | 0.999645 | Mean dependent var | 7.843870 | |
| Adjusted R-squared | 0.999616 | S.D. dependent var | 0.541833 | |
| S.E. of regression | 0.010619 | Akaike info criterion | −6.162741 | |
| Sum squared resid | 0.005413 | Schwarz criterion | −5.976865 | |
| Log likelihood | 168.3126 | Durbin–Watson stat | 1.395173 | |
| F-statistic | 33833.55 | Prob(F-statistic) | 0.000000 | |

expenditure value is to see if past consumption expenditure influences current consumption expenditure. If so, that will show the inertia factor mentioned previously.

It is clear from this table that lagged consumption affects current consumption expenditure, *ceteris paribus*. This may be due to inertia. The coefficients in Tables 6.2 and 6.7 look different at face value, but they really are not, for if you divide both sides by $(1 - 0.2765) = 0.7235$ you will obtain coefficient values that are about the same as in Table 6.2.[17]

Do we have autocorrelation in the revised model? Here we cannot use the Durbin–Watson $d$ test because, as noted earlier, this test is not applicable if the model contains lagged value(s) of the dependent variable, which is the case here.

Assuming first-order autocorrelation, Durbin has developed an alternative test for such models, called Durbin's **h statistic**.[18]

Under the null hypothesis that $\rho = 0$, in large samples, the $h$ statistic follows the standard normal distribution, that is, $h \sim N(0,1)$. Now from the properties of the normal distribution we know that the probability that $|h| > 1.96$ is about 5%, where $|h|$ means the absolute value of $h$. For our example, the $h$ value is about 5.43, which exceeds the 5% critical $h$ value, leading to the conclusion that model (6.15) also suffers from first-order autocorrelation.

Instead of using this test, we will use the BG test, for it allows for lagged value(s) of regressand as regressors. Using the BG test, and using two lagged values of the residuals, there still was evidence of autocorrelation; the estimated $p$ values of 0.09 ($F$ test) and 0.07 (chi-square test) (Table 6.8).

Whether we use model (6.1) or (6.15), it seems we have serial correlation in our data.

---

17  In the long-run when consumption expenditure stabilizes, $LC_t = LC_{t-1}$. Therefore, if you transfer $0.2765 \, LC_t$ to the left-hand side, you will get about $0.7235 \, LC_t$. Then dividing through by 0.7235 you will get results comparable to Table 6.2.

18  For a discussion of this test, see Gujarati/Porter, *op cit.*, p. 465.

**Table 6.8  BG test of autocorrelation for autoregressive consumption function.**

**Breusch–Godfrey Serial Correlation LM Test:**

| | | | |
|---|---|---|---|
| F-statistic | 2.544893 | Prob. F(2,46) | 0.0895 |
| Obs*R-squared | 5.280090 | Prob. Chi-Square(2) | 0.0714 |

Test Equation:
Dependent Variable: RESID
Method: Least Squares
Sample: 1948 2000
Included observations: 53
Presample missing value lagged residuals set to zero.

| | Coefficient | Std. Error | t-Statistic | Prob. |
|---|---|---|---|---|
| C | −0.024493 | 0.055055 | −0.444876 | 0.6585 |
| LINC | 0.036462 | 0.070518 | 0.517061 | 0.6076 |
| LW | 0.009814 | 0.020666 | 0.474868 | 0.6371 |
| R | −8.02E−06 | 0.000879 | −0.009121 | 0.9928 |
| LC(−1) | −0.045942 | 0.081647 | −0.562685 | 0.5764 |
| RESID(−1) | 0.354304 | 0.159237 | 2.225013 | 0.0310 |
| RESID(−2) | −0.136263 | 0.155198 | −0.877992 | 0.3845 |

| | | | |
|---|---|---|---|
| R-squared | 0.099624 | Mean dependent var | 2.05E−16 |
| Adjusted R-squared | −0.017816 | S.D. dependent var | 0.010202 |
| S.E. of regression | 0.010293 | Akaike info criterion | −6.192213 |
| Sum squared resid | 0.004873 | Schwarz criterion | −5.931986 |
| Log likelihood | 171.0936 | Durbin–Watson stat | 1.924355 |
| F-statistic | 0.848298 | Prob(F-statistic) | 0.539649 |

**A technical note:** Since we have a lagged dependent variable as one of the regressors and serial correlation, the estimated coefficients in Eq. (6.15) may be biased as well as inconsistent. One solution to this problem is to use an **instrumental variable (IV)**, or **instrument**, for the lagged regressand in such a way that the chosen IV is correlated (possibly highly) with the regressand but uncorrelated with the error term. This topic is rather involved and we have devoted an entire chapter to IV estimation (see Chapter 19). One suggested solutions is to use the lagged value of income as instrument for the lagged value of consumption expenditure. But we will have more to say about this in Chapter 19.

To get rid of autocorrelation in the error term we can use one or more of the remedial methods discussed above, or we can use the Newey–West method and obtain robust or HAC standard errors. This gives the results shown in Table 6.9.

Comparing the results in Tables 6.6 and 6.9, it is evident that the standard errors of the coefficients in Table 6.6 were underestimated. Again keep in mind that the HAC correction procedure is valid in large samples only.

Model (6.15) is not the only way in which the original model can be re-specified. Instead of including the lagged value of the regressand among the explanatory variables, we could introduce the lagged value(s) of the explanatory variable, LDPI. Or we could include both.[19]

---

**19**  For details, see Gujarati/Porter, *op cit.*, Chapter 17.

**Table 6.9  HAC standard errors of the autoregressive consumption function.**

Dependent Variable: LC
Method: Least Squares
Sample (adjusted): 1948 2000
Included observations: 53 after adjustments
Newey–West HAC Standard Errors & Covariance (lag truncation=3)

|          | Coefficient | Std. Error | t-Statistic | Prob.  |
|----------|-------------|------------|-------------|--------|
| C        | −0.316023   | 0.069837   | −4.525140   | 0.0000 |
| LINC     | 0.574832    | 0.090557   | 6.347768    | 0.0000 |
| LW       | 0.150289    | 0.021847   | 6.879011    | 0.0000 |
| R        | −0.000675   | 0.001157   | −0.583479   | 0.5623 |
| LC(−1)   | 0.276562    | 0.100655   | 2.747633    | 0.0084 |

| | | | |
|---|---|---|---|
| R-squared | 0.999645 | Mean dependent var | 7.843870 |
| Adjusted R-squared | 0.999616 | S.D. dependent var | 0.541833 |
| S.E. of regression | 0.010619 | Akaike info criterion | −6.162741 |
| Sum squared resid | 0.005413 | Schwarz criterion | −5.976865 |
| Log likelihood | 168.3126 | Durbin–Watson stat | 1.395173 |
| F-statistic | 33833.55 | Prob(F-statistic) | 0.000000 |

## 6.5    Summary and conclusions

In this chapter we covered in some depth the topic of autocorrelation. Time series data are often plagued by autocorrelation. First we discussed the nature and consequences of autocorrelation, then we discussed the methods of detecting autocorrelation, and then we considered ways in which the problem of autocorrelation can be resolved.

Since we generally do not know the true error terms in a regression model, in practice we have to infer the nature of autocorrelation in a concrete application by examining the residuals, which are good proxies for the true error term if the sample size is reasonably large. We can plot the residuals, or use the Durbin–Watson or Breusch–Godfrey (BG) tests.

If the tests of autocorrelation suggest that autocorrelation exists in a given case, we can transform the original model so that in the transformed model we do not face autocorrelation. This is easier said than done, for we do not know the true structure of autocorrelation in the population from which the sample was drawn. We therefore try several transformations, such as the first-difference and generalized difference transformations. Very often this is a trial and error process.

If the sample size is reasonably large, we can use the robust standard errors or HAC standard errors, which do not require any special knowledge of the nature of autocorrelation. The HAC procedure simply modifies the OLS standard errors, without changing the values of the regression coefficients.

Since the OLS estimators are consistent despite autocorrelation, the thrust of the corrective methods discussed in this chapter is to estimate the standard errors of the regression coefficients as efficiently as possible so that we do not draw misleading conclusions about the statistical significance of one or more regression coefficients.

## Exercises

**6.1**  Instead of estimating model (6.1), suppose you estimate the following linear model:

$$C_t = A_1 + A_2 DPI_t + A_3 W_t + A_4 R_t + u_t \qquad (6.16)$$

(a)  Compare the results of this linear model with those shown in Table 6.2.

(b)  What is the interpretation of the various coefficients in this model? What is the relationship between the $A$ coefficients in this model and the $B$ coefficients given in Table 6.2?

(c)  Does this regression suffer from the autocorrelation problem? Discuss the tests you would conduct. And what is the outcome?

(d)  If you find autocorrelation in the linear model, how would resolve it? Show the necessary calculations.

(e)  For this model how would you compute the elasticities of C with respect to DPI, W, and R? Are these elasticities different from those obtained from regression (6.1)? If so, what accounts for the difference?

**6.2**  Reestimate regression (6.1) by adding time, $t$, as an additional regressor, $t$ taking values of 1, 2, ..., 54. $t$ is known as the trend variable.

(a)  Compare the results of this regression with those given in Table 6.2. Is there a difference between the two sets of results?

(b)  If the coefficient of the trend variable is statistically significant, what does it connote?

(c)  Is there serial correlation in the model with the trend variable in it? Show the necessary calculations.

**6.3**  Repeat Exercise 6.2 for the model given in Eq. (6.15) and comment on the results.

**6.4**  Re-run the regression in Table 6.7 using ln INC(−1) as a regressor in place of LC(−1), and compare the results with those in Table 6.7. What difference, if any, do you see? What may be logic behind this substitution? Explain.

# 7

# Regression diagnostic IV: model specification errors

One of the assumptions of the classical linear regression model (CLRM) is that the model used in analysis is "correctly specified". This is indeed a tall order, for there is no such thing as a perfect model. An econometric model tries to capture the main features of an economic phenomenon, taking into account the underlying economic theory, prior empirical work, intuition, and research skills. If we want to take into account every single factor that affects a particular object of research, the model will be so unwieldy as to be of little practical use.

By correct specification we mean one or more of the following:

1. The model does not exclude any "core" variables.
2. The model does not include superfluous variables.
3. The functional form of the model is suitably chosen.
4. There are no errors of measurement in the regressand and regressors.
5. Outliers in the data, if any, are taken into account.
6. The probability distribution of the error term is well specified.
7. What happens if the regressors are stochastic?
8. The Simultaneous Equation Problem: the simultaneity bias.

In what follows we will discuss the consequences of what happens if one or more of the specification errors are committed, how we can detect them, and what remedial measures we can take.

## 7.1 Omission of relevant variables

We do not deliberately set out to omit relevant variables from a model. But sometimes they are omitted because we do not have the data, or because we have not studied the underlying economic theory carefully, or because we have not studied prior research in the area thoroughly, or sometimes just because of carelessness. This is called **underfitting** a model. Whatever the reason, omission of important or "core" variables has the following consequences.[1]

---

1  For details, see Gujarati/Porter, *op cit.*, pp. 471–3.

1  If the left-out, or omitted, variables are correlated with the variables included in the model, *the coefficients of the estimated model are biased*. Not only that, the bias does not disappear as the sample size gets larger. In other words, the estimated coefficients of the misspecified model are biased as well as inconsistent.

2  Even if the incorrectly excluded variables are not correlated with the variables included in the model, the intercept of the estimated model is biased.

3  The disturbance variance $\sigma^2$ is incorrectly estimated.

4  The variances of the estimated coefficients of the misspecified model are biased. As a result, the estimated standard errors are also biased.

5  In consequence, the usual confidence intervals and hypothesis-testing procedures become suspect, leading to misleading conclusions about the statistical significance of the estimated parameters.

6  Furthermore, forecasts based on the incorrect model and the forecast confidence intervals based on it will be unreliable.

As you can see, the consequences of omitting relevant variables can be very serious.

Naturally, we would like to avoid such consequences. Now the trouble is that it is easy to document the consequences of misspecification if we are told what the true model is. For in that case we can estimate the "correctly" specified model and compare the results with the results of the misspecified model. But this brings us back to the question of what is the "correctly specified" model? Searching for a "correctly specified" model is like searching for the Holy Grail.

Where do we begin then? Besides being meticulous in specifying the model, the best we can do is to compare the chosen model with an alternative model that may be a candidate for consideration, perhaps a model suggested by peer reviewers.

## An illustrative example: wage determination revisited

In Chapter 1 we considered a model of hourly wage determination, using the CPS (Current Population Survey) 1995 data on 1,289 workers. The results of that model are given in Table 1.2, which for convenience we reproduce here in Table 7.1.

This table considered only gender, race, union status, education, and experience as the determinants of hourly wage. But it is a common experience that wages increase as work experience increases, holding other variables constant. But do wages increase at a slower or faster rate as work experience increases? To allow for this possibility, let us expand the wage model in Table 7.1 by adding to it the squared-experience as an additional regressor. The results are given in the Table 7.2

Comparing these results with those in Table 7.1, we see that the variable experience-squared is highly statistically significant ($p$ value practically zero). Interestingly, the coefficient of the experience-squared variable is negative, but that of experience is positive. What this suggests is that although hourly wages increase with more work experience, the rate of increase declines with more work experience.[2]

For the present purposes, it seems that by omitting the experience-squared variable from the model in Table 7.1 we have committed the bias of omitting a relevant

---

2  Holding the other variables constant, if you take the derivative of wage with respect to experience, you will obtain, after rounding, d*Wage* / d*Exper* = 0.4245 − 0.0124*Exper*, which shows that the rate of change of wage with respect to experience declines at the rate of 0.0124 per additional year of work experience.

**Table 7.1  Determinants of hourly wage rate.**

Dependent Variable: WAGERATE
Method: Least Squares
Sample: 1 1289
Included observations: 1289

|  | Coefficient | Std. Error | t-Statistic | Prob. |
|---|---|---|---|---|
| C | −7.183338 | 1.015788 | −7.071691 | 0.0000 |
| FEMALE | −3.074875 | 0.364616 | −8.433184 | 0.0000 |
| NONWHITE | −1.565313 | 0.509188 | −3.074139 | 0.0022 |
| UNION | 1.095976 | 0.506078 | 2.165626 | 0.0305 |
| EDUCATION | 1.370301 | 0.065904 | 20.79231 | 0.0000 |
| EXPERIENCE | 0.166607 | 0.016048 | 10.38205 | 0.0000 |

| | | | |
|---|---|---|---|
| R-squared | 0.323339 | Mean dependent var | 12.36585 |
| Adjusted R-squared | 0.320702 | S.D. dependent var | 7.896350 |
| S.E. of regression | 6.508137 | Akaike info criterion | 6.588627 |
| Sum squared resid | 54342.54 | Schwarz criterion | 6.612653 |
| Log likelihood | −4240.370 | Hannan–Quinn criter. | 6.597646 |
| F-statistic | 122.6149 | Durbin–Watson stat | 1.897513 |
| Prob(F-statistic) | 0.000000 | | |

**Table 7.2  Expanded wage function.**

Method: Least Squares
Sample: 1 1289
Included observations: 1289

|  | Coefficient | Std. Error | t-Statistic | Prob. |
|---|---|---|---|---|
| C | −8.419035 | 1.035710 | −8.128758 | 0.0000 |
| FEMALE | −3.009360 | 0.361432 | −8.326210 | 0.0000 |
| NONWHITE | −1.536077 | 0.504448 | −3.045066 | 0.0024 |
| UNION | 1.026979 | 0.501521 | 2.047728 | 0.0408 |
| EDUCATION | 1.323745 | 0.065937 | 20.07597 | 0.0000 |
| EXPERIENCE | 0.424463 | 0.053580 | 7.922076 | 0.0000 |
| EXPERSQ | −0.006183 | 0.001227 | −5.039494 | 0.0000 |

| | | | |
|---|---|---|---|
| R-squared | 0.336483 | Mean dependent var | 12.36585 |
| Adjusted R-squared | 0.333378 | S.D. dependent var | 7.896350 |
| S.E. of regression | 6.447128 | Akaike info criterion | 6.570562 |
| Sum squared resid | 53286.93 | Schwarz criterion | 6.598593 |
| Log likelihood | −4227.728 | Durbin–Watson stat | 1.901169 |
| F-statistic | 108.3548 | Prob(F-statistic) | 0.000000 |

variable(s) from the model. Although in Table 7.2 all the coefficients are individually and collectively statistically significant, their values are in several cases substantially different from those given in Table 7.1. This substantiates the points made earlier that in situations like these the OLS estimates given in Table 7.1 are biased.

But this model can be further modified if you *interact* (i.e. multiply) experience with gender. This refined model gives the results of Table 7.3.

**Table 7.3  Refinement of the wage model.**

Dependent Variable: W
Method: Least Squares
Sample: 1 1289
Included observations: 1289

|  | Coefficient | Std. Error | t-Statistic | Prob. |
|---|---|---|---|---|
| C | −9.200668 | 1.072115 | −8.581792 | 0.0000 |
| FEMALE | −1.433980 | 0.680797 | −2.106326 | 0.0354 |
| NONWHITE | −1.481891 | 0.503577 | −2.942730 | 0.0033 |
| UNION | 0.949027 | 0.501081 | 1.893958 | 0.0585 |
| EDUC | 1.318365 | 0.065801 | 20.03554 | 0.0000 |
| EXPER | 0.471974 | 0.056212 | 8.396344 | 0.0000 |
| EXPERSQ | −0.006274 | 0.001224 | −5.124559 | 0.0000 |
| EXPER*FEMALE | −0.084151 | 0.030848 | −2.727939 | 0.0065 |

| | | | | |
|---|---|---|---|---|
| R-squared | 0.340315 | Mean dependent var | 12.36585 | |
| Adjusted R-squared | 0.336711 | S.D. dependent var | 7.896350 | |
| S.E. of regression | 6.430992 | Akaike info criterion | 6.566322 | |
| Sum squared resid | 52979.16 | Schwarz criterion | 6.598357 | |
| Log likelihood | −4223.994 | Durbin–Watson stat | 1.892702 | |
| F-statistic | 94.40528 | Prob(F-statistic) | 0.000000 | |

This table shows that the interaction coefficient between gender and experience is statistically very significant. The negative value of this coefficient suggests that females earn less than their male counterparts with similar work experience. Whether this is due to gender discrimination is hard to tell, although it might be the case.

It seems that it is worth expanding the original model given in Table 7.1 by adding the experience-squared and the gender-experience variables to the model. We can establish this formally by using the $F$ test. For this purpose call the model in Table 7.1 the *restricted model* and the one in Table 7.3 the *unrestricted model*. Let $R_r^2$ and $R_{ur}^2$ represent the restricted and unrestricted $R^2$ values.

Now consider the following expression:

$$F = \frac{(R_{ur}^2 - R_r^2)/m}{(1-R_{ur}^2)/(n-k)}$$                (7.1)[3]

where $m$ = number of restrictions (2 in our example, for the restricted model excludes two variables), $n$ = number of observations, and $k$ = number of regressors in the unrestricted model ($m = [(n-k)-(n-k-2)=2]$).

The $F$ statistic in Eq. (7.1) follows the $F$ distribution with $m$ and $(n-k)$ degrees of freedom in the numerator and denominator, respectively.

Putting the appropriate values from Table 7.1 and Table 7.3, we obtain the following result:

---

3  Note that the formula given in Eq. (7.1) is valid only if the dependent variable in both models is the same. In this case, the $F$ test in Eq. (7.1) is equivalent to the $F$ test in Eq. (2.11). If that is not the case, use the $F$ test in Eq. (2.11). See also Eq. (1.18).

$$F = \frac{(0.3403 - 0.3233)/2}{(1 - .3403)/(1289 - 8)} \approx 16.67 \tag{7.2}$$

For 2 df in the numerator and 1,281 df in the denominator, this $F$ value is highly significant, suggesting that it is worth adding the two variables to the original model. In this sense, the original model is misspecified because it omits two relevant variables.

Again notice that as we go from Table 7.1 to 7.2 to 7.3, the coefficients of some variables change substantially. This reinforces the point made earlier that if we omit relevant variables from a model the coefficients in the (incorrectly specified) model are biased and there is no guarantee that this bias will disappear as the sample size increases. In our example, we have a reasonably large sample.

Observe that the $R^2$ value of 0.3403 in the expanded model may not seem much larger than the $R^2$ value of 0.3233 in the original model, but the incremental contribution of the two added variables is statistically quite significant, as the $F$ test shows.

## 7.2    Tests of omitted variables

Although we have illustrated the consequences of omitting relevant variables, how do we find out if we have committed the omission variable bias? There are several tests of detecting the omission of relevant variables, but we will consider only two here, namely, **Ramsey's RESET test** and the **Lagrange multiplier (LM) test**.[4]

### Ramsey's RESET test

Ramsey's regression specification error test, RESET for short, is a general test of model specification errors. To explain this test, once again let us revert to the wage determination model. We saw that in relation to Tables 7.2 and 7.3, the model in Table 7.1 was misspecified. Without worrying about the results in the other tables for now, let us concentrate on the results in Table 7.1.

We first explain the steps involved in the RESET and then consider the rationale behind it.

1   From the (incorrectly) estimated wage model given in Table 7.1, we first obtain the estimated, or fitted, values of the hourly wage rate; call it $\hat{Wage}_i$.

2   Reestimate the model in Table 7.1 including $\hat{Wage}_i^2$, $\hat{Wage}_i^3$ (and possibly higher powers of the estimated wage rate) as additional regressors.

3   The initial model in Table 7.1 is the restricted model and the model in Step 2 is the unrestricted model.

4   Under the null hypothesis that the restricted (i.e. the original model) is correct, we can use the $F$ test given in Eq. (7.1). This $F$ statistic has $m = 2$ df in the numerator and $(n - k) = (1289 - 8) = 1281$ df in the denominator, for in the regression in Step 2 we are estimating eight parameters, including the intercept.

5   If the $F$ test in Step 4 is statistically significant, we can reject the null hypothesis. That is, the restricted model is not appropriate in the present situation. By the same token, if the $F$ statistic is statistically insignificant, we do not reject the original model.

---

4   For details of the other tests, see Gujarati/Porter, *op cit.*, pp. 479–82.

**Table 7.4  RESET test of the wage model.**

Ramsey RESET Test:

| | | | |
|---|---|---|---|
| F-statistic | 20.12362 | Prob. F(2,1281) | 0.0000 |
| Log likelihood ratio | 39.87540 | Prob. Chi-Square(2) | 0.0000 |

Test Equation:
Dependent Variable: WAGE
Method: Least Squares
Sample: 1 1289
Included observations: 1289

| | Coefficient | Std. Error | t-Statistic | Prob. |
|---|---|---|---|---|
| C | 4.412981 | 2.453617 | 1.798561 | 0.0723 |
| FEMALE | −0.059017 | 0.797535 | −0.073999 | 0.9410 |
| NONWHITE | −0.195466 | 0.631646 | −0.309454 | 0.7570 |
| UNION | 0.124108 | 0.564161 | 0.219987 | 0.8259 |
| EDUCATION | 0.080124 | 0.302395 | 0.264966 | 0.7911 |
| EXPER | 0.000969 | 0.042470 | 0.022809 | 0.9818 |
| FITTED^2 | 0.044738 | 0.020767 | 2.154294 | 0.0314 |
| FITTED^3 | −0.000311 | 0.000601 | −0.517110 | 0.6052 |

| | | | |
|---|---|---|---|
| R-squared | 0.343951 | Mean dependent var | 12.36585 |
| Adjusted R-squared | 0.340366 | S.D. dependent var | 7.896350 |
| S.E. of regression | 6.413247 | Akaike info criterion | 6.560795 |
| Sum squared resid | 52687.19 | Schwarz criterion | 6.592830 |
| Log likelihood | −4220.433 | Durbin–Watson stat | 1.894263 |
| F-statistic | 95.94255 | Prob(F-statistic) | 0.000000 |

The idea behind this test is simple. If the original model is correctly specified, the added squared and higher powers of the estimated wage values should not add anything to the model. But if one or more coefficients of the added regressors are significant, this may be evidence of specification error.

Using *Eviews* 6, we obtained the results in Table 7.4. The important finding of this table is that the estimated $F$ value of 20.12 is highly statistically significant; its $p$ value is practically zero. As you can also see, the coefficient of the squared fitted values of the wage rate is statistically highly significant.[5]

Although simple to apply, the RESET test has two drawbacks. *First*, if the test shows that the chosen model is incorrectly specified, it does not suggest any specific alternative. *Second*, the test does not offer any guidance about the number of powered terms of the estimated values of the regressand to be included in the unrestricted model. There is no definite answer to this, although in practice we could proceed by trial and error and select the powered terms on the basis of information criteria, such as Akaike or Schwarz.

## The Lagrange multiplier (LM) test

We illustrate this test with our wage rate example.

---

5  The important $F$ statistic here is the $F$ value given in the Ramsey RESET test in the top part of this table.

1 From the original model given in Table 7.1, we obtain the estimated residuals, $e_i$.

2 If in fact the model in Table 7.1 is the correct model, then the residuals $e_i$ obtained from this model should not be related to the regressors omitted from that model, namely, $Exper^2$ and the interaction between gender and experience, $Exper \cdot Female$.

3 We now regress $e_i$ on the regressors in the original model and the omitted variables from the original model. Call this the *auxiliary regression*, auxiliary to the original regression.

4 If the sample size is large, it can be shown that $n$ (the sample size) times the $R^2$ obtained from the auxiliary regression follows the chi-square distribution with df equal to the number of regressors omitted from the original regression; two in the present case. Symbolically,

$$nR^2 \sim \chi^2_{(m)} \text{ (asymptotically)} \tag{7.3}$$

where $m$ is the number of omitted regressors from the original model.

5 If the computed $\chi^2$ value exceeds the critical chi-square value at the chosen level of significance, or if its $p$ value is sufficiently low, we reject the original (or restricted) regression. This is to say, that the original model was misspecified. See Table 7.5.

Therefore, we have

$$nR^2 = (1289)(0.0251) \approx 32.35 \sim \chi^2_2 \tag{7.4}$$

**Table 7.5  The LM test of the wage model.**

Dependent Variable: S1
Method: Least Squares
Date: 11/25/09 Time: 12:36
Sample: 1 1289
Included observations: 1289

|  | Coefficient | Std. Error | t-Statistic | Prob. |
|---|---|---|---|---|
| C | −2.017330 | 1.072115 | −1.881636 | 0.0601 |
| FE | 1.640895 | 0.680797 | 2.410258 | 0.0161 |
| NW | 0.083422 | 0.503577 | 0.165659 | 0.8685 |
| UN | −0.146949 | 0.501081 | −0.293264 | 0.7694 |
| ED | −0.051936 | 0.065801 | −0.789287 | 0.4301 |
| EX | 0.305367 | 0.056212 | 5.432437 | 0.0000 |
| EX^2 | −0.006274 | 0.001224 | −5.124559 | 0.0000 |
| EX*FE | −0.084151 | 0.030848 | −2.727939 | 0.0065 |

| | | | | |
|---|---|---|---|---|
| R-squared | 0.025089 | Mean dependent var | 5.44E−09 |
| Adjusted R-squared | 0.019761 | S.D. dependent var | 6.495492 |
| S.E. of regression | 6.430992 | Akaike info criterion | 6.566322 |
| Sum squared resid | 52979.16 | Schwarz criterion | 6.598357 |
| Log likelihood | −4223.994 | Durbin–Watson stat | 1.892702 |
| F-statistic | 4.709394 | Prob(F statistic) | .0.000031 |

*Note*: S1 (= $e_i$), residuals from the model in Table 7.1.

For 2 df the probability of obtaining a chi-square value of 32.35 or greater is extremely small, practically zero.

On the basis of the LM test, we can conclude that the original model in Table 7.1 was misspecified, thus reinforcing the conclusion based on the Ramsey's RESET test. Keep in mind that our sample of 1,289 observations is quite large so that the LM test in this case is valid.

## 7.3    Inclusion of irrelevant or unnecessary variables

Sometimes researchers add variables in the hope that the $R^2$ value of their model will increase in the mistaken belief that the higher the $R^2$ the better the model. This is called **overfitting** a model. But if the variables are not economically meaningful and relevant, such a strategy is not recommended because of the following consequences:[6]

1  The OLS estimators of the "incorrect" or overfitted model are all *unbiased* and *consistent*.

2  The error variance $\sigma^2$ is correctly estimated.

3  The usual confidence interval and hypothesis testing procedures remain valid.

4  However, the estimated coefficients of such a model are generally inefficient – that is, their variances will be larger than those of the true model.

Notice the asymmetry in the two types of specification error – underfitting and overfitting a model. In the former case the estimated coefficients are biased as well as inconsistent, the error variance is incorrectly estimated, and the hypothesis-testing procedure becomes invalid. In the latter case, the estimated coefficients are unbiased as well as consistent, the error variance is correctly estimated, and the hypothesis-testing procedure remains valid; the only penalty we pay for the inclusion of irrelevant or superfluous variables is that the estimated variances, and hence the standard errors, are relatively large and therefore probability inferences about the parameters are less precise.

One may be tempted to conclude that it is better to include unnecessary variables (the so-called "kitchen sink approach") than omit relevant variables. Such a philosophy is not recommended because the inclusion of unnecessary variables not only leads to loss of efficiency of the estimators but may also lead, unwittingly, to the problem of multicollinearity, not to mention the loss of degrees of freedom.

### An illustrative example

To give a glimpse of this, let us continue with our wage determination example by adding to the model in Table 7.1 the variable "age of the worker". We could not run this regression because of near perfect collinearity between age and work experience. This is because the variable "work experience" was defined as (age – years of schooling – 6).[7] This can be verified by regressing work experience on age, which gives the results shown in Table 7.6.

As you can see, the two variables are highly correlated, the correlation coefficient between them being 0.9705 (= $\sqrt{0.942016}$).

---

6  For details, see Gujarati/Porter, *op cit.*, pp. 477–82.
7  Presumably, education starts at age 6.

Table 7.6  Regression of experience on age.

Dependent Variable: EXPER
Method: Least Squares
Sample: 1 1289
Included observations: 1289

|  | Coefficient | Std. Error | t-Statistic | Prob. |
|---|---|---|---|---|
| C | −18.56877 | 0.269951 | −68.78564 | 0.0000 |
| AGE | 0.984808 | 0.006811 | 144.5984 | 0.0000 |

| | | | |
|---|---|---|---|
| R-squared | 0.942016 | Mean dependent var | 18.78976 |
| Adjusted R-squared | 0.941971 | S.D. dependent var | 11.66284 |
| S.E. of regression | 2.809491 | Akaike info criterion | 4.905434 |
| Sum squared resid | 10158.60 | Schwarz criterion | 4.913443 |
| Log likelihood | −3159.552 | Hannan–Quinn criter. | 4.908440 |
| F-statistic | 20908.71 | Prob(F-statistic) | 0.000000 |

This exercise suggests that we can include age or work experience as a regressor but not both.

## 7.4    Misspecification of the functional form of a regression model

In Chapter 2, on the functional form of regression models, we discussed the choice between linear and log-linear (Cobb–Douglas) production functions. In both cases we had data on output (as measured by GDP), labor input (as measured by hours of work), and capital (capital expenditure) for the 50 states in the USA and Washington, DC, for 1995. There we discussed the general procedure for comparing such models. Here we will discuss it with reference to the wage determination model.

In labor economics researchers often choose the log of wages as the regressand. This is because the distribution of wages across the population tends to be skewed, with many workers at the low end of the distribution and a few at the high end of the distribution. On the other hand, the distribution of log of wages tends to be more symmetrical and it also has homoscedastic variance (see Figures 3.1 and 3.2).

For our wage example, which is a better model: linear or log-linear? We have already given the results of the linear model in Table 7.3. Table 7.7 presents the results of the log model.

All the regressors are individually highly significant, as their $t$ statistics have very low $p$ values. Collectively also all the variables are highly significant, as the $F$ value of about 109 has a $p$ value that is practically zero.

Of course, the interpretation of the coefficients in Table 7.7 is different from that in Table 7.3 because the dependent variables in the two models are different. For example, the coefficient of 0.0948 suggests that if schooling increases by a year, the average hourly wage goes up by about 9.48%, *ceteris paribus*. (Recall the interpretation of the semi-log model discussed in Chapter 2.) It is left for the reader to interpret the other coefficients in this table.

Which is a better mode: the linear model in Table 7.3 or the log-linear model in Table 7.7?

**Table 7.7  Determinants of log of wages.**

Dependent Variable: LOG(WAGE)
Method: Least Squares
Sample: 1 1289
Included observations: 1289

|  | Coefficient | Std. Error | t-Statistic | Prob. |
|---|---|---|---|---|
| C | 0.732446 | 0.077613 | 9.437130 | 0.0000 |
| FEMALE | −0.148060 | 0.049285 | −3.004179 | 0.0027 |
| NONWHITE | −0.127302 | 0.036455 | −3.492000 | 0.0005 |
| UNION | 0.168485 | 0.036275 | 4.644705 | 0.0000 |
| EDUCATION | 0.094792 | 0.004764 | 19.89963 | 0.0000 |
| EXPER | 0.041946 | 0.004069 | 10.30778 | 0.0000 |
| EXPER^2 | −0.000637 | 8.86E−05 | −7.187309 | 0.0000 |
| EXPER*FEMALE | −0.005043 | 0.002233 | −2.258065 | 0.0241 |

| | | | |
|---|---|---|---|
| R-squared | 0.373017 | Mean dependent var | 2.342416 |
| Adjusted R-squared | 0.369591 | S.D. dependent var | 0.586356 |
| S.E. of regression | 0.465556 | Akaike info criterion | 1.315020 |
| Sum squared resid | 277.6474 | Schwarz criterion | 1.347055 |
| Log likelihood | −839.5302 | Durbin–Watson stat | 1.926178 |
| F-statistic | 108.8741 | Prob(F-statistic) | 0.000000 |

For the linear model $R^2$ is about 0.34 and for the log-linear model, it is 0.37. But we cannot compare these two $R^2$s because the dependent variables in the two models are different. How then do we compare the two models?

We follow the steps outlined in Chapter 2 (for brevity of writing, we let $W$ stand for the wage rate).

1  We compute the geometric mean of wages, which is about 10.406.[8]

2  We construct a new variable $W_i^* = W_i / 10.406$, that is, we divide wages by the geometric mean of wages.

3  We estimate the model in Table 7.3, using $W_i^*$ instead of $W_i$ as the regressand and obtain the RSS from this regression, call it $RSS_1$.

4  We reestimate the model in Table 7.3, using $\ln W_i^*$, instead of $\ln W_i$ as the regressand and obtain the $RSS$ (residual sum of squares) from this regression, call it $RSS_2$.

5  We then compute:

$$\frac{n}{2} \ln\left(\frac{RSS_1}{RSS_2}\right) \sim \chi_1^2 \qquad (7.5)$$

Note: Put the larger $RSS$ in the numerator.

That is, the expression on the left-hand side of Eq. (7.5) follows the chi-square distribution with 1 df. If the chi-square value computed from Eq. (7.5) is statistically significant, we can conclude that the model with the lower $RSS$ is the better model.

---

8  The GM $= (W_1 \cdot W_2 \cdot ... \cdot W_{1289})^{1/1,289} = e^{2.342416} \approx 10.406$ in the present example.

To save space, we will not produce all the results except to note that in the present case: $RSS_1 = 489.2574$ and $RSS_2 = 277.6474$. As a result:

$$\frac{1289}{2} \ln\left(\frac{489.2574}{277.6474}\right) \approx 365.11 \tag{7.6}$$

This chi-square value for 1 df is so large that we can confidently conclude that it is the log-linear model given in Table 7.7 that is superior to the linear model given in Table 7.3.

The conclusion then is that the functional form of the wage model given in Table 7.3 is misspecified.

## 7.5    Errors of measurement

One of the assumptions of CLRM is that the model used in the analysis is correctly specified. Although not explicitly spelled out, this presumes that the values of the regressand as well as regressors are accurate. That is, they are not guess estimates, extrapolated, interpolated or rounded off in any systematic manner or recorded with errors.

This ideal, however, is not very often met in practice for several reasons, such as non-response errors, reporting errors, missing data, or sheer human errors. Whatever the reasons for such errors, measurement errors constitute yet another specification bias, which has serious consequences, especially if there are such errors in the regressors.

### Errors of measurement in the regressand

Although we will not prove it here, if there are errors of measurement in the dependent variable, the following consequences ensue.[9]

1  The OLS estimators are still unbiased.

2  The variances and standard errors of OLS estimators are still unbiased.

3  But the estimated variances, and *ipso facto* the standard errors, are larger than in the absence of such errors.

In short, errors of measurement in the regressand do not pose a very serious threat to OLS estimation.

### Errors of measurement in the regressors

The situation here is more serious, for errors of measurement in the explanatory variable(s) render OLS estimators biased as well as inconsistent.[10] Even such errors in a single regressor can lead to biased and inconsistent estimates of the coefficients of the other regressors in the model. And it is not easy to establish the size and direction of bias in the estimated coefficients.

It is often suggested that we use **instrumental or proxy variables** for variables suspected of having measurement errors. The proxy variables must satisfy two

---

9  For details, see Gujarati/Porter, 5th edn, pp. 482–3.

10  For details, see Gujarati/Porter, *op cit.*, 483–6.

requirements – that they are highly correlated with the variables for which they are a proxy and also they are uncorrelated with the usual equation error $u_i$ as well as the measurement error. But such proxies are not easy to find; we are often in the situation of complaining about the bad weather without being able to do much about it. Therefore this remedy may not be always available. Nonetheless, because of the wide use of instrumental variables in many areas of applied econometrics, we discuss this topic at length in Chapter 19.[11]

All we can say about measurement errors, in both the regressand and regressors, is that we should be very careful in collecting the data and making sure that some obvious errors are eliminated.

## 7.6    Outliers, leverage and influence data

II

In Chapter 1 we discussed the basics of the linear regression model. You may recall that in minimizing the residual sum of squares (RSS) to estimate the regression parameters, OLS gives equal weight to every observation in the sample. But this may create problems if we have observations that may not be "typical" of the rest of the sample. Such observations, or data points, are known as **outliers, leverage** or **influence points**. It is important that we know what they are, how they affect the regression results, and how we detect them.

▲ **Outliers:** In the context of regression analysis, an outlier is an observation with a large residual ($e_i$), large in comparison with the residuals of the rest of the observations. In a bivariate regression, it is easy to detect such large residual(s) because of its rather large vertical distance from the estimated regression line. Remember that there may be more than one outlier. One can also consider the squared values of $e_i$, as it avoids the sign problem – residuals can be positive or negative.

▲ **Leverage:** An observation is said to exert (high) leverage if it is disproportionately distant from the bulk of the sample observations. In this case such observation(s) can pull the regression line towards itself, which may distort the slope of the regression line.

▲ **Influence point:** If a levered observation in fact pulls the regression line toward itself, it is called an influence point. The removal of such a data point from the sample can dramatically change the slope of the estimated regression line.

To illustrate some of these points, consider the data given in **Table 7.8**, which can be found on the companion website.

This table gives data on the number of cigarettes smoked per capita (in 100s), and deaths from the cancers of bladder, lung, kidney and leukemia (per 100,000 population) for 43 states and Washington, DC, for the year 1960.

To illustrate the outlier problem, we regress deaths from lung cancer on the number of cigarettes smoked. The results are given in Table 7.9.

Without implying causality, it seems that there is a positive relationship between deaths from lung cancer and the number of cigarettes smoked. If we increase the

---

11 For an interesting, but somewhat advanced, discussion of this topic see Joshua D. Angrist and Jörn-Steffen Pischke, *Mostly Harmless Econometrics: An Empiricist's Companion*, Princeton University Press, Princeton, NJ, 2009, Chapter 4.

**Table 7.9  Deaths from lung cancer and number of cigarettes smoked.**

Dependent Variable: LUNGCANCER
Method: Least Squares
Sample: 1 43
Included observations: 43

|  | Coefficient | Std. Error | t-Statistic | Prob. |
|---|---|---|---|---|
| C | 6.274073 | 2.085699 | 3.008140 | 0.0045 |
| CIG | 0.542076 | 0.081939 | 6.615623 | 0.0000 |

| R-squared | 0.516318 | Mean dependent var | 19.74000 |
|---|---|---|---|
| Adjusted R-squared | 0.504521 | S.D. dependent var | 4.238291 |
| S.E. of regression | 2.983345 | Akaike info criterion | 5.069362 |
| Sum squared resid | 364.9142 | Schwarz criterion | 5.151279 |
| Log likelihood | −106.9913 | Durbin–Watson stat | 2.662271 |
| F-statistic | 43.76646 | Prob(F-statistic) | 0.000000 |

number of cigarettes smoked by 1 unit, the average number of deaths from lung cancer goes up by 0.54 units.

### Detection of outliers

A simple method of detecting outliers is to plot the residuals and squared residuals from the estimated regression model. An inspection of the graph will give a rough and ready method of spotting outliers, although that may not always be the case without further analysis.

For the lung cancer regression, we obtain Figure 7.1. This figure shows that there are spikes in the residuals and squared residuals at several observations, such as #15, #17, #20, #25 and #32, the more pronounced being for observation #15 (Louisiana).

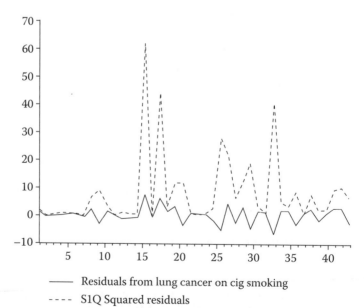

—— Residuals from lung cancer on cig smoking

- - - - S1Q Squared residuals

**Figure 7.1  Residuals and squared residuals of regression in Table 7.9.**

**Table 7.10  Regression results without Louisiana.**

Dependent Variable: LUNGCANCER
Method: Least Squares
Date: 11/07/11   Time: 20:35
Sample: 1 42
Included observations: 42

| Variable | Coefficient | Std. Error | t-Statistic | Prob. |
|----------|-------------|------------|-------------|-------|
| C | 5.622778 | 1.951918 | 2.880643 | 0.0063 |
| CIG | 0.561068 | 0.076428 | 7.341163 | 0.0000 |

| | | | |
|---|---|---|---|
| R-squared | 0.573982 | Mean dependent var | 19.60405 |
| Adjusted R-squared | 0.563331 | S.D. dependent var | 4.193696 |
| S.E. of regression | 2.771233 | Akaike info criterion | 4.922909 |
| Sum squared resid | 307.1892 | Schwarz criterion | 5.005656 |
| Log likelihood | −101.3811 | Durbin–Watson stat | 2.665938 |
| F-statistic | 53.89268 | | |
| Prob(F-statistic) | 0.000000 | | |

Consider the observation for Louisiana.  In the sample data it has one of the highest lung cancer deaths per $100,000$ population. Is it an outlying observation? Even if it is, it does not necessarily mean that it is a high leverage or influence point. For a (data) point to be influential, its removal from the sample must substantially change the regression results (the slope coefficient, its standard error, etc.). One way of finding this out is to see how the regression results change if we drop the Louisiana observation. The results are given in Table 7.10.

If you compare the regression coefficients in Tables 7.9 and 7.10, statistically they are not very different.  Thus despite the appearance, Louisiana may not be an outlier.

There are several other methods of detecting leverage and influence points, but these are somewhat involved and require the use of matrix algebra.[12] However, *Stata* has a routine that computes a leverage measure for every single observation in the sample.

There are other methods of detecting outliers, such as *recursive least squares* and *recursive residuals*, but the discussion of these methods will take us far afield, so we will not pursue them here.[13]

Our objective in discussing the topic of outliers is to warn the researcher to be on the lookout for them, because OLS estimates can be greatly affected by such outliers, especially if they are influential.

---

**12**  For an accessible discussion, see Samprit Chatterjee and Ali S. Hadi, *Regression Analysis by Example*, 4th edn, Wiley, New Jersey, 2006, Chapter 4.

**13**  See, for instance, Chatterjee and Hadi, *op cit.*, pp. 103–8.

## 7.7    Probability distribution of the error term

The classical normal linear regression model (CNLRM), an extension of CLRM, assumes that the error term $u_i$ in the regression model is normally distributed.[14] This assumption is critical if the sample size is relatively small, for the commonly used tests of significance, such as $t$ and $F$, are based on the normality assumption.

It is thus important that we check whether the error term is normally distributed. There are several tests of normality, but the most popularly used test is the **Jarque–Bera (JB)** test of normality. Before we present this test, it is important to keep in mind that the JB test is a *large sample* test and may not be appropriate in small samples. The formula for the test is as follows:

$$\text{JB} = n\left[\frac{S^2}{6} + \frac{(K-3)^2}{24}\right] \sim \chi_2^2 \tag{7.7}$$

where $n$ is the sample size, $S$ = skewness coefficient, and $K$ = kurtosis coefficient.[15] For a normally distributed variable $S = 0$ and $K = 3$. It is obvious from the JB statistic that if $S = 0$ and $K = 3$, its value is zero. Therefore, the closer is the value of JB to zero, the better is the normality assumption. Of course, we can always use the chi-square distribution to find the exact statistical significance (i.e. the $p$ value) of the JB statistic.

Since in practice we do not observe the true error term, we use its proxy, $e_i$. The null hypothesis is the *joint hypothesis* that $S = 0$ and $K = 3$. Jarque and Bera have shown that the statistic given in Eq. (7.7) follows the chi-square distribution with 2 df. There are two degrees of freedom because we are imposing two restrictions, namely, that skewness is zero and kurtosis is 3.

Therefore, if in an application the computed JB statistic (i.e. the chi-square statistic) exceeds the critical chi-square value, say, at the 5% level, we reject the hypothesis that the error term is normally distributed.

### JB test of the cigarette smoking and lung cancer example

Returning to our cigarette smoking and lung cancer example, the JB statistic for the residuals for the regression given in Table 7.9 is 0.4106 with a $p$ value of 0.41, and for the regression in Table 7.10, the JB statistic is 1.48 with a $p$ value of 0.47. Both these JB values suggest that the assumption of normality of the error term may be appropriate in both models, although the number of observations (43 and 42) is not very large.

### JB test of the wage determination model

In the linear wage model given in Table 7.3, the JB statistic of the residuals is about 4,130, a huge number, with a $p$ value practically zero. For the log wage model given in Table 7.7, the JB statistic of the residuals is also large, about 302, with a $p$ value of

---

14  Note that the normality assumption pertain to the error term, $u_t$, included in the population regression and not to the residual term, $e_i$, included in the sample regression, although we use the latter to learn about the former. This is because in practice we never observe $u_i$.

15  Just as the variance of a random variable is the second moment about the mean value of the variable, skewness is the third and kurtosis is the fourth moment, all measured from the mean value. Skewness is a measure of symmetry and kurtosis is a measure of tallness or flatness of the probability distribution.

almost zero.[16] The use of the JB statistic in both cases may be appropriate because we have a fairly large sample of 1,289 observations.

On the basis of the JB statistic, it would be hard to maintain that the error term in the wage regression is normally distributed.

It may be interesting to note here that the distribution of wages is highly non-normal, with $S$ being 1.84 and $K$ being 7.83 (the JB statistic is about 1900). On the other hand, the distribution of log of wages is normal, with an $S$ value of about 0.1 and a $K$ value of about 3.2 (the JB statistic is only 2.8) (see Exercise 7.8.).

### Non-normal error term

If the error term $u_i$ is not normally distributed, it can be stated that the OLS estimators are still best linear unbiased estimators (BLUE); that is, they are unbiased and in the class of linear estimators they have minimum variance. This is not a surprising finding, for in establishing the BLUE (recall the Gauss–Markov theorem) property we did not invoke the normality assumption.

What then is the problem? The problem is that for the purpose of hypothesis testing we need the **sampling**, or **probability**, **distributions** of the OLS estimators. The $t$ and $F$ tests that we have used all along assume that the probability distribution of the error term follows the normal distribution. But if we cannot make that assumption, we will have to resort to **large** or **asymptotic sample theory**.

Without going into technical details, under the assumptions of CLRM (not CNLRM) in large samples, the OLS estimators are not only **consistent** (i.e. they converge to their true values as the sample size increases indefinitely), but are also asymptotically **normally distributed** with the usual means and variances discussed in Chapter 1. *Interestingly, the t and F tests that we have used extensively so far are also approximately valid in large samples*, the approximation being quite good, as the sample size increases indefinitely.

Therefore, even though the JB statistic showed that the errors in both the linear wage model and the log-linear wage model may not be normally distributed, we can still use the $t$ and $F$ tests because our sample size of 1,289 observations is quite large.

## 7.8    Random or stochastic regressors

The CLRM, as discussed in Chapter 1, assumes that the regressand is random but the regressors are nonstochastic or fixed – that is, we keep the values of the regressors fixed and draw several random samples of the dependent variable. For example, in the regression of consumption expenditure on income, we assume that income levels are fixed at certain values and then draw random samples of consumers at the fixed levels of income and note their consumption expenditure. In regression analysis our objective is to predict the mean consumption expenditure at various levels of fixed income. If we connect these mean consumption expenditures the line (or curve) thus drawn represents the (sample) regression line (or curve).

---

**16**  For the linear wage model in Table 7.3 $S$ is about 2 and $K = 10.79$, and for the log wage model in Table 7.7, $S = -0.44$ and $K = 5.19$. In both cases the $S$ and $K$ measures are far from the normal values of 0 and 3, respectively.

Although the assumption of fixed regressors may be valid in several economic situations, by and large it may not be tenable for all economic data. In other words, we assume that both $Y$ (the dependent variable) and the $X$s (the regressors) are drawn randomly. This is the case of stochastic or random regressors. The important question that arises is whether the results of regression analysis based on fixed regressors also hold if the regressors are as random as the regressand. Although a detailed answer will be given in Chapter 19, for the topic is rather involved, we can make the following points.

If the stochastic regressors and the error term $u$ are independently distributed, the classical results discussed in Chapter 1 (the Gauss–Markov theorem) continue to hold *provided we stress the fact that our analysis is conditional on given values of the regressors*. If, on the other hand, the random regressors and the error term are uncorrelated, the classical results hold asymptotically – that is in large samples.[17]

But what happens if neither of these conditions holds? In other words, what happens if the regressors and the error term $u$ are correlated? We have already discussed the case of measurement errors in the regressor earlier and stated that in this situation we may have to resort to alternative estimating method(s), such as instrumental variables. But there are other situations where the regressors and the error term are correlated. Because of the importance of this topic, we discuss it at length in Chapter 19 on stochastic regressors and instrumental variables estimation. Suffice it to note here that in some situations we can find appropriate instruments, so that using them in lieu of the original stochastic regressors we can obtain consistent estimates of the parameters of interest.

## 7.9    The simultaneity problem

Our focus thus far has been on single-equation regression models, in that we expressed a single dependent variable $Y$ as a function of one or more explanatory variables, the $X$s. If there was any causality between $Y$ and the $X$s, it was implicitly assumed that the direction of causality ran from the $X$s to $Y$.

But there are many situations where such a unidirectional relationship between $Y$ and the $X$s cannot be maintained, for it is quite possible that some of the $X$s affect $Y$ but in turn $Y$ also affects one or more $X$s. In other words, there may be a feedback relationship between the $Y$ and $X$ variables. To take into account such feedback relationships, we will need more than one regression equation. This leads to a discussion of **simultaneous equation regression models** – that is, models that take into account feedback relationships among variables.[18] In what follows, we discuss briefly why OLS may not be appropriate to estimate a single equation that may be embedded in a simultaneous equation model containing two or more equations.

---

17  Remember that independence implies no correlation, but no correlation does not necessarily imply independence.

18  In the 1970s and 1980s the topic of simultaneous equation models was an integral part of every econometrics student's training. But of late, these models have lost favor because of their poor forecasting performance. Competing econometric models involving multi-equations, such as autoregressive moving average (ARMA) and vector autoregression (VAR), are increasingly replacing the traditional simultaneous equation models. However, the Federal Reserve Board and the US Department of Commerce and several private forecasting agencies still use them along with ARMA and VAR models.

## Simple Keynesian model of income determination

Every student of introductory macroeconomics knows the following Keynesian model of the determination of aggregate income. Here we replace the $Y$ and $X$ notation with the traditional macroeconomics mnemonics, namely $C$ for consumption expenditure, $Y$ for income and $I$ for investment:

Consumption Function:  $C_t = B_1 + B_2 Y_t + u_t; \ 0 < B_2 < 1$    (7.8)

Income Identity:        $Y_t = C_t + I_t$    (7.9)

The simple Keynesian model assumes a *closed economy* – that is, no foreign trade or government expenditure.[19]

When dealing with simultaneous equation models, we have to learn some new vocabulary. First, we have to distinguish between **endogenous** and **exogenous variables**. Endogenous variables are those variables whose values are determined in the model, and exogenous variables are those variables whose values are not determined in the model. In the simple Keynesian model $C$ and $Y$ are endogenous, or jointly dependent, variables, and $I$ is an exogenous variable. Sometimes, exogenous variables are called **predetermined variables,** for their values are determined independently or fixed, such as the tax rates fixed by the government.[20]

Another distinction is between **structural**, or **behavioral**, **equations** and **identities**. Structural equations depict the structure or behavior of a particular sector of the economy, such as the household sector. The consumption function in the Keynesian model tells us how the household sector reacts to changes in income. The coefficients in the structural equations are known as **structural coefficients**: $B_1$ and $B_2$ in our example. $B_2$ is the *marginal propensity to consume* (MPC) – that is the additional amount of consumption expenditure for an additional dollar's worth of income – which lies between 0 and 1.

Identities, like Eq. (7.9), are true by definition; in our example total income is equal to consumption expenditure and investment expenditure.

## The simultaneity bias

Suppose we want to estimate the consumption function given in Eq. (7.8) but neglect to take into account the second equation in the system. What are the consequences? To see them, suppose the error term $u$ includes a variable that cannot be easily measured, say, consumer confidence. Further suppose that consumers become upbeat about the economy because of a boom in the stock market or an impending tax cut. This results in an increase in the value of $u$. As a result of the increase

---

19  Of course, we can extend the model to include government expenditure and foreign trade, in which case it will be an *open economy* model.

20  It should be noted that the determination of which variables are endogenous and which are exogenous is up to the researcher. Variables such as weather, temperature, hurricanes, earthquakes and so on, are obviously exogenous variables. If we extend the simple Keynesian model to make investment as a function of interest rate, then investment becomes an endogenous variable and interest rate becomes exogenous. If we have another equation that gives interest rate as a function of the money supply, then interest rate becomes endogenous and money supply becomes exogenous. As you can see, the simple Keynesian model can be expanded very quickly. It is also clear that sometimes the classification of variables into endogenous and exogenous categories can become arbitrary, a criticism leveled against simultaneous equation modeling by the advocates of vector autoregression (VAR), a topic we discuss in Chapter 16.

in $u$, consumption expenditure increases. But since consumption expenditure is a component of income, this in turn will push up income, which in turn will push up consumption expenditure, and so on. So we have this sequence: $u \Rightarrow C \Rightarrow Y \Rightarrow C$. As you can see, income and consumption expenditure are *mutually interdependent*.

Therefore, if we disregard this interdependence and estimate Eq. (7.8) by OLS, the estimated parameters are not only biased (in small or finite samples), but are also inconsistent (in large samples). The reason for this is that in the consumption function, $Y_t$ and $u_t$ are correlated, which violates the OLS assumption that the regressor(s) and the error term are uncorrelated. The proof of this statement is given in the appendix to this chapter. This is similar to the case of stochastic regressor(s) correlated with the error term, a topic we have discussed earlier.

How then do we estimate the parameters of the consumption function? We can use the method of **indirect least squares** (ILS) for this purpose, which we now discuss.

## The method of indirect least squares (ILS)

There is an interesting way of looking at Eqs. (7.8) and (7.9). If you substitute Eq. (7.8) into Eq. (7.9), you will obtain, after simple manipulation, the following equation.

$$Y_t = \frac{B_1}{1-B_2} + \frac{1}{1-B_2} I_t + \frac{1}{1-B_2} u_t$$
$$= A_1 + A_2 I_t + v_t$$
(7.10)

Similarly, if you substitute Eq. (7.9) into Eq. (7.8), you will obtain:

$$C_t = \frac{B_1}{1-B_2} + \frac{B_2}{1-B_2} I_t + \frac{1}{1-B_2} u_t$$
$$= A_3 + A_4 I_t + v_t$$
(7.11)

Each of these equations expresses an endogenous variable as a function of exogenous, or predetermined, variable(s) and the error term. Such equations are called **reduced-form equations**.

Before proceeding further, it may be noted that the coefficients of the reduced form equations are called **impact multipliers**. They give the ultimate impact of a dollar's increase in investment (or any other variable on the right-hand side of the preceding equations) on consumption and income. Take, for instance, the coefficient of $I_t$ $(= B_2 / (1-B_2))$. Let us increase investment by one dollar. Then from Eq. (7.9), income will initially increase by one dollar. This will then lead to an increase in consumption of a $B_2$-dollar, which will then lead to a $B_2$ increase in income, which will then lead to $B_2^2$ increase in consumption and so on. The ultimate effect will be an increase in consumption of $B_2 / (1-B_2)$.[21] So if MPC $B_2 = 0.7$, the ultimate impact of a dollar's increase in investment expenditure on consumption expenditure will be $0.7 / 0.3 = \$2.33$. Of course, the higher the MPC, the higher is the impact on the consumption expenditure.

Now the reduced form equations can be estimated by OLS, for the exogenous variable $I$ and the error term are uncorrelated, by design. The key question now is whether

---

21   Thus we have a sequence like $B_2 + B_2^2 + B_2^3 + \ldots = B_2(1 + B_2 + B_2^2 + \ldots) = B_2 / (1-B_2)$, following the sum of an infinite geometric series. Keep in mind that $0 < B_2 < 1$.

we can obtain unique estimates of the structural coefficients from the reduced from coefficients. This is known as the **problem of identification**. Thus, if we can uniquely estimate the coefficients of the consumption function from the reduced form coefficients, we say that the consumption function is identified. So far as Eq. (7.9) is concerned, we do not have the problem of identification, for that equation is an identity and all its coefficients are known (= 1).

This process of obtaining the parameters of the structural equations from the reduced form coefficients is known as the **method of indirect least squares (ILS)**, because we obtain the estimates of the structural coefficients indirectly by first estimating the reduced form coefficients by OLS. Of course, if an equation is not identified, we cannot obtain the estimates of its parameters by OLS, or for that matter, by any other method.

Returning to the consumption function, you can verify that

$$B_1 = \frac{A_1}{A_2} \quad \text{and} \quad B_2 = \frac{A_4}{A_2} \tag{7.12}$$

So we can obtain unique values of the parameters of the consumption function from the reduced form coefficients. But note that the structural coefficients are non-linear functions of the reduced form coefficients.

In simultaneous equation models involving several equations it is tedious to obtain reduced form coefficients and then try to retrieve the structural coefficients from them. Besides, the method of indirect least squares is of no use if an equation is not identified. In that case we will have to resort to other methods of estimation. One such method is the method of **two-stage least squares (2SLS)**, which we discuss at some length in Chapter 19 on instrumental variables.

Before we illustrate ILS with a numerical example, it may be noted that the estimators of the structural coefficients obtained from ILS are *consistent estimators* – that is, as the sample size increases indefinitely, these estimators converge to their true values. But in small, or finite, samples, the ILS estimators may be biased. As noted before, the OLS estimators are biased as well as inconsistent.

## An illustrative example: aggregate consumption function for USA, 1960–2009

To illustrate the method of indirect least squares, we obtained data on consumption expenditure (PCE), investment expenditure (GDPI), and income($Y$) for the USA for 1960–2009; the data for 2009 are provisional. GDPI is gross domestic private investment and PCE is personal consumption expenditure. The data are in **Table 7.11**, which can be found on the companion website.

It should be pointed out that the data on income are simply the sum of consumption and investment expenditure, following the Keynesian income identity. We first estimate the two reduced form equations given in Eqs. (7.10) and (7.11), which are given by Tables 7.12 and 7.13.

Table 7.12 shows that if GDPI goes up by a dollar, on average, personal consumption goes up by about $4.45, showing the power of the multiplier.

From Table 7.13 we see that if GDPI increases by a dollar, on average, income increases by $5.45. Of this increase, $4.50 is for consumption expenditure and $1 for investment expenditure, thus satisfying the income identity.

**Table 7.12  Reduced form regression of PCE on GDPI.**

Dependent Variable: PCE
Method: Least Squares
Sample: 1960 2009
Included observations: 50

| Variable | Coefficient | Std. Error | t-Statistic | Prob. |
|---|---|---|---|---|
| C | −109.9016 | 102.0025 | −1.077440 | 0.2867 |
| GDPI | 4.450478 | 0.096194 | 46.26562 | 0.0000 |

| | | | |
|---|---|---|---|
| R-squared | 0.978067 | Mean dependent var | 3522.160 |
| Adjusted R-squared | 0.977610 | S.D. dependent var | 3077.678 |
| S.E. of regression | 460.5186 | Akaike info criterion | 15.14176 |
| Sum squared resid | 10179716 | Schwarz criterion | 15.21824 |
| Log likelihood | −376.5440 | Durbin–Watson stat | 0.555608 |
| F-statistic | 2140.508 | Prob(F-statistic) | 0.000000 |

**Table 7.13  Reduced form regression of income on GDPI.**

Dependent Variable: INCOME
Method: Least Squares
Date: 07/30/10 Time: 20:41
Sample: 1960 2009
Included observations: 50

| Variable | Coefficient | Std. Error | t-Statistic | Prob. |
|---|---|---|---|---|
| C | −109.9016 | 102.0025 | −1.077440 | 0.2867 |
| GDPI | 5.450478 | 0.096194 | 56.66127 | 0.0000 |

| | | | |
|---|---|---|---|
| R-squared | 0.985269 | Mean dependent var | 4338.266 |
| Adjusted R-squared | 0.984962 | S.D. dependent var | 3755.416 |
| S.E. of regression | 460.5186 | Akaike info criterion | 15.14176 |
| Sum squared resid | 10179716 | Schwarz criterion | 15.21824 |
| Log likelihood | −376.5440 | Durbin–Watson stat | 0.555608 |
| F-statistic | 3210.500 | Prob(F-statistic) | 0.000000 |

We can use the results in Tables 7.12 and 7.13 to estimate the original structural parameters of the consumption function, using Eq. (7.12). The reader is urged to verify the following consumption expenditure function, the empirical counterpart of Eq. (7.8).

$$\hat{C}_t = -20.1636 + 0.8165 Y_t \qquad (7.13)[22]$$

For comparison, we give the results of OLS in Table 7.14.

The results of ILS and OLS show that there is not much difference in the estimates of MPC, but the intercepts in the two regressions are different. Of course, there is no guarantee that in all applications OLS and ILS results will be similar. The advantage of

---

22  Since the structural coefficients are nonlinear functions of the reduced form coefficients, there is no simple way to obtain the standard errors of the structural coefficients.

**Table 7.14  OLS results of the regression of PCE on income.**

Dependent Variable: PCE
Method: Least Squares
Date: 07/31/10 Time: 10:00
Sample: 1960 2009
Included observations: 50

| Variable | Coefficient | Std. Error | t-Statistic | Prob. |
|---|---|---|---|---|
| C | −31.88846 | 18.22720 | −1.749498 | 0.0866 |
| INCOME | 0.819232 | 0.003190 | 256.7871 | 0.0000 |

| | | | |
|---|---|---|---|
| R-squared | 0.999273 | Mean dependent var | 3522.160 |
| Adjusted R-squared | 0.999257 | S.D. dependent var | 3077.678 |
| S.E. of regression | 83.86681 | Akaike info criterion | 11.73551 |
| Sum squared resid | 337614.8 | Schwarz criterion | 11.81200 |
| Log likelihood | −291.3879 | Hannan–Quinn criter. | 11.76464 |
| F-statistic | 65939.59 | Durbin–Watson stat | 0.568044 |
| Prob(F-statistic) | 0.000000 | | |

ILS is that it takes into account directly the simultaneity problem, whereas OLS simply ignores it.

We have considered a very simple example of simultaneous equation models. In models involving several equations, it is not easy to identify if all the equations in the system are identified. The method of ILS is too clumsy to identify each equation. But there are other methods of identification, such as the **order condition of identification** and the **rank condition of identification**. We will not discuss them here, for that will take us away from the main theme of this chapter, which is to discuss the major sources of specification errors. But a brief discussion of the order condition of identification is given in Chapter 19. An extended discussion of this topic can be found in the references.[23]

## 7.10  Dynamic regression models

Economic theory is often stated in *static* or *equilibrium* form. For example, elementary economics teaches us that the equilibrium price of a commodity (or service) is determined by the intersection of the relevant demand and supply curves. However, the equilibrium price is not determined instantaneously but by a process of trial and error, which takes time. This leads us to a discussion of **dynamic regression models**. Therefore, if we neglect to take into account the dynamic (i.e. time) aspect of a problem, we will be committing a specification error.

To motivate the discussion, we consider the celebrated *permanent income hypothesis* of Milton Friedman.[24] In simple terms, it states that the current consumption (expenditure) of an individual is a function of his or her *permanent* (i.e. life-long) income. But how does one measure the permanent income? Based on quarterly data, Friedman estimated permanent income as a weighted average of quarterly income going back

---

23  See, for instance, Gujarati/Porter, *op cit.*, Chapters 18–20.
24  Milton Friedman, *A Theory of Consumption Function*, Princeton University Press, New Jersey, 1957.

about 16 quarters. Letting $Y$ represent consumption expenditure and $X$ income, Friedman estimated the following type of model:

$$Y_t = A + B_0 X_t + B_1 X_{t-1} + B_2 X_{t-2} + \cdots + B_{16} X_{t-16} + u_t \qquad (7.14)$$

where $X_t$ is income in the current period (quarter), $X_{t-1}$ is income lagged one quarter, $X_{t-2}$ is income lagged two quarters, and so on. The $B$ coefficients are the weights attached to the income in the various quarters. We assume that the model (7.14) satisfies the usual OLS assumptions. For discussion purposes, we will call (7.14) the *consumption function*.

In the literature, model (7.14) is known as a **distributed lag model (DLM)** because the current value of the dependent variable $Y$ is affected by the current and lagged values of the explanatory variable $X$. This is not difficult to see. Suppose you get an increase in your salary this year. Assuming this increase is maintained, you will not necessarily rush to spend the increase in your income immediately. Rather, you are likely to spread it over a period of time.

Before we turn to the estimation of the DLM, it may be useful to interpret the model in (7.14). The coefficient $B_0$ is known as the **short-run** or **impact multiplier**, for it gives the change in the mean value of $Y$ following a unit change in $X$ in the same time period. If the change in $X$ is kept at the same level thereafter, $(B_0 + B_1)$ gives the change in mean $Y$ in the next period, $(B_0 + B_1 + B_2)$ in the following period, etc. These partial sums are called **interim** or **intermediate multipliers**. After $k$ periods (if that is the maximum lag length under consideration), we obtain:

$$\sum_0^k B_k = B_0 + B_1 + \cdots + B_k \qquad (7.15)$$

which is known as the **long-run** or **total multiplier**. It gives the ultimate change in mean consumption expenditure following a (sustained) unit increase in the income.

Thus, in the following hypothetical consumption function,

$$Y_t = \text{constant} + 0.4 X_t + 0.2 X_{t-1} + 0.15 X_{t-2} + 0.1 X_{t-3}$$

the impact multiplier will be 0.4, the interim multiplier will be (0.75) and the total, or long-run, multiplier will be 0.85. If, for example, income increases by $1000 in year $t$, and assuming this increase is maintained, consumption will increase by $400 in the first year, by another $200 in the second year, and by another $150 in the third year, with the final total increase being $750. Presumably, the consumer will save $250.

Returning to the model (7.14), we can estimate it by the usual OLS method.[25] But this may not be practical for several reasons. *First*, how do we decide how many lagged terms we use? *Second*, if we use several lagged terms, we will have fewer degrees of freedom to do meaningful statistical analyses, especially if the sample size is small. *Third*, in time series data successive values of the lagged term are likely to be highly correlated, which may lead to the problem of multicollinearity, which, as we noted in the chapter on multicollinearity, will lead to imprecise estimation of the regression coefficients.

---

25 Provided that the regressors (current and lagged) are **weakly exogenous**, that is, they are uncorrelated with the error term. In some cases a stronger assumption is needed in that the regressors are **strictly exogenous**, that is, they are independent of the past, current and future values of the error term.

To overcome some of these drawbacks of the DLM some alternatives have been suggested in the literature. We will discuss only one of these alternatives, namely the Koyck distributed lag model.[26]

## The Koyck distributed lag model[27]

To understand this model, let us express (7.14) in a more general form:

$$Y_t = A + B_0 X_t + B_1 X_{t-1} + B_2 X_{t-2} + \cdots + u_t \qquad (7.16)$$

This is called an **infinite DLM** because we have not defined the length of the lag; that is, we have not specified how far back in time we want to travel. By contrast, the model in (7.14) is a **finite DLM**, for we have specified the length of the lag: 16 lagged terms. The infinite DLM in (7.16) is for mathematical convenience, as we will show.

To estimate the parameters of (7.16), Koyck used the **Geometric Probability Distribution**. Assuming that all the $B$ coefficients in (7.16) have the same sign, which makes sense in our consumption function, Koyck assumed that they decline geometrically as follows:

$$B_k = B_0 \lambda^k, \quad k = 0, 1, \ldots; \quad 0 < \lambda < 1 \qquad (7.17)$$

where $\lambda$ is known as the *rate of decline or decay* and where $(1 - \lambda)$ is known as the *speed of adjustment*, that is, how fast consumption expenditure adjusts to the new income level.

Apart from $B_0$, the value of each $B_k$ depends on the value of $\lambda$: a value of $\lambda$ close to 1 would suggest that $B_k$ declines slowly, that is, $X$ values in distant past will have some impact on the current value of $Y$. On the other hand, a value of $\lambda$ close to zero would suggest that the impact of $X$ in the distant past will have little impact on the current $Y$.

What Koyck is assuming is that each successive $B$ coefficient is numerically smaller than each preceding $B$ (which follows from the assumption that $\lambda$ is less than 1), suggesting that as we go back into the distant past, the effect of that lag on $Y$ becomes progressively smaller. In the consumption function of (7.14) this makes good sense, for a person's consumption expenditure today is less likely to be affected by the distant past income than the recent past income.

How does this help us in estimating the infinite DLM? To see how, let us express (7.16) as

$$Y_t = A + B_0 X_t + B_0 \lambda X_{t-1} + B_0 \lambda^2 X_{t-2} + B_0 \lambda^3 X_{t-2} + \cdots + u_t \quad (7.18)$$

where use is made of (7.17).

However, (7.18) is not easy to estimate, for we still have to estimate an infinite number of coefficients and the adjustment coefficient $\lambda$ enters highly nonlinearly. But Koyck uses a clever trick to get around this problem. He lags (7.18) by one period to obtain:

$$Y_{t-1} = A + B_0 X_{t-1} + B_0 \lambda X_{t-2} + B_0 \lambda^2 X_{t-3} + \cdots + u_{t-1} \qquad (7.19)$$

He then multiplies (7.19) by $\lambda$ to obtain:

**26** For details, see Gujarati/Porter, Ch. 17. For an advanced discussion, see James H. Stock and Mark W. Watson (2011), *Introduction to Econometrics*, 3rd edn, Addison-Wesley, Boston, Ch. 15.

**27** L. M. Koyck (1954), *Distributed Lags and Investment Analysis*, North Holland Publishing Company, Amsterdam.

$$\lambda Y_{t-1} = \lambda A + \lambda B_0 X_{t-1} + \lambda^2 B_0 X_{t-2} + \lambda^3 B_0 X_{t-3} + \cdots + \lambda u_{t-1} \quad (7.20)$$

Subtracting (7.20) from (7.18), he obtains:

$$Y_t - \lambda Y_{t-1} = A(1-\lambda) + B_0 X_t + (u_t - \lambda u_{t-1}) \quad\quad\quad (7.21)$$

Rearranging (7.21), he finally obtains:

$$Y_t = A(1-\lambda) + B_0 X_t + \lambda Y_{t-1} + v_t \quad\quad\quad\quad\quad (7.22)$$

where $v_t = u_t - \lambda u_{t-1}$.

It is interesting to note that the lagged value of the dependent variable appears as a regressor in this model. Such models are called **autoregressive models,** for they involve the regression of the dependent variable upon its lagged value(s) among other independent explanatory variable(s).

A great advantage of the Koyck transformation is that instead of estimating an infinite number of parameters, as in (7.16), we now have to estimate only three parameters in model (7.22), a tremendous simplification of the original model. Are there any problems in estimating (7.22)? Before we answer that question, it is interesting to note that the short-run and long-run impacts of a unit change in $X$ on the mean value of $Y$ can be readily computed from (7.22). The short-run impact is given by the coefficient of $X$, $B_0$, and the long-run impact of a sustained unit change in $X$ is given by $B_0 /(1-\lambda)$.[28] Since $\lambda$ lies between 0 and 1, the long-run impact will be greater than the short-run impact, which makes sense because it takes time to adjust to the changed income.

The estimation of (7.22) poses formidable challenges: *First,* if the error term $u_t$ satisfies the classical assumptions (i.e. zero mean value, constant variance and no serial correlation), the composite error term $v_t$ in (7.22) may not satisfy the classical assumptions. As a matter of fact, it can be shown that the error term $v_t$ is serially correlated. *Second,* the lagged value of the dependent variable $Y$ appears as an explanatory variable in (7.22). Since $Y_t$ is a stochastic variable, so will $Y_{t-1}$. Since the classical OLS model assumes that the explanatory variables must either be nonstochastic, or if stochastic, they must be distributed independently of the error term, we must find out if the latter is the case. In (7.22) it can be shown that $Y_{t-1}$ and $v_t$ are correlated.[29] In this situation, the OLS estimators are not even consistent. *Third,* as noted in the chapter on autocorrelation, we cannot use the Durbin–Watson $d$ statistic to check for autocorrelation in $v_t$ if a lagged dependent variable appears as an explanatory variable in the model, as in (7.22), although Durbin himself has developed a test, the Durbin $h$ test, to test for serial correlation in this situation. For these reasons, the Koyck model, although elegant, poses formidable estimation problems. What then are the solutions?

First, since the error term $v_t$ is autocorrelated, the standard errors of the OLS estimators are not reliable, even though the OLS estimators are still consistent. But we can resolve this problem by using the **HAC** standard errors discussed in the chapter on autocorrelation.

But the more serious problem is the correlation between the lagged $Y_t$ and the error term $v_t$. As we know from previous discussion, in this situation the OLS estimators are not even consistent. One solution to this problem is to find a *proxy* for the

---

**28**   This is because in the long-run $Y^* = Y_t = Y_{t-1}$, so transferring $Y_{t-1}$ to the left-hand side of (7.22) and simplifying we obtain the long-run impact, as shown.
**29**   For a proof of this and the precedent statement, see Gujarati/Porter, 5th edn, p. 635.

lagged dependent variable, $Y_{t-1}$, such that it is highly correlated with $Y_{t-1}$ and yet uncorrelated with the error term $v_t$. Such a proxy is known as an **instrumental variable (IV)**, but it is not always easy to find IVs.[30] In the example discussed below we will show how we can find a proxy for the lagged consumption expenditure in our consumption example.

## An illustrative example

To illustrate the model (7.22), we use data on personal consumption expenditure (PCE) and disposable (i.e. after tax) income (DPI) for the USA for the period 1960 to 2009 (all data in 2005 dollars). (See data appendix on p. 149.)

For our example, using OLS we obtain the results in Table 7.15.

Because of the problems with the OLS standard errors in the presence of autocorrelation, we obtained robust standard errors (i.e. Newey–West standard errors) for our consumption function, which yielded the results in Table 7.16.

Although the estimated regression coefficients in the two tables are the same (as they should be under the HAC procedure), the estimated standard errors are somewhat higher under HAC. Even then, all the estimated coefficients are statistically highly significant, as reflected in the low $p$ values of the estimated $t$ values. This probably suggests that the problem of autocorrelation may not be very serious in the present case.

Accepting the results for the time being, we still have to resolve the possibility of correlation between the lagged PCE and the error term, it seems the short-run marginal propensity to consume (MPC) out of disposable income is about 0.43, but the long-run MPC is about 0.98.[31] That is, when consumers have had time to adjust to a dollar's increase in PDI, they will increase their mean consumption expenditure by almost a dollar in the long run, but in the short run, consumption increases by only about 43 cents.

**Table 7.15  OLS results of regression (7.22).**

Dependent Variable: PCE
Method: Least Squares
Date: 07/07/11 Time: 16:40
Sample (adjusted): 1961 2009
Included observations: 49 after adjustments

| Variable | Coefficient | Std. Error | t-Statistic | Prob. |
|---|---|---|---|---|
| C | −485.8849 | 197.5245 | −2.459872 | 0.0177 |
| DPI | 0.432575 | 0.081641 | 5.298529 | 0.0000 |
| PCE(−1) | 0.559023 | 0.084317 | 6.630052 | 0.0000 |

| | | | |
|---|---|---|---|
| R-squared | 0.998251 | Mean dependent var | 19602.16 |
| Adjusted R-squared | 0.998175 | S.D. dependent var | 6299.838 |
| S.E. of regression | 269.1558 | Akaike info criterion | 14.08773 |
| Sum squared resid | 3332462. | Schwarz criterion | 14.20355 |
| Log likelihood | −342.1493 | Hannan–Quinn criter. | 14.13167 |
| F-statistic | 13125.09 | Durbin–Watson stat | 0.708175 |
| Prob(F-statistic) | 0.000000 | | |

---

30  Chapter 19 is devoted to a discussion of the method of instrumental variable estimation.
31  This is obtained as $0.4325/(1 - \lambda) = 0.4325/0.441$, the value of $\lambda$ being about 0.5590.

**Table 7.16  Results of regression with robust standard errors.**

Dependent Variable: PCE
Method: Least Squares
Date: 07/07/11 Time: 16:46
Sample (adjusted): 1961 2009
Included observations: 49 after adjustments
HAC standard errors & covariance (Bartlett kernel, Newey–West fixed
bandwidth = 4.0000)

| Variable | Coefficient | Std. Error | t-Statistic | Prob. |
|----------|-------------|------------|-------------|-------|
| C | −485.8849 | 267.7614 | −1.814619 | 0.0761 |
| DPI | 0.432575 | 0.098339 | 4.398823 | 0.0001 |
| PCE(−1) | 0.559023 | 0.102057 | 5.477587 | 0.0000 |

| | | | | |
|---|---|---|---|---|
| R-squared | 0.998251 | Mean dependent var | 19602.16 |
| Adjusted R-squared | 0.998175 | S.D. dependent var | 6299.838 |
| S.E. of regression | 269.1558 | Akaike info criterion | 14.08773 |
| Sum squared resid | 3332462. | Schwarz criterion | 14.20355 |
| Log likelihood | −342.1493 | Hannan–Quinn criter. | 14.13167 |
| F-statistic | 13125.09 | Durbin–Watson stat | 0.708175 |
| Prob(F-statistic) | 0.000000 | | |

The estimated $\lambda$ of about 0.56 lies between 0 and 1, as expected. Thus the speed of adjustment of PCE to a change in DPI is not very slow or not very fast.

To see how quickly PCE adjusts to an increase in DPI, we can compute the so-called **median** and **mean** lag times. The median lag time is the time in which the first half, or 50%, of the total change in *PCE* follows a unit sustained change in *DPI*. The mean lag is the weighted average of all the lags involved, with the respective *B* coefficients serving as the weights.

For the Koyck model, it can be shown that these lags are as follows:

$$\text{Median lag} = -\frac{\log 2}{\log \lambda}$$

and

$$\text{Mean lag} = \frac{\lambda}{1-\lambda}$$

The reader can verify that for the present example the median and mean lags are about 1.19 and 1.27, respectively, noting that $\lambda$ is about 0.56. In the former case, about 50% of the total change in mean PCE is obtained in about 1.2 years and in the latter case the average lag is about 1.3 years.

As noted, the lagged DPI and the error term (7.22) are likely to be correlated, which would render the results in Table 7.16 suspect, for in this situation the OLS estimators are not even consistent. Can we find a proxy for the lagged PCE such that that proxy is highly correlated with it, but is uncorrelated with the error term in (7.22)? Since lagged PCE and lagged DPI are likely to be highly correlated, and since the latter by assumption is (weakly) exogenous, we can use lagged DPI as a proxy for lagged PCE.[32]

---

32  Calculations will show that the correlation coefficient between the two is about 0.998.

**Table 7.17  The results of regression (7.23) using HAC standard errors.**

Dependent Variable: PCE
Method: Least Squares
Date: 07/08/11 Time: 08:51
Sample (adjusted): 1961 2009
Included observations: 49 after adjustments
HAC standard errors & covariance (Bartlett kernel, Newey–West fixed
bandwidth = 4.0000)

| Variable | Coefficient | Std. Error | t-Statistic | Prob. |
|----------|-------------|------------|-------------|-------|
| C | −1425.511 | 372.3686 | −3.828224 | 0.0004 |
| DPI | 0.934361 | 0.175986 | 5.309287 | 0.0000 |
| DPI(−1) | 0.038213 | 0.177358 | 0.215455 | 0.8304 |

| | | | |
|---|---|---|---|
| R-squared | 0.996583 | Mean dependent var | 19602.16 |
| Adjusted R-squared | 0.996434 | S.D. dependent var | 6299.838 |
| S.E. of regression | 376.1941 | Akaike info criterion | 14.75736 |
| Sum squared resid | 6510013. | Schwarz criterion | 14.87318 |
| Log likelihood | −358.5553 | Hannan–Quinn criter. | 14.80130 |
| F-statistic | 6707.481 | Durbin–Watson stat | 0.351356 |
| Prob(F-statistic) | 0.000000 | | |

Therefore, instead of estimating (7.22), we can estimate

$$PCE_t = A + B_1 DPI_t + B_2 DPI_{t-1} + u_t \qquad (7.23)$$

which is a finite order DLM. The results of this regression, with HAC errors, are given in Table 7.17.

The lagged DPI coefficient in this regression is not statistically significant, which may be due to the fact that current and lagged DPI are so highly correlated. If you add the coefficients of current and lagged DPI, it is about 0.9725, which gives the long-run MPC.

It should be noted that the proxy we have chosen may not be the right one.[33] But as noted previously, and as will be discussed more fully in Chapter 19, finding appropriate proxies is not always easy.

## Autoregressive Distributed Lag Models (ARDL)

So far we have considered autoregressive and distributed lag models. But we can combine the features of these models in a more general dynamic regression model, known as the **Autoregressive Distributed Lag Models (ARDL)**.

To keep the discussion simple, we consider one dependent variable, or regressand, $Y$ and one explanatory variable, or regressor, $X$, although the discussion can be extended to models that contain more than one regressor and more than one dependent variable, a topic explored more fully in Chapters 13 and 16. Now consider the following model:

---

33  If we had data on consumer's wealth ($W$), we could use lagged $W$ for the lagged DPI, for they are likely to be highly correlated. However, it is not easy to find data on consumer wealth.

$$Y_t = A_0 + A_1 Y_{t-1} + A_2 Y_{t-2} + \cdots + A_p Y_{t-p}$$
$$+ B_0 X_t + B_1 X_{t-1} + B_2 X_{t-2} + \cdots + B_q X_{t-q} + u_t \qquad (7.24)$$

This equation can be written more compactly as:

$$Y_t = A_0 + \sum_{i=1}^{i=p} A_i Y_{t-i} + \sum_{i=0}^{i=q} B_i X_{t-i} + u_t \qquad (7.25)$$

In this model the lagged $Y$s constitute the autoregressive part and the lagged $X$s constitute the distributed part of the ARDL($p, q$) model, for there are $p$ autoregressive terms and $q$ distributed lag terms.

An advantage of such an ARLD model is that it not only captures the dynamic effects of the lagged $Y$s but also those of the lagged $X$s. If a sufficient number of lags of both variables are included in the model, we can eliminate autocorrelation in the error term, the choice of the number of lags included in the model being determined by Akaike or a similar information criterion. Such models are often used for forecasting and also for estimating the multiplier effects of the regressors in the model.

Before we consider the estimation and interpretation of this model, as well as the nature of the regressand, regressors and the error term, it may be useful to know why such models can be useful in empirical work.[34] One classic example is the celebrated **Phillips curve**. Based on historical data, Phillips found an inverse relationship between inflation and unemployment, although the initial Phillips curve has been modified in several ways.[35] Since current inflation is likely to be influenced by lagged inflation (because of inertia) as well as the current and past unemployment rates, it is appropriate to develop an ARDL model for forecasting and policy purposes.[36] For another example, consider the sale of a product in relation to advertising expenditure on that product. The sale of a product in the current time period is likely to depend on the sale of that product in the previous time periods as well as the expenditure on advertising in the current and previous time periods.

In our consumption function example we can also argue that current consumption expenditure is dependent on past consumption expenditures as well current and past levels of incomes, the number of lags being determined empirically using a suitable information criterion, such as the Akaike Information criterion.

To minimize the algebra, let us consider an ARDL (1,1) model for our consumption function.

$$Y_t = A_0 + A_1 Y_{t-1} + B_0 X_t + B_1 X_{t-1} + u_t, \quad A_1 < 1 \qquad (7.26)^{37}$$

where $Y$ = PCE and $X$ = DPI.

---

34  For a detailed but advanced discussion see David F. Henry (1995), *Dynamic Econometrics*, Oxford University Press.

35  For a chronology of the various forms of Phillips curve, see Gordon, R. J. (2008), The history of the Phillips curve: an American perspective', a keynote address delivered at the Australasian Meetings of the Econometric Society. See http://www.nzae.org.nz/conference/2008/090708/nr1217302437.pdf.

36  For a concrete example, see R. Carter Hill, William E. Griffiths and Guay C. Lim (2011), *Principles of Econometrics*, 3rd edn, Wiley, New York, pp. 367–369.

37  If the condition $A_1 < 1$ is violated, $Y$ will exhibit explosive behavior.

That is, personal consumption expenditure in the current period is related to personal consumption expenditure in the previous time period as well as on the current and one-period lagged disposable income.

An important feature of the model (7.26) is that it enables us to find the *dynamic* effects of a change in DPI on current and future values of PCE. The immediate effect, called the **impact multiplier**, of a unit change in DPI is given by the coefficient $B_0$ .If the unit change in DPI is sustained, it can be shown that the long-run multiplier is given by

$$\textbf{long-run multiplier} = \frac{B_0 + B_1}{1 - A_1} \qquad (7.27)$$

So if DPI increases by a unit (say, a dollar) and is maintained, the expected cumulative increase in PCE is given by (7.27).[38] In other words, if the unit increase in DPI is maintained, Equation (7.27) gives the long-run permanent increase in PCE.

To illustrate the ARDL(1,1) model for our consumption example, we have to make certain assumptions. *First*, the variables $Y$ and $X$ are *stationary*.[39] *Secondly*, given the values of regressors in Eq. (7.26), or more generally in Eq. (7.24), the expected mean value of the error term $u_t$ is zero. *Thirdly*, if the error term in Eq. (7.24) is serially uncorrelated, then the coefficients of the model (7.24), or in the present model (7.26), estimated by OLS will be consistent (in the statistical sense). However, if the error term is autocorrelated, the lagged $Y$ term in Eq. (7.26), or generally in Eq. (7.24), will also be correlated with the error term, in which case the OLS estimators will be inconsistent. So we need to find out if the error term is autocorrelated by any of the methods discussed in the chapter on autocorrelation. *Finally*, it is assumed that the $X$ variables are exogenous – at least weakly so. That is, they are uncorrelated with the error term.

Now let us return to our illustrative example. The results of model (7.26) are given in Table 7.18.

Assuming the validity of the model for the time being, the results show that the *impact multiplier* of a unit change in DPI on PCE is about 0.82. If this unit change is maintained, then the long-run multiplier, following Eq. (7.27), is about 0.9846.[40] As expected, the long-run multiplier is greater than the short-run multiplier. Thus a sustained one dollar increase in DPI will eventually increase mean PCE by about 98 cents.

To allow for the possibility of serial correlation in the error term, we re-estimated the model in Table 7.18 using the HAC procedure. The results are given in Table 7.19.

The HAC procedure does not change the estimated standard errors substantially, perhaps suggesting that the serial correlation problem in our example may not be serious.

We leave it to the reader to try different lagged values for $p$ and $q$ in the ARDL($p,q$) model for our data and compare the results with the ARDL(1,1) model.

---

38  For a derivation of this result, see Marno Verbeek (2008), *A Guide to Modern Econometrics*, 3rd edn, Wiley and Sons, Chichester, pp. 324–325.

39  Broadly speaking, a time series is stationary if its mean and variance are constant over time and the value of covariance between two time periods depends only on the distance between the two time periods and not the actual time at which the covariance is computed. This topic is discussed more thoroughly in Chapter 13.

40  Long-run multiplier = $(B_0 + B_1)/(1 - A_1) = (0.8245 - 0.6329)/(1 - 0.8053) = 0.9846$ (approx.)

**Table 7.18  OLS estimates of model (7.26).**

Dependent Variable: PCE
Method: Least Squares
Date: 08/14/11 Time: 13:35
Sample (adjusted): 1961 2009
Included observations: 49 after adjustments

| Variable | Coefficient | Std. Error | t-Statistic | Prob. |
|---|---|---|---|---|
| C | −281.2019 | 161.0712 | −1.745823 | 0.0877 |
| DPI | 0.824591 | 0.097977 | 8.416208 | 0.0000 |
| PCE(−1) | 0.805356 | 0.081229 | 9.914632 | 0.0000 |
| DPI(−1) | −0.632942 | 0.118864 | −5.324935 | 0.0000 |

| | | | | |
|---|---|---|---|---|
| R-squared | 0.998927 | Mean dependent var | 19602.16 | |
| Adjusted R-squared | 0.998855 | S.D. dependent var | 6299.838 | |
| S.E. of regression | 213.1415 | Akaike info criterion | 13.63990 | |
| Sum squared resid | 2044318. | Schwarz criterion | 13.79433 | |
| Log likelihood | −330.1775 | Hannan–Quinn criter. | 13.69849 | |
| F-statistic | 13962.93 | Durbin–Watson stat | 1.841939 | |
| Prob(F-statistic) | 0.000000 | | | |

**Table 7.19  OLS estimates of model (7.26) with HAC standard errors.**

Dependent Variable: PCE
Method: Least Squares
Date: 08/14/11 Time: 13:41
Sample (adjusted): 1961 2009
Included observations: 49 after adjustments
HAC standard errors & covariance (Bartlett kernel, Newey–West fixed bandwidth = 4.0000)

| Variable | Coefficient | Std. Error | t-Statistic | Prob. |
|---|---|---|---|---|
| C | −281.2019 | 117.3088 | −2.397107 | 0.0207 |
| PCE(−1) | 0.805356 | 0.071968 | 11.19044 | 0.0000 |
| DPI | 0.824591 | 0.114989 | 7.171026 | 0.0000 |
| DPI(−1) | −0.632942 | 0.119717 | −5.286977 | 0.0000 |

| | | | | |
|---|---|---|---|---|
| R-squared | 0.998927 | Mean dependent var | 19602.16 | |
| Adjusted R-squared | 0.998855 | S.D. dependent var | 6299.838 | |
| S.E. of regression | 213.1415 | Akaike info criterion | 13.63990 | |
| Sum squared resid | 2044318. | Schwarz criterion | 13.79433 | |
| Log likelihood | −330.1775 | Hannan–Quinn criter. | 13.69849 | |
| F-statistic | 13962.93 | Durbin–Watson stat | 1.841939 | |
| Prob(F-statistic) | 0.000000 | | | |

## Forecasting

How do we use the model (7.26) for forecasting? Suppose we want to forecast PCE for 1961, that is, one-period ahead of 1960 (our sample data ends in 1960). That is, we want to estimate $PCE_{1961}$. We can move the model one period ahead as follows:

$$PCE_{1961} = A_0 + A_1 Y_{1960} + B_0 X_{1961} + B_1 X_{1960} + u_{1961} \qquad (7.28)$$

Here we know the values of $Y_{1960}$ and $X_{1960}$. But we do not know the values of $X_{1961}$ and $u_{1961}$. We can guess-estimate $X_{1961}$ or obtain its value from any forecasting method discussed in Chapter 16 on economic forecasting. We can put the value of $u_{1961}$ at zero. Then, using the estimated values of the parameters from Table 7.19, we can estimate the estimated value of $PCE_{1961}$.

A similar procedure can be used for multi-period ahead forecasts of $PCE$. But we leave it to the reader to find the numerical values of $PCE$ for one-period-ahead and multi-period-ahead forecasts.

## Concluding comments

In this section we have discussed three dynamic regression models: autoregressive, distributed lag, and autoregressive and distributed lag models. We first considered an infinite order (DLM), but because it involves estimating an infinite number of parameters we converted it into an autoregressive model via the Koyck transformation. With a numerical example involving real personal consumption expenditure and real disposable income in the US for the period 1960–2009, we showed how these models are estimated, noting the assumptions underlying these models and some of the estimation problems.

We also discussed a simple autoregressive distributed lag model, ARDL(1,1), which combines the features of both autoregressive and distributed lag models and showed how we can compute the short-run and long-run multipliers following a permanent unit increase in the value of a regressor. We also discussed the assumptions underlying this model and some of the estimation procedures. We also discussed briefly how forecasts for future periods can be made based on the ARDL models.

The topic of dynamic regression models is vast and is mathematically complex. In this section we have just touched the essential features of such models. For further study of these models the reader is advised to consult the references.

## 7.11  Summary and conclusions

We have covered a lot of ground in this chapter on a variety of practical topics in econometric modeling.

If we omit a relevant variable(s) from a regression model, the estimated coefficients and standard errors of OLS estimators in the reduced model are biased as well as inconsistent. We considered the RESET and Lagrange Multiplier tests to detect the omission of relevant variables bias.

If we add unnecessary variables to a model, the OLS estimators of the expended model are still BLUE. The only penalty we pay is the loss of efficiency (i.e. increased standard errors) of the estimated coefficients.

The appropriate functional form of a regression model is a commonly encountered question in practice. In particular, we often face a choice between a linear and a log-linear model. We showed how we can compare the two models in making the choice, using the Cobb–Douglas production function data for the 50 states in the USA and Washington, DC, as an example.

Errors of measurement are a common problem in empirical work, especially if we depend on secondary data. We showed that the consequences of such errors can be very serious if they exist in explanatory variables, for in that case the OLS estimators are not even consistent. Errors of measurement do not pose a serious problem if they are in the dependent variable. In practice, however, it is not always easy to spot the errors of measurement. The method of instrumental variables, discussed in Chapter 19, is often suggested as a remedy for this problem.

Generally we use the sample data to draw inferences about the relevant population. But if there are "unusual observations" or outliers in the sample data, inferences based on such data may be misleading. Therefore we need to pay special attention to outlying observations. Before we throw out the outlying observations, we must be very careful to find out why the outliers are present in the data. Sometimes they may result from human errors in recording or transcribing the data. We illustrated the problem of outliers with data on cigarette smoking and deaths from lung cancer in a sample of 42 states, in addition to Washington, DC.

One of the assumptions of the classical normal linear regression model is that the error term included in the regression model follows the normal distribution. This assumption cannot always be maintained in practice. We showed that as long the assumptions of the classical linear regression model (CLRM) hold, and *if the sample size is large*, we can still use the $t$ and $F$ tests of significance even if the error term is not normally distributed.

Finally, we discussed the problem of simultaneity bias which arises if we estimate an equation that is embedded in system of simultaneous equations by the usual OLS. If we blindly apply OLS in this situation, the OLS estimators are biased as well as inconsistent. There are alternative methods of estimating simultaneous equations, such as the methods of indirect least-squares (ILS) or the two-stage least squares (2SLS). In this chapter we showed how ILS can be used to estimate the consumption expenditure function in the simple Keynesian model of determining aggregate income.

# Exercises

**7.1**    For the wage determination model discussed in the text, how would you find out if there are any outliers in the wage data? If you do find them, how would you decide if the outliers are influential points? And how would you handle them? Show the necessary details.

**7.2**    In the various wage determination models discussed in this chapter, how would you find out if the error variance is heteroscedastic? If your finding is in the affirmative, how would you resolve the problem?

**7.3**    In the chapter on heteroscedasticity we discussed robust standard errors or White's heteroscedasticity-corrected standard errors. For the wage determination models, present the robust standard errors and compare them with the usual OLS standard errors.

**7.4**    What other variables do you think should be included in the wage determination model? How would that change the models discussed in the text?

**7.5**    Use the data given in Table 7.8 to find out the impact of cigarette smoking on bladder, kidney, and leukemia cancers. Specify the functional form you use and present your results. How would you find out if the impact of smoking depends on the type of cancer? What may the reason for the difference be, if any?

**7.6**    Continue with Exercise 7.5. Are there any outliers in the cancer data? If there are, identify them.

**7.7** In the cancer data we have 43 observations for each type of cancer, giving a total of 172 observations for all the cancer types. Suppose you now estimate the following regression model:

$$C_i = B_1 + B_2 Cig_i + B_3 Lung_i + B_4 Kidney_i + B_5 Leukemia_i + u_i$$

where $C$ = number of deaths from cancer, $Cig$ = number of cigarettes smoked, $Lung$ = a dummy taking a value of 1 if the cancer type is lung, 0 otherwise, $Kidney$ = a dummy taking a value of 1 if the cancer type is kidney, 0 other wise, and $Leukemia$ = 1 if the cancer type is leukemia, 0 otherwise. Treat deaths from bladder cancer as a reference group.

(a) Estimate this model, obtaining the usual regression output.

(b) How do you interpret the various dummy coefficients?

(c) What is the interpretation of the intercept $B_1$ in this model?

(d) What is the advantage of the dummy variable regression model over estimating deaths from each type of cancer in relation to the number of cigarettes smoked separately?

*Note*: Stack the deaths from various cancers one on top of the other to generate 172 observations on the dependent variable. Similarly, stack the number of cigarettes smoked to generate 172 observations on the regressor.

**7.8** The error term in the log of wages regression in Table 7.7 was found to be non-normally distributed. However, the distribution of log of wages was normally distributed. Are these findings in conflict? If so, what may the reason for the difference in these findings?

**7.9** Consider the following simultaneous equation model:

$$Y_{1t} = A_1 + A_2 Y_{2t} + A_3 X_{1t} + u_{1t} \qquad (1)$$

$$Y_{2t} = B_1 + B_2 Y_{1t} + B_3 X_{2t} + u_{2t} \qquad (2)$$

In this model the $Y$s are the endogenous variables and the $X$s are the exogenous variables and the $u$s are stochastic error terms.

(a) Obtain the reduced form regressions.

(b) Which of the above equations is identified?

(c) For the identified equation, which method will you use to obtain the structural coefficients?

(d) Suppose it is known *a priori* that $A_3$ is zero. Will this change your answer to the preceding questions? Why?

**7.10** For the ARDL(1,1) model, the long-run multiplier is given in Eq. (7.27). Suppose for the illustrative example you estimate the following simple regression model:

$$PCE_t = C_1 + C_2 DPI_t + u_t$$

Estimate this regression and show that $C_2$ is equal to the long-run multiplier given in Eq. (7.27). Can you guess why this is so? Can you establish this formally?

# Inconsistency of the OLS estimators of the consumption function

The OLS estimator of the marginal propensity to consume is given by the usual OLS formula:

$$b_2 = \frac{\Sigma c_t y_t}{\Sigma y_t^2} = \frac{\Sigma C_t y_t}{\Sigma y_t^2} \tag{1}$$

where $c$ and $y$ are deviations from their mean values, e.g. $c_t = C_t - \bar{C}$.

Now substitute Eq. (7.8) into Eq. (1) to obtain:

$$b_2 = \frac{\Sigma(B_1 + B_2 Y_t + u_t) y_t}{\Sigma y_t^2} \tag{2}$$

$$= B_2 + \frac{\Sigma y_t u_t}{\Sigma y_t^2}$$

where use is made of the fact that $\Sigma y_t = 0$ and $\Sigma Y_t y_t / \Sigma y_t^2 = 1$.

Taking the expectation of Eq. (2), we obtain:

$$E(b_2) = B_2 + E\left[\frac{\Sigma y_t u_t}{\Sigma y_t^2}\right] \tag{3}$$

Since $E$, the expectations operator, is a linear operator, we cannot take the expectation of the nonlinear second term in this equation. Unless the last term is zero, $b_2$ is a biased estimator. Does the bias disappear as the sample increases indefinitely? In other words, is the OLS estimator consistent? Recall that an estimator is said to be consistent if its probability limit (plim) is equal to its true population value. To find this out, we can take the probability limit (plim) of Eq. (3):

$$p\lim(b_2) = p\lim(B_2) + p\lim\left[\frac{\Sigma y_t u_t / n}{\Sigma y_t^2 / n}\right] \tag{4}$$

$$= B_2 + \frac{p\lim(\Sigma y_t u_t / n)}{p\lim(\Sigma y_t^2 / n)}$$

where use is made of the properties of the plim operator that the plim of a constant (such as $B_2$) is that constant itself and the plim of the ratio of two entities is the ratio of the plim of those entities.

As the sample size $n$ increases indefinitely, it can be shown that

$$p\lim(b_2) = B_2 + \frac{1}{1 - B_2}\left(\frac{\sigma_u^2}{\sigma_y^2}\right) \tag{5}$$

where $\sigma_u^2$ and $\sigma_y^2$ are the (population) variances of $u$ and $Y$, respectively.

Since $B_2$ (MPC) lies between 0 and 1, and since the two variances are positive, it is obvious that $p\lim (b_2)$ will always be greater than $B_2$, that is, $b_2$ will overestimate $B_2$, no matter how large the sample is. In other words, not only is $b_2$ biased, but it is inconsistent as well.

## Data appendix

| obs | PCE | DPI | obs | PCE | DPI |
|-----|-----|-----|-----|-----|-----|
| 1960 | 9871.000 | 10865.00 | 1985 | 19037.00 | 21571.00 |
| 1961 | 9911.000 | 11052.00 | 1986 | 19630.00 | 22083.00 |
| 1962 | 10243.00 | 11413.00 | 1987 | 20055.00 | 22246.00 |
| 1963 | 10512.00 | 11672.00 | 1988 | 20675.00 | 22997.00 |
| 1964 | 10985.00 | 12342.00 | 1989 | 21060.00 | 23385.00 |
| 1965 | 11535.00 | 12939.00 | 1990 | 21249.00 | 23568.00 |
| 1966 | 12050.00 | 13465.00 | 1991 | 21000.00 | 23453.00 |
| 1967 | 12276.00 | 13904.00 | 1992 | 21430.00 | 23958.00 |
| 1968 | 12856.00 | 14392.00 | 1993 | 21904.00 | 24044.00 |
| 1969 | 13206.00 | 14706.00 | 1994 | 22466.00 | 24517.00 |
| 1970 | 13361.00 | 15158.00 | 1995 | 22803.00 | 24951.00 |
| 1971 | 13696.00 | 15644.00 | 1996 | 23325.00 | 25475.00 |
| 1972 | 14384.00 | 16228.00 | 1997 | 23899.00 | 26061.00 |
| 1973 | 14953.00 | 17166.00 | 1998 | 24861.00 | 27299.00 |
| 1974 | 14693.00 | 16878.00 | 1999 | 25923.00 | 27805.00 |
| 1975 | 14881.00 | 17091.00 | 2000 | 26939.00 | 28899.00 |
| 1976 | 15558.00 | 17600.00 | 2001 | 27385.00 | 29299.00 |
| 1977 | 16051.00 | 18025.00 | 2002 | 27841.00 | 29976.00 |
| 1978 | 16583.00 | 18670.00 | 2003 | 28357.00 | 30442.00 |
| 1979 | 16790.00 | 18897.00 | 2004 | 29072.00 | 31193.00 |
| 1980 | 16538.00 | 18863.00 | 2005 | 29771.00 | 31318.00 |
| 1981 | 16623.00 | 19173.00 | 2006 | 30341.00 | 32271.00 |
| 1982 | 16694.00 | 19406.00 | 2007 | 30838.00 | 32648.00 |
| 1983 | 17489.00 | 19868.00 | 2008 | 30479.00 | 32514.00 |
| 1984 | 18256.00 | 21105.00 | 2009 | 30042.00 | 32637.00 |

*Note*: The data in this table are 2005 chained dollars.
*Source*: US Department of Commerce. The data can also be found on the website of the Federal Reserve Bank of St Louis, USA.

# Regression models with cross-sectional data

# 8

# The logit and probit models

The dependent variable in most regression models is numerical, measured usually on a **ratio scale**. But in many applications the dependent variables are **nominal** in the sense that they denote categories, such as male or female, married or unmarried, employed or unemployed, in the labor force or not in the labor force.

Suppose we have data on adults, some of who smoke and some who do not. Further suppose we want to find out what factors determine whether a person smokes or not. So the variable smoking status is a nominal variable; you either smoke or you do not. How do we model such nominal variables? Can we use the traditional regression techniques or do we need specialized techniques?

Regression models involving nominal scale variables are an example of a broader class of models known as **qualitative response regression models**. There are a variety of such models, but in this chapter we will consider the simplest of such models, namely the **binary** or **dichotomous** or **dummy** dependent variable regression models. In subsequent chapters we will consider other types of qualitative response regression models.

The aim of this chapter is to show that although binary variable regression models can be estimated with the least-squares method, such models are usually estimated by specialized methods, such as **logit** and **probit**. First we will show why the least-squares method is not appropriate and then consider the logit and probit models. We begin with an example.

## 8.1 An illustrative example: to smoke or not to smoke

The data used here is a random sample of 1,196 US males.[1] These data are provided in **Table 8.1**, which can be found on the companion website.

The variables used in the analysis are as follows:

*Smoker* = 1 for smokers and 0 for nonsmokers

*Age* = age in years

*Education* = number of years of schooling

*Income* = family income

*Pcigs* = price of cigarettes in individual states in 1979

---

[1] These data are from the website of Michael P. Murray, *Econometrics: A Modern Introduction*, Addison-Wesley, Boston, 2006. See http://www.aw.-bc.com/murray. But the data were originally used by John Mullay, Instrumental-variable estimation of count data models: an application to models of cigarette smoking behavior, *The Review of Economics and Statistics*, 1997.

## 8.2 The linear probability model (LPM)

Since the dependent variable, smoker, is a nominal variable, it takes a value of 1 (for smoker) and 0 (for nonsmoker). Suppose we routinely apply the method of ordinary least-squares (OLS) to determine smoking behavior in relation to age, education, family income, and price of cigarettes. That is, we use the following model:

$$Y_i = B_1 + B_2 Age_i + B_3 Educ_i + B_4 Income_i$$
$$+ B_5 Pcigs + u_i$$

(8.1)

which, for brevity of expression, we write as:

$$Y_i = BX + u_i$$

(8.2)

where $BX$ is the right-hand side of Eq. (8.1).

Model (8.2) is called a **linear probability model** (**LPM**) because the conditional expectation of the depending variable (smoking status), given the values of the explanatory variables, can be interpreted as the *conditional probability* that the event (i.e. smoking) will occur.[2]

Using *Eviews*, we obtained the results in Table 8.2. Let us examine the results in this table.

Notice that all the variables, except income, are individually statistically significant at least at the 10% level of significance.

Age, education, and price of cigarettes have negative impact on smoking, which may not be a surprising result. Collectively all the explanatory variables are statistically significant, for the estimated $F$ value of $\approx 12.00$ has a $p$ value of almost zero. Recall that the $F$ value tests the hypothesis that all the slope coefficients are simultaneously equal to zero.

**Table 8.2  LPM model of to smoke or not to smoke.**

Dependent Variable: SMOKER
Method: Least Squares
Date: 12/06/08 Time: 21:54
Sample: 1 1196
Included observations: 1196

|  | Coefficient | Std. Error | t-Statistic | Prob. |
|---|---|---|---|---|
| C | 1.123089 | 0.188356 | 5.962575 | 0.0000 |
| AGE | −0.004726 | 0.000829 | −5.700952 | 0.0000 |
| EDUC | −0.020613 | 0.004616 | −4.465272 | 0.0000 |
| INCOME | 1.03E−06 | 1.63E−06 | 0.628522 | 0.5298 |
| PCIGS79 | −0.005132 | 0.002852 | −1.799076 | 0.0723 |

| | | | |
|---|---|---|---|
| R-squared | 0.038770 | Mean dependent var | 0.380435 |
| Adjusted R-squared | 0.035541 | S.D. dependent var | 0.485697 |
| S.E. of regression | 0.476988 | Akaike info criterion | 1.361519 |
| Sum squared resid | 270.9729 | Schwarz criterion | 1.382785 |
| Log likelihood | −809.1885 | Durbin–Watson stat | 1.943548 |
| F-statistic | 12.00927 | Prob(F-statistic) | 0.000000 |

2  If $P_i = \Pr(Y_i = 1)$ and $(1 - P_i) = \Pr(Y_i = 0)$, then the expected value of $Y_i = E(Y_i) = 1.P_i + 0.(1 - P_i) = P_i$.

Since we have estimated a linear probability model, the interpretation of the regression coefficients is as follows. If we hold all other variables constant, the probability of smoking decreases at the rate of $\approx 0.005$ as a person ages, probably due to the adverse impact of smoking on health. Likewise, *ceteris paribus*, an increase in schooling by one year decreases the probability of smoking by 0.02. Similarly, if the price of cigarettes goes up by a dollar, the probability of smoking decreases by $\approx 0.005$, holding all other variables constant. The $R^2$ value of $\approx 0.038$ seems very low, but one should not attach much importance to this because the dependent variable is nominal, taking only values of 1 and zero.

We can refine this model by introducing *interaction terms*, such as age multiplied by education, or education multiplied by income, or introduce a squared term in education or squared term in age to find out if there is nonlinear impact of these variables on smoking. But there is no point in doing that, because the LPM has several inherent limitations.

*First*, the LPM assumes that the probability of smoking moves linearly with the value of the explanatory variable, no matter how small or large that value is. *Secondly*, by logic, the probability value must lie between 0 and 1. But there is no guarantee that the *estimated* probability values from the LPM will lie within these limits. This is because OLS does not take into account the restriction that the estimated probabilities must lie within the bounds of 0 and 1. *Thirdly*, the usual assumption that the error term is normally distributed cannot hold when the dependent variable takes only values of 0 and 1. *Finally*, the error term in the LPM is heteroscedastic, making the traditional significance tests suspect.

For all these reasons, LPM is not the preferred choice for modeling dichotomous variables. The alternatives discussed in the literature are **logit** and **probit**.

## 8.3    The logit model

In our smoker example our primary objective is to estimate the probability of smoking, given the values of the explanatory variables. In developing such a probability function, we need to keep in mind two requirements: (1) that as $X_i$, the value of the explanatory variable(s) changes, the estimated probability always lies in the 0–1 interval, and (2) that the relationship between $P_i$ and $X_i$ is nonlinear, that is, "one which approaches zero at slower and slower rates as $X_i$ gets small and approaches one at slower and slower rates as $X_i$ gets very large".[3] The logit and probit models satisfy these requirements. We first consider the logit model because of its comparative mathematical simplicity.

Assume that in our example the decision of an individual to smoke or not to smoke depends on an *unobservable **utility index** $I_i^*$*, which depends on explanatory variables such as age, education, family income and price of cigarettes.[4] We express this index as:

$$I_i^* = BX + u_i \qquad\qquad (8.3)$$

where $i = i$th individual, $u$ = error term, and **BX** is as defined in Eq. (8.2).

---

3  John H. Aldrich and Forrest Nelson, *Linear Probability, Logit and Probit Models*, Sage Publications, 1984, p. 26.

4  The utility index is also known as a latent variable.

But how is the unobservable index related to the actual decision of smoking or not smoking? It is reasonable to assume that:

$Y_i = 1$ (a person smokes) if $I_i^* \geq 0$

$Y_i = 0$ (a person does not smoke) if $I_i^* < 0$

That is, if a person's utility index $I$ exceeds the threshold level $I^*$, he or she will smoke but if it is less that $I^*$, that individual will not smoke. Note that we are not suggesting that smoking is good or bad for health, although there is extensive medical research that suggests that smoking probably is bad for health.

To make this choice operational, we can think in terms of the probability of making a choice, say the choice of smoking (i.e. $Y = 1$):

$$\Pr(Y_i = 1) = \Pr(I^* \geq 0)$$
$$= \Pr[(BX + u_i) \geq 0] \tag{8.4}$$
$$= \Pr(u_i \geq -BX)$$

Now this probability depends on the (probability) distribution of $Y_i$, which in turn depends on the probability distribution of the error term, $u_i$.[5] If this probability distribution is symmetric around its (zero) mean value, then Eq. (8.4) can be written as:

$$\Pr(u_i \geq -BX) = \Pr(u_i \leq BX) \tag{8.5}$$

Therefore,

$$P_i = \Pr(Y_i = 1) = \Pr(u_i \leq BX) \tag{8.6}$$

Obviously $P_i$ depends on the particular probability distribution of $u_i$. Remember that the probability that a random variable takes a value less than some specified value is given by the **cumulative distribution function (CDF)** of that variable.[6]

The logit model assumes that the probability distribution of $u_i$ follows the **logistic probability distribution**, which for our example can be written as:

$$P_i = \frac{1}{1 + e^{-Z_i}} \tag{8.7}$$

where $P_i$ = probability of smoking (i.e. $Y_i = 1$) and

$$Z_i = BX + u_i \tag{8.8}$$

The probability that $Y = 0$, that is, the person is not a smoker, is given by

$$1 - P_i = \frac{1}{1 + e^{Z_i}} \tag{8.9}$$

*Note*: The signs of $Z_i$ in Eqs. (8.7) and (8.9) are different.

---

5  Note that $B$ is fixed or nonrandom and $X$ values are given. Therefore, the variation in $Y_i$ comes from the variation in $u_i$.

6  Recall from elementary statistics that the *cumulative distribution function* of a random variable $X$, $F(X)$, is defined as: $F(X) = \Pr(X \leq x)$, where $x$ is a particular value of $X$. Also recall that if you plot CDF, it resembles an elongated $S$.

It can be easily verified that as $Z_i$ ranges from $-\infty$ to $+\infty$, $P_i$ ranges between 0 and 1 and that $P_i$ is nonlinearly related to $Z_i$ (i.e. $X_i$), thus satisfying the requirements discussed earlier.[7]

How do we estimate model (8.7), for it is nonlinear not only in $X$ but also in the parameters, $B$s? We can use a simple transformation to make the model linear in the $X$s and the coefficients. Taking the ratio of Eqs. (8.7) and (8.9), that is the probability that a person is a smoker against the probability that he/she is not, we obtain:

$$\frac{P_i}{1-P_i} = \frac{1+e^{Z_i}}{1+e^{-Z_i}} = e^{Z_i} \tag{8.10}$$

Now $P_i/(1-P_i)$ is simply the **odds ratio** in favor of smoking – the ratio of the probability that a person is a smoker to the probability that he or she is not a smoker.

Taking the (natural) log of Eq. (8.10), we obtain a very interesting result, namely:

$$L_i = \ln\left(\frac{P_i}{1-P_i}\right) = Z_i = BX_i + u_i \tag{8.11}$$

In words, Eq. (8.11) states that the log of the odds ratio is a linear function of the $B$s as well as the $X$s. $L_i$ is know as the **logit** (log of the odds ratio) and hence the name **logit model** for models like (8.11). It is interesting to observe that the linear probability model (LPM) discussed previously assumes that $P_i$ is linearly related to $X_i$, whereas the logit model assumes that the log of the odds ratio is linearly related to $X_i$.

Some of the features of the logit model are as follows:

1  As $P_i$, the probability goes from 0 to 1, the logit $L_i$ goes from $-\infty$ to $+\infty$. That is, although the probabilities lie between 0 and 1, the logits are unbounded.

2  Although $L_i$ is linear in $X_i$, the probabilities themselves are not. This is contrast to with the LPM where the probabilities increase linearly with $X_i$.

3  If $L_i$, the logit, is positive, it means that when the value of the explanatory variable(s) increases, the odds of smoking increases, whereas it if is negative, the odds of smoking decreases.

4  The interpretation of the logit model in (8.11) is as follows: each slope coefficient shows how the log of the odds in favor of smoking changes as the value of the $X$ variable changes by a unit.

5  Once the coefficients of the logit model are estimated, we can easily compute the probabilities of smoking, not just the odds of smoking, from (8.7).

6  In the LPM the slope coefficient measures the marginal effect of a unit change in the explanatory variable on the probability of smoking, holding other variables constant. This is not the case with the logit model, for the marginal effect of a unit change in the explanatory variable not only depends on the coefficient of that variable but also on the level of probability from which the change is measured. But the latter depends on the values of all the explanatory variables in the model.[8]

---

7  The reason why $P_i$ is nonlinearly related to, say, income is that as income increases smokers will increase their consumption of cigarettes at a decreasing rate because of the law of diminishing returns. This is true of almost all normal commodities.

8  Calculus-minded readers can verify this if they take the (partial) derivative of Eq. (8.7) with respect to the relevant variables, noting that $Z_i = BX$. Note: use the chain rule: $\partial P_i/\partial X_i = \partial P_i/\partial Z_i \cdot \partial Z_i/\partial X_i$.

However, statistical packages such as *Eviews* and *Stata* can compute the marginal effects with simple instructions.

Now the question is: how do we estimate the parameters of the logit model?

## Estimation of the logit model

Estimation of the logit model depends on the type of data available for analysis. There are two types of data available: data at the individual, or micro, level, as in the case of the smoker example, and data at the group level. We will first consider the case of individual level data.

### Individual level data

For our smoker example, we have data on 1,196 individuals. Therefore, although the logit model is linear, it cannot be estimated by the usual OLS method. To see why, note that $P_i = 1$ if a person smokes, and $P_i = 0$ if a person does not smoke. But if we put these values directly in the logit $L_i$, we obtain expressions like $L_i = \ln(1/0)$ if a person smokes and $L_i = \ln(0/1)$ if a person does not smoke. These are undefined expressions. Therefore, to estimate the logit model we have to resort to alternative estimation methods. The most popular method with attractive statistical properties is the method of **maximum likelihood** (**ML**). We briefly discussed this method in Chapter 1, but further details of ML can be found in the references.[9] Most modern statistical packages have established routines to estimate parameters by the ML method.

We will first present the results of ML estimation for the smoker example, which are obtained from *Eviews* (Table 8.3).

**Table 8.3  Logit model of to smoke or not to smoke.**

Dependent Variable: SMOKER
Method: ML – Binary Logit (Quadratic hill climbing)
Sample: 1 1196
Included observations: 1196
Convergence achieved after 3 iterations
QML (Huber/White) standard errors & covariance

|  | Coefficient | Std. Error | z-Statistic | Prob. |
|---|---|---|---|---|
| C | 2.745077 | 0.821765 | 3.340462 | 0.0008 |
| AGE | −0.020853 | 0.003613 | −5.772382 | 0.0000 |
| EDUC | −0.090973 | 0.020548 | −4.427431 | 0.0000 |
| INCOME | 4.72E−06 | 7.27E−06 | 0.649033 | 0.5163 |
| PCIGS79 | −0.022319 | 0.012388 | −1.801626 | 0.0716 |

| | | | |
|---|---|---|---|
| McFadden R-squared | 0.029748 | Mean dependent var | 0.380435 |
| S.D. dependent var | 0.485697 | S.E. of regression | 0.477407 |
| Akaike info criterion | 1.297393 | Sum squared resid | 271.4495 |
| Schwarz criterion | 1.318658 | Log likelihood | −770.8409 |
| LR statistic | 47.26785 | Restr. log likelihood | −794.4748 |
| Prob(LR statistic) | 0.000000 | Avg. log likelihood | −0.644516 |
| Obs with Dep=0 | 741 | Total obs | 1196 |
| Obs with Dep=1 | 455 | | |

---

9  For an accessible discussion of ML, see Gujarati/Porter, *op cit.*

III

Let us examine these results. The variables age and education are highly statistically significant and have the expected signs. As age increases, the value of the logit decreases, perhaps due to health concerns – that is, as people age, they are less likely to smoke. Likewise, more educated people are less likely to smoke, perhaps due to the ill effects of smoking. The price of cigarettes has the expected negative sign and is significant at about the 7% level. *Ceteris paribus*, the higher the price of cigarettes, the lower is the probability of smoking. Income has no statistically visible impact on smoking, perhaps because expenditure on cigarettes may be a small proportion of family income.

The interpretation of the various coefficients is as follows: holding other variables constant, if, for example, education increases by one year, the average logit value goes down by $\approx 0.09$, that is, the log of odds in favor of smoking goes down by about 0.09. Other coefficients are interpreted similarly.

But the logit language is not everyday language. What we would like to know is the probability of smoking, given values of the explanatory variables. But this can be computed from Eq. (8.7). To illustrate, take smoker #2 from **Table 8.1** also. His data are as follows: age = 28, educ = 15, income = 12,500 and pcigs79 = 60.0. Inserting these values in Eq. (8.7), we obtain:

$$P = \frac{1}{1 + e^{-(-0.4935)}} \approx 0.3782$$

That is, the probability that a person with the given characteristics is a smoker is about 38%. From our data we know that this person is a smoker.

Now take a person with age, educ, income, and pcigs79 of 63, 10, 20,000, and 60.8, respectively. For this person, the probability of smoking is

$$P = \frac{1}{1 + e^{-(-0.7362)}} = 0.3227$$

That is, the probability of this person being a smoker is 32%. In our sample such a person is nonsmoker.

**Table 8.1** gives the probability of smoking for each person along with the raw data.

Can we compute the marginal effect of an explanatory variable on the probability of smoking, holding all other variables constant? Suppose we want to find out $\partial P_i / \partial Age_i$, the effect of a unit change in age on the probability of smoking, holding other variables constant. This was very straightforward in the LPM, but it is not that simple with logit or probit models. This is because the change in probability of smoking if age changes by a unit (say, a year) depends not only on the coefficient of the age variable but also on the level of probability from which the change is measured. But the latter depends on values of all the explanatory variables. For details of these computations the reader is referred to the references, although *Eviews* and *Stata* can do this job readily.[10]

The conventional measure of goodness of fit, $R^2$, is not very meaningful when the dependent variable takes values of 1 or 0. Measures similar to $R^2$, called **pseudo $R^2$**, are discussed in the literature. One such measure is the McFadden $R^2$, called $R^2_{McF}$. Like $R^2$, $R^2_{McF}$ lies between 0 and 1. For our example, its value is 0.0927.

Another goodness of fit measure is the **count $R^2$**, which is defined as

---

10  See, for instance, Gujarati/Porter, *op cit.*

$$\text{Count } R^2 = \frac{\text{number of correct predictions}}{\text{total number of observations}} \qquad (8.12)$$

Since the dependent variable takes a value of 1 or 0, if the predicted probability for an observation is greater than 0.5 we classify that observation as 1, but if is less than 0.5, we classify that as 0. We then count the number of correct predictions and the count $R^2$ as defined above (see Exercise 8.3).

It should be emphasized that in binary regression models goodness of fit measures are of secondary importance. What matters are the expected signs of the regression coefficients and their statistical and or practical significance. From Table 8.3 we can see that except for the income coefficient, all other coefficients are individually statistically significant, at least at the 10% level. We can also test the null hypothesis that all the coefficients are simultaneously zero with the **likelihood ratio (LR) statistic**, which is the equivalent of the $F$ test in the linear regression model.[11] Under the null hypothesis that none of the regressors are significant, the LR statistic follows the chi-square distribution with df equal to the number of explanatory variables: four in our example.

As Table 8.3 shows, the value of the LR statistic is about 47.26 and the *p value* (i.e. the exact significance level) is practically zero, thus refuting the null hypothesis. Therefore we can say that the four variables included in the logit model are important determinants of smoking habits.

▲ **Technical Note 1**: Table 8.3 gives two log likelihood statistics – unrestricted likelihood (= −770.84) and restricted likelihood (−794.47). The latter is obtained by assuming that there are no regressors in the model, only the intercept term, whereas the unrestricted likelihood is the value obtained with all the regressors (including the intercept) in the model. The likelihood ratio statistic (=λ) of about 47.27 shown in Table 8.3 is computed from the formula given in the Appendix to Chapter 1. For our example, the computed likelihood ratio of 47.27 is highly significant, for its *p* value is practically zero.[12] This is to say that it is the unrestricted model that includes all the regressors is appropriate in the present instance. To put it differently, the restricted model is not valid in the present case.

▲ **Technical Note 2**: Note that the Huber/White standard errors reported in Table 8.3 are not necessarily robust to heteroscedasticity but are robust to certain misspecification of the underlying probability distribution of the dependent variable.

*Model refinement*

The logit model given in Table 8.3 can be refined. For example, we can allow for the interaction effect between the explanatory variables. Individually education has negative impact and income has positive impact on the probability of smoking, although the latter effect is not statistically significant. But what is the combined influence of education and income on the probability of smoking? Do people with a higher level of

---

11　In the maximum likelihood Appendix to Chapter 1 we have discussed why we use the LR statistic.

12　As noted in the Appendix to Chapter 1, under the null hypothesis that the coefficients of all regressors in the model are zero, the LR statistic follows the chi-square distribution with df equal to the number of regressors (excluding the intercept), 4 in our example.

Table 8.4  **The logit model of smoking with interaction.**

Dependent Variable: SMOKER
Method: ML – Binary Logit (Quadratic hill climbing)
Sample: 1 1196
Included observations: 1196
Convergence achieved after 10 iterations
Covariance matrix computed using second derivatives

|  | Coefficient | Std. Error | z-Statistic | Prob. |
|---|---|---|---|---|
| C | 1.093186 | 0.955676 | 1.143887 | 0.2527 |
| AGE | −0.018254 | 0.003794 | −4.811285 | 0.0000 |
| EDUC | 0.039456 | 0.042511 | 0.928140 | 0.3533 |
| INCOME | 9.50E−05 | 2.69E−05 | 3.535155 | 0.0004 |
| PCIGS79 | −0.021707 | 0.012530 | −1.732484 | 0.0832 |
| EDUC*INCOME | −7.45E−06 | 2.13E−06 | −3.489706 | 0.0005 |

| | | | |
|---|---|---|---|
| McFadden R-squared | 0.037738 | Mean dependent var | 0.380435 |
| S.D. dependent var | 0.485697 | S.E. of regression | 0.475290 |
| Akaike info criterion | 1.288449 | Sum squared resid | 268.8219 |
| Schwarz criterion | 1.313968 | Log likelihood | −764.4926 |
| LR statistic | 59.96443 | Restr. log likelihood | −794.4748 |
| Prob(LR statistic) | 0.000000 | Avg. log likelihood | −0.639208 |
| Obs with Dep=0 | 741 | Total obs | 1196 |
| Obs with Dep=1 | 455 | | |

education and higher level of income smoke less or more than people with other characteristics?

To allow for this, we can introduce the multiplicative or interactive effect of the two variables as an additional explanatory variable. The results are given in Table 8.4.

These results are interesting. In Table 8.3 individually education had a significant negative impact on the logit (and therefore on the probability of smoking) and income had no statistically significant impact. Now education by itself has no statistically significant impact on the logit, but income has highly significant positive impact. But if you consider the interactive term, education multiplied by income, it has significant negative impact on the logit. That is, persons with higher education who also have higher incomes are less likely to be smokers than those who are more educated only or have higher incomes only. What this suggests is that the impact of one variable on the probability of smoking may be attenuated or reinforced by the presence of other variable(s).

The reader is encouraged to see if there are any other interactions among the explanatory variables.

## Logit estimation for grouped data

Suppose we group the smoker data into 20 groups of approximately 60 observations each. For each group we find out the number of smokers, say $n_i$. We divide $n_i$ by 60 to get an estimate of the (empirical) probability of smokers for that group, say, $p_i$. Therefore, we have 20 estimated $p_i$s. We can then use these probabilities to estimate the logit regression Eq. (8.11) by OLS.

Unless the data are already available in grouped form, forming groups in the manner suggested in the preceding paragraph has problems. *First*, we have to decide how many groups to form. If we form too few groups, we will have very few $p_i$ to estimate Eq. (8.11). On the other hand, if we form too many groups, we will have only a few observations in each group, which might make it difficult to estimate the $p_i$s efficiently.

*Second*, even if we have the "right" number of groups, one problem with the grouped logit estimation is that the error term in Eq. (8.11) is heteroscedastic. So we will have to take care of heteroscedasticity by suitable transformation or use White's robust standard errors, a topic discussed in Chapter 5.

We will not illustrate the grouped logit estimation with the smoker data for the reasons discussed above. Besides, we have data at the micro-level and we can use the ML method to estimate the logit model, as we have shown earlier (but see Exercise 8.4).

## 8.4    The probit model

In the LPM the error term has non-normal distribution; in the logit model the error term has the logistic distribution. Another rival model is the **probit model**, in which the error term has the normal distribution. Given the assumption of normality, the probability that $I_i^*$ is less than or equal to $I_i$ can be computed from the **standard normal cumulative distribution function (CDF)**[13] as:

$$P_i = \Pr(Y = 1 \mid X) = \Pr(I_i^* \le I_i) = \Pr(Z_i \le BX) = F(BX) \tag{8.13}$$

where $\Pr(Y|X)$ means the probability that an event occurs (i.e. smoking) given the values of the $X$ variables and where $Z$ is the standard normal variable (i.e. a normal variable with zero mean and unit variance). $F$ is the standard normal CDF, which in the present context can be written as:

$$F(BX) = \frac{1}{\sqrt{2\pi}} \int_{-\infty}^{BX} e^{-z^2/2}\, dz \tag{8.14}$$

Since $P$ represents the probability that a person smokes, it is measured by the area of the standard CDF curve from $-\infty$ to $I_i$. In the present context, $F(I_i)$ is called the **probit function**.

Although the estimation of the utility index $BX$ and the $B$s is rather complicated in the probit model, the method of maximum likelihood can be used to estimate them. For our example, the ML estimates of the probit model are given in Table 8.5.

Although the numerical values of the logit and probit coefficients are different, qualitatively the results are similar: the coefficients of age, education, and price of cigarettes are individually significant at least at the 10% level. The income coefficient, however, is not significant.

There is a way of comparing the logit and probit coefficients. Although the standard logistic distribution (the basis of the logit) and the standard normal distribution (the basis of probit) both have a mean value of zero, their variances are different: 1 for

---

13  If a variable $X$ follows the normal distribution with mean $\mu$ and variance $\sigma^2$, its probability density function (PDF) is $f(X) = (1/\sigma\sqrt{2\pi})e^{-(X-\mu)^2/2\sigma^2}$ and its cumulative distribution function (CDF) is $F(X_0) = \int_{-\infty}^{X_0}(1/\sigma\sqrt{2\pi})e^{-(X-\mu)^2/2\sigma^2}\, dX$, where $X_0$ is a specified value of $X$. If $\mu = 0$ and $\sigma^2 = 1$, the resulting PDF and CDF represent the standard normal PDF and CDF, respectively.

## Table 8.5  Probit model of smoking.

Dependent Variable: SMOKER
Method: ML – Binary Probit (Quadratic hill climbing)
Sample: 1 1196
Included observations: 1196
Convergence achieved after 6 iterations
Covariance matrix computed using second derivatives

|  | Coefficient | Std. Error | z-Statistic | Prob. |
|---|---|---|---|---|
| C | 1.701906 | 0.510575 | 3.333315 | 0.0009 |
| AGE | −0.012965 | 0.002293 | −5.655439 | 0.0000 |
| EDUC | −0.056230 | 0.012635 | −4.450266 | 0.0000 |
| INCOME | 2.72E−06 | 4.40E−06 | 0.618642 | 0.5362 |
| PCIGS79 | −0.013794 | 0.007696 | −1.792325 | 0.0731 |

| | | | |
|---|---|---|---|
| McFadden R-squared | 0.030066 | Mean dependent var | 0.380435 |
| S.D. dependent var | 0.485697 | S.E. of regression | 0.477328 |
| Akaike info criterion | 1.296970 | Sum squared resid | 271.3598 |
| Schwarz criterion | 1.318236 | Log likelihood | −770.5881 |
| LR statistic | 47.77335 | Restr. log likelihood | −794.4748 |
| Prob(LR statistic) | 0.000000 | Avg. log likelihood | −0.644304 |
| Obs with Dep=0 | 741 | Total obs | 1196 |
| Obs with Dep=1 | 455 | | |

the standard normal distribution and $\pi^2/3$ for the logistic distribution, where $\pi \approx 22/7$, which is about 3.14. Therefore, if we multiply the probit coefficient by about 1.81 ($\approx \pi/\sqrt{3}$), you will get approximately the logit coefficient. For example, the probit coefficient of age is −0.0235. If you multiply this coefficient by 1.81, you will get $\approx$ −0.0233, which is directly comparable to the age coefficient in the logit model given in Table 8.3.

How do we interpret the coefficients of the probit model given in Table 8.5? For example, what is the marginal effect on the probability of smoking if age increases by a year, holding other variables constant? This marginal effect is given by the coefficient of the age variable, −0.0130, multiplied by the value of the normal density function evaluated for all the $X$ values for that individual.

To illustrate, consider the data for smoker number 1 in our sample, which are: age = 21, education = 12, income = 8,500, and pcigs 60.6. Putting these values in the standard normal density function given in footnote 13, we obtain: $f(BX) = 0.3983$. Multiplying this by −0.0130, we obtain −0.0051. This means that with the given values of the $X$ variables the probability that someone smokes decreases by about 0.005 if age increases by a year. Recall that we had a similar situation in computing the marginal effect of an explanatory variable on the probability of smoking in the logit model.

As you can see, computing the marginal effect of an explanatory variable on the probability of smoking of an individual in this fashion is a tedious job, although the *Stata* and *Eviews* statistical packages can do this job relatively quickly.

Incidentally, the probit estimates of the interaction effect as in the logit model are as shown in Table 8.6.

**Table 8.6 The probit model of smoking with interaction.**

Dependent Variable: SMOKER
Method: ML – Binary Probit (Quadratic hill climbing)
Sample: 1 1196
Included observations: 1196
Convergence achieved after 10 iterations
Covariance matrix computed using second derivatives

|  | Coefficient | Std. Error | z-Statistic | Prob. |
| --- | --- | --- | --- | --- |
| C | 0.682050 | 0.587298 | 1.161336 | 0.2455 |
| AGE | −0.011382 | 0.002332 | −4.880864 | 0.0000 |
| EDUC | 0.024201 | 0.025962 | 0.932180 | 0.3512 |
| INCOME | 5.80E−05 | 1.62E−05 | 3.588406 | 0.0003 |
| PCIGS79 | −0.013438 | 0.007723 | −1.739941 | 0.0819 |
| EDUC*INCOME | −4.55E−06 | 1.28E−06 | −3.551323 | 0.0004 |

| | | | |
| --- | --- | --- | --- |
| McFadden R-squared | 0.038139 | Mean dependent var | 0.380435 |
| S.D. dependent var | 0.485697 | S.E. of regression | 0.475190 |
| Akaike info criterion | 1.287917 | Sum squared resid | 268.7082 |
| Schwarz criterion | 1.313436 | Log likelihood | −764.1745 |
| Hannan–Quinn criter. | 1.297531 | Restr. log likelihood | −794.4748 |
| LR statistic | 60.60065 | Avg. log likelihood | −0.638942 |
| Prob(LR statistic) | 0.000000 | | |
| Obs with Dep=0 | 741 | Total obs | 1196 |
| Obs with Dep=1 | 455 | | |

As you can see, the results in Tables 8.4 and 8.6 are quite similar. But you will have to use the conversion factor of about 1.81 to make the probit coefficients directly comparable with the logit coefficients.[14]

In passing it may be noted that we can also estimate the probit model for grouped data, called grouped probit, similar to the grouped logit model. But we will not pursue it here.

## Logit vs. probit

Logit and probit models generally give similar results; the main difference between the two models is that the logistic distribution has slightly fatter tails; recall that the variance of a logistically distributed random variable is about $\pi^2/3$, whereas that of a (standard) normally distributed variable it is 1. That is to say, the conditional probability $P_i$ approaches 0 or 1 at a slower rate in logit than in probit. But in practice there is no compelling reason to choose one over the other. Many researchers choose the logit over the probit because of its comparative mathematical simplicity.

## 8.5 Summary and conclusions

In this chapter we discussed the simplest possible qualitative response regression model in which the dependent variable is binary, taking the value of 1 if an attribute is present and the value of 0 if that attribute is absent.

14 A similar conversion factor for comparing LPM and logit models is given in Exercise 8.1.

Although binary dependent variable models can be estimated by OLS, in which case they are known as linear probability models (LPM), OLS is not the preferred method of estimation for such models because of two limitations, namely, that the estimated probabilities from LPM do not necessarily lie in the bounds of 0 and 1 and also because LPM assumes that the probability of a positive response increases linearly with the level of the explanatory variable, which is counterintuitive. One would expect the rate of increase in probability to taper off after some point.

Binary response regression models can be estimated by the logit or probit models.

The logit model uses the logistic probability distribution to estimate the parameters of the model. Although seemingly nonlinear, the log of the odds ratio, called the logit, makes the logit model linear in the parameters.

If we have grouped data, we can estimate the logit model by OLS. But if we have micro-level data, we have to use the method of maximum likelihood. In the former case we will have to correct for heteroscedasticity in the error term.

Unlike the LPM, the marginal effect of a regressor in the logit model depends not only on the coefficient of that regressor but also on the values of all regressors in the model.

An alternative to logit is the probit model. The underlying probability distribution of probit is the normal distribution. The parameters of the probit model are usually estimated by the method of maximum likelihood.

Like the logit model, the marginal effect of a regressor in the probit model involves all the regressors in the model.

The logit and probit coefficients cannot be compared directly. But if you multiply the probit coefficients by 1.81, they are then comparable with the logit coefficients. This conversion is necessary because the underlying variances of the logistic and normal distribution are different.

In practice, the logit and probit models give similar results. The choice between them depends on the availability of software and the ease of interpretation.

# Exercises

**8.1**   To study the effectiveness of price discount on a six-pack of soft drink, a sample of 5,500 consumers was randomly assigned to 11 discount categories as shown in Table 8.7.[15]

  (a)  Treating the redemption rate as the dependent variable and price discount as the regressor, see whether the logit model fits the data.[16]

  (b)  See whether the probit model does as well as the logit model.

  (c)  Fit the LPM model to these data.

  (d)  Compare the results of the three models. Note that the coefficients of LPM and Logit models are related as follows:

Slope coefficient of LPM = 0.25* Slope coefficient of Logit

Intercept of LPM = 0.25* slope coefficient of Logit + 0.5.

---

**15**  The data are obtained from Douglas Montgomery and Elizabeth Peck from their book, *Introduction to Linear Regression Analysis*, John Wiley & Sons, New York, 1982, p. 243 (notation changed).

**16**  The redemption rate is the number of coupons redeemed divided by the number of observations in each price discount category.

**Table 8.7  The number of coupons redeemed and the price discount.**

| Price Discount (cents) | Sample size | Number of coupons redeemed |
|---|---|---|
| 5 | 500 | 100 |
| 7 | 500 | 122 |
| 9 | 500 | 147 |
| 11 | 500 | 176 |
| 13 | 500 | 211 |
| 15 | 500 | 244 |
| 17 | 500 | 277 |
| 19 | 500 | 310 |
| 21 | 500 | 343 |
| 23 | 500 | 372 |
| 25 | 500 | 391 |

**8.2   Table 8.8** (available on the companion website) gives data on 78 homebuyers on their choice between adjustable and fixed rate mortgages and related data bearing on the choice.[17]

The variables are defined as follows:

Adjust = 1 if an adjustable mortgage is chosen, 0 otherwise.
Fixed rate = fixed interest rate
Margin = (variable rate – fixed rate)
Yield = the 10-year Treasury rate less 1-year rate
Points = ratio of points on adjustable mortgage to those paid on a fixed rate mortgage
Networth = borrower's net worth

  (a)  Estimate an LPM of adjustable rate mortgage choice.
  (b)  Estimate the adjustable rate mortgage choice using logit.
  (c)  Repeat (b) using the probit model.
  (d)  Compare the performance of the three models and decide which is a better model.
  (e)  Calculate the marginal impact of Margin on the probability of choosing the adjustable rate mortgage for the three models.

**8.3**   For the smoker data discussed in the chapter, estimate the count $R^2$.

**8.4**   Divide the smoker data into 20 groups. For each group compute $p_i$, the probability of smoking. For each group compute the average values of the regressors and estimate the grouped logit model using these average values. Compare your results with the ML estimates of smoker logit discussed in the chapter. How would you obtain the heteroscedasticity-corrected standard errors for the grouped logit?

---

17  These data are obtained from the website of R. Carter Hill, William E. Griffiths and Guay C. Lim, *Principles of Econometrics*, 3rd edn, John Wiley & Sons, 2008.

# 9

# Multinomial regression models

In Chapter 8 we considered the logit and probit models in which the objective was to choose between two discrete choices: to smoke or not to smoke. Such models are called *dichotomous* or *binary regression models*. But there are many occasions where we may have to choose among several discrete alternatives. Such models are called **multinomial regression models (MRM)**. Some examples are:

1 Transportation choices: car, bus, railroad, bicycle
2 Choice of cereal brands
3 Choice of Presidential candidate: Democrat, Republican, or Independent
4 Choice of education: high school, college, postgraduate
5 Choice of MBA School: Harvard, MIT, Chicago, Stanford
6 Choice of job: do not work, work part time, or work full time.
7 Buying a car: American, Japanese, European

Of course, many more examples can be cited in which a consumer is faced with several choices.

How do we estimate models that involve choosing among several alternatives? In what follows we will consider some of the techniques that are commonly used in practice. But before we proceed, it may be noted that there are several names for such models: **polytomous** or **polychotomous (multiple category) regression models**. For discussion purposes we will use the term **multinomial models** for all these models.

## 9.1    The nature of multinomial regression models

At the outset we can distinguish between **nominal or unordered MRM** and **ordered MRM**. For example, the transportation choice is nominal MRM because there is no particular (natural) order among the various options. On the other hand, if one is responding to a questionnaire which makes a statement and asks you to respond on a three-response scale, such as do not agree, somewhat agree, completely agree, it is an example of an ordered MRM.

In this chapter we consider the nominal MRMs and discuss ordered MRMs in the next chapter.

Even within the nominal MRMs we have to distinguish three cases:

1 Nominal MRM for chooser-specific data
2 Nominal MRM for choice-specific data

3 Nominal MRM for chooser-specific and choice-specific data, or mixed nominal MRM

Note that we are using the term "chooser" to represent an individual or decision maker who has to choose among several alternatives. We use the term "choice" to represent the *alternatives* or *options* that face an individual. The context of the problem will make clear which term we have in mind.

## Nominal MRM for chooser or individual-specific data

In this model the choices depend on the characteristics of the chooser, such as age, income, education, religion, and similar factors. For example, in educational choices, such as secondary education, a two-year college education, a four-year college education and graduate school, age, family income, religion, and parents' education are some of the variables that will affect the choice. These variables are specific to the chooser.

These types of model are usually estimated by **multinomial logit** (MLM) or **multinomial probit models** (MPM).[1] The primary question these models answer is: *How do the choosers' characteristics affect their choosing a particular alternative among a set of alternatives?* Therefore MLM is suitable when regressors vary across individuals.

## Nominal MRM for choice-specific data

Suppose we have to choose among four types of cracker: Private label, Sunshine, Keebler, and Nabisco. We have data on the prices of these crackers, the displays used by these brands and the special features used by these brands. In other words, we have *choice-specific characteristics*. However, in this model we do not have individual-specific characteristics. Such models are usually estimated by **conditional logit** (CLM) or **conditional probit** (CPM) **models**. The main questions such models answer is: *how do the characteristics or features of various alternatives affect individuals' choice among them*? For example, do people buy cars based on features, such as color, shape, commercial advertising, and promotional features? Therefore, CLM or CPM is appropriate when regressors vary across alternatives.

The difference between MLM and CLM has been well summarized by Powers and Xie as follows:[2]

> In the standard multinomial logit model, explanatory variables are invariant with outcome categories, but their parameters vary with the outcome. In the conditional logit model, explanatory variables vary by outcome as well as by the individual, whereas their parameters are assumed constant over all outcome categories.

## Mixed MRM

Here we have data on both chooser-specific and choice-specific characteristics. Such models can also be estimated by the conditional logit model by adding appropriate

---

1  Because of their comparative mathematical complexity, in practice MLM are more frequently used than the MPM. Therefore, we will confine our discussion largely to MLM.

2  See Daniel A. Powers and Yu Xie, *Statistical Methods for Categorical Data Analysis*, 2d ed., Emerald Publishers, UK, 2008, p. 256.

dummy variables. For example, in choosing cars, features of the cars as well as the income and age of individuals may affect their choice of car.

Since the topic of multi-choice models is vast, we will only consider the basic essentials of MLM, CLM and MXL (mixed logit model) and refer the reader to references for additional discussion of these models.[3]

## 9.2    Multinomial logit model (MLM): school choice

To illustrate MLM, we consider an example about school choice. The data consists of 1,000 secondary school graduates who are facing three choices: no college, a 2-year college, and a 4-year college, which choices we code as 1, 2, and 3.[4] Note that we are treating these as nominal variables, although we could have treated them as ordered. See **Table 9.1** on the companion website.

How does a high school graduate decide among these choices? Intuitively, we could say that the choice will depend on the satisfaction (or utility in economist's jargon) that a student gets from higher education. He or she will choose the alternative that gives him or her the highest possible satisfaction. That choice, therefore, will have the highest probability of being chosen.

To see how this can be done, let

$Y_{ij} = 1$, if the individual $i$ chooses alternative $j$ ($j$ = 1, 2 and 3 in the present case)

= 0, otherwise

Further, let

$$\pi_{ij} = \Pr(Y_{ij} = 1)$$

where Pr stands for probability.

Therefore, $\pi_{i1}$, $\pi_{i2}$, $\pi_{i3}$ represent the probabilities that individual $i$ chooses alternative 1, 2, or 3, respectively – that is alternatives of no college, a 2-year college and a 4-year college. If these are the only alternatives an individual faces, then, obviously,

$$\pi_{i1} + \pi_{i2} + \pi_{i3} = 1 \tag{9.1}$$

This is because the sum of the probabilities of mutually exclusive and exhaustive events must be 1. We will call the $\pi$s the **response probabilities**.

This means that in our example if we determine any two probabilities, the third one is determined automatically. In other words, we *cannot* estimate the three probabilities independently.

Now what are the factors or variables that determine the probability of choosing a particular option? In our school choice example we have information on the following variables:

---

3  For a comprehensive discussion with several examples, see J. Scott Long and Jeremy Freese, *Regression Models for Categorical Dependent Variables Using Stata*, Stata Press, 2nd edn, Stata Corporation LP, College Station, Texas and William H. Greene, *Econometric Analysis*, 6th ed., Pearson/Prentice-Hall, New Jersey, 2008, Ch. 23.

4  The data are originally from the National Education Longitudinal Study of 1988 and are reproduced in R. Carter Hill, William E. Griffiths, and Guay C. Lim, *Principles of Econometrics*, 3rd edn, John Wiley & Sons, New York, 2008.

$X_2$ = hscath = 1 if Catholic school graduate, 0 otherwise

$X_3$ = grades = average grade in math, English, and social studies on a 13 point grading scale, with 1 for the highest grade and 13 for the lowest grade. Therefore, higher grade-point denotes poor academic performance

$X_4$ = faminc = gross family income in 1991 in thousands of dollars

$X_5$ = famsiz = number of family members

$X_6$ = parcoll= 1 if the most educated parent graduated from college or had an advanced degree

$X_7$ = 1 if female

$X_8$ = 1 if black

We will use $X_1$ to represent the intercept.

Notice some of the variables are qualitative or dummy ($X_2, X_6, X_7, X_8$) and some are quantitative ($X_3, X_4, X_5$). Also note that there will be some random factors that will also affect the choice, and these random factors will be denoted by the error term in estimating the model.

Generalizing the bivariate logit model discussed in Chapter 8, we can write the multinomial logit model (MLM) as:

$$\pi_{ij} = \frac{e^{\alpha_j + \beta_j X_i}}{\sum_{j=1}^{3} e^{\alpha_j + \beta_j X_i}} \tag{9.2}$$

Notice that we have put the subscript $j$ on the intercept and the slope coefficient to remind us that the values of these coefficients can differ from choice to choice. In other words, a high school graduate who does not want to go to college will attach a different weight to each explanatory variable than a high school graduate who wants to go to a 2-year college or a 4-year college. Likewise, a high school graduate who wants to go to a 2-year college but not to a 4-year college will attach different weights (or importance if you will) to the various explanatory variables.

Also, keep in mind that if we have more than one explanatory variable in the model, $X$ will then represent a vector of variables and then $\beta$ will be a vector of coefficients. So, if we decide to include the seven explanatory variables listed above, we will have seven slope coefficients and these slope coefficients may differ from choice to choice. In other words, the three probabilities estimated from Eq. (9.2) may have different coefficients for the regressors. *In effect, we are estimating three regressions.*

As we noted before, we cannot estimate all the three probabilities independently. The common practice in MLM is to choose one category or choice as the **base, reference** or **comparison category** and set its coefficient values to zero. So if we choose the first category (no college) and set $\alpha_1 = 0$ and $\beta_1 = 0$, we obtain the following estimates of the probabilities for the three choices:

$$\pi_{i1} = \frac{1}{1 + e^{\alpha_2 + \beta_2 X_i} + e^{\alpha_3 + \beta_3 X_i}} \tag{9.3}$$

$$\pi_{i2} = \frac{e^{\alpha_2 + \beta_2 X_i}}{1 + e^{\alpha_2 + \beta_2 X_i} + e^{\alpha_3 + \beta_3 X_i}} \tag{9.4}$$

$$\pi_{i3} = \frac{e^{\alpha_3 + \beta_3 X_i}}{1 + e^{\alpha_2 + \beta_2 X_i} + e^{\alpha_3 + \beta_3 X_i}} \tag{9.5}$$

It should be noted that although the same regressors appear in each (response) probability expression their coefficients will not be necessarily the same. Again keep in mind that if we have more than one regressor, the $X$ variables will represent a vector of variables and $\beta$ will represent a vector of coefficients.

If you add the three probabilities given in Eqs. (9.3), (9.4), and (9.5), you will get a value of 1, as it should because we have three mutually exclusive choices here.

The probability expressions given in Eqs. (9.3), (9.4), and (9.5) are highly nonlinear. But now consider the following expressions:

$$\ln\left(\frac{\pi_{i2}}{\pi_{i1}}\right) = \alpha_2 + \beta_2 X_i \tag{9.6}$$

$$\ln\left(\frac{\pi_{i3}}{\pi_{i1}}\right) = \alpha_3 + \beta_3 X_i \tag{9.7}$$

$$\pi_{i1} = 1 - \pi_{i2} - \pi_{i3} \tag{9.8}[5]$$

Expressions (9.6) and (9.7) are familiar from the bivariate logit model discussed in Chapter 8. That is, the logits are linear functions of the explanatory variable(s). Remember that logits are simply the logs of the **odds ratio**. And the odds tell by how much alternative $j$ is preferred over alternative $l$.

The question that arises now is: why not estimate the bivariate logits using the techniques we learned in Chapter 8? This is, however, not a recommended procedure for various reasons. *First*, each of the bivariate logits will be based on different sample size. Thus, if we estimate (9.6), observations for school choice 3 will be dropped. Similarly, if we estimate (9.7), observations for school choice 2 will be dropped. *Second*, individual estimation of the bivariate logits will not necessarily guarantee that the three estimated probabilities will add up to one, as they should. *Third*, the standard errors of the estimated coefficients will generally be smaller if all the logits are estimated together than if we were to estimate each logit independently.

It is for these reasons that models (9.6) and (9.7) are estimated simultaneously by the method of **maximum likelihood** (**ML**). For our example we first show the ML estimates obtained from *Stata* (Table 9.2) and then discuss the results.

At the outset note that we have chosen pschoice = 1 (no college) as the base category, although one can choose any category as the base category. If we choose another base, the coefficients given above will change. *But no matter what the choice of the base category, the estimated probabilities of the three choices will remain the same.*

The coefficients given in the above table are to be *interpreted in relation to the reference category*, 1 in the present example.

*Stata* output is divided into two panels: The first panel gives the values of the various coefficients of school choice 2 (2-year college) in relation to school choice 1 (no college). That is, it gives estimates of the logit (9.6) and the second panel of the table

---

5 From Eq. (9.6) $\ln \pi_{i2} - \ln \pi_{i1} = \alpha_2 + \beta_2 X_i$ and from Eq. (9.7) $\ln \pi_{i3} - \ln \pi_{i1} = \alpha_3 + \beta_3 X_i$. Therefore, $\ln(\pi_{i2} / \pi_{i3}) = (\alpha_2 - \alpha_3) + (\beta_2 - \beta_3)X_i$, which gives the log of the odds of choosing choice 2 over choice 3.

**Table 9.2  Multinomial logistic model of school choice.**

Multinomial logistic regression

Number of obs = 1000
LR chi2 (14) = 377.82
Prob > chi2 = 0.0000
Pseudo R2 = 0.1855

Log likelihood = −829.74657

| psechoice | Coef. | Std. Err. | z | P>|z| | [95% Conf. Interval] | |
|---|---|---|---|---|---|---|
| **2** | | | | | | |
| hscath | −.9250111 | 7103556 | −0.00 | 1.000 | −1.39e+07 | 1.39e+07 |
| grades | −.2995178 | .0558307 | −5.36 | 0.000 | −.4089439 | −.1900917 |
| faminc | .0098115 | .0041953 | 2.34 | 0.019 | .0015888 | .0180342 |
| famsiz | −.0971092 | .0726264 | −1.34 | 0.181 | −.2394543 | .045236 |
| parcoll | .5264485 | .2899096 | 1.82 | 0.069 | −.0417638 | 1.094661 |
| female | .1415074 | .1961643 | 0.72 | 0.471 | −.2429676 | .5259824 |
| black | .5559303 | .4296774 | 1.29 | 0.196 | −.286222 | 1.398083 |
| _cons | 2.268805 | .5782357 | 3.92 | 0.000 | 1.135484 | 3.402126 |
| **3** | | | | | | |
| hscath | 31.86893 | 5023750 | 0.00 | 1.000 | −9846337 | 9846400 |
| grades | −.6983134 | .0574492 | −12.16 | 0.000 | −.8109118 | −.5857151 |
| faminc | .0148592 | .0041223 | 3.60 | 0.000 | .0067797 | .0229387 |
| famsiz | −.0665881 | .0720734 | −0.92 | 0.356 | −.2078494 | .0746732 |
| parcoll | 1.024194 | .2773905 | 3.69 | 0.000 | .4805189 | 1.56787 |
| female | −.0575686 | .1964295 | −0.29 | 0.769 | −.4425633 | .3274262 |
| black | 1.495133 | .4170371 | 3.59 | 0.000 | .6777555 | 2.312511 |
| _cons | 5.008016 | .5671225 | 8.83 | 0.000 | 3.896476 | 6.119556 |

(psechoice==1 is the base outcome)

gives similar information for school choice 3 (a 4-year college) in relation to choice 1 (no college). That is, it gives estimates of the logit (9.7).

Before we interpret these results, let us look at the statistical significance of the estimated coefficients. Since the sample size is quite large, we use $z$ (standard normal) rather than the $t$ statistic to test the statistical significance.[6] The above table gives the $z$ values as well as the $p$ values (the exact level of significance) of these $z$ values. In Panel 1 grades, family income, and parental education and in Panel 2 grades, family income, parental education, and black variables are statistically significant.

In multiple regressions we use $R^2$ as a measure of goodness of fit of the chosen model. The $R^2$ value lies between 0 and 1. The closer is $R^2$ to 1, the better is the fit. But the usual $R^2$ does not work well for MLM.[7] However, a *pseudo $R^2$* measure is developed by McFadden, which is defined as:

$$pseudo\ R^2 = 1 - \frac{\ln L_{\text{fit}}}{\ln L_0} \tag{9.9}$$

---

**6** Recall that as the sample size increases indefinitely the $t$ distribution converges to the normal distribution.

**7** This is generally true of all nonlinear (in the parameter) regression models.

where $L_{ft}$ = likelihood ratio for the fitted model and $L_0$ = likelihood ratio for the model without any explanatory variables. For our example the *pseudo $R^2$* is about 0.1855.

Instead of the *pseudo $R^2$* we can use the likelihood ratio test, which is generally computed when we use the ML method. Under the null hypothesis that none of slope coefficients are statistically significant, the computed LR follow the chi-square $(\chi^2)$ distribution with df equal to the total number of slope coefficients estimated, 14 in the present case. The estimated LR of $\approx 377$ is highly statistically significant, its $p$ value being practically zero. This suggests that the model we have chosen gives a good fit, although not every slope coefficient is statistically significant.

How do we interpret the results given in the preceding table? There are various ways of interpreting these results, which are described below.

## Interpretation in terms of odds

Take, for example, Eq. (9.6), which gives the log of the odds (i.e. logit) in favor of school choice 2 over school choice 1 – that is, a 2-year college over no college. A positive coefficient of a regressor suggests increased odds for choice 2 over choice 1, holding all other regressors constant. Likewise, a negative coefficient of a regressor implies that the odds in favor of no college are greater than a 2-year college. Thus, from Panel 1 of Table 9.2 we observe that if family income increases, the odds of going to a 2-year college increase compared to no college, holding all other variables constant. Similarly, the negative coefficient of the grades variable implies that the odds in favor of no college are greater than a 2-year college, again holding all other variables constant (remember how the grades are coded in this example.) Similar interpretation applies to the second panel of the Table 9.2.

To be concrete, let us interpret the coefficient of grade point average. *Holding other variables constant*, if the grade point average increases by one unit, the logarithmic chance of preferring a 2-year college over no college goes down by about 0.2995. In other words, −0.2995 gives the change in $\ln(\pi_{2i} / \pi_{1i})$ for a unit change in the grade average. Therefore, if we take the anti-log of $\ln(\pi_{2i} / \pi_{1i})$, we obtain $\pi_{2i} / \pi_{1i} = e^{-0.2995} = 0.7412$. That is, the odds in favor of choosing a 2-year college over no college are only about 74%. This outcome might sound counterintuitive, but remember a higher grade point on a 13-point scale means poor academic performance. Incidentally, the odds are also known as the **relative risk ratios (LRR)**.

## Interpretation in terms of probabilities

Once the parameters are estimated, one can compute the three probabilities shown in Eqs. (9.3), (9.4), and (9.5), which is the primary objective of MLM. Since we have 1,000 observations and 7 regressors, it would be tedious to estimate these probabilities for all the individuals. However, with appropriate command, *Stata* can compute such probabilities. But this task can be minimized if we compute the three probabilities at the mean values of the eight variables. The estimated probabilities for 1,000 individuals are given in the data table.

To illustrate, for individual #10, a white male whose parents did not have advanced degrees and who did not go to a Catholic school, had an average grade of 6.44, family income of 42.5, and family size 6, his probabilities of choosing option 1 (no college), or option 2 (a 2-year college) or option 3 (a 4-year college) were, respectively, 0.2329, 0.2773 and 0.4897; these probabilities add to 0.9999 or almost 1 because of rounding errors. Thus, for this individual the highest probability was about 0.49 (i.e. a 4-year college). This individual did in fact choose to go to a 4-year college.

Of course, it is not the case that the estimated probabilities actually matched the choices actually made by the individuals. In several cases the actual choice was different from the estimated probability of that choice. That is why it is better to calculate the choice probabilities at the mean values of the variables. We leave it for the reader to compute these probabilities.[8]

## Marginal effects on probability

We can find out the impact of a unit change in the value of a regressor on the choice probability, holding all other regressors values constant. That is, we can find out $\partial \pi_{ij} / \partial X_{ik}$, which is the partial derivative of $\pi_{ij}$ with respect to the $k$th explanatory variable. However, the marginal impact calculations are complicated. Not only that, the marginal impact of $X_k$ on the choice probability may have a different sign than the sign of the coefficient of $X_k$. This happens because in MLM all the parameters (not just the coefficient of $X_k$) are involved in the computation of the marginal impact of $X_k$ on the choice probability.[9]

It is for this reason that in practice it is better to concentrate on the odds or relative risk ratios.

## A word of caution in the use of MLM: the independence of irrelevant alternatives (IIA)

A critical assumption of MLM is that the error term in estimating $\pi_{ij}$, the choice probability for individual $i$ for alternative $j$, is independent of the error term in estimating $\pi_{ik}$, the choice probability for individual $i$ for alternative $k$ ($k \neq j$). This means that the alternatives facing an individual must be sufficiently different from each other. This is what is meant by IIA. *Stated differently, IIA requires that in comparing alternative $j$ and $k$, the other alternatives are irrelevant.*

To see how the IIA assumption can be violated, we can consider the classic "red bus, blue bus" paradox. Suppose a commuter has two choices: travel by car or travel by bus. The choice probability here is $\frac{1}{2}$. Therefore, the ratio of the two probabilities is 1.

Now suppose another bus service is introduced that is similar in all attributes, but that it is painted in red color whereas the previous bus was painted in blue color. In this case one would expect the choice probability to be $\frac{1}{3}$ for each mode of transportation. In practice, though, commuters may not care whether it is the red bus or the blue one. The choice probability for the car is still $\frac{1}{2}$, but the probability for each bus choice is $\frac{1}{4}$. As a result, the ratio of the choice probability for car and that for bus service is 2 instead of 1. Obviously, the assumption of IIA is violated because some of the choices are not independent, as required by IIA.

---

**8** The *mean* values for the explanatory variables for 1,000 observations are as follows: school choice 2.305, choice of Catholic school, 0.019, grade, 6.53039, family income, 51.3935, family size, 4.206, parents' higher education, 0.308, female, 0.496, black, 0.056, school choice 1, 0.222, school choice 2, 0.251, and school choice 3, 0.527.

**9** This can be seen from the following expression: $\partial \pi_{ij} / \partial X_{ik} = \pi_{ij}(\beta_j - \sum_{j=2}^{J} \pi_{ij}\beta_j)$.

The upshot of this example is that MLM models should not be considered if the alternatives are close substitutes.[10]

## 9.3    Conditional logit model (CLM)

As noted previously, MLM is appropriate when regressors vary across individuals and CLM is appropriate when regressors vary across choices. In CLM we cannot have regressors that vary across individuals.[11] Intuitively, we can see why. Suppose we have to choose among four alternatives for transportation to work, say, auto, train, water taxi, and bike, each with its own characteristics. If we also want to include the characteristics of an individual, such as, say, income, it will not be possible to estimate the coefficient of income because the income value of that individual will remain the same for all four means of transportation.

To estimate CLM, we rewrite (9.2) as follows:

$$\pi_{ij} = \frac{e^{\alpha + \beta X_{ij}}}{\sum_{m=1}^{m=J} e^{\alpha + \beta X_{im}}} \tag{9.10}$$

where $\pi_{ij}$ is the probability associated with the $j$th choice or alternative.

Note the critical difference between Eqs. (9.2) and (9.10): in Eq. (9.2) $\alpha$ and $\beta$ differ from choice to choice, hence the $j$ subscript on them, whereas in Eq. (9.10) there is no subscript on them. That is, in Eq. (9.10) there is a single intercept and a single slope coefficient (or a vector of slope coefficients if there is more than one regressor). Another difference between the MLM and CLM is that the regressors have two subscripts ($i$ and $j$) in CLM, whereas in MLM there is only subscript ($i$). In the MLM the $i$ subscript varies from individual to individual (e.g. the income variable in the school choice model), but remains the same across the alternatives. In CLM, on the other hand, the $j$ subscript for an individual varies across the alternatives.

Like the MLM, CLM is also estimated by the method of maximum likelihood. As in the MLM, and for ease of interpretation, CLM can be expressed in logit form as:

$$\log\left(\frac{\pi_{ij}}{\pi_{ik}}\right) = (X_{ij} - X_{ik})' \beta \tag{9.11}$$

This equation states that the log-odds between alternatives $j$ and $k$ is proportional to the difference between the subject's values on the regressors, the difference being weighted by the estimated regression coefficient or coefficients if there is more than one regressor, in which case $\beta$ will represent a vector of coefficients.

Before we proceed further, we consider a concrete example.

---

10  Hausman and McFadden have developed a test of the IIA hypothesis, but Long and Freese, *op cit.*, (p. 244) do not encourage this test. One can allow for correlation in the error terms of the choice probabilities by considering the *multinomial probit model.* But because it is complicated, in practice researchers prefer MLM.

11  But if we consider mixed MLM (=MXL), we can allow for individual characteristic by making use of appropriate dummy variables, as discussed in Section 9.4.

## Choice of travel mode

A common problem facing a traveler is to decide the means of transportation. This problem was studied by Greene and Hensher, among others.[12] The data here consists of 840 observations on 4 modes of travel for 210 individuals. The variables used in the analysis are as follows:

Mode = Choice: air, train, bus or car

Time = Terminal waiting time, 0 for car

Invc = In-vehicle cost–cost component

Invt = Travel time in vehicle

GC = Generalized cost measure[13]

Hinc = Household income

Psize = Party size in mode chosen

See **Table 9.3** on the companion website.

Time, invc, invt, and GC are choice-specific variables, for they vary among choices. Hinc and Psize are individual-specific variables and they cannot be included in the CLM because their values remain the same across the modes of transportation. Of course, if we consider the **mixed model,** we can include both choice-specific and individual-specific variables

We will first consider the CLM which only includes the choice-specific variables. As in the case of MLM, we use the method of maximum likelihood to estimate CLM. As in the MLM, we also estimate this model, treating one means of transportation as the reference choice.[14] We use car as the reference choice and consider the other choices in relation to car.

Using the clogit routine in Stata 10, we obtained the results shown in Table 9.4. Before interpreting these results, notice that all estimated coefficients are highly statistically significant, for their $p$ values are practically zero. The likelihood ratio statistic of about 213 is also highly significant; if we were to maintain that all the slope coefficients are simultaneously equal to zero, we can reject this hypothesis overwhelmingly.

The negative coefficients of termtime, invect, and traveltime make economic sense. If for instance, the travel mode that has longer waiting time at the terminal than travel by car, people will tend to choose less that mode of travel. Similarly, if the travel time is greater for one means of transportation than car, that mode of transportation is less likely to be chosen by the individual. The positive sign of travel cost, which includes the *opportunity cost*, also makes sense in that people will choose that mode of transportation that has lower opportunity cost than the car.

Air, train, and bus in Table 9.4 are choice-specific constants.

Another way of looking at the results presented in the preceding table is in terms of the odds ratios, which are shown in Table 9.5.

---

12 For a discussion of this study and the data, see http://pages.stern.nyu.edu/~wgreene/Text/econometric analysis.htm.

13 This equals the sum of Invc and Invt and the opportunity cost of the individual's time.

14 Remember that the sum of the probabilities of the four means of travel must be 1. Hence, we cannot estimate all the probabilities independently. Once we estimate probabilities of three modes of transportation (any three will do), the probability of the fourth mode is determined automatically.

**Table 9.4  Conditional logit model of travel mode.**

| Conditional (fixed-effects) logistic regression | | | Number of obs = 840 | | | |
|---|---|---|---|---|---|---|
| | | | LR chi2(7) = 213.23 | | | |
| | | | Prob > chi2 = 0.0000 | | | |
| Log likelihood = −184.50669 | | | Pseudo R2 = 0.3662 | | | |

| choice | Coef. | Std. Err. | z | P>\|z\| | [95% Conf. Interval] | |
|---|---|---|---|---|---|---|
| termtime | −.1036495 | .0109381 | −9.48 | 0.000 | −.1250879 | −.0822112 |
| invehiclec~t | −.0849318 | .0193825 | −4.38 | 0.000 | −.1229208 | −.0469428 |
| traveltime | −.0133322 | .002517 | −5.30 | 0.000 | −.0182654 | −.008399 |
| travelcost | .0692954 | .0174331 | 3.97 | 0.000 | .0351272 | .1034635 |
| air | 5.204743 | .9052131 | 5.75 | 0.000 | 3.430558 | 6.978928 |
| train | 4.360605 | .5106654 | 8.54 | 0.000 | 3.359719 | 5.36149 |
| bus | 3.763234 | .5062595 | 7.43 | 0.000 | 2.770984 | 4.755485 |

**Table 9.5  Conditional logit model of travel mode: odds ratios.**

| Conditional (fixed-effects) logistic regression | | | Number of obs = 840 | | | |
|---|---|---|---|---|---|---|
| | | | LR chi2(7) = 213.23 | | | |
| | | | Prob > chi2 = 0.0000 | | | |
| Log likelihood = −184.50669 | | | Pseudo R2 = 0.3662 | | | |

| choice | Odds Ratio | Std. Err. | z | P>\|z\| | [95% Conf. Interval] | |
|---|---|---|---|---|---|---|
| termtime | .9015412 | .0098612 | −9.48 | 0.000 | .8824193 | .9210774 |
| invehiclec~t | .9185749 | .0178043 | −4.38 | 0.000 | .8843337 | .954142 |
| traveltime | .9867563 | .0024837 | −5.30 | 0.000 | .9819004 | .9916362 |
| travelcost | 1.071753 | .0186839 | 3.97 | 0.000 | 1.035751 | 1.109005 |
| air | 182.134 | 164.8701 | 5.75 | 0.000 | 30.89387 | 1073.767 |
| train | 78.30446 | 39.98738 | 8.54 | 0.000 | 28.78109 | 213.0422 |
| bus | 43.08757 | 21.81349 | 7.43 | 0.000 | 15.97435 | 116.22 |

The interpretation of the odds ratios is as follows. Take, for example, the value of ≈ 0.99 of travel time. For any mode of transportation, holding other modes constant, increasing travel time by 1 minute decreases the odds of using that mode by a factor of 0.98 or 2%. Likewise, for any mode of transportation, holding the other modes constant, increasing the terminal time by 1 minute decreases the odds of that model by a factor of ≈ 0.90 or about 10%.

The alternative-specific constants, or intercepts, usually are not of interest except for estimating probabilities. The positive and statistically significant values of these constants suggest that the threshold values of travel by air, train and bus are distinct from the that of travel by car.

*Stata*'s **predict** command can be used to predict probabilities for each alternative for each individual, where the predicted probabilities sum to 1 for each individual. Remember that each traveler has a choice of four means of transportation. For example, the probabilities of traveling by air, train, bus, and car for the first traveler in our sample are: 0.06, 0.28, 0.12, and 0.54, respectively, the sum of these probabilities being 1. These probabilities would suggest that this traveler would probably choose travel by car. In actuality, he did choose to travel by car. Of course, this will not necessarily be true of all other travelers.

In addition to the odds ratio, we can also compute the marginal, or incremental, effect of a unit change in the value of a regressor on the choice probabilities, holding all other regressors constant. You will recall that in the multinomial logit model (MNL) all the (slope) parameters are involved in determining the marginal effect of a regressor on the probability of choosing the $m$th alternative. In the conditional logit model (CLM), on the other hand, the sign of $B_m$, the coefficient of the $m$th regressor, is the sign of the marginal effect of that regressor on the choice probability. The actual computations of these marginal effects can be done using the **asclogit routine** of *Stata*, which we do not pursue here.

## 9.4    Mixed logit (MXL)

As noted, in the MLM we consider only the subject-specific attributes, whereas in CLM we consider only the choice-specific attributes or characteristics. But in MXL we can include both sets of characteristics. In our travel data, we also have information about household income (hinc) and party size (psize), the number of people traveling together. These are subject-specific characteristics. To incorporate them in the analysis, MXL proceeds as follows:

Interact the subject-specific variables with the three modes of transportation, air, train, and bus, keeping in mind that car is the reference mode of transportation. In other words, multiply the subject-specific variables and the three modes of transportation as follows:

air*hinc, train*hinc, bus*hinc, air*psize, train*psize, and bus*psize.

Then use the clogit command of *Stata* to obtain Table 9.6.

Again to help us interpret these numbers, we will compute the odds ratio (Table 9.7).

The odds ratio for terminal time, in-vehicle time, and travel time show that a unit increase in each of these values reduces the attractiveness of that means of transportation compared with travel by car. If you look at the odds ratio of the interaction variables, we see, for instance, that a unit increase in family income, decreases the odds of travelling by train by about 5.75% [(1 − 0.94250) × 100], holding all else constant. Similarly, if the party size increases by one member, the odds of travelling by air decreases by about 60.25% [(1 − 0.3975) × 100], *ceteris paribus*.

We leave it for the reader to interpret the other odds coefficient.

## 9.5    Summary and conclusions

In this chapter we considered three models, multinomial logit (MNL), conditional logit (CL), and mixed logit (MXL) models. Faced with several choices in a variety of situations, these models attempt to estimate the choice probabilities, that is, probabilities of choosing the best alternative, best in the sense of maximizing the utility or satisfaction of the decision maker.

**Table 9.6  Mixed conditional logit model of travel mode.**

Iteration 0: log likelihood = −186.1019
Iteration 1: log likelihood = −172.82527
Iteration 2: log likelihood = −172.46893
Iteration 3: log likelihood = −172.46795
Iteration 4: log likelihood = −172.46795
Conditional (fixed-effects) logistic regression        Number of obs = 840
                                                        LR chi2(12) = 237.31
                                                        Prob > chi2 = 0.0000
Log likelihood = −172.46795                             Pseudo R2 = 0.4076

| choice | Coef. | Std. Err. | z | P>|z| | [95% Conf. Interval] | |
|---|---|---|---|---|---|---|
| termtime | −.1011797 | .0111423 | −9.08 | 0.000 | −.1230182 | −.0793412 |
| invehiclec~t | −.00867 | .0078763 | −1.10 | 0.271 | −.0241073 | .0067673 |
| traveltime | −.0041307 | .0008928 | −4.63 | 0.000 | −.0058806 | −.0023808 |
| air | 6.03516 | 1.138187 | 5.30 | 0.000 | 3.804355 | 8.265965 |
| train | 5.573527 | .7112915 | 7.84 | 0.000 | 4.179422 | 6.967633 |
| bus | 4.504675 | .7957919 | 5.66 | 0.000 | 2.944952 | 6.064399 |
| airXinc | .0074809 | .0132027 | 0.57 | 0.571 | −.0183959 | .0333577 |
| trainXinc | −.0592273 | .0148923 | −3.98 | 0.000 | −.0884157 | −.0300388 |
| busXinc | −.0208984 | .0163505 | −1.28 | 0.201 | −.0529448 | .0111481 |
| airXpartys | −.9224203 | .2585064 | −3.57 | 0.000 | −1.429084 | −.415757 |
| trainXparty | .2162726 | .233638 | 0.93 | 0.355 | −.2416494 | .6741945 |
| busXparty | −.1479247 | .3427697 | −0.43 | 0.666 | −.819741 | .5238915 |

**Table 9.7  Mixed conditional logit model of travel mode: odds ratios.**

Conditional (fixed-effects) logistic regression        Number of obs = 840
                                                        LR chi2(12) = 237.31
                                                        Prob > chi2 = 0.0000
Log likelihood = −172.46795                             Pseudo R2 = 0.4076

| choice | Odds Ratio | Std. Err. | z | P>|z| | [95% Conf. Interval] | |
|---|---|---|---|---|---|---|
| termtime | .9037706 | .0100701 | −9.08 | 0.000 | .8842476 | .9237247 |
| invehiclec~t | .9913675 | .0078083 | −1.10 | 0.271 | .976181 | 1.00679 |
| traveltime | .9958778 | .0008891 | −4.63 | 0.000 | .9941366 | .997622 |
| air | 417.8655 | 475.609 | 5.30 | 0.000 | 44.89628 | 3889.223 |
| train | 263.3614 | 187.3268 | 7.84 | 0.000 | 65.32806 | 1061.707 |
| bus | 90.43896 | 71.97059 | 5.66 | 0.000 | 19.00974 | 430.2639 |
| airXinc | 1.007509 | .0133018 | 0.57 | 0.571 | .9817723 | 1.03392 |
| trainXinc | .9424926 | .0140359 | −3.98 | 0.000 | .9153803 | .9704078 |
| busXinc | .9793185 | .0160124 | −1.28 | 0.201 | .9484324 | 1.01121 |
| airXpartys | .3975557 | .1027707 | −3.57 | 0.000 | .2395283 | .6598406 |
| trainXparty | 1.241441 | .2900477 | 0.93 | 0.355 | .7853314 | 1.962452 |
| busXparty | .862496 | .2956375 | −0.43 | 0.666 | .4405457 | 1.688586 |

In MLM the choice probabilities are based on individual characteristics, whereas in CLM these probabilities are based on choice-specific characteristics. In the MXL we incorporate both the individual and choice-specific characteristics.

All these models are estimated by the method of maximum likelihood, for these models are highly nonlinear.

Once these models are estimated, we can interpret the raw coefficients themselves or convert them into odds ratios, as the latter are easy to interpret. We can also assess the marginal contribution of regressors to the choice probability, although these calculations can sometimes be involved. However, statistical packages, such as *Stata*, can compute these marginal effects with comparative ease.

The main purpose of discussing these topics in this chapter was to introduce the beginner to the vast field of multi-choice models. The illustrative example in this chapter shows how one can approach these models. Once the basics are understood, the reader can move on to more challenging topics in this field by consulting the references.[15] It is beyond the scope of this book to cover the more advanced topics. But we will discuss one more topic in this area, the topic of **ordinal** or **ordered logit** in the next chapter.

In closing, a warning is in order. The models discussed in this chapter are based on the assumption of IIA, *independence of irrelevant alternatives*, which may not always be tenable in every case in practice. Recall the "red bus, blue bus" example we discussed earlier. Although one can use the Hausman-type tests to assess IIA, they do not always work well in practice. However, there are alternative techniques to deal with the IIA problem, for which we refer the reader to the Long-Freese and Greene texts cited earlier.

## Exercises

Several data sets are available on the websites of the books listed in the footnotes in this chapter. Access the data of your interest and estimate the various models discussed in this chapter so that you can be comfortable with the techniques discussed in the preceding pages.

---

15 See, Christiaan Heij, Paul de Boer, Philip Hans Franses, Teun Kloek and Herman K. van Dijk, *Econometrics Methods with Applications in Business and Economics*, Oxford University Press, Oxford, UK, 2004, Ch. 6; A. Colin Cameron and Pravin K. Trivedi, *Microeconometrics: Methods and Applications*, Cambridge University Press, New York, 2005, Ch. 15; Philip Hans Franses and Richard Papp, *Quantitative Models in Marketing Research*, Cambridge University Press, Cambridge, U.K., 2001, Chapter 5.

# 10

# Ordinal regression models

In Chapter 1 we discussed four types of variables that are commonly encountered in empirical analysis: *ratio scale, interval scale, ordinal scale*, and *nominal scale*. The earlier chapters largely discussed regression models that dealt with interval scale or ratio scale variables. In Chapter 8 we discussed binary nominal scale variables and in Chapter 9 we considered multi-category nominal scale variables. In this chapter we discuss regression models that involve ordinal scale variables.

In our travel example, discussed in the previous chapter, we considered four means of transportation – air, train, bus, and car. Although we labeled these means of transportation 1, 2, 3, and 4, we did not attribute ordinal properties to these numbers. They are simply nominal or category labels.

However, in many applications in the social and medical sciences the response categories are *ordered* or *ranked*. For example, in the Likert-type questionnaires the responses may be "strongly agree", "agree", "disagree", or "strongly disagree". Similarly, in labor market studies we may have workers who work full time (40+ hours per week), or who work part time (fewer than 20 hours per week) or who are not in the workforce. Another example is bond ratings provided by companies, such as Moody's or S&P. Corporate bonds are rated as B, B+, A, A+, A++, and so on, each higher rating denoting higher creditworthiness of the entity issuing the bonds.

Although there is clear ranking among the various categories, we cannot treat them as interval scale or ratio scale variables. Thus we cannot say that the difference between full-time work and part-time work or between part-time work and no work is the same. Also, the ratio between any two categories here may not be practically meaningful.

Although MLM models can be used to estimate ordinal-scale categories, they do not take into account the ordinal nature of the dependent variable.[1] The **ordinal logit** and **ordinal probit** are specifically developed to handle ordinal scale variables. Because of the mathematical complexity of the ordinal probit model, we will only discuss the ordinal logit model in this chapter. In practice it does not make a great difference whether we use ordinal probit or ordinal logit models.[2]

---

1  There are also technical reasons. Compared to MLM, ordinal logit or ordinal probit models are more parsimonious in that we need to estimate fewer parameters.

2  Several statistical packages have routines to estimate both these models. The difference between the two models lies in the probability distribution used to model the error term. The error term in the ordinal probit model is assumed to be normally distributed, whereas the error term in the ordinal logit model is assumed to follow the logistic distribution.

## 10.1    Ordered multinomial models (OMM)

Suppose we have the following model:

$$Y_i^* = B_1 X_{i1} + B_2 X_{i2} + \ldots + B_k X_{ik} + u_i$$

$$= \sum_{n=1}^{k} B_n X_{in} + u_i \qquad (10.1)$$

where $Y_i^*$ is unobserved, the $X$s are the regressors and $u_i$ is the error term.

$Y_i^*$ is often known as a **latent** or **index** variable. For example, it may denote the creditworthiness of a company, or happiness index of an individual. Although we cannot observe it directly, the latent variable depends on one or more regressors, such as diet, weight, or height of an individual in a medical study.[3]

Further suppose we have $n$ independent individuals (or observations) and they face *J-ordered* alternatives, such that

$$Y_i = 1, \text{if } Y_i^* \le a_1$$

$$Y_i = 2, \text{if } a_1 \le Y_i^* \le a_2$$

$$Y_i = 3, \text{if } a_2 \le Y_i^* \le a_3 \qquad (10.2)$$

$$\vdots$$

$$Y_i = J, \text{if } a_{j-1} \le Y_i^*$$

where $a_1 < a_2 < a_3 \ldots < a_{J-1}$.

That is, we observe an individual $Y_i$ in one of the $J$ ordered categories, these categories being separated by the **threshold parameters or cutoffs**, the $a$s. In other words, the threshold parameters demarcate the boundaries of the various categories. Returning to the bond rating example, if a bond is rated B, it will be in a lower category than a bond rated B+, which will lie below the category that gets an A− rating, and so on.

The ordered logit model estimates not only the coefficients of the $X$ regressors but also the threshold parameters. But note that the slope coefficients of the $X$ regressors are the same in each category; it is only that their intercepts (cutoffs) differ. In other words, we have *parallel regression lines*[4], but they are anchored on different intercepts.

That is why OLM are also known as **proportional odds models**.[5]

## 10.2    Estimation of ordered logit model (OLM)

The method of estimation, as in all multinomial regression models, is by the method of maximum likelihood. The underlying estimation principle is simple: we want to estimate

---

3   The latent variable is treated as continuous and the observed responses represent crude measurement of that variable. Even though we classify people as liberal or conservative, there is conceivably a continuum of conservative or liberal ideology.

4   More correctly, parallel regression surfaces.

5   For further details, see Daniel A. Powers and Yu Xie, *Statistical Methods for Categorical Data Analysis*, 2nd edn, Emerald Publishers, UK, 2008, p. 229.

$$Pr(Y_i \leq j) = Pr(B_1X_{1i} + B_2X_{2i} + \ldots + B_kX_{ki} + u_i \leq a_j)$$
$$= Pr(u_i \leq a_j - B_1X_{1i} - B_2X_{2i} - \ldots - B_kX_{ki}) \qquad (10.3)$$

That is, Eq. (10.3) gives the (cumulative) probability that $Y_i$ falls in a category $j$ and below (i.e. in category 1, 2, ..., or $j$).

Recall that to compute the probability that a random variable takes a value equal to or less than a given number, we use the *cumulative distribution function* (CDF) of probability distribution, the main question being: which probability distribution? As noted elsewhere, if the error term $u_i$ is assumed to follow the logistic distribution, we obtain the ordered logit model (OLM), but if it follows the normal distribution, we obtain the ordered probit model (OPM). For reasons stated earlier, we will estimate OLM.[6]

Models for ordered responses use cumulative probabilities as shown in Eq. (10.3). Now to compute such probabilities, we use

$$\frac{\exp(a_j - BX)}{1 + \exp(a_j - BX)} \qquad (10.4)[7]$$

which is the CDF of the logistic probability distribution. Note that $BX$ stands for $\Sigma_1^k B_k X_k$.

Now the effect of a regressor on the ordered dependent variable is nonlinear, as it gets channeled through a nonlinear CDF (logit in our case).[8] This makes interpretation of the OLM somewhat complicated. To make the interpretation easier, we can make use of the odds ratio.

Since the outcomes on the left-hand side of Eq. (10.2) reflect the ordering of the response scale, it is customary to consider the odds ratio defined by

$$\frac{Pr[Y_i \leq j | X]}{Pr[Y_i > j | X)} = \frac{Pr[Y_i \leq j | X]}{Pr[1 - Pr(Y_i \leq j | X)]} \qquad (10.5)$$

where

$$Pr[Y_i \leq j | X) = \sum_{m=1}^{j} Pr[Y_i = m | X] \qquad (10.6)$$

which denotes the cumulative probability that the outcome is less than or equal to $j$.

Now if we use the logistic CDF given in Eq. (10.4) to compute the odds ratio in Eq. (10.5) and take the log of this odds ratio (i.e. logit), we obtain, after simplification,

---

6  The following discussion is based on John Fox, *Applied Regression Analysis, Linear Models, and Related Methods,* Sage Publications, California, 1997, pp. 475–7, and Alan Agresti, *An Introduction to Categorical Data Analysis,* 2nd edn, Wiley, New York, 2007.

7  The PDF of a standard logistic distribution of variable $Y$ has mean of zero and a variance of $\pi^2 / 3$ and is given by $f(Y) = \exp(Y) / [1 + \exp(Y)]^2$ and its CDF is given by $F(Y) = \exp(Y) / [1 + \exp(Y)]$.

8  CDFs are elongated S-shaped curves, which are obviously nonlinear.

$$\text{logit}[\Pr(Y_i \le j)] = \ln\frac{\Pr_i(Y_i \le j)}{\Pr(Y_i > j)} = \ln\frac{\Pr(Y_i \le j)}{[1-\Pr(Y_i \le j)]}$$

$$= a_j - \sum_{n=1}^{K} B_n X_{in} \quad j = 1, 2, \ldots, (J-1)$$

(10.7)

(See the Appendix to this chapter for a derivation of this equation.)

Thus Eq. (10.7) gives a sequence of logits (or log odds; three such logits in the example discussed in Section 10.3), which all have the same regressors and the same (slope) coefficients but different intercepts. It is interesting to observe that the logit in Eq. (10.7) is linear in $a$ as well as $B$.

From Eq. (10.7) it is clear that all the regressors have the same impact on the (ordered) dependent variable, given by their $B$ coefficients, and the classification into the ordered categories shown in Eq. (10.2) depends on the cutoff or intercept coefficient, $a_j$. Notice that the $B$ coefficient has no $j$ subscript on it.

It is also clear from Eq. (10.7) why OLM is called a proportional-odds model because for given $X$ values any two cumulative log odds (i.e. logits) say, at categories $l$ and $m$, differ only by the constant $(a_l - a_m)$. Therefore, the odds are proportional, hence the name proportional odds model.

Before we proceed further, let us illustrate the ordered logit model with a concrete example.

## 10.3 An illustrative example: attitudes toward working mothers[9]

The 1977 and 1989 *General Social Survey* asked respondents to evaluate the following statement: *A working mother can establish just as warm and secure of relationship with her child as a mother who does not work.* Responses were recorded as: 1 = strongly disagree, 2 = disagree, 3 = agree, and 4 = strongly agree. In all 2,293 responses were obtained. For each respondent we have the following information: yr89 = survey year 1989, gender, male = 1, race, white = 1, age = age in years, ed = years of education, prst = occupational prestige.

Using the *ologit* command of *Stata 10*, we obtained the results in Table 10.1.

Before we interpret the results, let us look at the overall results. Recall that under the null hypothesis that all regressor coefficients are zero, the LR test follows the chi-square distribution with degrees of freedom equal to the number of regressors, 6 in the present case. In our example this chi-square value is about 302. If the null hypothesis were true, the chances of obtaining a chi-square value of as much as 302 or greater is practically zero. So collectively all the regressors have strong influence on the choice probability.

The model also gives the Pseudo $R^2$ of 0.05. This is not the same as the usual $R^2$ in OLS regression – that is, it is not a measure of the proportion of the variance in the regressand explained by the regressors included in the model. Therefore, the Pseudo $R^2$ value should be taken with a grain of salt.

---

9 The following data were obtained from http://www.stata-press.com/data/lf2/ordwarm2.dta, but the original data appear on http://www.ats.ucla.edu/stat/stata/dae.

## Table 10.1  OLM estimation of the warmth model.

ologit warm yr89 male white age ed prst
Iteration 0: log likelihood = −2995.7704
Iteration 1: log likelihood = −2846.4532
Iteration 2: log likelihood = −2844.9142
Iteration 3: log likelihood = −2844.9123
Ordered logistic regression          Number of obs = 2293
LR chi2(6) =                          301.72
Prob > chi2 =                         0.0000
Log likelihood = −2844.9123           Pseudo R2 = 0.0504

| warm | Coef. | Std. Err. | z | P>|z| | [95% Conf. Interval] | |
|------|-------|-----------|---|-------|----------|----------|
| yr89 | .5239025 | .0798988 | 6.56 | 0.000 | .3673037 | .6805013 |
| male | −.7332997 | .0784827 | −9.34 | 0.000 | −.8871229 | −.5794766 |
| white | −.3911595 | .1183808 | −3.30 | 0.001 | −.6231815 | −.1591374 |
| age | −.0216655 | .0024683 | −8.78 | 0.000 | −.0265032 | −.0168278 |
| ed | .0671728 | .015975 | 4.20 | 0.000 | .0358624 | .0984831 |
| prst | .0060727 | .0032929 | 1.84 | 0.065 | −.0003813 | .0125267 |
| /cut1 | −2.465362 | .2389126 | | | −2.933622 | −1.997102 |
| /cut2 | −.630904 | .2333155 | | | −1.088194 | −.173614 |
| /cut3 | 1.261854 | .2340179 | | | .8031873 | 1.720521 |

*Note*: cut1, cut2 and cut3, are respectively, the intercepts for the second, third and the fourth category, the intercept for the lowest category being normalized to zero.

The statistical significance of an individual regression coefficient is measured by the Z value (the standard normal distribution $Z$). All the regression coefficients, except prst, are individually highly statistically significant, their $p$ values being practically zero. Prst, however, is significant at the 7% level.

### Interpretation of the regression coefficients

The regression coefficients given in the preceding table are ordered log-odds (i.e. logit) coefficients. What do they suggest? Take, for instance, the coefficient of the education variable of $\approx 0.07$. If we increase the level of education by a unit (say, a year), the ordered log-odds of being in a higher warmth category increases by about $\approx 0.07$, holding all other regressors constant. This is true of warm category 4 over warm category 3 or of warm category 3 over 2 or warm category 2 over category 1. Other regression coefficients given in the preceding table are to be interpreted similarly.

Based on the regression results, you can sketch the regression lines for the four categories:[10] if the assumption of the proportional odds model is valid, the regression lines will be all parallel. By convention, one of the categories is chosen as the reference category and its intercept value is fixed at zero.

In practice it is often useful to compute the odds-ratios to interpret the various coefficients. This can be done easily by exponentiating (i.e. raising e to a given power) the estimated regression coefficients. To illustrate, take the coefficient of the education variable of 0.07. Exponentiating this we obtain $e^{0.07} = 1.0725$. This means if we

---

10  Actually you can do it only for a regressor at a time; there is no way to visualize the regression surface involving six regressors on a two-dimensional surface.

Table 10.2  **Odds ratios of the warm example.**

```
ologit warm yr89 male white age ed prst, or
Iteration 0: log likelihood = −2995.7704
Iteration 1: log likelihood = −2846.4532
Iteration 2: log likelihood = −2844.9142
Iteration 3: log likelihood = −2844.9123
Ordered logistic regression          Number of obs = 2293
LR chi2(6) =                         301.72
Prob > chi2 =                        0.0000
Log likelihood = −2844.9123          Pseudo R2 = 0.0504
```

| warm | Odds Ratio | Std. Err. | z | P>|z| | [95% Conf. Interval] | |
|------|-----------|-----------|-----|-------|--------------|----------|
| yr89 | 1.688605 | .1349175 | 6.56 | 0.000 | 1.443836 | 1.974867 |
| male | .4803214 | .0376969 | −9.34 | 0.000 | .4118389 | .5601915 |
| white | .6762723 | .0800576 | −3.30 | 0.001 | .5362357 | .8528791 |
| age | .9785675 | .0024154 | −8.78 | 0.000 | .9738449 | .983313 |
| ed | 1.06948 | .0170849 | 4.20 | 0.000 | 1.0365131 | .103496 |
| prst | 1.006091 | .003313 | 1.84 | 0.065 | .9996188 | 1.012605 |
| /cut1 | −2.465362 | .2389126 | −2.933622 | −1.997102 | | |
| /cut2 | −.630904 | .2333155 | −1.088194 | −.173614 | | |
| /cut3 | 1.261854 | .2340179 | .8031873 | 1.720521 | | |

increase education by a unit, the odds in favor of higher warmth category over a lower category of warmth are greater than 1. We need not do these calculations manually, for packages like *Stata* can do this routinely by issuing the command in Table 10.2. (Note: 'or' stands for odds ratio.)

As you can see from these odds ratios, the odds of getting higher warmth ranking are lower if you are a male or a white person. The odds are about even for education and parental education. The odds are higher for year 1989 compared to year 1977.

### Predicting probabilities

After estimating the ordered logit model in *Stata*, if you issue the command **Predict** (followed by the names of the four variables), you will get the estimated probabilities for all the 2,293 participants in the survey. For each participant there will be four probabilities, each for the four warmth categories. Of course, for each participant the sum of these four probabilities will be 1, for we have four mutually exclusive warmth categories. We will not present all the estimated probabilities, for that will consume a lot of space.

### Marginal effect of a regressor

It can be seen from Eq. (10.1), that the marginal effect of the $j$th regressor on $Y_i^*$ is as follows:

$$\frac{\partial Y_i^*}{\partial X_{ij}} = B_j \qquad (10.8)$$

That is, holding all other variables constant, for a unit increase in $X_{ij}$, $Y_i^*$ is expected to change by $B_j$ units. But as Long notes, "Since the variance of $y^*$ cannot be estimated from the observed data, the meaning of a change of $\beta_k y^*$ is unclear".[11] Also, as Wooldridge notes,

> ...we must remember that $\beta$, by itself, is of limited interest. In most cases we are not interested in $E(y^* \mid x) = x\beta$, as $y^*$ is an abstract construct. Instead we are interested in the response probabilities $P(y = j \mid x)$ ...[12]

However, one can use the *Stata* routine to compute $B^*$ standardized coefficient to assess the impact of regressor on the logits.[13]

## 10.4    Limitation of the proportional odds model[14]

To sum up, the proportional odds model estimates one equation over all levels of the regressand, or the dependent variable, the only difference being in their intercepts (the cutoff points). That is why we obtain parallel regression lines (surfaces) for the various levels. This may be a drawback of the proportional log-odds model. Therefore, it is important that we test this assumption explicitly.

### Informal test of constant B coefficient

Since we have $J$ categories of ordered responses, we can compute $J - 1$ binary logit regressions on the odds of being in a higher vs. lower category of $Y$. Thus, if the $Y$s are ordered as in Eq. (10.2), the log-odds (i.e. logits) of a response greater than $j$ vs. less than $j$ can be expressed as:

$$\ln\left[\frac{\Pr(Y_i > j)}{\Pr(Y_i \le j)}\right] = a_j - B_j X, \quad j = 1, 2, \ldots, J - 1 \tag{10.9}$$

This amounts to estimating separate binary logit models for $J - 1$ response variables. So in all we will have $J - 1$ estimates of $B_j$. Therefore, the assumption of parallel regressions means:

$$B_1 = B_2 = \ldots = B_{J-1} = B \tag{10.10}$$

An examination of these coefficients will suggest whether all the estimated $B$ coefficients are the same. If they do not seem the same, then we can reject the hypothesis of parallel regressions. Of course, we can test the hypothesis in Eq. (10.10) more formally, which is what the omodel and Brant tests do.

### Formal test of parallel regression lines

The tests **omodel** and **Brant**, developed by Long and Freese (*op cit.*), can be used to test the assumption of parallel regression lines. We will not discuss the actual mechanics of these tests, but they can be downloaded in *Stata*.

The omodel test gave the results in Table 10.3.

---

11  See J. Scott Long, *Regression Models for Categorical and Limited Dependent Variables*, Sage Publications, California, 1997, p. 128.

12  Jeffrey M. Wooldridge, *Econometric Analysis of Cross Section and Panel Data*, MIT Press, Cambridge, Massachusetts, 2002, pp. 505–6.

13  On this, see Scott Long, *op cit.*

14  The following discussion is based on Scott Long, *op cit.*, pp. 141–5.

**Table 10.3 Test of the warmth parallel regression lines.**

omodel logit warm yr89 male white age ed prst
Iteration 0: log likelihood = −2995.7704
Iteration 1: log likelihood = −2846.4532
Iteration 2: log likelihood = −2844.9142
Iteration 3: log likelihood = −2844.9123
Ordered logit estimates      Number of obs = 2293
     LR chi2(6) = 301.72
     Prob > chi2 = 0.0000
Log likelihood = −2844.9123      Pseudo R2 = 0.0504

| warm | Coef. | Std. Err. | z | P>|z| | [95% Conf. Interval] | |
|------|-------|-----------|---|-------|----------|----------|
| yr89 | .5239025 | .0798988 | 6.56 | 0.000 | .3673037 | .6805013 |
| male | −.7332997 | .0784827 | −9.34 | 0.000 | −.8871229 | −.5794766 |
| white | −.3911595 | .1183808 | −3.30 | 0.001 | −.6231815 | −.1591374 |
| age | −.0216655 | .0024683 | −8.78 | 0.000 | −.0265032 | −.0168278 |
| ed | .0671728 | .015975 | 4.20 | 0.000 | .0358624 | .0984831 |
| prst | .0060727 | .0032929 | 1.84 | 0.065 | −.0003813 | .0125267 |
| _cut1 | −2.465362 | .2389126 | (Ancillary parameters) | | | |
| _cut2 | −.630904 | .2333155 | | | | |
| _cut3 | 1.261854 | .2340179 | | | | |

Approximate likelihood-ratio test of proportionality of odds
across response categories:
chi2(12) = 48.91
Prob > chi2 = 0.0000

The null hypothesis in Eq. (10.10) can be tested by the chi-square test. In the present instance, as Table 10.3 shows, the chi-square value of 48.91 (for 12 df) is highly significant, thus leading to the rejection of the null hypothesis. In other words, the proportionality assumption in the present example does not hold and so the proportional odds model is not appropriate. What then?

## Alternatives to proportional odds model

If the assumption of parallel regression lines is violated, one alternative is to use the MLM discussed in the previous chapter or other alternatives that we do not pursue here. But an accessible discussion of the alternatives can be found in the Long–Freese book, Section 5.9.

We conclude this chapter by illustrating another example of OLM.

## Decision to apply for graduate school

College seniors were asked if they are (1) unlikely, (2) somewhat likely, or (3) very likely to apply to graduate school, which are coded as 1, 2, and 3, respectively. Based on hypothetical data on 400 college seniors along with information about three variables **pared** (equal to 1 if at least one parent has graduate education), **public** (1 if the undergraduate institution is a public university), and **GPA** (student's grade point average), we obtained the OLM of Table 10.4.[15]

---

15 These data are from: http://www.ats.ucla.edu/stat/stata/dae/ologit.dta.

### Table 10.4  OLM estimation of application to graduate school.

```
ologit apply pared public gpa
Iteration 0: log likelihood = −370.60264
Iteration 1: log likelihood = −358.605
Iteration 2: log likelihood = −358.51248
Iteration 3: log likelihood = −358.51244
Ordered logistic regression              Number of obs = 400
                                         LR chi2(3) = 24.18
                                         Prob > chi2 = 0.0000
Log likelihood = −358.51244              Pseudo R2 = 0.0326
```

| apply | Coef. | Std. Err. | z | P>|z| | [95% Conf. Interval] | |
|---|---|---|---|---|---|---|
| pared | 1.047664 | .2657891 | 3.94 | 0.000 | .5267266 | 1.568601 |
| public | −.0586828 | .2978588 | −0.20 | 0.844 | −.6424754 | .5251098 |
| gpa | .6157458 | .2606311 | 2.36 | 0.018 | .1049183 | 1.126573 |
| /cut1 | 2.203323 | .7795353 | .6754622 | 3.731184 | | |

Before we interpret the results, notice that the regressors **pared** and **GPA** are statistically significant, but public institution is not. Since we have three choices, we will have only two cutoff points, both of which are significant, suggesting that all three categories of intentions are distinct.

## Interpretation of results

It is easy to interpret the results if we obtain the odds ratios, which are given in Table 10.5. As this table shows, the OR of **pared** of 2.85 suggests that if we increase **pared** by 1 unit (i.e. going from 0 to 1), the odds of high apply vs. the combined middle and low apply are 2.85 times greater than if neither parent went to college, *ceteris paribus*. For a one unit increase in **gpa**, the odds of the low and middle categories of apply versus the high category of apply are 1.85 times greater than if **gpa** did not increase, *ceteris paribus*.

### Table 10.5  Odds ratios for Table 10.4.

```
ologit apply pared public gpa,or
Iteration 0: log likelihood = −370.60264
Iteration 1: log likelihood = −358.605
Iteration 2: log likelihood = −358.51248
Iteration 3: log likelihood = −358.51244
Ordered logistic regression              Number of obs = 400
                                         LR chi2(3) = 24.18
                                         Prob > chi2 = 0.0000
Log likelihood = −358.51244              Pseudo R2 = 0.0326
```

| apply | Odds Ratio | Std. Err. | z | P>|z| | [95% Conf. Interval] | |
|---|---|---|---|---|---|---|
| pared | 2.850982 | .75776 | 3.94 | 0.000 | 1.69338 | 4.799927 |
| public | .9430059 | .2808826 | −0.20 | 0.844 | .5259888 | 1.690644 |
| gpa | 1.851037 | .4824377 | 2.36 | 0.018 | 1.11062 | 3.085067 |
| /cut1 | 2.203323 | .7795353 | .6754622 | 3.731184 | | |
| /cut2 | 4.298767 | .8043146 | 2.72234 | 5.875195 | | |

**Table 10.6   Test of the proportional odds assumption of intentions to apply to graduate school.**

omodel logit apply pared public gpa
Iteration 0: log likelihood = −370.60264
Iteration 1: log likelihood = −358.605
Iteration 2: log likelihood = −358.51248
Iteration 3: log likelihood = −358.51244
Ordered logit estimatesNumber of obs = 400
LR chi2(3) = 24.18
Prob > chi2 = 0.0000
Log likelihood = −358.51244Pseudo R2 = 0.0326

| apply | Coef. | Std. Err. | z | P>|z| | [95% Conf. Interval] | |
|---|---|---|---|---|---|---|
| pared | 1.047664 | .2657891 | 3.94 | 0.000 | .5267266 | 1.568601 |
| public | −.0586828 | .2978588 | −0.20 | 0.844 | −.6424754 | .5251098 |
| gpa | .6157458 | .2606311 | 2.36 | 0.018 | .1049183 | 1.126573 |
| _cut1 | 2.203323 | .7795353 | (Ancillary parameters) | | | |
| _cut2 | 4.298767 | .8043146 | | | | |

Approximate likelihood-ratio test of proportionality of odds
across response categories:
chi2(3) = 4.06
Prob > chi2 = 0.2553

Because of the proportional odds assumption, the same odds (1.85) hold between low apply and the combined categories of middle and high apply.

As we remarked about the limitation of the proportional odds model in the warmth example, it is important to find out if in the present example the proportional odds assumption hold. Towards that end, we can use the omodel command in *Stata*. Applying this command, we obtained the results in Table 10.6.

The test of the proportionality is given by the chi-square statistic, which in this example has a value of 4.06, which for 3 df has a rather high probability of approximately 0.26. Therefore, unlike the warmth example discussed earlier, in the present case it seems that the proportional-odds assumption seem to hold.

It may be noted that the Brant test is similar to the Omodel test so we will not present results based on the former.

## 10.5   Summary and conclusions

In Chapter 9 we discussed the multinomial logit model as well as the conditional logit model, and in this chapter we discussed the ordinal logit model. These are all models of discrete dependent variables, but each has its special features. In MLM the dependent variable is nominal, but the nominal outcome is determined by characteristics that are specific to the individual. In CLM the nominal outcome depends on the characteristics of the choices rather than on the characteristics of the individual. In OLM we deal with discrete variables that can be ordered or ranked.

We discussed the limitations of MLM and CLM in the previous chapters. The assumption of proportional odds in OLM is often violated in many an application. But if this assumption is valid, and if the data are truly ordinal, OLM is preferred to MLM because we estimate a single regression for each ordered category; the only difference is that the intercepts differ between categories. Therefore OLM is more economical than MLM in terms of the number of parameters estimated.

Even then, we need to test explicitly the assumption of proportionality in any concrete application by applying tests, such as Omodel or Brant.

## Exercises

**10.1** In the illustrative example (warmth category), the assumptions of the proportional odds model is not tenable. As an alternative, estimate a multinomial logit model (MLM) using the same data. Interpret the model and compare it with the proportional odds model.

**10.2 Table 10.7** (available on the companion website) gives data on a random sample of 40 adults about their mental health, classified as well, mild symptom formation, moderate symptom formation, and impaired in relation to two factors, socio-economic status (SES) and an index of life events (a composite measure of the number and severity of important events in life, such as birth of a child, new job, divorce, or death in a family for occurred within the past three years).[16]

   (a)  Quantify mental health as well = 1, mild = 2, moderate = 3, and impaired = 4 and estimate an ordinal logit model based on these data.

   (b)  Now reverse the order of mental health as 1 for impaired, 2 for moderate, 3 for mild, and 4 for well and reestimate the OLM.

Compare the two models and find out if how we order the response variables makes a difference.

## Appendix

## Derivation of Eq. (10.4)

The cumulative probability of the logit model can be written as:

$$\Pr(Y_i \le j \mid X) = \frac{\exp(a_j - BX)}{1 + \exp(a_j - BX)} \tag{1}$$

A similar expression applies for the cumulative probability $\Pr(Y_i \ge j \mid X)$, but $\Pr(Y_i \ge j \mid X) = 1 - \Pr(Y_i < j \mid X)$. Therefore,

$$\frac{\Pr(Y_i \le j \mid X)}{\Pr(Y_i > j \mid X)} = \frac{\Pr(Y_i \le j \mid X)}{1 - \Pr(Y_i \le j \mid X)}$$

$$= \frac{\exp(a_j - BX)}{1 + \exp(a_j - BX)} \Big/ \frac{1}{1 + \exp(a_j - BX)} \tag{2}$$

$$= \exp(a_j - BX)$$

Taking logs on both sides of (2), we obtain Eq. (10.7).

---

16  These data are from Alan Agresti, *op cit.*, Table 6.9, p. 186.

# 11

# Limited dependent variable regression models

In the logit and probit models we discussed previously the dependent variable assumed values of 0 and 1, 0 representing the absence of an attribute and 1 representing the presence of that attribute, such as smoking or not smoking, or owning a house or not owning one, or belonging or not belonging to a union. As noted, the logit model uses the logistic probability distribution and the probit the normal distribution. We saw in Chapter 8 how one estimates and interprets such models, using the example of cigarette smoking.

But now consider this problem: how many packs of cigarettes does a person smoke, given his or her socio-economic variables? Now this question is meaningful only if a person smokes; a nonsmoker may have no interest in this question. In our smoker example discussed in Chapter 8 we had a sample of 1,196 people, of which about 38% smoked and 62% did not smoke. Therefore we can obtain information about the number of packs smoked for only about 38% of the people in the sample.

Suppose we only consider the sample of smokers and try to estimate a demand function for the number of packs of cigarettes smoked per day based on socio-economic information of the smokers only. How reliable will this demand function be if we omit 62% of the people in our sample of 1,196? As you might suspect, such a demand function may not be reliable.

The problem here is that we have a **censored sample**, a sample in which information on the regressand is available only for some observations but not all, although we may have information on the regressors for all the units in the sample. It may be noted that the regressand can be **left-censored** (i.e. it cannot take a value below a certain threshold, typically, but not always, zero) or it may be **right-censored** (i.e. it cannot take a value above a certain threshold, say, people making more than one million dollars of income), or it can be both left- and right-censored.

A closely related but somewhat different model from the censored sample model is the **truncated sample model**, in which information on both the regressand and regressors is not available on some observations. This could be by design, as in the New Jersey negative income tax experiment where data for those with income higher than 1.5 times the 1967 poverty line income were not included in the sample.[1]

Like the censored sample, the truncated sample can be left-censored, right-censored or both right- and left-censored.

---

1  See J. A. Hausman and D. A. Wise, *Social Experimentation*, NBER Economic Research Conference Report, University of Chicago Press, Chicago, 1985.

How then do we estimate such models, which are also known as **limited dependent variable regression models** because of the restriction put on the values taken by the regressand? Initially we will discuss the censored regression model and then discuss briefly the truncated regression model. As in the various models in this book, our emphasis will be on practical applications.

## 11.1    Censored regression models

A popularly used model in these situations is the **Tobit model**, which was originally developed by James Tobin, a Nobel laureate economist.[2] Before we discuss the Tobit model, let us first discuss OLS (ordinary least squares) applied to a censored sample. See **Table 11.1**, available on the companion website.

### OLS estimation of censored data

For this purpose we use the data collected by Mroz.[3] His sample gives data on 753 married women, 428 of whom worked outside the home and 325 of whom did not work outside the home, and hence had zero hours of work.

Some of the socio-economic variables affecting the work decision considered by Mroz are age, education, experience, squared experience, family income, number of kids under age 6, and husband's wage. **Table 11.1** gives data on other variables considered by Mroz.

Applying OLS to hours of work in relation to the socio-economic variables for all the observations, we obtained the results in Table 11.2.

The results in this table are to be interpreted in the framework of the standard linear regression model. As you know, in the linear regression model each slope coefficient gives *the marginal effect* of that variable on the *mean* or average value of the dependent variable, holding all other variables in the model constant. For example, if husband's wages go up by a dollar, the average hours worked by married women declines by about 71 hours, *ceteris paribus*. Except for education, all the other coefficients seem to be highly statistically significant. But beware of these results, for in our sample 325 married women had zero hours of work.

Suppose, instead of using all observations in the sample, we only use the data for 428 women who worked. The OLS results based on this (censored) sample are given in Table 11.3.

If you compare the results in Tables 11.2 and 11.3, you will see some of the obvious difference between the two.[4] The education variable now seems to be highly significant, although it has a negative sign. But we should be wary about these results also.

This is because OLS estimates of censored regression models, whether we include the whole sample (Figure 11.1) or a subset of the sample (Figure 11. 2), are *biased* as

---

2  James Tobin (1958) Estimation of Relationship for Limited Dependent Variables. *Econometrica*, vol. 26, pp. 24–36.

3  See T. A. Mroz, (1987) The sensitivity of an empirical model of married women's hours of work to economic and statistical assumptions. *Econometrica*, vol. 55, pp. 765–99. Recall that we used these data in Chapter 4 while discussing multicollinearity.

4  In the traditional regression model the mean value of the error term $u_i$ is is assumed to be zero, but there is no guarantee that this will be the case if we only use a subset of the sample values, as in this example.

Table 11.2  OLS estimation of the hours worked function.

Dependent Variable: HOURS
Method: Least Squares
Sample: 1 753
Included observations: 753

|  | Coefficient | Std. Error | t-Statistic | Prob. |
|---|---|---|---|---|
| C | 1298.293 | 231.9451 | 5.597413 | 0.0000 |
| AGE | −29.55452 | 3.864413 | −7.647869 | 0.0000 |
| EDUC | 5.064135 | 12.55700 | 0.403292 | 0.6868 |
| EXPER | 68.52186 | 9.398942 | 7.290380 | 0.0000 |
| EXPERSQ | −0.779211 | 0.308540 | −2.525480 | 0.0118 |
| FAMINC | 0.028993 | 0.003201 | 9.056627 | 0.0000 |
| KIDSLT6 | −395.5547 | 55.63591 | −7.109701 | 0.0000 |
| HUSWAGE | −70.51493 | 9.024624 | −7.813615 | 0.0000 |

| | | | | |
|---|---|---|---|---|
| R-squared | 0.338537 | Mean dependent var | 740.5764 |
| Adjusted R-squared | 0.332322 | S.D. dependent var | 871.3142 |
| S.E. of regression | 711.9647 | Akaike info criterion | 15.98450 |
| Sum squared resid | 3.78E+08 | Schwarz criterion | 16.03363 |
| Log likelihood | −6010.165 | Hannan–Quinn criter. | 16.00343 |
| F-statistic | 54.47011 | Durbin–Watson stat | 1.482101 |
| Prob(F-statistic) | 0.000000 | | |

Table 11.3  OLS estimation of hours function for working women only.

Dependent Variable: HOURS
Method: Least Squares
Sample: 1 428
Included observations: 428

|  | Coefficient | Std. Error | t-Statistic | Prob. |
|---|---|---|---|---|
| C | 1817.334 | 296.4489 | 6.130345 | 0.0000 |
| AGE | −16.45594 | 5.365311 | −3.067100 | 0.0023 |
| EDUC | −38.36287 | 16.06725 | −2.387644 | 0.0174 |
| EXPER | 49.48693 | 13.73426 | 3.603174 | 0.0004 |
| EXPERSQ | −0.551013 | 0.416918 | −1.321634 | 0.1870 |
| FAMINC | 0.027386 | 0.003995 | 6.855281 | 0.0000 |
| KIDSLT6 | −243.8313 | 92.15717 | −2.645821 | 0.0085 |
| HUSWAGE | −66.50515 | 12.84196 | −5.178739 | 0.0000 |

| | | | | |
|---|---|---|---|---|
| R-squared | 0.218815 | Mean dependent var | 1302.930 |
| Adjusted R-squared | 0.205795 | S.D. dependent var | 776.2744 |
| S.E. of regression | 691.8015 | Akaike info criterion | 15.93499 |
| Sum squared resid | 2.01E+08 | Schwarz criterion | 16.01086 |
| Log likelihood | −3402.088 | Hannan–Quinn criter. | 15.96495 |
| F-statistic | 16.80640 | Durbin–Watson stat | 2.107803 |
| Prob(F-statistic) | 0.000000 | | |

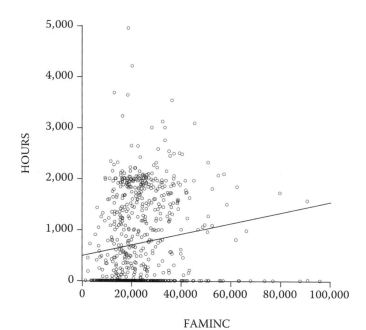

Figure 11.1  Hours worked and family income, full sample.

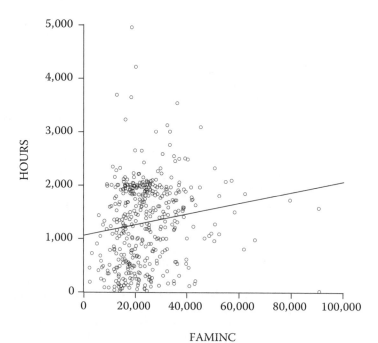

Figure 11.2  Hours vs. family income for working women.

well as *inconsistent* – that is, no matter how large the sample size is, the estimated parameters will not converge to their true values.[5] The reason for this is the fact that in censored as well as truncated regression models the conditional mean of the error term, $u_t$, is nonzero and the error is correlated with the regressors. As we know, if the error term and the regressors are correlated, the OLS estimators are biased as well as inconsistent.

To give a glimpse of why the OLS estimates may be biased as well as inconsistent, we plot hours worked against family income in Figure 11.1 and hours worked and family income only for working women in Figure 11.2.

In Figure 11.1 there are several observations (actually 325) that lie on the horizontal axis because for these observations the hours worked are zero.

In Figure 11.2, none of the observations lie on the horizontal axis, for these observations are for 428 working women. The slope coefficients of the regression lines in the two figures will obviously be different.

A popularly used model to deal with censored samples is the Tobit model, which we now discuss.

## 11.2    Maximum likelihood (ML) estimation of the censored regression model: the Tobit model

One of the popularly used censored sample regression model is the Tobit model. There are several variants of the Tobit model, but we consider here the simplest one, the so-called standard Tobit model.[6] We will continue with the Mroz data.

To see how the censored observations are dealt with, we proceed as follows: Let

$$Y_i^* = B_1 + B_2 Age_i + B_3 Edu_i + B_4 Exp_i + B_5 Kids6_i$$
$$+ B_6 Faminc_i + B_7 Huswage_i + u_i \tag{11.1}$$

where $Y_i^*$ are *desired* hours of work. Now

$$Y_i = 0 \quad \text{if } Y_i^* \le 0$$
$$= Y_i^* \text{ if } Y_i^* > 0 \tag{11.2}$$

where $u_i \sim N(0, \sigma^2)$ and where $Y_i$ are the realized or actual hours worked.[7] The regressors are, respectively, age in years, education in years of schooling, work experience in years, number of kids under age 6, family income in thousands of dollars, and husband's hourly wage.

The variable $Y_i^*$ is called a **latent variable**, the variable of primary interest. Of course, we do not actually observe this variable for all the observations. We only

---

5  For a rigorous proof, see Jeffrey M. Wooldridge, *Introductory Econometrics: A Modern Approach*, South-Western, USA,4th edn, 2006, Ch. 17. See also Christiaan Heij, Paul de Boer, Philip Hans Franses, Teun Kloek, and Herman K. van Dijk, *Econometric Methods with Applications in Business and Economics*, Oxford University Press, Oxford, UK, 2004, Chapter 6.

6  A detailed, but somewhat advanced discussion  can be found in A. Colin Cameron and Pravin K. Trivedi, *Microeconometrics: Methods and Applications*, Cambridge University Press, New York, 2005, Chapter 16.

7   One can use the logistic or the extreme value probability distribution in lieu of the normal distribution.

observe it for those observations with positive hours of work because of censoring. Recall that we discussed the concept of latent variables in the previous chapter.[8]

Notice that we are assuming that the error term is normally distributed with zero mean and constant (or homoscedastic) variance. We will have more to say about this assumption later.

Before we proceed further, it is useful to note the difference between the probit model and the Tobit model. In the probit model, $Y_i = 1$ if $Y_i^*$ is greater than zero, and it is equal to zero if the latent variable is zero. In the Tobit model $Y_i$ may take any value as long as the latent variable is greater than zero. That is why the Tobit model is also known as Tobin's probit.

To estimate a model where some observations on the regressand are censored (because they are not observed), the Tobit model uses the method of **maximum likelihood (ML)**, which we have encountered on several occasions.[9] The actual mechanics of Tobit ML method is rather complicated, but *Stata*, *Eviews* and other software packages can estimate this model very easily.[10]

Using *Eviews6* we obtained the results in Table 11.4 for our example.

## Interpretation of the Tobit estimates

How do we interpret these results? If you only consider the signs of the various regressors, you will see that they are the same in Tables 11.2 and 11.3. And qualitatively they make sense. For example, if the husband's wages go up, on average, a woman will work less in the labor market, *ceteris paribus*. The education variable is not significant in Table 11.2, but it is in Table 11.3, although it has a negative sign. In Table 11.4 it is significant and has a positive sign, which makes sense.

The slope coefficients of the various variables in Table 11.4 give the marginal impact of that variable on the *mean value of the latent variable, $Y_i^*$,* but in practice we are interested in the marginal impact of a regressor on the mean value of $Y_i$, the actual values observed in the sample.

Unfortunately, unlike the OLS estimates in Table 11.2, we *cannot interpret the Tobit coefficient of a regressor as giving the marginal impact of that regressor on the mean value of the observed regressand.* This is because in the Tobit type censored regression models a unit change in the value of a regressor has two effects: (1) the effect on the mean value of the observed regressand, and (2) the effect on the probability that $Y_i^*$ is actually observed.[11]

Take for instance the impact of age. The coefficient for age of about −54 in Table 11.4 means that, holding other variables constant, if age increases by a year, its direct impact on the hours worked per year will be a decrease by about 54 hours per year and the probability of a married woman entering the labor force will also decrease. So we have to multiply −54 by the probability that this will happen. Unless we know the latter, we will not able to compute the aggregate impact of an increase in age on the

---

8  In the present context we can interpret the latent variable as a married woman's propensity or desire to work.

9  There are alternative to ML estimation, some of which may be found in the book by Greene, *op cit.*

10  The details of Tobin's ML method can be found in Christiaan Heij, *op cit.*

11  That is, $\partial[Y_i^* \mid X_i] / \partial X_i = B_i x \Pr(0 < Y_i^* < \infty)$ and the latter probability depends on all the regressors in the model and their coefficients.

**Table 11.4  ML estimation of the censored regression model.**

Dependent Variable: HOURS
Method: ML - Censored Normal (TOBIT) (Quadratic hill climbing)
Sample: 1 753
Included observations: 753
Left censoring (value) at zero
Convergence achieved after 6 iterations
Covariance matrix computed using second derivatives

|          | Coefficient | Std. Error | z-Statistic | Prob. |
|----------|-------------|------------|-------------|--------|
| C        | 1126.335    | 379.5852   | 2.967279    | 0.0030 |
| AGE      | −54.10976   | 6.621301   | −8.172074   | 0.0000 |
| EDUC     | 38.64634    | 20.68458   | 1.868365    | 0.0617 |
| EXPER    | 129.8273    | 16.22972   | 7.999356    | 0.0000 |
| EXPERSQ  | −1.844762   | 0.509684   | −3.619422   | 0.0003 |
| FAMINC   | 0.040769    | 0.005258   | 7.754009    | 0.0000 |
| KIDSLT6  | −782.3734   | 103.7509   | −7.540886   | 0.0000 |
| HUSWAGE  | −105.5097   | 15.62926   | −6.750783   | 0.0000 |

Error Distribution
SCALE:C(9)            1057.598       39.06065      27.07579     0.0000
Mean dependent var   740.5764       S.D. dependent var      871.3142
S.E. of regression   707.2850       Akaike info criterion   10.08993
Sum squared resid    3.72E+08       Schwarz criterion       10.14520
Log likelihood       −3789.858
Avg. log likelihood  −5.033012
Left censored obs         325       Right censored obs            0
Uncensored obs            428       Total obs                   753

*Note*: The scale factor is the estimated scale factor σ, which may be used to estimate the standard deviation of the residual, using the known variance of the assumed distribution, which is 1 for the normal distribution, $\pi^2 / 3$ for the logistic distribution and $\pi^2 / 6$ for the extreme value (Type I) distribution.

hours worked. *And this probability calculation depends on all the regressors in the model and their coefficients.*

Interestingly, the slope coefficient gives directly the marginal impact of a regressor on the latent variable, $Y_i^*$, as noted earlier. Thus, the coefficient of the age variable of −54 means if age increases by a year, the *desired* hours of work will decrease by 54 hours, *ceteris paribus*. Of course, we do not actually observe the desired hours of work, for it is an abstract construct.

In our example we have 753 observations. It is a laborious task to compute the marginal impact of each regressor for all the 753 observations. In practice, one can compute the marginal impact at the *average value* of each regressor.

Since the probability of $Y^*$ must lie between zero and one, the *product* of each slope coefficient multiplied by this probability will be smaller (in absolute value) than the slope coefficient itself. As a result, the marginal impact of a regressor on the mean value of the *observed* regressand will be smaller (in absolute value) than indicated by the value of the slope coefficient given in Table 11.4. The sign of the marginal impact will depend on the sign of the slope coefficient, for the probability of observing $Y_i^*$ is always positive. Packages like *Stata* and *Eviews* can compute the marginal impact of each regressor.

### Statistical significance of the estimated coefficients

Table 11.4 presents the standard errors, the $Z$-statistics (standard normal distribution values) and the *p values* of each estimated coefficient.[12] As the table shows all the coefficients are statistically significant at the 10% or lower level of significance.

For the Tobit model there is no conventional measure of $R^2$. This is because the standard linear regression model estimates parameters by minimizing the residual sum of squares (RSS), whereas the Tobit model maximizes the likelihood function. But if you want to compute an $R^2$ equivalent to the conventional $R^2$, you can do so by squaring the coefficient of correlation between the actual $Y$ values and the $Y$ values estimated by the Tobit model.

The test of the omitted variables or superfluous variables can be conducted in the framework of the usual large sample tests, such as the likelihood ratio, Wald, or Lagrange Multiplier (L). Try this by adding the experience-squared variable to the model or father's education and mother's education variables to the model.

### Caveats

In the Tobit model it is assumed that the error term follows the normal distribution with zero mean and constant variance (i.e. homoscedasticity).

#### Non-normality of error term

In the censored regression models under non-normality of the error term the estimators are not consistent. Again, some remedial methods are suggested in the literature. One is to change the error distribution assumption. For example, *Eviews* can estimate such regression models under different probability distribution assumptions for the error term (such as logistic and extreme value). For a detailed discussion, see the books by Maddala and Wooldridge.[13]

#### Heteroscedasticity

In the usual linear regression model, if the error term is heteroscedastic, the OLS estimators are consistent, though not efficient. In Tobit-type models, however, the estimators are *neither consistent nor efficient*. There are some methods to deal with this problem, but a detailed discussion of them would take us far afield.[14] However, statistical packages, such as *Stata* and *Eviews*, can compute *robust* standard errors, as shown in Table 11.5.

As you can see, there are no vast differences in the estimated standard errors in the two tables, but this need not always be the case.

---

12  Because of the large sample size, we use the standard normal than the $t$ distribution.

13  For detailed, but somewhat advanced, discussion, see G. S. Maddala, *Limited Dependent and Qualitative Variables in Econometrics*, Cambridge University Press, Cambridge, UK, 1983, and Wooldridge, J. M., *Econometric Analysis of Cross Section and Panel Data*, MIT Press, Cambridge, MA, 2002.

14  For an advanced discussion, see Maddala and Wooldridge, *op cit.*

**Table 11.5  Robust estimation of the Tobit model.**

Dependent Variable: HOURS
Method: ML – Censored Normal (TOBIT) (Quadratic hill climbing)
Sample: 1 753
Included observations: 753
Left censoring (value) at zero
Convergence achieved after 6 iterations
QML (Huber/White) standard errors & covariance

|  | Coefficient | Std. Error | z-Statistic | Prob. |
|---|---|---|---|---|
| C | 1126.335 | 386.3109 | 2.915618 | 0.0035 |
| AGE | −54.10976 | 6.535741 | −8.279056 | 0.0000 |
| EDUC | 38.64634 | 20.30712 | 1.903094 | 0.0570 |
| EXPER | 129.8273 | 17.27868 | 7.513728 | 0.0000 |
| EXPERSQ | −1.844762 | 0.536345 | −3.439505 | 0.0006 |
| FAMINC | 0.040769 | 0.005608 | 7.269982 | 0.0000 |
| KIDSLT6 | −782.3734 | 104.6233 | −7.478004 | 0.0000 |
| HUSWAGE | −105.5097 | 16.33276 | −6.460007 | 0.0000 |

Error Distribution
SCALE:C(9)          1057.598        42.80938    24.70482        0.0000
Mean dependent var  740.5764    S.D. dependent var      871.3142
S.E. of regression  707.2850    Akaike info criterion   10.08993
Sum squared resid   3.72E+08    Schwarz criterion       10.14520
Log likelihood      −3789.858   Avg. log likelihood     −5.033012
Left censored obs        325    Right censored obs             0
Uncensored obs           428    Total obs                    753

## 11.3  Truncated sample regression models

Earlier we discussed the difference between censored and truncated sample regression models. Having discussed the censored sample regression model, we now turn our attention to truncated sample regression models.

In truncated samples if we do not have information on the regressand, we do not collect information on the regressors that may be associated with the regressand. In our illustrative example, we do not have data on hours worked for 325 women. Therefore we may not consider information about socio-economic variables for these observations, even though we have that information on them in the current example.

Why, then, not estimate the hours function for the sub-sample of 428 working women only using the method of OLS? As a matter of fact, we did that in Table 11.2. However, the OLS estimators are inconsistent in this situation. Since the sample is truncated, the assumption that the error term in this model is normally distributed with mean $\mu$ and variance $\sigma^2$ distributed cannot be maintained. Therefore, we have to use what is known as the **truncated normal distribution**. In that case we have to use a nonlinear method of estimation, such as the ML method.

Using ML, we obtain the results in Table 11.6. If you compare these results with the OLS results give in Table 11.2, you will see the obvious differences, although the signs of the coefficients are the same.

**Table 11.6  ML estimation of the truncated regression model.**

Dependent Variable: HOURS
Method: ML – Censored Normal (TOBIT) (Quadratic hill climbing)
Sample (adjusted): 1 428
Included observations: 428 after adjustments
Truncated sample
Left censoring (value) at zero
Convergence achieved after 6 iterations
QML (Huber/White) standard errors & covariance

| | Coefficient | Std. Error | z-Statistic | Prob. |
|---|---|---|---|---|
| C | 1864.232 | 397.2480 | 4.692867 | 0.0000 |
| AGE | −22.88776 | 7.616243 | −3.005125 | 0.0027 |
| EDUC | −50.79302 | 20.77250 | −2.445205 | 0.0145 |
| EXPER | 73.69759 | 22.42240 | 3.286784 | 0.0010 |
| EXPERSQ | −0.954847 | 0.575639 | −1.658761 | 0.0972 |
| FAMINC | 0.036200 | 0.006947 | 5.210857 | 0.0000 |
| KIDSLT6 | −391.7641 | 193.4270 | −2.025385 | 0.0428 |
| HUSWAGE | −93.52777 | 19.11320 | −4.893360 | 0.0000 |

Error Distribution

| | | | |
|---|---|---|---|
| SCALE:C(9) | 794.6310 | 56.36703 | 14.09744 |
| 0.0000 | | | |

| | | | |
|---|---|---|---|
| Mean dependent var | 1302.930 | S.D. dependent var | 776.2744 |
| S.E. of regression | 696.4534 | Akaike info criterion | 15.78988 |
| Sum squared resid | 2.03E+08 | Schwarz criterion | 15.87524 |
| Log likelihood | −3370.035 | Avg. log likelihood | −7.873913 |
| Left censored obs | 0 | Right censored obs | 0 |
| Uncensored obs | 428 | Total obs | 428 |

*Note*: The standard errors presented in this table are robust standard errors.

If you compare the results of the censored regression given in Table 11.5 with the truncated regression given in Table 11.6, you will again see differences in the magnitude and statistical significance of the coefficients. Notice particularly that the education coefficient is positive in the censored regression model, but is negative in the truncated regression model.

## Interpretation of the truncated regression coefficients

As in the Tobit model, an individual regression coefficient measures the marginal effect of that variable on the mean value of the regressand for *all* observations – that is, including the non-included observations. But if we consider only the observations in the (truncated) sample, then the relevant (partial) regression coefficient has to be multiplied by a factor which is smaller than 1. Hence, the within-sample marginal effect of a regressor is smaller (in absolute value) than the value of the coefficient of that variable, as in the case of the Tobit model.

## Tobit vs. truncated regression model

Now, between censored and truncation regression models, which is preferable? Since the Tobit model uses more information (753 observations) than the truncated regression model (428 observations), estimates obtained from Tobit are expected to be more efficient.[15]

## 11.4  Summary and conclusions

In this chapter we discussed the nature of censored regression models. The key here is the concept of a *latent variable*, a variable which, although intrinsically important, may not always be observable. This results in a censored sample in which data on the regressand is not available for several observations, although the data on the explanatory variables is available for all the observations.

In situations like this OLS estimators are biased as well as inconsistent. Assuming that the error term follows the normal distribution with zero mean and constant variance, we can estimate censored regression models by the method of maximum likelihood (ML). The estimators thus obtained are consistent.

The slope coefficients estimated by ML need to be interpreted carefully. Although we can interpret the slope coefficient as giving the marginal impact of a variable on the mean value of the *latent* variable, holding other variables constant, we cannot interpret it so with respect to the *observed value* of the latent variable. Here we have to multiply the slope coefficient by the probability of observing the latent variable. And this probability depends on all the explanatory variables and their coefficients. However, modern statistical software packages do this relatively easily.

One major caveat is that the ML estimators are consistent only if the assumptions about the error term are valid. In cases of heteroscedasticity and non-normal error term, the ML estimators are inconsistent. Alternative methods need to be devised in such situations. Some solutions are available in the literature. We can, however, compute robust standard errors, as illustrated by a concrete example.

The truncated regression model differs from the censored regression model in that in the former we observe values of the regressors only if we have data on the regressand. In the censored regression model, we have data on the regressors for all the values of the regressand including those values of the regressand that are not observed or set to zero or some such limit.

In practice, censored regression models may be preferable to the truncated regression models because in the former we include all the observations in the sample, whereas in the latter we only include observations in the truncated sample.

Finally, the fact that we have software to estimate censored regression models does not mean that Tobit-type models are appropriate in all situations. Some of the situations where such models many not be applicable are discussed in the references cited in this chapter.

## Exercises

11.1 Include the Faminc-squared variable in both the censored and truncated regression models discussed in the chapter and compare and comment on the results.

---

15  Technically, this is the result of the fact that the Tobit likelihood function is the sum of the likelihood functions of truncated regression model and the probit likelihood function.

**11.2** Expand the models discussed in this chapter by considering interaction effects, for example, education and family income.

**11.3** The data given in Table 11.1 includes many more variables than are used in the illustrative example in this chapter. See if adding one or more variables to the model in Tables 11.4 and 11.6 substantially alters the results given in these tables.

# 12

# Modeling count data: the Poisson and negative binomial regression models

In many a phenomena the regressand is of the **count type**, such as the number of visits to a zoo in a given year, the number of patents received by a firm in a year, the number of visits to a dentist in a year, the number of speeding tickets received in a year, the number of cars passing through a toll booth in a span of, say, 5 minutes, and so on. The underlying variable in each case is discrete, taking only a finite non-negative number of values.

Sometimes count data also include rare or infrequent occurrences, such as getting hit by lightning in a span or a week, winning Mega Lotto in two successive weeks, having one or more traffic accidents in a span of a day, and the number of appointments to the Supreme Court made by a President in a year. Of course, several more examples can be cited.

A unique feature of all these examples is that they take a finite number of non-negative integer, or count, values. Not only that, in many cases the count is 0 for several observations. *Also note that each count example is measured over a certain finite time period*. To model such phenomena, we need a probability distribution that takes into account the unique features of count data. One such probability distribution is the *Poisson probability distribution*. Regression models based on this probability distribution are known as **Poisson Regression Models (PRM)**. An alternative to PRM is the **Negative Binomial Regression Model (NBRM)**, which is based on the *Negative binomial probability distribution* and is used to remedy some of the deficiencies of the PRM. In what follows we first discuss the PRM and then consider the NBRM.

## 12.1 An illustrative example

Before we discuss the mechanics of PRM, let us consider a concrete example.

### Patents and R&D expenditure

A topic of great interest to students of Industrial Organization is the nature of the relationship between the number of patents received and the expenditure on research and development (R&D) by manufacturing firms. To explore this relationship, **Table 12.1** (available on the companion website) gives data on the number of patents received by a sample of 181 international manufacturing firms and the amount of their R&D

expenditure for the year 1990.[1] The table also gives dummy variables representing five major industries – aerospace, chemistry, computers, machines and instruments, and motor vehicles; food, fuel, metal and others being the reference category. Also given in the table are country dummies for two major countries, Japan and USA, the comparison group being European countries. The R&D variable is expressed in logarithmic form, as the figures for individual industries vary considerably.

If you examine the patent data you will see that they vary considerably, from a low of 0 to a high of 900. But most of them are at the lower end.

Our objective is to determine the influence of R&D, industry category and the two countries on the mean or average number of patents received by the 181 firms.[2] As a starting point, and for comparative purposes, suppose we fit a linear regression model (LRM), regressing patents, on the log of R&D (LR90), the five industry dummies and the two country dummies. The OLS regression results are given in Table 12.2.

As expected, there is a positive relationship between the number of patents received and R&D expenditure, which is highly statistically significant. Since the R&D variable is in the logarithmic form and the patent variable is in the linear form, the R&D coefficient of 73.17 suggests that if you increase R&D expenditure by 1%, the average number of patents received will increase by about 0.73, *ceteris paribus*.[3]

Of the industrial dummies, only the dummies for the chemistry and vehicles industries are statistically significant: Compared to the reference category, the average level of patents granted in the chemistry industry is higher by 47 patents and the average level of patents granted in the vehicles industry is lower by 192. Of the country dummies, the US dummy is statistically significant, but its value of about −77 suggests that on average US firms received 77 fewer patents than the base group.

The OLS regression, however, may not be appropriate in this case because the number of patents granted per firm per year is usually small, despite some firms obtaining a large number of patents. This can be seen more vividly if we tabulate the raw data (Table 12.3).

It is clear from this table that a preponderance of firms received fewer than 200 patents; actually much fewer than this number. This can also be seen from the following histogram of Figure 12.1.

This histogram shows the highly *skewed* distribution of the patent data, which can be confirmed by the coefficient of skewness, which is about 3.3, and the coefficient of kurtosis is about 14. Recall that for a normally distributed variable the skewness coefficient is zero and kurtosis is 3. The Jarque–Bera (JB) statistic clearly rejects the hypothesis that patents are normally distributed. Recall that in large samples the JB static follows the chi-square distribution with 2 df. In the present case the estimated JB value of 1,308 is so large that the probability of obtaining such a value or greater is practically zero.

---

1  These data are obtained from the website of Marno Verbeek, *A Guide to Modern Econometrics,* 3rd edn, Join Wiley & Sons, UK, 2008, but the original source is: M. Cincera, Patents, R&D, and technological spillovers at the firm level: some evidence from econometric count models for panel data. *Journal of Applied Econometrics,* vol. 12, pp. 265–80, 1997. The data can be downloaded from the archives of the *Journal of Applied Econometrics.*

2  Recall that in most regression analysis we try to explain the mean value of the regressand in relation to the explanatory variables or regressors.

3  Recall our discussion of semi-log models in Chapter 2.

**Table 12.2  OLS estimates of patent data.**

Dependent Variable: P90
Method: Least Squares
Sample: 1 181
Included observations: 181

|  | Coefficient | Std. Error | t-Statistic | Prob. |
|---|---|---|---|---|
| C | −250.8386 | 55.43486 | −4.524925 | 0.0000 |
| LR90 | 73.17202 | 7.970758 | 9.180058 | 0.0000 |
| AEROSP | −44.16199 | 35.64544 | −1.238924 | 0.2171 |
| CHEMIST | 47.08123 | 26.54182 | 1.773851 | 0.0779 |
| COMPUTER | 33.85645 | 27.76933 | 1.219203 | 0.2244 |
| MACHINES | 34.37942 | 27.81328 | 1.236079 | 0.2181 |
| VEHICLES | −191.7903 | 36.70362 | −5.225378 | 0.0000 |
| JAPAN | 26.23853 | 40.91987 | 0.641217 | 0.5222 |
| US | −76.85387 | 28.64897 | −2.682605 | 0.0080 |

| | | | |
|---|---|---|---|
| R-squared | 0.472911 | Mean dependent var | 79.74586 |
| Adjusted R-squared | 0.448396 | S.D. dependent var | 154.2011 |
| S.E. of regression | 114.5253 | Akaike info criterion | 12.36791 |
| Sum squared resid | 2255959. | Schwarz criterion | 12.52695 |
| Log likelihood | −1110.296 | Durbin–Watson stat | 1.946344 |
| F-statistic | 19.29011 | Prob(F-statistic) | 0.000000 |

*Note*: P(90) is the number of patents received in 1990 and LR(90) is the log of R&D expenditure in 1990. Other variables are self-explanatory.

**Table 12.3  Tabulation of patent raw data.**

Tabulation of P90
Sample: 1 181
Included observations: 181
Number of categories: 5

| # Patents | Count | Percent | Cumulative Count | Cumulative Percent |
|---|---|---|---|---|
| [0, 200) | 160 | 88.40 | 160 | 88.40 |
| [200, 400) | 10 | 5.52 | 170 | 93.92 |
| [400, 600) | 6 | 3.31 | 176 | 97.24 |
| [600, 800) | 3 | 1.66 | 179 | 98.90 |
| [800, 1000) | 2 | 1.10 | 181 | 100.00 |
| Total | 181 | 100.00 | 181 | 100.00 |

Obviously, we cannot use the normal probability distribution to model count data. The **Poisson probability distribution (PPD)** is often used to model count data, especially to model rare or infrequent count data. How this is done is explained below.

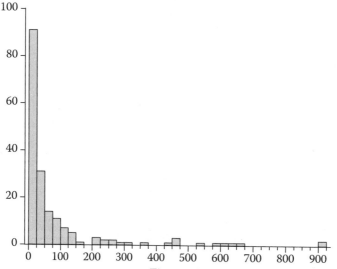

Figure 12.1  Histogram of raw data.

## 12.2   The Poisson regression model (PRM)

If a discrete random variable $Y$ follows the Poisson distribution, its probability density function (PDF) is given by

$$f(Y \mid y_i)=\Pr(Y=y_i)=\frac{e^{-\lambda_i}\lambda_i^{y_i}}{y_i!}, \quad y_i=0,1,2... \tag{12.1}$$

where $f(Y \mid y_i)$ denotes the probability that the discrete random variable $Y$ takes non-negative integer value $y_i$, and where $y_i!$ (read as $y_i$ factorial) stands for $y! = y \times (y-1) \times (y-2) \times ... \times 2 \times 1$ with $0! = 1$ and where $\lambda$ is the parameter of the Poisson distribution. Note that the Poisson distribution has a single parameter, $\lambda$, unlike a normal distribution which has two parameters, mean and variance.

It can be proven that

$$E(y_i)=\lambda_i \tag{12.2}$$

$$\mathrm{var}(y_i)=\lambda_i \tag{12.3}$$

*A unique feature of the Poisson distribution is that the mean and the variance of a Poisson-distributed variable are the same.* This property, which is known as **equidispersion**, is a *restrictive* feature of the Poisson distribution, *for in practice the variance of count variables is often greater than its mean.* The latter property is called **overdispersion**.

The Poisson regression model can be written as:

$$y_i = E(y_i)+u_i = \lambda_i + u_i \tag{12.4}$$

where the *ys* are *independently* distributed as Poisson random variables with mean $\lambda_i$ for each individual, expressed as

$$\lambda_i = E(y_i \mid X_i) = \exp[B_1 + B_2 X_{2i} + ... + B_k X_{ki}] = \exp(\boldsymbol{BX}) \tag{12.5}$$

where exp($BX$) means e raised to the power of the expression $BX$, the latter being a short-hand for the multiple regression shown in the brackets.

The $X$ variables are the regressors that might determine the mean value of the regressand. Therefore, *ipso facto*, it also determines the variance value if the Poisson model is appropriate. For example, if our count variable is the number of visits to the Bronx Zoo in New York in a given year, this number will depend on variables such as income of the visitor, admission price, distance from the museum, and parking fees.

Taking the exponential of $BX$ will guarantee that the mean value of the count variable, $\lambda$, will be positive.

For estimation purposes, our model can be written as

$$\Pr[Y = y_i \mid X] = \frac{e^{-\lambda}\lambda_i^{y_i}}{y_i!}$$

$$= \frac{e^{-BX}\lambda_i^{y_i}}{y_i!}, y_i = 0, 1, 2, \ldots \qquad (12.6)$$

This model is nonlinear in parameters, necessitating nonlinear regression estimation. This can be accomplished by the **method of maximum likelihood** (ML). We will not discuss the details of ML estimation in the context of the Poisson regression model, for the details are somewhat technical and can be found in the references.[4] However, a heuristic discussion of ML is given in the appendix to Chapter 1.

We first present the ML estimates of the patent data and then discuss the results and some of the limitations of the model; see Table 12.4.

The estimated *mean* value of the $i$th firm is therefore:

$$\hat{\lambda}_i = e^{\hat{B}X} = \exp[-0.74 + 0.86 LR90_i - 0.79 Aerosp_i + 0.77 Chemist_i$$

$$+ 0.46 Computer_i + 0.64 Machines_i - 1.50 Vehicles_i \qquad (12.7)$$

$$- 0.0038 Japan_i - 0.41 US_i]$$

A log-transformation of Eq. (12.7) gives:

$$\ln \hat{\lambda}_i = \hat{B}X = -0.74 + 0.86 LR90_i - 0.79 Aerosp_i + 0.77 Chemist_i$$

$$+ 0.46 Computer_i + 0.64 Machines_i - 1.50 Vehicles_i \qquad (12.8)$$

$$- 0.0038 Japan_i - 0.41 US_i$$

## Interpretation of the results

First, notice that in nonlinear models like PRM the $R^2$ is not particularly meaningful. It is the LR, the likelihood ratio, statistic that is important. Its value in the present instance is 21,482, which is highly significant because its $p$ value, or exact level of significance, is practically zero. This suggests that the explanatory variables are collectively important in explaining the conditional mean of patents, which is $\lambda_i$.

Another way of stating this is to compare the restricted log-likelihood with the unrestricted log-likelihood function. The former is estimated under the hypothesis that

---

4  An accessible reference is: J. Scott Long, *Regression Models for Categorical and Limited Dependent Variables*, Sage Publications, Thousand Oaks, California, 1997.

**Table 12.4  Poisson model of patent data (ML estimation).**

Dependent Variable: P90
Method: ML/QML – Poisson Count (Quadratic hill climbing)
Sample: 1 181
Included observations: 181
Convergence achieved after 6 iterations
Covariance matrix computed using second derivatives

|  | Coefficient | Std. Error | z-Statistic | Prob. |
|---|---|---|---|---|
| C | −0.745849 | 0.062138 | −12.00319 | 0.0000 |
| LR90 | 0.865149 | 0.008068 | 107.2322 | 0.0000 |
| AEROSP | −0.796538 | 0.067954 | −11.72164 | 0.0000 |
| CHEMIST | 0.774752 | 0.023126 | 33.50079 | 0.0000 |
| COMPUTER | 0.468894 | 0.023939 | 19.58696 | 0.0000 |
| MACHINES | 0.646383 | 0.038034 | 16.99479 | 0.0000 |
| VEHICLES | −1.505641 | 0.039176 | −38.43249 | 0.0000 |
| JAPAN | −0.003893 | 0.026866 | −0.144922 | 0.8848 |
| US | −0.418938 | 0.023094 | −18.14045 | 0.0000 |

| | | | | |
|---|---|---|---|---|
| R-squared | 0.675516 | Mean dependent var | 79.74586 |
| Adjusted R-squared | 0.660424 | S.D. dependent var | 154.2011 |
| S.E. of regression | 89.85789 | Akaike info criterion | 56.24675 |
| Sum squared resid | 1388804. | Schwarz criterion | 56.40579 |
| Log likelihood | −5081.331 | LR statistic | 21482.10 |
| Restr. log likelihood | −15822.38 | Prob(LR statistic) | 0.000000 |
| Avg. log likelihood | −28.07365 | | |

*Note*: LR90 is the logarithm of R&D expenditure in 1990.

there are no explanatory variables in the model except the constant term, whereas the latter includes the explanatory variables. Since the restricted LR is −15,822 and the unrestricted LR is −5,081, numerically the latter is greater (i.e. less negative) than the former.[5] Since the objective of ML is to maximize the likelihood function, we should choose the unrestricted model, that is, the model that includes the explanatory variables include in the above table.

Now let us interpret the estimated coefficients given in Eq. (12.8). The LR90 coefficient of 0.86 suggests that if R&D expenditure increases by 1%, the average number of patents given a firm will increase by about 0.86%. (Note that R&D expenditure is expressed in logarithmic form.) In other words, the elasticity of patents granted with respect to R&D expenditure is about 0.86% (see Eq. (12.8)).

What is the interpretation of the machines dummy coefficient of 0.6464? From Chapter 2 we know how to interpret the dummy coefficient in a semi-log model. The average number of patents in the machines industry is higher by $100[e^{0.6464} - 1] = 100(1.9086 - 1) = 90.86\%$ compared to the comparison category. In

---

5  As shown in the Appendix to Chapter 1, the LR statistic λ is computed as 2(ULLF – RLLF), where ULLF and RLLF are the unrestricted and restricted log-likelihood functions. The LR statistic follows the chi-square distribution with df equal to the number of restrictions imposed by the null hypothesis: seven in the present example. For our example, λ = 2[−5081 − (−15,822)] = 21,482.10, which is the value in Table 12.4.

similar fashion, the coefficient of the US dummy of $-0.4189$ means the average number of patents in the USA is lower by $100[e^{-0.4189} - 1] = 100(0.6577 - 1) = -34.23\%$ compared to the base group.

If you examine the results given in Table 12.4, you will see that, except for the Japan dummy, the other variables are highly statistically significant.

## Marginal impact of a regressor

Another way to interpret these results is to find the marginal impact of a regressor on the mean value of the count variable, the number of patents in our example.

It can be shown that the marginal impact of a *continuous* regressor, say, $X_k$, on this mean value is:

$$\frac{\partial E(y_i | X_k)}{\partial X_k} = e^{BX} B_k = E(y_i | X_k) B_k \qquad (12.9)[6]$$

As Eq. (12.9) shows, the marginal impact of the regressor $X_k$ depends not only on its coefficient $B_k$ but also on the expected value of $Y (= P90)$, which depends on the values of all the regressors in the model. Since we have 181 observations, we will have to do this calculation for each observation. Obviously this is a laborious task. In practice, the marginal impact is computed at the mean values of the various regressors. *Stata* and other statistical packages have routines to compute the marginal impact of continuous regressors.

How about computing the marginal impact of a dummy regressor?

Since a dummy variable takes a value of 1 and zero, we cannot differentiate $\lambda_i$ with respect to the dummy variable. However, we can compute the percentage change in mean patents obtained by considering the model when the dummy variable takes the value of 1 and when it takes the value of 0.[7]

## Computing the estimated probabilities

How do we compute the probability of obtaining, say, $m$ patents, given the values of the regressors? This probability can be obtained from Eq. (12.6) as:

$$\Pr(Y_i = m | X) = \frac{\exp(-\hat{\lambda}_i)\hat{\lambda}_i^m}{m!}, \quad m = 0, 1, 2, \ldots \qquad (12.10)$$

where $\hat{\lambda} = \hat{B}X$.

In principle we can compute such probabilities for each observation for each value $m$ or for an $m$ of particular interest. Of course, this is a tedious computation. Software such as *Stata* can compute these probabilities relatively easily.

## 12.3 Limitation of the Poisson regression model

The Poisson regression results for the patent and R&D given in Table 12.4 should not be accepted at face value. The standard errors of the estimated coefficients given in

---

6  Using the chain rule of calculus, we obtain: $\partial E(Y | X)/\partial X_k = (\partial e^{XB}/\partial XB) \cdot (\partial XB/\partial X_k) = e^{XB}B_k$. Remember that the derivative of an exponential function is the exponential function itself.

7  For details, consult Long, *op cit.*

that table are valid only if the assumption of the Poisson distribution underlying the estimated model is correct. Since the PPD assumes that the conditional mean and the conditional variance of the distribution, given the values of the $X$ regressors, are the same, it is critical that we check this assumption: the assumption of equidispersion.

If there is overdispersion, the PRM estimates, although consistent are inefficient with standard errors that are downward biased. If this is the case, the estimated $Z$ values are inflated, thus overestimating the statistical significance of the estimated coefficients.

Using a procedure suggested by Cameron and Trivedi, which is incorporated in *Eviews*, the assumption of equidispersion can be tested as follows:

1  Estimate the Poisson regression model, as in Table 12.4, and obtain the predicted value of the regressand, $\hat{P90}_i$.

2  Subtract the predicted value $\hat{P90}_i$ from the actual value $P90_i$, to obtain the residuals, $e_i = P90_i - \hat{P90}_i$.

3  Square the residuals, and subtract from them $P90_i$, i.e. $e_i^2 - P90i$.

4  Regress the result from Step 3 on $\hat{P90}_i^2$.

5  If the slope coefficient in this regression is statistically significant, reject the assumption of equidispersion. In that case reject the Poisson model.

6  If the regression coefficient in Step 5 is positive and statistically significant, there is overdispersion. If it is negative, there is under-dispersion. In any case, reject the Poisson model. However, if this coefficient is statistically insignificant you need not reject the PRM.

Using this procedure, we obtained the results in Table 12.5. Since the slope coefficient in this regression is positive and statistically significant, we can reject the Poisson assumption of equidispersion. Actually, the results show overdispersion.[8] Therefore the reported standard errors in Table 12.4 are not reliable; actually they underestimate the true standard errors.

There are two ways of correcting the standard errors in Table 12.4: one by the method of **quasi-maximum likelihood estimation (QMLE)** and the other by the

**Table 12.5  Test of equidispersion of the Poisson model.**

Dependent Variable: (P90-P90F)^2-P90
Method: Least Squares
Sample: 1 181
Included observations: 181

|          | Coefficient | Std. Error | t-Statistic | Prob.  |
|----------|-------------|------------|-------------|--------|
| P90F^2   | 0.185270    | 0.023545   | 7.868747    | 0.0000 |

| | | | |
|---|---|---|---|
| R-squared | 0.185812 | Mean dependent var | 7593.204 |
| Adjusted R-squared | 0.185812 | S.D. dependent var | 24801.26 |
| S.E. of regression | 22378.77 | Akaike info criterion | 22.87512 |
| Sum squared resid | 9.01E+10 | Schwarz criterion | 22.89279 |
| Log likelihood | −2069.199 | Durbin–Watson stat | 1.865256 |

*Note*: P90F is the predicted value of P90 from Table 12.4 and P90F^2 = P90F squared.

---

8  This test is also valid for underdispersion, in which case the slope coefficient will be negative. That is, the conditional variance is less than the conditional mean, which also violates the Poisson assumption.

**Table 12.6  Comparison of MLE, QMLE and GLM standard errors (SE) of the patent example.**

| Variable | MLE SE (Table12.4) | QMLE SE | GLM SE |
|----------|--------------------|---------|--------|
| Constant | 0.0621 | 0.6691 | 0.4890 |
|  | (−12.0031) | (−1.1145) | (−1.5250) |
| LR90 | 0.0080 | 0.0847 | 0.0635 |
|  | (107.2322) | (10.2113) | (13.6241) |
| ARROSP | 0.0679 | 0.3286 | 0.5348 |
|  | (−11.7210) | (−2.42350) | (−1.4892) |
| CHEMIST | 0.0231 | 0.2131 | 0.1820 |
|  | (33.5007) | (3.6350) | (4.2563) |
| COMPUTER | 0.0239 | 0.2635 | 0.1884 |
|  | (19.5869) | (1.7791) | (2.4885) |
| MACHINES | 0.0380 | 0.3910 | 0.2993 |
|  | (16.9947) | (1.6568) | (2.1592) |
| VEHICLES | 0.0391 | 0.2952 | 0.3083 |
|  | (−38.4324) | (−5.0994) | (−4.8829) |
| Japan | 0.0268 | 0.3259 | 0.2114 |
|  | (−0.1449) | (−0.0119) | (−0.0184) |
| US | 0.0230 | 0.2418 | 0.1817 |
|  | (−18.1405) | (−1.7318) | (−2.3047) |

*Note*: Figures in parentheses are the estimated Z values.

method of **generalized linear model** (GLM). The mathematics behind these methods is complicated, so we will not pursue it. But we will report the standard errors computed by these two methods along with the standard errors reported in Table 12.4 so the reader can see the differences in the estimated standard errors. In all cases the estimates of the regression coefficients remain the same, as in Table 12.4.

But before we do that, it may be noted that even though QMLE is robust to general misspecification of the conditional distribution of the dependent variable, P90 in our example, it does not possess any efficiency properties, whereas GLM directly corrects for overdispersion and may therefore be more dependable.

As you can see from Table 2.6, the standard errors shown in Table 12.4, which are obtained by the method of maximum likelihood, underestimate the standard errors substantially, and thereby inflate the estimated Z values a great deal. The other two methods show that in several cases the regressors are statistically insignificant, thus showing the extent to which MLE underestimated the standard errors.

The main point to note is that if one uses the Poisson Regression Model it should be subjected to overdispersion test(s), as in Table 12.5. If the test shows overdispersion, we should at least correct the standard errors by QMLE and GLM.

If the assumption of equidispersion underlying the PRM cannot be sustained, and even if we correct the standard errors obtained by ML, as in Table 12.6, it might be better to search for alternatives to PRM. One such alternative is the **Negative Binomial**

Regression Model (NBRM), which is based on the *Negative Binomial Probability Distribution* (NBPD).[9]

## 12.4   The Negative Binomial Regression Model (NBRM)

The assumed equality between the mean and variance of a Poisson-distributed random variable is a major shortcoming of the PRM. For the NBPD it can be shown that

$$\sigma^2 = \mu + \frac{\mu^2}{r}; \quad \mu > 0, r > 0 \tag{12.11}$$

where $\sigma^2$ is the variance, $\mu$ is the mean and $r$ is a parameter of the model.[10]

Equation (12.11) shows that for the NBPD the variance is always larger than the mean, in contrast to the Poisson PDF in which mean equals variance. It is worth adding that as $r \to \infty$ and $p \to 1$ the NBPD approaches the Poisson PDF, assuming the mean $\mu$ stays constant. *Note: p* is the probability of success.

Because of the property (12.11), NBPD is more suitable to count data than the PPD.

Using *Eviews6* we obtained Table 12.7. If you compare these results of the negative Binomial regression given in Table 12.7 with those of the Poisson regression in Table 12.4, you will again see the differences in the estimated standard errors.

Incidentally, the shape parameter given in the table gives an estimate of the extent to which the conditional variance exceeds the conditional mean. The shape parameter is equal to the natural log of the variance, $\ln \lambda_i$. Taking the antilog of this, we obtain 1.2864, which suggests that the (conditional) variance is greater by about 0.28 than the conditional mean.

## 12.5   Summary and conclusions

In this chapter we discussed the Poisson regression model which is often used to model count data. The PRM is based on the Poisson probability distribution. A unique feature of the PPD is that the mean of a Poisson variable is the same as its variance. This is also a restrictive feature of PPD.

We used patent data for 181 manufacturing firms for 1990 on the number of patents each firm received along with information on the R&D expenditure incurred by these firms, the industry in which these firms operate (represented by dummy variables) and dummies for two major countries, Japan and USA.

Being a nonlinear model, we estimated PRM by the method of maximum likelihood. Except for the Japan dummy, all the other variables were statistically significant.

But these results may not be reliable because of the restrictive assumption of the PPD that its mean and variance are the same. In most practical applications of PRM the variance tends to be greater than the mean. This is the case of overdispersion.

---

9  Consult any standard textbook on probability to learn more about the negative binomial probability distribution. Suffice it to say here that in the binomial probability distribution we look for the number of successes, $r$, in $n$ trials, where the probability of success is $p$. In the negative binomial probability distribution we look for the number of failures before the $r$th success in $n$ trials, where the probability of success is $p$.

10  For the NBPD the parameters are $p$ (the probability of success) and $r$ (the number of successes), the same parameters as that of the Binomial PDF.

**Table 12.7  Estimation of the NBRM of patent data.**

Dependent Variable: P90
Method: ML – Negative Binomial Count (Quadratic hill climbing)
Sample: 1 181
Included observations: 181
Convergence achieved after 6 iterations
Covariance matrix computed using second derivatives

|          | Coefficient | Std. Error | z-Statistic | Prob.  |
|----------|-------------|------------|-------------|--------|
| C        | −0.407242   | 0.502841   | −0.809882   | 0.4180 |
| LR90     | 0.867174    | 0.077165   | 11.23798    | 0.0000 |
| AEROSP   | −0.874436   | 0.364497   | −2.399022   | 0.0164 |
| CHEMIST  | 0.666191    | 0.256457   | 2.597676    | 0.0094 |
| COMPUTER | −0.132057   | 0.288837   | −0.457203   | 0.6475 |
| MACHINES | 0.008171    | 0.276199   | 0.029584    | 0.9764 |
| VEHICLES | −1.515083   | 0.371695   | −4.076142   | 0.0000 |
| JAPAN    | 0.121004    | 0.414425   | 0.291981    | 0.7703 |
| US       | −0.691413   | 0.275377   | −2.510791   | 0.0120 |

Mixture Parameter
| | | | | |
|---|---|---|---|---|
| SHAPE:C(10) | 0.251920 | 0.105485 | 2.388217 | 0.0169 |
| R-squared | 0.440411 | Mean dependent var | 79.74586 | |
| Adjusted R-squared | 0.410959 | S.D. dependent var | 154.2011 | |
| S.E. of regression | 118.3479 | Akaike info criterion | 9.341994 | |
| Sum squared resid | 2395063. | Schwarz criterion | 9.518706 | |
| Log likelihood | −835.4504 | Hannan–Quinn criter. | 9.413637 | |
| Restr. log likelihood | −15822.38 | LR statistic | 29973.86 | |
| Avg. log likelihood | −4.615748 | Prob(LR statistic) | 0.000000 | |

## III

We used a test suggested by Cameron and Trivedi to test for overdispersion and found that for our data there indeed was overdispersion.

To correct for overdispersion, we used the methods of Quasi Maximum Likelihood Estimation (QMLE) and Generalized Linear Model (GLM). Both these methods corrected the standard errors of the PRM, which was estimated by the method of maximum likelihood (ML). As a result of these corrections, it was found that several standard errors in the PRM were severely underestimated, resulting in the inflated statistical significance of the various regressors. In some cases, the regressors were found to be statistically insignificant, in strong contrast with the original PRM estimates.

Since our results showed overdispersion, we used an alternative model, the Negative Binomial Regression Model (NBRM). An advantage of NBRM model is that it allows for overdispersion and also provides a direct estimation of the extent of overestimation of the variance. The NBRM results also showed that the original PRM standard errors were underestimated in several cases.

## Exercises

**12.1  Table 12.1** also gives data on patents and other variables for the year 1991. Replicate the analysis discussed in this chapter using the data for 1991.

**12.2** **Table 12.8** (see the companion website) gives data on the extramarital affairs of 601 people and is obtained from Professor Ray Fair's website: http://fairmodel.econ.yale.edu/rayfair/pdf/1978ADAT.ZIP. The data consists of:

y = number of affairs in the past year

z1 = sex

z2 = age

z3 = number of years married

z4 = number of children

z5 = religiousness

z6 = education

z7 = occupation

z8 = self-rating of marriage

See if the Poisson and/or Negative Binomial Regression Model fits the data and comment on your results.

**12.3** Use the data in **Table 12.1**. What is the mean number of patents received by a firm operating in the computer industry in the USA with an LR value of 4.21? (Hint: Use the data in Table 12.4). For your information, a firm with these characteristics in our sample had obtained 40 patents in 1990.

# Topics in time series econometrics

# 13

# Stationary and nonstationary time series

In regression analysis involving time series data, a critical assumption is that the time series under consideration is stationary. Broadly speaking, a time series is stationary if its mean and variance are constant over time and the value of covariance between two time periods depends only on the distance or gap between the two periods and not the actual time at which the covariance is computed.[1]

A time series is an example of what is called a **stochastic process**, which is a sequence of random variables ordered in time.[2]

## 13.1    Are exchange rates stationary?

To explain what all this means, we consider a concrete economic time series, namely the exchange rate between the US dollar and the euro (EX), defined as dollars per unit of euro. The exchange rate data are daily from 4 January 2000 to 8 May 2008, for a total of 2,355 observations. These data are not continuous, for the exchange rate markets are not always open every day and because of holidays. These data are provided in **Table 13.1**, which can be found on the companion website.

In Figure 13.1 we have shown the log of the daily dollar/euro exchange rate (*LEX*). The idea behind plotting the log of the exchange rate instead of the exchange rate is that the change in the log of a variable represents a relative change (or rate of return), whereas a change in the variable itself represents an absolute change. For comparative purposes, it is the former that is generally more interesting.

A look at this figure suggests that the *LEX* series is not stationary, for it is generally drifting upward, albeit with a great deal of variation. This would suggest that neither the mean nor the variance of this time series is stationary. *More formally, a time series is said to be stationary if its mean and variance are constant over time and the value of the covariance between two time periods depends only on the distance between the two*

---

1  A time series with these characteristics is known as weakly or covariance stationary. A time series is strictly stationary if all moments of its probability distribution and not just the first two (i.e. mean and variance) are invariant over time.   If, however, the stationary process is normal, the weakly stationary stochastic process is also strictly stationary, for the normal process is fully specified by its two moments, mean and variance.

2  The term "stochastic" comes from the Greek word *stokhos*, which means a target or bull's-eye. Anyone who throws darts at a dartboard knows that the process of hitting the bull's eye is a random process; out of several darts, a few will hit the bull, but most of them will be spread around it in a random fashion.

LEX

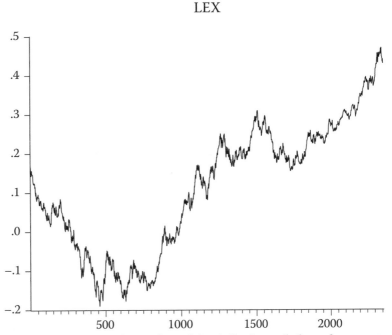

**Figure 13.1** *LEX*: **the logarithm of the dollar/euro daily exchange rate.**

IV

*time periods and not the actual time at which the covariance is computed.* Such a time series is known as **weakly stationary** or **covariance stationary**.[3]

## 13.2    The importance of stationary time series

Why should we worry whether a time series is stationary or not? There are several reasons. *First*, if a time series is nonstationary, we can study its behavior only for the period under consideration, such as the one in our dollar/euro exchange rate. Each time series will therefore be a particular episode. As a result, it is not possible to generalize it to other time periods. For forecasting purposes, therefore, nonstationary time series will be of little practical value.

*Second*, if we have two or more nonstationary time series, regression analysis involving such time series may lead to the phenomenon of **spurious** or **nonsense regression**. That is, if you regress a nonstationary time series on one or more nonstationary time series, you may obtain a high $R^2$ value and some or all of the regression coefficients may be statistically significant on the basis of the usual $t$ and $F$ tests. Unfortunately, in cases of nonstationary time series these tests are not reliable, for they assume that the underlying time series are stationary. We will discuss the topic of spurious regression in some detail in the next chapter.

---

**3**  As noted earlier, it is said to be strictly stationary if all the moments of its probability distribution and not just the mean and variance are time invariant.

## 13.3    Tests of stationarity

For the reasons just stated, it is important to find out if a time series is stationary. There are basically three ways to examine the stationarity of a time series: (1) graphical analysis, (2) correlogram, and (3) unit root analysis. We discuss the first two in this section and take up the last one in the next section.

### Graphical analysis

A rough and ready method of testing for stationarity is to plot the time series, as we have done in Figure 13.1. Very often such an informal analysis will give some initial clue whether a given time series is stationary or not. Such an intuitive feel is the starting point of more formal tests of stationarity. And it is worth remembering that "Anyone who tries to analyse a time series without plotting it first is asking for trouble".[4]

### Autocorrelation function (ACF) and correlogram

Figure 13.2 plots *LEX* at time $t$ against its value lagged one period. This figure shows very high correlation between current *LEX* and *LEX* lagged one day. But it is quite possible that correlation may persist over several days. That is, the current *LEX* may be correlated with *LEX* lagged several days. To see how far back the correlation extends, we can obtain the so-called **autocorrelation function** (ACF). The ACF at lag $k$ is defined as:

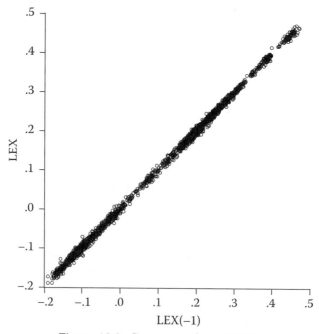

**Figure 13.2   Current vs. lagged *LEX*.**

4  Chris Chatfield, *The Analysis of Time Series: An Introduction*, 6th edn, Chapman & Hall/CRC Press, 2004, p. 6.

$$\rho_k = \frac{\gamma_k}{\gamma_0} = \frac{\text{covariance at lag } k}{\text{variance}} \qquad (13.1)$$

In practice, we compute the ACF from a given sample, denoted as $\hat{\rho}_k$, which is based on the sample covariance at lag $k$ and the sample variance. The actual formulae need not detain us, for modern software packages compute them routinely.

The main practical question is about the length of the lag, $k$. We can use the Akaike or Schwarz information criterion to determine the lag length.[5] But a rule of thumb is to compute ACF up to one-quarter to one-third the length of the time series. We have 2,355 observations. One quarter of this would be about 589 lags. We will not show the ACF at all these lags, but consider only the first 30 lags to give you some idea about the nature of the ACF. A plot of $\hat{\rho}_k$ against $k$, the lag length, is called the (sample) **correlogram**. For the time being, neglect the column of partial correlation (PAC), which we will need in Chapter 16 on time series forecasting.

For the dollar/euro exchange rate the correlogram is given in Table 13.2.

Before we proceed further, we should mention a special type of time series, namely a **purely random**, or **white noise**, time series. Such a time series has constant mean, constant (i.e. homoscedastic) variance, and is serially uncorrelated; its mean value is often assumed to be zero. Recall that the error term $u_t$ entering the classical linear regression model is assumed to be a white noise (stochastic) process, which we denoted as $u_t \sim IID(0, \sigma^2)$, that is $u_t$ is independently and identically distributed with zero mean and constant variance. If in addition, $u_t$ is also normally distributed, it is called a **Gaussian white noise process**. For such a time series the ACF at various lags hovers around zero and the correlogram shows no discernible pattern.

Returning to our example, let us concentrate on the ACF column and its graphic representation (i.e. correlogram) given in the first column. As you can see, even up to 30 days lag the correlation coefficient is very high, about 0.95. Not only that, the estimated autocorrelation coefficients, $\rho_k$, decline very slowly. This is in strong contrast to the correlogram of a white noise time series (see Table 13.5).

We can test the statistical significance of each autocorrelation coefficient by computing its standard error. The statistician Bartlett has shown that if a time series is purely random, the sample autocorrelation, $\hat{\rho}_k$, is approximately (i.e. in large samples) distributed as follows:

$$\hat{\rho} \sim N(0, 1/n) \qquad (13.2)$$

That is, in large samples $\hat{\rho}$ is approximately normally distributed with mean zero and variance equal to one over the sample size. Our sample size is 2,355. Therefore, the variance is 1/2,355 or about 0.00042 and the standard error is $\sqrt{0.00042} = 0.0206$. Therefore, following the properties of the normal distribution, the 95% confidence interval for $\rho_k$ is $[0 \pm 1.96(0.0206)]$ or $(-0.0404$ to $0.0404)$.

None of the estimated correlations lies in this interval. Therefore we can conclude that all the estimated autocorrelation coefficients shown in the table are statistically significant. This conclusion does not change even if we compute ACF up to 150 lags! This is a very strong indication that *LEX* is nonstationary.

Instead of assessing the statistical significance of an individual autocorrelation coefficient, we can also find out if the sum of autocorrelation coefficients squared is

---

5  We discussed these criteria in Chapter 2.

**Table 13.2 Sample correlogram of dollar/euro exchange rate.**

| Autocorrelation | Partial Correlation | | ACF | PAC | Q-Stat | Prob |
|---|---|---|---|---|---|---|
| ******* | ******* | 1 | 0.998 | 0.998 | 2350.9 | 0.000 |
| ******* | \|   \| | 2 | 0.997 | 0.004 | 4695.7 | 0.000 |
| ******* | \|   \| | 3 | 0.995 | −0.017 | 7034.2 | 0.000 |
| ******* | \|   \| | 4 | 0.994 | 0.012 | 9366.6 | 0.000 |
| ******* | \|   \| | 5 | 0.992 | −0.014 | 11693. | 0.000 |
| ******* | \|   \| | 6 | 0.991 | 0.012 | 14013. | 0.000 |
| ******* | \|   \| | 7 | 0.989 | −0.020 | 16326. | 0.000 |
| ******* | \|   \| | 8 | 0.988 | −0.018 | 18633. | 0.000 |
| ******* | \|   \| | 9 | 0.986 | 0.006 | 20934. | 0.000 |
| ******* | \|   \| | 10 | 0.984 | 0.001 | 23228. | 0.000 |
| ******* | \|   \| | 11 | 0.983 | 0.001 | 25516. | 0.000 |
| ******* | \|   \| | 12 | 0.981 | −0.024 | 27796. | 0.000 |
| ******* | \|   \| | 13 | 0.979 | −0.019 | 30070. | 0.000 |
| ******* | \|   \| | 14 | 0.978 | −0.001 | 32337. | 0.000 |
| ******* | \|   \| | 15 | 0.976 | 0.016 | 34597. | 0.000 |
| ******* | \|   \| | 16 | 0.974 | −0.007 | 36850. | 0.000 |
| ******* | \|   \| | 17 | 0.973 | −0.010 | 39097. | 0.000 |
| ******* | \|   \| | 18 | 0.971 | 0.020 | 41336. | 0.000 |
| ******* | \|   \| | 19 | 0.969 | −0.011 | 43569. | 0.000 |
| ******* | \|   \| | 20 | 0.968 | −0.005 | 45795. | 0.000 |
| ******* | \|   \| | 21 | 0.966 | −0.006 | 48014. | 0.000 |
| ******* | \|   \| | 22 | 0.964 | 0.006 | 50226. | 0.000 |
| ******* | \|   \| | 23 | 0.963 | −0.005 | 52431. | 0.000 |
| ******* | \|   \| | 24 | 0.961 | −0.016 | 54629. | 0.000 |
| ******* | \|   \| | 25 | 0.959 | −0.020 | 56820. | 0.000 |
| ******* | \|   \| | 26 | 0.957 | 0.009 | 59003. | 0.000 |
| ******* | \|   \| | 27 | 0.955 | 0.001 | 61179. | 0.000 |
| ******* | \|   \| | 28 | 0.954 | 0.007 | 63349. | 0.000 |
| ******* | \|   \| | 29 | 0.952 | −0.009 | 65511. | 0.000 |
| ******* | \|   \| | 30 | 0.950 | 0.012 | 67666. | 0.000 |

statistically significant. This can be done with the aid of the **Q statistic** developed by Box and Pierce, which is defined as

$$Q = n \sum_{k=1}^{m} \hat{\rho}_k^2 \tag{13.3}$$

where $n$ is the sample size (2,355 in our example), and $m$ is the total number of lags used in calculating ACF, 30 in the present example. The $Q$ statistic is often used to test whether a time series is purely random, or white noise.

In large samples, $Q$ is *approximately* distributed as the chi-square distribution with $m$ df. If in an application the computed $Q$ value exceeds the critical $Q$ value from the chi-square distribution at the chosen level of significance, we can reject the null hypothesis that the all the true $\rho_k$ are zero; at least some of them must be nonzero.

The last column of Table 13.1 gives the $p$ (probability) value of $Q$. As the table shows, the $Q$ value up to 30 lags is 67,666 and the probability of obtaining such a $Q$ value is practically zero. That is, our time series is nonstationary.

To summarize, there is strong evidence that the dollar/euro time series is nonstationary.

## 13.4    The unit root test of stationarity

Without going into the technicalities, we can express the unit root test for our dollar/euro exchange rate as follows:[6]

$$\Delta LEX_t = B_1 + B_2 t + B_3 LEX_{t-1} + u_t \tag{13.4}$$

where $\Delta LEX_t = LEX_t - LEX_{t-1}$, that is, the first difference of the log of the exchange rate, $t$ is the time or trend variable taking value of 1, 2, till the end of the sample, and $u_t$ is the error term.

In words, we regress the first differences of the log of exchange rate on the trend variable and the one-period lagged value of the exchange rate.

The null hypothesis is that $B_3$, the coefficient of $LEX_{t-1}$ is zero. This is called the **unit root hypothesis**.[7] The alternative hypothesis is: $B_3 < 0$.[8] A nonrejection of the null hypothesis would suggest that the time series under consideration is nonstationary.

It would seem that we can test the null hypothesis that $B_3 = 0$ by the usual $t$ test. Unfortunately, we cannot do that because the $t$ test is valid only if the underlying time series is stationary. However, we can use a test developed by statisticians Dickey and Fuller, called the $\tau$ **(tau) test** whose critical values are calculated by simulations and modern statistical packages, such as *Eviews* and *Stata*, produce them routinely. In the literature the tau test is know as the **Dickey–Fuller (DF)** test.

In practice we estimate Eq. (13.4) by OLS, look at the routinely calculated $t$ value of the coefficient of $LEX_{t-1}$ (= $B_3$), *but use the DF critical values* to find out if it exceeds the DF critical value. If in an application the computed $t$ (= tau) value of the estimated $B_3$ is greater (in absolute value) that the critical DF value, we reject the unit root hypothesis – that is, we conclude that the time series under study is stationary. In that case the conventional $t$ test is valid. On the other hand, if it does not exceed the critical tau value, we do not reject the hypothesis of unit root and conclude that the time series is nonstationary. The reason for considering the absolute tau value is that in general the coefficient $B_3$ is expected to be negative.[9]

Let us return to our illustrative example. The results of estimating (13.4) are given in Table 13.3.

---

6  For an accessible discussion, see Gujarati/Porter, *op cit.*, Chapter 21.

7  To see intuitively why the term *unit root* is used, we can proceed as follows: Let $LEX_t = B_1 + B_2 t + C LEX_{t-1} + u_t$. Now subtract $LEX_{t-1}$ from both sides of this equation, which gives $(LEX_t - LEX_{t-1}) = B_1 + B_2 t + C LEX_{t-1} - LEX_{t-1} + u_t$. Collecting terms, we obtain $\Delta LEX_t = B_1 + B_2 t + B_3 LEX_{t-1} + u_t$, where $B_3 = (C - 1)$. If $C = 1$, $B_3$ in regression (13.4) will be zero. Hence the name *unit root*.

8  We rule out the possibility that $B_3 > 0$, for in that case $C > 1$, in which case the underlying time series is explosive.

9  Note $B_3 = (C - 1)$. So if $C < 1$, $B_3 < 0$.

**Table 13.3  Unit root test of the dollar/euro exchange rate.**

Dependent Variable: Δ(LEX)
Method: Least Squares
Date: 11/24/08 Time: 17:00
Sample (adjusted): 2 2355
Included observations: 2354 after adjustments

|         | Coefficient | Std. Error | t-Statistic | Prob.  |
|---------|-------------|------------|-------------|--------|
| C       | −0.000846   | 0.000292   | −2.897773   | 0.0038 |
| t       | 1.21E−06    | 3.22E−07   | 3.761595    | 0.0002 |
| LEX(−1) | −0.004088   | 0.001351   | −3.026489   | 0.0025 |

| | | | | |
|---|---|---|---|---|
| R-squared | 0.005995 | Mean dependent var | 0.000113 | |
| Adjusted R-squared | 0.005149 | S.D. dependent var | 0.005926 | |
| S.E. of regression | 0.005911 | Akaike info criterion | −7.422695 | |
| Sum squared resid | 0.082147 | Schwarz criterion | −7.415349 | |
| Log likelihood | 8739.512 | Durbin–Watson stat | 1.999138 | |
| F-statistic | 7.089626 | Prob(F-statistic) | 0.000852 | |

Look at the coefficient of LEX lagged one period. Its $t$ (=tau) value is −3.0265. If you look at the conventionally computed $p$ or probability value of this coefficient, it is 0.0025, which is very low. Hence you would be tempted to conclude that the estimated coefficient of about −0.004 is statistically different from zero and so the US/EU time series is stationary.[10]

However, the DF critical values are: −3.9619 (1% level), −3.4117 (5% level) and −3.1277 (10% level). The computed $t$ value is −3.0265. In *absolute* terms, 3.0265 is smaller than any of DF critical $t$ values in absolute terms. Hence, we conclude that the US/EU time series is not stationary.

To put it differently, for us to reject the null hypothesis of unit root, the computed $t$ value of $LEX_{t-1}$ must be more negative than any of the critical DF values. On the basis of the DF critical value the probability of obtaining a *tau* (= $t$) value of −3.0265 is about 12%. As can be seen from the preceding table, the conventional $t$ statistic shows that −3.0264 is significant at the 0.0025 level. It is evident that the conventionally computed significance level of the estimated $t$ value can be very misleading when it is applied to a time series which is nonstationary.

## Some practical aspects of the DF test

The DF test can be performed in three different forms:

$$\text{Random walk:} \Delta LEX_t = B_3 LEX_{t-1} + u_t \tag{13.5}$$

$$\text{Random walk with drift:} \Delta LEX_t = B_1 + B_3 LEX_{t-1} + u_t \tag{13.6}$$

Random walk with drift around a deterministic trend:

$$\Delta LEX_t = B_1 + B_2 t + B_3 LEX_{t-1} + u_t \tag{13.7}$$

---

10  In this case $(C-1) = -0.004$, which gives $C = 0.996$, which is not exactly equal to 1. This would suggest that the LEX series is stationary.

In each case the null hypothesis is that $B_3 = 0$ (i.e. unit root) and the alternative hypothesis is that $B_3 < 0$ (i.e. no unit root). However, the critical DF values are different for each of these models. Which model holds in an application is an empirical question. But guard against model specification errors. If model (13.7) is the "correct" model, fitting either model (13.5) or (13.6) would constitute a model specification error: here the omission of an important variable(s).

Which of the Equations (13.5), (13.6), and (13.7) should we use in practice? Here are some guidelines:[11]

1   Use Eq. (13.5) if the time series fluctuates around a sample average of zero.

2   Use Eq. (13.6) if the times series fluctuates around a sample average that is nonzero.

3   Use Eq. (13.7) if the time series fluctuates around a linear trend. Sometimes the trend could be quadratic.

In the literature, model (13.5) is called a **random walk model without drift** (i.e. no intercept), model (13.6) is called a **random walk with drift** (i.e. with an intercept), $B_1$ being the drift (or shift) parameter, and model (13.7) is a **random walk model with drift and deterministic trend**, so called because a deterministic trend value $B_2$ is added for each time period. We will have more to say about the deterministic trend shortly.

Let us find out if regression (13.7) characterizes LEX. The results are given in Table 13.4.

The *Eviews* output given in this table is divided into two parts. The lower part gives the usual OLS output of Eq. (13.7). It shows that all the estimated coefficients are individually "highly" statistically significant on the basis of the $t$ test and also the $F$ value is "highly" significant, suggesting that collectively all the regressors are significant determinants of LEX.[12]

For the present purposes the important coefficient is that of the lagged LEX value. The $t$ value of this coefficient is significant at the 0.0025 level, whereas if you look at the tau value of this coefficient given in the upper half of the above table, it is significant at about the 0.125 level, which is much higher than the critical 1%, 5%, and 10% critical tau values. In other words, on the basis of the tau test, the coefficient of the lagged LEX is not different from zero, thus suggesting that the LEX time series is nonstationary. This reinforces the conclusion based on the simple graphic picture as well as the correlogram.

This exercise shows how misleading the conventional $t$ and $F$ tests can be if we are dealing with a nonstationary time series.

## Augmented Dickey–Fuller (ADF) test

In Models (13.5), (13.6), and (13.7) it was assumed that the error term $u_t$ is uncorrelated. But if it is correlated, which is likely to be the case with model (13.7), Dickey and Fuller have developed another test, called the **augmented Dickey–Fuller**

---

11   See R. Carter Hill, William E. Griffiths and Guay C. Lim, *Principles of Econometrics*, 3rd edn, John Wiley & Sons, New York, 2008, p. 336.

12   We also estimated the model with both linear and quadratic trend terms, but the quadratic trend term was not statistically significant, its $p$ value being 26%.

**Table 13.4 Unit root test of dollar/euro exchange rate with intercept and trend terms.**

Null Hypothesis: LEX has a unit root
Exogenous: Constant, Linear Trend
Lag Length: 0 (Automatic based on SIC, MAXLAG=0)

| | | | | t-Statistic | Prob.* |
|---|---|---|---|---|---|
| Augmented Dickey–Fuller test statistic | | | | −3.026489 | 0.1251 |
| Test critical values: | 1% level | | | −3.961944 | |
| | 5% level | | | −3.411717 | |
| | 10% level | | | −3.127739 | |

*MacKinnon (1996) one-sided p-values.
Augmented Dickey–Fuller Test Equation
Dependent Variable: D(LEX)
Method: Least Squares
Date: 01/26/10 Time: 12:04
Sample (adjusted): 2 2355
Included observations: 2354 after adjustments

| | Coefficient | Std. Error | t-Statistic | Prob. |
|---|---|---|---|---|
| LEX(−1) | −0.004088 | 0.001351 | −3.026489 | 0.0025 |
| C | −0.000846 | 0.000292 | −2.897773 | 0.0038 |
| @TREND(1) | 1.21E−06 | 3.22E−07 | 3.761595 | 0.0002 |

| | | | | |
|---|---|---|---|---|
| R-squared | 0.005995 | Mean dependent var | 0.000113 | |
| Adjusted R-squared | 0.005149 | S.D. dependent var | 0.005926 | |
| S.E. of regression | 0.005911 | Akaike info criterion | −7.422695 | |
| Sum squared resid | 0.082147 | Schwarz criterion | −7.415349 | |
| Log likelihood | 8739.512 | Durbin–Watson stat | 1.999138 | |
| F-statistic | 7.089626 | Prob(F-statistic) | 0.000852 | |

*Note*: @Trend is *Eviews'* command to generate the trend variable. D is *Eviews'* symbol for taking first differences.

**(ADF) test.** This test is conducted by "augmenting" the three equations by adding the lagged values of the dependent variable $\Delta LEX_t$ as follows:

$$\Delta LEX_t = B_1 + B_2 t + B_3 LEX_{t-1} + \sum_{i=1}^{m} \alpha_i \Delta LEX_{t-i} + \varepsilon_t \qquad (13.8)$$

where $\varepsilon_t$ is a pure white noise error term and where $m$ is the maximum length of the lagged dependent variable, which is determined empirically.[13] The objective is to make the residuals from Eq. (13.7) purely random.

As in the DF test, the null hypothesis is that $B_3$ in Eq. (13.8) is zero.

For our illustrative example we used $m = 26$. Even then, the conclusion that the dollar/euro exchange rate time series is nonstationary did not change.

---

13 But notice that if we introduce too many lags, they will consume a lot of degrees of freedom, which might be a problem in small samples. For annual data we may include one or two lags, while for monthly data we may include 12 lags. Of course, the purpose of introducing the lagged $\Delta LEX$ terms is to make the resulting error term free of serial correlation.

In sum, *it seems the evidence is overwhelming that the dollar/euro exchange rate is nonstationary.*

Is there a way we could make the dollar/euro exchange rate stationary? The answer follows.

## 13.5   Trend stationary vs. difference stationary time series

As Figure 13.1 shows, the dollar/euro exchange rate time series has generally been upward trending. A common practice to make such a trending time series stationary is to remove the trend from it. This can be accomplished by estimating the following regression:

$$LEX_t = A_1 + A_2 t + v_t \qquad (13.9)$$

where $t$ (time) is a **trend variable** taking chronological values, 1, 2, ..., 2,355, and $v_t$ is the error term with the usual properties.[14] After running this regression, we obtain

$$\hat{v} = LEX_t - a_1 - a_2 t \qquad (13.10)$$

The estimated error term in Eq. (13.10), $\hat{v}_t$, now represents the **detrended** LEX time series, that is LEX with the trend removed.

*The procedure just described is valid if the original LEX series has a **deterministic trend**.* The residuals obtained from regression (13.10) are shown in Figure 13.3.

This figure very much resembles Figure 13.1. If you subject the series in Figure 13.3 to unit root analysis, you will find that the detrended LEX series is still nonstationary.[15] Therefore the de-trending procedure just outlined will not make a

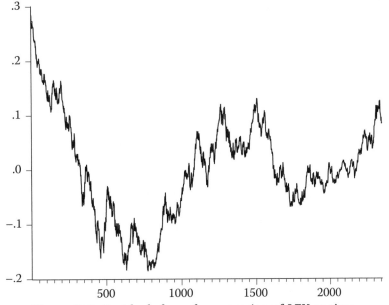

**Figure 13.3  Residuals from the regression of *LEX* on time.**

---

**14**  A quadratic trend could also be added.

**15**  Even if you add the quadratic trend term, $t^2$, to Eq. (13.9), the residuals from this regression still show that they are nonstationary.

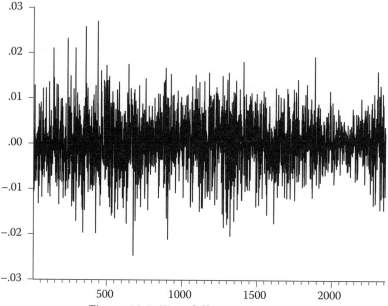

**Figure 13.4  First differences of LEX.**

nonstationary time series stationary, because such a procedure is valid only if the series contains a deterministic trend. What then?

If a time series becomes stationary if we detrend it in the manner suggested, it is called a **trend stationary (stochastic) process (TSP)**. It may be pointed out here that a process with a deterministic trend is nonstationary but not a unit root process.

Instead of detrending a time series in the manner suggested above, suppose we take the first differences of LEX (subtract the preceding value of LEX from its current value). This gives us Figure 13.4.

Unlike Figure 13.1, we do not see a discernible trend in the first differences of LEX. If we obtain the correlogram of the first differences of LEX, we obtain Table 13.5.

As you can see, up to 30 lags, none of the autocorrelation coefficients are statistically significant at the 5% level; neither is the $Q$ statistic.

An application of the unit root tests also showed that there is no unit root in the first differences of LEX. That is, it is the first difference of the LEX series that is stationary.

If a time series becomes stationary after we take its first differences, we call such a time series a **difference stationary (stochastic) process (DSP)**.[16]

It is important to note that if a time series is DSP but we regard it as TSP, this is called **under-differencing**. On the other hand, if a time series is TSP and we treat it as DSP, this is called **over-differencing**. In Figure 13.3 we in fact under-differenced the LEX series.

The main conclusion we reach is that the LEX time series is difference stationary.

---

16　Occasionally we may have to difference a time series more than once to make it stationary.

**Table 13.5  Correlogram of first differences of LEX.**

|    | AC     | PAC    | Q-Stat  | Prob  |
|----|--------|--------|---------|-------|
| 1  | 0.002  | 0.002  | 0.0113  | 0.915 |
| 2  | −0.001 | −0.001 | 0.0125  | 0.994 |
| 3  | −0.017 | −0.017 | 0.6673  | 0.881 |
| 4  | 0.051  | 0.052  | 6.9213  | 0.140 |
| 5  | −0.036 | −0.037 | 10.017  | 0.075 |
| 6  | 0.016  | 0.016  | 10.643  | 0.100 |
| 7  | 0.020  | 0.022  | 11.582  | 0.115 |
| 8  | −0.024 | −0.028 | 12.970  | 0.113 |
| 9  | 0.003  | 0.008  | 12.997  | 0.163 |
| 10 | −0.013 | −0.015 | 13.379  | 0.203 |
| 11 | −0.003 | −0.004 | 13.396  | 0.268 |
| 12 | 0.012  | 0.016  | 13.735  | 0.318 |
| 13 | 0.034  | 0.030  | 16.482  | 0.224 |
| 14 | −0.003 | −0.001 | 16.501  | 0.284 |
| 15 | −0.032 | −0.031 | 18.857  | 0.220 |
| 16 | 0.011  | 0.010  | 19.140  | 0.261 |
| 17 | 0.002  | 0.000  | 19.148  | 0.320 |
| 18 | 0.021  | 0.022  | 20.222  | 0.320 |
| 19 | 0.019  | 0.021  | 21.085  | 0.332 |
| 20 | 0.022  | 0.017  | 22.193  | 0.330 |
| 21 | −0.035 | −0.032 | 25.141  | 0.241 |
| 22 | 0.041  | 0.041  | 29.088  | 0.142 |
| 23 | 0.033  | 0.032  | 31.619  | 0.108 |
| 24 | 0.038  | 0.037  | 35.079  | 0.067 |
| 25 | −0.007 | −0.004 | 35.189  | 0.085 |
| 26 | 0.008  | 0.001  | 35.341  | 0.104 |
| 27 | −0.015 | −0.013 | 35.903  | 0.117 |
| 28 | −0.028 | −0.027 | 37.786  | 0.103 |
| 29 | −0.014 | −0.015 | 38.230  | 0.117 |
| 30 | 0.012  | 0.010  | 38.570  | 0.136 |

IV

## Integrated time series

In the time series literature you will often come across the term "**integrated time series**". If such a time series becomes stationary after differencing it once, it is said to be **integrated of order one**, denoted as I(1). If it has to be differenced twice (i.e. difference of difference) to make it stationary, it is said to be **integrated of order two**, denoted as I(2). If it has to be differenced *d* times to make it stationary, it is said to be **integrated of order *d***, denoted as I(d). *A stationary time series is I(0), that is, integrated of order zero.* Therefore the terms "stationary time series" and "time series integrated of order zero" mean the same thing. By the same token, if a time series is integrated, it is nonstationary.

It may be added that an I(0) series fluctuates around its mean with constant variance, while an I(1) series meanders wildly. Another way of putting this is that an I(0) series is **mean reverting**, whereas an I(1) series does not show such a tendency. It can drift away from the mean permanently. That is why an I(1) series is said to have a **stochastic trend**. As a result, the autocorrelations in a correlogram of an I(0) series decline to zero very rapidly as the lag increases, whereas for an I(1) series they decline to zero very slowly, as the correlogram of the LEX series in Table 13.2 shows clearly.

Most nonstationary economic time series generally do not need to be differenced more than once or twice.

*To sum up, a nonstationary time series is known variously as an integrated time series or a series with stochastic trend.*

Before we conclude this chapter, we will discuss briefly a special type of nonstationary time series that figures prominently in the finance literature, namely the **random walk time series**.

## 13.6    The random walk model (RWM)

It is often said that asset prices, such as stock prices and exchange rates, follow a random walk, that is, they are nonstationary.[17] We distinguish two types of random walk: (1) random walk without drift (i.e. no constant term or intercept) and (2) random walk with drift (i.e. a constant term is present).

### Random walk without drift

Consider the following model:

$$Y_t = Y_{t-1} + u_t \tag{13.11}$$

where $Y_t$ is, say, today's stock price and $Y_{t-1}$ is yesterday's price, and where $u_t$ is a white noise error term with zero mean and variance $\sigma^2$.

We can think of Eq. (13.11) as a regression of $Y$ at time $t$ on its value lagged one period. Believers in the **efficient market hypothesis** maintain that stock prices are random and therefore there is no scope for profitable speculation in the stock market.[18]

By successive substitution in Eq. (13.11), it can be shown that

$$Y_t = Y_0 + \sum u_t \tag{13.12}$$

where $Y_0$ is the initial stock price.

Therefore,

$$E(Y_t) = E(Y_0) + E(\Sigma u_t) = Y_0 \tag{13.13}$$

since the expectation of each $u_t$ is zero.

By successive substitution, it can also be shown that (see Exercise 13.1):

---

17  The term *random walk* is often compared with a drunkard's walk. On leaving a bar, the drunkard moves a random distance $u_t$ at time $t$ and, continuing to walk indefinitely, will eventually meander farther and farther away from the bar. The same can be said about stock prices. Today's stock price is equal to yesterday's stock price plus a random shock.

18  Technical analysts, or chartists as they are called, do not believe in such a hypothesis and believe that they can predict stock price patterns from historically observed stock prices.

$$var(Y_t) = t\sigma^2 \tag{13.14}$$

From the preceding discussion we see that the mean of $Y$ is equal to its initial, or starting, value, which is constant, but as $t$, the time horizon, increases indefinitely, the variance of $Y$ also increases indefinitely, thus violating one of the conditions of stationarity that the variance is a finite constant.

*In short, the random walk model without drift is a particular, and important, case of a nonstationary stochastic process.*

Interestingly, if we write Eq. (13.11) as

$$Y_t - Y_{t-1} = \Delta Y_t = u_t \tag{13.15}$$

where $\Delta$ is the first difference operator.

*Therefore, even though $Y_t$ is nonstationary, its first difference is stationary. To put it differently, the RWM without drift is a difference stationary process.*

## Random walk with drift

Now let us revise Eq. (13.11) and write it as

$$Y_t = \delta + Y_{t-1} + u_t \tag{13.16}$$

where $\delta$ (delta) is known as the **drift parameter**, which is basically an intercept in the RWM.

For the RWM with drift, it can be shown that

$$E(Y_t) = Y_0 + \delta t \tag{13.17}$$

$$var(Y_t) = t\sigma^2 \tag{13.18}$$

As you can see, for the RWM with drift both the mean and variance increase over time, again violating the condition of stationary time series.

Let us rewrite Eq. (13.16) as

$$Y_t - Y_{t-1} = \Delta Y_t = \delta + u_t \tag{13.19}$$

which is the first difference of a RWM with drift. It is easy to verify that

$$E(\Delta Y_t) = \delta \tag{13.20}$$

$$var(\Delta Y_t) = \sigma^2 \tag{13.21}$$

$$cov(\Delta Y_t, \Delta Y_{t-s}) = E(u_t u_{t-s}) = 0 \tag{13.22}$$

because $u_t$ is the white noise error term.

What all this means is that although the RWM with drift is a nonstationary time series, its first difference is a stationary (stochastic) process. To put it differently, RWM with drift is an I(1) process, whereas its first difference is an I(0) process. Here the constant $\delta$ acts like a linear trend because in each period the level of $Y_t$ shifts, on average, by the amount $\delta$.

IV

### An example: closing daily prices of IBM stock, 4 January 2000 to 20 August 2002

To see whether IBM prices over the sample period followed a random walk, we first plotted the log of the closing daily prices of the stock, giving Figure 13.5 (see **Table 13.6** on the companion website).

Visually, it seems the logs of IBM prices are nonstationary.

Can we verify this statistically? You might be tempted to run the following regression (let $Y$ represent the log of daily closing IBM prices):

$$Y_t = B_1 + B_2 Y_{t-1} + u_t \tag{13.23}$$

and test the hypothesis that $B_2 = 1$ with the usual $t$ test. However, in cases of nonstationary time series, the $t$ test is severely biased toward zero. To circumvent this, we manipulate Eq. (13.23) as follows: Subtract $Y_{t-1}$ from both sides of this equation to obtain:

$$Y_t - Y_{t-1} = B_1 + B_2 Y_{t-1} - Y_{t-1} + u_t$$

that is

$$\tag{13.24}$$

$$\Delta Y_t = B_1 + \lambda Y_{t-1} + u_t$$

where $\lambda = B_2 - 1$.

So instead of estimating Eq. (13.23), we estimate Eq. (13.24) and test the hypothesis that $\lambda = 0$ against the alternative hypothesis that $\lambda < 0$.[19] If $\lambda = 0$, then $B_2 = 1$ and $Y$ is a random walk (with drift), that is, it is nonstationary. Technically, the $Y$ time series has a unit root. On the other hand, if $\lambda < 0$, we can conclude that $Y_t$ is stationary.[20]

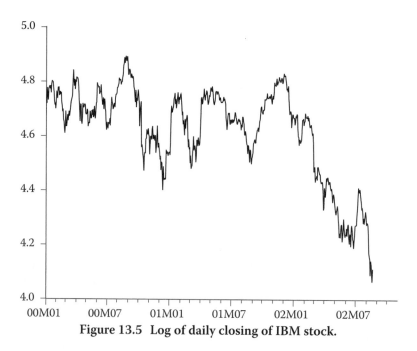

**Figure 13.5  Log of daily closing of IBM stock.**

---

19  We are essentially performing a unit root analysis.
20  If $\lambda = (B_2 - 1)$ for stationarity, $B_2$ must be less than 1. For this to happen $\lambda$ must be negative.

After you estimate regression (13.24), you cannot test the null hypothesis that $\lambda = 0$ with the usual $t$ test because the $t$ value of the estimated coefficient of $Y_{t-1}$ does not follow the $t$ distribution even in large samples.

As noted earlier, in situations like this, we use the Dickey–Fuller tau statistic, whose critical values have been formulated by them and have since been expanded by MacKinnon, which are now incorporated in several econometric packages.

Using *Eviews 6*, we obtained the results shown in Table 13.7. The second part of this table gives the usual OLS output. The $t$ value of the lagged closing price of the IBM coefficient is $-1.0026$ with $p$ value of about 0.30, suggesting that this coefficient is not different from zero, and thus supporting the hypothesis that the IBM closing stock prices are a random walk or that the IBM price series is nonstationary.

If you look at the first part of this output, you will find that the $p$ value of the Dickey–Fuller tau value of the lagged closing price of IBM coefficient is about 0.75, again supporting the random walk hypothesis. But note how the level of significance of the usual $t$ statistic and the tau statistic can differ substantially.

### Are the first differences of IBM closing prices stationary?

Since we know that the first differences of the log IBM stock prices are stationary because the first differences of an RW model are stationary, it would not surprise us to

**Table 13.7  Unit root test of IBM daily closing prices.**

Null Hypothesis: LCLOSE has a unit root
Exogenous: Constant
Lag Length: 0 (Automatic based on AIC, MAXLAG=0)

|  |  |  | t-Statistic | Prob.* |
|---|---|---|---|---|
| Augmented Dickey–Fuller test statistic |  |  | −1.026066 | 0.7455 |
| Test critical values: | 1% level |  | −3.439654 |  |
|  | 5% level |  | −2.865536 |  |
|  | 10% level |  | −2.568955 |  |

*MacKinnon (1996) one-sided p-values.
Augmented Dickey–Fuller Test Equation
Dependent Variable: D(LCLOSE)
Method: Least Squares
Date: 01/25/10  Time: 12:03
Sample (adjusted): 1/04/2000 8/20/2002
Included observations: 686 after adjustments

|  | Coefficient | Std. Error | t-Statistic | Prob. |
|---|---|---|---|---|
| LCLOSE(−1) | −0.006209 | 0.006051 | −1.026066 | 0.3052 |
| C | 0.027766 | 0.027984 | 0.992236 | 0.3214 |

| | | | |
|---|---|---|---|
| R-squared | 0.001537 | Mean dependent var | −0.000928 |
| Adjusted R-squared | 0.000077 | S.D. dependent var | 0.026385 |
| S.E. of regression | 0.026384 | Akaike info criterion | −4.429201 |
| Sum squared resid | 0.476146 | Schwarz criterion | −4.415991 |
| Log likelihood | 1521.216 | Hannan–Quinn criter. | −4.424090 |
| F-statistic | 1.052811 | Durbin–Watson stat | 2.099601 |
| Prob(F-statistic) | 0.305223 | | |

*Note*: In this table, $D$ stands for first difference and Lclose is the log of daily IBM price at the close of the stock market in the USA.

**Table 13.8  Unit root test of first differences of IBM daily closing prices.**

Null Hypothesis: D(LCLOSE) has a unit root
Exogenous: None
Lag Length: 0 (Automatic based on SIC, MAXLAG=0)

|  |  |  | t-Statistic | Prob.* |
|---|---|---|---|---|
| Augmented Dickey–Fuller test statistic |  |  | −27.65371 | 0.0000 |
| Test critical values: | 1% level |  | −2.568342 |  |
|  | 5% level |  | −1.941286 |  |
|  | 10% level |  | −1.616388 |  |

*MacKinnon (1996) one-sided p-values.
Augmented Dickey–Fuller Test Equation
Dependent Variable: D(LCLOSE,2)
Method: Least Squares
Date: 01/26/10  Time: 11:15
Sample (adjusted): 1/05/2000 8/20/2002
Included observations: 685 after adjustments

|  | Coefficient | Std. Error | t-Statistic | Prob. |
|---|---|---|---|---|
| D(LCLOSE(−1)) | −1.057102 | 0.038226 | −27.65371 | 0.0000 |

| | | | |
|---|---|---|---|
| R-squared | 0.527857 | Mean dependent var | 0.000116 |
| Adjusted R-squared | 0.527857 | S.D. dependent var | 0.038349 |
| S.E. of regression | 0.026351 | Akaike info criterion | −4.433187 |
| Sum squared resid | 0.474941 | Schwarz criterion | −4.426575 |
| Log likelihood | 1519.367 | Hannan–Quinn criter. | −4.430629 |
| Durbin–Watson stat | 1.989376 | | |

find that that is indeed the case. If you estimate the correlogram of the first differences, you will find that the correlations hover around zero, which is typically the case of a white noise time series.

If we do a formal unit root analysis, we obtain the results in Table 13.8. These results suggest that we can reject the unit root hypothesis in the first differences of the logged IBM stock price series. The estimated tau ($= t$) is more highly significantly negative than even the 1% critical tau value. In this case the tau and $t$ statistics are the same.

Earlier we noted that we cannot use a nonstationary time series for forecasting purposes. Can we use the first-differenced *LEX* or IBM stock prices for forecasting? How do we then relate the forecast first-difference series to the original (undifferenced) time series? We will take up this task in a later chapter (see Chapter 16 on ARIMA models).

## 13.7  Summary and conclusions

Although we have studied only two financial economic time series, the ideas and techniques discussed in this chapter are applicable to other economic and financial time series, for most economic time series in level form are nonstationary. Such series often exhibit an upward or downward trends over a sustained period of time. But such a trend is often stochastic and not deterministic. This has important implications for regression analysis, for regressing a nonstationary time series on one or more nonstationary time series may often lead to the phenomenon of spurious or meaningless regression. As we will show in the next chapter, only in the case of cointegrated time series may we avoid spurious correlation, even if the underlying series are nonstationary.

We looked at three diagnostic tools to find out if a time series is stationary. The simplest of these is a **time series plot** of the series. Such a plot of a time series is a very valuable tool to get a "feel" about the nature of the time series. More formally, we can examine the correlogram of the time series over several lags. The correlogram will suggest if the correlation of the time series over several lags decays quickly or slowly. If it does decay very slowly, perhaps the time series is nonstationary.

A test that has become popular is the unit root test. If on the basis of the Dickey–Fuller test or the augmented Dickey–Fuller test, we find one or more unit roots in a time series, it may provide yet further evidence of nonstationarity.

Since traditional regression modeling is based on the assumption that the time series used in analysis are stationary, it is critical that we subject a time series to stationarity tests discussed above.

If a time series has deterministic trend, it can be made stationary by regressing it on the time or trend variable. The residuals from his regression will then represent a time series that is trend-free.

However, if a time series has a stochastic trend, it can be made stationary by differencing it one or more times.

## Exercises

**13.1** Verify Eqs. (13.13) and (13.14).

**13.2** Verify Eqs. (13.17) and (13.18).

**13.3** For the IBM stock price series estimate model (13.7) and comment of the results.

**13.4** Suppose in Eq. (13.7) $B_3 = 0$. What is the interpretation of the resulting model?

**13.5** Would you expect quarterly US real GDP series to be stationary? Why or why not? Obtain data on the quarterly US GDP from the website of the Federal Reserve Bank of St Louis to support your claim.

**13.6** Repeat 13.5 for the Consumer Price Index (CPI) for the USA.

**13.7** If a time series is stationary, does it mean that it is a white noise series? In the chapter on autocorrelation, we considered the Markov first-order autoregressive scheme, such as:

$$u_t = \rho u_{t-1} + \varepsilon_t$$

where $u_t$ is the error term in the regression model, $\rho$ is the coefficient of autocorrelation, and $\varepsilon_t$ is a white noise series. Is $u_t$ a white noise series? Is it stationary, if so, under what conditions? Explain.

# 14

# Cointegration and error correction models

In the previous chapter we stated that if we regress a nonstationary time series on one or more nonstationary series, we might obtain a high $R^2$ value and one or more regression coefficients that are statistically significant on the basis of the usual and $t$ and $F$ tests. But these results are likely to be *spurious* or misleading because the standard linear regression procedures assume that the time series involved in the analysis are stationary in the sense defined in the previous chapter. If this is not the case, the resulting regression may be a **spurious regression**.

In this chapter we show how a spurious regression may arise and the reasons for it. We also show what can be done if we encounter a spurious regression.

In this chapter we also explain the phenomenon of **cointegration**, a situation in which the regression of one nonstationary time series on one or more nonstationary time series may *not* result in a spurious regression. If this happens, we say the time series under study are **cointegrated**, that is, there is a long-term or equilibrium relationship between them. We show this with concrete examples and explain the conditions under which cointegration can occur.

## 14.1 The phenomenon of spurious regression

If a trending variable is regressed on one or more trending variables we often find significant $t$ and $F$ statistics and a high $R^2$, but there is really no true relationship between them because each variable is growing over time. This is known as the problem of spurious or false regression. Very often the clue that the relationship is spurious is found in the low Durbin–Watson $d$ statistic.

Here are some examples of spurious regressions:[1]

1 Egyptian infant mortality rate ($Y$), 1971–1990, annual data, on Gross aggregate income of American farmers ($I$) and Total Honduran money supply ($M$)

$$\hat{Y} = 179.9 - .2952\, I - .0439\, M,\ R^2 = .918,\ D/W = .4752,\ F = 95.17$$
$$(16.63)\ (-2.32)\ (-4.26) \quad \text{Corr} = .8858,\ -.9113,\ -.9445$$

2 US Export Index ($Y$), 1960–1990, annual data, on Australian males' life expectancy ($X$)

---

1 See http://www.eco.uc3m.es/jgonzalo/teaching/timeseriesMA/examplesspuriousregression.pdf

$$\hat{Y} = -2943. + 45.7974\, X,\, R^2 = .916,\, D/W = .3599,\, F = 315.2$$
$$(-16.70)\,(17.76) \qquad Corr = .9570$$

3  US Defense Expenditure $(Y)$, 1971–1990, annual data, on Population of South Africa $(X)$

$$\hat{Y} = -368.99 + .0179\, X,\, R^2 = .940,\, D/W = .4069,\, F = 280.69$$
$$(-11.34)\,(16.75) \qquad Corr = .9694$$

4  Total Crime Rates in the US $(Y)$, 1971–1991, annual data, on Life expectancy in South Africa $(X)$

$$\hat{Y} = -24569 + 628.9\, X,\, R^2 = .811,\, D/W = .5061,\, F = 81.72$$
$$(-6.03)\,(9.04) \qquad Corr = .9008$$

5  Population of South Africa $(Y)$, 1971–1990, annual data, on Total R&D expenditure in the US $(X)$

$$\hat{Y} = 21698.7 + 111.58\, X,\, R^2 = .974,\, D/W = .3037,\, F = 696.96$$
$$(59.44)\,(26.40) \qquad Corr = .9873$$

*Note*: Corr is coefficient of correlation.

In each of these examples, there is no logical reason for the observed relationship among the variables. It so happens that all the variables in these examples seem to be trending over time.

## 14.2  Simulation of spurious regression

Consider the following two random walk series without drift:

$$Y_t = Y_{t-1} + u_t \tag{14.1}$$
$$X_t = X_{t-1} + v_t \tag{14.2}$$

where $u_t$ and $v_t$ each are NIID(0, 1), that is, each error term is normally and independently distributed with zero mean and unit variance (i.e. standard normal distribution). We obtained 500 observations for each series from the standard normal distribution.

We know from the discussion in the previous chapter that both these series are nonstationary, that is, they are I(1) or exhibit stochastic trends.

Since $Y_t$ and $X_t$ are uncorrelated I(1) processes, there should not be any relationship between the two variables. But when we regressed $Y_t$ on $X_t$, we obtained the following results:

$$\hat{Y}_t = -13.2556 + 0.3376 X_t \tag{14.3}$$
$$t = (-21.3685)\,(7.6122) \quad R^2 = 0.1044;\; d = 0.0123$$

This regression shows that both the intercept and slope coefficients are highly significant, for their $t$ values are so high. Thus this regression shows a significant relationship between the two variables, although there should not be any. This in a nutshell is the phenomenon of spurious regression, first pointed out by the statistician Yule.[2]

That there is something "fishy" about the results given in Eq. (14.3) is suggested by the extremely low Durbin–Watson statistic. According to Granger and Newbold, an $R^2 > d$ is *a good rule of thumb to suspect that the estimated regression is spurious.*[3] All the examples discussed above seem to be in accord with this rule. Note that the Durbin–Watson $d$ statistic is often used to measure first-order serial correlation in the error term, but it can also be used as an indicator that a time series is nonstationary.

## 14.3    Is the regression of consumption expenditure on disposable income spurious?

**Table 14.1** (which may be found on the companion website) gives quarterly data on personal consumption expenditure (PCE) and personal disposable (i.e. after-tax) income (PDI) for the USA for the period 1970–2008, for a total of 156 observations. All the data are in billions of 2000 dollars.

Let us first plot the data, as shown in Figure 14.1. As we have done frequently, we have plotted the data on a logarithmic scale so that changes in the variables represent relative changes, or percentage changes after multiplication by 100.

This figure shows that both LPDI and LPCE are trending series, which suggests that these series are not stationary. They seem to be I(1), that is, they have stochastic trends. This can be confirmed by unit root analysis, as shown in Tables 14.2 and 14.3.

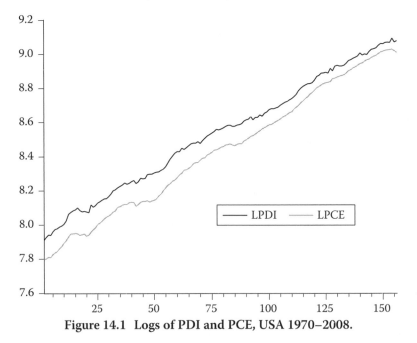

**Figure 14.1  Logs of PDI and PCE, USA 1970–2008.**

2  G. U. Yule, Why do we sometimes get nonsense correlation between time series? A study in sampling and the nature of series. *Journal of the Royal Statistical Society,* vol. 89, 1926, pp. 1–64.

3  C. W. J. Granger and P. Newbold, Spurious regression in econometrics. *Journal of Econometrics,* vol. 2, 1974, pp. 111–20.

**Table 14.2  Unit root analysis of the LPDI series.**

Null Hypothesis: LPDI has a unit root
Exogenous: Constant, Linear Trend
Lag Length: 1 (Automatic based on AIC, MAXLAG=1)

|  |  |  | t-Statistic | Prob.* |
|---|---|---|---|---|
| Augmented Dickey–Fuller test statistic | | | −2.774807 | 0.2089 |
| Test critical values: | 1% level | | −4.018748 | |
| | 5% level | | −3.439267 | |
| | 10% level | | −3.143999 | |

*MacKinnon (1996) one-sided p-values.
Augmented Dickey–Fuller Test Equation
Dependent Variable: D(LPDI)
Method: Least Squares
Date: 01/27/10 Time: 09:14
Sample (adjusted): 1970Q3 2008Q4
Included observations: 154 after adjustments

|  | Coefficient | Std. Error | t-Statistic | Prob. |
|---|---|---|---|---|
| LPDI(−1) | −0.11133 | 0.040123 | −2.774807 | 0.0062 |
| D(LPDI(−1)) | −0.12236 | 0.080488 | −1.520277 | 0.1305 |
| C | 0.894817 | 0.318753 | 2.807246 | 0.0057 |
| @TREND(1970Q1) | 0.001 | 0.0003 | 2.703094 | 0.0077 |

| | | | | |
|---|---|---|---|---|
| R-squared | 0.08339 | Mean dependent var | 0.0075 |
| Adjusted R-squared | 0.06506 | S.D. dependent var | 0.0098 |
| S.E. of regression | 0.0095 | Akaike info criterion | −6.44516 |
| Sum squared resid | 0.0136 | Schwarz criterion | −6.36628 |
| Log likelihood | 500.2774 | Durbin–Watson stat | 1.97578 |
| F-statistic | 4.548978 | Prob(F-statistic) | 0.0044 |

*Note*: D stands for first-difference and @trend is the trend variable

We have used the augmented Dickey–Fuller (ADF) test by including one lagged term of first difference of lagged LPD. The coefficient of primary interest is the coefficient of lagged LPD, which is −0.11133, which on the basis of the usual $t$ test is significant at the 0.006 level, but on the basis of the tau statistic it is significant at the 0.20 level, indicating that the LPD time series is nonstationary.

Here too the LPCE series is nonstationary on the basis of the ADF test, although the usual $t$ test declares otherwise.

It seems that both LPCE and LPDI series have a unit root, or stochastic trend. Therefore, if we regress LPCE on LPDI, we might get a spurious regression. Before we consider this possibility, let us present the results of this regression (Table 14.4).

Before we interpret the results, notice that $R^2 > d = 0.3672$. This raises the possibility that this regression might be spurious, which might be due to regressing one stochastic trend series on another stochastic trend series. Of course, if we interpret the Durbin–Watson on its own, it would suggest that the error term in this regression suffers from first-order autocorrelation.

The results at their face value suggest that the elasticity of personal consumption expenditure of 1.08 with respect to PDI is greater than one – a one percent increase in

Table 14.3  Unit root analysis of the LPCE series.

Null Hypothesis: LPCE has a unit root
Exogenous: Constant, Linear Trend
Lag Length: 1 (Automatic based on AIC, MAXLAG=1)

|  |  |  | t-Statistic | Prob.* |
|---|---|---|---|---|
| Augmented Dickey–Fuller test statistic |  |  | −2.038416 | 0.5754 |
| Test critical values: | 1% level |  | −4.018748 |  |
|  | 5% level |  | −3.439267 |  |
|  | 10% level |  | −3.143999 |  |

*MacKinnon (1996) one-sided p-values.
Augmented Dickey–Fuller Test Equation
Dependent Variable: D(LPCE)
Method: Least Squares
Date: 01/27/10  Time: 09:19
Sample (adjusted): 1970Q3 2008Q4
Included observations: 154 after adjustments

|  | Coefficient | Std. Error | t-Statistic | Prob. |
|---|---|---|---|---|
| LPCE(−1) | −0.0503 | 0.024686 | −2.038416 | 0.0433 |
| D(LPCE(−1)) | 0.313333 | 0.079964 | 3.9184 | 0 |
| C | 0.398477 | 0.192288 | 2.072292 | 0.0399 |
| @TREND(1970Q1) | 0 | 0.0002 | 1.975799 | 0.05 |

| R-squared | 0.111128 | Mean dependent var | 0.0078 |
|---|---|---|---|
| Adjusted R-squared | 0.09335 | S.D. dependent var | 0.0068 |
| S.E. of regression | 0.0065 | Akaike info criterion | −7.22165 |
| Sum squared resid | 0.0063 | Schwarz criterion | −7.14277 |
| Log likelihood | 560.0671 | Durbin–Watson stat | 2.104952 |
| F-statistic | 6.251045 | Prob(F-statistic) | 0.001 |

Table 14.4  Regression of LPCE on LPDI.

Dependent Variable: LPCE
Method: Least Squares
Sample: 1970Q1 2008Q4
Included observations: 156

|  | Coefficient | Std. Error | t-Statistic | 1Prob. |
|---|---|---|---|---|
| C | −0.84251 | 0.033717 | −24.98747 | 0 |
| LPDI | 1.086822 | 0.00395 | 275.2413 | 0 |

| R-squared | 0.997971 | Mean dependent var | 8.430699 |
|---|---|---|---|
| Adjusted R-squared | 0.997958 | S.D. dependent var | 0.366642 |
| S.E. of regression | 0.01657 | Akaike info criterion | −5.35003 |
| Sum squared resid | 0.04227 | Schwarz criterion | −5.31093 |
| Log likelihood | 419.3021 | Durbin–Watson stat | 0.367187 |
| F-statistic | 75757.76 | Prob(F-statistic) | 0 |

PDI leads to more than a one percent increase in personal consumption expenditure. This elasticity seems high.

Because of the possibility of spurious regression, we should be wary of these results.

Since both the time series are trending, let us see what happens if we add a trend variable to the model. Before we do that it may be worth noting that the trend variable is a catch-all for all other variables that might affect both the regressand and regressor(s). One such variable is population, because as population increases the aggregate consumption expenditure and aggregate disposable income also increase. If we had quarterly data on population, we could have added that variable as an additional regressor instead of the trend variable. Better yet, we could have expressed consumption expenditure and personal disposable income on a per capita basis. So keep in mind that the trend variable may be a surrogate for other variables. With this caveat, let us see what happens if we add the trend variable to our model.

Compared to the results in Table 14.4, there are changes. The elasticity of LPCE with respect LPID is now much less than unity, although it is still statistically significant on the basis of the usual $t$ test and the trend variable is also statistically significant. Therefore, allowing for linear trend, the relationship between the two variables is strongly positive. But notice again the low Durbin–Watson value, which suggests that the results are plagued by autocorrelation. Or maybe this regression too is spurious.

## 14.4  When a spurious regression may not be spurious

Underlying the regression in Table 14.5 is the population regression model:

$$lPCE_t = B_1 + B_2 lPDI_t + B_3 t + u_t \tag{14.4}$$

where $t$ is time or trend.

Rewrite this model as:

$$u_t = lPCE_t - B_1 - B_2 lPDI - B_3 t \tag{14.5}$$

After estimating (14.4), suppose we subject the estimated $u_t (= e_t)$ to unit root analysis and find that it is stationary, that is, it is I(0). This is an intriguing situation, for although the log of PCE and log of PDI are individually I(1), that is, that they have stochastic trends, their (linear) combination as shown in Eq. (14.5) is I(0). This linear combination, so to speak, cancels out the stochastic trends in the two series. In that

Table 14.5  Regression of LPCE on LPDI and trend.

Dependent Variable: LPCE
Method: Least Squares
Sample: 1970Q1 2008Q4
Included observations: 156

|  | Coefficient | Std. Error | t-Statistic | Prob. |
|---|---|---|---|---|
| C | 1.675338 | 0.487797 | 3.4345 | 0.001 |
| LPDI | 0.770241 | 0.061316 | 12.56176 | 0 |
| @TREND | 0.0024 | 0.0005 | 5.172271 | 0 |

| | | | | |
|---|---|---|---|---|
| R-squared | 0.998273 | Mean dependent var | 8.430699 |
| Adjusted R-squared | 0.998251 | S.D. dependent var | 0.366642 |
| S.E. of regression | 0.01534 | Akaike info criterion | −5.49835 |
| Sum squared resid | 0.03598 | Schwarz criterion | −5.4397 |
| Log likelihood | 431.8712 | Durbin–Watson stat | 0.261692 |
| F-statistic | 44226.49 | Prob(F-statistic) | 0 |

case the regression of lPCE on LPDI is not spurious. If this happens, we say that the variables lPCE and lPDI are **cointegrated**. This can be seen clearly in Figure 14.1, for even though the two series are stochastically trending, they do not drift apart substantially. It is as if two drunkards are meandering aimlessly, but they keep pace with each other.

Economically speaking, two variables will be cointegrated if they have a long-run, or equilibrium, relationship between them. In the present context economic theory tells us that there is a strong relationship between consumption expenditure and personal disposable income. Remember that PCE is about 70% of PDI.

The point of all this discussion is that not all time series regressions are spurious. Of course, we need to test this formally. As Granger notes, "A test for cointegration can be thought of as a pre-test to avoid 'spurious regression' situations".[4]

In the language of cointegration theory, regression like (14.4) is known as a **cointegrating regression** and the slope parameters $B_2$ and $B_3$ are known as **cointegrating parameters**.

## 14.5  Tests of cointegration

Although there are several tests of cointegration, we consider here the test we have already discussed in the previous chapter, the DF and ADF unit root tests on the residuals estimated from the cointegrating regression, as modified by the Engle–Granger (EG) and Augmented Engle–Granger (AEG) test.[5]

### The EG and AEG tests

To use the DF or ADF test, we estimate a regression like (14.4), obtain residuals from this regression, and use these tests. However, since we only observe $e_t$ and not $u_t$, the DF and ADF critical significance values need to be adjusted, as suggested by Engle and Granger.[6] In the context of testing for cointegration, the DF and ADF tests are known as **Engle–Granger** (EG) and **augmented Engle–Granger** (AEG) tests, which are now incorporated in several software packages.

Let us apply these tests to the PCE-PDI regression (14.4). The results of this regression are already shown in Table 14.5. Let us first run the EG test with no intercept and no trend term, which gives the results of Table 14.6.

This output clearly shows that the residuals from regression (14.4) are stationary, for the computed *tau* value of the lagged residual term far exceeds any of the critical values in the table. The results did not change materially if we add several lagged $D(S_3)$ terms. Notice also how the Durbin–Watson value has changed.

### Unit root tests and cointegration tests

Notice the difference between the unit root and cointegration tests. Tests for unit roots are performed on single time series, whereas cointegration deals with the

---

4  C. W. Granger, Developments in the study of co-integrated economic variables, *Oxford Bulletin of Economics and Statistics*, vol. 48, 1986, p. 226.

5  A test with better statistical properties is Johansen's cointegration test. But this test is mathematically somewhat complex. The interested reader may consult some of the textbooks mentioned in this chapter.

6  R. F. Engle and C. W. Granger, Co-integration and error correction: representation, estimation, and testing, *Econometrica*, vol. 55, 1987, pp. 251–76.

**Table 14.6  Unit root test on residuals from regression (14.4).**

Null Hypothesis: S3 has a unit root
Exogenous: None
Lag Length: 0 (Automatic based on SIC, MAXLAG=0)

|  |  |  | t-Statistic | Prob.* |
|---|---|---|---|---|
| Augmented Dickey–Fuller test statistic |  |  | −3.392603 | 0.001 |
| Test critical values: | 1% level |  | −2.579967 |  |
|  | 5% level |  | −1.942896 |  |
|  | 10% level |  | −1.615342 |  |

*MacKinnon (1996) one-sided p-values.
Augmented Dickey–Fuller Test Equation
Dependent Variable: D(S3)
Method: Least Squares
Date: 01/29/10  Time: 10:44
Sample (adjusted): 1970Q2 2008Q4
Included observations: 155 after adjustments

|  | Coefficient | Std. Error | t-Statistic | Prob. |
|---|---|---|---|---|
| S3(−1) | −0.13599 | 0.040085 | −3.392603 | 0.001 |

| | | | |
|---|---|---|---|
| R-squared | 0.06781 | Mean dependent var | 0 |
| Adjusted R-squared | 0.06781 | S.D. dependent var | 0.0078 |
| S.E. of regression | 0.0075 | Akaike info criterion | −6.93014 |
| Sum squared resid | 0.0088 | Schwarz criterion | −6.91051 |
| Log likelihood | 538.0859 | Durbin–Watson stat | 2.388956 |

*Note*: $S_3$ represents the residual term from regression (14.4). Also note that in this regression there is no intercept because the mean value of the residuals in an OLS regression is zero.

relationship among a group of variables, each having a unit root. In practice, it is better to test each series for unit roots, for it is quite possible that some of the series in a group may have more than one unit root, in which case they will have to be differenced more than once to make them stationary.

If two time series $Y$ and $X$ are integrated of different orders then the error term in the regression of $Y$ and $X$ is not stationary and this regression equation is said to be *unbalanced*. On the other hand, if the two variables are integrated of the same order, then the regression equation is said to be *balanced*.

## 14.6  Cointegration and error correction mechanism (ECM)

After allowing for deterministic trend, we have shown that log PCE and log PDI series are cointegrated, that is, they have a long-term, or equilibrium, relationship. But how is this equilibrium achieved, for in the short-run there may be disequilibrium?

We can treat the error term in Eq. (14.5) as the "equilibrating" error term that corrects deviations of LPCE from its equilibrium value given by the cointegrating regression (14.4). Dennis Sargan called this the **error correction mechanism (ECM)**, a term that was later popularized by Engle and Granger.[7]

An important theorem, known as **Granger Representation Theorem**, states that if two variables $Y$ and $X$ are cointegrated, the relationship between the two can be expressed as an ECM. To see the importance of this, we continue with the PCE-PDI example. Now consider the following model:

$$\Delta lPCE_t = A_1 + A_2 \Delta lPDI_t + A_3 u_{t-1} + v_t \qquad (14.6)$$

where $\Delta$, as usual, is the first-difference operator, $u_{t-1}$ is the lagged value of the error correction term from Eq. (14.5), and $v_t$ is a white noise error term.

We know that Eq. (14.4) gives the long-run relationship between lPCE and lPDI. On the other hand, Eq. (14.6) gives the short-run relationship between the two. Just as $B_2$ in Eq. (14.4) gives the long-run impact of lPDI on lPCE, $A_2$ in Eq. (14.6) gives the immediate, or short-run, impact of $\Delta LPDI$ on $\Delta LPCE$.

Model (14.6), called the **error correction model (ECM)**, postulates that changes in LPCE depend on changes in lPDI and the lagged equilibrium error term, $u_{t-1}$.[8] If this error term is zero, there will not be any disequilibrium between the two variables and in that case the long-run relationship will be given by the cointegrating relationship (14.4) (no error term here). But if the equilibrium error term is nonzero, the relationship between LPCE and LPDI will be out of equilibrium.

To see this, let $\Delta lPDI = 0$ (no change in lPDI) and suppose $u_{t-1}$ is positive. This means $LPCE_{t-1}$ is too high to be in equilibrium – that is, $LPCE_{t-1}$ is above its equilibrium value $(B_1 + B_2 LPDI_{t-1})$. Since $A_3$ in Eq. (14.6) is expected to be negative, the term $A_3 u_{t-1}$ is negative and, therefore $\Delta lPCE_t$ will be negative to restore the equilibrium. That is, if $LPCE_t$ is above its equilibrium value, it will start falling in the next period to correct the equilibrium error; hence the name ECM.

By the same token, if $lPCE_t$ is below its equilibrium value (i.e. if $u_{t-1}$ is negative), $A_3 u_{t-1}$ will be positive, which will cause $\Delta LPCE_t$ to be positive, leading $lPCE$ to rise in period $t$.

Thus the absolute value of $A_3$ will decide how quickly the equilibrium is reached. Note that in practice we estimate $u_{t-1}$ by its sample counterpart $e_{t-1}$.

It is interesting to note that Eq. (14.6) incorporates both the short-run and long-run dynamics. Also note that in Eq. (14.6) all the variables are I(0), or stationary. So Eq. (14.6) can be estimated by OLS.

To see all this theory in practice, we return to our illustrative example. The empirical counterpart of Eq. (14.6) is shown in Table 14.7.

### Interpretation of the results

First, note that all coefficients in this table are individually statistically significant at the 6% or lower level. The coefficient of about 0.31 shows that a 1% increase in $\ln(LPDI_t / LPDI_{t-1})$ will lead on average to a 0.31% increase in $\ln(LPCE_t / LPCE_{t-1})$.

---

7 See J. D. Sargan, Wages and prices in the United Kingdom: a study in econometric methodology, in K. F. Wallis and D. F. Hendry (eds.), *Quantitative Economics and Economic Analysis*, Basil Blackwell, Oxford, UK, 1984.

8 We use the lagged error term because it is the error made in the previous period that will be used to correct the imbalance in the current time period.

**Table 14.7  Error correction model of lPCE and lPDI.**

Dependent Variable: D(LPCE)
Method: Least Squares
Date: 01/28/10 Time: 20:51
Sample (adjusted): 1970Q2 2008Q4
Included observations: 155 after adjustments

|  | Coefficient | Std. Error | t-Statistic | Prob. |
|---|---|---|---|---|
| C | 0.0055 | 0.0006 | 8.646287 | 0 |
| D(LPDI) | 0.313476 | 0.052866 | 5.929625 | 0 |
| S1(−1) | −0.0583 | 0.031487 | −1.850423 | 0.0662 |

| | | | | |
|---|---|---|---|---|
| R-squared | 0.187863 | Mean dependent var | 0.0078 | |
| Adjusted R-squared | 0.177177 | S.D. dependent var | 0.0068 | |
| S.E. of regression | 0.0061 | Akaike info criterion | −7.33019 | |
| Sum squared resid | 0.0057 | Schwarz criterion | −7.27128 | |
| Log likelihood | 571.0895 | Durbin–Watson stat | 1.716035 | |
| F-statistic | 17.58023 | Prob(F-statistic) | 0 | |

Note: S1(−1) is the error term $u_{t-1}$ in Eq. (14.5). $D$ stands for first difference.

This is the short-run consumption–income elasticity. The long-run value is given by the cointegrating regression Eq. (14.5), which is about 0.77.

The coefficient of the error-correction term of about −0.06 suggests that only about 6% of the discrepancy between long-term and short-term PCE is corrected within a quarter, suggesting a slow rate of adjustment to equilibrium. One reason the rate of adjustment seems low is that our model is rather simple. If we had the necessary data on interest rate, wealth of consumer, and so on, probably we might have seen a different result.

To further familiarize the reader with concept of cointegration and ECM we consider another example.

## 14.7  Are 3-month and 6-month Treasury Bill rates cointegrated?

Figure 14.2 plots the constant maturity 3-month and 6-month US Treasury Bill (T-bill) rates from January 1981 to January 2010, for a total 349 observations. See **Table 14.8** on the companion website.

Since the two treasury bills seem to be so closely aligned, we would expect that the two rates are cointegrated, that is, there is a stable equilibrium relationship between the two, even though they both exhibit trends. This is what we would expect from financial economics theory, for if the two rates are not cointegrated, arbitrageurs will exploit any discrepancy between the short and the long rates.

But let us see if that is the case. We first test each series for stationarity. Including intercept, trend and five lagged terms, it was found that the TB3 series was stationary at about the 5% level. Under the same structure, the TB6 series was also found to be stationary at about the 5% level. Therefore it seems that both time series are stationary.

Now let us find out if the two series are cointegrated. After some experimentation, it was found that the two series were related as in Table 14.9.

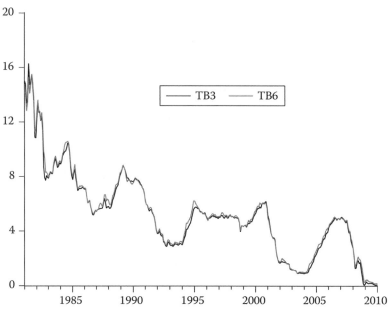

**Figure 14.2  Monthly three and six months Treasury Bill rates.**

Applying the unit root test to the residuals from this regression, we found that they were stationary, suggesting that TB6 and TB3 are cointegrated, albeit around a quadratic trend. We therefore obtained the ECM model of Table 14.10.

In this regression S1(−1) is the lagged error (correction) term from the regression in Table 14.9. Since the TB rates are in percentage form, the findings here suggest that if the 6-month TB rate was higher than the 3-month TB rate more than expected in the

**Table 14.9  Relationship between TB3 and TB6.**

Dependent Variable: TB6
Method: Least Squares
Date: 02/03/10 Time: 12:06
Sample: 1981M01 2010M01
Included observations: 349

|  | Coefficient | Std. Error | t-Statistic | Prob. |
|---|---|---|---|---|
| C | 0.606465 | 0.07682 | 7.894596 | 0 |
| TB3 | 0.958401 | 0.00631 | 151.9409 | 0 |
| @TREND | −0.003 | 0.0005 | −4.893455 | 0 |
| @TREND^2 | 0 | 0 | 3.533231 | 0.001 |

| | | | | |
|---|---|---|---|---|
| R-squared | 0.99595 | Mean dependent var | 5.352693 | |
| Adjusted R-squared | 0.995915 | S.D. dependent var | 3.075953 | |
| S.E. of regression | 0.19659 | Akaike info criterion | −0.404 | |
| Sum squared resid | 13.33346 | Schwarz criterion | −0.35981 | |
| Log likelihood | 74.49716 | Durbin–Watson stat | 0.363237 | |
| F-statistic | 28283.37 | Prob(F-statistic) | 0 | |

**Table 14.10  Error correction model for TB3 and TB6.**

Dependent Variable: D(TB6)
Method: Least Squares
Date: 02/03/10 Time: 12:26
Sample (adjusted): 1981M02 2010M01
Included observations: 348 after adjustments

|  | Coefficient | Std. Error | t-Statistic | Prob. |
|---|---|---|---|---|
| C | −0.002 | 0.00573 | −0.384308 | 0.701 |
| D(TB3) | 0.877882 | 0.014735 | 59.57784 | 0 |
| S1(−1) | −0.19968 | 0.029234 | −6.830361 | 0 |

| | | | |
|---|---|---|---|
| R-squared | 0.911494 | Mean dependent var | −0.04 |
| Adjusted R-squared | 0.910981 | S.D. dependent var | 0.35623 |
| S.E. of regression | 0.106285 | Akaike info criterion | −1.6368 |
| Sum squared resid | 3.897314 | Schwarz criterion | −1.60359 |
| Log likelihood | 287.8026 | Durbin–Watson stat | 1.663899 |
| F-statistic | 1776.513 | Prob(F-statistic) | 0 |

last month, this month it will be reduced by about 0.20 percentage points to restore the equilibrium relationship between the two rates.[9]

From the cointegrating regression given in Table 14.9, we see that after allowing for deterministic trends, if the 3-month TB rate goes up by one percentage point, the 6-month TB rate goes up by about 0.95 percentage point – a very close relationship between the two. From Table 14.10 we observe that in the short run a one percentage point change in the 3-month TB rate leads on average to about 0.88 percentage point change in the 6-month TB rate, which shows how quickly the two rates move together.

A question: why not regress TB-3 month on TB-6 month rate? If two series are cointegrated, and if the sample size is large, it matters little which is the regressand. Try to regress TB-3 month and TB-6 month rate and see what happens. Matters are different if we are studying more than two time series.

## Some caveats about the Engle–Granger approach

It is important to point out some drawbacks of the EG approach. First, if you have more than three variables, there might be more than one cointegrating relationship. The EG two step procedure does not allow for estimation of more than one cointegrating regression. It may be noted here that if we are dealing with $n$ variables, there can be at most $(n-1)$ cointegrating relationships. To find that out, we will have to use tests developed by Johansen. But we will not discuss the Johansen methodology because it is beyond the scope of this book.[10]

Another problem with the EG test is the order in which variables enter the cointegrating regression. When we have more than two variables, how do we decide which is the regressand and which ones are the regressors? For example, if we have three variables $Y, X,$ and $Z$ and suppose we regress $Y$ on $X$ and $Z$ and find cointegration.

---

9  See any textbook on money and banking and read up on the term structure of interest rates.

10  The details can be found in S. Johansen, Statistical analysis of cointegrating vectors, *Journal of Economic Dynamics and Control*, vol. 12, 1988, pp. 231–54. This is an advanced reference.

There is no guarantee that if we regress $X$ on $Y$ and $Z$ we will necessarily find cointegration.

Another problem with the EG methodology in dealing with multiple time series is that we not only have to consider finding more than one cointegrating relationship, but then we will also have to deal with the error correction term for each cointegrating relationship. As a result, the simple, or bivariate, error correction model will not work. We have to then consider what is known as the **vector error correction model** (**VECM**), which is briefly discussed in Chapter 16.

All these problems can be handled if we use the Johansen methodology. But a fuller discussion of this methodology is beyond the scope of this book.

## 14.8    Summary and conclusions

In this chapter we first examined the phenomenon of spurious regression which arises if we regress a nonstationary time series on another nonstationary time series.

After citing several examples of spurious regression, we conducted a Monte Carlo simulation study by artificially creating two random walk series, which are I(1), or nonstationary, by nature. When we regressed one of these series on the other, we obtained a "meaningful" relationship between the two, but we know *a priori* that there should not be any relationship between the two series to begin with.

There is a unique case where a regression of a nonstationary series on another nonstationary series does not result in spurious regression. This is the situation of cointegration. If two time series have stochastic trends (i.e. they are nonstationary), a regression of one on the other may cancel out the stochastic trends, which may suggest that there is a long-run, or equilibrium, relationship, between them, even though individually the two series are nonstationary.

We discussed the tests of cointegration, which are modifications of the Dickey–Fuller (DF) and augmented Dickey–Fuller (ADF) tests and known as Engle–Granger (EG) and augmented Engle–Granger (AEG) tests.

We illustrated cointegration by considering two examples. In the first, we considered the relationship between personal consumption expenditure (PCE) and personal disposable income (PDI), both expressed in real terms. We showed that individually the two economic time series are stationary around deterministic trends. We also showed that the two series are cointegrated.

Keep in mind that unit root and nonstationarity are not synonymous. A stochastic process with a deterministic trend is nonstationary but not unit root.

The second example we discussed in this chapter relates to the relationship between 3-month and 6-month US Treasury Bills. Using monthly data from January 1981 to January 2010 we showed that the two series are stationary around a quadratic trend. We also showed that the two series are cointegrated, that is, there is a stable relationship between the two.

In this chapter we also discussed some of the shortcomings of the EG methodology and noted that once we go beyond two time series, we will have to use Johansen methodology to test for cointegrating relationships among multiple variables.

# Exercises

**14.1** Consider the relationship between PCE and PDI discussed in the text.

(a) Regress PCE on an intercept and trend and obtain the residuals from this regression. Call it $S_1$.

(b) Regress PDI on an intercept and trend and obtain residuals from this regression. Call it $S_2$.

(c) Now regress $S_1$ on $S_2$. What does this regression connote?

(d) Obtain the residuals from the regression in (c) and test whether the residuals are stationary. If they are, what does that say about the long-term relationship between PCE and PDI?

(e) How does this exercise differ from the one we discussed in this chapter?

**14.2** Repeat the steps in Exercise 14.1 to analyze the Treasury Bill rates, but make sure that you use the quadratic trend model. Compare your results with those discussed in the chapter.

**14.3** Suppose you have data on real GDP for Mexico and the USA. *A priori*, would you expect the two time series to be cointegrated? Why? What does trade theory have to say about the relationship between the two? Obtain quarterly data on the two time series and analyze them from the perspective of cointegration.[11]

---

11  The data can be obtained from *World Development Indicators*, published by the World Bank. The data are revised frequently. See http://www.worldbank.org/data/.

# 15

# Asset price volatility: the ARCH and GARCH models

Financial time series, such as stock prices, interest rates, foreign exchange rates, and inflation rates, often exhibit the phenomenon of **volatility clustering**. That is, periods of turbulence in which their prices show wide swings and periods of tranquility in which there is relative calm. As Philip Franses notes:

> Since such financial time series reflect the result of trading among buyers and sellers at, for example, stock markets, various sources of news and other exogenous economic events may have an impact on the time series pattern of asset prices. Given that news can lead to various interpretations, and also given that specific economic events like an oil crisis can last for some time, we often observe the large positive and large negative observations in financial time series to appear in clusters.[1]

One only has to consider the behavior of US stock markets in the wake of the escalating oil prices in the first half of 2008; within a span of one year oil prices increased by more than 100%. On 6 June 2008 the Dow Jones Index dropped by almost 400 points in the wake of a ten dollar increase in the price of a barrel of oil that day; the price jumped to $139 a barrel, when two days earlier it had dropped to $122 a barrel. Towards the end of October 2008, oil price dropped to around $67 a barrel. Such gyrations in oil prices have led to wide swings in stock prices.

On 29 September 2008 the Dow Jones Index fell by about 777.7 (the "lucky sevens"?) points in the wake of the sub-prime mortgage loans crisis that led to the bankruptcies of several financial institutions. Although the US Government announced a bailout plan of $700 billion on 3 October 2008, on 6 October the stock market fell by almost 800 points before recovering and closing down by some 369 points. This time the culprit was crisis in the credit markets. In October 2008 there were several days when the Dow Jones Index went up or down by more than 300 points, indicating that the stock market had become more volatile. In varying degrees this pattern seems to have continued through 2009 and 2010. For instance, the Dow Jones Index fell by 261 points on 16 July 2010 after rising for six trading days in a row.

Such swings in oil prices and credit crises have serious effects on both the real economy and the financial markets. An average investor is not only concerned about the rate of return on his or her investment, but also about the risk of investment as well as

---

1 Philip Hanes Franses, *Time Series Models for Business and Economic Forecasting*, Cambridge University Press, New York, 1998, p. 155.

the variability, or *volatility*, of risk. It is, therefore, important to measure asset price and asset returns volatility.[2]

A simple measure of asset return volatility is its variance over time. If we have data for stock returns over, say, a period of 1,000 days, we can compute the variance of daily stock returns by subtracting the mean value of stock returns from their individual values, square the difference and divide it by the number of observations. By itself it does not capture volatility clustering because it is a measure of what is called **unconditional variance**, which is a single number for a given sample. It does not take into account the past history of returns. That is, it does not take into account *time-varying volatility* in asset returns. A measure that takes into account the past history is known as **autoregressive conditional heteroscedasticity**, or ARCH for short.

## 15.1    The ARCH model

We usually encounter heteroscedasticity, or unequal variance, in cross-sectional data because of the heterogeneity among individual cross-section units that comprise cross-sectional observations, such as families, firms, regions, and countries.

We also usually observe autocorrelation in time series data. But in time series data involving asset returns, such as returns on stocks or foreign exchange, we observe **autocorrelated heteroscedasticity**. That is, heteroscedasticity observed over different periods is autocorrelated. In the literature such a phenomenon is called **autoregressive conditional heteroscedasticity (ARCH)**. In what follows we explore the nature of ARCH, illustrating it with an example. We also consider several extensions of the ARCH model.

To set the stage, consider the behavior of the *daily* dollar/euro exchange rate from 1 January 2004 to 8 May 2008, first discussed in Chapter 13. These rates are not continuous because of holidays, market closures, and so on.

To get a glimpse of the daily dollar/euro exchange rate (EX), Figure 15.1 plots the log of EX (LEX) for the sample period. It is common practice in financial econometrics to plot the log of the exchange rate than the exchange rate itself, because changes in logs represent relative changes or percentage changes if the relative changes are multiplied by 100.

As you can see, initially the EU was depreciating against the dollar, but later it showed a steady appreciation against the dollar.[3] But a closer look at the figure suggests that the initial depreciation and then appreciation of EU was not smooth, which is apparent from the jagged nature of the graph. This would suggest that there is considerable volatility of the dollar/euro exchange rate.

This can be seen more vividly if we plot the *changes* in the LEX (Figure 15.2); as noted, changes in the log values represent relative changes, or percentage changes if multiplied by 100. For the purpose of discussion, we will refer to the log-changes in asset prices as asset returns, in the present case daily returns on the dollar/euro

---

2  It may be noted that asset prices are generally nonstationary, but the asset returns are stationary. But this does not preclude asset returns being volatile. In Chapter 13 we discussed the nature of stationary and nonstationary time series.

3  In 2010 the EU again started depreciating against the dollar, perhaps reflecting weakness in the EU economies relative to the US economy.

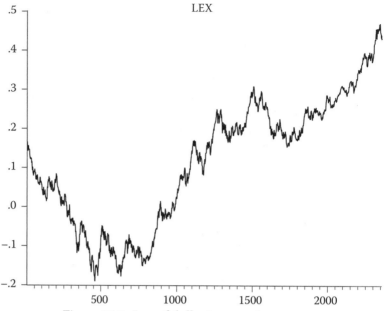

**Figure 15.1  Log of dollar/euro exchange rate.**

exchange rate, as our data are daily (in the following figure D(LEX) denotes change in the log of the dollar/euro exchange rate).

If you draw a horizontal line through 0.00, you will see clearly the volatility of log-exchange rate changes: the *amplitude* of the change swings wildly from time to time. Not only that, it seems there is a persistence in the swings that lasts for some

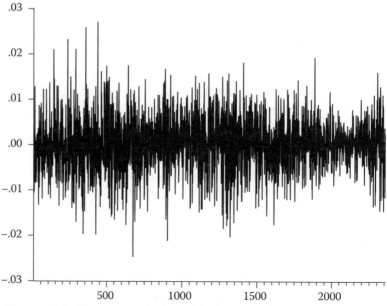

**Figure 15.2  Changes in the log of daily dollar/euro exchange rates.**

time. That is, these swings seem to be autocorrelated. This is the heuristic idea behind ARCH.

The variance of a random variable is a measure of the variability in the values of the random variable. For our data, the mean of the daily exchange rate returns is about 0.000113 or about 0.0113% and its variance is about 0.0000351. But this variance does not capture the volatility of the daily exchange rate return seen in Figure 15.2. This is because the variance is measured as the sum of squared deviation of individual returns from their mean value divided by the number of observations.[4] As such, it does not take into account the variation in the amplitudes noticed in Figure 15.2.

A simple way to measure the volatility is to run the following regression:

$$RET_t = c + u_t \tag{15.1}$$

where RET is daily return and where $c$ is a constant and $u_t$ represents the error term.[5] Here we measure return as log changes in the exchange rate over successive days.

The constant $c$ in this case measures simply the mean value of daily exchange rate returns. Notice that we have not introduced any explanatory variables in Eq. (15.1), for asset returns are essentially unpredictable.

The regression results are as follows:

$$\hat{RET}_t = 0.000113$$
$$se = (0.000122) \tag{15.2}$$

As you can see, 0.000113 is the mean daily return, as noted before. For our purpose, this regression is not important. But if you obtain residuals from this regression ($e_t$) (which are simply the deviations of daily returns from their mean value) and square them, you get the plot in Figure 15.3.

This shows wide swings in the squared residuals, which can be taken as an indicator of underlying volatility in the foreign exchange returns. Observe that not only are there clusters of periods when volatility is high and clusters of periods when volatility is low, but these clusters seem to be "autocorrelated". That is, when volatility is high, it continues to be high for quite some time and when volatility is low, it continues to be low for a while.

How do we measure this volatility? The ARCH model and its subsequent extensions attempt to answer this question.

Consider the following simple linear regression model:

$$Y_t \mid I_{t-1} = \alpha + \beta X_t + u_t \tag{15.3}$$

This states that, conditional on the information available up to time ($t-1$), the value of the random variable $Y_t$ (exchange rate return here) is a function of the variable $X_t$ (or a vector of variables if there are more $X_t$ variables) and $u_t$.

In Eq. (15.3) we assume that

---

4  More accurately, it should be divided by the degrees of freedom ($n-1$), but in large samples it makes little difference if we divide it by $n$.

5  There are two ways of measuring returns. (1) $[(EX_t - EX_{t-1})/EX_{t-1}] \times 100$ and (2) $(\ln EX_t - \ln EX_{t-1}) \times 100$, where $EX$ is the exchange rate and $t$ is time. Since our data are daily over a substantial number of days, there will not be much difference between the two rates of return.

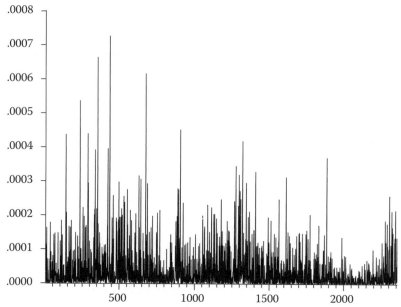

**Figure 15.3  Squared residuals from regression (15.2).**

$$u_t \mid I_{t-1} \sim iid\, N(0, \sigma_t^2) \tag{15.4}$$

That is, given the information available up to time $(t-1)$, the error term is independently and identically normally distributed with mean value of 0 and variance of $\sigma_t^2$. In the classical normal linear regression model it is assumed that $\sigma_t^2 = \sigma^2$ – that is, homoscedastic variance.

But to take into account the ARCH effect, and following Engle, we will let

$$\sigma_t^2 = \lambda_0 + \lambda_1 u_{t-1}^2 \tag{15.5}$$

That is, we assume that the error variance at time $t$ is equal to some constant plus a constant multiplied by the squared error term in the previous time period.[6] Of course, if $\lambda_1$ is zero, the error variance is homoscedastic, in which case we work in the framework of the classical normal linear regression model. It is assumed that the coefficients in this equation are positive because the variance cannot be a negative number. Also, it is assumed that $0 \leq \lambda_1 < 1$ for reasons that will be explained shortly.

After taking mathematical expectation on both sides of Eq. (15.3) $\alpha + \beta X_t$ is the conditional **mean equation**. And Eq. (15.5) is called the (conditional) **variance equation**, both conditional on the information set $I_{t-1}$. Equation (15.5) is known as the **ARCH (1)** model, for it includes only one lagged squared value of the error term. But this model can be easily extended to an **ARCH ($p$)** model, where we have $p$ lagged squared error terms, as follows:

$$\sigma_t^2 = \lambda_0 + \lambda_1 u_{t-1}^2 + \lambda_2 u_{t-2}^2 + \ldots + \lambda_p u_{t-p}^2 \tag{15.6}$$

---

6  R. F. Engel, Autoregressive conditional heteroscedasticity with estimates of the variance of United Kingdom inflation, *Econometrica*, vol. 50, pp. 987–1007, 1982. Engle was first to develop the ARCH model. Among other writings, he got the Nobel prize in economics for this contribution.

If there is an ARCH effect, it can be tested by the statistical significance of the estimated $\lambda$ coefficients. If we are considering an ARCH (1) model, as in (15.5), we can use the $t$ test to test the statistical significance of the estimated $\lambda$ coefficient. If it significantly different from zero, we can conclude that there is an ARCH effect.

To test the ARCH effect in (15.6), we can use the $F$ test to test the hypothesis that

Null hypothesis: $H_0: \lambda_1 = \lambda_2 = \ldots = \lambda_p = 0$ \hfill (15.7)

Alternative Hypothesis: $H_1$: At least one $\lambda$ coefficient is statistically significantly different from zero.

Alternatively, to test Eq. (15.7), we can use the chi-square test as follows:

$$(n-r)R^2 \sim \chi_p^2 \hfill (15.8)$$

where $r$ = number of coefficients estimated. That is, the estimated $R^2$ times the degrees of freedom $(n - r)$ follows the chi-square distribution with $p$ degrees of freedom.[7] If the estimated chi-square value is statistically significant at the chosen level of significance, we can conclude that there is significant ARCH effect. Alternatively, if the $p$ value (the exact level of significance) is sufficiently low, we can reject the null hypothesis.

Note that since a variance cannot be negative, in Eq. (15.6) we expect the $\lambda$ coefficients to be positive.

Since the $u$s are not directly observable, we first estimate Eq. (15.3) and estimate $u$ as

$$\hat{u}_t = Y_t - \hat{\alpha}_t - \beta \hat{X}_t \hfill (15.9)$$

and then estimate the following model:

$$\hat{u}_t^2 = \lambda_0 + \lambda_1 \hat{u}_{t-1}^2 + \lambda_2 \hat{u}_{t-1}^2 + \ldots + \lambda_p \hat{u}_{t-p}^2 + \varepsilon_t \hfill (15.10)$$

That is, we regress the squared residuals at time $t$ on its lagged values going up to $p$ previous period, the value of the $p$ being determined empirically. Notice that in practice we replace $\sigma_t^2$ by $u_t^2$ which is replaced by its estimate, $\hat{u}_t^2$.

As you can see, the AR part of the ARCH model is so-called because in Eq. (15.10) we are regressing squared residuals on its lagged values going back to $p$ periods. The CH part of ARCH is because variance in Eq. (15.10) is conditional on the information available up to time $(t - 1)$.

## Estimation of the ARCH model: the least-squares approach

Once we obtain the squared error term from the chosen model, we can easily estimate Eq. (15.10) by the usual least squares method. Of course, we have to decide about the number of lagged terms in Eq. (15.10). This can be done on the basis of some criterion, such as the Akaike or Schwarz information criterion, which is built into statistical packages such as *Eviews* and *Stata*. We choose a model that gives the lowest value on the basis of these criteria. This is the counterpart of the highest $R^2$ in the linear regression model. Sometimes there is a conflict in the two information criteria, but most of the time they give qualitatively similar conclusions.

---

7  If $n$ is very large relative to $r$, the left-hand side of Eq. (15.8) can be written as $nR^2$.

**Table 15.1  OLS estimates of ARCH (8) model of dollar/euro exchange rate returns.**

Dependent Variable: Return
Method: Least Squares
Sample (adjusted): 10 2355
Included observations: 2346 after adjustments
Convergence achieved after 3 iterations

|       | Coefficient | Std. Error | t-Statistic | Prob. |
|-------|-------------|------------|-------------|-------|
| C     | 0.000118    | 0.000124   | 0.949619    | 0.3424 |
| AR(1) | 0.005585    | 0.020678   | 0.270107    | 0.7871 |
| AR(2) | −0.001528   | 0.020671   | −0.073936   | 0.9411 |
| AR(3) | −0.018031   | 0.020670   | −0.872340   | 0.3831 |
| AR(4) | 0.053298    | 0.020660   | 2.579725    | 0.0099 |
| AR(5) | −0.035622   | 0.020648   | −1.725156   | 0.0846 |
| AR(6) | 0.016990    | 0.020662   | 0.822254    | 0.4110 |
| AR(7) | 0.021674    | 0.020653   | 1.049456    | 0.2941 |
| AR(8) | −0.028401   | 0.020656   | −1.374958   | 0.1693 |

| | | | | |
|---|---|---|---|---|
| R-squared | 0.005679 | Mean dependent var | 0.000118 | |
| Adjusted R-squared | 0.002275 | S.D. dependent var | 0.005921 | |
| S.E. of regression | 0.005915 | Akaike info criterion | −7.418928 | |
| Sum squared resid | 0.081756 | Schwarz criterion | −7.396830 | |
| Log likelihood | 8711.403 | Durbin–Watson stat | 1.998549 | |
| F-statistic | 1.668334 | Prob(F-statistic) | 0.101121 | |

*Note*: Return is obtained as differences in LEX (see Footnote 4).

To illustrate, using the dollar/euro exchange rate data we estimated an ARCH (8) model, which gave the results in Table 15.1.

We chose an ARCH (8) model for illustrative purposes. In practice one rarely goes for higher-order ARCH models because they consume too many degrees of freedom (i.e. too many parameters need to be estimated). Besides, more economical models, such as GARCH, can be easily estimated. We will discuss the GARCH model shortly.

A drawback of the least squares approach to estimate an ARCH model is that there is no guarantee that all the estimated ARCH coefficients will be positive, which is evident from the results in Table 15.1. Remember that the (conditional) variance must be positive. Another reason the least squares method is not appropriate for estimating the ARCH model is that we need to estimate both the mean function and the variance function simultaneously. This can be done with the **method of maximum likelihood.**

## Estimation of the ARCH model: the maximum likelihood approach

As noted, one advantage of the ML method is that we can estimate the mean and variance functions simultaneously, instead of separated as under OLS. The mathematical details of the ML method are somewhat involved, but statistical packages, such as *Stata* and *Eviews*, have built-in routines to estimate the ARCH models.

Returning to our example, the ML estimates of the ARCH (8) model are given in Table 15.2. The first part of the table gives the estimate of the mean equation and the second half gives estimates of the coefficients of the variance equation. As you can see,

#### Table 15.2  ML estimation of the ARCH (8) model.

Dependent Variable: Return
Method: ML – ARCH (Marquardt) – Normal distribution
Sample (adjusted): 2 2355
Included observations: 2354 after adjustments
Convergence achieved after 6 iterations
Presample variance: backcast (parameter = 0.7)GARCH = C(2) + C(3)*RESID(−1)^2 +
C(4)*RESID(−2)^2 + C(5)*RESID(−3)^2 + C(6)*RESID(−4)^2 + C(7)*RESID(−5)^2 +
C(8)*RESID(−6)^2 +C(9)*RESID(−7)^2 + C(10)*RESID(−8)^2

|  | Coefficient | Std. Error | z-Statistic | Prob. |
|---|---|---|---|---|
| C | 0.000168 | 0.000116 | 1.455799 | 0.1454 |

| | Variance Equation | | | |
|---|---|---|---|---|
| C | 2.16E−05 | 1.57E−06 | 13.76329 | 0.0000 |
| RESID(−1)^2 | 0.003934 | 0.014396 | 0.273266 | 0.7846 |
| RESID(−2)^2 | 0.016995 | 0.020147 | 0.843548 | 0.3989 |
| RESID(−3)^2 | 0.030077 | 0.016471 | 1.826061 | 0.0678 |
| RESID(−4)^2 | 0.058961 | 0.022441 | 2.627397 | 0.0086 |
| RESID(−5)^2 | 0.061412 | 0.025193 | 2.437648 | 0.0148 |
| RESID(−6)^2 | 0.088779 | 0.023935 | 3.709209 | 0.0002 |
| RESID(−7)^2 | 0.058567 | 0.020293 | 2.886032 | 0.0039 |
| RESID(−8)^2 | 0.076195 | 0.023278 | 3.273296 | 0.0011 |

| | | | |
|---|---|---|---|
| R-squared* | −0.000088 | Mean dependent var | 0.000113 |
| Adjusted R-squared | −0.003928 | S.D. dependent var | 0.005926 |
| S.E. of regression | 0.005938 | Akaike info criterion | −7.435345 |
| Sum squared resid | 0.082649 | Schwarz criterion | −7.410860 |
| Log likelihood | 8761.401 | Hannan–Quinn criter. | −7.426428 |
| Durbin–Watson stat | 1.995120 | | |

*The negative $R^2$ is not important in the present situation, as the mean equation has no explanatory variables.

all the lagged variance coefficients are positive, as expected; the first three coefficients are not individually statistically significant, but the last five are. It seems there is an ARCH effect in the dollar/euro exchange rate return. That is, the error variances are autocorrelated. As we show below, this information can be used for the purpose of forecasting volatility.

## 15.2  The GARCH model

Some of the drawbacks of the ARCH ($p$) model are as follows: *first*, it requires estimation of the coefficients of $p$ autoregressive terms, which can consume several degrees of freedom. *Secondly*, it is often difficult to interpret all the coefficients, especially if some of them are negative. *Thirdly*, the OLS estimating procedure does not lend itself to estimate the mean and variance functions simultaneously. Therefore, the literature suggests that an ARCH model higher than ARCH (3) is better estimated by the

GARCH model (**Generalized Autoregressive Conditional Heteroscedasticity**) model,[8] originally proposed by Tim Bollerslev.

In its simplest form, in the GARCH model we keep the mean equation (15.3) the same, but modify the variance equation as follows:

$$\sigma_t^2 = \lambda_0 + \lambda_1 u_{t-1}^2 + \lambda_2 \sigma_{t-1}^2 \tag{15.11}$$

Notice that here the conditional variance at time $t$ depends not only on the lagged squared error term at time $(t-1)$ but also on the lagged variance term at time $(t-1)$.

This is known as the **GARCH (1,1)** model. Although we will not prove it, it can be shown that ARCH $(p)$ model is equivalent to GARCH $(1, 1)$ as $p$ increases. Notice that in the ARCH $(p)$ given in Eq. (15.6) we have to estimate $(p + 1)$ coefficients, whereas in the GARCH (1,1) model given in Eq. (15.11) we have to estimate only three coefficients.

The GARCH (1,1) model can be generalized to the **GARCH ($p$,$q$)** model with $p$ lagged squared error terms and $q$ lagged conditional variance terms, but in practice GARCH (1,1) has proved useful to model returns on financial assets.

Returning to our exchange rate example, the results of GARCH (1,1) model are given in Table 15.3.

Comparing the ARCH (8) with GARCH (1,1), we see how GARCH (1,1) in effect captures the eight lagged squared error terms in Table 15.2. This is not surprising, for we have already mentioned that GARCH (1,1) is a short-cut method of modeling an infinite ARCH process.

**Table 15.3  GARCH (1,1) model of the dollar/euro exchange rate.**

Dependent Variable: Z
Method: ML – ARCH (Marquardt) – Normal distribution
Sample (adjusted): 2 2355
Included observations: 2354 after adjustments
Convergence achieved after 9 iterations
Presample variance: backcast (parameter = 0.7)GARCH = C(2) + C(3)*RESID(−1)^2 + C(4)*GARCH(−1)

|  | Coefficient | Std. Error | z-Statistic | Prob. |
|---|---|---|---|---|
| C | 0.000198 | 0.000110 | 1.797740 | 0.0722 |

|  | Variance Equation | | | |
|---|---|---|---|---|
| C | 7.72E−08 | 5.02E−08 | 1.538337 | 0.1240 |
| RESID(−1)^2 | 0.022788 | 0.004063 | 5.609174 | 0.0000 |
| GARCH(−1) | 0.975307 | 0.004377 | 222.8494 | 0.0000 |

| R-squared | −0.000205 | Mean dependent var | 0.000113 |
|---|---|---|---|
| Adjusted R-squared | −0.001482 | S.D. dependent var | 0.005926 |
| S.E. of regression | 0.005931 | Akaike info criterion | −7.472999 |
| Sum squared resid | 0.082659 | Schwarz criterion | −7.463205 |
| Log likelihood | 8799.720 | Hannan–Quinn criter. | −7.469433 |
| Durbin–Watson stat | 1.994884 | | |

*Note:* Z =d(lex) = first difference of log of LEX.

---

8  Tim Bollerslev, Generalized autoregressive conditional heteroscedasticity, *Journal of Econometrics*, vol. 31, 1986, pp. 307–27.

As you can see, in the variance equation both the lagged squared error term and the lagged conditional variance term are individually highly significant. Since lagged conditional variance affects current conditional variance, there is clear evidence that there is a pronounced ARCH effect.

*To sum up*, there is clear evidence that the dollar/euro exchange rate returns exhibit considerable time-varying and time-correlated volatility, whether we use the ARCH or the GARCH model.

## 15.3 Further extensions of the ARCH model

The original ARCH ($p$) has been extended in several directions. We consider a few of these variants, using our example.

### The GARCH-M model

As noted before, an average investor is interested not only in maximizing the return on his or her investment, but also in minimizing the risk associated with such investment. Therefore one can modify the mean equation given in (15.3) by explicitly introducing the risk factor, the conditional variance, to take into account the risk. That is, we now consider the following mean function:

$$Y_t = \alpha + \beta X_t + \gamma \sigma_t^2 + u_t \tag{15.12}$$

where $\sigma_t^2$ is the conditional variance, as defined in Eq. (15.11).

This is called the GARCH-M (1,1) model. See how the risk factor, as measured by the conditional variance, enters the conditional mean function.

Using *Eviews*, we obtained the results in Table 15.4.

The mean equation in this table now includes the risk factor, the conditional variance. This risk factor is statistically significant, suggesting that not only is there an ARCH effect, but also that the mean return is directly affected by the risk factor.

### Graphs of conditional variances of ARCH (8) and GARCH (1.1) models

Since investors generally dislike uncertainty, it would be useful to forecast (conditional) volatility. To see how this is done, return to Eq. (15.11) and suppose we want to estimate volatility for the next period – that is,

$$\sigma_{t+1}^2 = \lambda_0 + \lambda_1 u_t^2 + \lambda_2 \sigma_t^2 \tag{15.13}$$

The estimates of the $\lambda$ coefficients are given in Table 15.3. Using these estimates, we can forecast conditional variance for the following and for subsequent periods.

Equation (15.13) can be easily generalized to give forecast volatility for $j$ step or $j$ periods ahead as:

$$\sigma_{t+j}^2 = \lambda_0 + (\lambda_1 + \lambda_2)\sigma_{t+j-1}^2 \tag{15.14}$$

In the long run, the so-called **steady state variance** can be obtained by equating all variance terms to obtain:

$$\sigma^2 = \frac{\lambda_0}{(1 - \lambda_1 - \lambda_2)} \tag{15.15}$$

**Table 15.4  GARCH-M (1,1) model of dollar/euro exchange rate return.**

Dependent Variable: RET
Method: ML – ARCH (Marquardt) – Normal distribution
Date: 10/18/08 Time: 15:50
Sample (adjusted): 2 2355
Included observations: 2354 after adjustments
Convergence achieved after 14 iterations
Presample variance: backcast (parameter = 0.7)GARCH = C(3) + C(4)*RESID(−1)^2 +
C(5)*GARCH(−1)

|  | Coefficient | Std. Error | z-Statistic | Prob. |
|---|---|---|---|---|
| GARCH | −0.188763 | 0.095900 | −1.968318 | 0.0490 |
| C | 0.078320 | 0.031583 | 2.479842 | 0.0131 |

|  | Variance Equation | | | |
|---|---|---|---|---|
| C | 0.000803 | 0.000495 | 1.621984 | 0.1048 |
| RESID(−1)^2 | 0.022472 | 0.003982 | 5.642678 | 0.0000 |
| GARCH(−1) | 0.975473 | 0.004327 | 225.4335 | 0.0000 |

| | | | | |
|---|---|---|---|---|
| R-squared | 0.001512 | Mean dependent var | 0.013049 |
| Adjusted R-squared | −0.000189 | S.D. dependent var | 0.592711 |
| S.E. of regression | 0.592767 | Akaike info criterion | 1.736635 |
| Sum squared resid | 825.3740 | Schwarz criterion | 1.748878 |
| Log likelihood | −2039.020 | Hannan–Quinn criter. | 1.741094 |
| F-statistic | 0.889015 | Durbin–Watson stat | 1.998503 |
| Prob(F-statistic) | 0.469582 | | |

If $(\lambda_1 + \lambda_2) < 1$, Eq. (15.15) gives the long-term volatility level of the GARCH(1,1) model. From Table 15.4 we see that for our example the estimated $(\lambda_1 + \lambda_2) = 0.998$, which is less than 1, but not by much.

Figure 15.4 gives some idea about the conditional variances estimated from the ARCH (8) and GARCH (1,1) models: these two conditional variance series are quite similar in appearance, which is not surprising because the GARCH model captures higher-order ARCH terms, not only in ARCH(8) but beyond.

Since these two graphs are similar, and since the GARCH(1,1) model is more economical, in practice we can concentrate on the GARCH model. What is important to note is that forecasting conditional volatility can aid an investor in making his or her investment decisions.

## Further extensions of ARCH and GARCH models

In the preceding pages we have touched upon only a few variants of the ARCH and GARCH models. But there are more, with acronyms like AARCH, SAARCH, TARCH, NARCH, NARCHK and EARCH. It is beyond the scope of this book to delve into all these esoteric models, not only because they will take us far afield but also because some of the mathematics is quite involved. The interested reader may pursue the literature for further references.[9]

---

9  See, for example, Walter Enders, *Applied Econometric Time Series*, 2nd edn, Wiley, 2004; Chris Brooks, *Introductory Econometrics of Finance*, Cambridge University Press, 2002; and I. Gusti Ngurah Agung, *Time Series Data Analysis Using Eviews*, John Wiley & Sons (Asia), 2009.

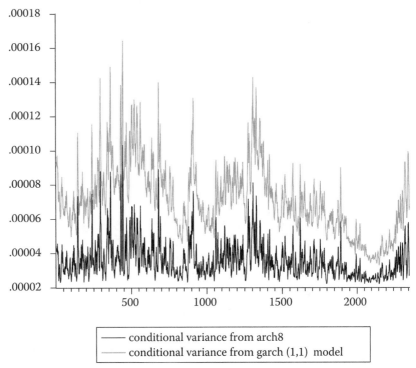

Figure 15.4  Comparison of the ARCH (8) and GARCH (1,1) models.

## 15.4   Summary and conclusions

A distinguishing feature of financial time series such as stock prices, inflation rates, and exchange rates is that they often exhibit volatility clustering – that is, periods in which their prices or the return on them show wide swings for extended time periods and periods over which there is relative calm. This results in correlation in error variance over time. To take into account such correlation, financial econometricians have developed several models, beginning with ARCH (autoregressive conditional heteroscedasticity). With daily data on the dollar/euro exchange rate over an extended time period, we showed how the ARCH model takes into account volatility in asset prices and asset returns.

Later incarnations of the ARCH model include GARCH, GARCH-M (GARCH in mean), TGARCH (threshold GARCH), and EGARCH (exponential GARCH), each introducing more versatility (and complexity) in the estimation of volatility. Fortunately, software packages exist which can estimate these models with comparative ease.

Apart from the technical aspect of volatility, the topic is of practical interest to investors at all levels, for an investor is not only interested in obtaining a higher rate of return, but also a steady (i.e. less volatile) rate of return.

## Exercise

**15.1** Collect data on a stock index of your choice over a period of time and find out the nature of volatility in the index. You may use ARCH, GARCH, or any other member of the ARCH family to analyze the volatility.

### Useful websites

The following websites provide several interesting data sets and references to other websites that provide all kinds of macro- and micro-economic data:

**WebEc**: A most comprehensive library of economic facts and figures: http://www.helsinki.fi/WebEc

**Bureau of Economic Analysis (BEA)**: Excellent source of data on all kinds of economic activities: http://www.bea.gov/

**Business Cycle Indicators**: Data on 256 economic time series: http://www.globalexposure.com/bci.html

**FRED Database**: Federal Reserve Bank of St Louis, historical economic and social data, which include interest rates, monetary and business cycle indicators, exchange rates, and so on. http://www.stls.frb.org.fed/

**World Bank Data and Statistics**: http://www.worldbank.org/data

**Various economic data sets**: http://economy.com/freelunch

**Economic Time Series Data**: http://economagic.com/

**World Economic Indicators**: http://devdata.worldbank.org/

# 16

# Economic forecasting

There are several areas in which economic forecasts have proved useful:[1]

1 Operations planning and control (e.g. inventory management, production planning, sales force management and the like)

2 Marketing (e.g. response of sales to different marketing schemes)

3 Economics (key economic variables, such as GDP, unemployment, consumption, investment and interest rates)

4 Financial asset management (e.g. asset returns, exchange rates and commodity prices)

5 Financial risk management (e.g. asset return volatility)

6 Business and government budgeting (revenue forecasts)

7 Demography (fertility and mortality rates)

8 Crisis management (probabilities of default, currency devaluations, military coups, and so forth)

Based on past and current information, the objective of forecasting is to provide quantitative estimate(s) of the likelihood of the future course of the object of interest (e.g. personal consumption expenditure). For this purpose we develop econometric models and use one or more methods of forecasting its future course.

Although there are several methods of forecasting, we will consider three prominent methods of forecasting in this chapter: (1) regression models, (2) the **autoregressive integrated moving average** (ARIMA) models, popularized by statisticians Box and Jenkins and known as the **Box–Jenkins (BJ) methodology**,[2] and (3) the **vector autoregression** (VAR) models, advocated by Christopher Sims.[3]

---

1 See Francis X. Diebold, *Elements of Forecasting*, Thompson-South-Western Publishers, 4th edn, 2007, Chapter 1.

2 G. P. Box and G. M. Jenkins, *Time Series Analysis: Forecasting and Control*, revised edn, Holden Day, San Francisco, 1976.

3 Another method of forecasting that was popular in the 1970s and 1980s is the method of simultaneous equation models. But this method has fallen out of favor because of its poor forecasting performance since the OPEC oil embargos in the 1970s, although it is still used by governmental agencies and the Federal Reserve Board. For a discussion of this method, see Gujarati/Porter, *op cit.*, Chapters 18–20.

## 16.1    Forecasting with regression models

We have devoted a considerable amount of space in this book to various aspects of regression analysis, but so far we have said little about the use of regression models for forecasting purposes. For many users of regression analysis in business and government, forecasting is probably the most important purpose of estimating regression models. The topic of business and economic forecasting is vast and several specialized books are written about this topic.[4] We will only discuss the salient aspects of forecasting using regression models. To keep things simple, and to use graphs, we will first consider the following bivariate regression:

$$PCE_t = B_1 + B_2 PDI_t + u_t \qquad\qquad (16.1)$$

where $PCE$ = per capita personal consumption expenditure and $PDI$ = per capita personal disposable (i.e. after-tax) income in chained 2005 dollars, and $u$ is the error term. We will call this regression the *consumption function*. The slope coefficient in this regression represents the **marginal propensity to consume** (**MPC**) – that is, the incremental consumption expenditure for an additional dollar's increase in income. To estimate this regression, we obtained aggregate data on these variables for the US for 1960–2008. See **Table 16.1** on the companion website.

To estimate the consumption function, initially we use the observations from 1960–2004 and save the last four observations, called the *holdover sample*, to evaluate the performance of the estimated model. We first plot the data to get some idea of the nature of the relationship between the two variables (Figure 16.1). This figure shows

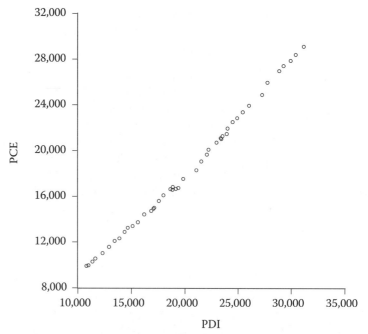

**Figure 16.1  Per capita PCE and PDI, USA, 1960–2004.**

4  See, for instance, Diebold, *op cit.*, Michael K. Evans, *Practical Business Forecasting*, Blackwell Publishing, Oxford, UK., 2003, and Paul Newbold and Theodore Bos, *Introductory Business and Economic Forecasting*, 2nd edn, South-Western Publishing Company, Cincinnati, Ohio, 1994.

**Table 16.2  Estimates of the consumption function, 1960–2004.**

Dependent Variable: PCE
Method: Least Squares
Date: 07/20/10 Time: 16:45
Sample: 1960 2004
Included observations: 45

| Variable | Coefficient | Std. Error | t-Statistic | Prob. |
|---|---|---|---|---|
| C | −1083.978 | 193.9579 | −5.588729 | 0.0000 |
| PDI | 0.953768 | 0.009233 | 103.2981 | 0.0000 |

| | | | |
|---|---|---|---|
| R-squared | 0.995986 | Mean dependent var | 18197.91 |
| Adjusted R-squared | 0.995893 | S.D. dependent var | 5515.914 |
| S.E. of regression | 353.4907 | Akaike info criterion | 14.61702 |
| Sum squared resid | 5373095. | Schwarz criterion | 14.69731 |
| Log likelihood | −326.8829 | Durbin–Watson stat | 0.299775 |
| F-statistic | 10670.51 | Prob(F-statistic) | 0.000000 |

that there is almost a linear relationship between PCE and PDI. Fitting a linear regression model to the data, we obtained the results in Table 16.2.

These results show that if PDI increases by a dollar, the average consumption expenditure goes up by about 95 cents, that is, the MPC is 0.95. By the standard statistical criteria, the estimated model looks good, although there is strong evidence of positive serial correlation in the error term because the Durbin–Watson value is so low. We will return to this point later.

To guard against the possibility of spurious regression, we subjected the residuals from regression (16.1) to unit root tests and found that the there was no evidence of unit root, even though individually PCE and DPI time series were nonstationary (verify this).

From this table, you will see that the *estimated* mean consumption expenditure function is:

$$P\hat{C}E_t = -1083.978 + 0.9537 PDI_t \tag{16.2}$$

What do we do with this "historical" regression? We can use it to forecast the future value(s) personal consumption expenditure. Suppose we want to find out $E(PCE_{2005}|PDI_{2005})$, that is the population or true mean personal consumption expenditure value in 2005 given the value of total household expenditure ($X$) for 2005, which is $31,318 (note that our sample regression is based on the period 1960–2004).

Before we undertake this task, we need to learn some special terms used in forecasting such as: (1) point and interval forecasts, (2) *ex post* (after the fact) and *ex ante* (viewed in advance or anticipated) forecasts, and (3) conditional and unconditional forecasts. We discuss these terms briefly.

1 **Point forecasts** and **interval forecasts**: in point forecasts we provide a single value for each forecast period, whereas in interval forecasts we obtain a range, or an interval, that will include the realized value with some probability. In other words, the interval forecast provides a margin of uncertainty about the point forecast.

Estimation period    *Ex-post* forecast period    *Ex-ante* forecast period

1960–2004              2005–2008                2009 forward

**Figure 16.2  Types of forecasting.**

2 *Ex post* and *ex ante* **forecasts**: to understand the distinction, consider Figure 16.2.[5]

In the estimation period we have data on all the variables in the model, in the *ex post* forecast period we also know the values of the regressand and regressors (this is the holdover period). We can use these values to get some idea about the performance of the fitted model. In the *ex ante* forecast we estimate the values of the depend variable beyond the estimation period but we may not know the values of the regressors with certainty, in which case we may have to estimate these values before we can forecast.

3 **Conditional and unconditional forecasts**: in conditional forecasts, we forecast the variable of interest *conditional* on the assumed values of the regressors. Recall that all along we have conducted our regression analysis, conditional on the given values of the regressors. This type of conditional forecasting is also known as **scenario analysis** or **contingency analysis**.

In unconditional forecasts, we know the values of the regressors with certainty instead of picking some arbitrary values of them, as in conditional forecasting. Of course, that is a rarity; it actually involves what Diebold calls the **forecasting the right-hand side variables** (i.e. regressors) **problem**.[6] For the present purposes we will work with conditional forecasts.

With these preliminaries, let us estimate the point forecast of consumption expenditure for 2005, given the value of per capita *PDI* for 2005 of $31,318 billions.

Now it can be shown that the best mean prediction of $Y_{2005}$ given the $X$ value is given by:

$$
\begin{aligned}
\hat{PCE}_{2005} &= b_1 + b_2 PDI_{2005} \\
&= -1083.978 + 0.9537(31318) \\
&= 28783.998 \\
&\approx 28784
\end{aligned}
\tag{16.3}
$$

That is, the best mean predicted value of personal consumption expenditure in 2005, is $28,784 billion, given the value of PDI $31,378 billion. From Table 16.1 we see that the actual value of PCE for 2005 was $29,771 billion. So the actual value was greater than the estimated value by $987 billion. We can call this the **forecast error**. Naturally, we do not expect the estimated regression line to forecast the actual values of the regressand without some error.

Since the PCE figure given in Eq. (16.3) is an estimate, it is subject to error as we just noted. So what we need is an estimate of the *forecast error* that we are likely to make in

5  The following discussion is based on Robert S. Pindyck and Daniel L. Rubinfeld, *Econometric Models and Economic Forecasts*, 3rd edn, McGraw-Hill, New York, 1991, Chapter 8.
6  For solutions to this problem, see Diebold, *op cit.*, p. 223.

using the figure in Eq. (16.3) as the true mean value of consumption expenditure for 2005. Now it can be shown that if the error term in Eq. (16.1) is normally distributed, then, letting $Y = PCE$ and $X = PDI$, it can be shown that $\hat{Y}_{2005}$ is normally distributed with mean equal to $(B_1 + B_2 X_{2005})$ and

$$\text{var}(\hat{Y}_{2005}) = \sigma^2 \left[ \frac{1}{n} + \frac{(X_{2005} - \bar{X})^2}{\Sigma(X_i - \bar{X})^2} \right] \tag{16.4}$$

where $\bar{X}$ is the sample mean of the $X$ values in our sample period of 1960–2004, $\sigma^2$ is the variance of the error term $u$ and $n$ is the sample size.

Since we do not observe the true variance of $u$ we estimate it from the sample as $\hat{\sigma}_2 = \Sigma e_t^2 / (n-2)$, following our discussion in Chapter 1.

Using this information, and given the $X$ value for 2005, we can establish, say, a 95% confidence interval for true $E(Y_{2005})$ as follows:

$$\Pr[\hat{Y}_{2005} - t_{\alpha/2} se(\hat{Y}_{2005}) \le E(Y_{2005}) \le \hat{Y}_{2005} + t_{\alpha/2} se(\hat{Y}_{2005})]$$
$$= 95\% \tag{16.5}$$

where $se(\hat{Y}_{2005})$ is the standard error obtained from Eq. (16.4), and where $\alpha = 5\%$. Notice that in establishing this confidence interval, we are using the $t$ distribution than the normal distribution because we are estimating the true error variance. This all follows from the linear regression theory discussed in Chapter 1.

Using Eq. (16.4), we obtain $se(\hat{Y}_{2005})$ (verify this). Therefore, the 95% confidence interval for $E(Y_{2005})$ is ($28,552 billion, $29,019 billion), although the single best estimate is $28,784 billion. (Note: $t_{\alpha/2} \approx 2.02$, for 43 df).

We will have to compute such confidence interval for each $E(Y|X)$ in our sample. If we connect such confidence intervals, we obtain what is known as a **confidence band**. This tedious calculation can be avoided if we use a software package such as *Stata* or *Eviews*. Using *Eviews*, we obtain the confidence band for our example (Figure 16.3).

The solid line in this figure is the estimated regression line (curve) and the two broken lines show the 95% confidence band for it. If you look at the formula for the

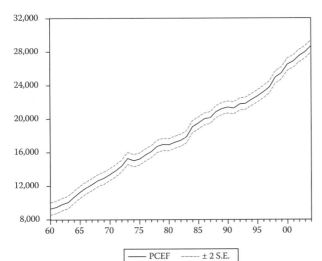

Figure 16.3  Forecast band for mean PCE.

variance of the estimated mean values, you will see that this variance increases as $X$ value against which the forecast is made moves further away from it mean value. In other words, the forecast error will increase as we move further away from the mean value of the regressor. This would suggest forecasting $E(Y|X)$ for $X$ values much greater than the mean value of $X$ will lead to substantial forecast errors.

The accompanying table gives some measures of the quality of the forecast, namely, the **root mean square, mean absolute error, mean absolute percentage error** and the **Theil Inequality Coefficient**, whose value lies between 0 and 1 – the closer it is to zero, the better is the model. These measures are discussed briefly in the Appendix to this chapter. These forecasting performance measures are useful if we are comparing two or more methods of forecasting, as we will discuss shortly.

We can extend this analysis to multiple regressions also, but in that case we need to use matrix algebra to express forecast variancs. We leave this topic for the references.

In the regression results given in Table 16.2 we found that the Durbin–Watson statistic was significant, suggesting that the error term suffers from first-order positive serial correlation. It can be shown that if we can take into account serial correlation in the error term, the forecast error could be made smaller, but we will not go into the mathematics of it.[7] However, *Eviews* can estimate model (16.1) by allowing for autocorrelation in the error term. For example, if we assume that the error term follows the first-order autoregressive scheme [AR(1)] discussed in Chapter 6, namely, $u_t = \rho u_{t-1} + \varepsilon_t$; $-1 \le \rho \le 1$, where $\rho$ is the coefficient of (first-order) autocorrelation and $\varepsilon$ is the white noise error term, we obtain the results in Table 16.3.

Compared with the model in Table 16.2 we see that the marginal propensity to consume has changed slightly, but its standard error is much higher. From this table we also see that the coefficient of the first-order autocorrelation is about 0.81.[8]

**Table 16.3  Consumption function with AR(1).**

Dependent Variable: PCE
Method: Least Squares
Date: 07/20/10 Time: 20:34
Sample (adjusted): 1961 2004
Included observations: 44 after adjustments
Convergence achieved after 8 iterations

| Variable | Coefficient | Std. Error | t-Statistic | Prob. |
|---|---|---|---|---|
| C | −1592.481 | 611.4801 | −2.604305 | 0.0128 |
| PDI | 0.975013 | 0.025965 | 37.55095 | 0.0000 |
| AR(1) | 0.812635 | 0.079793 | 10.18430 | 0.0000 |

| | | | |
|---|---|---|---|
| R-squared | 0.998872 | Mean dependent var | 18387.16 |
| Adjusted R-squared | 0.998817 | S.D. dependent var | 5429.892 |
| S.E. of regression | 186.7336 | Akaike info criterion | 13.36299 |
| Sum squared resid | 1429647. | Schwarz criterion | 13.48464 |
| Log likelihood | −290.9858 | Durbin–Watson stat | 2.433309 |
| F-statistic | 18158.75 | Prob(F-statistic) | 0.000000 |

7  See Robert S. Pindyck and Daniel L. Rubinfeld, *op cit.*, pp. 190–2.
8  Readers are encouraged to try higher order AR schemes, such as AR(2), AR(3), to see if the results given in Table 16.3 change.

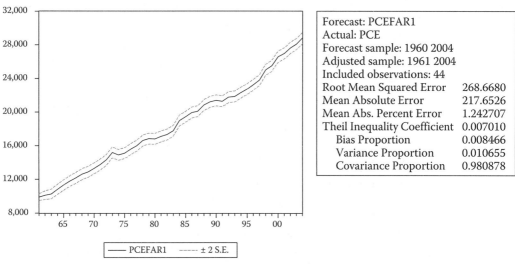

**Figure 16.4  95% confidence band for PCE with AR(1).**

Using the results in Table 16.3, we obtain the 95% confidence band for the estimated regression line – see Figure 16.4. If you compare this figure with Figure 16.3, you will see that the model in Table 16.3 does slightly better than the model in Table 16.1 because it does take into account explicitly serial correlation of the first order, supporting the statement made earlier that if we take into account serial correlation the forecast interval (band) will be narrower than without it. This can be seen by comparing the performance statistics accompanying the two figures.

## 16.2    The Box–Jenkins methodology: ARIMA modeling

The basic idea underlying the BJ methodology to forecasting is to analyze the probabilistic, or stochastic, properties of economic time series on their own under the philosophy "let the data speak for themselves". Unlike traditional regression models, in which the dependent variable $Y_t$ is explained by $k$ explanatory variables $X_1, X_2, X_3, ..., X_k$, the BJ time series models allow $Y_t$ to be explained by the past, or lagged, values of $Y_t$ itself and the current and lagged values of $u_t$, which is an uncorrelated random error term with zero mean and constant variance $\sigma^2$ – that is, a *white noise error term*.

The BJ methodology has several ways of forecasting a time series, which we discuss sequentially. We will first discuss the different BJ approaches in general terms and then consider a specific example, namely the dollar/euro exchange rate we first considered in Chapter 13.

The BJ methodology is based on the *assumption that the time series under study is stationary*. We discussed the topic of stationarity in Chapter 13 and pointed out the importance of studying stationary time series. Let us represent a stationary time series symbolically as $Y_t$.

### The autoregressive (AR) model

Consider the following model:

$$Y_t = B_0 + B_1 Y_{t-1} + B_2 Y_{t-2} + \ldots + B_p Y_{t-p} + u_t \qquad (16.6)$$

where $u_t$ is a white noise error term.

Model (16.6) is called an autoregressive model of order $p$, **AR ($p$)**, for it involves regressing $Y$ at time $t$ on its values lagged $p$ periods into the past, the value of $p$ being determined empirically using some criterion, such as the Akaike information criterion. Recall that we discussed autoregression when we discussed the topic of autocorrelation in Chapter 6.

## The moving average (MA) model

We can also model $Y_t$ as follows:

$$Y_t = C_0 + C_1 u_t + C_2 u_{t-1} + \ldots + C_q u_{t-q} \qquad (16.7)$$

That is, we express $Y_t$ as a weighted, or moving, average of the current and past white noise error terms. Model (16.7) is known as the **MA ($q$)** model, the value of $q$ being determined empirically.

## The autoregressive moving average (ARMA) model

We can combine the AR and MA models and form what is called the **ARMA ($p,q$)** model, with $p$ autoregressive terms and $q$ moving average terms. Again, the values of $p$ and $q$ are determined empirically.

## The autoregressive integrated moving average (ARIMA) model

As noted, the BJ methodology is based on the assumption that the underlying time series is *stationary* or can be made stationary by differencing it one or more times. This is known as the **ARIMA ($p,d,q$) model**, where $d$ denotes the number of times a time series has to be differenced to make it stationary. In most applications $d = 1$ – that is, we take only the first differences of the time series. Of course, if a time series is already stationary, then an ARIMA ($p,d,q$) becomes an ARMA ($p,q$) model.

The practical question is to determine the appropriate model in a given situation. To answer this question, the BJ methodology follows a four-step procedure:

**Step 1: Identification**: Determine the appropriate values of $p$, $d$ and $q$. The main tools in this search are the **correlogram and partial correlogram**.

**Step 2: Estimation**: Once we identify the model, the next step is to estimate the parameters of the chosen model. In some cases we can use the method ordinary least-squares (OLS), but in some cases we have to resort to nonlinear (in parameter) estimation methods. Since several statistical packages have built-in routines, we do not have to worry about the actual mathematics of estimation.

**Step 3: Diagnostic checking**: BJ ARIMA modeling is more an art than science because considerable skill is required to choose the right ARIMA model, for we may not be absolutely sure that the chosen model is the correct one. One simple test of this is to see if the residuals from the fitted model are white noise; if they are, we can accept the chosen model, but if they are not, we will have to start afresh. *That is why the BJ methodology is an iterative process.*

**Step 4: Forecasting**: The ultimate test of a successful ARIMA model lies in its forecasting performance, within the sample period as well as outside the sample period.

## 16.3    An ARMA model of IBM daily closing prices, 3 January 2000 to 31 October 2002

In Chapter 13 we showed that the logs of the IBM daily closing prices (LCLOSE) were nonstationary, but the first differences of these prices (DLCLOSE) were stationary. Since the BJ methodology is based on stationary time series, we will work with DLCLOSE instead of LCLOSE to model this time series, where DLCLOSE stands for the first differences of LCLOSE.

To see which ARMA model fits DLCLOSE, and following the BJ methodology, we show the correlogram of this series up to 50 lags (Table 16.4), although the picture does not change much if we consider more lags.

This correlogram produces two types of correlation coefficient: **autocorrelation (AC)** and **partial autocorrelation (PAC)**. The ACF (autocorrelation function) shows correlation of current DLCOSE with its values at various lags. The PACF (partial autocorrelation function) shows the correlation between observations that are $k$ periods apart after controlling for the effects of intermediate lags (i.e. lags less than $k$).[9] The BJ methodology uses both these correlation coefficients to identity the type of ARMA model that may be appropriate in a given case.

Some theoretical patterns of ACF and PACF are shown in Table 16.5. Notice that the ACFs and PACFs of AR($p$) and MA($q$) have opposite patterns: in the AR($p$) case the ACF declines geometrically or exponentially but the PCAF cuts off after a certain number of lags. The opposite happens to an MA($q$) process.

Keep in mind that in a concrete application we may not observe the neat patterns shown in Table 16.5. Some trial and error is unavoidable in practical applications.

Returning to our example, we see that both ACF and PAC functions alternate between negative and positive values and do not exhibit an exponential decay for any sustained period.

A careful examination of the correlogram shows that neither the ACF nor PACF shows the neat pattern described in Table 16.5. To see which correlations are statistically significant, recall that the standard error of a (sample) correlation coefficient is given by $\sqrt{1/n} = \sqrt{1/739} \approx 0.037$, where $n$ is the sample size (see Eq. (13.2)). Therefore the 95% confidence interval for the true correlation coefficients is about $0 \pm 1.96(0.037)$ = (−0.0725 to 0.0725). Correlation coefficients lying outside these bounds are statistically significant at the 5% level. On this basis, it seems both ACF and PACF correlations at lags 4, 18, 22, 35 and 43 seem to be statistically significant (see the confidence bands in the preceding figure).

Since we do not have the clear-cut pattern of the theoretical ACF and PACF outlined in Table 16.5, we can proceed by trial and error.

First, suppose we fit an AR model at lags 4, 18, 22, 35 and 43. The results are shown in Table 16.6. As you can see, the coefficients of AR(35) and AR(43) are not individually statistically significant. However, it should be noted that when the residuals from the preceding regression were tested for serial correlation, we did not find any up to five lags. So the model in Table 16.6 may be a candidate for further consideration.

---

9  This is akin to the partial regression coefficient in a multiple regression. In a $k$ variable regression model the coefficient $B_k$ of the $k$th regressor gives the impact of that variable on the regressand after holding, or allowing, for the influence of the other regressors in the model.

**Table 16.4  ACF and PACF of DCLOSE of IBM stock prices.**

Sample: 1/03/2000 10/31/2002
Included observations: 686

| Autocorrelation | Partial Correlation | | AC | PAC | Q-Stat | Prob |
|---|---|---|---|---|---|---|
| .\|.  \| | .\|.  \| | 1 | −0.059 | −0.059 | 2.4132 | 0.120 |
| .\|.  \| | .\|.  \| | 2 | −0.058 | −0.061 | 4.7046 | 0.095 |
| .\|.  \| | .\|.  \| | 3 | −0.016 | −0.024 | 4.8875 | 0.180 |
| .\|*  \| | .\|*  \| | 4 | 0.083 | 0.077 | 9.6393 | 0.047 |
| .\|.  \| | .\|.  \| | 5 | −0.007 | 0.001 | 9.6706 | 0.085 |
| .\|.  \| | .\|.  \| | 6 | 0.017 | 0.026 | 9.8727 | 0.130 |
| .\|.  \| | .\|.  \| | 7 | 0.017 | 0.023 | 10.080 | 0.184 |
| .\|.  \| | .\|.  \| | 8 | −0.044 | −0.047 | 11.446 | 0.178 |
| .\|.  \| | .\|.  \| | 9 | 0.018 | 0.016 | 11.665 | 0.233 |
| .\|.  \| | .\|.  \| | 10 | 0.036 | 0.031 | 12.574 | 0.248 |
| .\|.  \| | .\|.  \| | 11 | −0.050 | −0.049 | 14.292 | 0.217 |
| .\|.  \| | .\|.  \| | 12 | −0.012 | −0.007 | 14.396 | 0.276 |
| .\|.  \| | .\|.  \| | 13 | 0.038 | 0.030 | 15.415 | 0.282 |
| .\|.  \| | .\|.  \| | 14 | 0.012 | 0.010 | 15.519 | 0.344 |
| .\|.  \| | .\|.  \| | 15 | 0.021 | 0.036 | 15.821 | 0.394 |
| .\|.  \| | .\|.  \| | 16 | 0.052 | 0.056 | 17.695 | 0.342 |
| .\|.  \| | .\|.  \| | 17 | 0.050 | 0.058 | 19.455 | 0.303 |
| *\|.  \| | *\|.  \| | 18 | −0.103 | −0.089 | 26.984 | 0.079 |
| .\|.  \| | .\|.  \| | 19 | 0.002 | −0.013 | 26.987 | 0.105 |
| .\|.  \| | .\|.  \| | 20 | 0.030 | 0.010 | 27.609 | 0.119 |
| .\|.  \| | .\|.  \| | 21 | −0.025 | −0.033 | 28.064 | 0.138 |
| *\|.  \| | *\|.  \| | 22 | −0.109 | −0.103 | 36.474 | 0.027 |
| .\|.  \| | .\|.  \| | 23 | −0.011 | −0.031 | 36.561 | 0.036 |
| .\|.  \| | .\|.  \| | 24 | 0.011 | 0.001 | 36.651 | 0.047 |
| *\|.  \| | *\|.  \| | 25 | −0.069 | −0.066 | 40.020 | 0.029 |
| *\|.  \| | *\|.  \| | 26 | −0.068 | −0.075 | 43.369 | 0.018 |
| .\|.  \| | .\|.  \| | 27 | −0.030 | −0.039 | 43.998 | 0.021 |
| .\|.  \| | .\|.  \| | 28 | −0.025 | −0.026 | 44.444 | 0.025 |
| .\|.  \| | .\|.  \| | 29 | 0.006 | −0.007 | 44.470 | 0.033 |
| .\|.  \| | .\|.  \| | 30 | 0.071 | 0.066 | 48.139 | 0.019 |
| .\|.  \| | .\|.  \| | 31 | −0.005 | 0.021 | 48.154 | 0.025 |
| .\|.  \| | .\|.  \| | 32 | −0.036 | −0.018 | 49.115 | 0.027 |
| .\|.  \| | .\|.  \| | 33 | −0.029 | −0.043 | 49.731 | 0.031 |
| .\|.  \| | .\|.  \| | 34 | 0.004 | −0.009 | 49.744 | 0.040 |
| *\|.  \| | *\|.  \| | 35 | −0.079 | −0.069 | 54.268 | 0.020 |
| .\|.  \| | .\|.  \| | 36 | 0.008 | −0.012 | 54.317 | 0.026 |
| .\|.  \| | .\|.  \| | 37 | −0.050 | −0.057 | 56.155 | 0.023 |
| *\|.  \| | .\|.  \| | 38 | −0.070 | −0.059 | 59.698 | 0.014 |
| .\|.  \| | .\|.  \| | 39 | 0.046 | 0.057 | 61.247 | 0.013 |
| .\|.  \| | .\|.  \| | 40 | −0.019 | −0.036 | 61.514 | 0.016 |
| .\|.  \| | .\|.  \| | 41 | −0.003 | 0.023 | 61.520 | 0.021 |

Table 16.4 (*continued*)

| Autocorrelation | Partial Correlation | | AC | PAC | Q-Stat | Prob |
|---|---|---|---|---|---|---|
| .\|. | .\|. | 42 | −0.035 | 0.004 | 62.392 | 0.022 |
| .\|* | .\|. | 43 | 0.076 | 0.058 | 66.617 | 0.012 |
| .\|. | .\|. | 44 | 0.006 | −0.001 | 66.640 | 0.015 |
| .\|. | .\|. | 45 | 0.020 | 0.017 | 66.937 | 0.019 |
| .\|. | .\|. | 46 | −0.026 | −0.041 | 67.432 | 0.021 |
| .\|. | .\|. | 47 | 0.032 | 0.007 | 68.185 | 0.023 |
| .\|. | .\|. | 48 | 0.001 | −0.006 | 68.186 | 0.029 |
| .\|. | .\|. | 49 | −0.000 | −0.015 | 68.186 | 0.036 |
| .\|. | .\|. | 50 | −0.014 | −0.015 | 68.327 | 0.043 |

Table 16.5   Typical patterns of ACF and PACF.

| Type of model | Typical pattern of ACF | Typical pattern of PACF |
|---|---|---|
| AR($p$) | Decays exponentially or with damped sine wave pattern or both | Significant spikes through lags $p$ |
| MA($q$) | Significant spikes through lags $q$ | Declines exponentially |
| ARMA($p,q$) | Exponential decay | Exponential decay |

Table 16.6   An AR (4,18,22,35,43) model of DCLOSE.

Dependent Variable: D(LCLOSE)
Method: Least Squares
Sample (adjusted): 3/03/2000 8/20/2002
Included observations: 643 after adjustments
Convergence achieved after 3 iterations

| | Coefficient | Std. Error | t-Statistic | Prob. |
|---|---|---|---|---|
| C | −0.000798 | 0.000966 | −0.825879 | 0.4092 |
| AR(4) | 0.096492 | 0.039101 | 2.467745 | 0.0139 |
| AR(18) | −0.073034 | 0.039623 | −1.843242 | 0.0658 |
| AR(22) | −0.084777 | 0.039642 | −2.138565 | 0.0329 |
| AR(35) | −0.055990 | 0.039381 | −1.421768 | 0.1556 |
| AR(43) | 0.052378 | 0.039310 | 1.332428 | 0.1832 |

| | | | |
|---|---|---|---|
| R-squared | 0.032112 | Mean dependent var | −0.000811 |
| Adjusted R-squared | 0.024515 | S.D. dependent var | 0.026409 |
| S.E. of regression | 0.026084 | Akaike info criterion | −4.445734 |
| Sum squared resid | 0.433385 | Schwarz criterion | −4.404059 |
| Log likelihood | 1435.303 | Durbin–Watson stat | 2.089606 |
| F-statistic | 4.226799 | Prob(F-statistic) | 0.000869 |

*Note*: AR(4,18,22,3543) denotes the lagged terms included in the model.

Table 16.7  An AR (4,18,22) model of DCLOSE.

Dependent Variable: D(LCLOSE)
Method: Least Squares
Sample (adjusted): 2/03/2000 8/20/2002
Included observations: 664 after adjustments
Convergence achieved after 3 iterations

|  | Coefficient | Std. Error | t-Statistic | Prob. |
|---|---|---|---|---|
| C | 0.000937 | 0.000944 | −0.992942 | 0.3211 |
| AR(4) | 0.101286 | 0.038645 | 2.620899 | 0.0090 |
| AR(18) | 0.082566 | 0.039024 | −2.115760 | 0.0347 |
| AR(22) | 0.091977 | 0.039053 | −2.355157 | 0.0188 |

| | | | | |
|---|---|---|---|---|
| R-squared | 0.027917 | Mean dependent var | −0.000980 |
| Adjusted R-squared | 0.023499 | S.D. dependent var | 0.026416 |
| S.E. of regression | 0.026104 | Akaike info criterion | −4.447488 |
| Sum squared resid | 0.449720 | Schwarz criterion | −4.420390 |
| Log likelihood | 1480.566 | Durbin–Watson stat | 2.102050 |
| F-statistic | 6.318233 | Prob(F-statistic) | 0.000315 |

Since AR(35) and AR(43) coefficients were not significant, we can drop these from consideration and reestimate the model with only AR(4), AR(18) and AR(22) terms, which gives the results in Table 16.7. The residuals from this regression also seem to be randomly distributed.

If we have to choose between the two preceding models, we can use the Akaike or Schwarz information criterion to make the choice. Although there is not a big difference in the values of the two criteria in the two tables, numerically the information values are slightly more negative for the model in Table 16.7 than in Table 16.6; remember that on the basis of the information criteria, we choose the model with the lowest value of these criteria – in the present instance the value that is most negative.

On this basis it seems that the model in Table 16.7 is preferred over the one in Table 16.6. Also, the model in Table 16.7 is more parsimonious than the one Table 16.6, for we have to estimate only four instead of six parameters.

Initially we tried the counterpart of Table 16.6, using five lagged MA terms at lags 4, 18, 22, 35 and 43, but the coefficients of lags 35 and 43 were not statistically significant. Therefore we estimated the MA equivalent of Table 16.7, and obtained the results in Table 16.8. The residuals from this regression were randomly distributed.

Which model should we choose? AR(4,18,22) or MA(4,18,22)?

Since the values of the Akaike and Schwarz information criteria were lowest for the MA model, we can choose this over the AR model, although the difference between the two is not very great.

Recall that the MA model is simply a weighted average of the stochastic error term. But since the first differences of the log closing prices of IBM are stationary, it makes sense to use the MA model.

But before we sign off on the MA model, let us see if we can develop a model using both AR and MA terms. After some experimentation, we obtained the model in Table 16.9.

Using the Akaike and Schwarz criteria, it seems this is the "best" model. The residuals from this model were tested for unit root and it was found that there was no unit

**Table 16.8  An MA (4,18,22) model of DLCOSE.**

Dependent Variable: D(LCLOSE)
Method: Least Squares
Sample (adjusted): 1/04/2000 8/20/2002
Included observations: 686 after adjustments
Convergence achieved after 7 iterations
MA Backcast: 12/03/1999 1/03/2000

|         | Coefficient | Std. Error | t-Statistic | Prob.  |
|---------|-------------|------------|-------------|--------|
| C       | −0.000887   | 0.000878   | −1.011247   | 0.3123 |
| MA(4)   | 0.086628    | 0.038075   | 2.275167    | 0.0232 |
| MA(18)  | −0.099334   | 0.038682   | −2.567953   | 0.0104 |
| MA(22)  | −0.112227   | 0.038958   | −2.880715   | 0.0041 |

| R-squared          | 0.027366 | Mean dependent var    | −0.000928 |
|--------------------|----------|-----------------------|-----------|
| Adjusted R-squared | 0.023088 | S.D. dependent var    | 0.026385  |
| S.E. of regression | 0.026079 | Akaike info criterion | −4.449579 |
| Sum squared resid  | 0.463828 | Schwarz criterion     | −4.423160 |
| Log likelihood     | 1530.206 | Durbin–Watson stat    | 2.104032  |
| F-statistic        | 6.396312 | Prob(F-statistic)     | 0.000282  |

**Table 16.9  ARMA [(4,22),(4,22)] model of DLCLOSE.**

Dependent Variable: D(LCLOSE)
Method: Least Squares
Sample (adjusted): 2/03/2000 8/20/2002
Included observations: 664 after adjustments
Convergence achieved after 12 iterations
MA Backcast: 1/04/2000 2/02/2000

|         | Coefficient | Std. Error | t-Statistic | Prob.  |
|---------|-------------|------------|-------------|--------|
| C       | −0.000985   | 0.001055   | −0.934089   | 0.3506 |
| AR(4)   | −0.229487   | 0.061210   | −3.749152   | 0.0002 |
| AR(22)  | −0.641421   | 0.062504   | −10.26202   | 0.0000 |
| MA(4)   | 0.361848    | 0.060923   | 5.939484    | 0.0000 |
| MA(22)  | 0.618302    | 0.055363   | 11.16808    | 0.0000 |

| R-squared          | 0.048013 | Mean dependent var    | −0.000980 |
|--------------------|----------|-----------------------|-----------|
| Adjusted R-squared | 0.042235 | S.D. dependent var    | 0.026416  |
| S.E. of regression | 0.025852 | Akaike info criterion | −4.465365 |
| Sum squared resid  | 0.440423 | Schwarz criterion     | −4.431493 |
| Log likelihood     | 1487.501 | Durbin–Watson stat    | 2.111835  |
| F-statistic        | 8.309156 | Prob(F-statistic)     | 0.000002  |

root, suggesting that the residuals from this model are stationary. Also, on the basis of the Breusch–Godfrey test of autocorrelation discussed in Chapter 6, it was found that, using five lags, there was no serial correlation in the residuals.

*To sum up*, it would seem that ARMA (4,22,4,22) is probably an appropriate model to depict the behavior of the first differences of the logs of daily closing IBM prices over the sample period.

## Forecasting with ARIMA

Once a particular ARMA model is fitted, we can use it for forecasting, for this is the primary objective of such models. There are two types of forecast: **static** and **dynamic**. In static forecasts, we use the actual current and lagged values of the forecast variable, whereas in dynamic forecasts, after the first period forecast, we use the previously forecast values of the forecast variable.

Using the model in Table 16.9, the static forecast is shown in Figure 16.5.[10] This figure gives the actual and forecast values of logs of closing IBM prices, as well as the confidence interval of forecast. The accompanying table gives the same measures of the quality of the forecast that we saw before, namely, the **root mean square, mean absolute error, mean absolute percentage error** and the **Theil Inequality Coefficient**. For our example, this coefficient is practically zero, suggesting that the fitted model is quite good. This can also be seen from Figure 16.5, which shows how closely the actual and forecast values track each other.

The picture of the dynamic forecast is given in Figure 16.6. *Eviews* output gives the same measures of forecast quality as in the previous figures.

On the basis of the Theil coefficient, the dynamic forecast does not do as well as the static forecast. Also the 95% confidence band increases rapidly as we travel along the time axis. The reason for this is that we use the previous forecast values in computing subsequent forecasts and if there is an error in the previously forecast value(s), that error will be carried forward.

Before proceeding further, the reader is encouraged to acquire more recent data and see if the pattern observed in the current sample continues to hold in the new sample. Since the ARIMA modeling is an iterative process, the reader may want to try other ARIMA models to see if they can improve on the models discussed in this section.

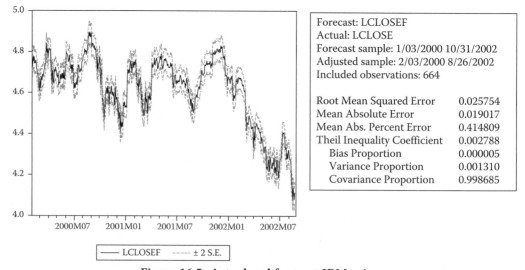

Forecast: LCLOSEF
Actual: LCLOSE
Forecast sample: 1/03/2000 10/31/2002
Adjusted sample: 2/03/2000 8/26/2002
Included observations: 664

| | |
|---|---|
| Root Mean Squared Error | 0.025754 |
| Mean Absolute Error | 0.019017 |
| Mean Abs. Percent Error | 0.414809 |
| Theil Inequality Coefficient | 0.002788 |
| Bias Proportion | 0.000005 |
| Variance Proportion | 0.001310 |
| Covariance Proportion | 0.998685 |

— LCLOSEF    ----- ± 2 S.E.

**Figure 16.5  Actual and forecast IBM prices.**

---

10  Although Table 16.6 is based on the first differences of IBM log closing prices, the forecasts given in the following figures are for the level of log closing prices. *Eviews* does this automatically.

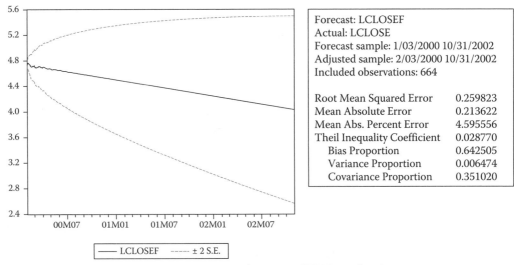

Figure 16.6  Dynamic forecast of IBM stock prices.

## 16.4    Vector autoregression (VAR)

In the classical simultaneous equation models involving $m$ endogenous (i.e. dependent) variables, there are $m$ equations, one for each endogenous variable.[11] Each equation may contain one or more endogenous variables and some exogenous variables. Before these equations can be estimated, we have to make sure that the **problem of identification** is solved, that is, whether the parameters or set of parameters can be consistently estimated. In achieving identification, often arbitrary restrictions are imposed by excluding some variables from an equation, which may be present in the other equations in the system.

This practice was severely criticized by Sims, who argued that if there are $m$ endogenous variables, they should all be treated on an equal footing; there should not be any distinction between endogenous and exogenous variables.[12] So each equation should have the same number of regressors. It is for this reason that Sims developed the VAR model.

### A bivariate VAR[13]

To explain the ideas behind VAR, we will first consider a system of two variables. In Chapter 14 we discussed the relationship between 3-month and 6-month T-bills (Treasury Bills) from the point of view of cointegration. Here we discuss it from the

---

11  In this book we do not discuss the simultaneous equations models, for they are no longer used as extensively as they were in the 1960s and 1970s. For an overview, see Gujarati/Porter, *op cit.*, Chapters 18–20.

12  C. A. Sims, Macroeconomics and reality, *Econometrica*, 1980, vol. 48, pp. 1–48.

13  In mathematics a vector is any quantity possessing direction. For our purpose, we can arrange the values of a variable in a column, called a column vector. Since in VAR we are dealing with more than one variable, we can arrange the values of each variable in a column. As we are dealing with such columned or vector values, we call the system of studying such column vectors a VAR system.

point of view of forecasting the two rates, using the VAR methodology. For this purpose, consider the following two equations:

$$TB3_t = A_1 + \sum_{j=1}^{j=p} B_j TB3_{t-j} + \sum_{j=1}^{j=p} C_j TB6_{t-j} + u_{1t} \tag{16.8}$$

$$TB6_t = A_2 + \sum_{j=1}^{j=p} D_j TB3_{t-j} + \sum_{j=1}^{j=p} E_j TB6_{t-j} + u_{2t} \tag{16.9}$$

where *TB3* and *TB6* are three and six-month T-bill rates, and where the *us* are white noise error terms, called **impulses** or **innovations** or **shocks** in the language of VAR.

Notice these features of the bivariate VAR given in the preceding equations:

1 The bivariate system resembles a simultaneous equation system, but the fundamental difference between the two is that each equation contains only its own lagged values and the lagged values of the other variables in the system. But no current values of the two variables are included on the right-hand side of these equations.

2 Although the number of lagged values of each variable can be different, in most cases we use the same number of lagged terms in each equation.

3 The bivariate VAR system given above is known as a VAR(*p*) model, because we have *p* lagged values of each variable on the right-hand side. If we had only one lagged value of each variable on the right-hand side, it would be a VAR(1) model; if two-lagged terms, it would be a VAR(2) model; and so on.

4 Although we are dealing with only two variables, the VAR system can be extended to several variables. Suppose we introduce another variable, say, the Federal Funds rate. Then we will have a three-variable VAR system, each equation in the system containing *p* lagged values of each variable on the right-hand side of each equation.

5 But if we consider several variables in the system with several lags for each variable, we will have to estimate several parameters, which is not a problem in this age of high-speed computers and sophisticated software, but the system becomes quickly unwieldy.

6 In the two-variable system of Eqs. (16.8) and (16.9), there can be at most one *cointegrating*, or *equilibrium*, relationship between them. If we have a three-variable VAR system, there can be at most two cointegrating relationships between the three variables. In general, an *n*-variable VAR system can have at most $(n-1)$ cointegrating relationships.

Finding out how many cointegrating relationships exist among *n* variables requires the use of Johansen's methodology, which is beyond the scope of this book. However, software packages such as *Stata* and *Eviews* can handle this relatively easily.

The cointegrating relationship may have some theoretical basis. In our example, it is the **term structure of interest rates**: the relationship between short and long-term interest rates.

Since our objective here is to introduce the basics of VAR, we will stick with the two-variable VAR system.

Since we have 349 monthly observations on the two Treasury bill rates, we have plenty of leeway about the number of lagged terms we can introduce in the model. Introducing too few lagged terms will lead to specification errors. Introducing too many lagged terms will consume several degrees of freedom, not to mention the problem of collinearity. So we will have to proceed by trial and error and settle on the number of lagged terms on the basis of the Akaike or Schwarz information criteria.

Since financial markets are supposed to be efficient, we need not introduce too many lagged terms in the two equations. This is especially so in the interest rate markets because of arbitrage operations.

Whatever the choice of the lagged terms introduced in the two equations, *a critical requirement of VAR is that the time series under consideration are stationary.* Here we have three possibilities:

*First*, both TB3 and TB6 time series are individually I(0), or stationary. In that case we can estimate each equation by OLS.

*Second*, both TB3 and TB6 are I(1) then we can take the first differences of the two variables, which, as we know, are stationary. Here too we can use OLS to estimate each equation individually.

*Third*, if the two series are I(1), but are cointegrated, then we have to use the **error correction mechanism (ECM)** that we discussed in Chapter 14. Recall that ECM combines the long-run equilibrium with short-run dynamics to reach that equilibrium. Since we are dealing with more than one variable in a VAR system, the multivariate counterpart of ECM is known as the **vector error correction model (VECM)**.

Now the estimation of the VAR system given in Eqs. (16.8) and (16.9), using the VECM approach, involves three steps:

*Step 1*: We first estimate the cointegrating relation between the two rates. From Chapter 14 we know that the cointegrating relation is given by

$$TB6_t = B_1 + B_2 TB3_t + B_3 t + B_4 t^2 + u_t \qquad (16.10)$$

The results of this regression are given in Table 16.10. These results show that, allowing for linear and quadratic trends, there is a statistically significant positive relationship between the two rates. If TB3 goes up by 1 percentage point, on average, TB6 goes up by about 0.96 percentage points, *ceteris paribus*. The results also show that both the interest rates have been trending downward, but they are trending down at an increasing rate, which is clear from Figure 14.2.

*Step 2*: From this regression we obtain the residuals, $e_t$, which are given by the relation:

$$e_t = TB6_t - 0.6064 - 0.9584 \ TB3_t + 0.0026t - 0.0000043t^2 \quad (16.11)$$

Provided that $e_t$ is stationary, we know that $e_t$ in Eq. (16.11) is the *error correction (EC) term.*[14]

---

**14** To establish that $e_t$ is stationary, use the unit root test. This involves regressing $\Delta e_t$ on $e_{t-1}$ and testing the hypothesis that the slope coefficient in this regression is zero (i.e. there is a unit root). Using the data the reader can verify that the unit root hypothesis can be convincingly rejected, thus establishing that the error term in Eq. (16.10) is indeed stationary.

Table 16.10  Relationship between TB6 and TB3.

Dependent Variable: TB6
Method: Least Squares
Sample: 1981M01 2010M01
Included observations: 349

|  | Coefficient | Std. Error | t-Statistic | Prob. |
|---|---|---|---|---|
| C | 0.606465 | 0.076820 | 7.894596 | 0.0000 |
| TB3 | 0.958401 | 0.006308 | 151.9409 | 0.0000 |
| @TREND | −0.002585 | 0.000528 | −4.893455 | 0.0000 |
| @TREND^2 | 4.43E−06 | 1.25E−06 | 3.533231 | 0.0005 |

| | | | | |
|---|---|---|---|---|
| R-squared | 0.995950 | Mean dependent var | 5.352693 |
| Adjusted R-squared | 0.995915 | S.D. dependent var | 3.075953 |
| S.E. of regression | 0.196590 | Akaike info criterion | −0.403995 |
| Sum squared resid | 13.33346 | Schwarz criterion | −0.359811 |
| Log likelihood | 74.49716 | Durbin–Watson stat | 0.363237 |
| F-statistic | 28283.37 | Prob(F-statistic) | 0.000000 |

*Step 3*: Now we estimate (16.8) and (16.9) using the EC term as follows, which is the VEC model:

$$\Delta TB6_t = \alpha_1 + \alpha_2 e_{t-1} + v_{1t} \tag{16.12}$$

$$\Delta TB3_t = \alpha_3 + \alpha_4 e_{t-1} + v_{2t} \tag{16.13}$$

You will see how VEC ties short-run dynamics to long-run relations via the EC term. In these two equations, the slope coefficients are known as **error correction coefficients**, for they show how much $\Delta TB6$ and $\Delta TB3$ adjust to "equilibrating" error in the previous period, $e_{t-1}$.

Notice carefully how the short-term behavior of the two TB rates is linked to their long-term relationship via the EC term. If, for example, $\alpha_2$ is positive, TB6 was below its equilibrium value in the previous period and hence in the current period it must be adjusted upward. On the other hand, if it is negative, TB6 was above its equilibrium value so that in the current period it will be adjusted downward. Similar comments apply to TB3.

It should be noted that the slope coefficients in the preceding two regressions will have opposite signs because there is only one equilibrium relation between the two rates.

The results of regressions, given in shortened form, are as follows:

$$\Delta TB6_t = -0.0400 - 0.0545 e_{t-1}$$
$$t \qquad = (-2.0928)(-0.5582) \tag{16.14a}$$

$$\Delta TB3_t = -0.0430 + 0.1962 e_{t-1}$$
$$t \qquad = (-2.0714)(1.5523) \tag{16.14b}$$

where figures in parentheses are *t* ratios.

The slope coefficients in both these VEC models are statistically insignificant, indicating that the two interest rates adjust to each other very quickly.

You might wonder that we started the VAR model given in Eqs. (16.8) and (16.9), with one lagged term for each variable, and ended with the VEC model given in Eqs. (16.12) and (16.13) – they do not look alike. But this difference is more apparent than real, for we can show that they are in fact equivalent.

To see this, look at Eq. (16.12):

$$\Delta TB6_t = \alpha_1 + \alpha_2 e_{t-1} + v_{1t}$$

$$(TB6_t - TB6_{t-1}) = \alpha_1 + \alpha_2 [TB6_{t-1} - 0.6064 - 0.9584 TB3_{t-1}$$

$$+ 0.0026(t-1) - 0.000004(t-1)^2] + v_{1t}$$

$$TB6_t = \alpha_1 + (\alpha_2 + 1)TB6_{t-1} - 0.6064\alpha_2$$

$$-0.9584\alpha_2 TB3_{t-1} + 0.0026\alpha_2 (t-1)$$

$$-0.000004\alpha_2 (t-1)^2 + v_{1t}$$

(16.15)

Collecting terms, it can be seen that Eq. (16.15) is precisely of the form Eq. (16.9). A similar equation can be written for $TB3_t$.

The point of this exercise is to show that we are in fact estimating a VAR model, but we explicitly take into account the error correction mechanism following Granger's Representation Theorem, albeit in the context of multivariate time series.

## Forecasting with VAR

The primary interest in time series models is forecasting. We showed earlier how ARIMA models can be used for forecasting. We now consider VAR for the same purpose. But unlike ARIMA, which dealt with a univariate time series, we now deal with two or more time series simultaneously.

We continue with our TB3 and TB6 time series to show how VAR forecasting is done. For simplicity, and with a slight change in notation, we consider a VAR (1) model, which is:

$$TB3_t = A_1 + A_2 TB3_{t-1} + A_3 TB6_{t-1} + A_4 t + u_t$$ (16.16)

$$TB6_t = B_1 + B_2 TB3_{t-1} + B_3 TB6_{t-1} + B_4 t + u_{2t}$$ (16.17)

where $t$ is the trend variable.[15]

Having estimated the two-variable VAR, we denote the estimated values of the coefficients by $a$s and $b$s. We obtained these estimates using the sample data from time period 1 to end of time period $(t)$. Now suppose we want to forecast the values of TB3 and TB6 beyond sample period, $t + 1, t + 2, ..., (t + n)$, where $n$ is specified.

We can proceed as following, using TB3. The forecast for time $(t + 1)$ is given by

$$TB3_{t+1} = A_1 + A_2 TB3_t + A_3 TB6_t + A_4 (t+1) + u_{t+1}$$ (16.18)

Since we do not know what the value of the error term in period $(t + 1)$ will be, we put it equal to zero because $u$ is random anyhow. We do not know the parameter values either, but we can use the estimated values of these parameters from the sample data. So we actually estimate

---

15  If need be, we can also add the quadratic trend, $t^2$, but for simplicity of discussion I have omitted this term.

$$T\hat{B}3_{t+1} = a_1 + a_2 TB3_t + a_3 TB6_t + a_4(t+1) \qquad (16.19)$$

Thus, to forecast TB3 in period $t + 1$, we use the actual values of TB3 and TB6 in period $t$, which is the last observation in the sample. Note that, as usual, a hat over a symbol represents an estimated value.

We follow the same procedure to forecast TB6 in period $(t + 1)$, namely,

$$T\hat{B}6_{t+1} = b_1 + b_2 TB3_t + b_3 TB6_t + b_4(t+1) \qquad (16.20)$$

To forecast TB3 for period $t + 2$, we follow the same procedure, but modify it as follows:

$$T\hat{B}3_{t+2} = a_1 + a_2 T\hat{B}3_{t+1} + a_3 T\hat{B}6_{t+1} + a_4(t+2) \qquad (16.21)$$

Notice carefully that in this equation we use the forecast values of TB3 and TB6 from the previous period and not the actual values because we do not know them.

As you can sense, this procedure produces dynamic forecasts. Also, note that if we make a forecast error in the first period, that error will be carried forward because, after the first period of forecast, we use the forecast value in the previous period as input on the right-hand side of the above equation.

Of course, this way of forecasting manually is very tedious. But packages like *Stata* can do this easily, using the **fcast** command. To save space we will not present the results for our example. It may be noted that the **fcast** command will also compute confidence intervals for the forecast values.

## 16.5    Testing causality using VAR: the Granger causality test

VAR modeling has been used to shed light on the notion of **causality**, a deeply philosophical question with all kinds of controversies. As we noted in our discussion of regression analysis, the distinction between the dependent variable $Y$ and one or more $X$ variables, the regressors, does not necessarily mean that the $X$ variables "cause" $Y$. Causality between them, if any, must be determined externally, by appealing to some theory or by some kind of experimentation.[16]

However, in regressions involving time series data the situation may be different because, as one author puts it,

> ...time does not run backward. That is, if event $A$ happens before event $B$, then it is possible that $A$ is causing $B$. However, it is not possible that $B$ is causing $A$. In other words, events in the past can cause events to happen today, future events cannot.[17]

This line of thinking is probably behind the so-called **Granger causality test**.

### Granger causality test

To explain the Granger causality test, we will look at the consumption function example discussed in Section 16.1 from the point of Granger causality. The question we now ask is: What is the relationship between per capita personal consumption expenditure

---

16  Experimental economics is a growing field of research. For an overview, see James H. Stock and Mark W. Watson, *Introduction to Econometrics*, 2nd edn, Pearson/Addison Wesley, Boston, 2007, Chapter 13. Very soon you will see books on "Experimetrics".

17  Gary Koop, *Analysis of Economic Data*, John Wiley & Sons, New York, 2000, p. 175.

(PCE) and per capita personal disposable income (PDI), both expressed in real term (2005 chained dollars)? Does $PCE \rightarrow PDI$ or does $PDI \rightarrow PCE$, where the arrow points to the direction of causality? For empirical purposes, we will use the logs of these variables because the slope coefficients can be interpreted as elasticities.

The Granger test involves estimating the following pairs of regressions:

$$LPCE_t = \sum_{i=1}^{m} \alpha_i LPCE_{t-i} + \sum_{j=1}^{m} \beta_j LPDI_{t-j} + \lambda_1 t + u_{1t} \qquad (16.22)$$

$$LPDI_t = \sum_{i=1}^{m} \gamma_i LPDI_{t-i} + \sum_{i=1}^{m} \delta_j LPCE_{t-j} + \lambda_2 t + u_{2t} \qquad (16.23)$$

where L stands for logarithm and $t$ is the time or trend variable and where it is assumed that the error terms $u_{1t}$ and $u_{2t}$ are uncorrelated.

Notice that the two equations represent a **bivariate** VAR. Each equation contains the lags of both variables in the system; the number of lagged terms included in each equation is often a trial and error process.

Now we distinguish four cases.

1 *Unidirectional causality from LPCE to LPDI ($LPCE \rightarrow LPDI$)* occurs if the estimated $\delta_j$ in Eq. (16.23) are statistically different from zero as a group and the set of estimated $\beta_j$ coefficients in Eq. (16.22) is not different from zero.

2 *Unidirectional causality from LPDI to LPCE ($LPDI \rightarrow LPCE$)* is indicated if the set of $\beta_j$ coefficients in Eq. (16.22) is statistically different from zero and the set of $\delta_j$ is not statistically different from zero.

3 *Feedback* or *bilateral causality* is indicated when the sets of LPCE and LPDI coefficients are statistically significantly different from zero in both regressions.

4 *Independence* is suggested when the sets of LPCE and LPDI coefficients are not statistically significant in either of the regressions.

To implement the test, consider regression (16.22). We proceed as follows:

1 Regress current LPCE on all lagged LPCE terms and other variables, if any (such as trend), but do not included the lagged LPDI terms in this regression. We call this the **restricted regression**.[18] From this regression we obtain the restricted residual sum of squares, $RSS_r$.

2 Now reestimate Eq. (16.22) including the lagged LPDI terms. This is the unrestricted regression. From this regression obtain the unrestricted residual sum of squares, $RSS_{ur}$.

3 The null hypothesis $H_0$ is that: $\beta_1 = \beta_2 = \ldots = \beta_m = 0$ – that is, the lagged LPDI terms do not belong in the regression.

4 To test the null hypothesis, we apply the $F$ test, which is:

$$F = \frac{(RSS_r - RSS_{ur})/m}{RSS_{ur}/(n-k)} \qquad (16.24)$$

18 Recall from Chapter 2 our discussion of the restricted and unrestricted regression and the $F$ test.

which has $m$ and $(n - k)$ df, where $m$ is the number of lagged *LPDI* terms, $k$ is the number of parameters estimated in the unrestricted regression, and $n$ is the sample size.

5   If the computed $F$ value exceeds the critical $F$ value at the chosen level of significance, we reject the null hypothesis. In this case the LPDI lagged terms belong in the LPCE equation, which is to say LPD causes LPCE.

These steps can be repeated for Eq. (16.23) to find out if LPCE causes LPDI.

Before we implement the Granger test, we need to consider several factors:

1   The number of lagged terms to be introduced in the Granger causality tests is an important practical question, *for the direction of causality may depend critically on the number of lagged terms included in the model.* We will have to use the Akaike, Schwarz or similar criterion to determine the length of the lags. Some trial and error is inevitable.

2   We have assumed that the error terms entering the Granger test are uncorrelated. If this is not the case, we will have to use appropriate error transformation as discussed in the chapter on autocorrelation.

3   We have to guard against "spurious" causality. When we say that LPCE causes LPDI (or vice versa), it is quite possible that there is a "lurking" variable, say interest rate, that causes both LPCE and LPDI. Therefore the causality between LPCE and LPDI may in fact be due to the omitted variable, the interest rate. One way to find this out is to consider a three-variable VAR, one equation for each of the three variables.

4   The critical assumption underlying the Granger causality test is that the variables under study, such as LPCE and LPDI, are *stationary*. In our case, it can be shown that both LPCE and LPDI are individually nonstationary. So, strictly speaking, we cannot use the Granger test.

5   However, while individually nonstationary, it is possible that the variables in question are cointegrated. In that situation, as in the case of univariate nonstationary variables, we will have to use the *error correction mechanism* (ECM). This is because if LPCE and LPDI are cointegrated, then *following the Granger Representation Theorem, either LPCE must cause LPDI or LPDI must cause LPCE.*[19]

To see if LPCE and LPDI are cointegrated, we estimated the (cointegrating) regression of Table 16.11. This regression shows that the elasticity of PCE with respect to PDI is about 0.71, which is statistically significant. The trend coefficient, which is also statistically significant, suggests that the rate of growth in LPCE is about 0.76% per year.

When the residuals from this regression were tested for unit root, it was found that the residuals were stationary.[20] Therefore we can conclude that the two time series, while individually nonstationary, are cointegrated.

In view of this finding we can conduct the Granger causality test, but we must use the error correction mechanism. This can be done as follows:

---

19   See Gary Koop, *Analysis of Financial Data*, John Wiley & Sons, West Sussex, England 2006, Chapter 11.

20   This was with no intercept and trend.

**Table 16.11  Regression of LPCE on LPDI and trend.**

Dependent Variable: LPCE
Method: Least Squares
Date: 07/21/10 Time: 13:30
Sample: 1960 2004
Included observations: 45

| Variable | Coefficient | Std. Error | t-Statistic | Prob. |
|---|---|---|---|---|
| C | 2.589374 | 0.476107 | 5.438637 | 0.0000 |
| LPDI | 0.709795 | 0.050779 | 13.97807 | 0.0000 |
| @TREND | 0.007557 | 0.001156 | 6.537171 | 0.0000 |

| | | | | |
|---|---|---|---|---|
| R-squared | 0.998228 | Mean dependent var | 9.762786 |
| Adjusted R-squared | 0.998143 | S.D. dependent var | 0.311154 |
| S.E. of regression | 0.013408 | Akaike info criterion | −5.721653 |
| Sum squared resid | 0.007550 | Schwarz criterion | −5.601209 |
| Log likelihood | 131.7372 | Hannan–Quinn criter. | −5.676753 |
| F-statistic | 11827.74 | Durbin–Watson stat | 0.619973 |
| Prob(F-statistic) | 0.000000 | | |

$$\Delta LPCE_t = \alpha_1 + \alpha_2 \Delta LPCE_{t-1} + \ldots + \alpha_p \Delta LPCE_{t-p}$$
$$+ \beta_1 \Delta LPDI_{t-1} + \ldots + \beta_q \Delta LPDI_{t-q} + \lambda e_{t-1} + v_t \tag{16.25}$$

where $\Delta$, as usual, is the first difference operator and where $e_{t-1}$ is the lagged residual term from the cointegrating regression given in Table 16.11, which is nothing but the error correction (EC) term.

As is clear from Eq. (16.25), there are now two sources of causation for LPCE: (1) through the lagged values of LPDI and/or (2) through the lagged value of the cointegrating vector (i.e. the EC term). The standard Granger test neglects the latter source of causation.

Therefore the null hypothesis $H_0$: $\beta_1 = \beta_2 = \ldots = \beta_q = \lambda = 0$ can be rejected if any of these coefficients are nonzero or if $\lambda \neq 0$. In other words, even if all the β coefficients are zero, but the coefficient of the lagged EC term is nonzero, we can reject the hypothesis that LPDI does not cause LPCE. This is because the EC term includes the impact of LPDI.

To test the null hypothesis that lagged LPDIs do not cause LPCE, we proceed as follows:

1  Estimate Eq. (16.25) by OLS and obtain the residual sum of squares from this regression (RSS); call it the unrestricted RSS$_{ur}$, because we include all the terms in the regression.

2  Re-estimate Eq. (16.25), dropping all the lagged terms of LPDI and the EC term. Obtain the RSS from this reduced regression; call it RSS restricted, RSS$_r$.

Now apply the $F$ test, as in Eq. (16.24), and reject the null hypothesis if the computed $F$ value exceeds the critical $F$ value at the chosen level of significance.

Note that the difference between the standard Granger causality test and the "extended" causality test is due to the presence of the EC term in Eq. (16.25).

**Table 16.12  Granger causality with EC.**

Dependent Variable: D(LPCE)
Method: Least Squares
Date: 07/21/10 Time: 13:45
Sample (adjusted): 1962 2004
Included observations: 43 after adjustments

| Variable | Coefficient | Std. Error | t-Statistic | Prob. |
|---|---|---|---|---|
| C | 0.013772 | 0.004440 | 3.101368 | 0.0036 |
| D(LPCE(−1)) | 0.579602 | 0.240720 | 2.407785 | 0.0209 |
| D(LPDI(−1)) | 0.135031 | 0.241895 | 0.558220 | 0.5799 |
| S2(−1) | 0.511126 | 0.192531 | 2.654766 | 0.0114 |

| | | | | |
|---|---|---|---|---|
| R-squared | 0.248628 | Mean dependent var | 0.025026 | |
| Adjusted R-squared | 0.190830 | S.D. dependent var | 0.016628 | |
| S.E. of regression | 0.014958 | Akaike info criterion | −5.478748 | |
| Sum squared resid | 0.008726 | Schwarz criterion | −5.314915 | |
| Log likelihood | 121.7931 | Hannan–Quinn criter. | −5.418331 | |
| F-statistic | 4.301676 | Durbin–Watson stat | 1.831083 | |
| Prob(F-statistic) | 0.010274 | | | |

*Note: D (=Δ) is the first-difference operator.*

The practical question in estimating Eq. (16.25) is the number of lagged terms in this equation. Since we have annual data, we decided to include only one lagged term of each variable on the right-hand side.[21] The results are as follows:

Notice that the lagged error term $\Delta LPDI(-1)$ is not significant, but the EC term is highly significant. We re-estimated the model in Table 16.12, dropping the lagged LPDI and EC terms and on the basis of the $F$ test it was found that both the lagged LPDI and EC terms belong in the model. This would suggest that LPCE is caused either by the lagged LPDI term or the lagged EC term or both.

We repeated the above exercise with LPDI as the dependent variable (i.e. Eq. (16.23)) to find out if lagged LPCE or lagged EC or both caused LPDI. The conclusion was that they indeed caused LPDI.

What all this says is that there is bilateral causality between LPCE and LPDI. At the macroeconomics level, this finding should not be surprising, for aggregate income and aggregate consumption are mutually dependent.

## 16.6  Summary and conclusions

The primary goal of this chapter was to introduce the reader to four important topics in time series econometrics, namely, (1) forecasting with linear regression models, (2) univariate time series forecasting with Box–Jenkins methodology, (3) multivariate time series forecasting using vector autoregression, and (4) the nature of causality in econometrics.

Linear regression models have long been used in forecasting sales, production, employment, corporate profits and a host of other economic topics. In discussing

---

21  We also introduced two lagged terms of LPCE and LDPI, but the substantive results did not change.

forecasting with linear regression, we distinguished between point and interval forecasts, *ex post* and *ex ante* forecasts, and conditional and unconditional forecasts. We illustrated these with an example relating real per capita consumption expenditure in relation to real per capita disposable income in the USA for the period 1960–2004 and saved the observations for 2005 to 2008 to see how the fitted model performs in the post the estimation period. We briefly discussed forecasting with autocorrelated errors.

We then discussed the ARIMA method of forecasting, which is popularly known as the Box–Jenkins (BJ) methodology. In the BJ approach to forecasting, we analyze a time series strictly on the basis its past history or purely moving average of random error term or both. The name ARMA is a combination of AR (autoregressive) and MA (moving average) terms. It is assumed that the time series under study is stationary. If it is not stationary, we make it stationary by differencing it one or more times.

ARIMA modeling is a four-step procedure: (1) Identification, (2) Estimation, (3) Diagnostic checking and (4) Forecasting. In developing an ARIMA model, we can look at the features of some of the standard ARIMA models and try to modify them in a given case. Once a model is identified, it is estimated. To see if the fitted model is satisfactory, we subject it to various diagnostic tests. The key here is to see if the residuals from the chosen model are white noise. If they are not, we start the four-step procedure once again. Thus the BJ methodology is an iterative procedure.

Once an ARIMA model is finally chosen, it can be used for forecasting future values of the variable of interest. This forecasting can be static as well as dynamic.

To deal with forecasting two or more time series, we need to go beyond the BJ methodology. Vector autoregressive models (VARs) are used for this purpose. In VAR we have one equation for each variable and each equation contains only the lagged values of that variable and the lagged values of all other variables in the system.

As in the case of the univariate time series, in VAR we also require the time series to be stationary. If each variable in the VAR is already stationary, each equation in it can be estimated by OLS. If each variable is not stationary, we can estimate VAR only in the first differences of the series; rarely do we have to difference a time series more than once. However, if individual variables in VAR are nonstationary, but are cointegrated, we can estimate VAR by taking into account the error correction term, which is obtained from the cointegrating regression. This leads to vector error correction model (VECM).

We can use the estimated VAR model for forecasting. In such forecasting we not only use information on the variable under consideration but also all the variables in the system. The actual mechanics is tedious, but software packages now do this routinely.

VAR modes can also be used to shed light on causality among variables. The basic idea behind VAR causality testing is that the past can cause the present and the future, but not the other way round. Granger causality uses this concept. In the PCE and PDI example, if the lagged values of PDI better forecast the current values of PCE than the lagged values of PCE alone, we may contend that PDI (Granger) causes PCE. Similarly, if the lagged values of PCE better forecast the current values of PDI than the lagged values of PDI alone, we may say that PCE (Granger) causes PDI. These are instances of unilateral causality. But it is quite possible that there is bilateral causality between the two in that PCE causes PDI and PDI causes PCE.

In establishing causality, we must make sure that the underlying variables are stationary. If they are not, we have to difference the variables and run the causality test on the differenced variables. However, if the variables are nonstationary, but are integrated, we need to use the error correction term to account for causality, if any.

## Exercises

**16.1** Estimate regression (16.1) using the logs of the variables and compare the results with those obtained in Table 16.2. How would you decide which is a better model?

**16.2** Refer to the IBM stock price ARIMA model discussed in the text. Using the data provided, try to come up with an alternative model and compare your results with those given in the text. Which model do you prefer, and why?

**16.3** Replicate your model used in the preceding exercise using more recent data and comment on the results

**16.4** Suppose you want to forecast employment at the national level. Collect quarterly employment data and develop a suitable forecasting model using ARIMA methodology. To take into account seasonal variation, employment data are often presented in seasonally adjusted form. In developing your model, see if it makes a substantial difference if you use seasonally adjusted vs. the raw data.

**16.5** Develop a suitable ARIMA model to forecast the labor force participation rate for females and males separately. What considerations would you take into account in developing such a model? Show the necessary calculations and explain the various diagnostic tests you use in your analysis.

**16.6** Collect data on housing starts and develop a suitable ARIMA model for forecasting housing starts. Explain the procedure step by step.

**16.7** Refer to the 3-month and 6-month Treasury Bills example discussed in the text. Suppose you also want to include the Federal Funds Rate (FFR) in the model. Obtain the data on FFR for comparable time period and estimate a VAR model for the three variables. You can obtain the data from the Federal Reserve Bank of St Louis.
    (*a*) How many cointegrating relationships do you expect to find among the three-variables?[22] Show the necessary calculations.
    (*b*) Suppose you find two cointegrating relationships. How do you interpret them?
    (*c*) Would you have to include one or two error correction terms in estimating the VAR?
    (*d*) What is the nature of causality among the three variables? Show the necessary calculations.

---

22  Consult the manuals for *Stata* or *Eviews* to learn about Johansen's method of estimating the number of cointegrating vectors in multivariate time series.

# Measures of forecast accuracy[23]

Measures of forecast accuracy are based on forecast errors. Some of the commonly used measures are as follows. Let

$Y_t$ = value of the forecast variable $Y$ at time $t$.

$Y_{t+h,t}$ = forecast value of $Y$ $h$ periods ahead, forecast being made at time $t$

$Y_{t+h}$ = actual value of $Y$ at time $(t + h)$

$e_{t+h,t}$ = forecast error

$\dfrac{Y_{t+h} - Y_{t+h,t}}{Y_{t+h}} = p_{t+h,t}$ percentage forecast error

Then the various measures of forecast accuracy are as follows:

$$\textbf{Mean Error (ME)} = \frac{1}{T} \sum_{1}^{T} e_{t+h,t} \tag{1}$$

which is the average error made in forecasting $Y$ over the forecast horizon, 1 to $T$. The lower the value of ME, the better is the accuracy of the forecast.

$$\textbf{Error Variance (EV)} = \frac{\sum_{1}^{T} (e_{t+h,t} - ME)^2}{T} \tag{2}$$

which measures the dispersion of forecast errors.

The lower the value of EV, the better is the accuracy of the forecast

Neither ME nor EV provides an overall accuracy measure of forecast, but the following measures do.

$$\textbf{Mean Squared Error (MSE)} = \frac{1}{T} \sum_{1}^{T} e^2_{t+h,t} \tag{3}$$

$$\textbf{Mean Squared Percent Error (MSPE)} = \frac{1}{T} \sum_{1}^{T} p^2_{t+h,t} \tag{4}$$

$$\textbf{Root Mean Square Error (RMSE)} = \sqrt{\frac{1}{T} \sum_{1}^{T} e^2_{h+t,t}} \tag{5}$$

$$\textbf{Root Mean Square Percent Error} = \sqrt{\frac{1}{T} \sum_{1}^{T} p^2_{t+h,t}} \tag{6}$$

$$\textbf{Mean Absolute Error} = \frac{1}{T} \sum_{1}^{T} |e_{t+h,t}| \tag{7}$$

---

23  For details, see Francis X. Diebold, *op cit.*, pp. 260–3.

$$\text{Mean Absolute Percent Error} = \frac{1}{T} \sum_{t=1}^{t=T} |P_{t+h,t}| \qquad (8)$$

*Note*: Measures (5) and (6) preserve the units in which the variables are measured. If the forecast errors are measured in dollars, MSE, for example, will be measured in squared dollars, but RMSE will be measured in dollars.

$$\text{Theil's U-Statistic} = \frac{\sum_{t=1}^{t=T} (Y_{t+1} - Y_{t+1,t})^2}{\sum_{t=1}^{t=T} (Y_{t+1} - Y_t)^2} \qquad (9)$$

which is the ratio of the 1-step ahead MSE obtained from a forecasting method compared to the MSE of a random walk forecast in which $Y_{t+1} = Y_t$.

$$\text{Theil Inequality Coefficient} = \frac{\sqrt{\sum_{t=T+1}^{T+h} (\hat{Y}_t - Y_t)^2 / h}}{\sqrt{\sum_{t=T+1}^{T+h} \hat{Y}_t^2 / h} + \sqrt{\sum_{t=T+1}^{T+h} Y_t^2 / h}}$$

This coefficient lies between 0 and 1, 0 indicating perfect fit.

# 17

# Panel data regression models

The regression models discussed in the preceding 16 chapters primarily used either cross-sectional or time series data. Each of these types of data has its unique features. In this chapter we discuss the **panel data regression models** – that is, models that study the same group of entities (individuals, firms, states, countries, and the like) over time.[1]

Some well-known examples of panel data sets are:

1  **The Panel Study of Income Dynamics (PSID):** This is conducted by the Institute of Social Research at the University of Michigan. Started in 1968, each year the institute collects data on some 500 families abut various socioeconomic and demographic variables.

2  **Survey of Income and Program Participation (SIPP):** This survey is conducted by the Bureau of the Census of the US Department of Commerce. Four times a year respondents are interviewed about their economic conditions.

3  **The German Socio-Economic Panel (GESOEP):** It studied 1,761 individuals every year between 1984 and 2002. It collected information on each individual about year of birth, gender, life satisfaction, marital status, labor earnings, and annual hours of work.

4  **National Longitudinal Survey of Youth (NLSY):** NLSY, conducted by the US Department of Labor, is a set of surveys designed to gather information at multiple points in time on the labor market activities and other significant life events of several groups of men and women.

There are several such surveys that are conducted by governments and private agencies in many countries.

## 17.1  The importance of panel data

In discussing the advantages of panel data over pure cross-sectional data or pure time series data, Baltagi lists the following factors:[2]

1  Since panel data deals with individuals, firms, states, countries and so on over time, there is bound to be *heterogeneity* in these units, which may be often unobservable. The panel data estimation techniques can take such heterogeneity

---

1  For more details and examples on panel data regression models, see Gujarati/Porter, *op cit.*, Chapter 16.
2  Badi H. Baltagi, *Econometric Analysis of Panel Data*, John Wiley & Sons, New York, 1995, pp. 3–6.

explicitly into account by allowing for **subject-specific** variables, as we shall show shortly. We use the term **subject** generically to include microunits such as individuals, firms or states.

2  By combining time series of cross-sectional observations, panel data gives "more informative data, more variability, less collinearity among variables, more degrees of freedom and more efficiency".

3  By studying the repeated cross-sections of observations, panel data are better suited to study the dynamics of change. Spells of unemployment, job turnover, duration of unemployment, and labor mobility are better studied with panel data.

4  Panel data can better detect and measure effects that cannot be observed in pure cross-sectional or time series data. Thus the effects of minimum wage laws on employment and earnings can be better studied if we follow successive waves of increases in federal and/or state minimum wages.

5  Phenomena such as economies of scale and technological change can be better studied by panel data than by pure cross-sectional or pure time series data.

## 17.2    An illustrative example: charitable giving

**Table 17.1** (available on the companion website) gives data on charitable giving by 47 individuals over the period 1979–1988.[3]

The variables are defined as follows:

*Charity*: The sum of cash and other property contributions, excluding carry-overs from previous years

*Income*: Adjusted gross income

*Price*: One minus the marginal income tax rate; marginal tax rate is defined on income prior to contributions

*Age*: A dummy variable equal to 1 if the taxpayer is over 64, and 0 otherwise

*MS*: A dummy variable equal to 1 if the taxpayer is married, 0 otherwise

*DEPS*: Number of dependents claimed on the tax return

These data were obtained from the 1979–1988 *Statistics of Income* (SOI) Panel of Individual Tax Returns.

One of the goals of this study was to find out the effect, if any, of the marginal tax rate on charitable giving.

Before we proceed to the analysis, it may be noted that the panel data in this example is called a **balanced panel** because the number of time observations (10) is the same for each individual. If that were not the case, it would be an example of an **unbalanced panel**. The data here are also called a **short panel**. In a short panel the number of cross-sectional or individual units $N$ (here 47) is greater than the number of time periods, $T$ (here 10). In a **long panel**, on the other hand, $T$ is greater than $N$.

Suppose we want to estimate a model of charity giving in relation to the variables listed above. Call it the *charity function*. How do we proceed? We have five options:

---

3  These data are obtained from Edward W. Frees, *Longitudinal and Panel Data Analysis and Applications in the Social Sciences*, Cambridge University Press, New York, 2004.

1 **Individual time series of charity functions**: We can estimate by OLS 47 time series charity functions, one for each individual using the data for 10 years. Although in principle we can estimate these functions, we will have very few degrees of freedom to do meaningful statistical analysis. This is because we have to estimate six coefficients in all, five for the five explanatory variables and one for the intercept. Besides, these individual charity functions neglect the information about the other individuals' charity contributions because they all operate in the same regulatory environment.

2 **Cross-sectional charity functions**: We can estimate by OLS 10 cross-sectional charity functions, one for each year. There will be 47 observations per year to estimate such functions. But again, we neglect the dynamic aspect of charitable giving, for the charitable contributions made by individuals over the years will depend on factors like income and marital status.

3 **Pooled OLS charity function**: We can pool all 470 observations ($47 \times 10$) and estimate a "grand" charity function, neglecting the dual nature of time series and cross-sectional data. Not only would we be neglecting this if we were to run a pooled model, but such a pooling assumes that the coefficients of the charity function remain constant across time and cross-section. The pooled OLS estimation is also known as the *constant coefficient model*, for we are assuming that coefficients across time and cross-section remain the same.

4 **Fixed effects least-squares dummy variable (LSDV) model**: As in Option 3, we pool all 470 observations, but allow each individual to have his or her individual intercept dummy. A variant of this is the **within estimator**, which we will explain shortly.[4]

5 **The random effects model**: Instead of allowing each individual to have their own (fixed) intercept value as in LSDV, we assume that the intercept values of the 47 individuals are random drawings from a much larger population of individuals. As a matter of fact, the SOI Panel is a subset of the IRS Individual Tax Model File.

We now discuss Options 3, 4 and 5 sequentially.

## 17.3  Pooled OLS regression of charity function

Consider the following charity function:

$$C_{it} = B_{1i} + B_2 Age_{it} + B_3 Income_{it} + B_4 Price_{it}$$
$$+ B_5 Deps_{it} + B_6 MS_{it} + u_{it} \qquad (17.1)$$
$$i = 1, 2, \ldots, 47; \quad t = 1, 2, \ldots, 10$$

where $C$ is charitable contribution. Notice that we have put two subscripts on the variables: $i$, representing the cross-section unit, and $t$, the time. It is assumed that the

---

4 Another variant is the first-difference transformation, which we will not discuss here because it has some estimation problems if we have more than two time periods. For a brief discussion of this method, see Gujarati/Porter, *op cit.*, pp. 601–2.

**Table 17.2  OLS estimation of the charity function.**

Dependent Variable: CHARITY
Method: Least Squares
Sample: 1 470
Included observations: 470

|  | Coefficient | Std. Error | t-Statistic | Prob. |
|---|---|---|---|---|
| C | −4.674219 | 1.298134 | −3.600722 | 0.0004 |
| AGE | 1.547275 | 0.216955 | 7.131788 | 0.0000 |
| INCOME | 1.035779 | 0.128944 | 8.032766 | 0.0000 |
| PRICE | 0.483092 | 0.207703 | 2.325875 | 0.0205 |
| DEPS | 0.175368 | 0.042642 | 4.112556 | 0.0000 |
| MS | −0.008036 | 0.184849 | −0.043476 | 0.9653 |

| | | | |
|---|---|---|---|
| R-squared | 0.224488 | Mean dependent var | 6.577150 |
| Adjusted R-squared | 0.216131 | S.D. dependent var | 1.313659 |
| S.E. of regression | 1.163067 | Akaike info criterion | 3.152681 |
| Sum squared resid | 627.6639 | Schwarz criterion | 3.205695 |
| Log likelihood | −734.8801 | Durbin–Watson stat | 0.701077 |
| F-statistic | 26.86280 | Prob(F-statistic) | 0.000000 |

regressors are nonstochastic, or if stochastic, are uncorrelated with the error term. It is also assumed that the error term satisfies the usual classical assumptions.

*A priori*, we would expect age, income, price, and marital status to have a positive impact on charitable giving and the number of dependents to have a negative impact. The reason the price variable, as defined, is included in the model is that it represents the opportunity cost of giving charitable contributions – the higher the marginal tax, the lower the opportunity cost.

Using *Eviews 6*, we obtained the results of Table 17.2. Assuming that pooling of the data is valid (a big assumption), the results show that Age, Income, and Price have significant positive impact on charitable donation, and MS has negative but statistically insignificant effect on charitable contributions. Surprisingly, DEPS has a positive and significant impact on charitable giving. The low Durbin–Watson in the present instance is probably more an indication of specification error than spatial or serial correlation.[5]

The possibility that the model is misspecified stems from the fact that by lumping together different individuals at different times, we *camouflage* the **heterogeneity** (individuality or uniqueness) that may exist among the 47 individuals. Perhaps the uniqueness of each individual is subsumed in the composite error term, $u_{it}$. As a result, it is quite possible that the error term is correlated with some of the regressors included in the model. If that is indeed the case, the estimated coefficients in Table 17.2 may be biased as well as inconsistent.

---

5  *Eviews* computes the Durbin–Watson statistic by computing the first-order serial correlation on the stacked set of residuals.

## 17.4 The fixed effects least squares dummy variable (LSDV) model

One way we can take into account the heterogeneity that may exist among 47 individuals is to allow each individual to have his or her own intercept, as in the following equation:

$$C_{it} = B_{1i} + B_2 Age_{it} + B_3 Income_{it} + B_4 Price_{it}$$
$$+ B_5 Deps_{it} + B_6 MS_{it} + u_{it} \qquad (17.2)$$
$$i = 1,2,\ldots,47; \quad t = 1,2,\ldots,10$$

Notice that we have added the subscript $i$ to the intercept to indicate that the intercept of the 47 individuals may be different. The difference may be due special features of each individual, such as education or religion.

Equation (17.2) is known as the **fixed effects regression model** (FEM). The term "fixed effects" is due to the fact that each taxpayer's intercept, although different from the intercepts of the other taxpayers, does not vary over time, that is, it is **time-invariant**. If we were to write the intercept as $B_{1it}$, the intercept of each taxpayer would be **time-variant**. But note that in Eq. (17.2) we assume that the slope coefficients are time-invariant.

But how do we make Eq. (17.2) operational? This can be done easily by introducing **differential intercept dummies**, which we first discussed in Chapter 3 on dummy variables. Specifically, we modify Eq. (17.1) as follows:

$$C_{it} = B_1 + B_2 D_{2i} + B_3 D_{3i} + \ldots + B_{46} D_{46i} + B_{47} Age_{it}$$
$$+ B_{48} Income_{it} + B_{49} Price_{it} + B_{50} DEPS_{it} + B_{51} MS_{it} + u_{it} \qquad (17.3)$$

where $D_{2i} = 1$ for individual 2, 0 otherwise; $D_{3i} = 1$ for individual 3, 0 otherwise; and so on.

It is important to note that we have used only 46 dummies to represent 47 individuals to avoid the **dummy variable trap** (perfect collinearity). In this case the 46 dummies will represent the **differential intercept dummy coefficients** – that is, they will show by how much the intercept coefficient of the individual that is assigned a dummy variable will differ from the benchmark category. We are treating the first individual as the **benchmark** or **reference category**, although any individual can be chosen for that purpose.

The first thing to notice about the results in Table 17.3 is that the table does not produce the values of the individual differential intercept coefficients, although they are taken into account in estimating the model. However, the differential intercept coefficients can be easily obtained (see Exercise 17.1). Secondly, if you compare the OLS pooled regression results with the FEM results, you will see substantial differences between the two, not only in the values of the coefficients, but also in their signs.

For example, in the pooled regression the coefficient of DEPS is not only positive (contrary to *a priori* expectation), but is also highly significant. The MS coefficient on the other hand is negative, although it is not statistically significant. Why should marital status have a negative sign?

These results, therefore, cast doubt on the pooled OLS estimates. If you examine the individual differential intercept dummies, you will find that several of them are

**Table 17.3 OLS charity regression with individual dummy coefficients.**

Sample: 1 10
Periods included: 10
Cross-sections included: 47
Total panel (balanced) observations: 470

| | Coefficient | Std. Error | t-Statistic | Prob. |
|---|---|---|---|---|
| C | −2.089970 | 1.131118 | −1.847704 | 0.0654 |
| AGE | 0.102249 | 0.208039 | 0.491490 | 0.6233 |
| INCOME | 0.838810 | 0.111267 | 7.538725 | 0.0000 |
| PRICE | 0.366080 | 0.124294 | 2.945265 | 0.0034 |
| DEPS | −0.086352 | 0.053483 | −1.614589 | 0.1072 |
| MS | 0.199833 | 0.263890 | 0.757257 | 0.4493 |

**Effects Specification**
Cross-section fixed (dummy variables)

| | | | |
|---|---|---|---|
| R-squared | 0.763177 | Mean dependent var | 6.577150 |
| Adjusted R-squared | 0.734282 | S.D. dependent var | 1.313659 |
| S.E. of regression | 0.677163 | Akaike info criterion | 2.162215 |
| Sum squared resid | 191.6735 | Schwarz criterion | 2.621666 |
| Log likelihood | −456.1204 | Hannan–Quinn criter. | 2.342975 |
| F-statistic | 26.41239 | Durbin–Watson stat | 1.234015 |
| Prob(F-statistic) | 0.000000 | | |

statistically highly significant (see Exercise 17.1), suggesting that the pooled estimates hide the heterogeneity among the 47 charitable donors.

We can provide a test to find out if the fixed effects model is better than the OLS pooled model given in Table 17.2. Since the pooled model neglects the heterogeneity effects that are explicitly taken into account in the fixed effects model, the pooled model is a restricted version of the fixed effects model. Therefore, we can use the restricted $F$ test that we discussed in Chapter 7, which is:

$$F = \frac{(R_{ur}^2 - R_r^2)/m}{(1 - R_{ur}^2)/(n-k)} \tag{17.4}$$

where $R_{ur}^2$ and $R_r^2$ are unrestricted and restricted coefficients of determination, $m$ is the number of parameters omitted from the restricted model (46 here), $n$ is the number of observations in the sample, and $k$ is the number of parameters estimated in the unrestricted regression (here a total of 52). The restricted and unrestricted $R^2$ values are obtained from Tables 17.2 and 17.3, respectively.

Using the appropriate numbers from Tables 17.2 and 17.3, we obtain the following $F$ value:

$$F = \frac{(0.7632 - 0.2245)/46}{(1 - 0.7632)/419} = 20.672$$

For 46 df in the numerator and 418 df in the denominator, this $F$ is highly significant, confirming that the fixed effects model is superior to the pooled regression model.

Before proceeding further, some features of the fixed effects model are worth noting. First, the model (17.3) is known as a **one-way fixed effects** model, for we have allowed the intercepts to differ among cross-sections (the 47 individuals), but not over time. We can introduce nine time dummies to represent 10 years (again to avoid the dummy variable trap) along with the 46 cross-section dummies. In that case the model that emerges is called a **two-way fixed effects model**.

Of course, if we add these time dummies, in all we have to estimate 46 cross-section dummies, nine time dummies, the common intercept and five slope coefficients of the five regressors: in all, a total of 61 coefficients. Although we have 470 observations, we will lose 61 degrees of freedom.

We have assumed that the slope coefficients of the charity function remain the same. But it is quite possible that these slope coefficients may be different for all 47 individuals. To allow for this possibility, we can introduce **differential slope coefficients**, multiplying the five slope coefficients by 46 differential intercept dummies, which will consume another 230 degrees of freedom. Nothing prevents us from interacting the 10 time dummies with the five explanatory variables, which will consume another 50 degrees of freedom. Ultimately, we will be left with very few degrees of freedom to do meaningful statistical analysis.

## 17.5    Limitations of the fixed effects LSDV model

Although easy to implement, the LSDV model has the following limitations:

1  Every additional dummy variable will cost an additional degree of freedom. Therefore, if the sample is not very large, introducing too many dummies will leave few observations to do meaningful statistical analysis.

2  Too many additive and multiplicative dummies may lead to the possibility of multicollinearity, which make precise estimation of one or more parameters difficult.

3  To obtain estimates with desirable statistical properties, we need to pay careful attention to the error term $u_{it}$. The statistical results presented in Tables 17.2 and 17.3 are based on the assumption that the error term follows the classical assumptions, namely $u_{it} \sim N(0, \sigma^2)$. Since the index $i$ refers to cross-sectional observation and $t$ to time series observations, the classical assumption regarding $u_{it}$ may have to be modified. There are several possibilities:

   (a)  We can assume that the error variance is the same for all cross-sectional units or we can assume that the error variance is heteroscedastic.[6]

   (b)  For each subject, we can assume that there is no autocorrelation over time or we can assume autocorrelation of the AR (1) type.

   (c)  At any given time, we can allow the error term of individual #1 to be noncorrelated with the error term for say, individual #2, or we can assume that there is such correlation.[7]

Some of the problems associate with LSDV can be alleviated if we consider the alternative that we discuss below.

---

6  *Stata* provides heteroscedasticity-corrected standard errors for the panel data regression models.

7  This can be accomplished by the so-called seemingly unrelated regression (SURE) model. This model was originally developed by Arnold Zellner, An efficient method of estimating seemingly unrelated regressions and tests for aggregation bias, *Journal of the American Statistical Association*, vol. 57, 1962, pp. 348–68.

## 17.6    The fixed effect within group (WG) estimator

Since the LSDV model may involve estimating several coefficients, one way to eliminate the fixed effect in $B_{1i}$ in Eq. (17.2) is to express both the regressand and the regressors in this equation as deviations from their respective (group) mean values and run the regression on the mean-corrected variables. To see what this does, start with Eq. (17.2):

$$C_{it} = B_{1i} + B_2 Age_{it} + B_3 Income_{it} + B_4 Price_{it} + B_5 Deps_{it} + B_6 MS_{it} + u_{it}$$

Summing this equation on both sides and dividing by $T (= 10)$ we obtain:

$$\frac{1}{10} \sum_{t=1}^{10} C_{it} = \frac{1}{10} [\sum_{t=1}^{10} (B_{1_i} + B_2 Age_{it} + B_3 Income_{it} + B_4 Price_{it} \quad (17.4)$$
$$+ B_5 Deps_{it} + B_6 MS_{it} + u_{it})]$$

Since the parameters do not change over time, this reduces to

$$\overline{C}_i = B_{1i} + B_2 \overline{Age}_i + B_3 \overline{Income}_i + B_4 \overline{Price}_i$$
$$+ B_5 \overline{Deps}_i + B_6 \overline{MS}_i + \overline{u}_i \quad (17.5)$$

where a bar over a variable represents its average value over 10 years. For our example, we will have 47 averaged values of each variable, each average value taken over a period of 10 years.

Subtracting (17.5) from (17.2), we obtain:

$$C_{it} - \overline{C}_i = B_2 (Age_{it} - \overline{Age}_i) + B_3 (Income_{it} - \overline{Income}_i)$$
$$+ B_4 (Price_{it} - \overline{Price}_i) + B_5 (Deps_{it} - \overline{Deps}_i) \quad (17.6)$$
$$+ B_6 (MS_{it} - \overline{MS}_i) + (u_{it} - \overline{u}_i)$$

See how the fixed or individual effect intercept term $B_{1i}$ drops out.

As you can see from Eq. (17.6), we are essentially running mean-corrected regressands on mean-corrected regressors. Since the average value of the mean-corrected variables is zero, there is no intercept term in Eq. (17.6).

The OLS estimators obtained from Eq. (17.6) are known as **within group (WG) estimators**, because they use the (time) variation within each cross-sectional unit. Compared to the pooled estimators given in Table 17.2, the WG estimators provide consistent estimators of the slope coefficients, although they are not efficient (i.e. they have larger variances).[8]

Interestingly, the estimators obtained from the LSDV method and the within group method are identical, because *mathematically the two models are identical*. This can be seen in following Table 17.4 (the results are obtained from Stata 10).

Although more economical than the LSDV model, one drawback of the WG estimator is that in removing the fixed, or individual, effects (i.e. $B_{1i}$), it also removes the

---

8   This is because when we express variables as deviations from their mean values, the variation in the mean-corrected values will be much smaller than the variation in the original values of the variables. In that situation the variation of the disturbance term $u_{it}$ may be relatively large, thus leading to higher standard errors of the estimated coefficients.

## Table 17.4 Within group estimators of the charity function.

R-squared = 0.1350
Adj R-squared = 0.1257

| chard | Coef. | Std. Err. | t | P>|t| |
|---|---|---|---|---|
| aged | .1022493 | .197458 | 0.52 | 0.605 |
| incd | .8388101 | .1056075 | 7.94 | 0.000 |
| prid | .3660802 | .1179726 | 3.10 | 0.002 |
| depd | −.0863524 | .0507623 | −1.70 | 0.090 |
| msd | .1998327 | .250468 | 0.80 | 0.425 |
| cons | 3.15e-09 | .0296465 | 0.00 | 1.000 |

*Note*: The standard errors shown in this table are slightly different from those shown in Table 17.3.[9] Note also the value of the constant term is practically zero, as it should be.

effect of time-invariant regressors that may be present in the model. For example, in a panel data regression of wages on work experience, age, gender, education, race, and so on, the effect of gender and race will be wiped out in the mean-corrected values of the regressors, for gender and race will not vary for an individual over time. So we will not be able to assess the impact such time-invariant variables on wages.

Before moving on, we present the robust standard errors of FEM (Table 17.5), using White's procedure, which we have discussed in earlier chapters.

## Table 17.5 Fixed effects model with robust standard errors.

Method: Panel Least Squares
Periods included: 10
Cross-sections included: 47
Total panel (balanced) observations: 470
White period standard errors & covariance (d.f. corrected)

| | Coefficient | Std. Error | t-Statistic | Prob. |
|---|---|---|---|---|
| C | −2.089970 | 1.710019 | −1.222191 | 0.2223 |
| AGE | 0.102249 | 0.113897 | 0.897738 | 0.3698 |
| INCOME | 0.838810 | 0.145653 | 5.758977 | 0.0000 |
| PRICE | 0.366080 | 0.146602 | 2.497102 | 0.0129 |
| DEPS | −0.086352 | 0.069186 | −1.248111 | 0.2127 |
| MS | 0.199833 | 0.712740 | 0.280373 | 0.7793 |

**Effects Specification**
Cross-section fixed (dummy variables)

| | | | |
|---|---|---|---|
| R-squared | 0.763177 | Mean dependent var | 6.577150 |
| Adjusted R-squared | 0.734282 | S.D. dependent var | 1.313659 |
| S.E. of regression | 0.677163 | Akaike info criterion | 2.162215 |
| Sum squared resid | 191.6735 | Schwarz criterion | 2.621666 |
| Log likelihood | −456.1204 | Durbin–Watson stat | 1.234015 |
| F-statistic | 26.41239 | Prob(F-statistic) | 0.000000 |

9  The reason for this is that the estimate of the usual error variance $\hat{\sigma}^2 = RSS/(NT-2)$ has to be adjusted as $\hat{\sigma}^2 = RSS/(NT-N-2)$ because we have to estimate $N$ means in computing group averages. However, the standard statistical packages take this into account.

If you compare these results with those given in Table 17.3 you will find that the standard errors were substantially underestimated in Table 17.3.

## 17.7    The random effects model (REM) or error components model (ECM)

In the fixed effects model it is assumed that the individual specific coefficient $B_{1i}$ is fixed for each subject, that is, it is time-invariant. In the random effects model it is assumed that $B_{1i}$ is a random variable with a mean value of $B_1$ (no $i$ subscript here) and the intercept of any cross-section unit is expressed as:

$$B_{1i} = B_1 + \varepsilon_i \tag{17.7}$$

where $\varepsilon_i$ is a random error term with mean 0 and variance $\sigma_\varepsilon^2$.

In terms of our illustrative example, this means that the 47 individuals included in our sample are a drawing from a much larger universe of such individuals and that they have a common mean value for the intercept ($= B_1$). Differences in the individual values of the intercept for each individual donor to charity are reflected in the error term $\varepsilon_i$. Therefore, we can write the charity function (17.1) as:

$$
\begin{aligned}
C_{it} = B_1 + B_2 Age_{it} + B_3 Income_{it} + B_4 Price_{it} + B_5 Deps_{it} \\
+ B_6 MS_{it} + w_{it}
\end{aligned}
\tag{17.8}
$$

where

$$w_{it} = \varepsilon_i + u_{it} \tag{17.9}$$

The composite error term $w_{it}$ has two components: $\varepsilon_i$, which is the cross-section or individual-specific error component and $u_{it}$, which is the combined time series and cross-section error component.[10]

Now you can see why the REM model is also called an **error components model** (**ECM**): the composite error term consists of two (or more) error components.[11]

The usual assumptions of ECM are that

$$
\begin{aligned}
& \varepsilon_i \sim N(0, \sigma_\varepsilon^2) \\
& u_{it} \sim N(0, \sigma_u^2) \\
& E(\varepsilon_i u_{it}) = 0; \quad E(\varepsilon_i \varepsilon_j) = 0 \quad (i \neq j) \\
& E(u_{it} u_{is}) = E(u_{it} u_{ij}) = E(u_{it} u_{js}) = 0 \quad (i \neq j; t \neq s)
\end{aligned}
\tag{17.10}
$$

That is, individual error components are not correlated with each other and are not autocorrelated across both cross-section and time series units. *It is also critical to note that $w_{it}$ is not correlated with any of the explanatory variables included in the model.* Since $\varepsilon_i$ is a part of $w_{it}$, it is possible that the latter is correlated with one or more regressors. If that turns out to be the case, the REM will result in inconsistent estimation of the regression coefficients. The **Hausman test**, which will be explained shortly,

---

10  $u_{it}$ is sometimes called the idiosyncratic term because it varies over cross-section (i.e. individual) as well as time.

11  If we introduce time dummies, there will be time-specific error components (see Exercise 17.2).

will show in a given application if $w_{it}$ is correlated with the regressors – that is, whether REM is the appropriate model.

As a result of the assumptions in Eq. (17.10), it follows that

$$E(w_{it}) = 0 \qquad (17.11)$$

$$\text{var}(w_{it}) = \sigma_\varepsilon^2 + \sigma_u^2 \qquad (17.12)$$

Now if $\sigma_\varepsilon^2 = 0$, there no difference between Eq. (17.1) and Eq. (17.8), in which case we can simply pool all the observations and run the pooled regression, as in Table 17.2. This is so because in this situation there are either no subject-specific effects or they have all been accounted for by the explanatory variables.

Although Eq. (17.12) shows that the composite error term is homoscedastic, it can be shown that $w_{it}$ and $w_{is}$ ($t \neq s$) are correlated – that is, the error terms of a given cross-sectional unit at two different times are correlated. The correlation coefficient between the two can be shown as:

$$\rho = corr(w_{it}, w_{is}) = \frac{\sigma_\varepsilon^2}{\sigma_\varepsilon^2 + \sigma_u^2}; \quad t \neq s \qquad (17.13)$$

Two points about this correlation should be noted. *First*, for any cross-sectional unit $\rho$ remains the same no matter how far apart the two time periods are; and *secondly*, $\rho$ remains the same for all cross-sectional units.

If we do not take into account $\rho$, the OLS estimators of random effects model are inefficient. Therefore we will have to use the method of **generalized least squares (GLS)** to obtain efficient estimates. Software packages like *Stata* can compute robust or *panel-corrected standard errors*.

Before we present the REM results for the charity example, it may be pointed out that in contrast to the fixed effects model (dummy variable, within or first-difference version), in REM we can include time-invariant variables, such as gender, geographic location or religion. They do not get washed out as in the FEM model.

Returning to our illustrative example, we obtain the REM of Table 17.6.

As in the FEM, the estimated coefficients have the expected signs, although DEPS and MS are individually statistically insignificant. From the effects specification box, we see that $\sigma_u^2 = (0.9309)^2 = 0.8665$ and $\sigma_\varepsilon^2 = (0.6771)^2 = 0.4584$. Then from Eq. (17.13), we obtain $\rho = 0.4584/1.3893 = 0.3299$, which gives the extent of correlation of a cross-sectional unit at two different time periods, and this correlation stays the same across all cross-sectional units. This $\rho$ value differs slightly from the one shown in Table 17.6 due to rounding error.

## 17.8    Fixed effects model vs. random effects model

Comparing the fixed effect estimators given in Table 17.3 and the random effects estimators given in Table 17.6, you will see substantial differences between the two. So which model is better in the present example: fixed effects or random effects?

The answer to this question depends on the assumption we make about the likely correlation between the cross-section specific error component $\varepsilon_i$ and the $X$ regressors. If it assumed that $\varepsilon_i$ and the regressors are uncorrelated, REM may be appropriate, but if they are correlated, FEM may be appropriate. In the former case we

**Table 17.6  Random effects model of the charity function with white standard errors.**

Dependent Variable: CHARITY
Method: Panel EGLS (Cross-section random effects)
Sample: 1 10
Periods included: 10
Cross-sections included: 47
Total panel (balanced) observations: 470
Swamy and Arora estimator of component variances
White period standard errors & covariance (d.f. corrected)

|  | Coefficient | Std. Error | t-Statistic | Prob. |
|---|---|---|---|---|
| C | −2.370567 | 1.386444 | −1.709817 | 0.0880 |
| AGE | 0.277063 | 0.127176 | 2.178577 | 0.0299 |
| INCOME | 0.852996 | 0.126574 | 6.739099 | 0.0000 |
| PRICE | 0.370199 | 0.140054 | 2.643253 | 0.0085 |
| DEPS | −0.036254 | 0.064181 | −0.564874 | 0.5724 |
| MS | 0.199669 | 0.472666 | 0.422432 | 0.6729 |

**Effects Specification**

|  |  |  | S.D. | Rho |
|---|---|---|---|---|
| Cross-section random |  |  | 0.930938 | 0.6540 |
| Idiosyncratic random |  |  | 0.677163 | 0.3460 |

**Weighted Statistics**

| R-squared | 0.132701 | Mean dependent var | 1.474396 |
|---|---|---|---|
| Adjusted R-squared | 0.123355 | S.D. dependent var | 0.731733 |
| S.E. of regression | 0.685116 | Sum squared resid | 217.7944 |
| F-statistic | 14.19881 | Durbin–Watson stat | 1.094039 |
| Prob(F-statistic) | 0.000000 | | |

**Unweighted Statistics**

| R-squared | 0.136789 | Mean dependent var | 6.577150 |
|---|---|---|---|
| Sum squared resid | 698.6427 | Durbin–Watson stat | 0.341055 |

also have to estimate fewer parameters. So how do we decide in a given situation which is the appropriate model?

A test devised by Hausman, which is incorporated in packages such as *Stata* and *Eviews*, can be used to answer this question. The null hypothesis underlying the Hausman test is that FEM and REM do not differ substantially. His test statistic has an asymptotic (i.e. large sample) $\chi^2$ distribution with df equal to number of regressors in the model. As usual, if the computed chi-square value exceeds the critical chi-square value for given df and the level of significance, we conclude that REM is not appropriate because the random error terms $\varepsilon_i$ are probably correlated with one or more regressors. In this case, FEM is preferred to REM.

For our example, the results of the Hausman test are given in Table 17.7. The Hausman test strongly rejects the REM, for the *p* value of the estimated chi-square statistics is very low. The last part of this table compares the fixed effects and random effects coefficient of each variable. As the last probability column of the table shows, the differences in the Age and DEPS coefficients are statistically highly significant.

Table 17.7  **Results of the Hausman test.**

Correlated Random Effects – Hausman Test
Equation: Untitled
Test cross-section random effects

| Test Summary | Chi-Sq. Statistic | Chi-Sq. d.f. | Prob. |
|---|---|---|---|
| Cross-section random | 15.964273 | 5 | 0.0069 |

Cross-section random effects test comparisons:

| Variable | Fixed | Random | Var(Diff.) | Prob. |
|---|---|---|---|---|
| AGE | 0.102249 | 0.277063 | 0.003539 | 0.0033 |
| INCOME | 0.838810 | 0.852996 | 0.000830 | 0.6224 |
| PRICE | 0.366080 | 0.370199 | 0.000087 | 0.6595 |
| DEPS | −0.086352 | −0.036254 | 0.000487 | 0.0232 |
| MS | 0.199833 | 0.199669 | 0.016167 | 0.9990 |

Basically, the Hausman test examines $(b_{RE} - b_{FE})^2$ – that is, the squared difference between regression coefficients estimated from REM and FEM.

Since the REM model does not seem appropriate in the present example, we can revert to the FEM model. Another alternative is to continue with REM but use **instrumental variables (IV)** for the individual effect that may be correlated with other regressors in the model. But the use of instrumental variables with panel data is a complicated subject and we will not pursue it in this book, although we will discuss the IV method in some detail in Chapter 19. However, it may be noted that the **Hausman–Taylor estimator** and the **Arellano–Bond estimator** use the instrumental variables to estimate REM models. For a somewhat accessible discussion of these estimators, see the references.[12]

## Some guidelines about REM and FEM

Here are some general guidelines about which of the two models may be suitable in practical applications:[13]

1  If $T$ (the number of time observations) is large and $N$ (the number of cross-section units) is small, there is likely to be little difference in the values of the parameters estimated by FEM and REM. The choice then depends on computational convenience, which may favor FEM.

2  In a short panel ($N$ large and $T$ small), the estimates obtained from the two models can differ substantially. Remember that in REM $B_{1i} = B_1 + \varepsilon_i$, where $\varepsilon_i$ is the cross-sectional random component, whereas in FEM $B_{1i}$ is treated as fixed. In the latter case, statistical inference is conditional on the observed cross-sectional units in the sample. This is valid if we strongly believe that the cross-sectional

---

12  See Gary Koop, *Introduction to Econometrics*, John Wiley & Sons, Chichester, England, 2008, pp. 267–8. For an advanced discussion, see Cameron/Trivedi *op cit.*, pp. 765–6.

13  See G. G. Judge, R. C. Hill, W. E. Griffiths, H. Lutkepohl and T. C. Lee, *Introduction to the Theory and Practice of Econometrics*, 2nd edn, John Wiley & Sons, New York, 1985, pp. 489–91.

units in the sample are not random drawings from a larger population. In that case, FEM is appropriate. If that is not the case, then REM is appropriate because in that case statistical inference is unconditional.

3 If $N$ is large and $T$ is small, and if the assumptions underlying REM hold, REM estimators are more efficient than FEM.

4 Unlike FEM, REM can estimate coefficients of time-invariant variables, such as gender and ethnicity. The FEM does control for such time-invariant variables, but it cannot estimate them directly, as is clear from the LSDV or WG estimator models. On the other hand, FEM controls for all time-invariant variables, whereas REM can estimate only those time-invariant variables that are explicitly introduced in the model.

## 17.9    Properties of various estimators[14]

In this chapter we have discussed several methods of estimating (linear) panel regression models, such as pooled estimators, fixed effects estimators (both LSDV and within-group estimator), and random effects. What are their statistical properties? We will concentrate on the **consistency property**, since panel data usually involve a large number of observations.

**Pooled estimators**: If the slope coefficients are constant across subjects, and if the error term in Eq. (17.1) is uncorrelated with the regressors, *pooled estimators are consistent*. However, it is very likely that the error terms are correlated over time for a given subject. Therefore, we must use **panel-corrected standard errors** for hypothesis testing. Otherwise, the routinely computed standard errors may be underestimated.

It may added that if the fixed effects model is appropriate, but we use the pooled model, the estimated coefficients will be inconsistent, as we saw in our charity example.

**Fixed effects estimators**: Even if the underlying model is pooled or random-effects, the fixed effects estimators are always consistent.

**Random effects estimators**: The random effects model is consistent even if the true model is pooled. But if the true model is fixed effects, the random effects estimators are inconsistent.

## 17.10    Panel data regressions: some concluding comments

As noted at the outset, the topic of panel data modeling is vast and complex. We have barely scratched the surface. Among the topics that we have not discussed at any length, the following may be mentioned.

1 Hypothesis testing with panel data.

2 Heteroscedasticity and autocorrelation in ECM.

3 Unbalanced panel data.

4 Dynamic panel data models in which the lagged value(s) of the regressand appears as an explanatory variable.

---

14   The following discussion draws on Cameron/Trivedi, *op cit.*, Chapter 21.

5  Simultaneous equations involving panel data.

6  Qualitative dependent variables and panel data.

7  Unit roots in panel data (on unit roots, see Chapter 13).

One or more of these topics can be found in the references cited in this chapter, and the reader is urged to consult them to learn more about this topic. These references also cite several empirical studies in various areas of business and economics that have used panel data regression models. The beginner is well advised to read some of these applications to get a feel for how researchers have actually implemented such models.[15]

## 17.11  Summary and conclusions

Panel data regression models are based on panel data, which are observations on the same cross-sectional, or individual, units over several time periods.

Panel data have several advantages over purely cross-sectional or purely time series data. These include: (a) increase in the sample size, (b) study of dynamic changes in cross-sectional units over time, and (c) study of more complicated behavioral models, including study of time-invariant variables.

However, panel models pose several estimation and inference problems, such as heteroscedasticity, autocorrelation, and cross-correlation in cross-sectional units at the same point in time.

The two prominently used methods to deal with one or more of these problems are the fixed effects model (FEM) and the random effects model (REM), also know as the error components model (ECM).

In FEM, the intercept in the regression model is allowed to differ among individuals to reflect the unique feature of individual units. This is done by using dummy variables, provided we take care of the dummy variable trap. The FEM using dummy variables is known as the least squares dummy variable model (LSDV). FEM is appropriate in situations where the individual-specific intercept may be correlated with one or more regressors. A disadvantage of the LSDV is that it consumes a lot of degrees of freedom when $N$ (the number of cross-sectional units) is very large.

An alternative to LSDV is to use the within-group (WG) estimator. Here we subtract the (group) mean values of the regressand and regressor from their individual values and run the regression on the mean-corrected variables. Although it is economical in terms of the degrees of freedom, the mean-corrected variables wipe out time-invariant variables (such as gender and race) from the model.

An alternative to FEM is REM. In REM we assume that the intercept value of an individual unit is a random drawing from a much larger population with a constant mean. The individual intercept is then expressed as a deviation from the constant mean value. REM is more economical than FEM in terms of the number of parameters estimated. REM is appropriate in situations where the (random) intercept of each cross-sectional unit is uncorrelated with the regressors. Another advantage of REM is that we can introduce time-invariant regressors. This is not possible in FEM because all such variables are collinear with the subject-specific intercept.

15  For further details and concrete applications, see Paul D. Allison, *Fixed Effects Regression Methods for Longitudinal Data, Using SAS*. SAS Institute, Cary, North Carolina, 2005.

The Hausman test can be used to decide between FEM and ECM.

Some specific problems with panel data model need to be kept in mind. The most serious problem is the problem of attrition, whereby for one reason or another, members of the panel drop out over time so that in the subsequent surveys (i.e. cross-sections) fewer original subjects remain in the panel. Also, over time subjects may refuse or be unwilling to answer some questions.

## Exercises

**17.1** Table 17.8 gives the LSDV estimates of the charity example. If you examine the raw data given in Table 17.1, can you spot some pattern regarding individuals that have significant intercepts? For example, are married taxpayers likely to contribute more than single taxpayers?

**Table 17.8  Panel estimation of charitable giving with subject-specific dummies.**

Dependent Variable: CHARITY
Method: Least Squares
Date: 03/26/10   Time: 20:11
Sample: 1 470
Included observations: 470

|  | Coefficient | Std. Error | t-Statistic | Prob. |
|---|---|---|---|---|
| AGE | 0.102249 | 0.208039 | 0.491490 | 0.6233 |
| INCOME | 0.838810 | 0.111267 | 7.538725 | 0.0000 |
| PRICE | 0.366080 | 0.124294 | 2.945265 | 0.0034 |
| DEPS | −0.086352 | 0.053483 | −1.614589 | 0.1072 |
| MS | 0.199833 | 0.263890 | 0.757257 | 0.4493 |
| SUBJECT=1 | −3.117892 | 1.139684 | −2.735752 | 0.0065 |
| SUBJECT=2 | −1.050448 | 1.148329 | −0.914762 | 0.3608 |
| SUBJECT=3 | −1.850682 | 1.175580 | −1.574272 | 0.1162 |
| SUBJECT=4 | −1.236490 | 1.146758 | −1.078248 | 0.2815 |
| SUBJECT=5 | −1.437895 | 1.157017 | −1.242761 | 0.2147 |
| SUBJECT=6 | −2.361517 | 1.176887 | −2.006580 | 0.0454 |
| SUBJECT=7 | −4.285028 | 1.153985 | −3.713244 | 0.0002 |
| SUBJECT=8 | −1.609123 | 1.120802 | −1.435689 | 0.1518 |
| SUBJECT=9 | −0.027387 | 1.242987 | −0.022033 | 0.9824 |
| SUBJECT=10 | −1.635314 | 1.086465 | −1.505170 | 0.1330 |
| SUBJECT=11 | −2.262786 | 1.159433 | −1.951632 | 0.0516 |
| SUBJECT=12 | −1.042393 | 1.189056 | −0.876656 | 0.3812 |
| SUBJECT=13 | −2.382995 | 1.100684 | −2.165013 | 0.0310 |
| SUBJECT=14 | −2.231704 | 1.201993 | −1.856669 | 0.0641 |
| SUBJECT=15 | −0.776181 | 1.113080 | −0.697328 | 0.4860 |
| SUBJECT=16 | −4.015718 | 1.178395 | −3.407788 | 0.0007 |
| SUBJECT=17 | −1.529687 | 1.172385 | −1.304765 | 0.1927 |
| SUBJECT=18 | −1.921740 | 1.178960 | −1.630029 | 0.1038 |
| SUBJECT=19 | −1.643515 | 1.207427 | −1.361170 | 0.1742 |
| SUBJECT=20 | 0.304418 | 1.159808 | 0.262473 | 0.7931 |

Table 17.8 (*continued*)

|  | Coefficient | Std. Error | t-Statistic | Prob. |
|---|---|---|---|---|
| SUBJECT=21 | −2.990338 | 1.101186 | −2.715562 | 0.0069 |
| SUBJECT=22 | −2.719506 | 1.161885 | −2.340599 | 0.0197 |
| SUBJECT=23 | −2.261796 | 1.144438 | −1.976338 | 0.0488 |
| SUBJECT=24 | −1.843015 | 1.163838 | −1.583568 | 0.1140 |
| SUBJECT=25 | −1.665241 | 1.166410 | −1.427664 | 0.1541 |
| SUBJECT=26 | −3.446773 | 1.139505 | −3.024799 | 0.0026 |
| SUBJECT=27 | −2.252749 | 1.172809 | −1.920816 | 0.0554 |
| SUBJECT=28 | −1.832946 | 1.227824 | −1.492841 | 0.1362 |
| SUBJECT=29 | −2.925355 | 1.095088 | −2.671344 | 0.0078 |
| SUBJECT=30 | −1.428511 | 1.140020 | −1.253058 | 0.2109 |
| SUBJECT=31 | −1.740051 | 1.133678 | −1.534872 | 0.1256 |
| SUBJECT=32 | −0.900668 | 1.107655 | −0.813130 | 0.4166 |
| SUBJECT=33 | −2.058213 | 1.157546 | −1.778083 | 0.0761 |
| SUBJECT=34 | −1.060122 | 1.114322 | −0.951360 | 0.3420 |
| SUBJECT=35 | −2.866338 | 1.146888 | −2.499232 | 0.0128 |
| SUBJECT=36 | −0.986984 | 1.174292 | −0.840493 | 0.4011 |
| SUBJECT=37 | −1.394347 | 1.188862 | −1.172841 | 0.2415 |
| SUBJECT=38 | −5.404498 | 1.132293 | −4.773054 | 0.0000 |
| SUBJECT=39 | −3.190405 | 1.140833 | −2.796558 | 0.0054 |
| SUBJECT=40 | −2.838580 | 1.179427 | −2.406745 | 0.0165 |
| SUBJECT=41 | −2.398767 | 1.180879 | −2.031340 | 0.0429 |
| SUBJECT=42 | −2.068558 | 1.085109 | −1.906314 | 0.0573 |
| SUBJECT=43 | −2.434273 | 1.152611 | −2.111964 | 0.0353 |
| SUBJECT=44 | −2.530733 | 1.189329 | −2.127867 | 0.0339 |
| SUBJECT=45 | −0.481507 | 1.200597 | −0.401056 | 0.6886 |
| SUBJECT=46 | −3.304275 | 1.132833 | −2.916826 | 0.0037 |
| SUBJECT=47 | −3.089969 | 1.221833 | −2.528962 | 0.0118 |

| | | | |
|---|---|---|---|
| R-squared | 0.763177 | Mean dependent var | 6.577150 |
| Adjusted R-squared | 0.734282 | S.D. dependent var | 1.313659 |
| S.E. of regression | 0.677163 | Akaike info criterion | 2.162215 |
| Sum squared resid | 191.6735 | Schwarz criterion | 2.621666 |
| Log likelihood | −456.1204 | Durbin–Watson stat | 1.430014 |

**17.2** Expand the LSDV model by including the time dummies and comment on the results.

**17.3** From the website of the Frees book cited earlier, obtain panel data of your liking and estimate the model using the various panel estimation techniques discussed in this chapter.

# 18

# Survival analysis

In this chapter we discuss a statistical technique that goes by various names, such as **duration analysis** (e.g. the length of time a person is unemployed or the length of an industrial strike), **event history analysis** (e.g. a longitudinal record of events in a person's life, such as marriage), **reliability or failure time analysis** (e.g. how long a light bulb lasts before it burns out), **transition analysis** (from one qualitative state to another, such as from marriage to divorce), **hazard rate analysis** (e.g. the conditional probability of event occurrence), or **survival analysis** (e.g. time until death from breast cancer). For brevity of exposition, we will christen all these terms by the generic name of survival analysis (SA).

The primary goals of survival analysis are: (1) to estimate and interpret survivor or hazard functions (to be discussed shortly) from survival data and (2) to assess the impact of explanatory variables on survival time.

The topic of survival analysis is vast and mathematically complex. In this chapter our objective is to provide an exposure to this subject and illustrate it. For further study of this subject, readers are advised to consult the references.[1]

## 18.1   An illustrative example: modeling recidivism duration

To set the stage, we consider a concrete example. This example relates to a random sample of 1,445 convicts released from prison between July 1977 and June 1978 and the time (duration) until they return to prison.[2] The data were obtained retrospectively by examining records in April 1984. Because of different starting times, the censoring times vary from 70 to 81 months.

The variables used in the analysis are defined as follows:

Black = 1 if black

Alcohol = 1 if alcohol problems

1  See D. Hosmer and S. Lemeshow, *Applied Survival Analysis*, John Wiley & Sons, New York, 1999; David G. Kleinbaum, *Survival Analysis: A Self-Learning Text*, Springer-Verlag, New York, 1996; Daniel A. Powers and Yu Xie, *Statistical Methods for Categorical Data Analysis*, 2nd edn, Emerald Group Publishing, UK, 2008, Chapter 6; M. Cleves, W. M. Gould and R. G. Gutierrez, *An Introduction to Survival Analysis using Stata*, Stata Press, College Station, Texas, 2002; Jeffrey Wooldridge, *Econometric Analysis of Cross Section and Panel Data*, MIT Press, MA, 2002, Chapter 20.

2  The data come from C. F. Chung, P. Schmidt and A. D. Witte, Survival analysis: a survey, *Journal of Quantitative Criminology*, vol. 7, 1991, pp. 59–98, and are reproduced from Wooldridge, *op cit.*; they can be downloaded from http://www.stata.com/data/jwooldridge/eacsap/recid.dta.

Drugs = 1 if drug history

Super = 1 if release supervised

Married = 1 if married when incarcerated

Felon = 1 if felony sentence

Workprg =1 if in prison work program

Property = 1 if property crime

Person = 1 if crime against person

Priors = number of prior convictions

Educ = years of schooling

Rules = number of rules violations in prison

Age = in months

Tserved = time served, rounded to months

Follow = length of follow period, months

Durat = maximum time until rearrest

Cens = 1 if duration right censored

The variable of interest in this study is *Durat*, the maximum time until a released convict commits a crime and returns to prison. We want to find out how Durat is related to the regressors, also called **covariates**, listed above, although we may not include all these variables in the analysis because of collinearity among some variables. See **Table 18.1** on the companion website.

Before we answer this question, it is essential that we know some of the terminology used in survival analysis.

## 18.2    Terminology of survival analysis

**Event**: "An event consists of some qualitative change that occurs at a specific point in time.... The change must consist of a relatively sharp disjunction between what precedes and what follows."[3] An obvious example is death. Less obvious, but nonetheless important, events are job changes, promotions, layoffs, retirement, convictions and incarcerations, admission into a nursing home or hospice facilities, and so on.

**Duration spell**: It is the length of time before an event occurs, such as the time when an unemployed person is re-employed, or the length of time after divorce a person gets re-married, or the length of time between successive children, or the length of time before a released prisoner is rearrested.

**Discrete time analysis**: Some events occur only at discrete times. For example, presidential elections in the USA take place every four years and the Census of Population is conducted every 10 years. The unemployment rate in the USA is published once a month. There are specialized techniques to handle such discrete events, such as discrete-time event history.

---

**3**  Paul D. Allison, *Event History Analysis: Regression for Longitudinal Event Data*, A Sage University Paper, Sage Publications, California, 1984, p. 9.

**Continuous time analysis**: In contrast to discrete time analysis, continuous time SA analysis treats time as continuous. This is often done for mathematical and statistical convenience, for very few events are observed along a time continuum. In some cases events can be observed in a small window of time, such as the weekly unemployment benefit claims. The statistical techniques used to handle continuous time SA are different from those used to handle discrete time SA. However, there are no hard and fast rules about which approach may be appropriate in a given situation.

**The cumulative distribution function (CDF) of time**: Suppose a person is hospitalized and let $T$ denote the time (measured in days or weeks) until he or she is discharged from the hospital. If we treat $T$ as a continuous variable, the distribution of the $T$ is given by the CDF,

$$F(t) = \Pr(T \leq t) \tag{18.1}$$

which gives the probability that the event (discharge from hospital) has occurred by duration $t$. If $F(t)$ is differentiable, its *density function* can be expressed as

$$f(t) = \frac{\mathrm{d}F(t)}{\mathrm{d}t} = F'(t) \tag{18.2}$$

**The survivor function $S(t)$**: The probability of surviving past time $t$, defined as:

$$S(t) = 1 - F(t) = \Pr(T > t) \tag{18.3}$$

**The hazard function**: Consider the following function:

$$h(t) = \lim_{h \to 0} \frac{\Pr(t \leq T \leq t + h \mid T \geq t)}{h} \tag{18.4}$$

where the expression in the numerator of this function is the conditional probability of leaving the initial state (e.g. hospital stay) in the (time) interval $\{t, t + h\}$, given survival up to time $t$. Equation (18.4) is known as the *hazard function. It gives the instantaneous rate of leaving the initial state per unit of time.*
Now by the definition of conditional probability,

$$
\begin{aligned}
\Pr(t \leq T \leq t + h \mid T \geq t) &= \frac{\Pr(t \leq T \leq t + h)}{\Pr(T \geq t)} \\
&= \frac{F(t + h) - F(t)}{1 - F(t)}
\end{aligned}
\tag{18.5}
$$

Since

$$\lim_{h \to 0} \frac{F(t + h) - F(t)}{h} = F'(t) = f(t) \tag{18.6}$$

we can write

$$h(t) = \frac{f(t)}{1 - F(t)} = \frac{f(t)}{S(t)} \tag{18.7}$$

In simple words, *the hazard function is the ratio of the density function to the survivor function for a random variable*. Simply stated, it gives the probability that someone fails at time $t$, given that they have survived up to that point, failure to be understood in the given context. Incidentally, note that Eq. (18.7) is also known as the **hazard rate function**, and we will use the terms "hazard function" and "hazard rate function" interchangeably.

Equation (18.7) is an important relationship, because regardless of the functional form we choose for the hazard function, $h(t)$, we can derive the CDF, $F(t)$, from it.

Now the question is: how do we choose $f(t)$ and $S(t)$ in practice? We will answer this question in the next section. In the mean time, we need to consider some special problems associated with SA.

1  **Censoring**: A frequently encountered problem in SA is that the data are often censored. Suppose we follow 100 unemployed people at time $t$ and follow them until time period $(t + h)$. Depending on the value we choose for $h$, there is no guarantee that all 100 people will still be unemployed at time $(t + h)$; some of them will have been re-employed and some dropped out of the labor force. Therefore, we will have a censored sample.

Our sample may be **right-censored** because we stop following our sample of the unemployed at time $t + h$. Our sample can also be **left-censored**, because we do not know how many of the 100 unemployed were in that status before time $t$. In estimating the hazard function we have to take into account this censoring problem. Recall that we encountered a similar problem when we discussed the censored and truncated sample regression models.

2  **Hazard function with or without covariates (or regressors)**: In SA our interest is not only in estimating the hazard function but also in trying to find out if it depends on some explanatory variables or covariates. The covariates for our illustrative example are as given in Section 18.1.

But if we introduce covariates, we have to determine if they are **time-variant** or **time-invariant**. Gender and religion are time-invariant regressors, but education, job experience, and so on, are time-variant. This complicates SA analysis.

3  **Duration dependence**: If the hazard function is not constant, there is duration dependence. If $dh(t)/dt > 0$, there is positive duration dependence. In this case the probability of exiting the initial state increases the longer is a person in the initial state. For example, the longer a person is unemployed, his or her probability of exiting the unemployment status increases in the case of positive duration dependence. The opposite is the case if there is negative dependency; in this case, $dh(t)/dt < 0$.

4  **Unobserved heterogeneity**: No matter how many covariates we consider, there may be intrinsic heterogeneity among individuals and we may have to account for this. Recall that we had a similar situation in the panel data regression models where we accounted for unobserved heterogeneity by including individual-specific (intercept) dummies, as in the fixed effects models.

With these preliminaries, let us show how survival analysis can be conducted.

## 18.3   Modeling recidivism duration

There are three basic approaches to analyzing survival data: **nonparametric, parametric**, and **partially parametric**, also known as **semi-parametric**.[4] In the nonparametric approach we do not make any assumption about the probability distribution of survival time, whereas in the parametric approach we assume some probability distribution.

The nonparametric approach is used in the analysis of **life tables**, which have been used for over 100 years to describe human mortality experience. Actuaries and demographers are obviously interested in life tables, but we will not pursue this topic in this chapter.[5] The parametric approach is largely used for continuous time data.

There are several parametric models that are used in duration analysis. Each depends on the assumed probability distribution, such as the **exponential, Weibull, lognormal**, and **loglogistic**. Since the (probability) density function of each of these distributions is known, we can easily derive the corresponding hazard and survival functions. We now consider some of these distributions and apply them to our illustrative example. In each of the distributions discussed below we assume that $h$, the hazard rate, can be explained by one or more covariates.

But before we consider these models, why not use the traditional normal linear regression model, regressing Durat on the explanatory variables listed earlier? The reason why the traditional regression methodology may not be applicable in survival analysis is that, "…the distributions for time to event might be dissimilar from the normal – they are almost certainly non-symmetric, they might be bimodal, and linear regression is not robust to these violations"[6] (but see Exercise 18.1).

## 18.4   Exponential probability distribution

Suppose the hazard rate $h(t)$ is constant and is equal to $h$. For our example, this would mean that the probability of recidivism does not depend on the duration (time) in the initial state. A constant hazard implies the following CDF and PDF:

$$F(t) = 1 - e^{-ht} \qquad (18.8)$$

$$f(t) = F'(t) = he^{-ht} \qquad (18.9)$$

Since

$$S(t) = 1 - F(t)$$
$$= 1 - [1 - e^{-ht}] = e^{-ht} \qquad (18.10)$$

which gives the survival function. Then from Eq. (18.7), it follows that

---

4   As Mittelhammer *et al.*, note, "A semiparametric model is a model whose DSP[data sampling process] is defined in terms of two components; one is fully determined once the values of a finite number of parameters are known (this is the parametric component), whereas the other is not amenable to being fully defined by the values of any finite collection of parameters (the nonparametric component)". See Ron C. Mittelhammer, George G. Judge and Douglas J. Miller, *Econometric Foundations*, Cambridge University Press, New York, 2000, p. 15.

5   For a brief description of life table analysis, see Hosmer and Lemeshow, *op cit.*, pp. 36–9.

6   See Cleves *et al.*, *op cit.*, p. 2.

**Table 18.2  Hazard rate using the exponential distribution.**

Exponential regression — log relative-hazard form
No. of subjects = 1445                   Number of obs = 1445
No. of failures = 552
Time at risk = 80013

                                          LR chi2 (8) = 185.13
Log likelihood = -1647.3304               Prob > chi2 = 0.0000

| | Haz. Ratio | Std. Err. | z | P>\|z\| | [95% Conf. Interval] | |
|---|---|---|---|---|---|---|
| black | 1.627119 | .1433317 | 5.53 | 0.000 | 1.369107 | 1.933753 |
| alcohol | 1.590821 | .1671353 | 4.42 | 0.000 | 1.294769 | 1.954567 |
| drugs | 1.375137 | .1345931 | 3.25 | 0.001 | 1.135099 | 1.665936 |
| felon | .5477735 | .0791362 | −4.17 | 0.000 | .4126947 | .7270649 |
| property | 1.52315 | .213146 | 3.01 | 0.003 | 1.157784 | 2.003816 |
| priors | 1.097332 | .0145236 | 7.02 | 0.000 | 1.069233 | 1.126171 |
| age | .9962639 | .0005034 | −7.41 | 0.000 | .9952777 | .997251 |
| tserved | 1.015066 | .0016809 | 9.03 | 0.000 | 1.011777 | 1.018366 |

$$h(t) = \frac{f(t)}{S(t)} = \frac{he^{-ht}}{e^{-ht}} = h \qquad\qquad (18.11)$$

That is, the hazard rate function is a constant, equal to $h$ (no time subscript here). This is the **memoryless property** of the exponential distribution.

Now we can incorporate regressors or covariates into duration models to see how they affect the hazard function. Using several regressors listed earlier, we obtain the results of Table 18.2 based on *Stata* (version 10); the estimation of the exponential distribution function is done by ML methods.[7]

## Interpretation of results

Before we interpret the results, it is very important to note that the coefficients presented in **Table 18.1** are **hazard** or **relative risk ratios**.

This ratio is expressed as $e^{\text{regression coefficient}}$, that is, as an exponential of a regression coefficient in the fitted model.

The table gives the hazard ratio for each covariate, its standard error, and the $Z$ value, or the Wald statistic, which is the ratio of the estimated coefficient divided by its standard error. This $Z$ value follows an asymptotic standard normal distribution and is used to test the null hypothesis that the true (or population) hazard ratio coefficient is zero.

Based on the $Z$ statistic, it can be seen that the variables black, alcohol, drugs, felon, property, priors, age, and time served are individually statistically highly significant. The likelihood ratio (LR) statistic of 185 is also highly significant, suggesting that the overall fit of the model is quite good. Recall that in the nonlinear model the equivalent of $R^2$ is given by the LR ratio.

The interpretation of hazard ratios is as follows:

---

7  Note that we have not included all the variables listed in Section 18.1 to avoid the problem of collinearity.

1 A hazard ratio of a covariate greater than 1 indicates increased hazard of experiencing the event of interest (re-arrest in the present example), holding the values of all other covariates constant. In our example, the hazard ratio of about 1.63 therefore suggests that black convicts have an increased hazard of being re-arrested compared to non-black convicts, by about 63%. Likewise, the hazard of being re-arrested is about 59% higher for a convict with an alcohol problem than a convict without that problem.

2 A hazard rate ratio of a covariate less than 1 indicates decreased hazard of experiencing the event of interest (again re-arrest in our example). Thus, the felon coefficient of about 0.55 suggests those convicted of felony charge have decreased hazard of re-arrest (45%) compared to convicts who are charged with other offenses, *ceteris paribus*.[8]

3 A hazard rate ratio of 1 suggests no association between the particular covariate and hazard. Thus, the length of time served in prison has no particular bearing on the hazard of re-arrest.

The reader will notice the similarity between hazard ratios and odds ratios. Like an odds ratio of 1, the hazard ratio of 1 means no effect. A hazard ratio of 20, like an odds ratio of 20, means that the group under consideration has 20 times the hazard of the comparison group.

Also keep in mind that the lower the hazard ratio, the higher the survival probability at time $t$, and vice versa.

Instead of estimating the hazard ratios, we can estimate the coefficients of the hazard rate by invoking the **nohr** (no hazard ratios) command in *Stata*. The results are given in Table 18.3.

**Table 18.3  Estimated coefficients of hazard rate.**

Exponential regression — log relative-hazard form
No. of subjects = 1445                    Number of obs = 1445
No. of failures = 552
Time at risk = 80013

LR chi2 (8) = 185.13
Log likelihood = −1647.3304              Prob > chi2 = 0.0000

| t | Coef. | Std. Err. | z | P>\|z\| | [95% Conf. Interval] | |
|---|---|---|---|---|---|---|
| black | .4868107 | .0880893 | 5.53 | 0.000 | .314159 | .6594625 |
| alcohol | .4642503 | .1050623 | 4.42 | 0.000 | .258332 | .6701687 |
| drugs | .3185534 | .0978762 | 3.25 | 0.001 | .1267196 | .5103871 |
| felon | −.6018934 | .1444689 | −4.17 | 0.000 | −.8850472 | −.3187395 |
| property | .4207805 | .1399377 | 3.01 | 0.003 | .1465078 | .6950533 |
| priors | .0928821 | .0132354 | 7.02 | 0.000 | .0669411 | .118823 |
| age | −.0037431 | .0005053 | −7.41 | 0.000 | −.0047335 | −.0027528 |
| tserved | .0149535 | .0016559 | 9.03 | 0.000 | .0117079 | .018199 |
| _cons | −4.498082 | .1713821 | −26.25 | 0.000 | −4.833985 | −4.16218 |

---

8 Since punishment for felony crime is more severe than some other crimes, felony convicts, once released from prison, may not want to go back to prison and face yet another harsher punishment.

A positive coefficient in this table means increased hazard and a negative coefficient means decreased hazard. Thus a hazard coefficient of about 0.49 for blacks means that black convicts have an increased hazard of recidivism. Literally interpreted, the coefficient of about 0.49 means that being a black convict increases the log of hazard by 0.49.

You might think that the results in Tables 18.2 and 18.3 are not comparable. Actually, they are. To see this, take the coefficient of black of 0.4868107 from Table 18.3. If you take the antilog of this coefficient, you will obtain 1.630165, the hazard ratio, which is about the same as in Table 18.2.

So the difference between Tables 18.2 and 18.3 is only in the way the results are presented, not in the results themselves.

## 18.5 Weibull probability distribution

A major drawback of the exponential probability distribution to model the hazard rate is that it assumes a constant hazard rate – that is, a rate that is independent of time. But if $h(t)$ is not constant, we have the situation of **duration dependence** – a positive duration dependence if the hazard rate increases with duration, and a negative duration dependence if this rate decreases with duration. In case of positive duration dependence the probability of leaving the initial state (e.g. unemployment) increases the longer one is in that state, assuming other things remaining the same.

A probability distribution that takes into account duration dependence is the **Weibull probability distribution**. For this distribution, it can be shown that

$$h(t) = \gamma \alpha t^{\,\alpha-1}; \quad \alpha > 0, \gamma > 0 \tag{18.12}$$

and

$$S(t) = e^{-(ht)^{\alpha}} \tag{18.13}$$

If $\alpha = 1$, we obtain the exponential (probability) distribution with $\gamma = h$. If $\alpha > 1$, the hazard rate increases monotonically, but if $\alpha < 1$, it decreases monotonically.

Fitting Weibull to our example, we obtain the results in Table 18.4. In this table $p$ represents $\alpha$. Since this value is less than 1 and is statistically significant, it indicates the risk of recidivism declining over time (negative duration dependence) of about 21% per week.

This finding therefore casts doubt on the results of recidivism based on the exponential probability distribution, even though the hazard rates shown in this table are not much different from those shown in Table 18.2. Since the log likelihood ratio based on the Weibull distribution of –1,630 is less negative than the log likelihood ratio of –1,647 based on the exponential distribution, the Weibull distribution gives a better fit.

Incidentally, if you want the coefficients rather than the hazard ratios, the results are given in Table 18.5.

Again, the difference between the two preceding tables is in the way the results are presented and not the results themselves.

**Table 18.4  Estimation of hazard function with Weibull probability distribution.**

Weibull regression — log relative-hazard form
No. of subjects = 1445                    Number of obs = 1445
No. of failures = 552
Time at risk = 80013

LR chi2 (8) = 170.11
Log likelihood = −1630.7151        Prob > chi2 = 0.0000

| _t | Haz. Ratio | Std. Err. | z | P>|z| | [95% Conf. Interval] | |
|---|---|---|---|---|---|---|
| black | 1.589062 | .1400574 | 5.25 | 0.000 | 1.336956 | 1.888706 |
| alcohol | 1.558327 | .1636645 | 4.22 | 0.000 | 1.268413 | 1.914506 |
| drugs | 1.357881 | .1329336 | 3.12 | 0.002 | 1.120807 | 1.6451 |
| felon | .5595468 | .0806046 | −4.03 | 0.000 | .4219082 | .7420871 |
| property | 1.504077 | .2089878 | 2.94 | 0.003 | 1.145507 | 1.974888 |
| priors | 1.094469 | .0145957 | 6.77 | 0.000 | 1.066233 | 1.123453 |
| age | .9964393 | .0005006 | −7.10 | 0.000 | .9954587 | .9974209 |
| tserved | 1.014259 | .0017029 | 8.43 | 0.000 | 1.010926 | 1.017602 |
| /ln_p | −.2147974 | .0388463 | −5.53 | 0.000 | −.2909347 | −.13866 |
| p | .8067049 | .0313375 | | | .7475645 | .8705239 |
| 1/p | 1.239611 | .0481543 | | | 1.148733 | 1.337677 |

**Table 18.5  Coefficients of hazard rate using Weibull.**

Weibull regression — log relative-hazard form
No. of subjects = 1445                    Number of obs = 1445
No. of failures = 552
Time at risk = 80013

LR chi2 (8) = 170.11
Log likelihood = −1630.7151        Prob > chi2 = 0.0000

| _t | Coef. | Std. Err. | z | P>|z| | [95% Conf. Interval] | |
|---|---|---|---|---|---|---|
| black | .4631437 | .0881384 | 5.25 | 0.000 | .2903955 | .6358918 |
| alcohol | .4436129 | .1050258 | 4.22 | 0.000 | .2377662 | .6494596 |
| drugs | .3059252 | .0978978 | 3.12 | 0.002 | .114049 | .4978014 |
| felon | −.5806281 | .1440534 | −4.03 | 0.000 | −.8629676 | −.2982887 |
| property | .4081794 | .1389475 | 2.94 | 0.003 | .1358473 | .6805116 |
| priors | .0902693 | .0133359 | 6.77 | 0.000 | .0641314 | .1164072 |
| age | −.003567 | .0005024 | −7.10 | 0.000 | −.0045516 | −.0025824 |
| tserved | .0141578 | .0016789 | 8.43 | 0.000 | .0108672 | .0174484 |
| _cons | −3.723363 | .2112758 | −17.62 | 0.000 | −4.137456 | −3.30927 |
| /ln_p | −.2147974 | .0388463 | −5.53 | 0.000 | −.2909347 | −.13866 |
| p | .8067049 | .0313375 | .7475645 | .8705239 | | |
| 1/p | 1.239611 | .0481543 | 1.148733 | 1.337677 | | |

## 18.6 The proportional hazard model

A model that is quite popular in survival analysis is the proportional hazard (PH) model, originally proposed by Cox.[9] The PH model assumes that the hazard rate for the $i$th individual can be expressed as:

$$h(t \mid X_i) = h_0(t)e^{BX_i} \tag{18.14}$$

In PH the hazard function consists of two parts in multiplicative form: (1) $h_0(t)$, called the **baseline hazard**, is a function of duration time, and (2) a part that is a function of explanatory variables ($X$ may represent one or more variables other than time) and the associated parameters $B$ (one or more parameters, depending on the number of explanatory variables).

A great advantage of the PH is that the ratio of the hazards for any two individuals, indexed by $i$ and $j$, depends only on the covariates or regressors but does not depend on $t$, the time, as can be seen from the following.

$$\frac{h(t \mid X_i)}{h(t \mid X_j)} = \frac{h_0(t)e^{BX_i}}{h_0(t)e^{BX_j}} = \frac{e^{BX_i}}{e^{BX_j}} = e^{B(X_i - X_j)} \tag{18.15}$$

which is constant,[10] assuming that the regressors $X_i$ and $X_j$ do not change over time, that is, the covariates are time-independent.

A reason for the wide use of the PH model is that time is not included among the explanatory variables, as a result of which the hazard rate is proportional to the baseline hazard rate for all individuals. This can be expressed as:

$$\frac{h(t \mid X_i)}{h_0(t)} = e^{BX_i} \tag{18.16}$$

Another reason for the popularity of the PH model is that we can obtain consistent estimates of the parameters of the covariates without estimating the parameters of the baseline hazard function. This can be accomplished by the method of **partial likelihood**. We will not go into the mathematical details of this method, for they are somewhat involved, but modern statistical packages do this easily.

Returning to our illustrative example, we can estimate the PH model by invoking the stcox command in *Stata* (Table 18.6).

Instead of the hazard ratios, if you are interested in the regression coefficients the results are as shown in Table 18.7. Notice that the Cox PH model does not have an intercept. This is because the intercept is absorbed in the baseline hazard $h_0(t)$.

The $Z$ statistic reported in the preceding two tables is the Wald statistic for testing the null hypothesis that the coefficient under consideration is zero. Under this null hypothesis, $Z$ follows an asymptotic standard normal distribution. As you can see from these tables, individually each regression coefficient is highly significant. The $p$ value reported in these tables is the two-sided $p$ value for the null hypothesis. The LR statistic is an overall measure of the goodness of fit of the estimated model, an equivalent of

---

9 D. R. Cox, Regression models and life tables, *Journal of the Royal Statistical Society*, series B, vol. 34, 1972, pp. 187–220.

10 What this says is that the ratio of the conditional probability that individual $i$ leaves the current state to the probability that individual $j$ does so is assumed to be the same for all $t$.

**Table 18.6  Cox PH estimation of recidivism.**

Cox regression — Breslow method for ties
No. of subjects = 1445                          Number of obs = 1445
No. of failures = 552
Time at risk = 80013

                                LR chi2 (8) = 161.02
Log likelihood = −3813.6724     Prob > chi2 = 0.0000

| _t | Haz. Ratio | Std. Err. | z | P>\|z\| | [95% Conf. Interval] | |
|---|---|---|---|---|---|---|
| black | 1.555061 | .1371039 | 5.01 | 0.000 | 1.308279 | 1.848395 |
| alcohol | 1.534183 | .1611062 | 4.08 | 0.000 | 1.248796 | 1.884789 |
| drugs | 1.349457 | .1321232 | 3.06 | 0.002 | 1.113831 | 1.634929 |
| felon | .5635607 | .0813093 | −3.97 | 0.000 | .4247478 | .7477394 |
| property | 1.520469 | .210447 | 3.03 | 0.002 | 1.159213 | 1.994305 |
| priors | 1.092879 | .0146367 | 6.63 | 0.000 | 1.064564 | 1.121946 |
| age | .9965673 | .0004983 | −6.88 | 0.000 | .9955911 | .9975445 |
| tserved | 1.013744 | .0017088 | 8.10 | 0.000 | 1.0104 | 1.017098 |

the $R^2$ value in the linear regression model. This value in the present instance is highly significant.

## Interpretation of the results

Take the hazard ratio of 0.997 (almost 1) for age. This means, if age increases by a year, then the hazard of recidivism declines by 1%, *ceteris paribus*. The coefficient of 1.555 for black people suggests that the hazard of recidivism is higher for black people by

**Table 18.7  Coefficients of the Cox PH model.**

failure _d: fail
analysis time _t: durat
Iteration 0: log likelihood = −3813.6724
Cox regression — Breslow method for ties
No. of subjects = 1445                          Number of obs = 1445
No. of failures = 552
Time at risk = 80013

                                LR chi2 (8) = 161.02
Log likelihood = −3813.6724     Prob > chi2 = 0.0000

| _t | Coef. | Std. Err. | z | P>\|z\| | [95% Conf. Interval] | |
|---|---|---|---|---|---|---|
| black | .4415151 | .0881662 | 5.01 | 0.000 | .2687125 | .6143177 |
| alcohol | .4279981 | .1050111 | 4.08 | 0.000 | .2221801 | .633816 |
| drugs | .2997025 | .0979084 | 3.06 | 0.002 | .1078056 | .4915995 |
| felon | −.5734802 | .1442779 | −3.97 | 0.000 | −.8562596 | −.2907008 |
| property | .4190185 | .1384093 | 3.03 | 0.002 | .1477413 | .6902958 |
| priors | .0888153 | .0133928 | 6.63 | 0.000 | .0625658 | .1150647 |
| age | −.0034386 | .0005 | −6.88 | 0.000 | −.0044187 | −.0024585 |
| tserved | .0136502 | .0016856 | 8.10 | 0.000 | .0103464 | .016954 |

about 55.5% as compared to others. Other coefficients are to be interpreted in a similar fashion.

Although quite popular, Cox's PH model gets a little complicated if some of the regressors included in the model are time-variant. Thus, if we had information on ex-in-mates' employment status in our example that was monitored, say, weekly, we would have a time-variant regressor. Although methods are available to deal with this problem, we will not pursue this topic in view of the introductory nature of survival analysis in this chapter. The reader is advised to consult the references for further study.[11]

It may be added that there are tests of the appropriateness of the PH model, but again we urge the reader to consult the references for these tests. An alternative to the PH model is the **accelerated failure time model (AFT)**. Again, the reader is advised to consult the references.

## 18.7    Summary and conclusions

The primary objective of this chapter was to introduce the reader to some fundamental concepts in survival analysis. Since specialized books and articles have been written on this topic, we cannot discuss all the details of all the SA models.

In this chapter we discussed three SA models, namely the exponential, the Weibull and the proportional hazard model. Using the data on recidivism, we showed the output of these models and how to interpret the output. The simplest of these models is the exponential or constant hazard model. But this model is a special case of the Weibull model. The proportional hazard model, quite popular in many fields, can be estimated without estimating the baseline hazard model. A drawback of the PH model is that it assumes that the covariates are time-invariant. However, the PH model can be extended to take into account time-varying covariates. Also, the proportional assumption of the PH model can be explicitly tested.

As noted, we did not discuss all the hazard models. In Table 18.8 we give the salient features of the Exponential and Weibull models, along with the lognormal and loglogistic models, which we have not discussed in this chapter. But they can be easily estimated with the aid of packages like *Stata*.

**Table 18.8  Salient features of some duration models.**

| Probability distribution | Hazard function | Survival function |
|---|---|---|
| Exponential | $h(t) = h$ | $S(t) = e^{-ht}$ |
| Weibull | $h(t) = \gamma \alpha t^{\alpha-1}$ | $S(t) = e^{-(ht)^{\alpha}}$ |
| Lognormal | $f(t) = (p/t)\phi[p\ln(ht)]$ | $S(t) = \Phi[-p\ln(ht)]^{*}$ |
| Loglogistic | $h(t) = \dfrac{\gamma\alpha(ht)^{\alpha-1}}{1+\gamma t^{\alpha}}$ $\alpha > 0, \gamma > 0$ | $S(t) = \dfrac{1}{1+(\gamma t)^{\alpha}}^{**}$ |

*Note*: *ln($t$) is normally distributed with mean −ln$h$ and standard deviation $1/p$
**ln($t$) has a logistic distribution with mean −ln $h$ and variance $\pi^2/3p^2$, where ln stands for natural log.

---

11  For an intuitive discussion, see Paul Allison, *op cit.*, pp. 36–8.

Also note that when $\alpha = 1$, the Weibull distribution reduces to the exponential distribution with $h = \gamma$.

## Exercises

**18.1** Using Durat as the dependent variable, estimate an OLS regression in relation to the regressors given in Table 18.1 and interpret your results.

How do these results compare with those obtained from the exponential, Weibull and PH models?

**18.2** Which of the regressors given in Section 18.1 are time-variant and which are time-invariant? Suppose you treat all the regressors as time-invariant. Estimate the exponential, Weibull and PH survival models and comment on your results.

**18.3** The Kleinbaum text cited in this chapter gives several data sets on survival analysis in Appendix B. Obtain one or more of these data sets and estimate appropriate SA model(s) so that you are comfortable in dealing with duration models.

**18.4** The book by Klein and Moeschberger gives several data sets from the fields of biology and health.[12] These data can be accessed from the website of the book. Pick one or more data sets from this book and estimate the hazard function using one or more probability distributions discussed in this chapter.

---

12 Joseph P. Klein and Melvin L. Moeschberger, *Survival Analysis: Techniques for Censored and Truncated Data* (Statistics for Biology and Health), Springer, New York, 2000.

# 19

# Stochastic regressors and the method of instrumental variables

Once I asked my students whether the following statements are true, false, or uncertain:

A.   More schooling leads to higher earnings.

B.   The higher the proportion of older people in the population the higher the poverty rate.

C.   More school districts in a community means more competition and better schools.

D.   Higher financial aid means more students will go to college.

E.   Higher score in the verbal part of the SAT implies higher score on the mathematics part of the SAT.

F.   Being a war veteran leads to higher lifetime earnings.

G.   On average women are paid less than men because of gender discrimination.

H.   A student's grade in an examination in econometrics depends on his or her effort.

I.   Increase in the money supply leads to higher inflation.

J.   Watching TV leads to autism.

Although there were a few students in my class who thought that some of these statements were true, a majority of them said that, "It depends...".

Take statement A. Is it formal schooling *per se* or schooling and innate ability that determine future earnings? So if we do not take into account student's ability, we may be inflating the contribution of education to earnings. Thus in a regression of earnings on education (as measured by years of schooling) the variable education is likely to be correlated with the regression error term, for that error term may include an ability variable. In this case we say that education is an *endogenous regressor*, or more formally, a *stochastic regressor*. As we show below, this will render the usual OLS regression results suspect.

As another case, consider statement D. For many students higher financial aid may be a necessary condition for higher education, but it may not be sufficient, for there are a variety of factors that are involved in deciding to go to college. Therefore a regression of the decision to go to college (via a logit or probit model) on financial aid may exaggerate the impact of the latter because it does not take into account the omitted variables from this regression, which may very well be correlated with financial aid. Thus financial aid may be a stochastic regressor.

The main point of all the preceding statements and many more like that is that if we have a stochastic regressor it may be correlated with the (regression) error term, which may render the standard OLS estimation inapplicable, or at least unreliable. In the rest of this chapter we study this problem a bit more formally and then consider some applications.

## 19.1    The problem of endogeneity

A critical assumption of the CLRM stated in Eq. (1.8) is that the expected value of the error term $u_i$, given the values of the regressors, is zero. Symbolically,

$$E(u_i \mid X_i) = 0 \qquad\qquad (19.1) = (1.8)$$

In other words this assumption states that the unobserved factors represented by the error term $u_i$ are not systematically related to the regressors or that the regressors are truly exogenous. Note that $X$ may contain one or more regressors.

With this and the other assumptions made in Chapter 1 we were able to establish that the OLS estimators are best linear unbiased estimators (BLUE). With the added assumption that the error term is normally distributed, we were able to show that OLS estimators are individually normally distributed with the mean and variances given in that chapter.

But what happens if assumption (19.1) fails – that is, there is correlation between the error term and one or more regressors? To put it another way, what happens if $X$ is a stochastic, or random, variable and is correlated with the error term? This is known as the case of an **endogenous regressor** – that is, a situation where the stochastic regressors are correlated with the error term.

To give a concrete example, consider the following regression of the crime rate on expenditure on police for the 50 states in the USA for 1992 in **Table 19.1**, which can be found on the companion website.

Using these data, we obtained the regression results in Table 19.2. Judged by the usual criteria, this regression looks impressive. The results suggest that increased expenditure on police leads to higher crime rates! If this were true, it is indeed bad news.

**Table 19.2  Crime rate regression.**

Dependent Variable: CRIME
Method: Least Squares
Sample: 1 50
Included observations: 50

| Variable | Coefficient | Std. Error | t-Statistic | Prob. |
|---|---|---|---|---|
| C | 3251.679 | 430.7541 | 7.548806 | 0.0000 |
| POLICE EXPENDITURE | 6.743364 | 1.490629 | 4.523839 | 0.0000 |

R-squared          0.298913          Mean dependent var     5085.200
*Note*: The crime rate is per 100,000 population.[1]

---

1  The crime categories are: assault with deadly weapon, arson, burglary, homicide, robbery, sex abuse, stolen auto, and theft from auto.

Of course, we should be skeptical about these results because they do not make practical sense. It seems that some explanatory variables that belong in this regression are left out and the police expenditure variable may very well be correlated with these left-out variables.

In their now famous book, *Freakonomics*, Steven Levitt and Stephen Dubner argue that to establish causality between crime and police

> ... we need a scenario in which more police are hired for reasons completely unrelated to rising crime. If, for instance, police were randomly sprinkled in some cities and not in others, we could look to see whether crime declines in the cities where the police happened to land.[2]

Levitt and Dubner point out that in the months leading up to election day, incumbent mayors harp upon their law-and-order credentials by hiring more police, even when the crime rate does not seem to be increasing.

The point of all this discussion is that whether $X$ causes $Y$ may very well depend on another variable $Z$ that may cause $Y$ indirectly through its influence on $X$, although $Z$ may not have any direct relationship with $Y$. Therefore, in a regression of $Y$ on $X$, if we do not take into account the influence of $Z$ on $X$ and relegate it to the equation error $u_i$, there is bound to be correlation between $X$ and the error term. In other words, the regressor $X$ is a stochastic variable, which violates the assumption in Eq. (19.1). We can show this with a *path diagram*, in which the arrow indicates the direction of association between variables (Figure 19.1).[3]

$$
\begin{array}{ccc}
X \rightarrow Y & X \rightarrow Y & Z \rightarrow X \rightarrow Y \\
u \nearrow & u \uparrow \nearrow & u \uparrow \nearrow \\
(a) & (b) & (c)
\end{array}
$$

**Figure 19.1  Relationships among variables.**

In Figure 19.1(a) there is no arrow between $X$ and $u$ (i.e. no correlation), which represents the classical OLS assumption. Here OLS regression of $X$ on $Y$ will produce *consistent* estimates of the regression coefficients. Figure 19.1(b) shows a correlation between the regressor and the error term, which is the case of stochastic regressor. In this case, as we show below, regression of $Y$ on $X$ will produce inconsistent estimates of regression coefficients, even in large samples. In Figure 19.1(c), changes in $Z$ do not affect $Y$ directly but indirectly through $X$. As we will show shortly, $Z$ is called an **instrumental variable** (**IV**), or simply an **instrument** and show how such variable(s) enable us to obtain consistent estimates of the regressor coefficients.

In what follows we first discuss the case of stochastic regressor and point out its consequences for OLS estimation and then show how the method of instrumental variable (IV) can be used in case we cannot rely on OLS.

---

2  Steven D. Levitt and Stephen J. Dubner, *Freakonomics*, William Morrow, New York, 2005, p. 126.

3  This figure is adapted from A. Colin Cameron and Pravin K. Trivedi, *Microeconometrics Using Stata*, Stata Press, College Station, Texas, pp. 172–3.

## 19.2   The problem with stochastic regressors

To explain the basic ideas without resorting to matrix algebra, we will consider the bivariate linear regression:

$$Y_i = B_1 + B_2 X_i + u_i \tag{19.2}$$

We assume that the regressor $X_i$ is random. We now distinguish three cases.[4]

1 *X and u are distributed independently*: In this case for all practical purposes we can continue to use OLS. As Greene notes:

> The conclusion, therefore, is that the important results we have obtained thus far for the least squares estimator, unbiasedness, and the Gauss–Markov theorem holds whether or not we regard $X$ as stochastic.[5]

2 *X and u are contemporaneously (i.e. at the same time) uncorrelated*: This is a weaker condition than #1. In this case the classical OLS results hold only *asymptotically* – that is in large samples (see Appendix 19A.1.)

3 *X and u are neither independently distributed nor are contemporaneously uncorrelated*: In this, the more serious case, *the OLS estimators are not only biased, but are also inconsistent*. Intuitively, the reason for this is:

> ... the least-squares estimation method is designed in such a way that the total variation in $Y$ [TSS] can always be divided into two parts, one representing the variation due to the explanatory variables [ESS] and the other representing the variation due to other factors. But when the explanatory variable and the disturbance are correlated, such a division is not valid since it does not allow for the *joint* effect of $X$ and $\varepsilon$ [$=u$] on $Y$.[6]

This can be easily shown in the case of the bivariate regression. The OLS estimator of $B_2$ in Eq. (19.2) is given as:

$$b_2 = \frac{\Sigma x_i y_i}{\Sigma x_i^2} = \frac{\Sigma x_i Y_i}{\Sigma x_i^2} \tag{19.3}$$

where $x_i = (X_i - \overline{X})$ and $y_i = (Y_i - \overline{Y})$.

Now substituting Eq. (19.2) into the right-hand side of Eq. (19.3), we obtain

---

4 The following discussion follows Jan Kmenta, *Elements of Econometrics*, 2nd edn, Macmillan Publishing Company, New York, 1986, pp. 334–41; William H. Greene, *Econometric Analysis*, 6th edn, Pearson/Prentice-Hall, 2008; and Russell Davidson and James G. MacKinnon, *Econometric Theory and Methods*, 2nd edn, Oxford University Press, New York, 2004.

5 Greene *op cit.*, p. 50.

6 Kmenta, *op cit.*, p. 340.

$$b_2 = \frac{\Sigma x_i (B_1 + B_2 X_i + u_i)}{\Sigma x_i^2}$$

$$= B_1 \frac{\Sigma x_i}{\Sigma x_i^2} + B_2 \frac{\Sigma x_i X_i}{\Sigma x_i^2} + \frac{\Sigma x_i u_i}{\Sigma x_i^2} \qquad (19.4)$$

$$= B_2 + \frac{\Sigma x_i u_i}{\Sigma x_i^2}$$

where use is made of the fact that $\Sigma x_i = 0$, because the sum of the deviations of a random variable from its mean value is always equal to zero, and also because $\Sigma x_i X_i / \Sigma x_i^2 = 1$ (see Exercise 19.1).

Now if we try to take the expectation of the preceding equation on both sides, we run into a problem, for

$$E\left(\frac{\Sigma x_i u_i}{\Sigma x_i^2}\right) \neq \frac{E(\Sigma x_i u_i)}{E(\Sigma x_i^2)} \qquad (19.5)$$

because the expectation operator, $E$, is a linear operator. Furthermore, the expectation of the product of $x_i$ and $u_i$ is not the product of the expectations, because they are not independent.[7]

The best we can do is to see how $b_2$ behaves as the sample size increases indefinitely. This we can do by using the concept of **probability limit**, or **plim** for short, which is the standard procedure to find out if an estimator is consistent; that is, if it approaches its true (population) value as the sample size increases indefinitely. So we proceed as follows:

IV

$$\text{plim}(b_2) = \text{plim}\left(B_2 + \frac{\Sigma x_i u_i}{\Sigma x_i^2}\right)$$

$$= B_2 + \text{plim}\left(\frac{\frac{1}{n}\Sigma x_i u_i}{\frac{1}{n}\Sigma x_i^2}\right) \qquad (19.6)$$

$$= B_2 + \frac{\text{plim}(\frac{1}{n}\Sigma x_i u_i)}{\text{plim}(\frac{1}{n}\Sigma x_i^2)}$$

$$= B_2 + \frac{\text{Population } \text{cov}(X_i, u_i)}{\text{Population } \text{var}(X_i)}$$

where use is made of the properties of plim,[8] $n$ is the sample size, and cov means covariance and var means variance.

As a result, we obtain:

$$b_2 - B_2 = \frac{\text{cov}(X_i, u_i)}{\text{var}(X_i)} \qquad (19.7)$$

---

7  Remember that $E(XY) = E(X)E(Y)$ only if $X$ and $Y$ are independent.

8  These properties are: $\text{plim}(X+Y) = \text{plim}X + \text{plim}Y$; $\text{plim}(XY) = \text{plim}X.\text{plim}Y$; $\text{plim}(X/Y) = \text{plim}X/\text{plim}Y$, and the plim of a constant is that constant itself.

This may be called the (**asymptotic**) **bias**.

Now if the covariance between the regressor and the error term is positive, $b_2$ will overestimate the true $B_2$, a positive bias. On the other hand, if the covariance term is negative, $b_2$ will underestimate $B_2$, a negative bias. And the bias, positive or negative, will not disappear no matter how large the sample is.

*The upshot of the preceding discussion is that if a regressor and the error term are correlated, the OLS estimator is biased as well as inconsistent. Now even if a single regressor in a multiple regression is correlated with the error term, OLS estimators of all the coefficients are inconsistent.*[9]

## 19.3 Reasons for correlation between regressors and the error term

Primarily there are four reasons why the regressor(s) may be correlated with the error term:

1 Measurement errors in the regressor(s)

2 Omitted variable bias

3 Simultaneous equation bias

4 Dynamic regression model with serial correlation in the error term.

It is important that we study these sources of correlation between regressor(s) and the error term to appreciate fully the method of instrumental variables.

### Measurement errors in the regressor(s)

In Chapter 7 we noted that if there are errors of measurement in the regressor(s) the OLS estimators are biased as well as inconsistent. To get a glimpse of this, we consider the celebrated *permanent income* hypothesis (PIH) of the late Nobel laureate Milton Friedman, which can be explained as follows?

$$Y_i = B_1 + B_2 X_i^* + u_i; \quad 0 < B_2 < 1 \tag{19.8}$$

where $Y$ = current, or observed, consumption expenditure, $X_i^*$ = permanent income and $u_i$ = disturbance, or error, term. $B_2$ here represents the *marginal propensity to consume* (MPC), that is, the increase in consumption expenditure for an additional dollar's worth of increase in the *permanent income*, that is, the average level of income you expect to be in the future.[10]

Of course, we do not have readily available measures of permanent income. So instead of using permanent income we use observed or current income, $X_i$, which may contain errors of measurement, say $w_i$. Therefore, we can write

$$X_i = X_i^* + w_i \tag{19.9}$$

That is, current income is equal to permanent income plus errors of measurement.

---

9 Recall that in multiple regressions the cross-product terms of the regressors are involved in the computation of the partial regression coefficients. Therefore an error in a regressor may affect the coefficients of the other regressors in the model.

10 We could make permanent consumption $(Y_i^*)$ as a function of permanent income $(X_i^*)$, but to keep the algebra simple we will not do so.

Therefore, instead of estimating Eq. (19.8), we estimate

$$Y_i = B_1 + B_2(X_i - w_i) + u_i$$
$$= B_1 + B_2 X_i + (u_i - B_2 w_i) \qquad (19.10)$$
$$= B_1 + B_2 X_i + v_i$$

where $v_i = u_i - B_2 w_i$, a compound of equation and measurement errors.

Now even if we assume that $w_i$ has zero mean, is serially uncorrelated, and is uncorrelated with $u_i$, we can no longer maintain that the composite error term $v_i$ is independent of the regressor $X_i$ because (assuming $E(v_i) = 0$) it can be shown that (see Exercise 19.2)

$$\text{cov}(v_i, X_i) = -B_2 \sigma_w^2 \qquad (19.11)$$

This result shows that in the regression (19.10) the regressor $X_i$ and the error term $v_i$ are correlated, which violates the crucial assumption of CLRM that the error term and the regressor(s) are uncorrelated.

As a result, it can be shown that the OLS estimate of $B_2$ in Eq. (19.8) is *not only biased but is also inconsistent*. It can be proved formally that (see Exercise 19.3)

$$\text{plim}(b_2) = B_2 \left[ \frac{1}{1 + \sigma_w^2 / \sigma_{X^*}^2} \right] \qquad (19.12)$$

where *plim* means the probability limit, which, as mentioned before, we use to establish the consistency property of an estimator.

Since the term inside the bracket is expected to be less than 1, $b_2$ will not converge to its true MPC value whatever the sample size. If $B_2$ is assumed positive, which makes sense in the present case, $b_2$ will be less than the true $B_2$ – that is, $b_2$ will underestimate $B_2$. More technically, it is biased toward zero.

As this exercise shows, errors of measurement in the regressor(s) can pose serious problems in estimating the true coefficient.[11]

How, then, can we measure the true MPC? If somehow we can find a proxy or a tool or an instrument for permanent income so that that proxy is uncorrelated with the error term but is correlated with the regressor (presumably highly), we may be able to measure the true MPC, at least in large samples. *This is the essence of the method of instrumental variable(s).* But how do we find a "good" proxy? We will answer this question shortly.

## Omitted variable bias

In Chapter 2 we discussed several cases of specification errors, such as the omission of relevant variables, incorrect functional form, and incorrect probabilistic assumption of the distribution of the error term and the like.

For example, consider the following model of wage determination – call it the wage function:

---

11 Incidentally note that errors of measurement in the regressand do not pose such a problem because those errors can be absorbed in the equation error and we can still obtained unbiased estimates of the regression coefficients, although the variances and standard errors of the estimators are larger than they would have been in the absence of measurement errors in the regressand.

$$Y_i = B_1 + B_2 X_{2i} + B_3 X_{3i} + u_i \tag{19.13}$$

where $Y$ is wages or earnings, $X_2$ is education as measured by years of schooling, and $X_3$ is (innate) ability.

Since direct measures of ability are hard to come by, suppose, instead of estimating Eq. (19.13), we estimate the following function:

$$Y_i = A_1 + A_2 X_{2i} + v_i \tag{19.14}$$

where $v_i$ is the error term.

That is, we omit the ability variable from the wage function. In this case, $v_i = u_i + B_3 X_{3i}$

Now it can be shown that (see Appendix 19A.2)

$$E(a_2) = B_2 + B_3 b_{32} \tag{19.15}$$

where $b_{32}$ is the slope coefficient in the regression of $X_3$ (the omitted variable) on $X_2$ (the variable included in the model).

In other words, in the present instance, the expected value of the estimated slope coefficient in Eq. (19.15) is equal to its true value ($B_2$) plus the slope coefficient of the left-out variable multiplied by $b_{32}$. That is, it is biased. And there is no reason to believe that this bias disappears as the sample size increases. In other words, the estimator is not even consistent. For other consequences of omitting relevant variables, see Chapter 7.

As in the case of the errors-in-regressor case, can we find an instrument for ability so that we can estimate Eq. (19.13) and obtain consistent estimate of the education coefficient $B_2$? Can we use mother's or father's education as a proxy for ability? We will take up this question shortly after we discuss the remaining two sources of errors between regressor(s) and the error term.

## Simultaneous equation bias

Consider the following pair of equations:

$$Y_i = B_1 + B_2 X_i + u_{1i} \tag{19.16}$$

$$X_i = A_1 + A_2 Y_i + u_{2i} \tag{19.17}$$

where $Y_i$ = crime rate in city $i$ and $X_i$ = expenditure on police in city $i$.

This is the "chicken or egg first"-type problem. Does the crime rate determine the number of police and hence expenditure on police or does expenditure on police determine the crime rate?

If you to estimate Eqs. (19.16) and (19.17) individually by OLS, you will find that $X_i$ and $u_{1i}$ in Eq. (19.16) are correlated. Likewise, if you estimate Eq. (19.17) by itself, you will find that $Y_i$ and $u_{2i}$ are correlated – a classic case of a stochastic regressor correlated with the error term (for proof, see Appendix 19A.3).

In the literature this situation is known as the **simultaneity bias**.

How do we handle this situation? As we show below, the technique of instrumental variable can be used to resolve the problem in many cases.

## Dynamic regression and serial correlation in the error term

Return to Friedman's permanent income hypothesis stated in Eq. (19.8). Since permanent income, $X_i^*$, is not directly observable, let us consider the following mechanism developed by Cagan and Friedman, known as the **adaptive expectations, progressive expectations,** or **error learning model:**[12]

$$X_t^* - X_{t-1}^* = \gamma(X_t - X_{t-1}^*) \qquad 0 < \gamma < 1 \qquad (19.18)$$

Equation (19.18) states that "economic agents will adapt their expectations in the light of past experience and that in particular they will learn from their mistakes".[13] More specifically, Eq. (19.18) states that expectations are revised each period by a fraction $\gamma$ of the gap between the current value of the variable and its previous expected value, that is between currently observed income and its expected or anticipated value in the previous period. Another way of expressing this is to write Eq. (19.18) as:

$$X_t^* = \gamma X_t + (1-\gamma)X_{t-1}^* \qquad (19.19)$$

which shows that the value of the permanent income at time $t$ is a weighted average of the actual value of income at time $t$ and its value expected in the previous period, with weights of $\gamma$ and $(1 - \gamma)$, respectively.

Substituting Eq. (19.19) into Eq. (19.8), we obtain, after suitable manipulation, the following model:

$$Y_t = \gamma B_1 + \gamma B_2 X_t + (1-\gamma)Y_{t-1} + v_t \qquad (19.20)$$

where

$$v_t = u_t - (1-\gamma)u_{t-1} \qquad (19.21)$$

In the literature model (19.20) is known as the **adaptive expectations model** and $\gamma$ is known as the **coefficient of expectations.**

Model (19.20) is also known as a **dynamic model** because it expresses the current consumption expenditure as a function of current or observed income and the lagged value of current consumption expenditure.

It is interesting how with the help of a dynamic model we have been able to get rid of the unobservable variable $X_t^*$. Since there is no such thing as a free lunch, in "simplifying" the permanent income hypothesis, we have created some estimation problems. First, $Y_t$ is random, so is $Y_{t-1}$. Therefore we have a stochastic regressor on the right-hand side of Eq. (19.20). Additionally, the error term $v_t$ is likely to be serially correlated, as it is a linear combination of the original error term, $u_i$.

As a matter of fact, it can be shown that

$$\text{cov}(v_t, v_{t-1}) = -\gamma\sigma_u^2 \qquad (19.22)$$

and also

IV

---

12  P. Cagan, "Monetary Dynamics of Hyperinflation", in M. Friedman (ed.), *Studies in the Quantitative Theory of Money*,  University of Chicago Press, Chicao, 1956 and Milton Friedman, *A Theory of Consumption Function*, National Bureau of Economic Research, Princeton University Press, Princeton, NJ, 1957. This model is based on the pioneering work of Koyck: L. M. Koyck, *Distributed Lags and Investment Analysis*, North-Holland Publishing Company, Amsterdam, 1954.

13  G. K. Shaw, *Rational Expectations: An Elementary Exposition*, St. Martin's Press, New York, 1984, p. 25.

$$\text{cov}(Y_{t-1}, v_t) = -\gamma \sigma_u^2 \tag{19.23}$$

As we have shown before, if a regressor is correlated with the error term, the OLS estimators are not only biased but are also inconsistent, regardless of the sample size.

*To summarize*, in all the four cases we have considered there is a strong possibility that the regressor(s) is (are) not only stochastic but also correlated with the error term. As a result, the OLS estimators are biased as well inconsistent. This suggests that we either abandon OLS or find a suitable alternative(s) which will produce estimators that are at least consistent. One of the alternatives prominently suggested in the literature is the method of instrumental variable(s), which we now discuss.

## 19.4    The method of instrumental variables

The main problem with the use of OLS in regression models that contain one or more regressors that are correlated with the error term is that the OLS estimators are biased as well as inconsistent. Can we find a "substitute" or "proxy" variables for the suspect stochastic regressors such that the proxy variables produce consistent estimators of the true (population) regression coefficients? If we can do that successfully, such variables are called **instrumental variables** or simply **instruments**. How do we find such instruments? How do we know they are good instruments? Are there formal ways to find out if the chosen instrument is indeed a good instrument?

To answer these questions, let us start with the simple linear regression given in Eq. (19.2). Suppose in this regression that regressor $X$ is stochastic and that it is correlated with the error term $u$. Suppose a variable $Z$ is a candidate instrument for $X$. To be a valid instrument, $Z$ must satisfy the following criteria:

1   *Instrument relevance*: That is, $Z$ must be correlated, positively or negatively, with the stochastic variable for which it acts as an instrument, variable $X$ in the present case. The greater the extent of correlation between the two variables, the better is the instrument. Symbolically,

$$\text{cov}(X_i, Z_i) \neq 0 \tag{19.24}$$

2   *Instrument exogeneity*: $Z$ must not be correlated with the error term $u$. That is,

$$\text{cov}(Z_i, u_i) = 0 \tag{19.25}$$

3   *Not a regressor in its own right*. That is, it does not belong in the original model. If it does, the original model must be misspecified.

Before we proceed further, it may be noted that if we have a multiple regression with several regressors and some of them are correlated with the error term, we must find an instrument for each of the stochastic regressors. *In other words, there must be at least as many instruments as the number of stochastic regressors in the model*. But we will have more to say about this later.

As you can see, all these conditions may be hard to satisfy at the same time. So it is not easy to find good instruments in every application. That is why sometimes the idea of instrumental variables sounds chimerical, although there are examples of successful instruments.[14]

As an example of an interesting but somewhat questionable example of IV application, Caroline Hoxby wanted to find out the relationship between student performance and school competition. She estimated the following regression:

Test scores = $B_1$ + $B_2$ (Number of school districts) + error term

Suspecting that the regressor is stochastic, she used the number of streams in a school district as an instrument for the number of school districts, for she observed that areas with more school districts also had a lot of streams; presumably the streams made natural boundaries for the school districts.[15]

How does IV estimation work? The answer follows.

## IV estimation

To show how IV works, we will continue with the two-variable regression. As we know the OLS estimator of $B_2$ in Eq. (19.2) is:

$$b_2 = \frac{\Sigma x_i y_i}{\Sigma x_i^2}$$

where $x_i = X_i - \overline{X}$ and $y_i = Y_i - \overline{Y}$.

Now we use $Z$ as an instrument for $X$ in Eq. (19.2) and obtain:

$$b_2^{IV} = \frac{\Sigma z_i y_i}{\Sigma z_i x_i} \tag{19.26}$$

where $z_i = Z_i - \overline{Z}$.

*Caution*: Do not just put $z_i$ for $x_i$ in the formula for $b_2$ given above and note carefully that the denominator has both $z$ and $x$ terms.

Now noting that $Y_i = B_1 + B_2 X_i + u_i$ and, therefore,

$$y_i = B_2 x_i + (u_i - \overline{u})$$

we obtain

$$b_2^{IV} = \frac{\Sigma z_i [B_2 x_i + (u_i - \overline{u})]}{\Sigma z_i x_i}$$
$$= B_2 + \frac{\Sigma z_i (u_i - \overline{u})}{\Sigma z_i x_i} \tag{19.27}$$

You can see the similarity between the OLS and IV estimators. Of course, if $Z = X$, the IV estimator coincides with the OLS estimator.

The estimator of the intercept $B_1$, following the usual formula, is:

$$b_1 = \overline{Y} - b_2^{IV} \overline{X} \tag{19.28}$$

---

14  See, for instance, Jonathan Klick and Alexander Tabarrok, Using terror alert levels to estimate the effect of police on crime, *Journal of Law and Economics*, University of Chicago, vol. 48, 2005, pp. 267–79.

15  Caroline M. Hoxby, Does competition among public schools benefit students and taxpayers?, *American Economic Review*, 2000, vol. 90, pp. 1209–38.

In this expression the only difference from the usual OLS estimator of $B_1$ is that we use the slope coefficient estimated from the IV estimator.

Since we are assuming that in the population cov $(Z, u) = 0$, taking the probability limit of Eq. (19.27) it can be shown that[16]

$$\text{plim} b_2^{IV} = B_2 \tag{19.29}$$

that is, the IV estimator of $B_2$ is consistent (see Exercise 19.4). But it should be added that in finite, or small, samples this estimator is biased.

Although $b_2^{IV}$ is a consistent estimator of $B_2$, in small samples it is biased. Further, it can be shown that in large samples the IV estimator is distributed as follows:

$$b_2^{IV} \sim N\left( B_2, \frac{\sigma_u^2}{\Sigma x_i^2} \frac{1}{\rho_{XZ}^2} \right) \tag{19.30}$$

Notice that the variance of the IV estimator involves the squared (population) correlation between $X$ and its instrument $Z$. In words, in large samples the IV estimator $b_2^{IV}$ is normally distributed with mean equal to its population value and variance given above. By contrast, the usual OLS estimator has the variance

$$\text{var}(b_2) = \frac{\sigma_u^2}{\Sigma x_i^2} \tag{19.31}$$

Since $0 < \rho_{XZ}^2 < 1$, the variance of the IV estimator will be larger than the variance of the OLS estimator, especially so if $\rho_{XZ}^2$ is small. In other words, the IV estimator is less efficient than the OLS estimator. If $\rho_{XZ}^2$ is small it suggests that $Z$ is a **weak instrument** for $X$. On the other hand, if it is large, it suggests that it is a **strong instrument** for $X$.

To give some idea how far the variances of IV and OLS estimators can diverge, assume that $\rho_{zx} = 0.2$. In this case, variance of the IV estimator is 25 times as large as that of the OLS estimator. If $\rho_{zx} = 0.1$, it is 100 times larger. In the extreme case, if $\rho_{zx} = 0$, the variance of the IV estimator is infinite. Of course, if $\rho_{zx} = 1$, the two variances are the same, which is another way of saying that the variable $X$ is its own instrument. Note that in practice we estimate $\rho_{xz}$ by its sample counterpart, $r_{xz}$.

We can use the variance of the IV estimator given in Eq. (19.30) to establish confidence intervals and test hypotheses, assuming that our sample size is reasonably large. But notice that the variance of the IV estimator is heteroscedastic.[17] Therefore we will have to use the White-type robust standard errors that correct for heteroscedasticity. But modern software packages can obtain robust standard errors by invoking the appropriate command.

An interesting point to note about the preceding discussion is that in obtaining consistent estimates via the IV method we pay a price in terms of wider confidence intervals because of the larger variance of IV estimators, especially if the selected instrument is a weak proxy for the original regressor. Again, there is no such thing as a free lunch!

---

16 We are taking the probability limit because the second term in Eq. (19.27) involves sample quantities and not the population quantities.

17 This is true for the simple model considered here. For models involving several regressors, the formulas of variances and covariances are complicated, which the reader can find in the references.

## 19.5    Monte Carlo simulation of IV

To show how OLS can distort the results in cases of stochastic regressor(s) correlated with the error term, Cameron and Trivedi conducted a Monte Carlo simulation experiment.[18] They assumed the following:

$$Y_i = 0.5X_i + u_i \tag{19.32}$$

$$X_i = Z_i + v_i \tag{19.33}$$

$$Z_i \sim N(2,1); \quad u_i \sim N(0,1); \quad v_i \sim N(0,1); \quad \mathrm{cov}(u_i, v_i) = 0.8 \tag{19.34}$$

In words, the true slope coefficient in the regression of $Y_i$ on $X_i$ is assumed known and is equal to 0.5. Further, the regressor $X_i$ is equal to the instrumental variable $Z_i$ and the error term $v_i$. The authors assumed that $Z_i$ was distributed normally with mean 2 and variance 1. The error terms were jointly normally distributed, each with mean of 0 and variance of 1, and the correlation between the two error terms was assumed to be 0.8.

With this structure, they generated a sample size of 10,000 and obtained the following results:

| Method | OLS | IV |
|---|---|---|
| Constant | −0.804 | −0.017 |
| | (0.014) | (0.022) |
| $X$ | 0.902 | 0.510 |
| | (0.006) | (0.010) |
| $R^2$ | 0.709 | 0.576 |

*Note*: Figures in parentheses are robust standard errors, that is, standard errors corrected for heteroscedasticity.

These results are revealing. The true model given in Eq. (19.32) has no intercept in it, but the OLS results show that its value is −0.804 and that it is statistically significant ($t = -0.804/0.014 = -57.43$). Secondly, the OLS estimate of the slope coefficient is 0.902, whereas we know the true slope coefficient is 0.5.

The IV estimates, on the other hand, are very close to the true values; the intercept coefficient is statistically indifferent from zero and the slope coefficient of 0.51 is about the same as the true slope coefficient of 0.5. However, notice that the standard errors of the IV estimates are larger than the OLS standard errors, a point made earlier.

The Monte Carlo experiment of Cameron and Trivedi shows dramatically how OLS estimation can distort the true results.

*A note on Monte Carlo experiments*: In such experiments we assume a true model and generate several sets of artificial data that will produce several sets of parameter estimates; from these estimates we obtain their sampling distribution to see how they match with competing methods of estimating the parameters of interest.[19]

---

18   A. Colin Cameron and Pravin K. Trivedi, *Microeconometrics, op cit.*, pp. 102–3.

19   For a graphic presentation and other details of this procedure, see Peter Kennedy, *A Guide to Econometrics*, 6th edn, Blackwell Publishing, 2008, p. 23–5.

## 19.6    Some illustrative examples

Before we proceed to an extended numerical example of IV estimation, let us consider a few examples of IV application.

### Effect of police on crime using terror alert level

In Table 19.2 we found that the effect of police (as represented by expenditure on police) is positively related to the crime rate, which is counterintuitive. We raised the possibility that this result could be due to simultaneity bias. To assess the impact of police on crime, Jonathan Klick and Alexander Tabarrok used an interesting instrument that avoids the simultaneity problem.[20]

The instrument they used was the **alert level** that was instituted by the Department of Homeland Security (DHS) in the wake of 9/11. These alert levels are low (green), guarded (blue), yellow (elevated), orange (high), and red (severe). Their hypothesis was that the level of crime decreases on high alert days in Washington, DC because of increased police presence on the streets.

Based on the data for 506 days (12 March 2002 to 30 July 2003), during which there were 55,882 crimes (about an average of 110 per day), they first regressed the daily DC crime totals on the level of alert (Eq. 1) and then on the alert level and the log of mid-day public transport ridership (Eq. 2) as shown in Table 19.3.

*Note*: Alert is a dummy variable taking the value of 1 on high alert days and 0 on elevated alert days. The authors also included dummies representing the days of the week to control for day effects, but these coefficients are not reported. * and ** denote 5% and 1% significance levels, respectively.

As Eq. (1) shows, there was an average decline of about 7 crimes per day, and this effect is statistically significant. In Eq. (2) they include the log of mid-day ridership as a proxy for tourism. Allowing for this, total crimes decreased by about 6 per day, not a big difference from the effect in Eq. (1). The positive coefficient of the log-ridership coefficient suggests that a 10% increase in ridership increases total crimes by an average of 1.7 per day, not strong enough to counter the strong presence of police on high alert days.[21]

The reader is advised to read this article for further details. But the point to note is that sometimes one can find meaningful proxies to resolve the problem(s) created by stochastic regressors.

### Table 19.3  Crimes on high alert days.

|  | (1) | (2) |
|---|---|---|
| High alert | −7.316 (2.877)* | −6.046 (2.537)* |
| Log of mid-day ridership | – | 17.341 ( 5.309)** |
| $R^2$ | 0.14 | 0.17 |

---

20  See Klick and Tabarrok, *op cit.*

21  Recall our discussion of the lin-log model in Chapter 2. Multiply the coefficient 17.341 by 0.01, which gives 0.17341. Hence a 10% increase in ridership leads to about 1.7 increase in the crime rate.

## The permanent income hypothesis (PIH)

In discussing Friedman's permanent income hypothesis earlier, we showed that if regress PCE on current DPI in lieu of permanent income we are likely to obtained biased estimates of the marginal propensity to consume because of errors of measurement, and this bias does not diminish even if we increase the sample size indefinitely.

The difficulty here is that we do not know how to measure permanent income. One method of obtaining a measure of permanent income is to take a weighted average of past incomes over a certain period and take that as a (crude) measure of permanent income.

The literature is full of discussion on PIH in its various forms and the problems of measuring the permanent income.[22] For example, Fumo Hiyashi uses lagged variables such as lagged per capita exports and lagged per capita government spending as instruments for permanent income, as he argues these variables are correlated with consumers' permanent income.[23]

Friedman himself estimated permanent income as a moving average of current and past income with geometrically declining weights, restricting the lags to 17 terms. But with Cagan's adaptive expectations model, discussed earlier, it is not necessary to restrict the lags arbitrarily. The details of his strategy as well as the details of Cagan's model can be found in the references[24] (see also Exercise 19.5).

## Law enforcement spending and the crime rate

To illustrate the simultaneity problem, Barreto and Howland considered the following model (notations changed from the original).[25]

$$\text{Enforcement Spending}_i = A_1 + A_2 \text{Crimerate}_i + u_{1i} \qquad (19.35)$$

$$\text{Crime Rate}_i = B_1 + B_2 \text{Enforcement Spending}_i$$
$$+ B_3 \text{Gini}_i + u_{2i} \qquad (19.36)$$

where Gini is the Gini coefficient, a measure of income inequality. This coefficient lies between 0 (perfect equality) and 1 (complete inequality: one person owns all the income.) The closer this coefficient to 0, the greater the income equality. Contrarily, the closer it is to 1, the greater the income inequality.

In Eq. (19.36) $B_3$ is expected to be positive because more income inequality suggests higher crime rates, *ceteris paribus*. But notice that there is no logical reason to expect that Gini belongs in Eq. (19.35). We can treat Gini as an exogenous variable, determined outside the system, and so we do not expect it to be correlated with the error term, $u_{2i}$. But this is not the case with the other two variables, for they are mutually dependent.

---

22  For a survey on measurement errors in survey data, see J. Bound, C. Brown and N. Kathiowetz, "Measurement errors in survey data", in J. J. Heckman and E. E. Leamer (eds.), *Handbook of Econometrics*, vol. V., Amsterdam, North Holland, 2001, pp. 3705–843.

23  See Fumio Hayashi, The permanent income hypothesis: estimation and testing by instrumental variables, *Journal of Political Economy*, vol. 90, no. 5, 1982, pp. 895–916.

24  See Kenneth F. Wallis, *Topics in Applied Econometrics*, 2nd edn, University of Minnesota Press, 1980, Chapter 1; Gujarati/Porter, *op cit.*, Chapter 17.

25  Humberto Barreto and Frank M. Howland, *Introductory Econometrics: Using Monte Carlo Simulation with Microsoft Excel*, Cambridge University Press, New York, 2006, Chapter 24.

If we solve Eqs. (19.35) and (19.36) simultaneously, treating Gini as exogenous (a kind of instrument), we obtain:

$$\text{Enforcement Spending}_i = C_1 + C_2 Gini_i + u_{3i} \qquad (19.37)$$

$$\text{Crime Rate}_i = D_1 + D_2 Gini_i + u_{4i} \qquad (19.38)$$

where the coefficients in these equations are (nonlinear) combinations of the coefficients in Eqs. (19.35) and (19.36). Also, the error terms in these equations are (nonlinear) combinations of the error terms in Eqs. (19.35) and (19.36).

Equations (19.37) and (19.38) are known as **reduced form equations** in the language of simultaneous equation models.[26] Compared with the reduced form equations, Eqs. (19.35) and (19.36) are called the **structural equations**. In reduced form equations only exogenous or predetermined (i.e. lagged endogenous or lagged exogenous) variables appear on the right-hand side of the equations.

The coefficients of the reduced form equations are called the **reduced form coefficients**, whereas those in the structural equations are called the **structural coefficients**.

We can estimate reduced form equations by OLS. Once the reduced form coefficients are estimated, we may be able to estimate one or all of the structural coefficients. If we can estimate all the structural coefficients from the reduced form coefficients, we say the structural equations are **identified**; that is, we can obtain unique estimates of the structural coefficients. If this is not possible for one or more structural equations, we say that the equation(s) is (are) **unidentified**. If we obtain more than one estimate for one or more parameters of a structural equation, we say that equation is **overidentified**.

It may be noted that the method of obtaining the structural coefficients from the reduced form coefficients is known as the method of **indirect least squares** – we first estimate the reduced form coefficients and then try to retrieve the structural coefficients.

Shortly, we will discuss the method of **two-stage least squares** (2SLS) and show how it aids in finding instrumental variables.

Toward that purpose we now consider a numerical example.

## 19.7    A numerical example: earnings and educational attainment of youth in the USA

The National Longitudinal Survey of Youth 1979 (NLSY79) is a repeated survey of a nationally representative sample of young males and females between ages 14 to 21 in 1979. From 1979 until 1994 the survey was conducted annually, but since then it is conducted bi-annually. Originally the core sample consisted of 3,003 males and 3,108 females.

The NLSY cross-section data is provided in 22 subsets, each subset consisting of randomly drawn sample of 540 observations: 270 males and 270 females.[27] Data are collected on a variety of socio-economic conditions and is quite extensive. The major

---

26  For a detailed discussion of simultaneous equations, see Gujarati/Porter, *op cit.*, Chapters 18, 19 and 20. As noted elsewhere, this topic is no longer as prominent as it was in the 1960s and 1970s.

27  The data used here can be obtained from http://www.bls.gov/nls/. Some of the data can be downloaded and more extensive data can be purchased.

categories of data obtained pertain to gender, ethnicity, age, years of schooling, highest educational qualification, marital status, faith, family background (mother's and father's education and number of siblings), place of living, earning, hours, years of work experience, type of employment (government, private sector, self-employed), and the region of the country (North central, North eastern, Southern and Western).

We will use some of these data for 2002 (sample subset number 22) to develop an earnings function. Following the tradition established by Jacob Mincer, we consider the following earnings function:[28]

$$\ln Earn_i = B_1 + B_2 S_i + B_3\ Wexp_i + B_4\ Gender_i + \\ B_5\ Ethblack_i + B_6\ Ethhisp_i + u_i \qquad (19.39)$$

where $\ln Earn$ = log of hourly earnings in \$, $S$ = years of schooling (highest grade completed in 2002), $Wexp$ = total out-of-school work experience in years as of the 2002 interview, $Gender$ = 1 for female and 0 for men, $Ethblack$ = 1 for blacks, $Ethhis$ = 1 for Hispanic; non-black and non-Hispanic being the left-out, or reference, category.

As you can see, some variables are quantitative and some are dummy variables. A priori, based on prior empirical evidence, we expect $B_2 > 0$, $B_3 > 0$, $B_4 < 0$; $B_5 < 0$, and $B_6 < 0$.

For the purpose of this chapter our concern is with the education variable $S$ in the above model. If (native) ability and education are correlated, we should include both variables in the model. However, the ability variable is difficult to measure directly. As a result, it may be subsumed in the error term. But in that case the education variable may be correlated with the error term, thereby making education an endogenous or stochastic regressor. From our discussion of the consequences of stochastic regressor(s) it would seem that if we estimate Eq. (19.39) by OLS the coefficient of $S$ will be biased as well as inconsistent. This is so because we may not be able to find the true impact of education on earnings that does not net out the effect of ability. Naturally, we would like to find a suitable instrument or instruments for years of schooling so that we can obtain consistent estimate of its coefficient.

Before we search for the instrument(s), let us estimate Eq. (19.39) by OLS for comparative purposes. The regression results using *Stata 10* are given in Table 19.4.

All the estimated coefficients have the expected signs and under the classical assumptions all the coefficients are statistically highly significant, the sole exception being the dummy coefficient for Hispanics.

These results show that compared to male workers, female workers on average earn less than their male counterpart, *ceteris paribus*. The average hourly earnings of black workers is lower than that of non-black non-Hispanic workers, *ceteris paribus*, which is the base category. Qualitatively, the sign of the Hispanic coefficient is negative, but the coefficient is statistically insignificant.

Noting that the regression model is log-lin, we have to interpret the coefficients of quantitative and qualitative (i.e. dummy) variables carefully (see Chapter 2 on functional forms). For quantitative variables, schooling and work experience, the estimated coefficients represent **semi-elasticities**. Thus, if schooling increases by a year, the average hourly earnings go up by about 13%, *ceteris paribus*. Similarly, if work

---

**28** Jacob Mincer, *Schooling, Experience, and Earnings,* Columbia University Press, 1974. See also James J. Hickman, Lance J. Lochner and Petra E. Todd, *Fifty Years of Mincer Earnings Functions*, National Bureau of Economic Research, Working Paper No. 9732, May 2003.

Table 19.4 Earnings function, USA, 2000 data set.

```
regress lEarnings s female wexp ethblack ethhisp,robust
Linear regression      Number of obs = 540
                F(5, 534) = 50.25
                Prob > F = 0.0000
                R-squared = 0.3633
                Root MSE = .50515
```

| lEarnings | Coef. | Std. Err. | t | P>\|t\| | [95% Conf. Interval] | |
|---|---|---|---|---|---|---|
| | | | | | Robust | |
| S | .1263493 | .0097476 | 12.96 | 0.000 | .1072009 | .1454976 |
| female | −.3014132 | .0442441 | −6.81 | 0.000 | −.3883269 | −.2144994 |
| wexp | .0327931 | .0050435 | 6.50 | 0.000 | .0228856 | .0427005 |
| ethblack | −.2060033 | .062988 | −3.27 | 0.001 | −.3297381 | −.0822686 |
| ethhisp | −.0997888 | .088881 | −1.12 | 0.262 | −.2743881 | .0748105 |
| _cons | .6843875 | .1870832 | 3.66 | 0.000 | .3168782 | 1.051897 |

*Note*: Regress is *Stata*'s command for OLS regression. This command is followed first by the dependent variables and then the regressors. Sometimes additional options are given, such as *robust*, which computes robust standard errors – in the present case standard errors corrected for heteroscedasticity, a topic we have discussed in the chapter on heteroscedasticity.

experience goes up by 1 year, the average hourly earnings go up by about 3.2%, *ceteris paribus*.

To obtain the semi-elasticity of a dummy variable, we first take the anti-log of the dummy coefficient, subtract 1 from it, and multiply the difference by 100%. Following this procedure, for the female dummy coefficient we obtain a value of about 0.7397, which suggests that females on average earn about 26% less than the male workers. The semi-elasticities for black and Hispanic workers are about 0.81 and 0.90, respectively. This suggests that black and Hispanic workers on average earn less than the base category by about 19% and 10%, although the semi-elasticity for Hispanics is not statistically different from the base category.

As we have discussed, since the education variable does not necessarily take into account ability, it may be correlated with the error term, thus rendering it a stochastic regressor. If we can find a suitable instrument for schooling that satisfies the three requirements that we specified for a suitable instrument, we can use it and estimate the earnings function by the IV method. The question is what may be a proper instrument? This question is difficult to answer categorically. What we can do is to try one or more proxies and compare the OLS results given in Table 19.4 and see how far the OLS results are biased, if any.

In the data we have information on mother's and father's education (as measured by years of schooling), number of siblings, and the ASVAB verbal (word knowledge) and mathematics (arithmetic reasoning) scores.

In choosing a proxy or proxies we must bear in mind that such proxies must be uncorrelated with the error term but must be correlated (presumably highly) with the stochastic regressor(s) and must *not* be a candidate in their own right as regressors – in the latter case, the model used in the analysis will suffer from model specification errors. It is not always easy to accomplish these entire objectives in every case. So very often it is a matter of trial and error, supplemented by judgment or "feel" for the subject under study.

However, there are diagnostic tests which can tell us if the chosen proxy or proxies are appropriate, tests which we will consider shortly. The data gives information on mother's schooling (*Sm*), which we will use as the instrument for participant's school-ing. The thinking here is that *S* and *Sm* are correlated, a reasonable assumption. For our data the correlation between the two is about 0.40. We have to assume that *Sm* is uncorrelated with the error term. We also assume that *Sm* does not belong in the par-ticipant's earning function, which seems reasonable.

We accept for the time being the validity of *Sm* as an instrument, which will be tested after we present the details of IV estimation.

To use *Sm* as the instrument for *S* and estimate the earnings function, we proceed in two stages:

**Stage 1**: We regress the suspected endogenous variable (*S*) on the chosen instru-ment (*Sm)* and the other regressors in the original model and obtain the estimated value of *S* from this regression; call it *S*-hat.

**Step 2**: We then run the earnings regression on the regressors included in the origi-nal model but replace the education variable by its value estimated from the Step 1 regression.

This method of estimating the parameters of the model of interest is appropriately called the method of **two-stage least squares** (**2SLS**), for we apply OLS twice. There-fore *the IV method is also known as 2SLS.*

Let us illustrate this method (Table 19.5). Using the estimated *S*-hat value from this regression, we obtain the second stage regression 2SLS (Table 19.6).

Note that in this (log) earnings function, unlike the one reported in Table 19.4, we use *S-hat* (estimated from the first-stage of 2SLS) instead of *S* as the regressor. How-ever, *the standard errors reported in Table 19.6 are not correct* because they are based on the incorrect estimator of the variance of the error term, $u_i$. The formula to correct

**Table 19.5  First stage of 2SLS with *Sm* as instrument.**

regress s female wexp ethblack ethhisp sm

| Source | SS | df | MS | |
|--------|-----|-----|------|---|
| | | | | Number of obs = 540 |
| | | | | F( 5, 534) = 35.06 |
| Model | 822.26493 | 5 | 164.452986 | Prob > F = 0.0000 |
| Residual | 2504.73322 | 534 | 4.69051165 | R-squared = 0.2471 |
| | | | | Adj R-squared = 0.2401 |
| Total | 3326.99815 | 539 | 6.17253831 | Root MSE = 2.1658 |

| s | Coef. | Std. Err. | t | P>\|t\| | [95% Conf. Interval] | |
|-------|---------|-----------|-------|-------|----------|----------|
| female | −.0276157 | .1913033 | −0.14 | 0.885 | −.4034151 | .3481837 |
| wexp | −.1247765 | .0203948 | −6.12 | 0.000 | −.1648403 | −.0847127 |
| ethblack | −.9180353 | .2978136 | −3.08 | 0.002 | −1.503065 | −.3330054 |
| ethhisp | .4566623 | .4464066 | 1.02 | 0.307 | −.420266 | 1.333591 |
| Sm | .3936096 | .0378126 | 10.41 | 0.000 | .3193298 | .4678893 |
| _cons | 11.31124 | .6172187 | 18.33 | 0.000 | 10.09876 | 12.52371 |

IV

**Table 19.6  Second stage of 2SLS of the earnings function.**

regress lEarnings s_hat female wexp ethblack ethhisp

| Source | SS | df | MS | |
|--------|------|-----|------------|---|
| | | | | Number of obs = 540 |
| | | | | F(5, 534) = 24.26 |
| Model | 39.6153236 | 5 | 7.92306472 | Prob > F = 0.0000 |
| Residual | 174.395062 | 534 | .326582514 | R-squared = 0.1851 |
| | | | | Adj R-squared = 0.1775 |
| Total | 214.010386 | 539 | .397050809 | Root MSE = .57147 |

| lEarnings | Coef. | Std. Err. | t | P>\|t\| | [95% Conf. Interval] | |
|-----------|----------|-----------|-------|-------|-----------|-----------|
| S_hat | .140068 | .0253488 | 5.53 | 0.000 | .0902724 | .1898636 |
| female | −.2997973 | .0505153 | −5.93 | 0.000 | −.3990304 | −.2005642 |
| wexp | .0347099 | .0064313 | 5.40 | 0.000 | .0220762 | .0473437 |
| ethblack | −.1872501 | .0851267 | −2.20 | 0.028 | −.3544744 | −.0200258 |
| ethhisp | −.0858509 | .1146507 | −0.75 | 0.454 | −.3110726 | .1393708 |
| _cons | .4607716 | .4257416 | 1.08 | 0.280 | −.3755621 | 1.297105 |

the estimated standard errors is rather involved. So it is better to use software like *Stata* or *Eviews* that not only correct the standard errors, but also obtain the 2SLS estimates without explicitly going through the cumbersome two-step procedure.

To do this, we can use the **ivreg** (instrumental variable regression) command of *Stata*. Using this command, we obtain the results in Table 19.7.

Observe that the estimated coefficients in the preceding two tables are the same, but the standard errors are different. As pointed out, we should rely on the standard errors reported in Table 19.7. Also notice that with the ivreg command we need only one table, instead of two, as in the case of the rote application of 2SLS.

## 19.8  Hypothesis testing under IV estimation

Now that we have estimated the earnings function using the IV method, how do we test hypotheses about an individual regression coefficient (like the $t$ test in CLRM) and hypotheses about several coefficients collectively (like the $F$ test of CLRM)? For the time being, assume that the instrument we have chosen (*Sm*) is the appropriate instrument for schooling, although we will provide a test to find out if this is indeed correct in the following section.

As Davidson and MacKinnon note, "Because the finite sample distributions of IV estimators are almost never known, exact tests of hypotheses based on such estimators are almost never available".[29]

However, in large samples it can be shown the IV estimator is approximately normally distributed with mean and variance as shown in Eq. (19.30). Therefore, instead of using the standard $t$ test, we use the $z$ test (i.e. the standard normal distribution) as shown in Table 19.7. The $z$ values in this table are all individually highly statistically significant, save the coefficient of Hispanic.

---

29  Davidson and MacKinnon, *op cit.*, pp. 330–5.

**Table 19.7  One step estimates of the earnings function (with robust standard errors).**

. ivregress 2sls lEarnings female wexp ethblack ethhisp ( $S$ = $Sm$),robust
(Instrumental variables (2SLS) regression Number of obs = 540
Wald chi2(5) = 138.45
Prob > chi2 = 0.0000
R-squared = 0.3606
Root MSE = .50338

| lEarnings | Coef. | Std. Err. | z | P>|z| | [95% Conf. Interval] | |
|---|---|---|---|---|---|---|
| | | | | Robust | | |
| S | .140068 | .0217263 | 6.45 | 0.000 | .0974852 | .1826508 |
| female | −.2997973 | .043731 | −6.86 | 0.000 | −.3855085 | −.2140861 |
| wexp | .0347099 | .0055105 | 6.30 | 0.000 | .0239095 | .0455103 |
| ethblack | −.1872501 | .0634787 | −2.95 | 0.003 | −.3116661 | −.0628342 |
| ethhisp | −.0858509 | .0949229 | −0.90 | 0.366 | −.2718963 | .1001945 |
| _cons | .4607717 | .3560759 | 1.29 | 0.196 | −.2371241 | 1.158668 |

Instrumented: S
Instruments: female wexp ethblack ethhisp sm

To test joint hypotheses of two or more coefficients, instead of using the classical $F$ test we use the Wald test, which is a large sample test. The Wald statistic follows the *chi-square* statistic with degrees of freedom equal to the number of regressors estimated: 5 in Table 19.7. The null hypothesis, as in the usual $F$ test, is that all the regressor coefficients are zero simultaneously, that is, collectively none of the regressors have any bearing on (log) earnings. In our example the chi-square value is about 138 and the probability of obtaining such a chi-square value or greater is practically nil.

In other words, collectively all the regressors have important impact on hourly earnings.

## A caution on the use of $R^2$ in IV estimation

Although we have presented the $R^2$ for the IV regressions given in the preceding two tables, it does not have the same interpretation as in the classical linear regression model and sometimes it can actually be negative. Hence the reported $R^2$ in IV regressions should be taken with a grain of salt.[30]

## Diagnostic testing

Having presented the basics of IV estimation, we now consider several questions regarding the IV methodology. Because of their importance in practice, we discuss these questions sequentially.

A  How do we know that a regressor is truly endogenous?

B  How do we find out if an instrument is weak or strong?

---

30  The conventionally computed coefficient of determination is defined as $R^2 = 1 - RSS/TSS$, but in case of IV estimation RSS can be greater than TSS, making $R^2$ negative.

C  What happens if we introduce several instruments for a stochastic regressor? And how do we test the validity of all the instrument?

D  How do we estimate a model when there is more than one stochastic regressor?

In what follows we answer these questions sequentially.

## 19.9   Test of endogeneity of a regressor

We have been working on the assumption that $S$ in our example is endogenous. But we can test this assumption explicitly by using one of the variants of the Hausman test. This test is relatively simple, and involves two steps:

**Step 1:**   We regress the endogenous $S$ on all the (nonstochastic) regressors in the earnings function plus the instrumental variable(s) and obtain residuals from this regression; call it $S$-hat.

**Step 2:**   We then regress lEarnings on all the regressors, including the (stochastic) $S$ and the residuals from Step I. If in this regression the $t$ value of the residuals variable is statistically significant, we conclude that $S$ endogenous or stochastic. If it is not, then there is no need for IV estimation, for in that case $S$ is its own instrument.

Returning to our example, we obtain the results in Table 19.8.

The results of the second step regression are as given in Table 19.9.

Since the coefficient of *shat* is not statistically significant, it would seem that schooling is not an endogenous variable. But we should not take these results at face value because we have cross-sectional data and heteroscedasticity is usually a problem in such data. Therefore we need to find heteroscedasticity-corrected standard error, such as the HAC standard errors discussed the chapter on heteroscedasticity.

**Table 19.8  Hausman test of endogeneity of schooling: first step result.**

regress s female wexp ethblack ethhisp sm

| Source | SS | df | MS | |
|---|---|---|---|---|
| Model | 822.26493 | 5 | 164.452986 | Number of obs = 540 |
| Residual | 2504.73322 | 534 | 4.69051165 | F( 5, 534) = 35.06 |
| | | | | Prob > F = 0.0000 |
| | | | | R-squared = 0.2471 |
| | | | | Adj R-squared = 0.2401 |
| Total | 3326.99815 | 539 | 6.17253831 | Root MSE = 2.1658 |

| S | Coef. | Std. Err. | t | P>\|t\| | [95% Conf. Interval] | |
|---|---|---|---|---|---|---|
| female | −.0276157 | .1913033 | −0.14 | 0.885 | −.4034151 | .3481837 |
| wexp | −.1247765 | .0203948 | −6.12 | 0.000 | −.1648403 | −.0847127 |
| ethblack | −.9180353 | .2978136 | −3.08 | 0.002 | −1.503065 | −.3330054 |
| ethhisp | .4566623 | .4464066 | 1.02 | 0.307 | −.420266 | 1.333591 |
| sm | .3936096 | .0378126 | 10.41 | 0.000 | .3193298 | .4678893 |
| _cons | 11.31124 | .6172187 | 18.33 | 0.000 | 10.09876 | 12.52371 |

. predict shat,residuals

**Table 19.9  Hausman test of endogeneity of schooling: second step results.**

egress lEarnings s female wexp ethblack ethhisp shat

| Source | SS | df | MS | |
|---|---|---|---|---|
| | | | | Number of obs = 540 |
| | | | | F( 6, 533) = 50.80 |
| Model | 77.8586985 | 6 | 12.9764498 | Prob > F = 0.0000 |
| Residual | 136.151687 | 533 | .255444066 | R-squared = 0.3638 |
| | | | | Adj R-squared = 0.3566 |
| Total | 214.010386 | 539 | .397050809 | Root MSE = .50541 |

| lEarnings | Coef. | Std. Err. | t | P>|t| | [95% Conf. Interval] | |
|---|---|---|---|---|---|---|
| S | .140068 | .0224186 | 6.25 | 0.000 | .0960283 | .1841077 |
| female | −.2997973 | .044676 | −6.71 | 0.000 | −.38756 | −.2120346 |
| wexp | .0347099 | .0056879 | 6.10 | 0.000 | .0235365 | .0458834 |
| ethblack | −.1872501 | .0752865 | −2.49 | 0.013 | −.3351448 | −.0393554 |
| ethhisp | −.0858509 | .1013977 | −0.85 | 0.398 | −.2850391 | .1133373 |
| shat | −.0165025 | .0245882 | −0.67 | 0.502 | −.0648041 | .0317992 |
| _cons | .4607717 | .3765282 | 1.22 | 0.222 | −.2788895 | 1.200433 |

**Table 19.10  Hausman endogeneity test with robust standard errors.**

regress lEarnings s female wexp shat,vce(robust)
Linear regression                    Number of obs = 540
F( 4, 535) = 59.14
Prob > F = 0.0000
R-squared = 0.3562
Root MSE = .50747

| lEarnings | Robust | | | | | |
|---|---|---|---|---|---|---|
| | Coef. | Std. Err. | t | P>|t| | [95% Conf. Interval] | |
| S | .1642758 | .0209439 | 7.84 | 0.000 | .1231334 | .2054183 |
| female | −.3002845 | .0443442 | −6.77 | 0.000 | −.3873947 | −.2131744 |
| wexp | .0390386 | .0053869 | 7.25 | 0.000 | .0284565 | .0496207 |
| shat | −.0407103 | .022955 | −1.77 | 0.077 | −.0858034 | .0043828 |
| _cons | .0311987 | .3380748 | 0.09 | 0.927 | −.6329182 | .6953156 |

We can use the robust standard error command in *Stata* to obtain the heteroscedasticity-corrected standard errors, which are given in Table 19.10.

Now the coefficient of the *shat* variable is statistically significant, at about the 8% level, indicating that education (schooling) seems to be endogenous.

## 19.10  How to find whether an instrument is weak or strong

If an instrument used in the analysis is weak in the sense that it is poorly correlated with the stochastic regressor for which it is an instrument, the IV estimator can be severely biased and its sampling distribution is not approximately normal, even in large samples. As a consequence, the IV standard errors and the confidence intervals based on them are highly misleading, leading to hypotheses tests that are unreliable.

To see why this is the case, refer to Eq. (19.30). If $\rho_{xz}$ in this equation is zero, the variance of the IV estimator is infinite. If $\rho_{xz}$ is not exactly zero, but very low (the case of a weak instrument), the IV estimator is not normally distributed, even in large samples. But how do we decide in a given case whether an instrument is weak?

In the case of a single endogenous regressor a rule of thumb says that an $F$ statistic of less than 10 in the first step of the Hausman test suggests that the chosen instrument is weak. If it is greater than 10, it probably is not a weak instrument.[31] In the case of a single (stochastic) regressor, this rule translates into a a $t$ value of about 3.2 because of the relationship between the $F$ and $t$ statistics, namely, that $F_{1,k} = t_k^2$, where for the $F$ statistic has 1 df in the numerator and $k$ df in the denominator.

On that score, in our example $Sm$ (mother's schooling) seems to be a strong instrument for $S$ because the value of the $F$ statistic in the first stage of the two-stage procedure is about 35, which exceeds the threshold value of 10. But this rule of thumb, like most rules of thumb, should not be used blindly.

## 19.11  The case of multiple instruments

Since there are competing instruments, education may be correlated with more than one instrumental variable. To allow for this possibility, we can include more than one instrument in the IV regression. This is often done with the aid of **two-stage least squares (2SLS)** that we just discussed.

> **Step 1**: We regress the suspected variable on all the instruments, and obtain the estimated value of the regressor.
>
> **Step 2**: We then run the earnings regression on the regressors included in the original model but replace the education variable by its value estimated from the Step 1 regression.

We can replace this two-step procedure by a single step by invoking Stata's *ivreg* command by including several instruments simultaneously, as the following example demonstrates.

For our earnings regression, in addition to mother's education ($Sm$), we can include father's schooling ($Sf$), and the number of siblings as instruments in the regression of earnings on education ($S$), gender (*female* = 1), years of work experience (*wexp*), ethnicity (dummies for black and Hispanics).

> **Step 1**: Regress schooling ($S$) on all the original (nonstochastic) regressors and the instruments. From this regression we obtain the estimated value of $S$, say, $\hat{s}$.
>
> **Step 2**: We now regress earnings on gender, wexp, ethnic dummies, and $\hat{s}$, the latter estimated from Step 1.

See Table 19.11. Compared to a single instrument in Table 19.7, when we introduced multiple instruments, the coefficient of $S$ (education) has gone up a bit, but it is still

---

31  Why 10? The slightly technical answer for this can be found in James H. Stock and Mark W. Watson, *Introduction to Econometrics*, 2nd edn, Pearson/Addison Wesley, Boston, 2007, p. 466. If the $F$ statistic exceeds 10, it suggests that the small sample bias of the IV estimate is less than 10% of the OLS bias. Remember that in cases of stochastic regressor(s) OLS is biased in small as well as large samples.

**Table 19.11  Earnings function with several instruments.**

ivreg lEarnings female wexp ethblack ethhisp (S=sm sf siblings),robust
Instrumental variables (2SLS) regression            Number of obs = 540
F( 5, 534) = 26.63
Prob > F = 0.0000
R-squared = 0.3492
Root MSE = .51071

| lEarnings | Coef. | Std. Err. | t | P>\|t\| | [95% Conf. Interval] | |
|---|---|---|---|---|---|---|
| | | | | | | Robust |
| s | .1579691 | .0216708 | 7.29 | 0.000 | .1153986 | .2005396 |
| female | −.2976888 | .0441663 | −6.74 | 0.000 | −.3844499 | −.2109278 |
| wexp | .0372111 | .005846 | 6.37 | 0.000 | .0257271 | .0486951 |
| ethblack | −.1627797 | .0625499 | −2.60 | 0.010 | −.2856538 | −.0399056 |
| ethhisp | −.0676639 | .098886 | −0.68 | 0.494 | −.2619172 | .1265893 |
| _cons | .1689836 | .3621567 | 0.47 | 0.641 | −.542443 | .8804101 |

Instrumented: S
Instruments: female wexp ethblack ethhisp sm sf siblings

significantly higher than the OLS regression. But notice again that the relative standard error of this coefficient is higher than its OLS counterpart, again reminding us that IV estimators may be less efficient.

## Testing the validity of surplus instruments

Earlier we stated that the number of instruments must be at least equal to the number of stochastic regressor. So, technically for our earnings regression one instrument will suffice, as in Table 19.7 where we used *Sm* (mother's education) as an instrument. In Table 19.11 we have three instruments, two more than the absolute minimum. How do we know that they are valid in the sense they are correlated with education but are not correlated with the error term? In simple terms, are they relevant?

Before we provide an answer to this question, it is worth mentioning the following:

1  If the number of instruments (*I*) equals the number of endogenous regressors, say *K*, we say that the regression coefficients are **exactly identified**, that is, we can obtain unique estimates of them.

2  If the number of instruments (*I*) exceeds the number of regressors, *K*, the regression coefficients are **overidentified**, in which case we may obtain more than one estimate of one or more of the regressors.

3  If the number of instruments is less than the number of endogenous regressors, the regression coefficients are **underidentified**, that is, we cannot obtain unique values of the regression coefficients.[32]

---

32  The topic of identification is usually discussed in the context of simultaneous equation models. For details, see Gujarati/Porter, *op cit.*, Chapters 18, 19 and 20.

In the present example, if we use three instruments (*Sm, Sf, siblings*), we have two extra or surplus instruments. How do we find out the validity of the extra instrument? We can proceed as follows:[33]

1 Obtain the IV estimates of the earnings regression coefficients including all the (exogenous) variables in the model plus all the instruments, three in the present case.

2 Obtain residuals from this regression; call them *Res*.

3 Regress *Res* on all the original regressors, including the instruments, and obtain the $R^2$ value from this regression.

4 Multiply the $R^2$ value obtained in Step 3 by the sample size ($n = 540$). That is, obtain $nR^2$. If all the surplus instruments are valid, it can be shown that $nR^2 \sim \chi^2_m$, that is $nR^2$ follows the chi-square distribution with $m$ df, where $m$ is the number of surplus instruments; two in our case.

5 If the estimated chi-square value exceeds the critical chi-square value, say, the 5% level, we conclude that at least one surplus instrument is *not* valid.

We have already given the IV estimates of the earnings regression including the three instruments in Table 19.11. From this regression we obtained the following regression as per Step 3 above. The results are given in Table 19.12.

We need not worry about the coefficients in this table. The important entity here is $R^2$, which is 0.0171. Multiplying this by the sample size of 540, we obtain $nR^2 = 9.234$. The chi-square 1% significance value for 2 df is about 9.21. So the computed chi-square value is highly significant, which suggests that at least one surplus

**Table 19.12  Test of surplus instruments.**

regress Res female wexp ethblack ethhisp sm sf siblings

| Source | SS | df | MS | |
|--------|-----|----|----|----|
| | | | | Number of obs = 540 |
| | | | | F( 7, 532) = 1.32 |
| Model | 2.38452516 | 7 | .340646452 | Prob > F = 0.2366 |
| Residual | 136.894637 | 532 | .257320746 | R-squared = 0.0171 |
| | | | | Adj R-squared = 0.0042 |
| Total | 139.279162 | 539 | .258402898 | Root MSE = .50727 |

| Res | Coef. | Std. Err. | t | P>\|t\| | [95% Conf. Interval] | |
|-----|-------|-----------|---|---------|-----------------------|---|
| female | −.0067906 | .0449329 | −0.15 | 0.880 | −.0950584 | .0814771 |
| wexp | −.0001472 | .0047783 | −0.03 | 0.975 | −.0095339 | .0092396 |
| ethblack | −.0034204 | .0708567 | −0.05 | 0.962 | −.1426136 | .1357728 |
| ethhisp | −.0197119 | .1048323 | −0.19 | 0.851 | −.225648 | .1862241 |
| sm | −.0206955 | .0110384 | −1.87 | 0.061 | −.0423797 | .0009887 |
| sf | .0215956 | .0082347 | 2.62 | 0.009 | .0054191 | .0377721 |
| siblings | .0178537 | .0110478 | 1.62 | 0.107 | −.0038489 | .0395563 |
| _cons | −.0636028 | .1585944 | −0.40 | 0.689 | −.3751508 | .2479452 |

---

33 This discussion is based on R. Carter Hill, William E. Griffiths and Guay C. Lim, *Principles of Econometrics*, 3rd edn, John Wiley & Sons, New York, 2008, pp. 289–90.

instrument is not valid. We could throw away two of the three instruments, as we need just one to identify (i.e. estimate) the parameters. Of course, it is not a good idea to throw away instruments. There are procedures in the literature to use weighted least-squares to obtain consistent IV estimates. We leave the reader to discover more about this in the references (see the Stock and Watson text for additional details).

## 19.12 Regression involving more than one endogenous regressor

So far we have concentrated on a single endogenous regressor. How do we deal with a situation of two or more stochastic regressors? Suppose in our earnings regression we think that the regressor work experience (*wexp*) is also stochastic. Now we have two stochastic regressors, education (*S*) and *wexp*. We can use 2SLS method to handle this case.

Just as one instrument (*Sm*) sufficed to identify the impact of education on earnings, we need another instrument for *wexp*. We have a variable, *age*, in our data. So we can use it to proxy *wexp*. We can treat age as truly exogenous. To estimate the earnings regression with two stochastic regressors, we proceed as follows:

**Stage 1**: We regress each endogenous regressor on all exogenous variables and obtain the estimated values of these regressors.

**Stage 2**: We estimate the earnings function using all exogenous variables and the estimated values of the endogenous regressors from Stage 1.

Actually, we do not have to go trough this two-stage procedure, for packages like *Stata* can do this in one step. The results are given in Table 19.13.

This regression shows that the return to education per incremental year is about 13.4%, *ceteris paribus*. The regressors female and ethblack are individually highly significant, as before, but the work experience variable is not statistically significant.

**Table 19.13 IV estimation with two endogenous regressors.**

. ivregress 2sls lEarnings female ethblack ethhisp (s wexp = sm age)
Instrumental variables (2SLS) regression Number of obs = 540
Wald chi2(5) = 139.51
Prob > chi2 = 0.0000
R-squared = 0.3440
Root MSE = .50987

| lEarnings | Coef. | Std. Err. | z | P>\|z\| | [95% Conf. Interval] | |
|-----------|-------|-----------|-----|-------|----------------------|---|
| s | .1338489 | .0229647 | 5.83 | 0.000 | .0888389 | .1788589 |
| wexp | .0151816 | .0158332 | 0.96 | 0.338 | −.0158509 | .0462141 |
| female | −.3378409 | .0535152 | −6.31 | 0.000 | −.4427287 | −.2329531 |
| ethblack | −.215774 | .0787299 | −2.74 | 0.006 | −.3700818 | −.0614663 |
| ethhisp | −.1252153 | .1063871 | −1.18 | 0.239 | −.3337301 | .0832995 |
| _cons | .8959276 | .4964128 | 1.80 | 0.071 | −.0770236 | 1.868879 |

Instrumented: s wexp
Instruments: female ethblack ethhisp sm age

We have argued that IV estimation will give consistent estimates in case a regressor has serious measurement errors, even though the estimates thus obtained are inefficient. But if measurement errors are absent OLS and IV estimates are both consistent, in which case we should choose OLS because it is more efficient. Thus it behooves us to find out if the instruments chosen for consideration are valid.

A test developed by Durbin, Wu and Hausman (DWH), but popularly known as the **Hausman test**, is one that is used in applied econometrics to test the validity of instruments.[34]

Although the mathematics of the test is involved, the basic idea behind the DWH test is quite simple. We compare the differences between OLS and IV coefficients of all the variables in the model, and obtain, say, $m = (b^{OLS} - b^{IV})$. Under the null hypothesis that $m = 0$, it can be shown that $m$ is distributed as the chi-square distribution with degrees of freedom equal to the number of coefficients compared. If $m$ turns out to be zero, it would suggest that the (stochastic) regressor is not correlated with the error term and we can use OLS in lieu of IV, because OLS estimators are more efficient.

The results of the DWH test based on *Stata* are given in Table 19.14. In this table the column (b) gives the estimates of the model under IV (earniv) and column (B) gives the estimates obtained by OLS (earnols). The next column gives the difference between the two sets of coefficients ($m$) and the last column gives the standard error of the difference between the two estimates.

Table 19.14  **The DWH test of instrument validity for the earnings function.**

hausman earniv earnols1, constant

| | Coefficients | | | |
|---|---|---|---|---|
| | (b) | (B) | (b-B) | sqrt(diag(V_b-V_B)) |
| | earniv | earnols | Difference | S.E. |
| educ | .1431384 | .1082223 | .0349161 | .0273283 |
| female | −.2833126 | −.2701109 | −.0132017 | .0121462 |
| wexp | .0349416 | .029851 | .0050906 | .0040397 |
| ethblack | −.1279853 | −.1165788 | −.0114065 | .0138142 |
| ethhisp | −.0506336 | −.0516381 | .0010045 | .0141161 |
| asvab02 | .0044979 | .0093281 | −.0048302 | .0037962 |
| _cons | .1715716 | .483885 | −.3123135 | .2454617 |

b = consistent under Ho and Ha; obtained from ivreg
B = inconsistent under Ha, efficient under Ho; obtained from regress
Test: Ho: difference in coefficients not systematic
chi2(7) = (b−B)'[(V_b−V_B)^(−1)](b−B)
       = 1.63
Prob>chi2 = 0.9774

34  See Jerry Hausman, Specification tests in econometrics, *Econometrica*, vol. 46, no. 6, 1978, pp. 1251–71; James Durbin, Errors in variables, *Review of the International Statistical Institute*, vol. 22, no. 1, 1954, pp. 23–32, and Wu, De-Min, Alternative tests of independence between stochastic regressors and disturbances, *Econometrica*, vol. 41, no. 4, 1073, 733–50. See also A. Nakamura and M. Nakamura, On the relationship among several specification error tests presented by Durbin, Wu, and Hausman, *Econometrica*, vol. 49, November 1981, pp. 1583–8.

We do not reject the null hypothesis that the OLS and IV estimates are statistically the same, for the probability of obtaining a chi-square value of 1.63 or greater is about 98%. In this case we should choose the OLS estimators, as they are more efficient than the IV estimators.

Although we have not considered all the data given in Table 19.2, based on the model considered here, it seems that the education variable ($S$) is probably not correlated with the error term. But the reader is advised to try other models from the data given in Table 19.2 to see if they arrive at a different conclusion.

## 19.13 Summary and conclusions

One of the critical assumptions of the classical linear regression model is that the error term and regressor(s) are uncorrelated. But if they are correlated, then we call such regressor(s) stochastic or endogenous regressors. In this situation the OLS estimators are biased and the bias does not disappear even if the sample size increases indefinitely. In other words, the OLS estimators are not even consistent. As a result, tests of significance and hypothesis testing become suspect.

If we can find proxy variables such that they are uncorrelated with the error term, but are correlated with the stochastic regressors and are not candidates in their own right in the regression model, we can obtain consistent estimates of the coefficients of the suspected stochastic regressors. Such variables, if available, are called instrumental variables, or instruments for short.

In large samples IV estimators are normally distributed with mean equal to the true population value of the regressor under stress and the variance that involves the population correlation coefficient of the instrument with the suspect stochastic regressor. But in small, or finite, samples, IV estimators are biased and their variances are less efficient than the OLS estimators.

The success of IV depends on how strong they are – that is, how strongly they are correlated with the stochastic regressor. If this correlation is high, we say such IVs are strong, but if it is low, we call them weak instruments. If the instruments are weak, IV estimators may not be normally distributed even in large samples.

Finding "good" instruments is not easy. It requires intuition, introspection, familiarity with prior empirical work, or sometimes just luck. That is why it is important to test explicitly whether the chosen instrument is weak or strong, using tests like the Hausman test.

We need one instrument per stochastic regressor. But if we have more than one instrument for a stochastic regressor, we have a surfeit of instruments and we need to test their validity. Validity here means whether the surfeit instruments have high correlation with the regressor but are uncorrelated with the error term. Fortunately, several tests are available to test for this.

If there is more than one stochastic regressor in a model, we will have to find an instrument(s) for each stochastic regressor. Again, we need to test the instruments for their validity.

One practical reason why IVs have become popular is that we have excellent statistical packages, such as *Stata* and *Eviews*, which make the task of estimating IV regression models very easy.

The topic of IV is still evolving and considerable research is being done on it by various academics. It pays to visit their websites to learn more about the recent developments in the field. Of course, the Internet is a source of information on IV and other statistical techniques.

## Exercises

**19.1** Prove that $\Sigma x_i X_i / \Sigma x_i^2 = 1$, where $x_i = X_i - \overline{X}$.

**19.2** Verify Eq. (19.11).

**19.3** Verify Eq. (19.12).

**19.4** Verify Eq. (19.29).

**19.5** Return to the wage regression discussed in the text. Empirical evidence shows that the wage–work experience (*wexp*) profile is concave – wages increase with work experience, but at a diminishing rate. To see if this is the case, one can add the *wexp*$^2$ variable to the wage function (19.39). If *wexp* is treated as exogenous, so is *wexp*$^2$. Estimate the revised wage function by OLS and IV and compare your results with those shown in the text.

**19.6** Continue with the wage function discussed in the text. The raw data contains information on several variables besides those included in Eq. (19.39). For example, there is information on marital status (single, married, and divorced), ASVAB scores on arithmetic reasoning and word knowledge, faith (none, Catholic, Jewish, Protestant, other), physical characteristics (height and weight), category of employment (Government, private sector, self-employed) and region of the country (North central, North eastern, Southern, and Western). If you want to take into account some of these variables in the wage function, estimate your model, paying due attention to the problem of endogeneity. Show the necessary calculations.

**19.7** In his article, "Instrumental-Variable Estimation of Count Data Models: Applications to Models of Cigarette Smoking Behavior", *Review of Economics and Statistics* (1997, pp. 586–93), John Mullahy wanted to find out if a mother's smoking during pregnancy adversely affected her baby's birth weight. To answer this question he considered several variables, such as natural log of birth weight, gender (1 if the baby is male), parity (number of children the woman has borne), the number of cigarettes the mother smoked during pregnancy, family income, father's education, and mother's education.

The raw data can be found on the website of Michael Murray (http://www.aw-bc.com/murray/). Download this data set and develop your own model of the effect of mother's smoking during pregnancy on the baby's birth weight and compare your results with those of John Mullahy. State your reasons why you think that a standard logit or probit model is sufficient without resorting to IV estimation.

**19.8** Consider the model given in Equations (19.35) and (19.36). Obtain data on the crime rate, law enforcement spending and Gini coefficient for any country of your choice, or for a group of countries, or for a group of states within a country, and estimate the two equations by OLS. How would you use IV to obtain consistent estimates of the parameters of the two models? Show the necessary calculations.

**19.9** Consider the following model:

$$Y_t = B_1 + B_2 X_t + u_t \tag{1}$$

where $Y$ = monthly changes in the AAA bond rate, $X$ = monthly change in the three month Treasury bill rate (TB3), and $u$ = stochastic error term. Obtain monthly data on these variables from any reliable source (e.g. the Federal Reserve Bank of St. Louis) for the past 30 years.

(a) Estimate Eq. (1) by OLS. Show the necessary output.

(b) Since general economic conditions affect changes in both AAA and TB3, we cannot treat TB3 as purely exogenous. These general economic factors may very well be hidden in the error term, $u_t$. So TB3 and the error term are likely to be correlated. How would you use IV estimation to obtain an IV estimator of $B_2$? Which IV would you use to instrument TB3?

(c) Using the instrument you have chosen, obtain the IV estimate of $B2$ and compare this estimate with the OLS estimate of $B_2$ obtained in (a).

(d) Someone suggests to you that you can use past changes in TB3 as an instrument for current TB3. What may be the logic behind this suggestion? Suppose you use TB3 lagged one month as the instrument. Using this instrument, estimate Eq. (1) above and comment on the results.

IV

# Appendix 1

## Data sets used in the text

Entries headed **Table** are available either on the companion website or are included in the text. Entries headed **Section** describe data downloadable from third parties.

**Table 1.1** Wages and related data.
*W* (*Wage*): Hourly wage in dollars, which is the dependent variable.
The explanatory variables, or regressors, are as follows:
*FE* (*Female*): Gender, coded 1 for female, 0 for male
*NW* (*Nonwhite*): Race, coded 1 for nonwhite workers, 0 for white workers
*UN* (*Union*): Union status, coded 1 if in a union job, 0 otherwise
*ED* (*Education*): Education (in years)
*EX* (*Exper*): Potential work experience (in years), defined as age minus years of
    schooling minus 6. (It is assumed that schooling starts at age 6).
*Age*: Age in years

*Wind*: Coded 1 if not paid by the hour

**Table 2.1** Production data for the USA, 2005.
*Q* (Output): Value added, thousands of dollars
*L* (Labor input): Work hours in thousands
*Q* (Capital input): Capital expenditure in thousands of dollars

**Table 2.5** Data on Real GDP, USA, 1960–2007.
*RGDP* = Real GDP

**Table 2.8** Food expenditure and total expenditure for 869 US households in 1995.
*SFDHO* = Share of food expenditure on total expenditure
*EXPEND* = Total expenditure

**Table 2.15**
*GDP-cap* = Per worker GDP (1997)
*Index* = Corruption index (1998)

**Table 3.6** Gross private investment and gross private savings, USA, 1959–2007.
*GPI* = Gross Private Investment, billions of dollars
*GPS* = Gross Private Savings, billions of dollars

**Table 3.10** Quarterly retail fashion sales, 1986-I–1992-IV.
*Sales* = Real sales per thousand square feet of retail space

**Table 3.16** Effects of ban and sugar consumption on diabetes.
*Diabetes* = Diabetes prevalence in a country

*Ban* = 1 is some type of ban on genetically modified goods is present, 0 otherwise
*Sugar Sweet Cap* = Domestic supply of sugar and sweetener per capita, in kg.

**Table 4.2** Mroz data on married women's hours of work: data from *Stata*.
*Hours*: hours worked in 1975 (dependent variable)
*Kidslt6*: number of kids under age 6
*Kidsge6*: number of kids between ages 6–18
*Age*: woman's age in years
*Educ*: years of schooling
*Wage*: estimated wage from earnings
*Hushrs*: hours worked by husband
*Husage*: husband's age
*Huseduc*: husband's years of schooling
*Huswage*: husband's hourly wage, 1975
*Faminc*: family income in 1975
*Mtr*: federal marginal tax rate facing a woman
*motheduc*: mother's years of schooling
*fatheduc*: father's years of schooling
*Unem*: unemployment rate in county of residence
*exper*: actual labor market experience

**Table 4.9** Manpower needs for operating a US Navy bachelor officers' quarters in 25 establishments
*Y*: Monthly manhours needed to operate an establishment
*X1*: Average daily occupancy
*X2*: Monthly average number of check-ins
*X3*: Weekly hours of service desk operation
*X4*: Common use area (in square feet)
*X5*: Number of building wings
*X6*: Operational berthing capacity
*X7*: Number of rooms

**Table 5.1** Data on abortion rates in the 50 States of the USA, 1992.
*State* = name of the state (50 US states)
*ABR* = Abortion rate, number of abortions per thousand women aged 15–44 in 1992
*Religion* = the percentage of a state's population that is Catholic, Southern Baptist, Evangelist or Mormon
*Price* = the average price charged in 1993 in non-hospital facilities for an abortion at 10 weeks with local anesthesia (weighted by the number of abortions performed in 1992)
*Laws* = a variable that takes the value of 1 if a state enforces a law that restricts a minor's access to abortion, 0 otherwise
*Funds* = a variable that takes the value of 1 if state funds are available for use to pay for an abortion under most circumstances, 0 otherwise
*Educ* = the percentage of a state's population that is 25 years or older with a high school degree (or equivalent), 1990
*Income* = disposable income per capita, 1992

*Picket* = the percentage of respondents that reported experiencing picketing with physical contact or blocking of patients

**Table 6.1**  US consumption function, 1947–2000.
*C* = consumption expenditure
*DPI* = real disposable personal income
*W* = real wealth
*R* = real interest rate

**Table 7.8**  Data on cigarette smoking and deaths from various types of cancer in 43 US states and Washington, DC, 1960
*Cig* = Number of cigarettes smoked per capita (in hundreds)
*Deaths* = number of deaths from bladder, lung, kidney and leukemia

**Table 7.11**
*PCE* = Personal Consumption Expenditure, $ billions
*GDPI* = Gross Domestic Private Investment, $ billions
*Income* = Income, $ billions

**Table 8.1**  Data on smoking and other variables.
*Smoker* = 1 for smokers and 0 for non-smokers.
*Age* = age in years
*Education* = number of years of schooling
*Income* = family income
*Pcigs* = price of cigarettes in individual states in 1979

**Table 8.7**  Number of coupons redeemed and the price discount.
*Discount* = Price discount in cents.
*Sample size* = Number of discount coupons issued, 500 in each case
*Redeemed* = Number of coupons redeemed.

**Table 8.8**  Fixed vs. adjustable rate mortgages.
*Adjust* = 1 if an adjustable mortgage is chosen, 0 otherwise
*Fixed rate* = fixed interest rate
*Margin* = (variable rate – fixed rate)
*Yield* = the 10-year Treasury rate less 1-year rate
*Points* = ratio of points on adjustable mortgage to those paid on a fixed rate mortgage
*Networth* = borrower's net worth

**Table 9.1**  Data on school choice.
$Y$ = school choice, no college, a 2-year college or a 4-year college
$X_2$ = *hscath* = 1 if Catholic school graduate, 0 otherwise
$X_3$ = *grades* = average grade in math, English and social studies on a 13 point grading scale, with 1 for the highest grade and 13 for the lowest grade. Therefore, higher grade-point denotes poor academic performance
$X_4$ = *faminc* = gross family income in 1991 in thousands of dollars
$X_5$ = *famsiz* = number of family members
$X_6$ = *parcoll* = 1 if the most educated parent graduated from college or had an advanced degree
$X_7$ = female = 1 if female

$X_8$ = black = 1 if black

**Table 9.3**  Raw data for mode of travel.

*Mode* = Choice: air, train, bus or car
*Time* = Terminal waiting time, 0 for car
*Invc* = In-vehicle cost–cost component
*Invt* = Travel time in vehicle
*GC* = Generalized cost measure
*Hinc* = Household income
*Psize* = Party size in mode chosen

**Section 10.3**  Attitudes toward working mothers: load data from http://www.stata-press.com/data/lf2/ordwarm2.dta.

*response* = 1 (strongly disagree)
= 2 (disagree)
= 3 (agree)
= 4 strongly agree
*yr89* = survey year 1989
*gender* = 1 for male
*race* = 1 if white
*age* = age in years
*ed* = years of education
*prst* = occupational prestige

**Section 10.4**  OLM estimation of application to graduate school: download from http://www.ats.ucla.edu/stat/stata/dae/ologit.dta.

*Intention to go to graduate school* = 1 (unlikely), 2 (somewhat likely) or 3 (very likely)
*pared* = 1 if at least one parent has graduate education
*public* = 1 if the undergraduate institution is a public university
*GPA* = student's grade point average

**Table 10.7**  Mental impairment and related data.

*Mental health* = well, mild symptom formation, moderate symptom formation, and impaired
*SES* = socio-economic status
*Events* = index of life events

**Table 11.1**  Married women's hours of work and related data.
See **Table 4.2**.

**Table 12.1**  Data on patents and R&D expenditure for 181 firms.

*P91* = number of patents granted in 1991
*P90* = number of patents granted in 1990
*LR91* = log of R&D expenditure in 1991
*LR90* = log of R&D expenditure in 1990
*Industry* dummy = 5 dummies for 6 industries
*Country* dummy = 1 for US and 0 for Japan
*R&D* = R&D expenditure

**Table 12.8**  Ray Fair: extramarital affairs.
  *obs* = observation number
  *affair* = 1 if had at least one affair
  *naffair* = number of affairs
  *male* = 1 if male, 0 if female
  *age* = age in years
  *yrsmarr* = number of year married
  *kids* = number of kids
  *education* = years of schooling
  *relig* = religiousness: 1 = anti-religion, 2 = not at all, 3 = slightly, 4 = somewhat, 5 = very religious
  *ratemarr* = self-rating of marriage: 1 = very unhappy, 2 = somewhat unhappy, 3 = average, 4 = happier than average, 5 = very happy

**Table 13.1**  Daily data on euro/dollar exchange rates, 2000–2008.
  *LEX* = Daily data on euro/dollar exchange rates

**Table 13.6**  Daily closing prices of IBM stock January 2000 to August 2002.
  *LCLOSE* = logarithm of daily closing price of IBM

**Table 14.1**  PCE and DPI, USA, quarterly, 1970–2008.
  *PDI* = personal disposable income
  *PCE* = personal consumption expenditure

**Table 14.8**  Monthly 3-month and 6-month Treasury Bill rates, January 1981 to January 2010.
  *TB3* = Three-month Treasury Bill rate
  *TB6* = Six-month Treasury Bill rate

**Table 16.1**  Real per capita PCE and PDI, USA, 1960–2008.
  *PCE* = Per capita personal consumption expenditure
  *PDI* = Per capita personal disposable income

**Table 17.1**  Charitable giving.
  *Charity*: The sum of cash and other property contributions, excluding carry-overs from previous years
  *Income*: Adjusted gross income
  *Price*: One minus the marginal income tax rate; marginal tax rate is defined on income prior to contributions
  *Age*: A dummy variable equal to 1 if the taxpayer is over 64, and 0 otherwise
  *MS*: A dummy variable equal to 1 if the taxpayer is married, 0 otherwise
  *DEPS*: Number of dependents claimed on the tax return

**Table 18.1**  Modeling recidivism.
  1. *black* = 1 if black
  2. *alcohol* = 1 if alcohol problems
  3. *drugs* = 1 if drug history
  4. *super* = 1 if release supervised
  5. *married* = 1 if married when incarc.
  6. *felon* = 1 if felony sentence
  7. *workprg* = 1 if in N.C. pris. work prg.

8. *property* = 1 if property crime

9. *person* = 1 if crime against person

10. *priors* = # prior convictions

11. *educ* = years of schooling

12. *rules* = # rules violations in prison

13. *age* in months

14. *tserved* = time served, rounded to months

15. *follow length* = follow period, months

16. *durat* = max(time until return, follow)

17. *cens* = 1 if duration right censored

18. *ldurat* = log(durat)

**Table 19.1** Data on crime rate and expenditure on police, USA, 1992.
*Crime rate* = number of crimes per 100,000 population
*Expenditure* = police expenditure in dollars

**Section 19.7** Earnings and educational attainment of 540 youths in USA.
*ln Earn* = log of hourly earnings in $
*S* = years of schooling (highest grade completed in 2002)
*Wexp* = total out-of school work experience in years as of the 2002 interview
*Gender* = 1 for female and 0 for men
*Ethblack* = 1 for blacks
*Ethhis* = 1 for Hispanic; non-black and non-Hispanic being the left-out, or reference, category

# Appendix 2

## Statistical appendix

This appendix serves as a primer in basic statistical theory and should not substitute for a comprehensive background in statistics. The basic tools covered here are needed to understand the econometric theory described in the book. A brief overview of probability, random variables, probability distributions and their characteristics, and statistical inference are given. Four distributions will be mentioned that are particularly useful in econometrics: (1) the normal distribution; (2) the $t$ distribution; (3) the chi-square ($\chi^2$) distribution; and (4) the $F$ distribution.

## A.1 Summation notation

Several mathematical expressions are more practically expressed in shorthand, as with the Greek capital letter sigma ($\Sigma$) used for summation as such:

$$\sum_{i=1}^{n} X_i = X_1 + X_2 + X_3 + \ldots + X_n$$

The expression $\sum_{i=1}^{n} X_i$ means to take the sum of the variable $X$ from 1 (the first value) to $n$ (the last value).[1] Identical forms of this expression include

$$\sum_{i=1}^{n} X_i, \sum X_i \text{ and } \sum_{x} X.$$

### Properties of $\Sigma$

1  $\sum_{i=1}^{n} k = nk$, where $k$ is a constant.

   For example, $\sum_{i=1}^{4} 2 = (4)(2) = 8$

2  $\sum_{i=1}^{n} kX_i = k\sum_{i=1}^{n} X_i$

---

1 This appendix was written with the help of Professor Inas Kelly. In general, a capital letter with a subscript $i$ identifies it as a variable, able to take many values, rather than a constant.

For example, $\sum_{i=1}^{2} 2X_i = 2\sum_{i=1}^{2} X_i = (2)(X_1 + X_2) = 2X_1 + 2X_2$

**3** $\sum_{i=1}^{n}(X_i + Y_i) = \sum_{i=1}^{n} X_i + \sum_{i=1}^{n} Y_i$ where $X_i$ and $Y_i$ are variables.

For example, $\sum_{i=1}^{2}(X_i + Y_i) = \sum_{i=1}^{2} X_i + \sum_{i=1}^{2} Y_i = X_1 + X_2 + Y_1 + Y_2$

**4** $\sum_{i=1}^{n}(a + bX_i) = na + b\sum_{i=1}^{n} X_i$ where $a$ and $b$ are constants.

For example, $\sum_{i=1}^{3}(4 + 5X_i) = (3)(4) + (5)\sum_{i=1}^{3} X_i = 12 + 5X_1 + 5X_2 + 5X_3$

## A.2  Experiments

### Key concepts

▲ A **statistical** or **random experiment** refers to any process of observation or measurement that has more than one possible outcome and for which there is uncertainty about which outcome will materialize.

▲ The set of all possible outcomes of an experiment is referred to as the **population** or **sample space**.

▲ An **event** is a particular collection of outcomes and is a subset of the sample space. Events are *mutually exclusive* if the occurrence of one event prevents the simultaneous occurrence of another event. Two events are *equally likely* if the probabilities of their occurrences are the same. Events are *collectively exhaustive* if they exhaust all possible outcomes of an experiment.

▲ A variable whose numerical value is determined by the outcome of an experiment is called a **random**, or **stochastic, variable**. Random variables are generally denoted by capital letters (such as $X$, $Y$ and $Z$), and the values taken by these variables are typically denoted by small letters (such as $x$, $y$ and $z$). A **discrete random variable** takes a finite number of values or an infinite number of values pertaining to whole numbers. A **continuous random variable** takes any value in some interval of values.

▲ The **probability** that an event $A$ occurs, if an experiment results in $n$ mutually exclusive and equally likely outcomes and if $m$ of these outcomes are favorable to $A$, is $m/n$. That is, $P(A) = m/n = $ (number of outcomes favorable to $A$)/(total number of outcomes). Note that this classical definition of probability is not valid if the outcomes of an experiment are not finite or not equally likely.

These concepts will be clarified with a coin toss example.

### *Coin toss example*

Two fair coins are tossed. Let H denote a head and T denote a tail. The possible outcomes are two heads, two tails, one head and one tail, or one tail and one head, where each of these four outcomes is an event. In other words, the sample space is S = {HH,

HT, TH, TT}. Since it is not possible to, say, toss both HH *and* HT, the events are considered mutually exclusive. The probability of each event occurring is $\frac{1}{4}$. The four events are therefore equally likely. Since the four probabilities add up to 100%, or 1, the events in the sample space are collectively exhaustive.

## A.3    Empirical definition of probability

Table A.1 gives information on the distribution of ages for ten children in an orphanage.

This table is more concisely presented as shown in Table A.2. Note that in this table, the tabulated frequencies for a given age are combined.

A **frequency distribution**, as shown in Tables A.1 and A.2, shows how the random variable *age* is distributed. The second column shows the **absolute frequency**, the number of occurrences for a given event. The numbers in this column must add up to the total number of occurrences (10 in the present case). The **relative frequency**, shown in the third column, is equal to the absolute frequency divided by the total number of occurrences. The numbers in this column must add up to 1, as shown in the table.

The **empirical**, or **relative frequency**, **definition of probability**, involves approximating probabilities using relative frequencies, provided the number of observations

**Table A.1  Distribution of ages for ten children.**

| Age | Absolute frequency | Relative frequency |
|-----|--------------------|--------------------|
| 5   | 1                  | 1/10               |
| 7   | 1                  | 1/10               |
| 7   | 1                  | 1/10               |
| 7   | 1                  | 1/10               |
| 8   | 1                  | 1/10               |
| 8   | 1                  | 1/10               |
| 8   | 1                  | 1/10               |
| 8   | 1                  | 1/10               |
| 9   | 1                  | 1/10               |
| 10  | 1                  | 1/10               |
|     |                    | $\Sigma = 1$       |

**Table A.2  Distribution of ages for ten children (concise).**

| Age | Absolute frequency | Relative frequency |
|-----|--------------------|--------------------|
| 5   | 1                  | 1/10               |
| 7   | 3                  | 3/10               |
| 8   | 4                  | 4/10               |
| 9   | 1                  | 1/10               |
| 10  | 1                  | 1/10               |
|     |                    | $\Sigma = 1$       |

used in calculating the relative frequencies is reasonably large. Thus, for $n$ observations, if $m$ are favorable to event $A$, then $P(A)$, the probability of event $A$, is the ratio $m/n$, provided $n$ is reasonably large. Unlike the classical definition, the outcomes do not have to be mutually exclusive and equally likely.

## A.4    Probabilities: properties, rules, and definitions

1  $0 \leq P(A) \leq 1$

2  $P(A + B + C + \ldots) = P(A) + P(B) + P(C) + \ldots$
if $A$, $B$, $C$, $\ldots$ are mutually exclusive events.

3  $P(A + B + C + \ldots) = P(A) + P(B) + P(C) + \ldots = 1$
if $A$, $B$, $C$, $\ldots$ are mutually exclusive and collectively exhaustive events.

4  $P(ABC\ldots) = P(A)P(B)P(C), \ldots,$
if $A$, $B$, $C$, $\ldots$ are statistically independent events, meaning that the probability of their occurring together is equal to the product of their individual probabilities.[2] $P(ABC\ldots)$ is referred to as a **joint probability**.

5  $P(A + B) = P(A) + P(B) - P(AB),$
if $A$ and $B$ are not mutually exclusive events.

6  The complement of $A$, $A'$, is defined as:

$$P(A + A') = 1 \quad \text{and} \quad P(AA') = 0$$

7  $P(A \mid B) = P(AB)/P(B); P(B) > 0,$
where $P(A \mid B)$ is referred to as a conditional probability.

An application of conditional probability is provided by **Bayes' Theorem**, which states:

$$P(A \mid B) = \frac{P(B \mid A)P(A)}{P(B \mid A)P(A) + P(B \mid A')P(A')}$$

## A.5    Probability distributions of random variables

### Discrete random variables

The number of values of a discrete random variable is finite or countably infinite. Let the function f, the **probability mass function** (PMF), be defined by:

$$P(X = x_i) = f(x_i), \quad i = 1, 2, \ldots$$

Note that

$$0 \leq f(x_i) \leq 1$$

$$\sum_x f(x_i) = 1$$

---

2  Note that if $A$ and $B$ are mutually exclusive events, then $P(AB) = 0$.

## Continuous random variables

The number of values of a continuous random variable is infinite and defined over an interval or range. Let the function, $f$, the **probability density function** (PDF), be defined by:

$$P(x_1 < X < x_2) = \int_{x_1}^{x_2} f(x)dx$$

where $x_1 < x_2$ and $\int$ is the integral symbol of calculus, equivalent to the summation symbol $\Sigma$ but used for a continuous random variable in lieu of a discrete random variable.

Note that

$$\int_{-\infty}^{\infty} f(x)dx = 1$$

The **cumulative distribution function** (CDF), denoted by a capital $F(x)$, is associated with the PMF or PDF of a random variable as follows:

$$F(x) = P(X \leq x),$$

where $P(X \leq x)$ is the probability that a random variable $X$ takes a value less than or equal to $x$. (Note that for a continuous random variable, the probability that a random variable takes the exact value of $x$ is zero.)

## Properties of CDF

1  $F(-\infty) = 0$ and $F(\infty) = 1$, where $F(-\infty)$ and $F(\infty)$ are the limits of $F(x)$ as $x$ tends to $-\infty$ and $\infty$, respectively.

2  $F(x)$ is nondecreasing such that if $x_2 > x_1$, then $F(x_2) \geq F(x_1)$.

3  $P(X \geq k) = 1 - F(k)$, where $k$ is a constant.

4  $P(x_1 \leq X \leq x_2) = F(x_2) - F(x_1)$.

## Multivariate probability density functions

Thus far, we have been dealing with single variable (univariate) probability density functions, since we have been dealing with one variable, $X$. Now we will introduce $Y$ and give an example of the simplest multivariate PDF, a bivariate PDF. Table A.3 gives information on two random variables, average wage ($X$) and the number of DVDs owned ($Y$), for 200 individuals. The numbers shown in this table are absolute frequencies.

The relative frequencies for the values provided in Table A.3 are given in Table A.4. Note that all the probabilities within the table, called **joint probabilities**, or $f(X,Y)$, must add up to 1, or 100%.

Note the following:

1  $f(X,Y) \geq 0$ for all $X$ and $Y$.

2  As noted above, $\sum_x \sum_y f(X,Y) = 1$.

**Table A.3  Frequency distribution of two random variables.**

|  |  | X = Wage | | | |
|---|---|---|---|---|---|
|  |  | $10 | $15 | $20 | f(Y) |
| Y = Number of DVDs owned | 0 | 20 | 10 | 10 | 40 |
|  | 25 | 60 | 20 | 20 | 100 |
|  | 50 | 0 | 20 | 40 | 60 |
|  | f(X) | 80 | 50 | 70 | 200 |

**Table A.4  Relative frequency distribution of two random variables.**

|  |  | X = Wage | | | |
|---|---|---|---|---|---|
|  |  | $10 | $15 | $20 | f(Y) |
| Y = Number of DVDs owned | 0 | 0.10 | 0.05 | 0.05 | 0.20 |
|  | 25 | 0.30 | 0.10 | 0.10 | 0.50 |
|  | 50 | 0.00 | 0.10 | 0.20 | 0.30 |
|  | f(X) | 0.40 | 0.25 | 0.35 | 1.0 |

3  Marginal probabilities in Table A.4 are denoted by $f(X)$ and $f(Y)$. That is, the probability that $X$ assumes a given value regardless of the values taken by $Y$ is called the **marginal probability** of $X$, and the distribution of these probabilities is the marginal PDF of $X$. Therefore:

$$f(X) = \sum_{y} f(X,Y) \text{ for all } X$$

and

$$f(Y) = \sum_{x} f(X,Y) \text{ for all } Y.$$

4  **Conditional probability** refers to the probability that one random variable assumes a particular value, given that the other random variable has assumed a particular value. It is equal to the joint probability divided by the marginal probability. In shorthand:

$$f(Y \mid X) = \frac{f(X,Y)}{f(X)} \quad \text{and} \quad f(X \mid Y) = \frac{f(X,Y)}{f(Y)}$$

For example, in Table A.4, the probability that the number of DVDs owned is equal to 50 given that average wage is $20 is expressed as:[3]

$$f(Y = 50 \mid X = 20) = \frac{f(X = 20, Y = 50)}{f(X = 20)} = \frac{0.20}{0.35} = 0.5714$$

---

3  Note that this conditional probability of 57% is higher than the unconditional probability of having 50 DVDs, $P(Y = 50)$, of 30%, which is expected since we would expect people with higher wages to own more DVDs. As we will see shortly, this means that $X$ and $Y$ in this case are not statistically independent.

5  Two random variables X and Y are said to be **statistically independent** if and only if their joint PDF can be expressed as the product of their marginal PDFs for all combinations of X and Y values. In other words:

$$f(X,Y) = f(X)f(Y) \text{ for all } X \text{ and } Y.$$

We can see that in the example above, wage (X) and number of DVDs owned (Y) are *not* statistically independent.

## A.6    Expected value and variance

The **expected value** of a random variable, also called the first moment of the probability distribution, is the weighted average of its possible values, or the sum of products of the values taken by the random variable and their corresponding probabilities. It is also referred to as the population mean value, and is expressed as:

$$E(X) = \mu_x = \Sigma X f(X)$$

Using the values in Table A.2, the average age in the orphanage is:

$$\mu_x = \sum_X xf(X) = 5(0.10) + 7(0.30) + 8(0.40) + 9(0.10) + 10(0.10) = 7.7$$

Using the values in Table A.4, the average wage for the 200 individuals is:

$$\mu_x = \sum_X xf(X) = 10(0.40) + 15(0.25) + 20(0.35) = 14.75$$

The average number of DVDs for the 200 individuals is:

$$\mu_y = \sum_Y yf(Y) = (0)(0.20) + (25)(0.50) + (50)(0.30) = 27.5.$$

Note that a simple average is a special case of the more general form above, in which the weights or probabilities f(X) are equal for all values of X.

### Properties of expected value

1  $E(a) = a$, where $a$ is a constant.

2  $E(X + Y) = E(X) + E(Y)$

3  $E(X/Y) \neq E(X)/E(Y)$

4  $E(XY) \neq E(X)E(Y)$, unless X and Y are statistically independent random variables.[4]

5  $E(X^2) \neq [E(X)]^2$

6  $E(bX) = bE(X)$, where $b$ is a constant.

7  $E(aX + b) = aE(X) + E(b) = aE(X) + b$

Thus $E$ is a linear operator.

---

4  Careful: if X and Y are statistically independent, then $E(XY) = E(X)E(Y)$. Yet it does not follow that if $E(XY) = E(X)E(Y)$, then X and Y are statistically independent. You would still need to check that $f(X,Y) = f(X)f(Y)$ for all values of X and Y.

The expected value of two random variables in a bivariate PDF is expressed as:

$$E(XY) = \mu_{xy} = \sum_x \sum_y XY f(X,Y)$$

Using the values in Table A.4, the expected value of wage and DVDs for the 200 individuals is:

$$\mu_{xy} = \sum_x \sum_y XY f(X,Y)$$

$$= (10)(0)(0.10) + (10)(25)(0.30) + (10)(50)(0.00)$$

$$+ (15)(0)(0.05) + (15)(25)(0.10) + (15)(50)(0.10)$$

$$+ (20)(0)(0.05) + (20)(25)(0.10) + (20)(50)(0.20) = 437.5$$

A **conditional expected value** (as opposed to the unconditional one outlined above) is an expected value of one variable conditional on the other variable taking on a particular value, and is defined using conditional probability as:

$$E(X \mid Y) = \sum_X x f(X \mid Y)$$

Using the values in Table A.4, the expected value of wage given that the number of DVDs is 50 is:

$$E(X \mid Y = 50) = \sum_X x f(X \mid Y = 50) = \sum_X x \frac{f(X, Y = 50)}{f(Y = 50)}$$

$$= (10)\left(\frac{0.0}{0.3}\right) + (15)\left(\frac{0.1}{0.3}\right) + (20)\left(\frac{0.2}{0.3}\right) = 18.333$$

Imagine a sample is picked at random from the population we have been considering so far. The **sample mean** is defined as:

$$\bar{X} = \sum_{i=1}^{n} \frac{X_i}{n}$$

Note that this is a simple mean as each observation is given the same probability, equal to $1/n$. The sample mean is known as an estimator of $E(X)$. An **estimator** is a rule or formula that tells us how to go about estimating a population quantity.

The **variance** of a random variable, also called the second moment of the probability distribution, is a measure of dispersion around the mean, expressed as follows:

$$\text{var}(X) = \sigma_x^2 = E(X - \mu_x)^2 = \Sigma(X - \mu_x)^2 \cdot f(X)$$

Using the values in Table A.2, the variance of age in the orphanage is:

$$\sigma_x^2 = \sum_X (X - \mu_x)^2 f(X) = (5 - 7.7)^2 (0.10) + (7 - 7.7)^2 (0.30)$$

$$+ (8 - 7.7)^2 (0.40) + (9 - 7.7)^2 (0.10) + (10 - 7.7)^2 (0.10) = 1.61$$

Using the values in Table A.4, the variance of wage for the 200 individuals is:

$$\sigma_x^2 = \sum_X (X - \mu_x) f(X) = (10 - 14.75)^2 (0.40)$$

$$+ (15 - 14.75)^2 (0.25) + (20 - 14.75)^2 (0.35) = 18.688$$

**Properties of variance**

1  $\text{var}(k) = 0$, where $k$ is a constant.

2  $\text{var}(X + Y) = \text{var}(X) + \text{var}(Y)$, and $\text{var}(X - Y) = \text{var}(X) + \text{var}(Y)$, where $X$ and $Y$ are statistically independent random variables.

3  $\text{var}(X + b) = \text{var}(X)$, where $b$ is a constant.

4  $\text{var}(aX) = a^2\text{var}(X)$, where $a$ is a constant.

5  $\text{var}(aX + b) = a^2\text{var}(X)$, where $a$ and $b$ are constants.

6  $\text{var}(aX + bY) = a^2\text{var}(X) + b^2\text{var}(Y)$,
   where $X$ and $Y$ are statistically independent random variables, and $a$ and $b$ are constants.

7  $\text{var}(X) = E(X^2) - [E(X)]^2$, where $E(X^2) = \sum_X X^2 f(X)$.

The **standard deviation** of a random variable, $\sigma_x$, is equal to the square root of the variance. Using the values in Table A.2, the standard deviation of age in the orphanage is:

$$\sigma_x = \sqrt{\sigma_x^2} = \sqrt{1.61} = 1.269$$

The **sample variance** is an estimator of the population variance, $\sigma_x^2$, and is expressed as:

$$S_x^2 = \sum_{i=1}^{n} \frac{(X_i - \bar{X})^2}{n-1}$$

The denominator of the sample variance represents the **degrees of freedom**, equal to $(n - 1)$ since we lose one degree of freedom through calculating the sample mean using the same sample.

The **sample standard deviation** of a random variable, $S_x$, is equal to the square root of the sample variance.

## A.7    Covariance and correlation coefficient

The **covariance** is a measure of how two variables vary or move together in a multivariate PDF and is expressed as:

$$\text{cov}(X, Y) = \sigma_{xy} = E[(X - \mu_x)(Y - \mu_y)] = \sum_x \sum_y (X - \mu_x)(Y - \mu_y)f(X, Y)$$

Alternatively, we can write:

$$\text{cov}(X, Y) = \sigma_{xy} = E(XY) - \mu_x\mu_y = \sum_x \sum_y XYf(X, Y) - \mu_x\mu_y$$

Using the values in Table A.4, the covariance between wage for the 200 individuals ($X$) and number of DVDs owned ($Y$) is:

$$\sigma_{xy} = \sum_x \sum_y XYf(X, Y) - \mu_x\mu_y = (437.5) - (14.75)(27.5) = 31.875$$

### Properties of covariance

1  $E(XY) = E(X)E(Y) = \mu_x\mu_y = 0$,

   if $X$ and $Y$ are statistically independent random variables.

2  $\text{cov}(a + bX, c + dY) = bd\,\text{cov}(X,Y)$, where $a$, $b$, $c$ and $d$ are constants.

3  $\text{cov}(X,X) = \text{var}(X)$

4  $\text{var}(X + Y) = \text{var}(X) + \text{var}(Y) + 2\,\text{cov}(X,Y)$

   and

   $\text{var}(X - Y) = \text{var}(X) + \text{var}(Y) - 2\,\text{cov}(X,Y)$

Since the covariance is unbounded $[-\infty < \sigma_{xy} < \infty]$, a more useful measure in showing the relationship between two variables is the **correlation coefficient**, which takes a value between $-1$ and $1$ and is expressed as:

$$\rho = \frac{\text{cov}(X,Y)}{\sigma_x\sigma_y}$$

### Properties of correlation coefficient

1  The correlation coefficient always has the same sign as the covariance.

2  The correlation coefficient is a measure of linear relationship between two variables.

3  $-1 \leq \rho \leq 1$

4  The correlation coefficient is a pure number, devoid of any units.

5  If two variables are statistically independent, then their covariance and in turn their correlation coefficient is zero. *However*, if the correlation coefficient between two variables is zero, that does not necessarily mean that the two variables are statistically independent.

6  Correlation does not necessarily imply causality.

The **sample covariance** is an estimator of the population covariance, $\sigma_{xy}$, and is expressed as:

$$S_{xy} = \frac{\Sigma[(X_i - \overline{X})(Y_i - \overline{Y})]}{n-1}$$

Similarly, the **sample correlation coefficient** is an estimator of the population correlation coefficient, $\rho$, and is expressed as:

$$r = \frac{S_{xy}}{S_x S_y}$$

## A.8    Normal distribution

The most important probability distribution is the bell-shaped **normal distribution**. A normally distributed random variable is expressed as:

$$X \sim N(\mu_x, \sigma_x^2)$$

with a PDF distributed as:

$$f(x) = \frac{1}{\sigma_x \sqrt{2\pi}} \exp{-\frac{1}{2}\left(\frac{X - \mu_x}{\sigma_x}\right)^2}$$

## Properties of the normal distribution:

1  The normal distribution curve is symmetrical around its mean value $\mu_x$.

2  The PDF of a normally distributed random variable is highest at its mean value and tails off at its extremities.

3  Approximately 68% of the area under the normal curve lies between the values of $(\mu_x \pm \sigma_x)$; approximately 95% of the area lies between $(\mu_x \pm 2\sigma_x)$; and approximately 99.7% of the area lies between $(\mu_x \pm 3\sigma_x)$. The total area under the curve is 100%, or 1.

4  A normal distribution is fully described by its two parameters, $\mu_x$ and $\sigma_x$. Once the values of these two parameters are known, it is possible to calculate the probability of $X$ lying within a certain interval from the PDF of the normal distribution given above (or through using tables provided in a standard statistics textbook).

5  A linear combination of two normally distributed random variables is itself normally distributed.

If $X \sim N(\mu_x, \sigma_x^2)$ and $Y \sim N(\mu_y, \sigma_y^2)$, and if $W = aX + bY$, then

$$W \sim N(a\mu_x + b\mu_y, a^2\sigma_x^2 + b^2\sigma_y^2 + 2ab\sigma_{xy})$$

It is often useful to standardize variables that are normally distributed for ease of comparison. The variable $X$ is standardized by using the following transformation:

$$Z = \frac{X - \mu_x}{\sigma_x}$$

The resulting variable is normally distributed with a mean of zero and a variance of 1:

$$Z \sim N(0, 1)$$

The **Central Limit Theorem** (CLT) states that if $X_1, X_2, X_3, ..., X_n$ is a random sample drawn from *any* population (not necessarily a normally distributed one) with mean $\mu_x$ and variance $\sigma_x^2$, the sample mean $\overline{X}$ tends to be normally distributed with mean $\mu_x$ and variance $\sigma_x^2/n$ as the sample size increases indefinitely. That is,

$$\overline{X} \sim N\left(\mu_x, \frac{\sigma_x^2}{n}\right)$$

We would standardize $\overline{X}$ by using the following transformation:

$$Z = \frac{\overline{X} - \mu_x}{\sigma_x / \sqrt{n}} \sim N(0,1)$$

## A.9   Student's $t$ distribution

The $t$ distribution is used when the population variance is unknown. In the standardization of $\overline{X}$, the sample standard deviation, $S_x$, is used rather than the population standard deviation, $\sigma_x$:

$$t = \frac{\overline{X} - \mu_x}{S_x / \sqrt{n}} \sim N\left(0, \frac{k}{k-2}\right)$$

### Properties of the $t$ distribution

1. The $t$ distribution is symmetric around its mean.

2. The mean of the $t$ distribution is zero and its variance is $k/(k-2)$ when $k > 2$, where $k$ is equal to degrees of freedom, here equal to $n - 1$ (the denominator of the formula for sample variance).

3. Since the variance of the standard $t$ distribution is larger than the variance of the standard normal distribution, it has larger spread in the tails of the distribution. But as the number of observations increases, the $t$ distribution converges to the normal distribution.

## A.10   Chi-square ($\chi^2$) distribution

While the $Z$ and $t$ distributions are used for the sampling distributions of the sample mean, $\overline{X}$, the **chi-square ($\chi^2$) distribution** is used for the sampling distribution of the sample variance,

$$S_x^2 = \sum_{i=1}^{n} \frac{(X_i - \overline{X})^2}{n-1}$$

The square of a standard normal variable is distributed as a chi-square ($\chi^2$) probability distribution with one degree of freedom:

$$Z^2 = \chi^2_{(1)}$$

Now let $Z_1$, $Z_2$, $Z_3$, ..., $Z_k$ be $k$ independent standardized random variables (each with a mean of zero and a variance of one). Then the sum of the squares of these $Z$s follows a chi-square distribution:

$$\sum Z_i^2 = Z_1^2 + Z_2^2 + Z_3^2 + ... + Z_k^2 \sim \chi^2_{(k)}$$

### Properties of the chi-square distribution

1. Unlike the normal distribution, the chi-square distribution takes only positive values, and ranges from zero to infinity.

2. Unlike the normal distribution, the chi-square distribution is a skewed distribution yet becomes more symmetrical and approaches the normal distribution as degrees of freedom increase.

3. The expected value of a chi-square random variable is $k$ and its variance is $2k$, where $k$ is equal to degrees of freedom.

4  If $W_1$ and $W_2$ are two independent chi-square variables with $k_1$ and $k_2$ degrees of freedom, respectively, then their sum, $(W_1 + W_2)$, is also a chi-square variable with degrees of freedom equal to $(k_1 + k_2)$.

## A.11  *F* distribution

The *F* distribution, also known as a variance ratio distribution, is useful in comparing the sample variances of two normally distributed random variables that are independent of one another. Let $X_1, X_2, X_3, ..., X_n$ be a random sample of size *n* from a normal population with mean $\mu_x$ and variance $\sigma_x^2$, and let $Y_1, Y_2, Y_3, ..., Y_m$ be a random sample of size *m* from a normal population with mean $\mu_y$ and variance $\sigma_y^2$. The following ratio, used in determining whether the two population variances are equal, is distributed as an *F* distribution with $(n - 1)$ and $(m - 1)$ degrees of freedom in the numerator and denominator, respectively:

$$F = \frac{S_x^2}{S_y^2} = \frac{\Sigma_{i=1}^{n}(X_i - \overline{X})^2 / (n-1)}{\Sigma_{i=1}^{m}(Y_i - \overline{Y})^2 / (m-1)} \sim F_{n-1, m-1}$$

### Properties of the *F* distribution

1  Like the chi-square distribution, the *F* distribution is also skewed to the right and ranges between zero and infinity.

2  Like the *t* and chi-square distributions, the *F* distribution approaches the normal distribution as $k_1$ and $k_2$, the degrees of freedom for the numerator and denominator, respectively, increase in value.

3  The square of a *t*-distributed random variable with *k* degrees of freedom follows an *F* distribution with one degree of freedom in the numerator and *k* degrees of freedom in the denominator:

$$t_k^2 = F_{1,k}$$

4  For large denominator df, the numerator df times the *F* value is approximately equal to the chi-square value with the numerator df. That is

$$mF_{m,n} = \chi_\mu^2 \text{ as } n \rightarrow \infty.$$

where *m* and *n* are numerator and denominator df.

## A.12  Statistical inference

The concept of **statistical inference** refers to the drawing of conclusions about the nature of some population on the basis of a random sample that has been drawn from that population. This requires estimation and hypothesis testing. **Estimation** involves collecting a random sample from the population and obtaining an estimator, such as $\overline{X}$ (also known as a sample statistic). **Hypothesis testing** involves assessing the veracity of a value based on a prior judgment or expectation about what that value may be. For example, we may assume that the average female height in a population is 5'5", or 165 centimeters, and choose a random sample of females from the population to see whether or not the average height from that sample is *statistically different* from 165 cm. This is the essence of hypothesis testing. If this is what we are testing, we can set up the null ($H_0$) and alternative ($H_1$) hypotheses as follows:

$$H_0: \mu_x = 165 \text{ cm}$$

$$H_1: \mu_x \neq 165 \text{ cm}$$

As we will see shortly, this is a two-tailed test. If we are interested in testing whether or not the true population mean is *less than* 165 cm instead of simply not being equal to 165 cm, we can set up the null and alternative hypotheses as follows:

$$H_0: \mu_x = 165 \text{ cm}$$

$$H_1: \mu_x < 165 \text{ cm}$$

As we will see shortly, this is a one-tailed test.

There are two methods we can use for hypothesis testing – interval estimation and point estimation. In **interval estimation**, we set up a range around $\overline{X}$ where the true (population) value of the mean is likely to lie. The created interval is referred to as a **confidence interval**, where our confidence in our conclusions is based on the probability of committing Type I error, the probability of rejecting the null hypothesis when it is true.[5] Type I error is often denoted by $\alpha$. The interval is defined as:

$$P(L \leq \mu_x \leq U) = 1 - \alpha, \text{ where } 0 < \alpha < 1.$$

In calculating the lower ($L$) and upper ($U$) limits, recall that[6]

$$t = \frac{\overline{X} - \mu_x}{S_x / \sqrt{n}}$$

In creating a 95% confidence interval, the **critical $t$ value** for a reasonably large number of degrees of freedom is equal to 1.96.[7] Since the $t$ distribution is symmetrical, the $t$ values are −1.96 and 1.96. We can therefore create the interval as:

$$P(-1.96 \leq t \leq 1.96)$$

$$P\left(-1.96 \leq \frac{\overline{X} - \mu_x}{S_x / \sqrt{n}} \leq 1.96\right)$$

Rearranging, we have:

$$P\left(\overline{X} - 1.96 \frac{S_x}{\sqrt{n}} \leq \mu_x \leq \overline{X} + 1.96 \frac{S_x}{\sqrt{n}}\right) = 0.95$$

In **point estimation**, a single numerical value is used, such as $\overline{X}$, and is tested against a proposed (hypothesized) population mean. For example, if we collect

---

5  Type II error is the probability of not rejecting the null hypothesis when it is false, which is generally believed to be the milder of the two errors. (If someone is facing the death penalty, would you rather execute an innocent person – akin to Type I error – or not execute a guilty person?) It is not possible to minimize both types of error without increasing the number of observations. The power of the test, which is sometimes calculated, is equal to one minus the probability of committing Type II error.

6  We use the $t$ distribution rather than the $Z$ distribution because we generally assume that the population variance is unknown.

7  This value is obtained from the $t$ table, available in standard statistics textbooks.

information on heights for a random sample of 21 females and find the mean height, $\overline{X}$, to be 162 cm, with a sample standard deviation of 2, we can test the above two-tailed hypothesis using an $\alpha$ value of 5% by calculating the actual $t$ value and comparing it to the critical $t$ value (of 2.086 for 20 degrees of freedom). The actual $t$ value is:

$$t = \frac{\overline{X} - \mu_x}{S_x / \sqrt{n}} = \frac{162 - 165}{2 / \sqrt{20}} = -6.708$$

Since the value of −6.708 is greater in absolute value than 2.086, we can reject the null hypothesis (at the 95% confidence level) that the population mean is 165 cm, in favor of the alternative hypothesis that it is *not* 165 cm.

A 95% confidence interval around the sample mean would look like this:

$$P\left( \overline{X} - 1.96 \frac{S_x}{\sqrt{n}} \leq \mu_x \leq \overline{X} + 1.96 \frac{S_x}{\sqrt{n}} \right) = 0.95$$

$$P\left( 162 - 2.086 \frac{2}{\sqrt{20}} \leq \mu_x \leq 162 + 2.086 \frac{2}{\sqrt{20}} \right) = 0.95$$

$$P(161.067 \leq \mu_x \leq 162.933) = 0.95$$

Note that 165 lies outside the confidence interval. Thus, based on the 95% confidence interval one can reject the null hypothesis that the true population height is 165 cm in favor of the alternative hypothesis that the true population height is *not equal to* 165 cm.

If we were to conduct a one-tailed test for this example rather than a two-tailed test, the critical $t$ value (from the table) would be 1.725, and we would again reject the null hypothesis in favor of the alternative hypothesis that the population mean is *less than* 165 cm.

A 95% confidence interval for this one-tailed test would look like this:

$$P\left( -\infty < \mu_x \leq \overline{X} + 1.725 \frac{S_x}{\sqrt{n}} \right) = 0.95$$

$$P\left( -\infty < \mu_x \leq 162 + 1.725 \frac{2}{\sqrt{20}} \right) = 0.95$$

$$P(-\infty < \mu_x \leq 162.771) = 0.95$$

Note that 165 lies outside the confidence interval. Thus, based on the 95% confidence interval one can reject the null hypothesis that the true population height is 165 cm in favor of the alternative hypothesis that the true population height is *less* than 165 cm.

## Properties of point estimators

1 *Linearity*: An estimator is said to be a linear estimator if it is a linear function of the observations. For example

$$\overline{X} = \sum_{i=1}^{n} \frac{X_i}{n}$$

2   *Unbiasedness*: An estimator $\hat{\theta}$ is said to be an unbiased estimator of $\theta$ if the expected value of $\hat{\theta}$ is equal to $\theta$, that is, $E(\hat{\theta}) = \theta$. For example, $E(\overline{X}) = \mu_X$, where $\mu_X$ and $\overline{X}$ are the population and sample mean values of the random variable $X$.

3   *Minimum variance*: An estimator is a minimum variance estimator if its variance is the smallest of all competing estimators of that parameter. For example, $\text{var}(\overline{X})$ $< \text{var}(X_{\text{median}})$ since $\text{var}(X_{\text{median}}) = (\pi/2)\,\text{var}(\overline{X})$.

4   *Efficiency*: If we consider only unbiased estimators of a parameter, the one with the smallest variance is called the best, or efficient, estimator.

5   *Best linear unbiased estimator (BLUE)*: If an estimator is linear, is unbiased, and has minimum variance in a class of all linear unbiased estimators of a parameter, it is called a best linear unbiased estimator.

6   *Consistency*: An estimator is said to be a consistent estimator if it approaches the true value of the parameter as the sample size gets larger and larger.

Hypothesis testing may be conducted using the $F$ and chi-square distributions as well, examples of which will be illustrated in Exercises A.17 and A.21.

## Exercises

**A.1**   Write out what the following stand for:

(a)   $\sum_{i=3}^{4} x^{i-3}$

(b)   $\sum_{i=1}^{4} (2x_i + y_i)$

(c)   $\sum_{j=1}^{2}\sum_{i=1}^{2} x_i y_j$

(d)   $\sum_{i=31}^{100} k$

**A.2**   If a die is rolled and a coin is tossed, find the probability that the die shows an even number and the coin shows a head.

**A.3**   A plate contains three butter cookies and four chocolate chip cookies.
(a)   If I pick a cookie at random and it is a butter cookie, what is the probability that the second cookie I pick is also a butter cookie?
(b)   What is the probability of picking two chocolate chip cookies?

**A.4**   Of 100 people, 30 are under 25 years of age, 50 are between 25 and 55, and 20 are over 55 years of age. The percentages of the people in these three categories who read the *New York Times* are known to be 20, 70, and 40 per cent, respectively. If one of these people is observed reading the *New York Times*, what is the probability that he or she is under 25 years of age?

**A.5**   In a restaurant there are 20 baseball players: 7 Mets players and 13 Yankees players. Of these, 4 Mets players and 4 Yankees players are drinking beer.
(a)   A Yankees player is randomly selected. What is the probability that he is drinking beer?

(b)  Are the two events (being a Yankees player and drinking beer) statistically independent?

**A.6**  Often graphical representations called **Venn diagrams**, as in Figure A2.1, are used to show events in a sample space. The four groups represented in the figure pertain to the following racial/ethnic categories: W = White, B = Black, H = Hispanic, and O = Other. As shown, these categories are *mutually exclusive* and *collectively exhaustive*. What does this mean? Often in surveys, individuals identifying themselves as Hispanic will also identify themselves as either White or Black. How would you represent this using Venn diagrams? In that case, would the probabilities add up to 1? Why or why not?

**Figure A2.1  Venn diagram for racial/ethnic groups.**

**A.7**  Based on the following information on the rate of return of a stock, compute the expected value of $x$.

| Rate of return ($x$) | $f(x)$ |
|---|---|
| 0 | 0.15 |
| 10 | 0.20 |
| 15 | 0.35 |
| 30 | 0.25 |
| 45 | 0.05 |

**A.8**  You are given the following probability distribution:

|   |   | X | | |
|---|---|---|---|---|
|   |   | 2 | 4 | 6 |
| Y | 50 | 0.2 | 0.0 | 0.2 |
|   | 60 | 0.0 | 0.2 | 0.0 |
|   | 70 | 0.2 | 0.0 | 0.2 |

Compute the following:
(a)  $P[X = 4, Y > 60]$
(b)  $P[Y < 70]$
(c)  Find the marginal distributions of $X$ and $Y$.
(d)  Find the expected value of $X$.
(e)  Find the variance of $X$.
(f)  What is the conditional distribution of $Y$ given that $X = 2$?
(g)  Find $E[Y|X = 2]$.
(h)  Are $X$ and $Y$ independent? Why or why not?

**A.9** The table below shows a bivariate probability distribution. There are two variables, monthly income ($Y$) and education ($X$).

| | | X = Education | | |
| --- | --- | --- | --- | --- |
| | | High School | College | $f(Y)$ |
| Y = Monthly income | $1000 | 20% | 6% | |
| | $1500 | 30% | 10% | |
| | $3000 | 10% | 24% | |
| | $f(X)$ | | | |

    (*a*) Write down the marginal probability density functions (PDFs) for the variables *monthly income* and *education*. That is, what are $f(X)$ and $f(Y)$?

    (*b*) Write down the conditional probability density function, $f(Y|X = \text{College})$ and $f(X|Y = \$3000)$. (*Hint:* You should have *five* answers.)

    (*c*) What are $E(Y)$ and $E(Y|X = \text{College})$?

    (*d*) What is var($Y$)? Show your work.

**A.10** Using tables from a statistics textbook, answer the following.

    (*a*) What is $P(Z < 1.4)$?

    (*b*) What is $P(Z > 2.3)$?

    (*c*) What is the probability that a random student's grade will be greater than 95 if grades are distributed with a mean of 80 and a variance of 25?

**A.11** The amount of shampoo in a bottle is normally distributed with a mean of 6.5 ounces and a standard deviation of one ounce. If a bottle is found to weigh less than 6 ounces, it is to be refilled to the mean value at a cost of $1 per bottle.

    (*a*) What is the probability that a bottle will contain less than 6 ounces of shampoo?

    (*b*) Based on your answer in part (a), if there are 100,000 bottles, what is the cost of the refill?

**A.12** If $X \sim N(2,25)$ and $Y \sim N(4,16)$, give the means and variances of the following linear combinations of $X$ and $Y$:

    (*a*) $X + Y$ (Assume cov($X,Y$) = 0)

    (*b*) $X - Y$ (Assume cov($X,Y$) = 0)

    (*c*) $5X + 2Y$ (Assume cov($X,Y$) = 0.5)

    (*d*) $X - 9Y$ (Assume correlation coefficient between $X$ and $Y$ is –0.3)

**A.13** Let $X$ and $Y$ represent the rates of return (per cent) on two stocks. You are told that $X \sim N(18,25)$ and $Y \sim N(9,4)$, and that the correlation coefficient between the two rates of return is –0.7. Suppose you want to hold the two stocks in your portfolio in equal proportion. What is the probability distribution of the return on the portfolio? Is it better to hold this portfolio or to invest in only one of the two stocks? Why?

**A.14** Using statistical tables, find the critical $t$ values in the following cases (df stands for *degrees of freedom*):

    (*a*) df = 10, $\alpha$ = 0.05 (two-tailed test)

    (*b*) df = 10, $\alpha$ = 0.05 (one-tailed test)

    (*c*) df = 30, $\alpha$ = 0.10 (two-tailed test)

**A.15** Bob's Buttery Bakery has four applicants for jobs, all equally qualified, of whom two are male and two are female. If it has to choose two candidates at random, what is the probability that the two candidates chosen will be the same sex?

**A.16** The number of comic books sold daily by Don's Pictographic Entertainment Store is normally distributed with a mean of 200 and a standard deviation of 10.
- (a) What is the probability that on a given day, the comic bookstore will sell less than 175 books?
- (b) What is the probability that on a given day, the comic bookstore will sell more than 195 books?

**A.17** The owner of two clothing stores at opposite ends of town wants to determine if the variability in business is the same at both locations. Two independent random samples yield:

$$n_1 = 41 \, \text{days}$$
$$S_1^2 = \$2000$$
$$n_2 = 41 \, \text{days}$$
$$S_2^2 = \$3000$$

- (a) Which distribution ($Z, t, F$ or chi-square) is the appropriate one to use in this case? Obtain the ($Z, t, F$, or chi-square) value.
- (b) What is the probability associated with the value obtained? (*Hint*: Use an appropriate table from a statistics textbook.)

**A.18** (a) If $n=25$, what is the $t$-value associated with a (one-tailed) probability of 5%?
(b) If $X \sim N(20,25)$, what is $P(\overline{X} > 15.3)$ if $n = 9$?

**A.19** On average, individuals in the USA feel in poor physical health on 3.6 days in a month, with a standard deviation of 7.9.[8] Suppose that the variable *days in poor physical health* is normally distributed, with a mean of 3.6 and a standard deviation of 7.9 days. What is the probability that someone feels in poor physical health more than 5 days in a month? (*Hint*: Use statistical tables.)

**A.20** The size of a pair of shoes produced by Shoes R Us is normally distributed with an average of 8 and a population variance of 4.
- (a) What is the probability that a pair of shoes picked at random has a size greater than 6?
- (b) What is the probability that a pair has a size less than 7?

**A.21** It has been shown that, if $S_x^2$ is the sample variance obtained from a random sample of $n$ observations from a normal population with variance $\sigma_x^2$, then statistical theory shows that the ratio of the sample variance to the population variance multiplied by the degrees of freedom $(n - 1)$ follows a chi-square distribution with $(n - 1)$ degrees of freedom:

8  Data are from the 2008 *Behavioral Risk Factor Surveillance System*, available from the Centers for Disease Control.

$$(n-1)\left(\frac{S_x^2}{\sigma_x^2}\right) \sim \chi^2_{(n-1)}$$

Suppose a random sample of 30 observations is chosen from a normal population with $\sigma_x^2 = 10$ and gave a sample variance of $S_x^2 = 15$. What is the probability of obtaining such a sample variance (or greater)? (*Hint*: Use statistical tables.)

## Exponential and logarithmic functions

In Chapter 2 we considered several functional forms of regression models, one of them being the logarithmic model, either double-log or semi-log. Since logarithmic functional forms appear frequently in empirical work, it is important that we study some of the important properties of the logarithms and their inverse, the exponentials.

Consider the numbers 8 and 64. As you can see

$$64 = 8^2 \tag{1}$$

Written this way, the *exponent* 2 is the *logarithm* of 64 to the *base* 8. Formally, the logarithm of a number (e.g. 64) to a given base (e.g. 8) is the power (2) to which the base (8) must be raised to obtain the given number (64).

In general, if

$$Y = b^X \ (b > 0) \tag{2}$$

then

$$\log_b Y = X \tag{3}$$

In mathematics function (2) is called the *exponential function* and (3) is called the *logarithmic function*. It is clear from these equations that one function is the inverse of the other function.

Although any positive base can be used in practice, the two commonly used bases are 10 and the mathematical number e = 2.71828....

Logarithms to base 10 are called *common logarithms*. For example,

$$\log_{10} 64 \approx 1.81; \quad \log_{10} 30 \approx 1.48$$

In the first case $64 \approx 10^{1.81}$ and in the second case $30 \approx 10^{1.48}$.

Logarithms to base e are called *natural logarithms*. Thus,

$$\log_e 64 \approx 4.16 \quad \text{and} \quad \log_e 30 \approx 3.4$$

By convention, logarithms to base 10 are denoted by 'log' and to base e by 'ln'. In the preceding case we can write log 64 or log 30 or ln 64 and ln 30.

There is a fixed relationship between common and natural logs, which is

$$\ln X = 2.3026 \log X \tag{4}$$

That is, the natural log of the (positive) number $X$ is equal to 2.3026 times the log of $X$ to base 10. Thus,

$$\ln 30 = 2.3026 \log 30 = 2.3026(1.48) \approx 3.4, \text{ as before.}$$

In mathematics the base that is usually used is e.

*It is important to keep in mind that logarithms of negative numbers are not defined.*

Some of the important properties of logarithms are as follows: let $A$ and $B$ be some positive numbers. It can be shown that the following properties hold:

1.  $\ln(A \times B) = \ln A + \ln B$ $\qquad\qquad$ (5)

That is, the log of the product of two positive numbers $A$ and $B$ is equal to the sum of their logs. This property can be extended to the product of three or more positive numbers.

2.  $\ln\left(\dfrac{A}{B}\right) = \ln A - \ln B$ $\qquad\qquad$ (6)

That is, the log of the ratio of $A$ to $B$ is equal the difference in the logs of $A$ and $B$.

3.  $\ln(A \pm B) \neq \ln A \pm \ln B$ $\qquad\qquad$ (7)

That is, the log of the sum or difference of $A$ and $B$ is not equal to the sum or difference of their logs.

4.  $\ln(A^k) = k \ln A$ $\qquad\qquad$ (8)

That is, the log of $A$ raised to power $k$ is $k$ times the log of $A$.

5. $\ln e = 1$ $\qquad\qquad$ (9)

That is, the log of e to itself as a base is 1 (as is the log of 10 to base 10).

6.  $\ln 1 = 0$

That is, the natural log of the number 1 is zero; so is the common log of the number 1.

7.  If $Y = \ln X$, then $\dfrac{dY}{dX} = \dfrac{d(\ln X)}{dX} = \dfrac{1}{X}$ $\qquad\qquad$ (10)

That is, the derivative or rate of change of $Y$ with respect to $X$ is 1 over $X$. However, if you take the second derivative of this function, which gives the rate of change of the rate of change, you will obtain:

$$\frac{d^2 Y}{dX^2} = -\frac{1}{X^2}$$ $\qquad\qquad$ (11)

That is, although the rate of change of the log of a (positive) number is positive, the rate of change of the rate of change is negative. In other words, a larger positive number will have a larger logarithmic value, but it increases at a decreasing rate. Thus, $\ln(10) \approx 2.3026$ but $\ln(20) \approx 2.9957$. That is why the logarithmic transformation is called a *nonlinear transformation*. All this can be seen clearly from Figure A2.2.

8. Although the number whose log is taken is always positive, its logarithm can be positive as well as negative. It can be easily verified that if

$\qquad 0 < Y < 1, \ \ln Y < 0$

$\qquad Y = 1, \ \ln Y = 0$

$\qquad Y > 1, \ \ln Y > 0$

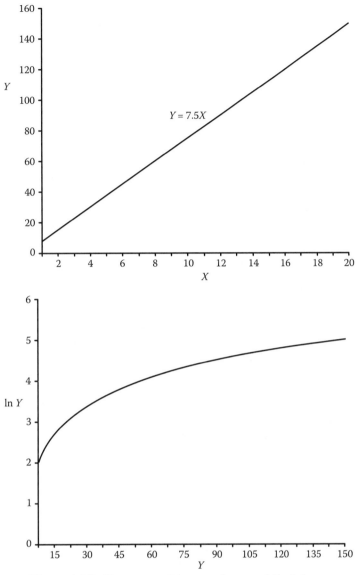

**Figure A2.2  Twenty positive numbers and their logs.**

## Logarithms and percentage changes

Economists are often interested in the percentage change of a variable, such as the percentage change in GDP, wages, money supply, and the like. Logarithms can be very useful in computing percentage changes. To see this, we can write (10) above as:

$$d(\ln X) = \frac{dX}{X}$$

Therefore, for a very small (technically, infinitesimal) change in $X$, the change in $\ln X$ is equal to the relative or proportional change in $X$. If you multiply this relative change by 100, you get the percentage change.

In practice if the change in $X$ (= $dX$) is reasonably small, we can approximate the change in $\ln X$ as a relative change in $X$, that is, for small changes in $X$, we can write

$$(\ln X_t - \ln X_{t-1}) \approx \frac{(X_t - X_{t-1})}{X_{t-1}}$$

$$= \text{relative change in } X,$$
$$\text{or percentage change if multiplied by } 100$$

## Some useful applications of logarithms

### Doubling times and the rule of 70

Suppose the GDP in a country is growing at the rate of 3% per annum. How long will take for its GDP to double? Let $r$ = percentage rate of growth in GDP and let $n$ = number of years it takes for GDP to double. Then the number of years ($n$) it takes for the GDP to double is given by the following formula:

$$n = \frac{70}{r} \tag{12}$$

Thus, it will take about 23 years to double the GDP if the rate of growth of GDP is 3% per annum. If $r$ = 8%, it will take about 8.75 years for the GDP to double. Where does the number 70 come from?

To find this, let GDP $(t + n)$ and GDP $(t)$ be the values of GDP at time $(t + n)$ and at time $t$ (it is immaterial where $t$ starts). Using the continuous compound interest formula of finance, it can be shown that

$$GDP(t + n) = GDP(t)e^{r \cdot n} \tag{13}$$

where $r$ is expressed in decimals and $n$ is expressed in years or any convenient time unit.

Now we have to find $n$ and $r$ such that

$$e^{r \cdot n} = \frac{GDP(t + n)}{GDP(t)} = 2 \tag{14}$$

Taking the natural logarithm of each side, we obtain

$$r \cdot n = \ln 2 \tag{15}$$

*Note*: There is no need to worry about the middle term in (14), for the initial level of GDP (or any economic variable) does not affect the number of years it takes to double its value.

Since

$$\ln (2) = 0.6931 \approx 0.70 \tag{16}$$

we obtain from (15)

$$n = \frac{0.70}{r} \tag{17}$$

Multiplying the right-hand side in the numerator and denominator by 100, we obtain the rule of 70. As you can see from this formula, the higher the value of $r$, the shorter the time it will take for the GDP to double.

## Some growth rate formulas

Logarithmic transformations are very useful in computing growth rates in variables that are functions of time-dependent variables. To show this, let the variable $W$ be a function of time, $W = f(t)$, where $t$ denotes time. Then the instantaneous (i.e. a point in time) rate of growth of $W$, denoted as $g_W$, is defined as:

$$g_W = \frac{dW/dt}{W} = \frac{1}{W}\frac{dW}{dt} \tag{18}$$

For example, let

$$W = X \cdot Z \tag{19}$$

where $W$ = nominal GDP, $X$ = real GDP, and $Z$ is the GDP price deflator. All these variables vary over time. Taking the natural log of the variables in (19), we obtain:

$$\ln W = \ln X + \ln Z \tag{20}$$

Differentiating this equation with respect to $t$ (time), we obtain:

$$\frac{1}{W}\frac{dW}{dt} = \frac{1}{X}\frac{dX}{dt} + \frac{1}{Z}\frac{dZ}{dt} \tag{21}$$

Or,

$$g_W = g_X + g_Z \tag{22}$$

In words, the instantaneous rate of growth of $W$ is equal to the sum of the instantaneous rates of growth of $X$ and $Z$. In the present instance, the instantaneous rate of growth of nominal GDP is the sum of the instantaneous rates of growth of real GDP and the GDP price deflator, a finding that should be familiar to students of economics.

*In general, the instantaneous rate of growth of a product of two or more variables is the sum of the instantaneous rates of growth of its components.*

Similarly, it can be shown that if we have

$$W = \frac{X}{Z} \tag{23}$$

then

$$g_W = g_X - g_Z \tag{24}$$

Thus, if $W$ = per capita income (measured by GDP), $X$ = GDP, and $Z$ = total population, then the instantaneous rate of growth of per capita income is equal to the instantaneous rate of growth of GDP minus the instantaneous rate of growth of the total population, a proposition well known to students of economic growth.

# Index

probability limit   323
probability mass function   359
probit model   161–2
problem of identification   133, 275
proportional hazard model   315–17
proportional odds models   181
  alternatives to   187
  limitations   186–7
proxy variables   124
PSID *see* Panel Study of Income Dynamics
*p* value   16

QMLE *see* quasi-maximum likelihood
  estimation
Q statistic   220–1
quadratic trend variable   39
qualitative response regression models   152
qualitative variables *see* dummy variables
quasi-maximum likelihood estimation   210–11

$R^2$ measure   43
Ramsey's RESET test   118–19
random component   2
random effects estimators   302
random effects model   298–302
random interval   12
random variables   361
  variance   251
random walk models   223, 228–31
rank condition of identification   135
ratio scale   3
recidivism duration   306–7, 310
reciprocal models   36–7
reduced form equations   334
reduced-form equations   132
reference category   48, 169
regressand   2
regression, standardized variables   41–3
regression coefficients   3–4
  interpretation of   184
  truncated   200
regression models   25–46
  choice of   40
  misspecification of functional
   form   122–4
regression parameter   3
regressors   2, 4
  correlation with error term   324–8
  endogenous   340–1, 345–6
  marginal effect   185–6
  marginal impact   209
  measurement errors   324

random   129–30
  stochastic   129–30
relative frequency   358
relative risk ratios   172, 311
REM *see* random effects model
residual   7
residual sum of squares   10, 198
response probabilities   168
restricted model   117
restricted regression   29
returns to scale   26
  constant   27
  testing   29
ridge regression   78
robust standard errors   92–3
RSS *see* residual sum of squares
rule of 70   378–9
RWM *see* random walk models

sample correlation coefficient   365
sample covariance   365
sample mean   363
sample regression function   7
sample regression model   7
sample space   357
sample standard deviation   364
sample variance   364
scale effect   5
scenario analysis   264
school choice   168–73
Schwarz's Information Criterion   44–45, 104
seasonal adjustment   58–64
semi-elasticities   31, 55, 90
semilog model   31
SER *see* standard error, of the regression
serial correlation   327
short panel   290
SIC *see* Schwarz's Information Criterion
significance   11
simultaneity   130–5
simultaneous equation bias   326
simultaneous equation regression
  models   130
SIPP *see* Survey of Income and Program
  Participation
skewness   53
smoking   152–9
software packages   11
specification bias   9
spurious correlation   99
spurious regression   217, 234–40
  non-spurious   239–40
  simulation   235–6
square transformation   90